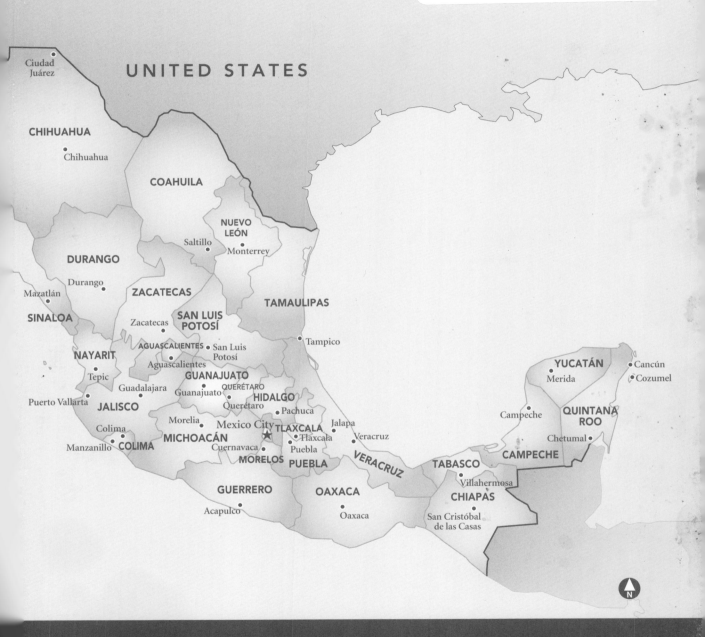

UNITED STATES

Ciudad
Juárez

CHIHUAHUA

Chihuahua

COAHUILA

NUEVO
LEÓN

Saltillo
Monterrey

DURANGO

Durango

Mazatlán

ZACATECAS

SINALOA

Zacatecas

SAN LUIS
POTOSÍ

TAMAULIPAS

AGUASCALIENTES   San Luis
Potosí

Tampico

NAYARIT

Aguascalientes

Tepic

Guadalajara

GUANAJUATO

Guanajuato

QUERÉTARO

Puerto Vallarta

JALISCO

Querétaro

HIDALGO

Querétaro

Morelia

Pachuca

YUCATÁN

Cancún

Merida

Cozumel

Colima

Mexico City

TLAXCALA

Jalapa

Campeche

QUINTANA
ROO

MICHOACÁN

Tlaxcala

Veracruz

Chetumal

Manzanillo

COLIMA

Cuernavaca

Puebla

CAMPECHE

MORELOS

PUEBLA

VERACRUZ

TABASCO

GUERRERO

OAXACA

Villahermosa

Acapulco

Oaxaca

CHIAPAS

San Cristóbal
de las Casas

N

Praise for *1,000 Mexican Recipes*
by Marge Poore

"Here is an amazing book that will become the *Joy of Cooking* for the Mexican kitchen. This encyclopedic work reveals the wonderful breadth and variety of Mexican cuisine. It explains in simple steps and with accessible ingredients how to cook all the great authentic, tasty dishes that make this one of the truly captivating cuisines of the world. Whether you want to make a perfect quesadilla, a scrumptious Mexican breakfast or give a huge fiesta—this book has it all. It has something for everyone. I found hundreds of recipes that I can't wait to cook. This cookbook is as useful and necessary as your stove—a masterpiece that is very helpful."

—Mark Miller, owner of Coyote Café (New Mexico), and author of
Coyote Café Cookbook, The Great Chile Book, and *The Great Salsa Book*

"A veritable bible of Mexican cooking. If you can't find it here, you won't find it anywhere!"

—Sharon Tyler Herbst, author of *The New Food Lover's Companion*

A book this size can seem daunting, but from the first page, Marge Poore's accessible approach and love for the subject welcome you graciously to her Mexico. She offers simple, straightforward, yet authentic snapshots of one of the world's most complex, diverse, and delightful cuisines. A delicious addition to the field. Salud!

—Cheryl Alters Jamison and Bill Jamison, James Beard award-winning
authors of *The Border Cookbook, Smoke & Spice,*
American Home Cooking, and *Best Places to Stay in Mexico*

"Marge Poore's collection of 1,000 mouthwatering recipes brings to mind the kind of inspirational cooking that is served in homes, restaurants, street stalls and markets throughout Mexico. Her colorful descriptions made me feel nostalgic for Mexico, uncontrollably hungry, and eager to dash into the kitchen with her book and start cooking."

—Elaine Gonzalez, Mexican chocolate historian and author, *The Art of Chocolate*

"What a fun culinary treasure trove! Marge Poore takes you adventuring into Mexico's hidden by-ways where wonderful dishes may be found. Her *1,000 Mexican Recipes* cookbook makes your mouth water, your tongue tingle, and every taste bud titillate! Extensive and well-written, this book should be on every "foodie's" cookbook shelf. "

—Sam'l P. Arnold, owner of The Fort restaurant (Colorado),
culinary historian, and author of *The Fort Cookbook*,
Frying Pans West, and *Eating Up the Santa Fe Trail*

"What a feat! This enormous and engaging work testifies to Marge Poore's vast knowledge of Mexico's culture and cuisine. The salsa section alone would make a worthwhile book. The remarkable breadth of the recipes make this volume a must for every food lover's library. I can't wait to start cooking from it."

—Janet Fletcher, Napa Valley food writer and author of
Fresh from the Farmers' Market

"Flavors are at saturation level in this epic of *1,000 Mexican Recipes*. The more than three decades Marge Poore has devoted to learning about the richness of this country's cuisine pays off in an appealing, usefully catalogued, must-have book. It's written for cooks of all skills, with recipes for all meals—everyday and entertaining. And it's practical in the way of savvy Mexican cooks (who shop in supermarkets, too), starting from scratch when important, taking advantage of short-cuts when they work."

—Jerry Anne Di Vecchio, Food and Wine Editor, *Sunset Magazine*

"This single book is so complete that you'll never need to buy another Mexican cookbook again. The recipes not only reflect the breadth of Mexican cooking, but are an expression of a person who has studied and traveled extensively throughout Mexico. It's both a useful cookbook and an enjoyable thumbnail travel guide to Mexico."

—Bruce Aidells, owner of Bruce Aidells' Sausage Company;
cooking instructor; and author of *The Complete Meat Cookbook*

1,000 MEXICAN *Recipes*

1,000
MEXICAN
Recipes

BY MARGE POORE

Hungry Minds™
New York, NY • Cleveland, OH • Indianapolis, IN

Published by
Hungry Minds, Inc.
909 Third Avenue
New York, NY 10022
www.hungryminds.com

For general information on Hungry Minds' products and services, please contact our Customer Care Department within the U.S. at 800-762-2974, outside the U.S. at 317-572-3993 or fax 317-572-4002.

For sales inquiries and reseller information, including discounts, premium and bulk quantity sales, and foreign-language translations, please contact our Customer Care Department at 800-434-3422, fax 317-572-4002, or write to Hungry Minds, Inc.,
Attn: Customer Care Department, 10475 Crosspoint Boulevard, Indianapolis, IN 46256.

Library of Congress Cataloging-in-Publication Data

Poore, Marge.
  1,000 Mexican Recipes / by Marge Poore.
     p.   cm.
   ISBN 0-7645-6487-0
   1. Cookery, Mexican. I. Title.
  TX716.M4 P66 2001
  641.5972—dc21
                                                                           2001024145

ISBN 0-7645-6487-0

HUNGRY MINDS, INC.
Cover Design by Edwin Kuo
Interior Design by Holly Wittenberg
Cover Illustration by Elizabeth Traynor

Manufactured in the United States of America
10 9 8 7 6 5 4 3 2 1

Key to Cover Illustration

1: garlic braid (or *ristra*)
2: de arbol chile *ristra*
3: dried herbs
4: *comal* (griddle)
5: calla lilies
6: talavera pottery
7: tortilla soup
8: tortillas
9: guacamole
10: red bell pepper
11: poblano chile
12: habanero chile
13: de arbol chiles
14: black beans; pinto beans

15: jalapeño chile
16: manzana chile
17: *güero* (yellow) chile
18: Cheese Enchiladas in Red Sauce
19: epazote
20: serrano chiles
21: yellow rice
22: red rice
23: zucchini blossoms
24: Shrimp Ceviche
25: Pork Roast (for mole)
26: tamales
27: Mexican Fried Sweet Pastries (*Churros*)

28: Basic Pot Beans
29: Mexican Sweet Buns
30: Mexican Wedding Cookies
31: Mexican Hot Chocolate
32: Mango-Orange Drink
33: Watermelon-Tequila Cooler
34: papaya
35: orange
36: lime
37: guava
38: mango
39: plantains

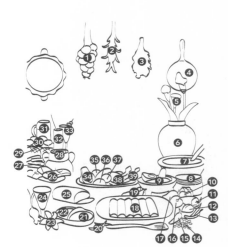

Dedication

To my husband, Bill.
Together, we discovered the magic of Mexico
and together the journey continues.

Contents

Acknowledgments

Thanks to everyone who encouraged and helped me along the way and gave me the confidence to write this book.

At Home—To my husband, Bill, whose support, suggestions, and enthusiasm for this project helped me in more ways than words can convey.

In the Kitchen—To my friends, Camille Tarantino, Helen Prince, Sandi Torrey, Marcie Atkinson, and Evie Leib, who gave a great deal of time and effort to help test, develop, and critique recipes for this book. I thank them very much for a job well done.

In the Classroom and on Tour—To my loyal cooking students who have kept me happily teaching classes for a long time, and to all those tour participants who traveled with me when I organized culinary trips to Mexico. I appreciate their enthusiasm, flexibility, and friendship.

In the Markets and Restaurants—To a host of home cooks, market vendors, and professional chefs in Mexico for being helpful in dozens of ways by answering questions, offering advice, and contributing recipes.

In My Inner Circle—To Donna Nordin and Joyce Jue, my partners and dear friends for twenty years as we worked together creating and running our Tahoe International Summer Cooking Classes, and to all the students who kept returning summer after summer for these special sessions. Very special thanks go to Jan Miller, computer expert and my personal tutor, for her technical knowledge and help in pulling the final manuscript together.

At the Final Gate—to Linda Ingroia, my editor at Hungry Minds, Edwin Kuo, the art director, Holly Wittenberg, the designer, Helen Chin, the production editor, and Brian Hahn, the editorial coordinator, who worked so hard to compile, organize, and design a mound of materials into a real book! I thank them for the amazing results.

Introduction

More than thirty years ago, I went to Mexico for the first time as a tourist, but soon after I began to travel there as a cook and a student of the cuisine. During those thirty years, I've traveled fifty to sixty times to various regions of Mexico. The markets, food, culture, crafts, architecture, history, and the people continued to lure me back again and again.

There was much to learn and I started in earnest to educate myself about Mexican cuisine. I took my first formal classes in Leon, Mexico under the direction of the school owners, Maria and Richard Merrill. Following that experience, I took cooking classes at every opportunity and began to teach Mexican cooking myself and to lead culinary tours to several locations in Mexico. Over time, I've had the pleasure and privilege to attend classes and travel with many well-known teachers and experts in the field of Mexican cuisine. Their names read like a list of "who's who" in Mexican cooking: Diana Kennedy, Patricia Quintana, Lula Bertran, Maria Dolores Torres Izabel, Carmen Ramírez Degollado, Rick Bayless, Ricardo Muñoz Zurita, Susana Trilling, Maria Marquez Merrill, Abigail Mendoza, and Marilyn Tausend, have all contributed to my continuing education. Learning about Mexican cuisine and the country is a fascinating lifelong endeavor.

Mexico is vast and varied. The cuisine, too, has enormous variety with many regional forms, as does the countryside, from north to south and east to west. The cuisine is one of the worlds oldest and greatest with native traditions that date back to the pre-Hispanic era, as far back as 1800 B.C.

The food reflects both Mexico's ancient past and the foreign influences that have contributed to the creation of its distinctive and exciting dishes. Mexico already had a developed cuisine long before the arrival of the Spanish in 1519. The foods of the ancient Mexican civilization—of corn, beans, chiles, squash, chocolate, tomatoes, avocados, peanuts, pecans, pineapple, vanilla, sunflowers, wild greens, herbs, and more—were prepared in many ways and cooked with turkey, quail, duck, venison, rabbit, other wild game, and fish. After the Spanish conquest of Mexico new food products such as pigs, chickens, cattle, sheep, wheat, rice, olives, almonds, certain fruits and vegetables were introduced and greatly influenced the evolution of Mexican cuisine. Many of the changes occurred during the Colonial Era from 1521 after the fall of the Aztec Empire and continued through Mexico's tumultuous history and their War of Independence ending in 1821. French influences came to Mexico during the reign of Emperor Maximilian from 1864 to 1867.

The fusion of Spanish and other European cuisines with native Mexican foods enriched not only the foods of Mexico, but also made a culinary impact on Europe and the rest of the world when tomatoes, chocolate, beans, corn, and much more found their way into European and other world markets. As Old World and New World ingredients mixed a culinary evolution slowly took place in Mexico, but the spicy full-flavored native traditions prevailed, and today Mexico's cuisine remains distinct and recognized as one of the world's greatest.

Patterns of change are part of history. A nation's cuisine goes through change, too. Food habits evolve as people move and carry their customs with them, and simultaneously are influenced by new experiences wherever they go. In the United States, as more people travel to Mexico and experience the vibrant flavors of Mexican foods, they often return home with a desire to cook some of the foods in their own kitchens. Studies show that spicy foods have moved into the mainstream, and people are enjoying a wider range of flavors and ethnic foods than ever before.

There has also been a noticeable trend in Mexico toward innovative cooking called *nueva cocina* (the new cuislne). Now, traditional foods are being prepared in surprising and satisfying ways. Many dishes are lightened and cooked with less fat, and more olive oil or vegetable oil is being used in place of lard. Salads as a separate course seem to be more prevalent and more cooked fresh vegetables add color and texture to contemporary entrée plates.

In recent travels to Mexico I have dined in many restaurants that feature *nueva cocina* and sampled a lot of creative contemporary dishes. The results are often exciting and beautifully presented, while still being true to the flavors of Mexico. Sometimes, as in all new endeavors, the food misses the mark and is disappointing. The best food seems to come from chefs who respect and understand the traditions of real Mexican cooking and know what combinations really work.

I find *nueva cocina* to be inspiring and I like cooking Mexican dishes in the new way, so *nueva cocina* recipes are scattered throughout the book.

Along with exciting new recipes, this book highlights classic recipes prepared nationwide and in different regions of Mexico. The recipes are as authentic as possible, given the constraints of cooking Mexican food in an American kitchen. Ingredients have become more available in recent years, so you may actually find items like banana leaves and cactus paddles in local specialty stores or even in a supermarket. In the event that they are not available, substitutions are suggested and a list of possible sources is included in the appendix. Time- and labor-saving ideas are also shared, to help you prepare good food in the time you have. With 1,000 recipes, there is something for everyone and always something new to try. You can cook Mexican food for special occasions or bring a little of Mexico into your kitchen whenever you cook.

I hope you will be continually inspired each time you see, smell, and taste the foods of Mexico and the delicious results of your cooking. Exploring Mexican cooking has been a pleasurable adventure for me for thirty years—one that continues every day.

Ingredients *for the* Mexican Pantry

Authentic Mexican cooking starts with tradition-ally used ingredients. Of course, substitutions can be made or ingredients left out and the dishes will still be flavorful, but to enjoy food as it was intended to be eaten, try to use authentic ingredients. This is not a comprehensive list of Mexican ingredients but describes items commonly used in Mexican cooking and in this book. A few of the ingredients may be unfamiliar or difficult to find, but are worth seeking in order to capture the flavors of authentic dishes. For hard to find items, see Mail-Order Sources (page 620).

Achiote: Reddish-orange seed of the annato tree used to season and color foods. A seasoning paste is also made from the seeds. Achiote is used exten-sively in the Yucatán region. The seeds and pre-pared seasoning paste are available in Latin American markets and some supermarkets.

Allspice: Aromatic spice that's used whole or ground to flavor many foods. Allspice trees grow mainly in the states of Tabasco, Veracruz, Oaxaca, and Chiapas.

Avocado: Avocados are native to Mexico and there are many varieties. The almost-black, pebbly-skinned Hass is preferred due to its creamy texture and rich flavor. To ripen avocados, store at room temperature for 2 to 3 days, or until barely soft when cupped in your hand and pressed lightly.

Banana leaves: Large flat leaves of the banana tree are widely used in Mexico to wrap tamales, or other foods that are baked or steamed. Asian or Mexican markets usually carry banana leaves, often frozen in large plastic packages. The leaves defrost quickly. To use, cut the size desired and remove the tough rib. To make the leaves pliable, pass quickly over a direct flame to impart a subtle aroma and smoky flavor, or rinse under hot running water and wrap in a damp towel for a few minutes.

Canela (cinnamon): Mexican name for the preferred cinnamon variety that comes from the light brown, soft bark of the true cinnamon tree. It is native to Sri Lanka (formerly Ceylon) and now grown in Mexico. Canela may be found ground or in sticks in Mexican stores and some supermarkets. (It is also known as Ceylon cinnamon.) Cinnamon commonly found in the United States is a darker, more bittersweet flavoring from the cassia tree and will lend a different taste to foods.

Chaya: This is a Mayan green leafy plant similar to spinach that's often used in the Yucatan but rarely available in the United States. The tender greens are used like spinach or Swiss chard, which are the recommended substitutes.

Chayote: Pear-shaped pale green vegetables related to squash. They are indigenous to Mexico and are also known as vegetable pears or mirlitons. Chayotes are used as a cooked vegetable just like summer squash. They are also stuffed and baked for desserts with raisins, nuts, and spices.

Cherimoya: Tropical dark green fruit with patterned skin that resembles thumbprints. Creamy white flesh with shiny black seeds. Used in sorbets and other desserts.

Chiles: Fresh and Dried—Listed in detail at the end of ingredients list.

Cilantro: Green herb, also called Chinese parsley, has a distinctive flavor that's essential in many fresh salsas and as a garnish. Very popular and widely used throughout the United States; easy to find.

Crema: Mexican cream that is thick and slightly sour, somewhat like French crème fraiche. It's used to garnish enchiladas, tacos, and other snacks. Make crema at home (page 17) or substitute plain sour cream diluted with a little milk.

Epazote: Important green herb used in bean dishes, tamales, some sauces and stews, and other dishes as well. In some regions of Mexico it's an essential flavor and worth seeking. Check Mexican markets, health food stores, gourmet stores, and spice and herb catalogs. It is also available dried.

Hierba Santa: Large leaf used in sauces and as a wrap for steaming fish and sometimes tamales. Also called *hoja santa, momo,* and *acuyo* in some regions. It has an anise-like flavor.

Huitlacoche (also *cuitlacoche*): Black fungus that grows on corn during the rainy season. This Mexican delicacy with an earthy mushroom taste has been discovered by many in the United States and can currently be found in some Mexican markets. It is used in crepes, soups, and with eggs.

Jicama: Large root vegetable with light brown skin and white flesh, shaped like a turnip, with a crisp sweet taste. Jicama is eaten raw, peeled and sliced, and is occasionally cooked.

Masa: Fresh dough made of specially processed dried corn that is used to make corn tortillas, tamales, and other masa dishes. Dried masa, called *masa harina,* is dehydrated into a flour, packaged, and sold in the flour section of most supermarkets.

Nopales: Paddles from the prickly pear cactus that are eaten as a vegetable throughout Mexico. The edible fruit of the plant is called a prickly pear, or *tuna.* *Nopalitos* refer to the sliced or diced cactus paddles.

Oregano: Many herbs in the oregano family are used in Mexico, but in general, what is referred to as Mexican oregano is an herb with more pronounced flavor than what is common in the United States. Found often as fresh leaves or in dried form in Mexican stores. Should be crumbled or crushed to release flavor.

Papalo: Green herb with a strong flavor used in central Mexico to season guacamole, tacos, and other foods.

Papaya: Fruit native to Central America and very common in Mexico. The Mexican variety is shaped like a hand-sized, slightly flat football, and has mixed dark green-yellow skin. The smooth pinkish-red flesh has a rich, lightly sweet taste. The gray-black seed pack in the center is often discarded but the peppery seeds are edible. (Smaller papayas from Hawaii can be substituted in recipes by weight.)

Piloncillo: Unrefined sugar, most often found in hard cones in Mexican markets and some supermarkets. Can be grated or ground in a food processor or softened in liquid. Dark brown sugar can be substituted.

Plantain: Known as *plátano macho,* this is a cooking or "vegetable" banana. Plantains are fried, baked, or mashed. The peel is thicker than that of a sweet banana and turns nearly black when ripe. Bananas, as we know them, are most often used in sweet desserts and fruit dishes.

Seville orange: Small bitter orange. The juice is important in the foods of Yucatán, Campeche, and Veracruz. Seldom found in Unites States markets. The usual substitution is grapefruit or orange juice mixed with lime juice.

Tamarind: Brown pods from the tamarind tree. The inside of the pods makes a tart juice that's used to flavor beverages, candies, and sauces.

Tomatillo: Small green fruit with a papery husk that looks like a green tomato and has a tart flavor. Used in cooked and raw sauces and salsas throughout Mexico.

Yuca: Edible root from a tropical plant that's used like potatoes, mainly in Yucatán, Campeche, Quintana Roo, and Chiapas. Often made into fritters or chips.

Chiles

The generic word chile is used for a large number of capsicum peppers—both fresh and dried—ranging from mild to extremely hot, that are used in cooking. (As a rule, the smaller the chile, the more concentrated the heat.) Most of the chiles used in this book can be found in Latin American markets and some supermarkets.

Fresh Chiles

Although the heat of fresh chiles ranges greatly, as a general rule, the following is a quick reference for the fresh chiles used in this book, from mild to very hot: Poblano, Anaheim or California, and New Mexico all range on the mildly spicy end, followed by Guëro, Jalapeño, then Serrano, with Habanero the most fiery.

Anaheim or California: Long, slender, and light green in color. Ranges from mild to quite hot. Roast and peel before using in chiles rellenos, sauces, and vegetable dishes. Also canned as whole green chiles and diced green chiles.

Guëro: Pale yellow, waxy, small hot chile. Also milder banana and Hungarian wax chiles, about 4 inches long—used in sauces, salads, and sometimes pickled.

Habanero: Small, very hot—maybe the hottest of all chiles—in shades of green, yellow, orange, and red. A lantern shape with indentations and irregularities. Closely related to the Scotch Bonnet chile.

Jalapeño: Dark green plump hot chile about 2 to 3 inches long with a rounded bottom. Used raw in salsas and cooked in sauces. Also pickled and canned.

New Mexico: Long green chile resembling Anaheim, but hotter, and used in the same ways as Anaheims.

Poblano: The most used fresh green chile. It's dark green and shiny with broad shoulders, tapering to a rounded or pointed bottom. Used extensively roasted, peeled, and stuffed for *rellenos*, and as a garnish when cut into thin strips or squares. Poblanos are also cooked in many dishes and pureed in many sauces.

Serrano: Small, slender, light green hot to very hot chile that is used mainly in fresh salsas or cooked sauces. Often used interchangeably with jalapeños.

Dried Chiles

Dried chiles are mainly used for cooked sauces. They range from shades of orange and red to dark red, brownish red, and black. They are generally toasted on a *comal*, griddle, or in a dry skillet for a brief time until they are fragrant and slightly blistered. When purchasing dried chiles in packages, always buy more than needed. Invariably, some will be moldy or in very poor condition and the whole chile or some part will have to be thrown away. If possible, buy dried chiles in bulk and look for those that are blemish free, and flexible with good color. The heat scale for the dried chiles used in this book: California, Ancho, and New Mexico are on the mild side, followed by Mulato, then Guajillo, then Cascabel, with Chile de arbol and Chipotle offering the most heat. The following dried chiles are used in this book.

Ancho: A dark red to almost-black dried poblano chile, with wrinkled skin. In some places it is called *pasilla*. It is wide at the top and tapered toward the tip, and 3 to 4 inches long. Anchos are mild to hot. They are toasted, then reconstituted in hot water to soften the skin, before being pureed in sauces. Sometimes after reconstituting, anchos are left whole and stuffed to make rellenos, or served in vinaigrette as part of a salad.

California: Shiny dried chile with smooth red skin, 4 to 5 inches long, mild to slightly hot. Used in cooked sauces and ground into chili powders.

Cascabel: Dried reddish brown chile that's mildly hot with a nutty flavor. Round in shape and cherry-sized or larger. Rattles when shaken.

Chile de arbol: Small, thin dried red chile that's very hot. Used in table sauces and cooked sauces.

Chipotle: Dried smoked jalapeño with a brown leathery skin; it's very hot. Often used canned in a seasoning mixture called adobo, and also pureed and made into a fiery chipotle sauce with a smoky taste. Chipotles are popular and a little goes a long way.

Guajillo: Medium to long dark red dried chile that's quite hot and very popular. Used extensively in cooked sauces.

Mulato: Very dark, almost black dried chile very similar to and often mistaken for an ancho. Used in moles.

Pasilla: Long, narrow, black chile that's also called *pasilla negra*. Be aware that in some places the name *pasilla* is used instead for fresh poblano chiles and dried anchos. (It can be confusing!)

Pure Ground Chili Powder and Chili Powder Blends: Unseasoned chili powders are labeled with the name of the chile, pure ground *ancho*, *pasilla*, California, New Mexico. Commercial chili powders are blends of ground chili, cumin, oregano, garlic, and other spices. Generally used in chili, beans, and stews.

Kitchen Equipment

Mexican cooking doesn't require a lot of special equipment, but a few things increase the efficiency and enjoyment of time spent in the kitchen. Below are some frequently used items that make Mexican cooking authentic and easier.

***Comal*, Griddle, Cast Iron Skillet:** Flat pans of clay or metal (*comals*) that sit on the heating unit of a stove are used to bake tortillas and other things that do not use oil. When a *comal* is not available, a griddle or skillet is used.

Electric Blender, Food Processor, Electric Mixer: These three will be in constant use when preparing salsas, sauces, beating egg whites for chile relleno batter or cakes, and lots of other things every time you cook. A blender may be the Mexican cook's best friend, not only for margaritas, but also for blending Mexican sauces better than food processors.

Fine-Mesh Strainers or Food Mill: Essential. Whatever type you prefer, because Mexican cooking frequently involves straining and mashing ingredients to make smoother sauces.

Juice Presser: Used by cooks, bartenders, and food vendors all over Mexico. Mexican cooks have individual presses for limes, oranges, and even a larger one to get fresh-squeezed grapefruit juice. These useful utensils are made of cast iron with a cup to hold a cut half lime, orange, or grapefruit, and a lever to press against the fruit to extract the juice, leaving seeds and inverted skin behind. An electric juicer or reamer utensil can also be used.

Mortar and Pestle (*molcajete* and *tejolote*): Grinding bowls and grinder from ancient times are still in use all over Mexico. They can be purchased in Mexico or in many Mexican markets in the United States. After rinsing well, (water only, no soap) they need to be cured: in the mortar with the pestle grind small amounts of rice several times until the resulting gray sandy grit is ground away. Rinse again, then use to grind nuts, seeds, herbs, spices, and to make salsa the ancient Mexican way.

Other kinds of heavy mortars and pestles are useful for some of the grinding jobs called for in Mexican cooking, especially when grinding small amounts of herbs, seeds, or spices.

Nonstick Skillets: Three sizes—8-, 10-, and 12-inch— are in constant use in my kitchen. They are relatively inexpensive and when they wear out, I toss them and get some new ones.

Spice Grinder: An electric coffee or spice grinder is necessary to pulverize seeds, nuts, whole spices, and herbs. I use a small electric coffee grinder reserved for food ingredients only.

Stovetop Grill Pan: If you don't have one, get one. It allows cooks to come pretty close to making foods with the grilled look and smoky taste of an outdoor grill, yet takes less effort to prepare, can be used year-round, and require very little fat. I prefer heavy-duty, high-quality nonstick grill pans with a handle.

Tamale Steamer: For a makeshift steamer, a metal colander lined with foil (to avoid contact with water) can be placed inside a large pot over several inches of water. Bring the water to a boil, place the tamales in the colander and cover with a clean kitchen towel. Then put the lid on the pot tightly to trap the steam. Work in batches so the tamales cook evenly, and quickly enough to seal in the filling.

Tortilla Press: Utensil with two hinged flat metal or wood plates with a handle that's pressed to flatten the dough for corn tortillas. I prefer the heavy metal type. Flour tortillas are commonly rolled with a rolling pin. Tortilla presses are often available in specialty cookware shops and many Mexican markets.

Techniques

Roasting, Peeling, and Seeding Fresh Chiles

It is important to roast, peel, and seed fresh large green chiles that are to be used for stuffing, cut into strips, diced, or puréed. Roasting chars and loosens the skin for easy removal. It also makes the chiles more flavorful and tender.

The two methods I find most successful for home cooking are to roast the chiles directly over a gas burner, or to roast them under a hot oven broiler. The most common large green chiles to roast and peel are the *poblano*, Anaheim, or New Mexico chiles. (To avoid skin or eye irritation, wear protective gloves when handling chiles or wash your hands thoroughly after.)

To roast: Hold the chiles, 1 at a time, with long tongs, directly over a gas flame, turning frequently until blistered and charred all over. Or, put the chiles on a large baking sheet, and broil as close to the preheated broiler as possible. Turn the chiles frequently until they are blistered and charred all over.

Immediately enclose the charred chiles in a plastic or paper bag and let steam about 5 minutes. (Put only 2 to 3 chiles in a bag at a time. They continue to generate heat, and if there is too much moisture in the bag, or, they steam too long, the bright color is lost and they get too soft.)

Rub off the blackened skin and rinse the chiles under running water. Cut the chiles open and remove the seeds and veins in either of the following ways:

If the chiles will be stuffed, leave the stems on. Make a slit down the side of the chile and the seed pod and remove the seeds and veins with a knife, leaving the whole chile intact.

If the chiles will be cut into strips or diced, remove the stem and scrape out the seeds and veins with your fingers or a small spoon. Rinse gently under running water to wash away any remaining seeds. Pat gently with a paper towel to remove excess moisture.

Roasting Tomatoes

Tomatoes are very often oven-roasted, broil-roasted, or roasted directly in a skillet or on a Mexican *comal*—a flat metal or clay griddle. Roasting tomatoes before adding them to a dish concentrates the flavor and adds extra body to the dish. Sometimes the skins are removed before you add the tomatoes to the dish, and sometimes not, for the charred skins will add flavor, too. Be sure to add to the dish any juices that accumulate in the roasting pan.

To oven roast, preheat the oven to 400°. Put the whole tomatoes on a foil-lined pan or baking sheet, and roast for about 40 minutes, or until the tomato skins are lightly charred and wrinkled, and the tomatoes are very soft.

To broil-roast, preheat the broiler. Put the tomatoes on a foil-lined baking sheet, and roast the tomatoes about 5 inches from the hot broiler, turning once or twice, for about 10 to 15 minutes, or until the tomatoes are charred and soft.

To pan-roast, heat a dry skillet or Mexican *comal*, over medium heat. Put the tomatoes directly on the hot pan surface, and roast, turning occasionally, until the skins blacken, and the tomatoes soften. Pan roasting is rather messy, so I do as restaurateur and cookbook author Rick Bayless does—I put a piece of foil on the pan before adding the tomatoes. It prevents having to clean burned tomato juices from the pan.

Toasting Dried Chiles

Dried chiles are used to add flavor, heat, and body to many sauces. Toasting is not always called for in a recipe, but when it is, it's an important step to give extra depth and flavor. After toasting, the dried chiles can either be ground into a powder, or soaked to soften the skin if they will be puréed for a sauce.

Wear protective gloves to avoid irritation from the chile oils in the veins and seeds of the chiles. Do not rub your eyes or nose.

To toast dried chiles: Wipe the dried chiles with damp paper towels to remove dust. If dried chiles are washed before roasting, they may be too wet to roast, so allow them to dry completely before roasting.

Cut the chiles open with kitchen scissors or a small sharp knife. Remove and discard the stems, seeds, and veins. Heat a dry skillet or *comal* over medium heat. Put the chiles in the heated pan and press to flatten with a wide spatula to make contact with the surface of the pan. Toast, turning 2 to 3 times, until aromatic and chiles take on some orange color. Do not let the chiles get any black spots, which indicates it is burned, or they will be bitter.

Toasting, Grinding, and Frying of Dried Herbs, Spices, Nuts, and Seeds

There are a few basic steps to follow when preparing certain ingredients for Mexican cooked sauces and seasoning pastes. The steps do take extra time, but are important to maximize the flavor of the ingredients and to reflect authentic Mexican tastes. Once you start cooking Mexican food frequently, the steps become almost automatic. When you see a recipe using certain chiles, nuts, herbs, seeds, or spices, you'll know that some toasting, grinding, and frying will be included in the preparation as described below.

Toasting Dried Herbs and Spices: Heat a *comal* (a traditional Mexican metal or clay pan), a griddle, or skillet until hot, then toast the herbs and/or spices, shaking the pan or stirring, until they release their aromas, generally about 10 to 15 seconds. Transfer to a plate; they're ready to use.

Toasting Nuts and Seeds: Heat a *comal*, griddle, or skillet until hot and toast the nuts or seeds until they turn to a pale brown, about 5 to 7 minutes. Watch carefully and keep them moving by shaking the pan or stirring to prevent burning. Transfer to a plate; they're ready to use.

Grinding, Blending, and Frying: Nowadays electric blenders and spice grinders do most of the grinding and blending of ingredients for seasoning pastes and sauces. Of course, some cooks still prefer to do some parts of the job by hand with a basalt mortar and pestle (*molcajete* and *tejolote*) or on a flat stone (*metate*). To them, the differences in the final sauce is worth the hard work.

After these steps are completed for cooked sauces, the remaining recipe ingredients are combined, and liquid is added if called for, such as broth, stock, or water. The frying step is next: Here, fat is heated in a deep pot (to control splatters) and the combined ingredients are quickly fried to intensify flavors and to reduce the sauce to the desired thickness.

Using Banana Leaves

Banana leaves are most commonly found frozen in packages in Mexican, Latin-American, and Asian markets. Frozen leaves thaw in about 5 to 10 minutes at room temperature.

The leaves tear easily, so handle them gently. To use, carefully unfold and separate the leaves. Using a damp towel, wipe off any white chalky residue from the surface of the leaves. Cut out the center vein, cutting from the pointed end toward the wide end to prevent tearing the leaf.

Using scissors, cut the leaf into the desired size for your recipe. If the leaf tears, it can be patched with smaller pieces when you wrap the food.

Then make the leaves more flexible, by running them briefly over a gas flame or an electric burner until flexible enough to fold, about 5 to 6 seconds on each side. Or, the leaves can be steamed in a large steamer over boiling water until they become pliable enough to fold, about 3 minutes. Put the leaves between two damp towels to keep them moist. Prepare just the number of leaves needed and store the remaining leaves in the freezer.

Using Fresh Cactus Paddles (Nopales)

The paddles that grow on the prickly pear cactus are called *nopales* and taste somewhat like green beans when cooked. *Nopales* are very common and used extensively in Mexican cooking in salads, soups, omelets, and as a filling for tacos and other snacks.

If you have the opportunity to gather *nopales* from a prickly pear cactus, or purchase cactus with spines still on, it is necessary to remove them.

Cutting and Removing Thorns from Cactus Paddles: Wear heavy protective gloves if cutting paddles from cactus plants. Cut young, small, thin paddles. They will be firm and have a better flavor. To remove the thorns, lay paddles on newspapers, outdoors, if possible. Wear gloves to protect hands and tongs to hold the paddles. Using a sharp knife, trim off the outside edge all around the paddles, then scrape the flat sides of the paddles with the knife blade to shave off all the tiny thorns that grow from the small bumps on the surface of the cactus paddles. Don't peel off the dark green outer skins. Rinse well. Cut off and discard the base of the paddle. The nopales are ready to cut into strips or squares, called *nopalitos,* or used whole, as recipe instructs. Roll up and discard the newspapers with the thorns and scraps inside.

Menus

South-of-the-Border-Meals from North-of-the-Border Kitchens

There are many opportunities to incorporate Mexican dishes into your daily meals. A simple salsa and toasted tortilla chips, or a flavorful Mexican soup or side dish can liven up just about any everyday meal, but many people also like to plan a complete Mexican menu and entertain around a Mexican theme. It's one of the most festive ways to bring a party atmosphere to the table, indoors or out.

The twelve menus that follow are designed to fit a certain kind of gathering and time of the day. I hope the menus will inspire you to use the recipes in this book and give you ideas for creating your own menus for everyday meals or when entertaining. You can mix and match from menu to menu or select an item or two and build a menu around them as you thumb through the many possibilities in each chapter of the book. Prepare the number of dishes you feel comfortable with and don't try to make too many things for any single event. *Buen Provecho!*

Easy Family Supper

Ham and Cheese Appetizer (page 70)

Chicken Tostadas (page 69)

Mexican Bread Pudding (page 565)
with Brown Sugar Syrup (page 583)

Easy Lazy Day Breakfast or Brunch

Strawberry Cooler (page 594)

Bean Burritos (page 104)

Mexican Scrambled Eggs (page 487)

Banana Bread (page 516)

Casual Hacienda-Style Supper

Mushroom and Epazote Tacos (page 94)

Tomato and Avocado Salad (page 165)

Lamb Shanks in Ancho Chile and Red Wine
Sauce (page 368)

Basic White Rice (page 472) with
Ranch Beans with Bacon (page 463)

Pineapple Cake (page 540)

Portable Mexican Picnic

Deviled Eggs, Mexican Style (page 130)

Turkey and Avocado Sandwiches (page 120)
on Oval Mexican Sandwich Rolls (page 521)

Marinated Black Bean Salad (page 206)

Jicama, Melon, Cucumber, and Tomato Salad
(page 186)

Chocolate Pecan Cookies (page 543)

Outdoor Summer Barbecue

Fresh Jamaica Cooler (page 596)
or Red Wine Punch (page 598)

Fresh Salsa Mexicana (page 24)
and Classic Guacamole (page 23) with
Toasted Corn Tortilla Chips (page 86)

Tequila-Lime Flank Steak with
Pickled Red Onions (page 330)

Basic Refried Beans (page 462)

Corn with Epazote and Poblano Chiles
(page 419)

Mangos with Strawberries (page 572)

Cozy Winter Dinner

Masa Potato and Cheese Snack, Oaxaca Style
(page 114)

Zucchini and Onion Soup (page 262)

Pork Roast with Peanut Mole (page 354)

White Beans with Roasted Garlic (page 469)

Pumpkin Flan (page 561)

Vegetarian Dinner

Melted Cheese Appetizer (page 66) or
Green Chiles with Cheese (page 88)

Greens with Grapefruit (page 181)

Vegetable Enchiladas (page 143)

Baked Sweet Potatoes with Pumpkin Seeds
(page 449)

Almond Macaroons (page 542)
and Coffee Ice Cream (page 569)

Gourmet Mexican Dinner

Margarita Mexicana (page 602)

Caviar and Serrano Chiles on Crisp Tortilla
Rounds (page 85)

Hearts of Palm and Shrimp Salad (page 200)

Walnut Soup (page 265)

Duck in Green Pumpkin Seed Sauce
(page 322) with Pineapple Salsa (page 41)

Basic White Rice (page 472)

Mexican Caramel Crepes (page 557)

Treats for an Afternoon Visit

White Wine Punch (page 599)

Apple-Raisin Turnovers (page 550)

Three Milks Cake (page 537)

Pecan Butter Cookies (page 544)

Mexican Coffee (page 588)

Festive Celebration Brunch

Tequila Sunrise (page 605)

Pineapple Boats (page 510)

Goat Cheese Quesadillas (page 102)

Bacon Guacamole (page 86) with
Toasted Corn Tortilla Chips (page 86)

Shrimp and Spinach Omelets (page 498)

Whole-Wheat Breakfast Cookies (page 520)

Mexican Christmas Dinner

Christmas Wine Punch (page 600)

Tamales with Shrimp (page 148)

Christmas Eve Salad (page 188)

Chicken in Mole Sauce from Puebla
(page 300)

Rice with Plantains (page 476)

Mexican Coffee Flan (page 560)

Fingers and Forks Party Buffet

Meatballs in Almond Sauce (page 72)

Shrimp Pinwheel with Jalapeño and Cilantro
Sauce (page 76)

Refried Beans with Cheese (page 87)

Masa Cups with Spicy Meat Filling
(page 109)

Cauliflower with Guacamole (page 127)

Pickled Jalapeños and Carrots (page 126)

Cactus Salad (page 170)

Pecan Bars with Chocolate Crust (page 545)

Salsas, Sauces, *and* Condiments

Fruit Salsas 39

Mango Salsa

Mango, Papaya, and
Poblano Chile Salsa

Mango-Avocado Salsa

Jicama-Mango Salsa

Banana Salsa

Melon Salsa

Pineapple Salsa

Pineapple, Jicama,
and Bell Pepper Salsa

Cooking Sauces 42

Basic Cooked Tomato Sauce

Basic Roasted Tomato Sauce

Tomato Sauce for
Stuffed Chiles

Tomato Sauce for
Folded Tortillas

Tomato Sauce for Tortas

Ranchera Sauce

Yucatán Tomato Sauce

Yucatán White Sauce

White Sauce with Tomatoes

Basic Cooked Tomatillo Sauce

Tomatillo Sauce with
Mushrooms and Carrots

Basic Red Chile Sauce

Ancho Chile Sauce
for Enchiladas

Ancho Chile and Red Pepper
Cream Sauce

Ancho Chile and
Red Wine Sauce

Chipotle and Tomatillo Sauce

Guajillo Chile Sauce

Guajillo Chile Sauce
with Cream

Chili Powder Enchilada Sauce

Serrano Chile Cream Sauce

Almond Sauce

Walnut Sauce

Red Pumpkin Seed Sauce

Green Pumpkin Seed Sauce

Red Sesame Seed Sauce

Black Bean Sauce

Easy Mole from Prepared Paste

Mole Sauce from Puebla

Oaxacan Red Mole

Peanut Mole

Yellow Mole

Red Bell Pepper Sauce

Red Onion Sauce

Fresh and cooked table salsas and sauces are absolutely basic to Mexican cooking, as are the many condiments that enhance the flavors and adorn almost every dish. Guacamole, pickled onions, spicy red and green table sauces, seasoning pastes, dry spice rubs, and creative fruit and vegetable salsas, all provide a sensory spark with every bite. Complex cooked sauces, such as *moles* and *pipianes*, are also integral to Mexican cooking—so important that it's said, "In Mexican cooking, the sauce is the dish." *Moles* (from *molli*, the ancient Nahuatl Aztec word for mixture or sauce), are the special sauces made of chiles, nuts, seeds, herbs, spices, tomatoes, tomatillos, bread, tortillas, and sometimes chocolate. *Moles* are celebration dishes and are made for special occasions, such as weddings and important holidays.

Sauces called *pipianes* get their name from pumpkin seeds (*pepitas*) that are toasted and finely ground to give the sauces a rich, nutty flavor. This chapter has recip██ ██r several basic *moles* and *pipianes* that are ███ made ahead for convenience and better flavor ██ poultry or meat usually

served with them can be cooked the day the dish is to be served and then simmered with the sauce.

There are more than 90 recipes in this chapter that give Mexican dishes their unique and distinctive flavors, textures, and colors. Although there are no absolute distinctions among the different types of Mexican "salsas," for convenience, most of the recipes in this chapter are categorized either as salsas and table sauces or cooking sauces.

Salsas resembling chopped salads, such as Fresh Salsa Mexicana (page 24), and smooth table sauces such as Classic Guacamole (page 23) are usually served cold or at room temperature when accompanying foods. Cooking sauces such as Basic Cooked Tomato Sauce (page 42) are usually served hot over meats, poultry, and other foods like enchiladas. Of course, if you are seeking a certain flavor for a dish, you can pair almost any salsa or sauce with any dish.

You will find yourself returning often to this chapter to select the right sauce, salsa, or condiment to compliment your meals.

Flavoring Basics and Condiments

Mixed Herb Bouquet
Hierbas de Olor

If you walk through a food market in Mexico, you'll often see women sitting at their vendor table, tying together various herb bouquets. When a recipe calls for a common mix, hierbas de olor, *this is what it means.*

1 bay leaf
1 sprig of thyme
1 sprig of marjoram
1 sprig of oregano

Tie the herbs together with kitchen string. Add it to the cooking pot. Remove and discard before serving. That's it!

Bitter Orange Juice Substitute
Naranja Agria

Makes ¾ cup

Bitter oranges (naranja agria), *sometimes called Seville oranges, are used a great deal in Yucatán cooking. The juice is used in the seasoning pastes* (recados) *of the region, in fresh salsas, and to flavor fish and other meats. This is a substitute for the real thing if Seville oranges are not available.*

¹/₂ cup fresh orange juice
¹/₄ cup fresh grapefruit juice
1 tablespoon fresh lime juice

Mix all of the juices together in a jar, cover, and store in the refrigerator. The juice is best used fresh or within 2 days.

Mexican Sour Cream
Crema

Makes **about 1 cup**

If Mexican crema *is not currently available where you live, this is an acceptable substitute. A good quality heavy cream combined with yogurt or buttermilk should thicken by standing at room temperature overnight. This homemade* crema *will stand up to cooking much better than commercial sour cream, which either dries out or curdles.*

2 tablespoons plain yogurt or buttermilk
1 cup heavy cream

Put the yogurt or buttermilk into a glass jar. Add the cream gradually, stirring, to make a smooth mixture. Cover with the lid, but do not tighten. Let stand at room temperature overnight. Remove the lid, stir gently, replace and tighten the lid, and refrigerate about 4 hours to finish thickening. Crema keeps about 10 days in the refrigerator.

Chipotle Mayonnaise or Crema
Mayonesa de Chipotle

Makes **about 1 cup**

Mayonnaise or thick Mexican crema can be mixed with prepared salsa de chipotle or canned chipotle peppers packed in adobo for this creamy spicy spread to use on tortas, tacos, quesadillas, added to salads, or whatever you like. Heat lovers really like this! The Mexican ingredients are available in Latin-American markets, and in the Mexican section of most supermarkets.

1 cup mayonnaise or Mexican crema
2 tablespoons chipotle salsa, or the adobo from canned chipotles

Mix the mayonnaise or crema with the chipotle salsa in a medium bowl. Store in a small jar, refrigerated. Mayonnaise mixture keeps for months, crema mixture for 1 to 2 weeks.

Avocado Butter
Mantequilla de Aguacate

Makes **2 to 3 servings**

Avocados are so plentiful in Mexico that it's no wonder buttery mashed avocado mixed with a bit of lime juice and salt is sometimes called "poor man's butter." Many times, my husband and I have purchased one avocado, one lime, and two bolillos (oval Mexican sandwich rolls) at the public market. With the aid of a pocket knife, we've feasted on this superb, simple fare while seated on a shady park bench. Smear avocado butter on sandwiches, steaks, or chicken.

1 large ripe avocado (Hass variety preferred), peeled and pitted
1 teaspoon fresh lime juice, or to taste
1/4 teaspoon salt, or to taste

Mix all the ingredients together in a small bowl. Use at once, or it will start to darken.

Tomato-Jalapeño Chile Butter
Mantequilla de Jitomate y Chile Jalapeño

Makes **about 1/2 cup**

Chef Francisco Cisneros of Guaymas Mexican restaurant in Tiburon, California shared this recipe with me. It goes into seafood sauces, or a small amount can be melted on grilled fish, chicken, or steaks.

1/4 pound unsalted butter, at room temperature
2 jarred pickled jalapeño chiles (en escabeche), seeded and chopped
2 tablespoons tomato paste
1/4 cup cilantro sprigs
Salt, to taste

Put all of the ingredients, except salt in a food processor and blend to combine. Add salt, if desired. Transfer to a bowl, cover and refrigerate, up to 5 days, or freeze in covered plastic container about 3 weeks.

Pickled Chipotle Chiles
Chipotles en Vinagre

Makes **about 3 cups**

In the regions of Puebla and Tlaxcala, smoky chipotle chiles are frequently pickled and used to season sauces, stews, and soups. Look for chipotles or another smoked jalapeño variety, chile mora, which is tan or reddish brown in color, pliable and about 2 inches in length. Pickled chiles keep in the refrigerator for 3 to 4 months.

3 to 4 ounces chipotle chiles
1 1/2 cups water
1 1/2 cups cider vinegar
3/4 cup *piloncillo* (Mexican raw sugar) or dark brown sugar
8 whole allspice berries
2 cloves
2 teaspoons sea salt
1 small carrot, peeled and thinly sliced
1/4 medium white onion, sliced

1. Bring 1½ cups water to a boil in a small saucepan. Meanwhile, rinse the chiles. Remove the stems and seeds, if desired.

2. When the water boils, put the chiles in the boiling water. Add the vinegar, sugar, allspice, cloves, and salt. Bring to a boil, then reduce the heat to medium-low, cover and simmer 30 minutes. Add the carrot and onion. Cook until the vegetables are tender, 6 to 8 minutes. Cool. Transfer to a jar with a lid and store in the refrigerator.

Pickled Red Onions
Cebollas Rojas en Escabeche

Makes **about 1 cup**

Traditional pickled red onions are usually blanched in boiling water before being marinated in vinegar, water, herbs and spices, but I really like to do a quick sauté in oil instead for more flavor, as in this recipe. Serve as a condiment with all meats, poultry, fish, on sandwiches, or as part of a salad.

3 tablespoons olive oil

1 large red onion, quartered lengthwise and thinly sliced

¹/₂ teaspoon dried oregano (Mexican variety preferred), crumbled

1¹/₂ tablespoons red wine vinegar

¹/₂ teaspoon sugar

¹/₂ teaspoon salt, or to taste

¹/₈ teaspoon freshly ground pepper, or to taste

Heat the oil in a medium skillet over medium heat. Add the onion and oregano. Cook, stirring, until the onion is barely tender, 2 to 3 minutes. Transfer to a bowl. Stir in the vinegar and sugar. Season with salt and pepper. Marinate for at least 1 hour or up to overnight. Serve the onions at room temperature, or sizzle the onions briefly in a hot skillet just before serving.

Basic Fresh Lard
Manteca

Makes **about 1 cup**

Lard—rendered pork fat—definitely has a place in Mexican cooking; it has been the favorite cooking fat of Mexican cooks for centuries, giving tamales a fluffier texture and refried beans an extra-rich traditional flavor. Although vegetable shortening and vegetable oil have been replacing lard in recent decades, some health experts say that lard actually has less cholesterol and saturated fat than butter. Even if you maintain a healthful diet, you can use lard in limited quantities and attain more authenticity in your Mexican cooking.

Fresh Mexican lard can sometimes be purchased from a Mexican meat market, or try making your own. Purchased Mexican lard should contain no stabilizers and should have a rich roasted taste when cooked.

To make it at home, I ask the butcher for pork fat trimmings or, if I have a pork roast, I trim off all the excess fat and render it. Discard the browned bits (cracklings) if any, that separate from the liquid fat, if you wish, or add them to scrambled eggs, salads, or other dishes.

1 pound fresh pork fat, cut into ¹/₂-inch pieces

Preheat the oven to 350°. Put the pork fat pieces into a heavy ovenproof saucepan (cast iron works well), and cook until the liquid fat separates out, and the remaining pork pieces (cracklings) are crisp and browned, about 45 to 50 minutes. Strain the fat into a glass container. Cover and refrigerate. The lard will keep fresh tasting for 6 to 8 weeks. Store the cracklings separately in the refrigerator up to 1 day, or discard.

Dry Rubs and Seasoning Pastes

Chili Rub
Especias para Carne

Makes **about 1 cup**

Prepare this dry seasoning mix and store it in the freezer. It's unbelievably easy to use and adds fabulous flavor to meats, poultry, or fish. New Mexico chili powder is sold in cellophane packages in Mexican markets or the Mexican section of many supermarkets. Try it on Lamb Steaks with Chili Rub (page 365), or another favorite of mine—rub it on pork tenderloin before roasting. (Use about ½ to 1 teaspoon per pound of meat.)

¹/₄ cup cumin seeds

1¹/₂ teaspoon coriander seeds

1 teaspoon anise seeds

2 tablespoons dried oregano (Mexican variety preferred), crumbled

¹/₄ cup New Mexico chili powder

2 tablespoons dark brown sugar

1 teaspoon salt, or to taste

1. In a dry medium skillet, over medium heat, toast the cumin, coriander, anise, and oregano until very aromatic, about 2 minutes. Stir and shake the pan constantly while toasting. Take care not to burn or the mixture may taste bitter. As soon as the mixture smells toasty and aromatic, transfer to a plate to cool. Grind to a powder in a spice grinder. (I use a coffee grinder reserved for spices.)

2. In a bowl, mix the ground seasonings with the chili powder, brown sugar, and salt. Can be stored in the freezer in a sealed plastic bag or container about 1 year. Use amount called for in recipes and keep the rest frozen.

Red Chile Paste
Adobo

Makes **about 1¹/₂ cups**

Adobo is a thick seasoning paste for meats, poultry, and fish, made of dried chiles, herbs, and spices. The paste is also used to thicken and flavor a number of traditional stews.

6 large ancho chiles, stems cut out, seeds and veins removed

2 whole medium garlic cloves, unpeeled

1 teaspoon dried oregano (Mexican variety preferred), crumbled

¹/₂ teaspoon ground cumin

¹/₂ teaspoon ground cinnamon (Mexican canela or Ceylon variety preferred)

¹/₈ teaspoon ground allspice

2 whole cloves

1 teaspoon salt

¹/₂ teaspoon sugar

2 tablespoons cider vinegar

1. In a dry skillet over medium heat, toast the chiles, pressing flat with a spatula and turning, about 8 to 10 seconds per side, or until aromatic and slightly blistered. Do not burn. Submerge the chiles in a bowl of hot water and soak about 25 to 30 minutes.

2. Toast the garlic cloves in the same skillet about 2 minutes, until some brown spots appear, and the garlic softens a little, about 5 minutes. Remove and discard the papery skin. Drain the chiles and put in a blender with the garlic. Add the other ingredients and ¼ cup of water. Purée until smooth. If the blender stalls, add only enough water to keep the blades working. Scrape down the sides of the blender jar often, and continue to blend. (The adobo should be thick and smooth with the consistency of thick ketchup.) Scrape the adobo into a container. The adobo is ready to use. The paste can be kept refrigerated for 2 to 3 weeks, or frozen up to 3 months.

Tamarind Paste

Tamarindo

Makes about 1 cup

Tamarind (tamarindo, the paste, is named after the pod) comes from the pods of a tree native to Asia and northern Africa. This tall handsome tree is widely grown in India and tropical regions of Mexico. The fruit inside the pods is made into a popular cold beverage in Mexico and new-wave Mexican chefs are using tamarind to glaze and flavor creative new dishes, and so can you. Tamarind is sour so it must be sweetened to make its tartness palatable.

Dense, sticky tamarind paste is available in Mexican or Asian markets labeled seedless tamarind paste, but it may contain seeds anyway. Don't worry, because the paste has to be strained.

¹/₂ cup seedless tamarind paste, firmly packed
¹/₂ cup dark brown sugar
³/₄ cup water

Put all of the ingredients in a small saucepan and cook, stirring, over medium heat until completely melted. With a spoon, push the mixture through a fine-mesh strainer into a bowl. Thick, stringy pulp and seeds will remain in the strainer, but push through as much as possible. The paste will be about as thick as apple sauce. Discard the seeds and remaining solids. Stir the paste to mix well and transfer to a covered container. The paste is ready to use or refrigerate indefinitely.

Yucatán Dry Spice Rub

Xak

Makes about ¹/₂ cup

It's very easy to make your own seasoning mixture to flavor poultry and meat Yucatán style. Chef Manuel Arjona, a native of Yucatán, and currently Executive Chef of Maya, a restaurant in Sonoma, California, shared this special seasoning combination with me.

2 (2¹/₂- to 3-inch) cinnamon sticks (Mexican canela or Ceylon variety preferred)
¹/₄ cup dried oregano (Mexican variety preferred), crumbled
2 teaspoons whole black peppercorns
2 teaspoons whole allspice berries
1¹/₂ teaspoons whole cloves
¹/₂ teaspoon cumin seeds

Put all of the ingredients in a spice grinder or a coffee grinder reserved for spices. Grind to a powder. If the mixture seems too grainy, sift it through a fine-mesh strainer. This spice rub can be stored indefinitely in a covered container at room temperature.

Yucatán Green Seasoning Paste
Recado de Bistec

Makes **about ⅓ cup**

From the Mexican name of this traditional Yucatán seasoning paste, which is dark green, you might conclude that it's intended to season steak, but it's also used to flavor, turkey, chicken, fish, and many other foods as well. The garlic-rich paste imparts a wonderful flavor that immediately conjures up the pleasure of eating in the Yucatán. I have found that an electric mini-chopper/grinder helps make the paste efficiently.

10 large garlic cloves, unpeeled

2 teaspoons black peppercorns

2 teaspoons whole allspice berries

½ teaspoon cumin seeds

¼ teaspoon whole cloves

1 tablespoon dried oregano (Mexican variety preferred), crumbled

½ teaspoon salt

¼ teaspoon ground cinnamon (Mexican canela or Ceylon variety preferred)

2 tablespoons cider vinegar

1. In a dry skillet, toast the garlic cloves, turning frequently until the skins are flecked with brown and the garlic feels slightly soft when pinched, 5 to 6 minutes. Peel the cloves and put them in a mini-chopper/grinder or blender and set aside.

2. In a spice grinder, pulverize the peppercorns, allspice berries, cumin seeds, and cloves. Transfer to the mini-chopper/grinder along with the oregano, salt, cinnamon, and vinegar. Blend to a thick paste. Add 1 teaspoon of water if the paste is too thick to blend. Scrape the paste into a container, cover, and let stand about 2 hours to blend the flavors. The paste is ready to use, or store up to 3 weeks in the refrigerator.

Yucatán Seasoning Pastes

Mounds and bars of colorful seasoning pastes (*recados*) are present in the public markets wherever you go in Yucatán, a southern state on the Gulf of Mexico. Traditionally, herbs, spices, and garlic are ground together with vinegar in a *molcajete* (basalt stone bowl). For convenience, the pastes can also be made in an electric blender or mini-chopper. The pastes are not difficult to make and can be refrigerated for several weeks or frozen for up to six months. Ready-made seasoning pastes can also be found in the United States sold in small packages in Mexican markets.

The recipes here for making and using the seasoning pastes will give authentic flavor to meat, poultry, and fish dishes prepared Yucatán style. Although you'll find several classic pastes detailed, the black paste (*recado de chilmole*), is not included in this book. The chiles for *recado de chilmole* are actually set afire to burn until black before grinding. The paste is used mainly with turkey for a dish called *chilmole*, and seems to be an acquired taste for many people in the United States.

Yucatán Red Seasoning Paste
Recado Rojo

Makes **about ⅓ cup**

Among the unique seasoning pastes of Yucatán called recados, *the red one is probably the most known since it's used in the preparation of the popular Mayan dishes* Cochinita Pibil *and* Pollo Pibil—*pork and chicken cooked in the traditional pibil style.* Pibil *is a Mayan word for pit-baked foods that are wrapped in banana leaves or other wrappings, covered, and cooked underground. Prepared paste called* Achiote Rojo *(spiced seasoning paste), can be purchased in many Mexican specialty markets. I use the commercial product as a base for building this paste.*

An important caution: Annatto seed in the anchiote paste is an effective dye and will stain, so protect your clothes when you make this recipe.

3 tablespoons prepared achiote seasoning paste
4 whole medium garlic cloves, unpeeled
1½ teaspoons dried oregano (Mexican variety preferred), crumbled
1 teaspoon cumin seeds
½ teaspoon black peppercorns
½ teaspoon salt
¼ teaspoon ground allspice
¼ teaspoon ground cloves

1. Put the achiote paste in a blender jar. In a dry skillet, toast the garlic cloves, turning frequently, until the skins are flecked with brown spots and the garlic feels slightly tender when pinched, 4 to 5 minutes. Peel the garlic, chop it, and add it to the blender.

2. In the same skillet, toast the oregano, cumin, and peppercorns until aromatic, 10 to 15 seconds. Add to the blender along with the salt, allspice, cloves, and water. Blend to a thick paste as smooth as possible. Add another 1 to 2 teaspoons of water if the mixture is too thick to blend. Scrape the paste into a bowl. The paste is ready to use. If made ahead, cover and refrigerate up to 3 weeks.

Vegetable Salsas and Table Sauces

Classic Guacamole
Guacamole

Makes **about 2 cups**

Guacamole is probably the best known Mexican sauce and is traditionally made in a molcajete *(basalt grinding bowl), and mashed with a* tejolote *(stone grinding tool or pestle). The word comes from* ahuacatl *(avocado) and* molli *(mixture), from the ancient Nahuatl Aztec language. Avocados are native to Mexico and abundant year round in different varieties. My favorite in the United States is the buttery pebbly skinned, dark green Hass variety (from California).*

Guacamole has many variations; one common way of serving it is with tomato. If you would like to try it, seed and finely chop 1 medium ripe tomato and gently stir it into the guacamole before serving.

Guacamole should be served within 4 hours after it's made for best color and freshest flavor.

2 large ripe avocados (Hass variety preferred)
¼ medium white onion, finely chopped
2 serrano chiles, finely chopped with seeds
¼ cup lightly packed chopped fresh cilantro
1 tablespoon fresh lime juice, or to taste
¼ teaspoon salt, or to taste

Cut the avocados in half and remove the seeds. Hold 1 avocado half in the palm of one hand and with the other hand, mash the avocado in its shell with a fork; then scoop the avocado into a bowl with a spoon, scraping out the creamy pulp. Discard the shell and repeat with the remaining avocado halves. Add the remaining ingredients and mix well. Cover tightly with plastic wrap to prevent discoloration.

Avocado and Tomatillo Sauce
Salsa de Aguacate y Tomatillo

Makes about 1¹/₂ cups

Smooth, creamy avocado sauce combined with tomatillos is another form of guacamole that I've had in Veracruz and Yucatán. Serve as a table sauce to spoon over poultry, fish, or whatever you like.

4 medium tomatillos, husked and rinsed

1 large ripe avocado (Hass variety preferred)

¹/₄ medium white onion, chopped

1 serrano chile (or more if you like), chopped with seeds

1 medium garlic clove, chopped

3 tablespoons coarsely chopped fresh cilantro

2 tablespoons fresh lime juice, or to taste

¹/₂ teaspoon salt, or to taste

In a small saucepan, cook the tomatillos in water to cover until they turn pale green and are slightly soft, 5 to 6 minutes. Drain and put them in a food processor. Cut the avocado in half. Remove seed. Peel and add to the processor along with the remaining ingredients. Process until smooth. Adjust seasoning. Serve within 4 hours for best color.

Fresh Salsa Mexicana
Salsa Fresca Mexicana

Makes about 2 cups

Fresh Mexican salsa is so well known that it has become a staple in many supermarkets, but when vine-ripened farmers' market tomatoes are in season, homemade salsa is still the best. This is the kind of fresh table salsa served all over Mexico.

3 large ripe tomatoes, finely chopped

¹/₂ medium white onion, finely chopped

2 to 3 serrano chiles, minced with seeds

3 tablespoons coarsely chopped fresh cilantro

2 tablespoons fresh lime juice, or to taste

¹/₂ teaspoon salt, or to taste

Mix all of the ingredients together in a medium bowl. Let stand about 15 minutes to blend the flavors. For the best taste and texture, serve within 3 hours of preparing.

Black Bean and Avocado Salsa
Salsa de Frijol Negro y Aguacate

Makes about 3 cups

Make this sauce when you have leftover black beans or use canned black beans. For the best appearance, the beans should be tender and cooked through, but not mushy. To maintain color and texture, add the avocado last.

2 cups cooked drained and rinsed black beans, or 1 (15-ounce) can, drained and rinsed

2 tablespoons finely chopped red or white onion

2 serrano chiles, minced with seeds

1 small tomato, seeded and finely chopped

1 tablespoon olive oil

1 tablespoon fresh lime juice

¹/₂ teaspoon salt, or to taste

1 avocado (Hass variety preferred), neatly diced (¹/₄ inch)

2 tablespoons chopped cilantro

In a bowl, mix all of the ingredients, except the avocado and cilantro. Shortly before serving, gently stir in the avocado and cilantro. Adjust seasoning. Serve with tortilla chips, seafood, or grilled chicken.

Corn and Black Bean Salsa
Salsa de Elote y Frijol Negro

Makes **about 3 cups**

Modern salsas are imaginative, colorful, and made of healthful ingredients with little or no added fat. Serve as a topping for tortilla chips, or spoon over grilled meat or fish. Canned black beans are a great convenience, but home-cooked beans are better.

1 large ear of corn, shucked

1 cup drained and rinsed black beans, canned or homemade

1 medium tomato, finely chopped

1/4 medium red onion, finely diced

2 jalapeño chiles, seeded and finely diced

2 tablespoons chopped fresh cilantro

2 tablespoons fresh lime juice

2 teaspoons olive oil

1/2 teaspoon ground cumin

1/4 teaspoon salt, or to taste

In a large pot of boiling water, cook the corn until just tender, 3 to 4 minutes. Cool under running water. With a sharp knife, cut the kernels off the cobs. Put the corn kernels in a large bowl. Serve within 4 hours, cold or at room temperature.

Fresh Corn Salsa
Salsa de Elote

Makes **about 3 cups**

The time to enjoy this salsa is whenever fresh corn is in season. Remember to wear protective gloves when handling hot chiles. Serve the corn salsa as a condiment with fish, chicken, or steak.

4 ears fresh corn, shucked

1/2 medium white onion, finely chopped

1 to 2 fresh serrano chiles, minced (with or without seeds)

1 ripe tomato, seeded and chopped

1/2 cup loosely packed chopped fresh cilantro

3 tablespoons fresh lime juice

1 teaspoon vegetable oil or olive oil

1/2 teaspoon salt, or to taste

In a large pot of boiling water, cook the corn until just tender, 3 to 4 minutes. Cool under running water. With a sharp knife, cut the kernels off the cobs. Put the corn kernels in a large bowl. Mix in the onion, chiles, tomato, cilantro, oil, and lime juice. Season to taste with salt. Serve cold or at room temperature.

Tomato and Corn Salsa
Salsa de Jitomate y Elote

Makes **about 3 cups**

Many farmers' markets are offering and home gardeners are growing tomatoes of various kinds and colors. This sauce is best when tomatoes are abundant and vine-ripened. It's a contemporary salsa that's great with traditional Mexican dishes like Stacked Beef Enchiladas (page 142) or Barbecued Pork Steaks Marinated in Red Chile Paste (page 350).

3 ripe tomatoes (2 red and 1 yellow, if available)
1 cup cooked white or yellow corn kernels (about 1 ear corn)
1/2 medium red bell pepper, finely diced
1 *guëro* (yellow) chile, seeded and finely chopped
1 tablespoon chopped fresh cilantro
2 teaspoon finely chopped fresh mint
1 tablespoon fresh lime juice
2 teaspoons olive oil
1/2 teaspoon cumin
1/2 teaspoon salt, or to taste

Mix all of the ingredients in a large bowl. Serve within 4 hours, cold or at room temperature.

Tomato and de Arbol Chile Sauce
Salsa de Jitomate y Chile de Arbol

Makes **about 1 cup**

Dried chiles de arboles are very hot, so caution your guests when they taste this cooked table sauce, which is especially popular in the state of Sonora in northern Mexico. Try it with grilled or roasted meats and poultry. The dried red chiles de arbol are found in cellophane packages in the Mexican section of most supermarkets and occasionally in bulk bins in some specialty gourmet stores.

3 whole chiles de arbol
1/2 pound (about 3 large) plum tomatoes, cored with skins on
2 medium garlic cloves, unpeeled
1 tablespoon vegetable oil
1/3 cup finely chopped white onion
1/2 teaspoon dried oregano (Mexican variety preferred), crumbled
1/2 teaspoon salt

1. In a small skillet, toast the chiles over medium heat, turning 2 to 3 times, until they are aromatic and turn to a lighter, somewhat orange color, about 30 seconds. Set the chiles aside to cool. In the same skillet, roast the tomatoes and the garlic, turning several times, until lightly charred in several places, about 10 minutes.

2. Coarsely chop the tomatoes, skins and all, and put them into a blender jar. Remove the outer skin from the garlic, chop and add to the blender jar. Break open the chiles, shake out most of the seeds, and cut or break the chiles into small pieces; add them to the blender jar. Blend to a purée. (There will still be some texture.)

3. Heat the oil in a small saucepan, and cook the onion and oregano until the onion begins to brown. Add the tomato mixture and the salt. Simmer the sauce, uncovered 5 minutes. Put the sauce into a small bowl and serve at the table.

Pasilla Chile Sauce
Salsa de Chile Pasilla

Makes **about 1 cup**

Pasilla (or pasilla negro) chiles are long, slender, and nearly black dried chiles. For this robust table sauce, there is really no substitute for the black chile that's quite easy to identify by its color and shape. Pasillas are grown in central Mexico and much of northern Mexico.

3 pasilla chiles, cut open, seeded, and veins
   removed
1 tablespoon cider vinegar
1 tablespoon canned tomato sauce
1 tablespoon chopped white onion
1/4 teaspoon cumin seeds
2 black peppercorns
2 teaspoons vegetable oil
1 Roma tomato, finely chopped
2 tablespoons chopped fresh cilantro
1/4 teaspoon salt, or to taste

Cut the chiles into pieces and submerge into a bowl of hot water to cover, and soak 20 minutes. Put the soaked chiles in a blender jar and discard the water. Add the vinegar, tomato sauce, onion, cumin seed, and peppercorns. Blend until smooth. (The sauce will be about as thick as ketchup.) Heat the oil in a small saucepan add the sauce and cook, stirring, 3 minutes to blend the flavors. Transfer to a bowl and cool to room temperature. Stir in the tomato, cilantro, and salt. Transfer to a medium bowl and serve.

Pasilla Chile and Tomato Sauce
Salsa de Chile Pasilla y Jitomate

Makes about 1 1/2 cups

Pasilla (or pasilla negro) chiles are dried black chiles that are called chilacas when they are fresh and are widely grown in central Mexico. The name pasilla is also given to ancho and poblano chiles in some parts of the United States, so be careful when selecting chiles. (I use the names I learned in Mexico.) Ancho or mulato chiles could be substituted for this sauce, but the flavor will be quite different. Serve as a table sauce or spoon over grilled fish or chicken.

10 pasilla chiles
3 teaspoons olive oil or vegetable oil
2 medium tomatoes, quartered
1/4 medium white onion, sliced
3 medium garlic cloves, thinly sliced
1/2 teaspoon dried oregano (Mexican variety
   preferred), crumbled
1/4 teaspoon dried thyme
1/2 teaspoon salt, or to taste

1. Heat a dry skillet over medium heat and toast the chiles, turning, until aromatic and slightly blistered. (Do not burn, or the chiles will be bitter.) Cut the chiles open and discard the seeds and veins. Submerge into a bowl of hot water to cover and soak 25 minutes.

2. Meanwhile, heat the oil in the same skillet and fry the tomatoes, onion, and garlic, stirring frequently, until starting to brown, 6 to 8 minutes. Transfer to a blender.

3. Drain the soaked chiles and add them to the blender with the oregano and thyme. Blend as smoothly as possible.

4. Pour the sauce through a strainer into a saucepan. Discard the bits of skin and debris left in the strainer. Add the salt and bring to a boil over medium heat. Reduce the heat to low, cover and simmer 15 minutes to blend the flavors. If the sauce thickens too much, add a little water or heated chicken broth to reach the consistency of heavy cream. Serve warm or at room temperature.

Pumpkin Seed Sauce with Tomatoes
Sikil-Pak

Makes **about 2 cups**

This typical Mayan nutty-tasting dip from Yucatán is made with raw green pumpkin seeds that are toasted and ground very fine. In this recipe the habanero chile *is cut in half, seeded, and added to the dip as is to lend its heat and flavor. If you leave the chile in the dip, warn your guests not to eat the chile! Also, be forewarned that the* habanero chile *is extremely hot, so wear protective gloves when handling it.*

1¹/₂ cups hulled raw green pumpkin seeds

3 medium tomatoes (about 1 pound), broil-roasted (page 8)

2 tablespoons chopped fresh cilantro

2 small green onions, green and white parts finely chopped

1 teaspoon salt, or to taste

1 habanero chile, cut in half, seeded and deveined (wear protective gloves)

1. In a large skillet, toast the pumpkin seeds over medium heat until fragrant, light brown, and popping in the pan. Remove to a plate to cool. When the seeds are cool, grind them very fine in a spice grinder. (I use a coffee grinder reserved for spices.) Transfer to a medium bowl and reserve.

2. Peel the broiled tomatoes and purée in a blender until smooth. Add to the bowl with the ground pumpkin seeds along with the cilantro, onions, salt, and habanero halves. The sauce should be thick enough to hold its shape on a spoon or on a chip for dipping. Let the sauce stand about 20 minutes. Remove the habanero halves, if desired. Serve the dip at room temperature with chips.

Sunflower Seed Sauce with Tomatoes
Salsa de Pepitas con Jitomate

Makes **about 1 cup**

Serve this easy blended sauce with crisp tortilla chips, or spoon a dollop on grilled fish or shrimp. Dry-roasted sunflower seeds are already salted and are available in most supermarkets or in health food stores.

¹/₂ cup dry-roasted sunflower seeds

¹/₄ teaspoon ground cumin

2 Roma tomatoes, cored and chopped with skins

1 serrano chile, chopped with seeds

1 tablespoon chopped fresh cilantro

2 teaspoons fresh lime juice

2 teaspoons olive oil

¹/₄ teaspoon salt, or to taste

Put all of the ingredients in a blender or food processor and blend until almost smooth. (There should be some texture.) Add salt. Transfer to a bowl and serve within 1 hour, at room temperature, or cover and refrigerate up to 4 hours.

Spicy Mayonnaise Dip
Mayonesa Picante

Makes **about 1 cup**

This is a good dip to serve with cold seafood, such as shrimp or crab. It also goes well with Fried Squid (page 83) or Appetizer Fish Balls (page 84). The mayonnaise can be made up to one day before serving.

³/₄ cup mayonnaise

2 teaspoons Dijon mustard

1 jalapeño or serrano chile, seeded and minced

1 tablespoon drained finely chopped capers

1 tablespoon chopped fresh cilantro or parsley

In a small bowl, stir together all of the ingredients. Store in the refrigerator for up to 3 days for best texture. Serve cold.

Cucumber and Jalapeño Salsa
Pepino y Jalapeño Salsa

Makes **about 1 cup**

This unusual salsa can be spooned over tostada *salads or served as a table salsa with seafood or chicken.*

1 medium cucumber, peeled, halved lengthwise, and finely diced (about 1/4 inch)
2 large jalapeño chiles, seeded and finely chopped
2 green onions, finely chopped
1/2 peeled carrot, coarsely shredded
1 tablespoon chopped fresh cilantro
1 teaspoon finely chopped fresh mint
1 1/2 teaspoons unseasoned rice vinegar
1 1/2 teaspoons olive oil
1/4 teaspoon salt, or to taste
1/8 teaspoon fresh pepper, or to taste

In a medium bowl mix all of the ingredients together. Serve the salsa cold within 3 to 4 hours for best flavor.

Fresh Serrano Chile Salsa
Salsa de Chile Serrano

Makes **about 1 cup**

A delightful woman from the state of Michoacan *mixed up this raw fresh salsa at an outdoor party near my home in California. She told me what was in it, and I matched her recipe*

exactly. Be forewarned. It's hot! Wear protective gloves when working with the chiles.

1/2 cup (8 to 10) serrano chiles, finely chopped and seeded (wear protective gloves)
1/4 cup finely chopped white onion
2 tablespoons fresh lime juice
2 Roma tomatoes, finely chopped
1/4 cup coarsely chopped fresh cilantro.
1 small garlic clove, minced
1/4 teaspoon salt, or to taste

In a bowl, mix the serranos, onion, and lime juice. Let marinate about 10 minutes. Add the remaining ingredients and mix well. Refrigerate. Serve cold.

Jicama-Cilantro Salsa
Salsa de Jicama y Cilantro

Makes **about 2 cups**

Here's a pale green, crisp, fresh-tasting salsa that goes very well with seafood of all kinds and lots of other things, too. If you'd like a touch of red in the salsa, add 2 to 3 finely chopped radishes.

1 small jicama (about 1 pound), peeled and finely diced
1 tablespoon finely chopped white onion
2 tablespoons chopped fresh cilantro
2 teaspoons finely chopped fresh mint
1 serrano chile, minced with seeds
1 tablespoon fresh lime juice
1/4 teaspoon salt, or to taste

In a medium bowl mix all of the ingredients together. Refrigerate. Serve cold.

Jalapeño-Cilantro Sauce
Salsa de Jalapeño y Cilantro

Makes **about 1 cup**

Los Pacos, a small restaurant in Oaxaca, gets credit for this spicy jalapeño sauce that can be served as a salad dressing or a dipping sauce.

2 large jalapeño chiles, stemmed, seeded, veins removed, and chopped
2 small garlic cloves, thinly sliced
³/₄ cup lightly packed coarsely chopped fresh cilantro
3 tablespoons fresh orange juice
3 tablespoons fresh lime juice
¹/₄ cup olive oil
¹/₂ teaspoon salt, or to taste

In a blender, purée all of the ingredients together until smooth. Pour into a small bowl. Use as a dipping sauce or salad dressing.

Fiery Cilantro-Mint Sauce
Salsa de Cilantro y Yerbabuena

Makes **about 1 cup**

This uncooked pale green sauce is perfect over sautéed fish fillets, shrimp, or chicken breasts, or as a dip for raw vegetables. Adjust chile heat to taste. Prepare this sauce shortly before using for freshest color and flavor.

1 cup packed cilantro sprigs
¹/₂ cup loosely packed stemmed parsley
1 tablespoon finely shredded mint leaves
2 tablespoons hulled raw green pumpkin seeds (pepitas)
2 to 3 serrano chiles, chopped with seeds
2 tablespoons unseasoned rice vinegar
2 tablespoons fresh lime juice
¹/₂ teaspoon salt
¹/₄ cup olive oil

Place all of the ingredients, except the olive oil, in a food processor. Process until the ingredients are finely chopped. Add the olive oil and process until thick and smooth, about 10 seconds. Scrape down the sides of the bowl and process another 5 seconds. Transfer to a serving bowl. Cover and refrigerate until shortly before serving, up to 3 hours, for best flavor and texture. Serve cold.

Pan-Roasted Red Salsa
Salsa Roja Asada

Makes **about 2 cups**

A rustic salsa of pan-roasted ingredients has a different, more intense flavor than a fresh salsa with raw ingredients. Try it spooned over plain grilled meats, poultry, or fish.

6 small plum tomatoes
2 (¹/₂-inch-thick) slices white onion
2 large jalapeño chiles, halved lengthwise and seeded
2 medium garlic cloves, unpeeled
¹/₂ teaspoon dried oregano (Mexican variety preferred), crumbled
¹/₄ teaspoon ground cumin
2 teaspoons olive oil
1 teaspoon unseasoned rice vinegar
¹/₂ teaspoon salt, or to taste

1. Heat a dry griddle or skillet over medium heat and pan-roast the tomatoes, onions, jalapeños and garlic, turning frequently, until all have charred spots on all sides and are softened. The roasting time varies with each piece. Remove the pieces to a plate, as they are ready, about 5 minutes for the garlic, 10 minutes for the chile, and 12 to 15 minutes for the onion and tomatoes.

2. When all are finished, finely chop the tomatoes, onions, and jalapeños, and put them in a bowl. Remove the outer skin from the garlic, and chop it very fine. Add it to the tomato mixture.

3. In a small dry skillet, toast the oregano until aromatic, about 45 seconds. Add to the bowl along with the cumin, olive oil, vinegar, and salt. Mix well. Serve at room temperature.

Poblano Chile Salsa
Salsa de Chile Poblano

Makes about 1¹/₂ cups

Poblano chiles are usually mild to slightly hot, but occasionally they pack a real bite, so wear protective gloves when peeling and chopping them. This versatile sauce can be served hot or cool with just about anything. I like it spooned over grilled chicken or steak or even mixed with green salads.

2 large poblano chiles, roasted and peeled
    (page 8)
2 tablespoons olive oil or vegetable oil
¹/₄ cup finely chopped white onion
1 small tomato, peeled and finely chopped
    or diced
1 teaspoon unseasoned rice vinegar
¹/₂ teaspoon salt, or to taste

1. Prepare the chiles. Remove the stems and seeds. Cut the chiles lengthwise into thin strips, ¹/₄-inch wide; then cut crosswise into ¹/₄-inch dice. Reserve.

2. Heat the oil in a medium skillet and cook the onion until softened, about 3 minutes. Add the tomato and cook, stirring, until heated through, about 1 minute. Add the reserved diced chiles, vinegar, and salt. Heat through and serve.

Yucatán Habanero Sauce
Ixni-Pec

Makes about 1 cup

Habanero chiles are considered to be one of the hottest chiles of all, but they have become popular with people who like hot and spicy food. Ixni-Pec (schnee-pec) is a habanero table sauce of the Yucatán. Warn your guests! Habanero chiles have become pretty common here in the states. Seville oranges (bitter oranges) are not widely available, but you can make a simple substitute that works well.

3 medium tomatoes, peeled and finely chopped
¹/₂ small white onion, finely chopped
1 to 2 habanero chiles, seeded, veins removed,
    and minced (wear protective gloves)
¹/₄ cup Seville orange juice or Bitter Orange Juice
    Substitute (page 17)
3 tablespoons chopped fresh cilantro
¹/₄ teaspoon salt, or to taste

In a medium bowl, mix all of the ingredients together. Serve chilled or at room temperature.

Cascabel Chile Sauce
Salsa de Chile Cascabel

Makes **about 1 cup**

Cascabel chiles are small, round dark-red dried chiles that rattle when shaken. A wonderful aroma is released when the chiles are toasted for this terrific table sauce. A spoonful is especially good drizzled over grilled fish, chicken, or roasted pork.

8 cascabel chiles
1 large ripe tomato, broil-roasted (page 8), and chopped
1 small garlic clove, finely chopped
¹/₄ teaspoon salt, or to taste

1. Toast the chiles in a dry skillet or on a *comal* over medium heat, turning, until aromatic and pliable, about 2 to 3 minutes. Cool; then cut the chiles open and remove the seeds and veins. Save about ½ teaspoon of seeds to toast, and discard the remaining seeds. Cut the chiles into pieces and put into a spice grinder. (I use a coffee grinder reserved for spices.)

2. Toast the chile seeds in the dry skillet until they just begin to color, about 2 minutes. Add them to the spice grinder and grind the chiles and seeds to a coarse powder. Transfer to a blender with the chopped tomato, garlic, and salt. Blend to a coarse sauce. Transfer to a bowl and serve as a table sauce.

Chihuahua Chile Salsa
Salsa de Chihuahua

Makes **about 1¹/₂ cups**

Chihuahua, known for silver mining, breweries, and cattle raising, is also meat country, and the beef grown there is considered some of the best in the country. Naturally, most restaurants feature all kinds of grilled meats, stews, and barbecues. This sassy salsa makes those smoky meats taste extra special.

2 large poblano chiles, roasted, peeled, seeded, and veins removed (page 8)
1 medium tomato, finely chopped
¹/₄ medium white onion, finely chopped
3 to 4 serrano chiles, minced with seeds
¹/₄ teaspoon salt, or to taste
2 tablespoons fresh lime juice
1 tablespoon canned tomato sauce
¹/₄ cup lightly packed coarsely chopped fresh cilantro

Prepare the chiles, then finely dice them. Put them in a medium bowl with all of the remaining ingredients. Serve at room temperature.

Yellow Chile Sauce
Salsa de Chile Güero

Makes **about 1 cup**

Yellow güero *chiles (*güero *meaning blonde or light-skinned) are usually quite mild, but occasionally they fool you. Regional names include,* caribe, *in parts of northern Mexico, and* xcatic, *in Yucatán. In the United States available varieties are generally called Hungarian or yellow wax peppers. When combined with tomatillos, as in this salsa, they make a great combination of flavor and color to serve with seafood.*

4 to 5 tomatillos (4 ounces) husked, rinsed, and quartered

3 *guëro* (yellow) chiles, seeded and chopped

1/4 cup coarsely chopped fresh cilantro

2 tablespoons chopped white onion

2 teaspoons vegetable oil or olive oil

1/2 teaspoon salt, or to taste

1/4 teaspoon sugar

Put the tomatillos in a small saucepan in enough water to cover. Bring to a boil and cook 2 minutes. Drain and rinse under cold running water to stop the cooking. Put in a food processor or blender along with the remaining ingredients. Process to a coarse purée. Transfer the salsa to a small serving bowl. Refrigerate and serve cold or serve at room temperature. The salsa is best served the day it's made.

Smoked Red Chile Sauce
Salsa de Chile Pasilla de Oaxaca

Makes **about 1 cup**

Although dried smoked pasilla de Oaxaca *chiles are unique to the region and are not yet available in this country, this is a wonderful salsa worth knowing. (If you travel to Oaxaca, bring back some of these dried chiles. They are usually legal to bring into the United States. Inquire at U.S. Customs about the current practice.) Substitute canned* chipotle chiles en adobo *and the salsa will still have a hot smoky taste. Serve as a spicy dip for chips, or as a table sauce with meat, poultry, or eggs.*

4 dried pasilla de Oaxaca chiles, stemmed, seeded, and veins removed, or 2 canned chipotles en adobo

2 teaspoons vegetable oil

1/2 medium white onion, chopped

1 medium garlic clove, chopped

1/2 teaspoon dried oregano (Mexican variety preferred), crumbled

4 Roma tomatoes, cored and chopped

1 tablespoon coarsely chopped fresh cilantro

1 teaspoon unseasoned rice vinegar

3/4 teaspoon salt, or to taste

1. Put the dried chiles in a small bowl and cover with hot water to cover and soak about 10 minutes. (If using canned chipotles, cut each into 3 to 4 pieces and set aside.)

2. Heat the oil in a small skillet and cook the onion, garlic, and oregano until they begin to brown, 3 to 4 minutes. Transfer to a blender or food processor. Drain the chiles and add to the blender. Blend to a coarse purée. Add the remaining ingredients. Blend until finely chopped with a uniform texture. Serve at room temperature.

"Drunken" Sauce
Salsa Borracha

Makes **about 2 cups**

There are many "drunken" sauces, and different ways to add spirits to foods in Mexican cooking. In addition to the tequila in this recipe, drunken sauces are also made with rum, brandy, or even beer. Tequila is a town in the state of Jalisco where tequila is distilled and often used in cooking as well as for drinking. Salsa borracha is pretty common in Jalisco, but is known in other regions, too.

This is an uncooked version of a table sauce that goes well with grilled meats and poultry.

4 dried ancho chiles, cut open and seeded
1/2 cup silver or white tequila
1/2 cup fresh orange juice
1 tablespoon fresh lime juice
1 tablespoon minced white onion
1 tablespoon olive oil
1/2 teaspoon salt, or to taste

In a dry skillet, over medium heat, toast the chiles by pressing them flat and turning once or twice until aromatic. Put the chiles into a bowl of hot water, cover and soak about 20 minutes. Drain the chiles and put them into a blender jar with the tequila, orange juice and lime juice. Blend until smooth. Add the onion, oil and salt. Blend briefly to combine. Put the sauce into a medium bowl and serve at room temperature.

Radish Salsa
Salsa de Rábanos

Makes **about 1 cup**

This crunchy salsa goes well with most meat dishes, or as a topping for tostadas *(crisp fried corn tortillas).*

1 bunch radishes, tops removed
2 tablespoons finely chopped white onion
1 small tomato, finely chopped
1 serrano chile, minced
1 tablespoon fresh lime juice
2 teaspoons vegetable oil or olive oil
1 tablespoon chopped fresh cilantro
1/4 teaspoon salt, or to taste

Rinse the radishes. Cut them into quarters and slice thinly. Put the sliced radishes in a medium bowl, and mix in all of the other ingredients. Cover and refrigerate 30 minutes to an hour. Serve cold.

Fresh Tomatillo Sauce
Salsa Verde Cruda

Makes **about 1 1/2 cups**

Chef Ricardo Muñoz of Mexico City is a skillful teacher and excellent chef who really knows Mexican cuisine. Raw tomatillo *salsa is typical around Mexico City. Serve as a table sauce or with chips within 2 to 4 hours for best flavor and texture. It's great with* quesadillas.

1 pound husked, rinsed, and coarsely chopped
    tomatillos
2 tablespoons chopped white onion
1 serrano chile, coarsely chopped with seeds
1 small garlic clove, sliced
1/2 cup loosely packed cilantro sprigs
1/2 teaspoon salt, or to taste

Put about half of each ingredient, except salt, into a blender. Blend to a coarse purée and until the tomatillos release their juices. Add the remaining half of the ingredients and blend until nearly smooth. (It should have some texture.) Transfer to a small serving bowl. Adjust seasoning. Serve cool or at room temperature.

Pan-Roasted Tomatillo Sauce
Salsa de Tomatillo

Makes about 1 cup

Pan-roasting the tomatillos and onion give this salsa a slightly smoky flavor. Serrano chiles punch up the heat and a touch of sugar balances the tartness of the tomatillos. It's a classic green salsa and one of my personal favorites.

¹/₂ pound fresh tomatillos, husked and rinsed
1 round slice (¹/₂-inch thick) white medium onion
¹/₄ teaspoon olive oil
2 small serrano chiles, chopped with seeds
¹/₂ cup loosely packed coarsely chopped fresh cilantro
¹/₄ teaspoon salt, or to taste
¹/₄ teaspoon sugar

1. Heat a large nonstick skillet over medium heat. Add the tomatillos and toast, turning, until charred in spots, about 5 to 6 minutes. In the same skillet, put the onion slice on a small piece of aluminum foil and pan roast at the same time. Drizzle the oil over the onion and turn it 2 or 3 times until browned and softened, about 5 minutes.

2. Transfer the tomatillos and onion to a blender. Add the remaining ingredients and purée until nearly smooth. (There should be some texture.) Transfer to a bowl. Adjust seasoning. Serve cold or at room temperature. Salsa will keep refrigerated up to 3 days.

Tomatillo and de Arbol Chile Sauce
Salsa de Chile de Arbol y Tomatillo

Makes about 1 cup

A fiery table salsa made with dried chiles de arbol *and tomatillos is popular in many areas of northern Mexico. Add a spoonful to meat, poultry, or fish for a blast of flavorful heat.*

¹/₂ pound fresh tomatillos, husked and rinsed
1 tablespoon vegetable oil
4 chiles de arbol
¹/₄ medium white onion, chopped
1 medium garlic clove, chopped
¹/₄ teaspoon dried oregano (Mexican variety preferred), crumbled
¹/₄ teaspoon ground cumin
¹/₄ teaspoon salt, or to taste
1 tablespoon chopped cilantro

1. Cook the tomatillos in boiling water to cover over medium heat until just tender, about 5 minutes. Drain the tomatillos and put them in a blender jar.

2. In a small skillet, heat the oil over medium heat until hot. Add the whole chiles and fry 8 to 10 seconds. Drain on a paper towel and let cool; then remove the stems, break the chiles into small pieces and add to the blender. In the same skillet, sauté the onion, garlic, oregano, and cumin until the onions begin to brown, about 3 minutes. Add to the blender and blend until smooth. Add the cilantro, and pulse a few times to mix. Serve at room temperature, or cover and refrigerate about 3 days.

Tomatillo and Chipotle Chile Sauce
Salsa de Tomatillo y Chile Chipotle

Makes about 1 cup

Serve this tomatillo table sauce on any number of appetizers or as a topping on fish fillets or grilled chicken. Canned chipotle chiles en adobo can be purchased in Mexican markets and many supermarkets.

1/2 pound (about 12) medium tomatillos, husked and rinsed

2 tablespoons chopped white onion

1/4 cup loosely packed chopped fresh cilantro

1 canned chipotle chile en adobo, seeds and veins removed, and chopped

3/4 teaspoon salt, or to taste

1/4 teaspoon sugar

Cook the tomatillos in boiling water to cover until just tender, about 5 minutes. Drain under cold running water to stop the cooking and place in a blender or food processor. Add the remaining ingredients and blend until almost smooth with a little texture. Transfer to a bowl. Serve at room temperature, or cover, refrigerate, and serve chilled.

Tomatillo and Pumpkin Seed Sauce
Salsa de Tomatillo y Pepitas

Makes about 1¹/₂ cups

Toasting the tomatillos and pumpkin seeds enhances the flavors in this sauce that's great for dipping or as a table sauce to spoon over meats or seafood.

1/2 pound tomatillos, husked and rinsed

1/2 cup hulled raw pumpkin seeds

2 teaspoons olive oil

1/4 medium white onion, finely chopped

1 medium garlic clove, chopped

1/4 teaspoon dried oregano (Mexican variety preferred), crumbled

2 jalapeño chiles, seeded and chopped

1/4 cup loosely packed coarsely chopped fresh cilantro

1/2 teaspoon salt, or to taste

1/4 teaspoon sugar

1. In a small dry skillet, over medium heat, toast the tomatillos, turning frequently, until slightly softened and charred in spots, about 8 minutes. Transfer to a blender. In the same skillet, toast the pumpkin seeds, stirring, until they pop around in the pan and brown lightly, 4 to 5 minutes. Put in the blender.

2. Heat the oil in the same skillet and cook the onion, garlic, and oregano slowly, stirring, until translucent and lightly browned, 4 to 5 minutes. Scrape into the blender. Add the jalapeños, cilantro, salt, sugar, and 2 tablespoons of water. Blend to a smooth sauce with some texture. Transfer the sauce to a medium bowl. If too thick, add about 1 teaspoon of water at a time to achieve a dipping consistency. Adjust seasoning. Serve at room temperature.

Note: Sauce will thicken as it sits. Stir it well to bring it together, and add a bit of water, if needed.

Oaxacan Green Tomatillo Sauce
Salsa de Tomatillo Oaxaqueno

Makes **about 2 cups**

Almost everyone likes this rustic and surprisingly tasty Oaxacan smooth salsa with pan-roasted tomatillos, garlic, and smoky chipotle chiles. Serve with chips or as a condiment with poultry, pork or fish.

1 pound small to medium tomatillos, husked and rinsed

2 large garlic cloves, unpeeled

2 tablespoons vegetable oil

1/2 medium white onion, chopped

1/2 teaspoon dried oregano (Mexican variety preferred), crumbled

2 canned chipotle chiles en adobo, seeded

1 to 2 teaspoons adobo sauce from the canned chiles

A loose handful of cilantro sprigs (largest stems removed)

1/2 teaspoon salt

1. On a *comal*, or in a heavy dry skillet (preferably cast iron), roast the tomatillos, over medium heat, turning frequently, until they are barely tender and the skins are covered with black and brown spots. At the same time, put the garlic in the skillet and roast the cloves until they feel slightly tender when pinched. The pan roasting will take about 15 to 20 minutes. The skillet may be covered for the last 2 to 3 minutes to steam the tomatillos if they don't feel a little tender when lightly pinched. Peel the outer paper skins from the garlic. Put the roasted tomatillos and garlic into a blender jar. Cover the jar and blend about 6 to 8 seconds to a coarse mixture.

2. In the same skillet used for roasting the tomatillos, heat the oil, and sauté the onion 3 to 4 minutes, until softened and beginning to brown. Stir in the oregano and cook until aromatic, about 30 seconds. Scrape the onion and oregano into the blender jar. Add the chipotle chiles and adobo sauce. Blend until smooth. Add cilantro and salt. Blend briefly. (There should still be a bit of texture.) Adjust seasoning. Transfer the salsa to a bowl. Serve at room temperature, or cover and refrigerate up to 2 days.

Note: Sauce will thicken as it sits. Stir it well to bring it together, and add a bit of water, if needed.

Mild Tomatillo and Sweet Pepper Sauce
Salsa de Tomatillo y Chiles Dulce

Makes **about 2 cups**

Tart tomatillos and colorful sweet bell peppers make a table sauce that pleases heat-timid palates. Serve with grilled or roasted meats.

1 tablespoon vegetable oil

1/2 pound tomatillos, husked, rinsed, and halved

1 (1/2-inch-thick) center slice of red onion

1 red bell pepper, seeded and chopped or diced

1 yellow bell pepper, seeded and chopped or diced

1 tablespoon chopped fresh cilantro

2 tablespoons fresh lime juice

1 tablespoon olive oil

1/2 teaspoon salt, or to taste

1/8 teaspoon freshly ground pepper, or to taste

Heat the vegetable oil in a large nonstick skillet over medium heat. Add the tomatillos, cut sides down, and pan-roast until lightly browned, about 4 minutes. Put in a blender jar and reserve. In the same skillet, pan-roast the onion slice until lightly browned on both sides, about 3 minutes per side. Remove to a cutting board and chop coarsely. Add to the blender jar with the tomatillos. Blend to a coarse purée and transfer to a bowl. Add the remaining ingredients and serve at room temperature.

Yucatán Cabbage Salsa
Salsa de Col Estilo Yucatán

Makes about 2 cups

A crisp, fiery salsa made with shredded cabbage, red onion, and habanero chile was brought to the table at Café Express in Merida, in the state of Yucatán. The salsa was fiercely hot, but hard to resist. This recipe is my interpretation of that salsa. Mix this salsa in a glass or ceramic bowl. (The cabbage and acids in the citrus juices may react with the metal of some bowls, such as aluminum, and alter the color and flavor.) Serve with grilled fish, pork, or chicken.

$1/4$ **medium cabbage, very finely shredded**

2 **tablespoons minced red onion**

1 **habanero chile, seeded, veins removed, and minced (wear protective gloves)**

3 **tablespoons fresh lime juice**

3 **tablespoons fresh orange juice**

$1/2$ **teaspoon salt, or to taste**

$1/4$ **teaspoon sugar**

$1/4$ **cup coarsely chopped fresh cilantro**

Put all of the ingredients in a medium glass or ceramic bowl, and mix well to combine. Cover and refrigerate the salsa about 2 hours before serving. Serve cold.

Zucchini Salsa
Salsa de Calabacitas

Makes about 1$1/2$ cups

I have discovered that young small zucchini make an excellent salsa that goes very well with grilled and roasted meats. Zucchini salsa is not traditional, but can we ever have too many ways to use this abundant, nutritious squash?

2 **tablespoons olive oil**

$1/2$ **medium red onion, finely chopped**

$1/2$ **teaspoon dried oregano (Mexican variety preferred), crumbled**

$1/2$ **teaspoon salt**

$1/8$ **teaspoon freshly ground pepper, or to taste**

1 **tablespoon white wine vinegar**

3 **small zucchini (about $1/2$ pound), finely diced**

1 **small tomato, seeded, and finely chopped**

1 **serrano chile, minced with seeds**

1 **tablespoon chopped fresh cilantro**

1. Heat 1 tablespoon of the oil in a medium skillet over medium-high heat and sauté the onion 1 minute. Add the oregano, salt, pepper, and vinegar. Cook about 30 seconds; then stir in the remaining 1 tablespoon of oil and the zucchini. Cook, stirring, 30 seconds more.

2. Immediately transfer the zucchini to a medium bowl and cool 10 minutes. Stir in the tomato, serrano, and cilantro. Serve the salsa at room temperature within 3 hours for best flavor, color, and texture.

Fruit Salsas

Mango Salsa
Salsa de Mango

Makes **about 2 cups**

Mangos appear as one of the more modern salsas, and aren't we lucky that this versatile delectable fruit is available almost everywhere! Choose ripe mangos with yellow skin and a blush of pink to red with no soft or bruised spots. The fruit should feel firm, but not hard, when held in the palm. Mango salsa is especially good with roasted, grilled, or fried poultry, fish, or pork.

2 large mangos, peeled and cut into $^1/_2$**-inch dice**
2 tablespoons finely chopped white onion
2 tablespoons red bell pepper, finely diced
2 serrano chiles, minced with seeds
$^1/_4$ **cup fresh lime juice**
1 tablespoon chopped fresh cilantro
1 tablespoon finely chopped fresh mint
$^1/_2$ **teaspoon salt, or to taste**

Put all of the ingredients into a medium bowl and toss gently to mix. Refrigerate and serve cold or serve at room temperature within 4 hours for the best texture and flavor.

Mango, Papaya, and Poblano Chile Salsa
Salsa de Mango, Papaya, y Chile Poblano

Makes **about 2**$^1/_2$ **cups**

This tropical salsa comes from Chef Manuel Arjona, a native of Yucatán, and currently Executive Chef of Maya, in Sonoma, California. Yucatán's hot climate and mix of Mayan,

Caribbean, and Spanish influences make cold, juicy tropical fruits popular and welcome in any form. The sauce is good with Fish Fillets Baked in Banana Leaves (page 382), or other grilled fish or chicken.

1 large poblano chile, roasted and peeled (page 8)
1 large ripe mango, finely diced
1 cup finely diced Mexican or Hawaiian papaya (see Note)
$^1/_2$ **cup fresh lime juice**
$^1/_2$ **teaspoon salt, or to taste**
$^1/_8$ **teaspoon freshly ground pepper, or to taste**

Remove the stem, seeds and veins from the roasted poblano chile. Neatly dice the chile into ½-inch pieces and put in a large bowl. Add the remaining ingredients and mix to combine. Serve cold.

Note: Mexican papayas are much larger and shaped differently than Hawaiian papayas, so 1 cup of diced papaya is about the right amount for the salsa, or use 1 whole Hawaiian papaya.

Mango-Avocado Salsa
Salsa de Mango y Aguacate

Makes **about 1**$^1/_2$ **cups**

This is an easy new salsa combining traditional Mexican ingredients. Serve it as a topping for crisp tortilla chips or as a condiment with poultry, pork, or seafood.

1 large mango, peeled and finely diced
1 ripe avocado, peeled and finely diced
2 green onions, very finely chopped
1 jalapeño chile, finely chopped
2 tablespoons fresh lime juice
$^1/_4$ **teaspoon salt, or to taste**

Put all the ingredients into a medium bowl, and stir gently to mix. Refrigerate. Serve cold.

Jicama-Mango Salsa
Salsa de Jicama y Mango

Makes **about 2 cups**

Young Mexican chefs are creating some exciting new style dishes, such as this condiment inspired by one I had at the Villa Maria restaurant in the Polanco district of Mexico City. Polanco is one of the most fashionable residential and shopping zones in the city where recently a host of top restaurants have opened. It was served on the plate in a small mound to accompany grilled shrimp. For the most appealing presentation, dice the mango and peppers into very tiny pieces.

1 medium jicama, peeled and coarsely shredded
1/2 ripe mango, peeled and cut into 1/8-inch dice
1/2 red bell pepper, cut into 1/8-inch dice
1 jalapeño chile, seeded, veins removed, and minced
2 teaspoons unseasoned rice vinegar
1/4 teaspoon salt, or to taste

Put the shredded jicama in a clean kitchen towel and press out the moisture. Put the jicama into a medium bowl. Add the mango, red pepper, jalapeño, and vinegar. Toss well. Add salt. Put the relish in a serving bowl to pass at the table, or spoon about 2 heaping tablespoons on each plate next to the appetizer or the meat it accompanies.

Banana Salsa
Salsa de Plátano

Makes **about 2 cups**

Bananas make a surprisingly good salsa that tastes fabulous with swordfish, sea bass, and shrimp. This salsa is not traditional, but is made with traditional New World ingredients. To help prevent the bananas from turning brown, be sure to add the lime juice as soon as the bananas are cut.

2 small firm bananas, peeled and finely diced
1 tablespoon fresh lime juice
2 tablespoons very finely diced red bell pepper
1 serrano chile, minced with seeds
1 tablespoon finely chopped fresh mint
1/4 teaspoon salt

In a medium bowl, gently mix the bananas with the lime juice. Add the remaining ingredients and stir to mix. Cover tightly with plastic wrap and refrigerate until shortly before serving. The salsa should be served within 2 to 3 hours for best color and flavor.

Melon Salsa
Salsa de Melon

Makes **about 2 cups**

Contemporary Mexican and American chefs are using basic ingredients in new ways, giving spark and excitement to traditional dishes. John Ash, Culinary Director of Fetzer Food and Wine Center in California, prepared a similar salsa in a cooking class. Cantaloupe and honeydew combine in a fresh melon salsa that's a beautiful addition to chicken and pork dishes.

1/4 medium cantaloupe, peeled, seeded, and
    finely diced (about 3/4 cup)
1/4 medium honeydew, peeled, seeded, and
    finely diced (about 3/4 cup)
1/4 medium red bell pepper, seeded, and finely diced
1/2 cup finely diced jicama
1 tablespoon minced white onion
1 tablespoon chopped fresh cilantro
1 tablespoon minced fresh mint
1 serrano chile, minced with seeds
2 tablespoons fresh lime juice
1/2 teaspoon salt, or to taste

Mix all of the ingredients together in a medium bowl. Cover and refrigerate until cold, about 1 hour. Serve chilled.

neapple Salsa
lsa de Piña

*eapple is native to Central and South
erica and is grown in most of Mexico's
pical regions and distributed throughout
xico year round. Many supermarkets in the
ited States offer pre-peeled fresh pineapple,
l in plastic containers or packages. They are
reat convenience to use for this salsa if you
pressed for time. Serve with Turkey Cutlets
h Almond Crust (page 312) or Duck in
en Pumpkin Seed Sauce (page 322).*

fresh pineapple, about 1¹/₂ pounds
medium red bell pepper, finely chopped
lapeño chiles, seeded, veins removed,
  and minced
:allion, minced
blespoon white wine vinegar
aspoon sugar
easpoon salt, or to taste
blespoons chopped fresh cilantro

Cut off both ends of the pineapple and then
off the hard thorny skin all the way around
: pineapple. Cut out the "eyes." Cut the pine-
ple in half lengthwise and cut out the center
re from each half. Cut the pineapple in ½-inch
eces and put them in a large bowl.
. Add the remaining ingredients and stir gently
) combine. Cover and refrigerate at least 1 hour
r up to 6 hours. Serve cold.

Pineapple, Jicama, and Bell Pepper Salsa
Salsa de Piña, Jicama, y Chile Dulce

Makes **about 2¹/₂ cups**

*This refreshing spicy-sweet fruit salsa goes espe-
cially well with pork, poultry, and seafood.*

¹/₂ fresh pineapple, about 1¹/₂ pounds
¹/₂ red bell pepper, finely diced
¹/₂ green bell pepper, finely diced
³/₄ cup finely diced jicama
2 tablespoons finely chopped white onion
2 serrano chiles, minced with seeds
2 tablespoons unseasoned rice vinegar
¹/₂ teaspoon salt, or to taste
¹/₈ teaspoon freshly ground pepper, or to taste
¹/₃ cup chopped fresh cilantro
2 teaspoons minced fresh mint

1. Cut off both ends of the pineapple and then
cut off the hard thorny skin and remove the
"eyes." Cut pineapple in half lengthwise and cut
out the center core from each piece. Cut the
pineapple in ½-inch pieces and put them in a
large bowl.

2. Add the remaining ingredients and stir gently
to combine. Cover and refrigerate at least 1 hour
or up to 6 hours. Serve cold.

Cooking Sauces

Basic Cooked Tomato Sauce
Salsa de Jitomate

Makes about 2 cups

This basic cooked tomato sauce and the other variations that follow are typical of tomato sauces from the Mexican kitchen, and are used for many dishes. It should be made with vine-ripened and flavorful tomatoes, otherwise, use good-quality canned tomatoes. This sauce has a little heat from serranos; discard some of the seeds for a milder sauce. The sauce keeps refrigerated up to 5 days, or frozen up to 3 months.

2 tablespoons vegetable oil

1/2 medium white onion, chopped

1/2 teaspoon dried oregano (Mexican variety preferred), crumbled

4 large ripe tomatoes, peeled and chopped, or 1 (141/2-ounce) can diced, peeled, no salt tomatoes

2 serrano chiles, finely chopped with seeds

1/2 teaspoon salt, or to taste

1/8 teaspoon freshly ground pepper, or to taste

1. In a medium saucepan, heat the oil over medium heat, and cook the onion and oregano, stirring frequently, until the onion is softened, about 4 minutes. Scrape into a blender jar. Add the tomatoes, chiles, salt, and pepper. Blend to a coarse purée.

2. Return the sauce to the same pan, and bring to a boil. Reduce the heat, cover, and simmer the sauce 10 minutes, stirring frequently, to blend the flavors. Serve.

Basic Roasted Tomato Sauce
Salsa de Jitomate Casera

Makes about 11/2 cups

This is a typical cooked tomato sauce to use in stews with vegetables, or to serve with meats or poultry dishes.

4 large ripe tomatoes, roasted (page 8)

1 tablespoon vegetable oil or olive oil

1/2 medium white onion, chopped

2 medium garlic cloves, chopped

1 to 2 serrano chiles, chopped

1/2 teaspoon dried oregano (Mexican variety preferred), crumbled

1/2 teaspoon ground cumin

1/4 teaspoon dried thyme

1/4 teaspoon salt, or to taste

1. Roast the tomatoes and reserve. Then, heat the oil in a small skillet over medium heat. Add the onion and cook, stirring, until it begins to brown, 4 to 5 minutes. Add the garlic and cook, stirring, 1 minute.

2. Transfer the onions and garlic to a blender jar or food processor. Add the roasted tomatoes and the juices that collected while roasting. Add the serranos, oregano, cumin, and thyme. Blend until almost smooth, with some texture.

3. Pour the sauce into a medium saucepan, and simmer, partially covered, over medium-low heat about 10 minutes, to blend the flavors. Season with salt. Serve.

Tomato Sauce for Stuffed Chiles
Salsa de Jitomate para Chiles Rellenos

Makes **about 3 cups**

Typical Chiles Rellenos *(pages 421–428), or stuffed chiles, are often served with this cooked tomato sauce. The brothy sauce is also good served with roasted pork or chicken. It can be made ahead, covered and refrigerated for several hours or overnight, for best flavor.*

4 large ripe tomatoes, peeled and chopped

2 tablespoons chopped white onion

2 medium garlic cloves, chopped

2 tablespoons vegetable oil

1/2 teaspoon dried oregano (Mexican variety preferred), crumbled

1/2 teaspoon ground cinnamon (Mexican canela or Ceylon variety preferred)

1/4 teaspoon dried thyme

1 bay leaf

3/4 cup canned fat-free reduced-sodium chicken broth

1/2 teaspoon salt

1/8 teaspoon freshly ground pepper, or to taste

1. Put the tomatoes, onion, and garlic in a blender and purée until smooth. Heat the oil in a medium saucepan then pour in the tomato mixture. Cook over medium-high heat, stirring, until the tomato juices reduce a little, 3 to 4 minutes.

2. Add the remaining ingredients. Reduce the heat to low and simmer, uncovered, stirring occasionally, 12 to 15 minutes, to blend the flavors. Serve hot.

Tomato Sauce for Folded Tortillas
Salsa de Jitomate para Entomatadas

Makes **about 2¹/₂ cups**

This is the sauce for a traditional dish of sauced and folded tortillas from Oaxaca called entomatadas *(Folded Tortillas in Tomato Sauce, page 144). The sauce is also very good spooned over chicken, pork, or stuffed chiles.*

5 to 6 medium tomatoes (about 2 pounds), peeled and chopped

1 tablespoon olive oil or vegetable oil

1 medium white onion, finely chopped

4 medium garlic cloves, finely chopped

1 teaspoon dried oregano (Mexican variety preferred), crumbled

1/2 teaspoon ground cinnamon (Mexican canela or Ceylon variety preferred)

1/4 teaspoon ground allspice

1/4 teaspoon crushed red pepper

1 teaspoon dark brown sugar

1 teaspoon salt, or to taste

1/8 teaspoon freshly ground pepper, or to taste

Put the tomatoes in a blender and blend until smooth. Reserve in the blender. In a large saucepan, heat the oil over medium heat and cook the onion, stirring, until softened, 3 to 4 minutes. Add the garlic and cook until it lightly browned. Add the puréed tomatoes and all the remaining ingredients. Bring to a boil, then reduce the heat to low and simmer until the sauce thickens a little, about 5 minutes. Adjust seasoning. The sauce is ready to use, or if made ahead, cover and refrigerate for 3 days, or freeze for 3 months.

Tomato Sauce for Tortas
Salsa de Jitomate para Tortas

Makes **about 2 cups**

This simple mild tomato sauce is used for tortas (sandwiches) called ahogadas, *such as Pork Sandwiches with Tomato Sauce (page 120), and can also be added to soups or some casseroles. The sauce freezes well and it's handy to have a container or two in the freezer.*

1 pound plum tomatoes, peeled and chopped
2 tablespoons chopped onion
1 medium garlic clove, finely chopped
1/4 teaspoon salt, or to taste
2 teaspoons olive oil

Put the tomatoes, onion, garlic, salt, and 1/4 cup water in a blender and blend until smooth. Heat the oil in a medium saucepan over medium heat until it shimmers. Add the tomato mixture gently to the hot oil (to minimize splattering), and bring to a boil. Reduce the heat to low, cover and cook, stirring frequently, about 12 minutes, or until the onion no longer tastes raw. The sauce is ready to use, or cover and refrigerate up to 5 days or freeze up to 3 months.

Ranchera Sauce
Salsa Ranchera

Makes **about 2 cups**

This is the sauce for the well-known Huevos Rancheros *(page 492). It is also used in meat dishes and some tortilla appetizers or casseroles.*

1 tablespoon vegetable oil
1/4 medium white onion, finely chopped
2 large garlic cloves, chopped
21/2 pounds medium tomatoes, oven-roasted (page 8)
2 to 3 serrano chiles, chopped with seeds
1/2 teaspoon salt, or to taste

1. In a medium skillet, heat the oil over medium heat and cook the onion and garlic, stirring, until they begin to brown, 4 to 5 minutes. Reserve in the pan off heat.

2. Prepare the tomatoes. Put the tomatoes with skins and juices in a blender. Add the serrano chiles and blend until smooth. Transfer the sauce to the skillet with the onion and cook over medium-low heat, partially covered, stirring frequently, to blend flavors, about 10 minutes. Add salt. The sauce is ready to use, or store the sauce in a covered container, refrigerated, up to 3 days, or freeze up to 3 months.

Yucatán Tomato Sauce
Salsa de Tomate Yucatecan

Makes **about 2 cups**

Make this sauce with the best and ripest tomatoes, and it will have a rich and marvelous flavor. Use this sauce with Huevos Motuleños *(page 501), a favorite Yucatán egg dish made with beans, peas, and ham; and with grilled chicken.*

6 medium-size ripe tomatoes
2 to 3 serrano chiles, chopped with seeds
3 tablespoons vegetable oil
1 large white onion, finely chopped
1/2 teaspoon salt
1/8 teaspoon freshly ground pepper, or to taste

1. Line a baking sheet with foil. Put the tomatoes on the baking sheet, and broil them under an oven broiler, about 5 inches from the heat until the skins are lightly charred, about 6 to 8 minutes. Turn the tomatoes over with tongs to char all sides as evenly as possible. Remove and discard the cores. Put the tomatoes in a blender jar with the skins on. Add the serrano peppers, and blend until smooth. Reserve in the jar.

2. In a medium pan, heat the oil over medium heat and cook the onion, stirring frequently, until it begins to brown, about 4 minutes. Add the reserved tomato mixture, salt, and pepper. Cook the sauce partially covered, stirring frequently, over medium-low heat about 15 minutes, or until thoroughly cooked and the flavors are blended. Adjust seasoning, if needed. The sauce keeps for 5 or 6 days refrigerated, or can be frozen up to 3 months.

Yucatán White Sauce
Yucatán Salsa Blanca

Makes **about 2 cups**

This is the traditional gravy to serve with Yucatán Stuffed Turkey Breast (page 318). The sauce is also good as a topping over cauliflower or broccoli.

2 tablespoons unsalted butter
2 tablespoons all-purpose flour
2 cups canned chicken broth or turkey broth
Salt, to taste

In a medium saucepan, melt the butter over medium heat. Stir in the flour and cook, stirring, about 1 minute. Remove the pan from and heat and add the broth all at once. Whisk to mix. Return the pan to the heat and whisk constantly until the sauce comes to a boil and thickens, about 6 to 8 minutes. Add salt, if needed.

White Sauce with Tomatoes
Salsa Blanca con Jitomates

Makes **about 3 cups**

Although Yucatán White Sauce (preceding recipe) is commonly served with Yucatán Stuffed Turkey Breast with White Sauce (page 318), I also serve the turkey with this sauce. My friends and students like it, and you will, too.

3 tablespoons unsalted butter
3 tablespoons all-purpose flour
2 tablespoons finely chopped white onion
2 tablespoons finely chopped green bell pepper
1 serrano chile, minced with seeds
2 cups canned fat-free reduced-sodium chicken broth
10 pimiento-stuffed green olives, sliced in thirds
1/2 teaspoon salt, or to taste
2 medium tomatoes, peeled, seeded, and diced (1/2-inch)

1. In a medium saucepan, melt the butter over medium heat. Stir in the flour and cook, stirring 1 minute. Stir in the onion and cook until the onion softens, 3 to 4 minutes.

2. Remove the pan from the heat and add the remaining ingredients except the tomatoes. Stir to mix and return the pan to the heat. Cook, uncovered, stirring frequently, until the sauce thickens, 8 to 10 minutes. Stir in the tomatoes. Bring to a boil, reduce heat to low and simmer 3 minutes. Cover and keep warm, or if made ahead, refrigerate up to 2 days.

Basic Cooked Tomatillo Sauce
Salsa Tomatillo

Makes about 2 cups

This is a quick salsa verde *for enchiladas and chilaquiles (a dish in which strips or triangles of corn tortilla are combined with shredded meats, cheese, or other ingredients mixed with a sauce), or to use whenever a recipe calls for a cooked green sauce.*

1 pound tomatillos, husks removed, rinsed and
    quartered
1/2 medium white onion, chopped
1 medium garlic clove, finely chopped
1 to 2 jalapeño chiles, seeded and chopped
1/2 cup loosely packed fresh cilantro
1/2 teaspoon dried oregano (Mexican variety
    preferred), crumbled
1/2 teaspoon ground cumin
1/4 teaspoon sugar
1/2 cup canned fat-free reduced-sodium
    chicken broth
1/2 teaspoon salt, or to taste

Put all of the ingredients except the chicken broth and the salt, in a blender jar, and blend to a smooth purée. Pour into a medium saucepan and stir in the chicken broth. Bring to a boil; then reduce the heat to low and simmer, partially covered, stirring occasionally, until the sauce thickens a bit and is completely cooked, about 15 minutes. Adjust seasoning. The sauce is ready to use; or cool, cover, and refrigerate up to 5 days, or freeze up to 3 months.

Tomatillo Sauce with Mushrooms and Carrots
Salsa Tomatillo con Hongos y Zarajorias

Makes about 1 1/2 cups

This cooked tomatillo sauce has the added colors, flavors, and texture of carrot and mushrooms. The sauce is good served over just about any meat, or for a vegetarian meal, over rice or pasta.

1/2 pound tomatillos, husked and rinsed
2 tablespoons chopped white onion
2 medium garlic cloves, finely chopped
1 serrano chile, finely chopped with seeds
1/2 teaspoon ground cumin
1/2 teaspoon sugar
1/4 teaspoon salt, or to taste
1 tablespoon olive oil
4 medium mushrooms, finely chopped
1 medium carrot, peeled and finely chopped

1. Bring to a boil 2 cups of water in a medium saucepan, and cook the tomatillos over high heat until barely tender, about 3 minutes. Drain the tomatillos and put them in a food processor or blender. Pulse to a coarse puree. The sauce should have some texture.

2. Heat the oil in a medium saucepan over medium heat. Add the sauce and stir in the mushrooms and carrot. Bring to a boil then reduce the heat to medium-low, and cook, partially covered but stirring occasionally, until the mushrooms and carrot are tender and the sauce thickens, 8 to 10 minutes. Serve hot.

Basic Red Chile Sauce
Salsa de Chile Rojo

Makes about 2¹/₂ cups

This sauce can be used whenever red chile sauce is called for, such as for enchiladas and chilaquiles. Use gloves with the chiles.

6 guajillo chiles (about 1¹/₂ ounces)

4 large ancho chiles (about 3 ounces)

2 teaspoons vegetable oil

¹/₂ medium onion, chopped

2 medium garlic cloves, chopped

1 teaspoon dried oregano (Mexican variety preferred), crumbled

¹/₂ teaspoon ground cumin

2 medium tomatoes, peeled, seeded, and chopped

³/₄ teaspoon salt, or to taste

1. Wipe the chiles with damp paper towels. With scissors, cut off the tops and cut each chile lengthwise in half. Remove the seeds and veins. On a comal or in a dry skillet toast the chiles about 3 seconds on each side, holding them down with a wide spatula until barely blistered and aromatic. Do not burn, or they will be bitter. Submerge the chiles in a bowl of hot water, and soak about 20 minutes.

Modified Mild & Quick

1 vg can mild sauce

1 onion

2 garlic cloves

oregano

cumin

tomatoes

salt

2. Meanwhile, heat the oil in a medium skillet over medium-low heat and cook the onion and garlic slowly until they start to brown, 5 to 6 minutes. Stir in the oregano and cumin and immediately transfer to a blender. Add the tomatoes to the blender. With tongs, lift the chiles from the soaking water and put them in the blender. Taste the chile water. If it has a pleasant taste and is not bitter, add ¹/₂ cup chile water to the blender, along with ¹/₄ cup of water. (If it is bitter, discard the chile water and add ³/₄ cup of water.) Blend the mixture 1 minute or until the sauce is as smooth as possible, scraping down the sides of the blender jar as needed. Pour the sauce through a strainer or a food mill into a medium bowl. Discard remaining bits of tough skin and seeds.

3. Transfer the puréed chile sauce to a saucepan and simmer the sauce 15 minutes over low heat, stirring occasionally, until completely cooked and flavors are blended. The sauce is ready to use, or cover and refrigerate for 5 days, or freeze up to 3 months.

Ancho Chile Sauce for Enchiladas
Salsa de Chile Ancho para Enchiladas

Makes about 4¹/₂ cups

This sauce is especially good with enchiladas, such as Stacked Beef Enchiladas (page 142). (I also use it with Tamales with Beef or Pork, page 148.) It can be mild to medium-hot, because the heat level of chiles is never certain. The sauce is also good served with grilled chicken or roasted pork. Wear protective kitchen gloves when handling the chiles.

8 large ancho chiles

2 medium tomatoes, peeled and coarsely chopped

2 medium garlic cloves, chopped

¹/₂ teaspoon dried oregano (Mexican variety preferred), crumbled

¹/₂ teaspoon ground cumin

¹/₂ teaspoon dried marjoram

1 cup beef broth or chicken broth, canned or homemade (depending on the meat that's used for the enchiladas)

1 tablespoon vegetable oil

¹/₂ teaspoon salt, or to taste

³/₄ cup heavy cream

1. Wipe the chiles with a damp paper towel. Cut the chiles open and remove the stems and seeds. Heat a dry skillet over medium heat and toast the chiles, turning, until they are aromatic, about 10 seconds. Do not burn, or chiles will be bitter. Put the chiles in a bowl, add hot water to cover, and soak about 20 minutes. Drain, discarding the water.

2. Put the chiles, tomatoes, onion, garlic, oregano, cumin, marjoram, and broth in a blender. Blend, in batches if necessary, to a smooth purée. The sauce should have the consistency of heavy cream. If too thick, add about

1 tablespoon water at a time, to reach the desired consistency.

3. In a saucepan, heat the oil over medium heat. Add the chile purée. Reduce the heat to medium-low, cover, and simmer the sauce, stirring frequently to blend the flavors, about 15 minutes. Stir in the cream and heat through completely, 3 to 4 minutes. The sauce is ready to use, or store in a covered container, refrigerated up to 3 days or freeze up to 3 months.

Ancho Chile and Red Pepper Cream Sauce
Crema de Chile Ancho

Best w/ Red meat

Makes about 1 cup

Modern Mexican chefs are experimenting with traditional ingredients to create new sauces. This sauce is very good with steak or vegetables such as cauliflower, broccoli, and green beans.

1 large ancho chile, rinsed, stemmed, seeded, and veins removed (page 8)

³/₄ cup chopped red bell pepper

¹/₄ teaspoon dried oregano (Mexican variety preferred), finely crumbled

¹/₄ teaspoon ground cumin

³/₄ cup heavy cream

¹/₄ cup chicken broth, canned or homemade

¹/₂ teaspoon salt, or to taste

1. Prepare chile. Then, cut the chile into small pieces. Put in a small saucepan with all of the remaining ingredients. Bring to a boil, then reduce heat to medium-low and cook, stirring frequently, until the red pepper is tender, 6 to 8 minutes. Transfer to a blender and purée.

2. Press purée through a fine-mesh strainer back into the saucepan. Cook 1 minute to heat through. (The sauce should have the consistency of heavy cream.) The sauce may be covered and refrigerated for up to 2 days. It does not freeze well.

Ancho Chile and Red Wine Sauce
Salsa de Chile Ancho y Vino Rojo

Makes **about 2 cups**

Ancho chiles and red wine make a surprisingly ideal marriage. Try this sauce with Lamb Shanks in Ancho Chile and Red Wine Sauce (page 368), and Beef Steaks with Red Chile and Wine Sauce (page 337).

2 large ancho chiles, toasted and seeded, and veins removed (page 9)

2 plum tomatoes, cut in half lengthwise

2 large garlic cloves, peeled

1 teaspoon Worcestershire sauce

1/2 teaspoon dried oregano (Mexican variety preferred), finely crumbled

1/4 teaspoon crushed red pepper

1 cup canned fat-free reduced-sodium chicken broth

1 tablespoon olive oil

1/3 cup dry red wine

1 tablespoon unsalted butter

1/2 teaspoon salt, or to taste

1. Prepare the chiles. Then, cut the toasted ancho chiles into pieces and soak in hot water to soften for 15 minutes. In a small, dry skillet, pan roast the tomatoes and garlic until the tomatoes are lightly charred on both sides, and the garlic is slightly soft with some brown spots, about 5 minutes. Transfer to a blender. Add the soaked chiles, Worcestershire, oregano, red pepper, and the chicken broth. Blend until very smooth. Reserve in the blender.

2. In a saucepan, heat the oil over medium heat. Pour in the puréed mixture and cook, stirring, 1 minute. Add the wine and cook, partially covered. Bring to a boil; reduce heat to medium-low and cook, stirring frequently until reduced and

thickened, about 10 minutes. Stir in the butter and salt. The sauce is ready to use, or store, covered, in the refrigerator for 3 days or freeze for 3 months.

Chipotle and Tomatillo Sauce
Salsa de Chipotle y Tomatillo

Makes **about 1 1/2 cups**

Chipotle chiles are dried smoked jalapeños that are often canned in a red sauce called adobo. *Canned* chipotle chiles en adobo *are available in most supermarkets and Mexican grocery stores. Chipotles are very hot with a smoky taste. Add it to stews and soups, or spoon it over meats, poultry, and many other foods.*

7 medium tomatillos, about 1/4 pound, husked and rinsed

2 canned chipotles chiles en adobo

1 teaspoon adobo sauce from the canned chiles

2 teaspoons vegetable oil

1/2 medium onion, chopped

1 medium garlic clove, thinly sliced

1/2 teaspoon dried oregano (Mexican variety preferred), crumbled

1 medium tomato, chopped

1/4 teaspoon salt, or to taste

1. In a small saucepan, bring 1 cup of water to a boil then cook the tomatillos, uncovered, until they change color and soften, about 5 minutes. Put the tomatillos and 1/2 cup of the cooking water into a blender. Reserve.

2. In a medium skillet, heat the oil over medium heat, and cook the onion until it begins to brown, about 4 minutes. Add the garlic, oregano, and tomato. Cook until the juices reduce and the mixture is nearly dry, about 5 minutes. Transfer to the blender with the tomatillos. Add the salt. Blend smooth, then return to the skillet and heat through, about 2 minutes. Serve hot.

Guajillo Chile Sauce
Salsa de Chile Guajillo

Makes **about 1¹/₂ cups**

This basic red chile sauce made from dried guajillo chiles is used in meat, poultry, or fish soups and stews. Guajillos are mild to moderate in heat with a pleasing flavor.

12 guajillo chiles, toasted and seeded (page 9)
2 teaspoons olive oil or vegetable oil
¹/₂ medium white onion, thinly sliced
3 medium garlic cloves, peeled and thinly sliced
1 teaspoon dried oregano (Mexican variety preferred), crumbled
¹/₂ teaspoon ground cumin
¹/₂ teaspoon salt, or to taste
¹/₂ cup water or broth to suit the dish being prepared

1. Prepare the chiles. Then, break or cut them into pieces and put them in a bowl. Cover with hot tap water and soak about 25 to 30 minutes.

2. Meanwhile, heat the oil in a medium skillet over medium-low heat and cook the onion and garlic slowly, stirring, until they start to brown, 4 to 5 minutes. Stir in the oregano, cumin, and salt, then scrape the skillet contents into a blender. Drain the chiles then add the chiles to the blender along with the water. Purée as smooth as possible. If too thick to blend, add water 1 tablespoon at a time, until the purée is the consistency of ketchup. Pour the sauce through a strainer into a heavy saucepan. Push the pulp through with a wooden spoon. Discard the bits of skin and debris in the strainer.

3. Cook the sauce, covered, over medium-low heat, stirring frequently 6 to 8 minutes to blend the flavors. The sauce is ready to use or store in a covered container in the refrigerator up to 3 days, or freeze up to 3 months.

Guajillo Chile Sauce with Cream
Salsa de Guajillo con Crema

Makes **about 2 cups**

Guajillo chiles are among the most common dried red chiles used to make sauces for enchiladas, crepes, or to serve with mushrooms, fish, or poultry. Adding cream to the sauce makes it rich and elegant. The sauce is also very good without the cream. Dilute with chicken broth to the desired consistency.

2 medium tomatoes, cored and chopped
8 guajillo chiles (2 ounces)
2 medium garlic cloves, unpeeled
1¹/₂ teaspoons dried oregano (Mexican variety preferred), toasted
1 teaspoon cumin seeds, toasted
1 tablespoon vegetable oil
²/₃ cup cream or half and half
¹/₂ teaspoon salt, or to taste

1. Put the tomato in a blender. In a dry skillet, toast the chiles, turning, until aromatic and the color looks orange in places. Do not burn. Break the toasted chiles into pieces, discarding the stems and seeds. Grind in a spice grinder to a powdery consistency. (I use a coffee grinder reserved for spices.) Transfer to the blender.

2. In the same dry skillet, pan-roast the garlic until speckled with brown in a few places, about 5 minutes. Peel and put in the blender. In the same skillet, toast the oregano and cumin seeds until aromatic, about 2 minutes. Add to the blender with ²/₃ cup of water. Process as smooth as possible. Pour through a strainer into a bowl, pressing to extract all the pulp. Discard the bits of skin and debris.

3. Heat the oil in a medium saucepan over medium heat. Pour in the sauce and cook, partially covered, stirring frequently, to blend the flavors, 6 to 8 minutes. Stir in the cream and season with salt. Cook over low heat, uncovered, until thick and smooth, 3 to 4 minutes. The sauce is ready to use, or store in a covered container up to 3 days, refrigerated, or frozen for 3 months.

Chili Powder Enchilada Sauce
Enchilada Salsa de Chili en Polvo

Makes about 2¹/₂ cups

Here's an easy, convenient sauce to serve hot with enchiladas. Prepared chili powder in cellophane packages can be used to make a convenient and easy enchilada sauce. Pure ground New Mexican or California chili powders are available in most supermarkets or Latin American markets. California chili powder is less spicy than New Mexican chili powder.

2 tablespoons vegetable oil

1 tablespoon all-purpose flour

1 (8-ounce) can tomato sauce

¹/₄ cup pure New Mexico or California chili powder

2 cups canned beef broth or chicken broth

1 teaspoon dried oregano (Mexican variety preferred), crumbled

¹/₂ teaspoon ground cumin

¹/₄ teaspoon salt, or to taste

Heat the oil in a medium saucepan over medium heat and cook the flour, stirring, 1 minute. Stir in the tomato sauce and chili powder until well combined. Add the remaining ingredients and bring to a boil, stirring, then reduce the heat to low and simmer the sauce 15 minutes, stirring occasionally. Sauce is ready to use or store, refrigerated in a covered container for up to 5 days or freeze up to 3 months.

Serrano Chile Cream Sauce
Salsa de Crema con Chile Serrano

Makes about 1¹/₂ cups

I like this contemporary (nueva style) spicy cream sauce with chicken or pork. It's also very good with firm white fish, such as swordfish or sea bass. Try it with carrots, broccoli, corn, or other vegetables.

2 to 3 fresh serrano chiles, sliced in thin rings with seeds (wear protective gloves)

2 medium shallots, peeled and coarsely chopped

2 large garlic cloves, thinly sliced

4 tablespoons unseasoned rice vinegar

1 cup canned fat-free reduced-sodium chicken broth

1 cup heavy cream

1¹/₂ teaspoons cornstarch

¹/₄ teaspoon salt, or to taste

1. Put the serranos, shallots, garlic, and vinegar in a heavy medium saucepan and bring to a boil over medium-high heat. Boil until liquid boils down to about 1 teaspoon, about 2 minutes. Add the broth and cream. Boil briskly, stirring occasionally, until reduced to about 1½ cups, about 10 minutes. (Watch to prevent boil-over.) Pour the sauce through a fine-mesh strainer into a medium bowl. Press solids with a spoon to extract the juices. Discard the solids. Return the sauce to the saucepan.

2. In small bowl mix about 2 tablespoons of the sauce with the cornstarch and stir into the sauce. Bring the sauce to a boil. Reduce heat and simmer over medium-low heat until the sauce thickens and coats the back of a wooden spoon, 3 to 4 minutes. Add the salt. The sauce is ready to use, or cover and refrigerate up to 3 days.

Almond Sauce
Salsa de Almendra

Makes **about 2¹/₂ cups**

Toasted almonds combined with chiles, tomato, onion, and spices, makes a versatile spicy sauce to serve over meat, poultry, or seafood. Salsa de almendra is a classic sauce found throughout the country.

1 pound (about 8) ripe plum tomatoes, rinsed and cored
4 whole chiles de arbol
2 teaspoons vegetable oil
²/₃ cup slivered almonds
¹/₂ medium white onion, finely chopped
1 teaspoon cumin seeds
¹/₂ teaspoon salt, or to taste
¹/₂ cup water

1. Preheat the oven to 450°. Put the tomatoes on a foil-lined baking pan, and roast in the middle of the oven until the tomatoes are lightly charred and soft but still juicy, about 25 minutes. Put the tomatoes, with skins and juices, into a blender and reserve.

2. In a medium skillet, over medium heat, toast the chiles, turning them, until aromatic, 10 to 12 seconds. Remove and discard the stems and let the chiles cool. In the same skillet, heat 1 teaspoon of the oil and toast the almonds slowly, over medium-low-to-low heat, stirring constantly, until golden brown, 4 to 6 minutes. With a slotted spoon, scoop the nuts onto a plate to cool.

3. Add the remaining teaspoon of oil to the skillet and cook the onion and the cumin seeds until the onion starts to brown, about 4 minutes. Scrape the onions and cumin seeds into the blender jar with the tomatoes. Add the toasted nuts.

4. Break the cooled chiles into small pieces, and add to the blender with about half of their seeds. Add the salt, and water. Blend until thick and smooth with the consistency of thick ketchup. If the sauce is too thick, add about 1 tablespoon of water at a time and blend. The sauce is ready to use in your recipe, or store, covered, in a container in the refrigerator up to 3 days, or freeze for 3 months.

Walnut Sauce
Nogada

Makes **about 2 cups**

Walnut sauce is classically made as a topping for one of Puebla's most famous dishes, Chiles en Nogada *(page 427). This elegant dish features stuffed poblano chiles coated with walnut sauce and sprinkled with pomegranate seeds. It is most often served in autumn during walnut harvest. The sauce is also appropriate to drizzle over fresh fruits. Mexican crema is widely available these days and I recommend it above sour cream for this sauce.*

1 cup walnut pieces
¹/₂ cup milk
1 cup Mexican crema or sour cream
¹/₄ teaspoon ground cinnamon (Mexican canela or Ceylon variety preferred)
¹/₄ teaspoon sugar, or to taste
¹/₄ teaspoon salt, or to taste

Bring 2 cups of water to a boil in a medium saucepan. Add the walnuts and soak them off the heat about 10 minutes to rid the nuts of some of the bitter tannins. Put the nuts in a strainer and rinse the nuts with cold running water. Transfer the nuts to a blender. Add the milk and blend until smooth. Transfer the nut mixture to a bowl. Stir in the remaining ingredients until well combined. Adjust seasoning. Cover and refrigerate until shortly before using, up to 3 days.

Red Pumpkin Seed Sauce
Pipian Rojo de Pepitas

Makes **about 2 cups**

Red pumpkin seed sauce belongs to the family of pipianes that includes cooked sauces flavored and thickened with pumpkin seeds or sesame seeds. It is a delicious accompaniment to red meats, chicken, or turkey. Mexicans use fresh lard to cook this sauce for the special, rich flavor it imparts. Vegetable oil can be used for a different, although still-satisfying flavor.

3 **ancho chiles, cut in half, stemmed; seeded, and veins removed**

/2 **cup green hulled pumpkin seeds (pepitas)**

4 **small plum tomatoes (6 ounces), cored and chopped**

/4 **medium white onion, chopped**

2 **medium garlic cloves, chopped**

/2 **teaspoon ground cumin**

/4 **teaspoon ground cinnamon (Mexican canela or Ceylon variety preferred)**

2 **whole cloves**

1/2 **cups chicken broth, canned or homemade**

tablespoon Basic Fresh Lard (page 19) or vegetable oil

/2 **teaspoon salt, or to taste**

1. In a dry medium skillet over medium heat toast the chile pieces until pliable and aromatic, 8 to 10 seconds. Put the chiles in a bowl and cover with hot water. Soak about 20 minutes or until softened.

2. In the same skillet, toast the pumpkin seeds, stirring, until they start to brown and pop around in the pan, about 1 minute. Transfer to a bowl to cool. When the seeds are cool, pulverize in a spice grinder to a fine powder. (I use a coffee grinder reserved for spices.) Reserve in a bowl.

3. Drain the chiles, discarding the liquid, and put in a blender. Add the tomatoes, onion, garlic, cumin, cinnamon, cloves, and 1 cup of the chicken broth. Blend until smooth. Add the reserved ground pumpkin seeds and blend as smooth as possible.

4. In a medium saucepan, heat the lard or oil over medium heat. Add the blended sauce, remaining chicken broth, and salt. Bring to a boil, stirring, then reduce the heat to low, cover, and simmer, stirring frequently to prevent sticking, until the flavors blend and the sauce thickens to the consistency of thick cream, about 15 minutes. Adjust seasoning. The sauce is ready to use, or store in a covered container for up to 3 days refrigerated, or freeze up to 3 months.

Green Pumpkin Seed Sauce
Pipian Verde

Makes **about 2 1/2 cups**

Sauces that are flavored and thickened with ground pumpkin seeds or sesame seeds are known as pipianes. *Tomatillos, fresh green chiles, onion, and herbs add depth to the bright, slightly tart, and nutty flavor of this sauce that's often used with chicken, duck, and seafood.*

3/4 cup hulled raw pumpkin seeds (pepitas)
1/2 cup lightly packed cilantro sprigs
1/2 pound tomatillos, husked, rinsed, and quartered
2 serrano chiles, chopped with seeds
3 tablespoons chopped white onion
1/2 teaspoon dried oregano (Mexican variety preferred), crumbled
1/2 teaspoon ground cumin
1/2 teaspoon salt
1/2 to 1 cup fat-free reduced-sodium chicken broth
1 tablespoon olive oil or vegetable oil

1. In a dry skillet toast the pumpkin seeds over medium heat, stirring, until they pop around in the pan, start to brown, and release their aromas, 3 to 4 minutes. Transfer to a bowl to cool. When they are cool, grind to a fine powder in a spice grinder. (I use a coffee grinder reserved for spices.) Put the ground pumpkin seeds in a blender. Add the cilantro, tomatillos, serrano chiles, onion, oregano, cumin, salt, and 1/2 cup of the broth. Purée as smooth as possible. If the sauce is too thick, add enough broth to make the mixture the consistency of heavy cream.

2. Heat the oil in a medium saucepan over medium heat. Add the sauce and cook, stirring, 2 minutes. Reduce the heat to low and simmer the sauce, uncovered, stirring frequently, 15 minutes. Adjust seasoning. The sauce is ready to use, or store, in a jar or plastic container, cover and refrigerate up to 3 days or freeze up to 3 months.

Red Sesame Seed Sauce
Pipian Rojo de Ajonjoli

Makes **about 3 cups**

Chef Roberto Santibanez of Fonda San Miguel in Austin, Texas, shared this traditional sauce flavored and thickened with toasted sesame seeds and ancho chiles. Serve with poultry, pork, or other meats.

6 ancho chiles
1/2 cup sesame seeds
1/4 teaspoon anise seeds
2 whole cloves
2 tablespoons olive oil or vegetable oil
1/4 medium white onion, chopped
1 large garlic clove, thinly sliced
1/2 teaspoon salt
1/4 teaspoon ground cinnamon (Mexican canela or Ceylon variety preferred)
2 to 2 1/2 cups chicken broth, canned or homemade

1. Wipe the chiles with a damp paper towel. Cut the chiles open. Discard stems, seeds, and veins. In a dry skillet over medium heat toast the chiles, turning them, until aromatic and slightly blistered, about 10 seconds. Put in a bowl, cover with hot water, and soak 20 minutes until softened. In the same skillet, toast the sesame seeds, stirring frequently, until they are fragrant and lightly colored. Do not burn. Cool in a bowl. When the seeds are cool put them in a spice grinder. (I use a coffee grinder reserved for spices.) Add the anise seeds and cloves. Grind to a powder. Reserve.

2. Heat 1 tablespoon of the oil in the same skillet and cook the onion and garlic over medium-low heat, stirring, until softened, 3 to 4 minutes. Transfer to a blender. Drain the chiles, discarding the liquid, and add them to the blender. Add the ground seed mixture, salt, cinnamon, and 1 1/2 cups of chicken broth. Blend as smooth as possible. If too thick to blend, add enough broth to reach the consistency of ketchup.

3. Heat the remaining tablespoon of oil in a medium saucepan over medium heat then add the sauce gently (to minimize splattering), and cook, stirring, for 3 minutes. Add the remaining broth, bring to a boil, then reduce the heat to low, cover and simmer 20 minutes to blend the flavors. Adjust seasoning. The sauce is ready to use or store in a covered container and refrigerate up to 3 days or freeze up to 3 months.

Black Bean Sauce
Salsa Cocida de Frijoles Negros

Makes **about 3 cups**

Flavoring puréed black beans with the traditional ingredients for moles *produces a really good sauce that tastes much like a mole but is not as complex and cooks in much less time. Serve with tamales, over meats, or poultry.*

2 ancho chiles, cut in half, stems, seeds, and veins removed

1 1/2 teaspoons dried oregano (Mexican variety preferred), crumbled

1 teaspoon cumin seeds

1 tablespoon sesame seeds

1/4 teaspoon ground cinnamon (Mexican canela or Ceylon variety preferred)

1/4 teaspoon ground allspice

1 medium tomato, peeled and chopped

1 cup cooked black beans, canned or homemade, drained and rinsed

1 cup canned fat-free reduced-sodium chicken broth

1 teaspoon dark brown sugar

1 teaspoon cider vinegar

1/2 teaspoon salt, or to taste

1 tablespoon olive oil or vegetable oil

1. In a small dry skillet over medium heat toast the chile pieces until pliable and aromatic, 12 to 15 seconds. Put the chile in a small bowl and cover with hot water. Soak about 20 minutes until softened. In the same skillet, toast the oregano, cumin, and sesame seeds, stirring, until aromatic, 30 to 40 seconds. Transfer to a spice grinder (or coffee grinder reserved for spices) and let cool; then grind to a powder, and put into a blender.

2. Drain the chiles, discarding the soaking water, and add the chiles to the blender along with the cinnamon, allspice, tomato, beans, chicken broth, sugar, vinegar, and salt. Blend as smooth as possible.

3. In a medium saucepan heat the oil over medium heat. Add the puréed sauce and cook, stirring frequently to prevent sticking, until the sauce is the consistency of ketchup, about 5 minutes. If the sauce is too thick, add a bit of broth or water to reach the desired consistency. Cover, reduce heat to low, and simmer 5 more minutes to blend flavors. Adjust seasoning. The sauce is ready to use, or cover and refrigerate up to 3 days or freeze up to 3 months.

Easy Mole from Prepared Paste
Mole Rapido

Makes about 3 cups

Mole paste containing all of the ingredients needed to make mole poblano *is commonly available in jars. I like to prepare the entire amount of an 8-ounce jar and cook the sauce one or two days in advance giving the flavors time to develop. Leftover sauce stored in a covered container, freezes very well for up to 6 months. Serve the sauce over roasted, fried, or grilled chicken or turkey breast.*

1 (8-ounce) jar prepared mole poblano paste
1 (14¹/₂-ounce) can fat-free reduced-sodium chicken broth
¹/₂ cup water

Pour the oil that has risen to the top of the jar of mole paste into a large saucepan. Heat the oil over medium heat and add the paste, stirring, until the paste softens, 3 to 4 minutes. Stir in the broth gradually. Stir in the water. Bring to a boil, reduce the heat to low, cover and simmer, stirring frequently, to prevent scorching, 15 minutes. The sauce should be thick and smooth with the consistency of ketchup. The sauce is ready to serve or in a covered container refrigerate 2 to 3 days or freeze for 6 months. If made ahead, reheat before serving over cooked poultry.

Mole Sauce from Puebla
Mole Poblano

Makes 7 to 8 cups

Mole Poblano is the best-known mole sauce from all of Mexico. The sauce is complex with ingredients that are roasted, toasted, fried, and blended before being simmered into the seductive dark and spicy sauce that's most often served over chicken or turkey. It's a labor of love to make this famous sauce from Puebla that legend tells us was first concocted by the nuns in the Convent of Santa Rosa. Every Mexican cook may vary the mole to her or his exacting standards. This delicious version is adapted from a recipe from Chef Ricardo Muñoz Zurita of Mexico City. It takes about 3 to 4 hours to make, but will be worth the effort.

4 cups chicken stock or canned chicken broth
6 mulato chiles
4 pasilla negro chiles
2 ancho chiles
Vegetable oil or lard for frying
³/₄ pound (5 or 6) plum tomatoes, cored
¹/₄ pound (3 or 4) small tomatillos, husked
2 (¹/₄-inch thick) round slices white onion
2 whole medium garlic cloves, peeled
1 (6- to 7-inch) corn tortilla, cut in quarters
1 slice (1 ounce) French bread
2 tablespoons raisins
1 cinnamon stick (Mexican canela or Ceylon variety preferred)
¹/₄ cup salted dry-roasted peanuts
¹/₄ cup slivered almonds
2 tablespoons hulled raw green pumpkin seeds
¹/₂ teaspoon cumin seeds
4 whole cloves
¹/₄ teaspoon whole allspice
2 teaspoons sugar
2 teaspoons salt
2 ounces Mexican chocolate (Ibarra or other brand)

1. Put the broth and 2 cups of water in a big pot. Bring to a boil, then reduce the heat to low and keep warm.

2. Wipe all the chiles clean with a damp cloth and split them in half lengthwise. Discard the stems, seeds, and veins. In a large dry nonstick skillet, toast the chiles, 2 to 3 at a time, until slightly blistered and aromatic, about 10 seconds per chile. Put the chiles in the pan with the broth as they are toasted. In the same skillet, heat 1 tablespoon of the oil and cook the tomatoes and tomatillos, turning frequently, until browned in a few spots, 5 to 6 minutes. Put the chiles in the pot with the broth.

3. In the skillet, cook the onion and garlic until they start to brown in spots, 4 to 5 minutes. Add to the broth. Fry the tortilla and bread until crisp and brown. Add to the broth. Add the raisins and cinnamon stick to the broth. Stir to mix and cook, uncovered, over low heat, until the chiles and vegetables are soft, about 20 minutes. When finished, remove pan from heat and let cool.

4. Meanwhile, put the roasted peanuts in a medium bowl. In a medium dry skillet, toast the almonds until they start to color and are aromatic, 2 to 3 minutes. Put in the bowl with the peanuts. In the skillet, toast the pumpkin seeds until they start to pop around in the pan. Add to the bowl. Toast the cumin seeds in the same skillet and add to the bowl. Cool the toasted nuts and seeds. When cool, pulverize all of the nuts and seeds to a powder in a spice grinder (or coffee grinder reserved for spices) along with the cloves and allspice. Grind in batches and reserve in a bowl.

5. Using a large slotted spoon transfer to a blender 2 to 3 cups of the cooked chiles and vegetables from the cooking pot. Add ¾ cup broth and purée as smooth as possible and pour into a large bowl. Repeat in batches until all are blended. Stir in the sugar, salt, and the ground nut mixture. Mix well.

6. In a large, heavy deep pot, heat 2 tablespoons oil. Add the blended mixture from the bowl. Bring to a boil, stirring, and cook 3 to 4 minutes. Reduce the heat to low and simmer, partially covered, 30 minutes. Stir frequently to prevent sticking. After 30 minutes, add the chocolate and stir, constantly to prevent scorching, until the chocolate melts. The sauce should have the consistency of heavy cream. If too thick, add more broth. Partially cover the pot, and simmer, stirring frequently, 15 more minutes. Adjust seasoning. The sauce is ready to use, or, in a covered container refrigerate up to 5 days, or freeze up to 3 months.

Note: Use protective kitchen gloves when preparing the chiles.

Oaxacan Red Mole
Mole Coloradito

Makes **about 4 cups**

Mexico's famous mole sauces come in countless variations and from different regions of the country. This red mole from Oaxaca is not too spicy. It's full of rich flavors with just a touch of chocolate. Serve over chicken or turkey. (The sauce is also used for tamales and enchiladas.) The sauce freezes well, so double the recipe if you wish.

6 guajillo chiles

4 ancho chiles

4 plum tomatoes (about 6 ounces)

3 tablespoons vegetable oil

1/2 medium white onion, chopped

4 medium garlic cloves, chopped

3 (1/2-inch) rounds of ripe plantain, peeled

2 (1/2-inch-thick) slices of sweet French bread

6 whole almonds

2 tablespoons sesame seeds

1 tablespoon dried oregano (Mexican variety preferred), crumbled

1 teaspoon cumin seeds

2 cups chicken broth, canned or homemade

1/2 teaspoon ground cinnamon (Mexican canela or Ceylon variety preferred)

1/2 teaspoon ground allspice

1/2 teaspoon salt, or to taste

1/8 teaspoon freshly ground pepper, or to taste

1/2 ounce Mexican chocolate or bittersweet chocolate

1. Wipe the chiles with damp paper towels. Cut open. Remove the stems, seeds, and veins. In a large dry skillet, toast the chiles in batches over medium heat, pressing down with a spatula until they turn orange in some places and are aromatic, about 10 seconds. Do not burn them. Soak the chiles, submerged, in a bowl of hot water about 45 minutes.

2. Meanwhile, preheat the broiler then broil the tomatoes until blistered and charred all over, about 2 minutes. Transfer with skins on to a large bowl and reserve. In a medium nonstick skillet heat 2 tablespoons of the oil over medium heat and cook the onion and garlic, stirring, until they begin to brown, about 3 minutes. Put in the bowl with the tomatoes. Fry the plantain and the bread in the same pan until brown on both sides, about 2 minutes. Reserve with the tomatoes.

3. In a small dry skillet, toast the almonds, stirring frequently, until they show some brown spots, about 3 minutes. Transfer to a small bowl and reserve. In the same skillet, toast the sesame seeds, stirring, until light brown, about 2 minutes. Reserve with the almonds. In the same pan toast the oregano and cumin. Reserve with the almonds.

4. Remove the chiles from the soaking water and put them in a blender jar with 1 cup of the chicken broth. (Discard the soaking water.) Blend the chiles as smooth as possible, adding 1 to 2 tablespoons of water if too thick to blend. Pour the chile purée through a strainer into a large bowl, pushing the pulp through with a wooden spoon and reserve. Discard the bits of skin.

5. To the same blender, add all of the remaining ingredients, except the chocolate. Add the remaining cup of broth. Blend until completely smooth. Add to the bowl of puréed chiles and mix well. Reserve.

6. Heat the remaining tablespoon of oil in a large heavy saucepan until it shimmers. Gently pour in the puréed sauce (to minimize splattering) and cook over medium-low heat, stirring frequently, 15 minutes. Add the chocolate and cook, stirring, until the chocolate melts, 3 to 4 minutes. The sauce should be the consistency of thick gravy. If too thick, add water or chicken broth, 1 tablespoon at a time, to reach the desired consistency. Reduce the heat to low, cover and simmer, stirring frequently to prevent scorching, about 20 minutes to blend the flavors. Adjust seasoning. The mole is ready to use, or cover and refrigerate for up to 3 days or freeze in a covered container for up to 6 months.

Peanut Mole
Mole de Cacahuate

Makes **about 3 cups**

Mole *is not just one dish or one sauce. There are regional* moles *made with different combinations of chiles, herbs, spices, nuts, seeds, fruits, tomatoes, and sometimes chocolate, and even more ingredients, all blended together to produce exceptional main dish sauces called* moles. *This orange-colored mole is thickened and flavored with roasted peanuts, guajillo chiles, and a long but flavorful list of other ingredients. Serve it with pork roast, chicken, or turkey.*

5 dried guajillo chiles (about 1 ounce)

3 tablespoons vegetable oil

3 tablespoons chopped white onion

2 medium garlic cloves, thinly sliced

1 (6- to 7-inch) corn tortilla, cut in quarters

2 plum tomatoes (6 ounces), cored and quartered

3/4 cup salted dry-roasted peanuts

2 tablespoons raisins

1 teaspoon dried oregano (Mexican variety preferred), crumbled

1/4 teaspoon ground cinnamon (Mexican canela or Ceylon variety preferred)

1/4 teaspoon ground allspice

2 cups canned fat-free reduced-sodium chicken broth

1 tablespoon cider vinegar

1/2 teaspoon salt, or to taste

1. Wipe the chiles with damp paper towels. Cut the chiles open and discard the stems, seeds, and veins. Put the chiles in a bowl of hot water and let soak 25 minutes.

2. Meanwhile, heat 2 tablespoons of the oil in a medium skillet over medium heat and cook the onion and garlic, stirring, until softened and starting to brown, 3 to 4 minutes. Transfer to a blender. In the same skillet, cook the tortilla pieces until crisp and lightly browned, 2 to 3 minutes. Add to the blender with the onion. In the same skillet, cook the tomatoes until the skins char a bit, 4 to 5 minutes. Add to the blender along with the peanuts, raisins, oregano, cinnamon, and allspice. Drain the chiles and add to the blender, discarding the liquid. Add 1¼ cups of the broth, vinegar, and salt to the blender and purée the mixture as smoothly as possible.

3. Pour the mixture through a strainer into a large bowl. Heat the remaining tablespoon of oil in a large heavy saucepan. Add the purée gently (to minimize splattering) and cook, stirring, about 1 minute. Add the remaining broth. Bring the mixture to a boil, stirring, reduce the heat to low, cover and simmer the sauce 20 to 25 minutes to blend the flavors, stirring frequently to prevent sticking to the bottom of the pan. The sauce should have the consistency of gravy. If too thick, add a little broth to reach the right consistency. Adjust seasoning. The sauce is ready to use, or cover and refrigerate for up to 3 days, or freeze in a covered container for 3 months. The sauce thickens as it sits. Thin with chicken broth to the desired consistency when reheating.

Yellow Mole
Mole Amarillo

Makes **about 3 cups**

Yellow mole is one of the traditional mole sauces of Oaxaca. Since the dried chiles (chilcostle and chilhuacle) *commonly used in Oaxaca are difficult, if not impossible, to find in the United States, guajillo chiles are often substituted to make the sauce. My modern version can serve as a guide until you eat the real thing in Oaxaca. Credit for adding yellow bell pepper to the mix goes to Chef Mark Miller of the Coyote Café in New Mexico, whose food always inspires me. The herb, hoja santa is difficult to find in many places. Fresh fennel makes a somewhat acceptable substitute, or just leave it out.*

4 guajillo chiles, stemmed, seeded, and veins
    removed

2 tablespoons olive oil

1 yellow bell pepper, coarsely chopped

1/2 medium onion, coarsely chopped

3 medium garlic cloves, thinly sliced

1/2 teaspoon sugar

1/2 teaspoon ground cumin

1/4 teaspoon ground allspice

1/8 teaspoon ground cloves, or 1 whole clove

6 tomatillos, husked, rinsed, and quartered

1 hoja santa leaf, coarsely chopped or substitute
    1/4 cup chopped fresh fennel

1/2 teaspoon salt, or to taste

1/8 teaspoon freshly ground pepper, or to taste

1. Submerge the chiles in a bowl of hot water and soak 30 minutes. Meanwhile, heat 1 tablespoon of the oil in a large skillet over medium-low heat and cook the yellow pepper and onion slowly, covered, stirring frequently, until they are limp and tender, 6 to 8 minutes. Stir in the garlic, sugar, cumin, allspice, and cloves. Immediately transfer the mixture to a blender.

2. Drain the soaked chiles, discarding the soaking water, and add to the blender along with the tomatillos and hoja santa. Add 1/4 cup of water and purée until smooth. If too thick to blend, add about 2 tablespoons water and blend again. Pour the sauce through a strainer into a large bowl, pushing with a wooden spoon to extract all the pulp. Discard the debris.

3. Heat the remaining tablespoon of oil in a saucepan. Pour the sauce into the pan. Add the salt and pepper. Cook, covered, stirring occasionally, about 10 minutes, to blend the flavors. The sauce is ready to use, or, refrigerate in a covered container, 3 to 4 days.

Red Bell Pepper Sauce
Salsa de Chile Dulce

Makes **about 1 cup**

Red bell peppers are referred to as sweet in Mexican cooking to distinguish them from fiery chiles. This puréed red bell pepper sauce has a mild flavor and is used to add eye-catching color to contemporary plates.

2 large red bell peppers, seeded and coarsely chopped
1 tablespoon paprika
1 teaspoon ground cumin
1 teaspoon olive oil
1/2 teaspoon salt, or to taste

Put all of the ingredients into a medium saucepan and add ¾ cup of water. Bring to a boil; reduce heat to medium, and cook, partially covered, until the peppers are very soft, about 10 minutes to 12 minutes. Transfer to a blender and purée until smooth. Pour the purée through a strainer back into the saucepan, using a spoon to press the contents. Discard the solids. The sauce should be as thick as heavy cream. The sauce is ready to use, or refrigerate in a covered container up to 3 days.

Red Onion Sauce
Salsa de Cebolla Roja

Makes **about 2 cups**

Cooked red onions take on an extra glow and a tart-sweet tang when red jalapeño jelly is added to the mix. The sauce is a take on Yucatán-style red onion salsas. At my house, we love it with pork roast and grilled chicken. Red jalapeño jelly is available in most supermarkets.

2 tablespoons olive oil or vegetable oil
2 large red onions, finely diced or minced
1¼ teaspoons salt, or to taste
1/8 teaspoon freshly ground pepper, or to taste
1/4 cup unseasoned rice vinegar
1 cup fresh orange juice
5 to 6 tablespoons red jalapeño jelly

In a stainless steel saucepan, heat the oil over medium heat. Add the onion and cook, stirring frequently, until it starts to brown, about 5 minutes. Add the salt and pepper. Reduce the heat to low and cook 5 minutes. Stir in the vinegar, orange juice, and jelly. Bring to a boil, and cook, stirring frequently, until the jelly is completely melted and the sauce reduces and is slightly thickened with a glossy appearance, 6 to 8 minutes. Serve hot, or store, refrigerated in a covered container, for 3 to 4 days. The sauce can be made ahead and reheated.

Appetizers *and* Snacks

Appetizers with Cheese, Meats, and Poultry 66

Melted Cheese Appetizer

Melted Cheese with Chorizo Sausage

Mushrooms with Melted Cheese

Baked Cheese with Green Sauce

Avocado and Cheese Appetizer

Chicken Wings with Tamarind and Chipotle

Yucatán Chicken and Bean Tortilla Snack

Chicken Tostadas

Smoked Turkey Tostadas

Shredded Beef Tostadas

Ham and Cheese Appetizer

Stuffed Mushrooms with Ham

Appetizer Meatballs

Meatballs in Almond Sauce

Appetizers with Fish 72

Spicy Baked Shrimp

Shrimp Ceviche

Shredded Shrimp Appetizer

Chilled Shrimp in Cilantro Salsa

Shrimp Salpicón

Shrimp, Puerto Vallarta Style

Fried Shrimp in Beer Batter

Shrimp Fritters

Shrimp Pinwheel with Jalapeño and Cilantro Sauce

Shrimp Cakes with Corn Salsa

Jalapeños with Shrimp Filling

Grilled Jalapeños with Tuna Stuffing

Tuna in Parsley Sauce

Mixed Seafood Cocktail

Marinated Fish Cocktail

Marinated Scallop Cocktail

Marinated Fried Fish Fillets

Return-to-Life Shellfish Cocktail

Oysters with Garlic and Lime

Steamed Clams, Baja Style

Clams Steamed in Beer

Clams in Red Chili Broth

Fried Squid

Swordfish Bites with Pineapple and Red Bell Pepper

Appetizer Fish Balls

Chopped Crab Appetizer

Caviar and Serrano Chiles on Crisp Tortilla Rounds

Chips, Dips, and Nachos 85

Fried Corn Tortilla Chips
and Strips

Toasted Corn Tortilla Chips

Crisp-Fried Whole Tortillas

Bacon Guacamole

Black Bean Dip

Refried Beans with Cheese

Green Chiles with Cheese

Almond and Cheese Dip

Olive and Tomato Dip

Yucatán Stuffed Cheese

Mushroom Appetizer Spread

Tuna, Capers, and Jalapeños

Bean and Cheese Nachos

Black Bean Nachos

Chorizo and Refried Bean
Nachos

Cheese, Jicama, and
Green Chile Nachos

Combination Nachos

Folded and Wrapped Tortilla Snacks 92

Crisp Rolled Chicken Taquitos

Crisp Rolled Flautas
with Chicken

Crisp Rolled Flautas
with Chorizo

Mushroom and Epazote Tacos

Creamy Mushroom Tacos

Cactus Tacos

Tacos with Steak, Cactus,
and Onions

Potato and Green Chile Tacos

Mashed Potato Tacos with
Red Salsa

Fish Tacos

Red Snapper Fish Tacos

Open-Faced Chicken and
Cheese Quesadillas

Chicken Quesadillas

Quesadillas with
Oven-Barbecued Beef

Quesadillas with Avocado

Quesadillas with Zucchini
and Cheese

Quesadillas with
Squash Blossoms

Quesadilla Stack with
Onions and Cheese

Quesadillas with Chiles
and Mushrooms

Goat Cheese Quesadillas

Chickpea Quesadillas
with Cheese

Yucatán Egg-Stuffed Tortillas
with Pumpkin Seed Sauce

Bean Burritos

Tijuana Pork Burritos

Grilled Chicken Burritos

Stuffed and Fried Flour Tortillas

These are the fun foods of Mexico that everyone loves to eat: very familiar ones like nachos, tacos, and quesadillas, plus *tortas* (Mexican sandwiches), and dozens of *antojitos*—irresistible finger foods made with both soft and crisp corn and flour tortillas.

To the uninitiated, the various folded and wrapped tortilla snacks made with corn and flour tortillas, can be confusing. So, here's a little primer of several kinds you'll find in this chapter:

Tacos are corn tortillas stuffed, then folded in half. They are usually served soft, but sometimes they are briefly fried to make them crisp.

Taquitos and flautas resemble each other closely: They are stuffed corn tortillas rolled into a cylinder, then fried. Taquitos are sometimes made with very small tortillas. Flautas are sometimes longer (like a flute), made with larger tortillas or with two overlapping tortillas, filled and then rolled into a cylinder. (In this book, the same size tortilla is used for both.)

Quesadillas—true to its name—always contains cheese. The tortillas are either folded in half (similar to a taco), or stacked like a sandwich. Either form is then toasted or fried to melt the cheese.

Burritos are always made with flour tortillas, are bountifully filled, and then one or both sides are tucked in and the tortilla is rolled to enclose the filling. Chimichangas are fried burritos.

Mexico is also known for the fantastic little Mexican snacks based on masa (corn tortilla dough)—such as *sopes*, *chalupas*, *garnachas*, and *picadas*—in which masa is formed into little tortilla cups or boats, that are crisp on the outside, soft on the inside, and topped with fillings of salsas, meats, cheeses, and other creative, flavorful combinations. Once you learn how to make the tortilla cups, you'll want to sample all the possibilities!

Mexican rolls are put to delicious use for tortas, such as Pork Sandwiches with Tomato Sauce (page 120), and Poblano Chile, Beans, and Cheese Sandwiches (page 123). The tortas are made with fillings reflecting a variety of regional flavors, and really are some of the best sandwiches in the world.

This chapter also contains recipes for easy dips and spreads and for delicious vegetable, meat, and seafood appetizers such as Fried Potato Chips with Lime and Chili (page 125), and Shrimp Cakes with Corn Salsa (page 77), to name just two. From all of these choices, you are bound to find some favorite recipes—to start off your meals, satisfy mid-day snacking urges, enliven any party or gathering.

Appetizers with Cheese, Meats, and Poultry

Melted Cheese Appetizer
Queso Fundido

Makes **4 servings**

The most common way to serve this simple but delicious appetizer that is popular throughout Mexico, is to place the plate of oven-melted cheese in the center of the table so guests can serve themselves. The cheese can also be melted in individual plates or ramekins and set at each place. Either way, you scoop a bit of cheese into a tortilla, roll it up, and eat! A bowl of Fresh Salsa Mexicana (page 24) accompanies the cheese.

3 cups shredded Monterey Jack cheese
8 (6- to 7-inch) corn or flour tortillas

1. Preheat the oven to 375°. Grease an 8-inch oven-proof plate or shallow earthenware casserole dish. Sprinkle the cheese evenly in the dish. Bake about 8 minutes, or until the cheese is melted and bubbling.

2. Meanwhile, warm the tortillas, 1 at a time, in a hot, dry skillet, turning once or twice until hot and pliable, about 2 minutes.

3. Wrap the hot tortillas in a napkin and put in a basket. Serve at once with the plate of melted cheese.

Melted Cheese with Chorizo Sausage
Queso Fundido con Chorizo

Makes **4 servings**

Bubbling, hot melted cheese (queso fundido) with crumbled spicy chorizo comes to the table in shallow earthenware dishes to be eaten with corn or flour tortillas. The cheese is scooped up with pieces of tortilla and eaten out of hand. This dish must be eaten as soon as it is served, because the melted cheese solidifies as it cools. Fresh Salsa Mexicana (page 24) should accompany the cheese and remember to warm the tortillas while the cheese is melting.

¹/₄ pound fresh bulk chorizo or other spicy sausage, casing removed
3 cups shredded Monterey Jack cheese
8 (6- to 7-inch) corn or flour tortillas

1. Preheat the oven to 375°. Cook the chorizo in a skillet, over medium-low heat breaking it up into small bits, about 4 minutes, or until well done. Transfer to a plate.

2. Grease an 8-inch ovenproof dish or shallow earthenware casserole dish. Spread the cheese in the dish, and bake until cheese starts to melt, about 4 minutes. Remove the cheese from the oven. Scatter the chorizo over the top, and return the dish to the oven until the chorizo is hot and the cheese is bubbling, 4 to 5 minutes.

3. Meanwhile, wrap the tortillas in foil and warm in the oven while the cheese is melting, or wrap in heavy plastic and warm in a microwave. Serve at once with the tortillas.

Mushrooms with Melted Cheese
Hongos con Queso

Makes **4 servings**

This variation of queso fundido *can be mild made with white button mushrooms or rich made with earthy portobellos or exotic porcini or shiitake mushrooms. Instead of wrapping the filling in soft, warm tortillas, serve this with crisp corn tortilla wedges. Each person can scoop or spoon the filling onto the chips. If fresh epazote is not available, fresh oregano can be substituted for a different herb flavor that also works well.*

Fried Corn Tortilla Chips (page 85)
1 tablespoon vegetable oil
1/2 medium white onion, chopped
1/2 pound fresh mushrooms, any kind, halved and
    thinly sliced
1 tablespoon chopped fresh epazote leaves
    (or substitute oregano)
1/4 teaspoon salt
1/8 teaspoon freshly ground pepper, or to taste
2 cups shredded Monterey Jack cheese

1. Prepare the tortilla chips. Then, preheat the oven to 375°. In a medium skillet, heat the oil over medium heat, and cook the onion until softened, 3 to 4 minutes. Add the mushrooms, epazote, salt, and pepper. Cook, stirring, until all the moisture has evaporated, 3 to 4 minutes.

2. Grease a shallow ovenproof earthenware plate or gratin dish, then transfer the mushrooms to the plate. Spread the cheese on top and bake until the cheese is melted and bubbly, about 6 to 8 minutes. Serve at once with the chips.

Baked Cheese with Green Sauce
Queso Asado con Salsa Verde

Makes 4 servings

Oaxaca cheese is available in many supermarkets and Mexican markets. For this appetizer, cheese is covered with salsa verde, *gently warmed in the oven, and immediately served with warm tortillas. You tear the tortilla into pieces and fold them around the cheese and sauce and pop the morsels into your mouth. This recipe is cooked in separate serving plates but you can also cook it on one large ovenproof plate for family-style eating.*

Basic Cooked Tomatillo Sauce (page 46)
1 (12-ounce) ball Oaxaca cheese, at room temperature
    (or substitute whole-milk mozzarella)
8 (6- to 7-inch) corn tortillas

1. Prepare the tomatillo sauce and keep it hot in a pan over low heat. Preheat the oven to 250°. Cut the cheese into 8 (1/4-inch-thick) slices.

2. Warm 4 ovenproof plates or individual round ramekins in the oven 3 to 4 minutes, or until warm to the touch, but not hot. Then, spread about 1/3 cup sauce on the bottom of each plate. Place 2 slices of cheese on the sauce in the center of each dish. Spoon about 1 tablespoon sauce over each piece of cheese and immediately put the dishes in the oven until the cheese is warm and soft but still holds its shape, about 3 minutes.

3. Meanwhile, wrap the tortillas in foil and warm in the oven while the cheese is melting, or wrap in heavy plastic and warm in a microwave. Serve the cheese and tortillas at once.

Avocado and Cheese Appetizer
Botana de Aguacate y Queso

Makes 4 servings

This is a sure-to-please appetizer. If you're short on time this botana *(quick snack) can be made with all store-bought ingredients. It's best, of course, with freshly made salsa and tortilla chips.*

1/2 cup Fresh Salsa Mexicana (page 24), or purchased
2 avocados (Hass variety preferred), peeled,
    and finely chopped or diced
1 cup Oaxaca cheese, fresh goat cheese,
    or other cheese of choice
1 bunch radishes, washed and trimmed
Toasted Corn Tortilla Chips (page 86),
    or purchased chips

Prepare the salsa and chips, if using homemade. Then, mix the avocado and salsa together in a serving bowl. Cut the cheese into strips. Put the bowl of avocado-salsa mixture in the center of a large serving plate. Surround with sliced cheese. Place the radishes on the plate at random. Put the chips in a basket to dip into the avocado mixture and serve.

Chicken Wings with Tamarind and Chipotle
Pollo con Tamarindo y Chipotle

Makes **24 appetizers**

Chicken wings are very popular as a finger food for informal parties or picnics. These are baked in a spicy contemporary tamarind barbecue sauce, similar to one from Santo Coyote Restaurant in Guadalajara.

Tamarind Paste (page 21)
2 medium garlic cloves, finely chopped
2 tablespoons ketchup
1 chipotle chile, seeded, veins removed
1 tablespoon frozen pineapple concentrate, undiluted
2 teaspoons honey
$1/2$ teaspoon dried oregano (Mexican variety preferred), crumbled
$1/2$ teaspoon dried thyme
$1/4$ teaspoon ground cumin
$1/2$ teaspoon salt
12 chicken wings, with tips removed, and cut at the joint

1. Prepare the tamarind paste. Then, measure out ½ cup and put into a blender. Add all of the remaining ingredients, except the chicken wings, to the blender. Purée until smooth. Transfer to a bowl and reserve.

2. Preheat the oven to 350°. Place the chicken wings in a single layer on a baking sheet. Bake, turning once, 30 minutes. Reduce the oven temperature to 325°. Brush the chicken with the marinade and continue baking until dark brown and tender, about 45 minutes more, basting with additional marinade every 15 minutes. Serve hot or at room temperature.

Yucatán Chicken and Bean Tortilla Snack
Panuchos

Makes **4 servings**

Panuchos are a common Yucatán snack. Small 4-inch corn tortillas, filled with mashed black beans and a slice of hard cooked egg, are fried and topped with shredded chicken or other meat and pickled onions. It might be difficult to slit open machine-made tortillas from the United States. Freshly baked tortillas tend to puff and create a space that is easier to slit, whereas commercial tortillas are more dense and don't separate readily. (If your tortillas won't open easily, lightly fry them, and layer everything else on top instead.)

1 cup Shredded Chicken (page 271)
1 cup Pickled Red Onions (page 19), at room temperature
8 soft (4-inch) corn tortillas
$1/2$ cup mashed black beans, canned or homemade
2 hard-cooked large eggs, peeled and thinly sliced

1. Prepare the chicken and the onions. Then, with a sharp knife, slit a pocket along one side of each tortilla by sliding the knife blade in an arc to create a space of about 2½ inches inside the tortillas. Spread about 1 tablespoon of mashed beans inside the pocket. Add 1 or 2 egg slices. Press closed.

2. Heat the oil over medium heat in a medium nonstick skillet and fry the filled tortillas until barely browned and stiff, 3 to 4 seconds on each side. Drain on paper towels. Transfer two tortillas to each of four plates. Top each *panucho* with ¼ of the shredded chicken and pickled onions. Serve at once.

Chicken Tostadas
Tostadas de Pollo

Makes **4 servings**

A tostada is a crisp-fried corn tortilla with a pile of good things on top. The tortillas can be fried 1 day in advance and stored in the cupboard in an airtight container.

4 (6- to 7-inch) corn tortillas
Vegetable oil for frying
1/2 teaspoon dried oregano (Mexican variety preferred), crumbled
1/2 teaspoon ground cumin
3/4 teaspoon salt
1/4 teaspoon freshly ground pepper, or to taste
4 skinless boneless chicken breast halves
2 cups coarsely shredded romaine or iceberg lettuce
1 cup coarsely shredded carrot
1 cup coarsely shredded peeled jicama
1 cup shredded Monterey Jack cheese
2 serrano chiles, minced with seeds
1/4 cup loosely packed chopped fresh cilantro
3 tablespoons olive oil
2 tablespoons unseasoned rice vinegar
1 cup Fresh Salsa Mexicana (page 24), or purchased
1/2 cup sour cream

1. In a medium skillet, heat about ½ cup of vegetable oil over medium-high heat. When the oil shimmers, fry the tortillas, 1 at a time, turning with tongs, until crisp and lightly browned on both sides, about 1 minute per side. Drain on paper towels. Set aside.

2. In a small bowl, combine the oregano, cumin, ½ teaspoon of the salt, and ⅛ teaspoon of the pepper. Rub the seasonings all over the chicken breasts. Remove all but 1 tablespoon of the oil from the skillet in which the tortillas were fried. Heat the oil left in the skillet and cook the chicken breasts until golden brown on both sides, 8 to 10 minutes total, depending upon the thickness of the breasts. Remove the chicken to a cutting board and let stand while preparing the salad.

3. In a large mixing bowl, toss together the lettuce, carrot, jicama, cheese, chiles, cilantro, olive oil, and vinegar. Season with the remaining ¼ teaspoon of salt and ⅛ teaspoon pepper. Toss again. To serve, place 1 tortilla on each of 4 serving plates. Pile the tossed vegetables equally on top, mounding a little in the centers. Slice the chicken breasts into thin strips and arrange on top of each salad. Garnish equally with salsa and sour cream.

Smoked Turkey Tostadas
Tostadas de Pavo

Makes **4 servings**

Wonderful tostadas can be made with deli-smoked turkey as the focal point of the tostada.

4 Crisp-Fried Whole Tortillas (page 86)
4 plum tomatoes, finely chopped
1 avocado (Hass variety preferred), peeled and chopped
2 green onions including the green, finely chopped
1 serrano chile, finely chopped with seeds
2 tablespoons chopped fresh cilantro
2 teaspoons fresh lime juice
2 teaspoons olive oil
Salt, to taste
1 cup finely shredded romaine or iceberg lettuce
6 ounces thinly sliced deli-smoked turkey, cut into thin strips
1/2 cup Mexican crema, sour cream, or mayonnaise

1. Prepare the fried tortillas. Reserve. In a medium bowl, toss together the tomatoes, avocado, green onions, chile, cilantro, lime juice, and olive oil. Season with salt. Reserve.

2. Put about ¼ cup of lettuce on each tostada. Divide the tomato mixture evenly on top of the lettuce and scatter the turkey on top of each tostada. Top each with a dollop of crema. Serve at once.

Shredded Beef Tostadas
Tostadas de Machaca

Makes **4 servings**

Shredded beef is easy to make and turns up all over in Mexican dishes in countless ways. Tossing the beef with salad ingredients and mounding it atop a crisp-fried corn tortillas to make tostadas, *is truly a fine treat. You can be flexible with the salad and add whatever suits you, using this recipe as a guide.*

4 Crisp-Fried Whole Tortillas (page 86)

2 cups Basic Shredded Beef (page 329)

2 cups finely shredded romaine lettuce

2 medium tomatoes, finely chopped

1/2 medium cucumber, peeled and thinly sliced crosswise

6 radishes, thinly sliced

1/4 cup coarsely chopped fresh cilantro

1/3 cup olive oil

2 tablespoons cider vinegar

1/2 teaspoon salt

1/8 teaspoon freshly ground pepper, or to taste

1 large avocado (Hass variety preferred), peeled, pitted, and sliced

1/2 cup fresh red salsa, purchased or homemade

1/2 cup crumbled queso fresco (fresh Mexican cheese)

1. Prepare the tortillas and the beef. Then, fry the tortillas (tostadas) and put 1 on each of 4 serving plates.

2. In a large salad bowl, put the shredded beef, lettuce, tomatoes, cucumber, radishes, and cilantro. Toss to combine.

3. In a small bowl, whisk together the olive oil, vinegar, salt, and pepper. Pour over the salad and toss to coat. Mound the salad equally on the tortillas. Arrange the sliced avocado equally on top. Add a portion of the salsa and cheese. Serve.

Ham and Cheese Appetizer
Sincronizadas

Makes **4 servings**

For a great treat, try this Mexican version of a grilled ham and cheese sandwich made with small flour tortillas. I had my first sincronizadas *in Leon, Mexico, where they were served as a light snack topped with fresh salsa and guacamole. At home, I cut them into wedges for an appetizer.*

8 (6- to 7-inch) flour tortillas

1/4 pound thinly sliced ham

1 1/2 cups shredded cheddar or Monterey Jack cheese

2 tablespoons vegetable oil

Fresh salsa or guacamole, purchased or homemade (optional)

1. Lay 1 tortilla on a flat surface. Cover with 2 slices ham to within 1/2 inch of the tortilla edge. Cut ham to fit, as needed. Cover the ham with about one quarter of the cheese. Top with another tortilla to create a sandwich. Place on a tray and repeat with remaining tortillas. Can be done ahead.

2. Heat a medium skillet and brush about 1 teaspoon of oil in the pan. Brown 1 sincronizada turning once with a wide spatula, until the cheese is melted and both sides are golden brown, about 1 minute per side. Transfer to a cutting board. Repeat until all are browned, brushing the pan with oil as needed. Cut into wedges and serve at once. Top the wedges with dollop of salsa or guacamole, if desired.

Stuffed Mushrooms with Ham
Hongos Rellenos con Jamon

Makes **16 appetizers**

Stuffed mushrooms are just the answer for a make-ahead party appetizer. This recipe is a twist on a snack of cooked mushrooms, onions, and chiles wrapped in corn tortillas that are sold by food vendors in central Mexico. It only takes a few minutes to finish the mushrooms under the hot broiler and they're ready to eat.

**16 medium brown cremini mushrooms,
    wiped clean**
2 tablespoons olive oil
1/4 cup very finely chopped white onion
**2 ounces very finely chopped deli-style sliced
    smoked ham**
**1 jarred pickled jalapeño (en escabeche), seeded,
    veins removed, and finely chopped**
1/2 cup grated Monterey Jack cheese
2 teaspoons mayonnaise

1. Remove the stems from the mushrooms. Finely chop the stems and reserve. Rub the mushroom caps with about 1 tablespoon of the oil. Heat a large nonstick skillet over medium heat and pan-roast the mushrooms, turning once until barely tender, 3 to 4 minutes. Transfer to a baking sheet and set aside.

2. In a small skillet, heat the remaining oil and cook the onion and reserved chopped mushroom stems, stirring, 3 minutes. Transfer to a medium bowl. When cool, add the remaining ingredients and mix well. Put about 1 rounded teaspoon of the ham mixture in each mushroom cap. If made ahead, cover and refrigerate up to overnight. To serve, preheat oven broiler and broil the mushrooms about 4 inches from the heat until hot and bubbly, 2 to 3 minutes. (Watch carefully to prevent burning.) Serve at once.

Appetizer Meatballs
Botana de Albondigas

Makes **about 24 meatballs**

One year, my husband and I rented a villa in Puerta Vallarta, and our delightful cook made these meatballs to dip into a spicy fresh tomato salsa, to accompany our cocktails. Here, little Mexican meatballs are simmered in broth instead of being fried. They are usually served warm with a fresh red or green salsa on the side for dipping.

1 1/2 pounds ground beef
1/2 small white onion, finely chopped
1/4 cup bread crumbs
1 large egg, beaten
1 tablespoon finely chopped fresh mint
1/2 teaspoon ground cumin
1/2 teaspoon salt
1/4 teaspoon freshly ground pepper, or to taste
1/4 cup prepared canned tomato sauce
Fresh Salsa Mexicana (page 24), or purchased
**4 cups canned beef broth, diluted with
    1/2 cup water**

1. In a large bowl, mix all of the ingredients together, except the tomato sauce and broth. With clean hands work the mixture together. Add just enough tomato sauce to hold the mixture together, making it moist but firm. Form into small meatballs 1 1/2-inch in diameter.

2. In a saucepan, bring the broth to a boil. Reduce the heat to medium-low and add the meatballs. Simmer about 25 minutes to completely cook meatballs. Remove the meatballs to a serving dish. Place a bowl of fresh salsa on the side. Serve with toothpicks.

Meatballs in Almond Sauce
Albondigas en Salsa Almendra

Makes **about 36 small meatballs**

Toasted ground almonds are used to thicken and flavor sauces throughout Mexico. This recipe features small ground turkey meatballs blanketed with a traditional pale red almond sauce—a great dish for parties.

Almond Sauce (page 52)
1 large egg, lightly beaten
1 large garlic clove, finely chopped
1/2 teaspoon ground cumin
1/2 teaspoon dried oregano (Mexican variety preferred), crumbled
1 teaspoon salt
1/4 teaspoon freshly ground pepper, or to taste
2 slices dry white bread, torn into pieces
2 tablespoons milk or water
1 1/4 pounds ground turkey meat
2 tablespoons vegetable oil

1. Prepare the almond sauce, then set it aside while making the meatballs. In a large mixing bowl, mix together the egg, garlic, cumin, oregano, salt, and pepper. Add the bread and the milk, and mix well until the bread is mushy. Add the turkey and mix thoroughly. (Mixture will be a bit sticky.) Form into small meatballs about 1-inch in diameter. Reserve on a plate.

2. Preheat the oven to 350°. In a large nonstick skillet, heat the oil over medium heat, and brown the meatballs, turning frequently, about 4 to 5 minutes. (Meatballs will not be completely done.) Transfer to an ovenproof casserole dish. Pour enough of the almond sauce over the meatballs to barely cover. (Save extra sauce for another use.) Cover the casserole dish and put it in the oven for about 25 minutes, or until the sauce is bubbling and the meatballs are cooked through. Serve with toothpicks.

Appetizers with Fish

Spicy Baked Shrimp
Camarones Picanté al Horno

Makes **6 servings**

Serve these spicy oven-baked shrimp with crisp tortilla chips and ice cold beer or margaritas. Pure chili powders are sold in cellophane packages in the Mexican section of many supermarkets and Mexican markets.

1 tablespoon pure ancho or pasilla chili powder
1/2 teaspoon dried oregano (Mexican variety preferred), crumbled
1/2 teaspoon ground cumin
1/4 teaspoon ground cinnamon (Mexican canela or Ceylon variety preferred)
1/8 teaspoon ground allspice
1/4 teaspoon salt
1 large garlic clove, finely chopped
1 tablespoon fresh lime juice
1 tablespoon vegetable oil or olive oil
1 pound (16 to 20) large shrimp, peeled and deveined, tails on

1. In a medium bowl, mix together all of the ingredients except the shrimp. Add the shrimp and toss to coat completely. Cover and refrigerate 1 hour or up to 6 hours.

2. Place the oven rack on the top level and preheat the oven to 500°. Oil a baking sheet. Remove shrimp from the refrigerator and place on the baking sheet in a single layer. Bake shrimp until pink and curled, and opaque inside, 4 to 5 minutes. Serve hot or at room temperature.

Shrimp Ceviche
Ceviche de Camarone

Makes **4 to 6 servings**

Traditionally, ceviche is "cooked" by the chemical action of the lime juice. (See Marinated Fish Cocktail, page 79.) Instead, for this ceviche the shrimp is briefly cooked in boiling water before marinating. People who are put off by the idea of eating raw fish like this method very much. Marinate the ceviche for 3 to 4 hours before serving.

1 pound (16 to 20) large shrimp, peeled and
   deveined
1 medium tomato, chopped
$1/4$ medium white onion, finely chopped
1 jarred pickled jalapeño chile (en escabeche),
   seeded and chopped
$1/2$ cup coarsely chopped fresh cilantro
$1/4$ cup fresh lime juice
$1/2$ teaspoon salt, or to taste
$1/4$ teaspoon freshly ground pepper, or to taste
1 large avocado (Hass variety preferred),
   cut into $1/2$-inch dice
2 teaspoons olive oil

Bring a medium pan of water to a boil. Cut the shrimp crosswise into thirds. Drop the shrimp into the boiling water until they just turn pink, about 45 seconds. Drain immediately and cool under running water. Put the shrimp in a glass or stainless steel bowl. Add the tomato, onion, jalapeño, cilantro, lime juice, salt, and pepper. Stir. Cover and refrigerate 3 to 4 hours. Shortly before serving, gently stir in the avocado and olive oil. Serve in small bowls, or cocktail glasses.

Shredded Shrimp Appetizer
Antojito de Camaron Deshebrado

Makes **4 servings**

Mazatlán, on the Pacific coast, attracts many tourists. The busy harbor is home to lots of shrimp boats and the restaurants reflect the abundance. At El Shrimp Bucket (a name anyone can understand), a festive place, shrimp is offered in just about every possible way, such as this tasty mixture to eat with chips or to roll up in a warm corn tortilla.

2 tablespoons olive oil
1 medium white onion, finely chopped
1 medium garlic clove, finely chopped
2 medium tomatoes, chopped
$3/4$ pound (14 to 18) medium shrimp, peeled,
   deveined, and very finely chopped
3 jarred pickled jalapeño chiles (en escabeche),
   seeded and finely chopped
$1/4$ teaspoon salt, or to taste
Lime wedges
(6- to 7-inch) warmed corn tortillas,
   or tortilla chips

Heat the oil in a medium skillet and cook the onion until softened, about 3 minutes Add the garlic and cook 1 minute. Add the tomatoes and cook, stirring frequently, until the juices are reduced and the mixture is nearly dry, 3 to 4 minutes. Add the chopped shrimp, jalapeños, and salt. Cook until shrimp pieces are pink, 3 to 4 minutes. Serve with lime wedges to squeeze over the shrimp when eaten with tortilla chips or soft, warm tortillas.

Chilled Shrimp in Cilantro Salsa
Camarones Frio en Salsa de Cilantro

Makes **6 as an appetizer**

Cold shrimp presented with a lively salsa makes for a simple but crowd-pleasing appetizer.

**1 pound (18 to 22) medium shrimp, peeled and
   deveined**
**1 serrano chile, stemmed, veins removed,
   and chopped with seeds**
1 small garlic clove, thinly sliced
1 green onion, chopped
¹/₂ cup lightly packed fresh cilantro
1 tablespoon unseasoned rice vinegar
¹/₄ cup olive oil
¹/₄ teaspoon salt, or to taste

1. In a large saucepan, bring to a boil about 2 quarts of water. Add the shrimp, reduce heat to low, and cook the shrimp until pink and curled, about 3 to 4 minutes. Drain the shrimp under cold running water and put them in a large bowl.

2. In a blender, purée as smooth as possible the serrano, garlic, onion, cilantro, vinegar, and oil. Season with salt. Put about 2 tablespoons sauce in the bowl with the shrimp. Toss well to coat. Arrange the shrimp on a serving platter in even rows. Put the remaining sauce in a small bowl for dipping. Serve the shrimp with cocktail picks and the remaining sauce.

Shrimp Salpicón
Salpicón de Camarones

Makes **8 to 10 appetizer servings**

A salpicón is made of ingredients that are diced or chopped into small pieces and mixed with a dressing or sauce. Serve this shrimp salpicón on crisp corn tortilla chips, or use as a filling for soft tacos. I also toss the salpicón with baby greens and a little olive oil for a new style salad.

**1 pound (18 to 22) medium shrimp, peeled and
   deveined**
**3 poblano chiles, roasted, peeled, seeded, and
   veins removed (page 8)**
2 serrano chiles, finely chopped with seeds
1 medium garlic clove, finely chopped
3 tablespoons fresh lime juice
1 tablespoon unseasoned rice vinegar
2 tablespoons olive oil
2 tablespoons chopped fresh cilantro
¹/₂ teaspoon salt, or to taste
¹/₈ teaspoon freshly ground pepper, or to taste

1. Cook the shrimp in boiling water to cover until pink and curled, about 3 to 4 minutes. Drain and cool under running water. Chop the shrimp into ¼-inch pieces. Put them in a medium glass or stainless steel bowl.

2. Dice the roasted poblano chiles into ¼-inch pieces and put them in the bowl with the shrimp. Add the remaining ingredients and toss well to mix. Cover and refrigerate until cold, about 1 hour. Serve.

Shrimp, Puerto Vallarta Style
Camarones Vallarta

Makes **4 servings**

For consecutive years, I arranged a special week for cooks in Puerto Vallarta. We stayed in beautiful seaside villas, and cooked, dined out, shopped, and lazed in the sun. During one of our cooking sessions, this shrimp dish evolved.

2 tablespoons olive oil
1 pound (18 to 22) medium shrimp, peeled and deveined
1 medium garlic clove, finely chopped
1/2 teaspoon salt
1/4 cup cider vinegar
2 ancho chiles, cut open, seeds and stems removed
1 teaspoon dried oregano (Mexican variety preferred), crumbled
1/2 cup coarsely chopped onion
1 teaspoon brown sugar
2 tablespoons hot tap water
1 tablespoon finely chopped fresh cilantro

1. In a medium skillet, heat the oil over medium heat, and cook the shrimp, garlic, and 1/4 teaspoon of the salt, stirring, until the shrimp are pink, 3 to 4 minutes. Remove the shrimp to a bowl, cover and refrigerate. Reserve the skillet for the sauce.

2. In a small skillet, heat the vinegar until warm. Cut or tear the ancho chiles into pieces and soak in the vinegar until soft, about 20 minutes. Remove the anchos then put them in a blender with the oregano, onion, sugar, and hot tap water. Discard the vinegar. Blend to a smooth purée. Heat the same skillet used for cooking the shrimp, and cook the puréed chile mixture, stirring, until thickened, about 5 minutes. Transfer to a bowl and cool. To serve, pool the sauce on a serving plate. Arrange the shrimp in an overlapping pattern on the sauce. Scatter cilantro on top. Serve as an appetizer with toothpicks.

Fried Shrimp in Beer Batter
Camarones Capeados

Makes **6 appetizer servings**

Restaurants, fast-food places, and food stalls in the fish markets in Baja all feature shrimp in many ways, and batter-fried shrimp is popular. Serve the shrimp with salsa, if you like.

1 cup all-purpose flour, plus extra to dust the shrimp
1 teaspoon salt
1 teaspoon sugar
1/2 teaspoon baking powder
1 cup (8 ounces) beer
1/2 teaspoon hot pepper sauce, such as Tabasco
Vegetable oil for frying
1 pound (16 to 20) large shrimp, peeled and deveined

1. In a medium bowl, mix the flour, salt, sugar, and baking powder. Add the beer and Tabasco. Whisk well until smooth. Set aside at room temperature about 1 hour.

2. In a medium saucepan, or deep-fryer, add oil to a depth of about 4 inches and heat until a drop of batter sizzles at once. Coat shrimp with batter. Using tongs, put shrimp into the hot fat and fry in batches until golden brown and crisp. Drain on paper towels and serve at once.

Shrimp Fritters
Tortitas de Camarones

Makes 12 to 16 small appetizers

This is an updated version of a recipe made with dried shrimp that's often served during Lent in the states of Chiapas and Oaxaca. Dried shrimp has a strong taste that many people don't like, so I use fresh, cooked shrimp.

1 to 1½ cups Fresh Salsa Mexicana (page 24), or purchased salsa
½ pound (36 to 40) small cooked shrimp, coarsely chopped
1 small jalapeño chile, seeded, veins removed, and minced
2 large eggs, separated
¼ teaspoon cream of tartar
¼ teaspoon salt
¼ cup flour plus 1 teaspoon to dust the shrimp
Vegetable oil for frying

1. Prepare the salsa, if using homemade. Then, put the chopped shrimp and jalapeño in a bowl and mix together. In a medium bowl, using an electric mixer, beat the egg whites with cream of tartar and salt until soft peaks form. In another small bowl, using the same beaters, beat the egg yolks until thick and pale. Gradually beat in the ¼ cup of flour. Fold the egg yolk mixture into the beaten egg whites. To the bowl with the shrimp add the remaining teaspoon of flour and toss to coat shrimp with flour. Fold the shrimp into the egg batter.

2. Pour oil to a depth of about ½ inch into a heavy frying pan, such as cast iron, and heat over medium-high heat until a tiny drop of batter sizzles immediately when put into the hot oil. Fry the battered shrimp by heaping tablespoons, turning once, until golden brown on both sides. Drain on paper towels. Serve at once with salsa for dipping.

Shrimp Pinwheel with Jalapeño and Cilantro Sauce
Camarones Frio con Salsa de Jalapeño y Cilantro

Makes 3 to 4 appetizer servings

Daiquiri Dick's—its real name—a beach-front restaurant in Puerto Vallarta, has long been a popular local gathering place to view spectacular sunsets while enjoying a margarita, cocktail, or other "sundowner." This cold shrimp dish is a great appetizer to share while gazing out at the horizon (or enjoying a summer night on the patio). The pink shrimp and pale green dipping sauce make a pretty picture, too.

16 large shrimp in the shell
½ teaspoon salt
Jalapeño-Cilantro Sauce (page 30)

1. In a medium skillet with a cover bring to a boil about 3 cups of water. Add the shrimp and salt. Reduce the heat to low, cover, and simmer until the shrimp are pink and cooked through, about 10 minutes. Drain the shrimp under cold running water. Peel and devein them, leaving the tail intact. Put the shrimp in a bowl, cover and refrigerate. While the shrimp cool, prepare the jalapeño sauce.

2. In a shallow 8-inch round soup plate with a rim, place an attractive smaller bowl that will fit in the center. Arrange the shrimp around the outside of the smaller bowl so they are touching in a tight circle, with the tails resting on the rim of the bowl. Fill the small bowl with dipping sauce. Refrigerate. Serve cold.

Shrimp Cakes with Corn Salsa
Tortas de Camarones con Salsa de Elote

Makes **4 servings**

Chapuline, a stylish and popular restaurant in Oaxaca prepares a number of dishes in the new style, called nueva cocina, *using traditional ingredients and presenting them in an updated way. This is my interpretation of the memorable appetizer shrimp cakes I had there.*

¹/₂ pound (9 to 12) medium shrimp, peeled and deveined

2 tablespoons minced white onion

1 tablespoon minced red bell pepper

1 serrano chile, finely chopped with seeds

¹/₂ teaspoon ground cumin

1 large egg, beaten

¹/₂ cup unseasoned bread crumbs

2 teaspoons fresh lime juice

¹/₄ teaspoon salt

3 tablespoons olive oil

Fresh Corn Salsa (page 25)

¹/₂ cup Mexican crema or sour cream

1. Coarsely chop the raw shrimp and put them in a bowl. Mix in the onion, red pepper, serrano, and cumin. Add the egg, bread crumbs, lime juice, and salt. Mix well and form into 8 (2-inch) patties about ¾-inch thick. Put the patties on an oiled platter, and refrigerate about 1 hour, or up to 6 hours before cooking.

2. In a large skillet, heat the oil until it shimmers, and cook the patties over medium heat until crisp and brown, about 3 minutes. Turn the patties, reduce the heat to medium-low and cook until completely cooked through, about 3 to 4 minutes. Put 2 patties on each of 4 plates. Put a dollop of crema or sour cream on top of the patties. Put about 2 tablespoons of corn salsa on the side of each serving.

Jalapeños with Shrimp Filling
Jalapeños Rellenos con Camarones

Makes **4 servings**

Jalapeño *chiles that are pickled and sold in cans or jars are called* jalapeños en escabeche. *These hot little demons are common appetizers and are presented with a variety of fillings. Here the jalapeños are stuffed with shrimp, topped with cheese and run under a broiler. These appetizers can be done ahead, then popped in the oven at the last minute.*

8 jarred pickled jalapeño chiles (en escabeche), cut in half lengthwise and seeded

12 medium cooked shrimp, chopped

1 tablespoon mayonnaise

¹/₂ tablespoon cocktail sauce

16 thin strips Monterey Jack cheese, 1-inch- × ¹/₂-inch

Place the oven rack on the top level and preheat the oven broiler. Meanwhile, put the jalapeños, cut sides up, in a single layer on a baking sheet. In a bowl, mix together the shrimp, mayonnaise, and cocktail sauce. Spoon a bit of the shrimp mixture into each jalapeño cavity. Top each with a strip of cheese. Run under the broiler until the cheese melts, about 2 to 3 minutes.

Grilled Jalapeños with Tuna Stuffing
Chiles Jalapeños Rellenos de Atún

Makes **24 appetizers**

Ricardo Muñoz, a talented chef from Mexico City, introduced me to this excellent appetizer. Fresh jalapeños are grilled, either on a stovetop grill pan or in a dry nonstick skillet, and then filled with a flavorful tuna mixture. Look for really large jalapeños that are often less hot than the smaller varieties, but don't count on it! Wear rubber gloves when cutting and seeding the chiles, and don't touch your face.

12 large fresh jalapeño chiles, halved lengthwise, seeded and veins removed

3 tablespoons olive oil

¼ cup finely chopped onion

2 medium garlic cloves, minced

2 medium tomatoes, peeled, seeded and finely chopped

1 (6-ounce) can white water-packed tuna, drained very well

1 tablespoon finely chopped fresh flat leaf parsley

2 tablespoons chopped raisins

1 tablespoon chopped capers

1 teaspoon sugar

½ teaspoon dried oregano (Mexican variety preferred), crumbled

¼ teaspoon salt

1. Brush the jalapeños all over with about 1 tablespoon of the olive oil. Heat a grill pan or nonstick skillet over medium heat until hot. Put the chiles, cut sides down on the pan, and cook 3 minutes. Turn and grill the skin sides until marked with brown from the pan, 3 to 4 minutes. Remove the jalapeños to a plate.

2. Heat the remaining oil in a medium skillet over medium-high heat. Cook the onion stirring,

until softened, about 3 minutes. Add the garlic and tomatoes. Cook, stirring frequently, until the mixture is nearly dry and paste-like, 3 to 4 minutes. Add the remaining ingredients, stirring to mix well. Reduce the heat to low and cook 2 to 3 minutes for flavors to blend. Adjust the seasoning, if needed. Stuff the chiles. Serve warm or at room temperature.

Tuna in Parsley Sauce
Atún en Salsa de Perejil

Makes **4 servings**

Tuna cooked with parsley, vinegar, and onions, is an unusual and tasty topping for crisp tortilla chips, first eaten in a sidewalk café in Colima City, between Guadalajara and Manzanilla. The tuna is also good with tossed salad greens. The contrast of cilantro and parsley with spicy jalapeño chiles, tart vinegar, extra-virgin olive oil, and tuna is a surprisingly good combination.

1 cup fresh parsley sprigs, lightly packed

1 tablespoon coarsely chopped fresh cilantro

2 jalapeño chiles, seeded, veins removed, and coarsely chopped

¼ cup white wine vinegar

¼ cup water

1 tablespoon extra-virgin olive oil

¼ cup finely chopped white onion

1 (6-ounce) can white water-packed tuna, drained and flaked with a fork

¼ teaspoon salt, or to taste

⅛ teaspoon freshly ground pepper, or to taste

1. Put the parsley, cilantro, jalapeños, vinegar, and water in a blender, and purée until very smooth. Reserve.

2. In a medium skillet, heat the olive oil over medium heat and cook the onion until softened, 3 to 4 minutes. Add the blended parsley mixture and cook until nearly dry, about 3 minutes. Add the tuna, salt and pepper. Reduce heat to medium-low and cook, stirring, 3 minutes, to blend the flavors. Transfer to a bowl. Cover and refrigerate until cold, about 2 hours. Serve with chips or as part of a salad.

Mixed Seafood Cocktail
Coctel de Mariscos

Makes **4 to 6 servings**

Mixed seafood cocktails are served on the street, in market food stalls, and restaurants throughout Mexico. It's quite common for restaurants to serve them in ice cream soda glasses easy filled to the brim. This easy cocktail from Campeche on the Gulf Coast contains shrimp and oysters mixed with avocado, onion, cocktail sauce, and fresh lime juice.

1/2 pound (9 to 12) medium shrimp in the shell

1 pint jar of small oysters with the liquid

1 cup prepared cocktail sauce or ketchup

1/2 cup spicy tomato juice, such as Snappy Tom

1 avocado (Hass variety preferred), peeled and diced

4 green onions, finely chopped

2 tablespoons fresh lime juice

1. Cook the shrimp in a pot of boiling salted water to cover. Cook until pink and curled, about 3 to 4 minutes. Drain and cool under cold running water. Peel and devein. Put in a large bowl and refrigerate.

2. In a saucepan, cook the oysters in the liquid from the jar for 1 minute. Drain, but do not rinse. Add the oysters to the bowl with the shrimp. Add the remaining ingredients to the bowl. Stir gently to mix. Cover and refrigerate 1 hour. Divide among 4 cocktail glasses. Serve cold.

Marinated Fish Cocktail
Ceviche

Makes **4 servings**

Ceviche, *while not originally of Mexican origin, is a classic spicy marinated fish cocktail found all along Mexico's extensive coastlines. The dish consists of raw fish marinated in fresh lime juice, which "cooks" the fish by the chemical action of the acid in the lime juice. The ice-cold marinated fish is then mixed with the other ingredients to complete the dish. Only absolutely fresh fish should be used for ceviche. Red snapper, rock cod, and sea bass are typical choices, as well as scallops, because they are firm fish that keep their texture.*

3/4 pound fresh firm white fish, such as snapper or sea bass

1/2 cup fresh lime juice

1 medium tomato, chopped

2 serrano chiles, minced with seeds

1/4 medium white onion, finely chopped

1/4 cup chopped fresh cilantro

1/4 teaspoon dried oregano (Mexican variety preferred), crumbled

1 avocado (Hass variety preferred), cut into 1/2-inch dice

1 tablespoon olive oil

1/2 teaspoon salt

1. Trim the fish of skin and fat. Remove all bones, and cut the fish into 1/2-inch pieces. Put the fish in a glass bowl or jar. Stir in the lime juice. Cover and refrigerate until the fish becomes firm and opaque, about 2 hours.

2. Drain the fish and transfer to a medium bowl. Add the remaining ingredients and stir gently to mix. Serve cold.

Marinated Scallop Cocktail
Ceviche de Callos

Makes 4 servings

Ceviche is raw seafood that is "cooked" while marinating for several hours in fresh lime juice. Some people prefer this version where the scallops or other firm, white-fleshed fish are blanched in boiling water for one minute before marinating. Serve ceviche ice cold with crisp tortilla chips.

8 ounces small calico or bay scallops

1/4 cup fresh lime juice

2 medium tomatoes, chopped

2 tablespoons finely chopped white onion

1 serrano chile, finely chopped with seeds

1 small garlic clove, finely chopped

1 tablespoons chopped fresh cilantro

1 avocado (Hass variety preferred), peeled, seeded, and diced

1 teaspoon unseasoned rice vinegar

1 1/2 tablespoons olive oil

1/4 teaspoon salt, or to taste

1 cup chopped romaine lettuce

1. Put the scallops in a medium pan of boiling water and cook 1 minute. Drain in a colander and cool under running water. Transfer the scallops to a medium bowl and mix with the lime juice. Cover and refrigerate 3 hours.

2. Drain the lime juice, and add the remaining ingredients to the scallops. Stir gently to mix. Cover and refrigerate until shortly before serving. To serve, put about 1/4 cup of chopped lettuce in each of 4 cocktail glasses, and divide the ceviche evenly among the 4 glasses. Serve cold with crisp corn tortilla chips.

Marinated Fried Fish Fillets
Pescado en Escabeche

Makes 4 to 6 servings

Escabeche is a method of pickling. In this dish, fish is sautéed and then soaked in a spicy marinade. The dish is common along the Gulf Coast of Mexico, especially in the states of Veracruz, Tabasco, and Yucatán. Serve the fish with sliced, buttered bolillos (oval Mexican sandwich rolls) or soft, warm corn tortillas. Since the entire process can be done in advance, it's a good choice when entertaining. Accompany the dish with radishes and sliced cucumbers, if desired.

3/4 cup unseasoned rice vinegar

1/4 cup water

2 medium garlic cloves, thinly sliced

2 serrano chiles, halved lengthwise with seeds

1/4 white onion, sliced

2 sprigs parsley

1 cinnamon stick (Mexican canela or Ceylon variety preferred)

3 whole cloves

2 bay leaves

1/2 teaspoon dried oregano (Mexican variety preferred)

1/2 teaspoon sugar

4 (6-ounce) fish fillets, such as snapper or rock cod

1/2 teaspoon salt

1/8 teaspoon freshly ground pepper, or to taste

2 tablespoons olive oil

8 pimiento-stuffed green olives, halved crosswise

2 jarred pickled jalapeño chiles (en escabeche), seeded, and thinly sliced lengthwise into strips

1 tablespoon capers, drained

1. In a small saucepan bring to a boil the vinegar, water, garlic, serrano chiles, onion, parsley, cinnamon stick, cloves, bay, oregano, and sugar. Reduce the heat to low and simmer, uncovered, for 3 minutes. Set aside off heat.

2. Season the fish with salt and pepper. In a large nonstick skillet, heat the olive oil and sauté the fish until light brown, about 3 minutes per side. Transfer the fish to an enamel or glass baking dish just large enough to hold the fish in one layer. Pour the marinade over the fish. Cover and refrigerate at least 4 hours or up to overnight. To serve, lift the fish from the marinade and place on a serving plate. Scatter the olives, jalapeño strips, and capers on top. Discard the marinade. Serve with tortillas or sliced crusty bread.

Return-to-Life Shellfish Cocktail
Vuelve de la Vida

Makes **4 servings**

One of the first Veracruz specialties I wanted to try was this famous shellfish cocktail. It is usually served in huge glass goblets packed with crab, shrimp, lobster, oysters, or whatever fresh shellfish is available. The whole thing is mixed with ketchup, citrus juices, onion, and cilantro, and garnished with avocado and lime wedges. The cocktail's title refers to its fabled ability to ease the after-effects of the night before. It's outstanding even without a hangover.

1¹/₄ cups ketchup
¹/₄ medium white onion, finely chopped
¹/₄ cup loosely packed chopped fresh cilantro
¹/₄ cup fresh lime juice
3 tablespoons fresh orange juice
2 pounds shellfish, such as cold cooked shrimp, crab, lobster, or raw clams or oysters, all cut into bite-size pieces
Salt, to taste
1 large avocado (Hass variety preferred), peeled and diced
Lime wedges

In a large bowl mix together the ketchup, onion, cilantro, lime juice, orange juice, and ½ cup water. Add the shellfish and stir to mix. Season to taste with salt. Divide among 4 large fat goblets. Top with diced avocado and garnish with lime wedges. Serve at once, cold.

Oysters with Garlic and Lime
Ostiones con Ajo y Limón

Makes **4 servings**

Oysters are plentiful along the coast of Baja, California where they are sometimes prepared on the beach over hot coals. This is one of my favorite ways to enjoy them as an appetizer. An oyster knife should be used to pry open fresh oysters.

20 medium-size oysters, in the shell
¹/₄ cup olive oil
¹/₂ medium white onion, minced
4 medium garlic cloves, minced
¹/₄ cup fresh lime juice
¹/₄ teaspoon hot pepper sauce, such as Tabasco
¹/₂ teaspoon salt
¹/₄ teaspoon freshly ground pepper, or to taste

1. Pry open the oysters over a bowl to catch and reserve the liquid. Place the bottom shells containing the oysters on a baking sheet and set aside. Discard the top shells.

2. Preheat the oven broiler. Heat the olive oil in a medium skillet over medium heat and cook the onion until softened, about 3 minutes. Add the garlic and cook about 3 minutes. Stir in the reserved oyster liquid, lime juice, hot pepper sauce, salt, and pepper. Heat through. Remove the pan from the heat. Spoon a little of the mixture over each oyster and broil the oysters until the edges of the oysters begin to curl, 2 to 3 minutes. Serve hot.

Steamed Clams, Baja Style
Almejas al Vapor

Makes 4 appetizer servings

Fresh little cockle clams are found in great abundance in San Quentin Bay on the coast of Baja, Mexico and they are often cooked right on the beach. You may not be cooking on a beach in Mexico, but here's a great way to savor small clams of any kind. Serve with good crusty bread to dip into the juices.

³/₄ cup sherry
¹/₄ cup water
¹/₄ onion, sliced
1 sprig parsley
1 tablespoon butter
24 small clams, scrubbed
Lime wedges

Put all of the ingredients except the lime wedges and rolls in a large pot, and cover with a tight lid to prevent steam from escaping. Bring to a boil over high heat until the clams pop open in about 5 minutes. (Discard any that don't open.) Serve hot in the shells with lime wedges to squeeze over the clams.

Clams Steamed in Beer
Almejas en Cerveza

Makes 4 servings

Beer adds flavor and aroma to steamed clams and is a popular way to steam clams along the Pacific coast of Mexico. I use a mild-flavored lager-style Mexican beer. Serve with crusty rolls.

24 small clams
¹/₂ bottle of beer (pale lager preferred)
2 green onions, cut into 2-inch pieces
1 tablespoon unsalted butter
Lime wedges

1. Scrub the clams and put them into a bowl. Cover the clams with cold salted water and refrigerate up to 6 hours before cooking. Drain off all the water and put the clams in a large saucepan. Add the beer, onions, and butter. Cover and bring to a boil. Cook until the shells open, 4 to 5 minutes. (Discard any that don't open.)

2. Transfer the clams to a serving bowl and pour in the broth, except for the last bit of sand or grit that has settled on the bottom. Serve hot with lime wedges to squeeze over the clams.

Clams in Red Chili Broth
Almejas en Salsa de Chili Rojo

Makes 4 servings

Small clams sometimes simply called steamers are easy to come by in Baja. This simple red chili broth gives the clams a wonderful taste to serve with bolillos (oval Mexican sandwich rolls) or other rolls to dip in the broth while eating the clams.

1 tablespoon vegetable oil
2 medium garlic cloves, peeled and thinly sliced
2 tablespoons finely chopped onion
24 small clams, scrubbed and rinsed
1 tablespoon pure ground ancho or pasilla chili powder
1 cup canned fat-free reduced-sodium chicken broth
¹/₄ cup vermouth or dry sherry
2 tablespoons chopped fresh cilantro
¹/₄ teaspoon salt, or to taste

In a large pot heat the oil over medium heat and sauté the garlic and onion 2 minutes. Add the chili powder and cook, stirring, about 30 seconds. Add the clams and all of the remaining ingredients. Cover and cook until the clams open, about 5 minutes. (Discard any that don't open.) Serve in shallow bowls with the broth.

Fried Squid
Calamares Fritos

Makes 4 servings

Fried squid rings are a popular snack in Baja, Mexico. Previously frozen, cleaned squid bodies are available at most fresh seafood counters in the United States so it's easy to fry up a few to serve with drinks before a Mexican meal. I prefer to cut rings from the whole body sections rather than buy precut rings, for better flavor. Spicy Mayonnaise Dip (page 28) is excellent to serve with this dish that is often referred to in Mexico as calamar *in Spanish and by the Italian word* calamari *in the United States. For tender squid, do not overcook.*

1 pound thawed previously frozen squid bodies
Vegetable oil for frying
1 cup all-purpose flour
1/2 cup fine bread crumbs
1/4 teaspoon salt, or to taste
Lime wedges

1. Rinse the squid tail sections, drain, and cut crosswise into 1/2- to 1-inch rings. Put the rings in a bowl. In a pie plate, mix together the flour and bread crumbs.

2. In a deep fryer or medium heavy skillet, heat about 1½ inches of oil until it shimmers. Dredge the squid in the flour mixture a few at a time, and fry in hot oil until golden, about 1 minute. Drain on paper towels. Sprinkle lightly with salt. Serve hot with lime wedges and a dipping sauce.

Swordfish Bites with Pineapple and Red Bell Pepper
Pes Espada con Piña y Chile Rojo Dulce

Makes 4 to 6 appetizer servings

Swordfish is found in temperate and tropical seas throughout much of the world. Along the Pacific coast of Mexico, swordfish is often grilled and served with salsas of various kinds. This recipe grills highly prized and expensive swordfish in small pieces and skewers the cooked fish with pineapple chunks and red bell pepper on cocktail picks. Accompany with a spicy salsa or dipping sauce. To save time, you can use fresh packaged pre-cut pineapple found in supermarkets.

Jalapeño-Cilantro Sauce (page 30)
2 (6- to 8-ounce) swordfish steaks, 1/2- to 3/4-inch thick
2 medium garlic cloves, minced
1 1/2 tablespoons olive oil
1/4 teaspoon salt
1/8 teaspoon freshly ground pepper, or to taste
1 medium fresh pineapple (about 1 1/2 pounds), rind removed, cored, and cut into 1-inch chunks—about 2 cups of pineapple chunks
2 red bell peppers, seeded, and cut into 3/4-inch squares

1. Prepare the salsa. Then, trim the skin from the swordfish, and cut the steaks into 1-inch pieces. Mix together the garlic, oil, salt, and pepper. Coat the fish on all sides with the mixture. Cover and refrigerate about 1 hour.

2. Skewer the pineapple and red pepper on cocktail picks, and put on a plate. Remove the fish from the refrigerator. Heat a stovetop grill pan over medium-high heat until hot and a few drops of water sizzle on the pan. Cook the swordfish chunks, turning, until light brown outside, about 3 to 5 minutes, or until just cooked through. Add the cooked fish to the skewers with the pineapple and peppers. Serve at room temperature with the jalapeño and cilantro salsa on the side.

Appetizer Fish Balls
Albondigas de Pescado

Makes **about 24 fish balls**

Fish balls are a popular item to serve as part of a buffet with a dipping sauce such as Spicy Mayonnaise Dip (page 28). The fish balls can be kept warm in a chafing dish. The fish mixture is also excellent for fish patties to make tortas (sandwiches), or to serve atop salads.

1 pound firm white fish fillets, such as cod, halibut or snapper.
2 thin slices—about 2 to 3 ounces fresh white bread (sandwich-type loaf)
2 tablespoons milk
2 tablespoons chopped white onion
1 tablespoon prepared red salsa
1 tablespoon chopped fresh parsley
2 large eggs
1/2 teaspoon salt
1/4 all-purpose flour
3/4 cup dry bread crumbs
Vegetable oil for frying

1. Remove any bones from the fish, cut fish into small pieces, and put in a food processor bowl. Tear the bread into small pieces and add to the processor along with the milk. Pulse 4 to 5 times to combine. Add the onion, salsa, parsley, 1 of the eggs, and salt. Process until smooth. Form the mixture into small balls, about 1 inch in diameter, put on a plate, cover and refrigerate about 1 hour.

2. Beat the remaining egg in a bowl with 1 teaspoon of water. Put the flour and bread crumbs on separate sheets of wax paper. Dredge the fish balls in flour, dip into the beaten egg, and roll in the bread crumbs. Put on a plate and refrigerate 2 to 3 hours.

3. In a deep skillet, or deep-fryer, pour in oil to a depth of about 2 inches. Heat until the oil shimmers and a small piece of bread sizzles at once. Cook the fish balls in batches without crowding, turning once or twice until golden brown all over. Drain on paper towels. Serve hot with toothpicks and a dipping sauce.

Chopped Crab Appetizer
Salpicón de Jaiba

Makes **8 appetizer servings**

A salpicón refers to foods with shredded or chopped ingredients mixed with citrus juices, vinegar, and oil. Blue crab is used for crab salpicón along the gulf coast in the state of Veracruz, and is usually served with a basket of small warm corn tortillas for do-it-yourself soft tacos. I serve crab salpicón as a topping for crisp corn tostadas or chips. Any variety of fresh or thawed frozen crab works well for this appetizer, but canned crab is a poor substitute. Guacamole is an excellent accompaniment.

3/4 pound picked-over fresh or thawed frozen crab meat
1 small white onion, chopped
1 medium tomato, finely chopped
1 to 2 serrano chiles, finely chopped with seeds
1/4 cup fresh lime juice
1 tablespoon unseasoned rice vinegar
2 tablespoons olive oil
2 tablespoons chopped fresh cilantro
1/2 teaspoon salt, or to taste

Drain the crab very well and put into a glass or ceramic bowl. Add the remaining ingredients, and toss to mix. Cover and refrigerate until cold, about 1 hour. Serve as a topping on crisp corn tostadas or chips.

Caviar and Serrano Chiles on Crisp Tortilla Rounds
Tostaditas con Caviar Picanté

Makes **6 servings**

My husband and I met Marta and Alfredo Rios during one of our many trips to Mexico, and were invited for dinner in their beautiful home in Satellite City, a suburb of Mexico City. One of the appetizers was ice-cold dark caviar sprinkled with chopped serrano chile and a dab of sour cream on small crisp tortilla rounds. We were amazed. The combination was unforgettable. It may be difficult to find good-quality 2-inch fried tortilla rounds (tostaditas), but it's pretty simple to cut your own from fresh corn tortillas and fry them until crisp. For the caviar, my favorites are beluga or sevruga.

6 (6- to 7-inch) fresh corn tortillas
Oil for frying
About 2 ounces caviar of choice
2 to 3 serrano chiles, seeded, veins removed, and minced
1/2 cup sour cream

1. Lay 1 corn tortilla on a flat surface. Using a round cookie cutter or glass, cut three 2½-inch rounds from the tortilla. Save the scraps to fry for snacks, or discard. Repeat with remaining tortillas.

2. Heat about 1 inch of oil in a skillet. Fry the tortilla rounds until crisp and lightly golden, 1 to 2 minutes. Drain on paper towels.

3. To assemble, put a tiny bit of caviar (¼ teaspoon) on each crisp tostadita. Add a sprinkle of minced serrano and a dab of sour cream. Arrange the tostaditas on a beautiful flat serving plate and serve.

Chips, Dips, and Nachos

Fried Corn Tortilla Chips and Strips
Tostaditos o Totopos

Makes **48 chips**

Crisp-fried tortilla chips are easy to make at home, and they're better than most commercial chips. I prefer homemade for nachos because the chips are flatter and hold the toppings better. Leftover tortillas that have dried out are ideal for making chips or cutting into thin strips for soups and casseroles containing tortilla strips called chilaquiles.

12 (6- to 7-inch) corn tortillas
1 cup vegetable oil
1/2 teaspoon salt, or to taste (optional)

1. Stack 3 tortillas on a cutting surface. With a large sharp knife, cut straight down through the stack into quarters. If making strips, cut across the tortillas to make strips the width you want for your dish.

2. In a medium skillet, heat the oil over medium-high heat until a wedge or strip of tortilla starts to sizzle immediately when dipped into the hot oil. Fry the tortilla pieces in batches about 2 minutes, or until crisp and lightly browned. Remove with a slotted spoon or tongs, and drain on paper towels. While the chips are still hot, sprinkle lightly with salt, if desired.

Toasted Corn Tortilla Chips
Tostaditas al Horno

Makes 4 to 8 dozen chips

Toasting tortilla chips in the oven uses almost no fat. The chips will be a bit more crunchy and drier than fried chips, but I like the results of oven-toasted chips, and often make them this way.

12 (6- to 7-inch) corn tortillas
1/4 cup vegetable oil
1/2 teaspoon salt, or to taste (optional)

1. Preheat the oven to 325°. Lay one tortilla on a cutting surface. Brush one side only with a thin film of vegetable oil, about 1/8 teaspoon. Repeat with the remaining tortillas and oil. Cut the tortillas into the desired size: quarters, sixths, or eighths.

2. Arrange as many tortilla wedges as will fit in a single layer on a large baking sheet. Bake on the middle rack of the oven about 10 minutes, or until the chips are crisp and lightly browned. Remove the chips from the oven and sprinkle lightly with salt, if desired. Repeat baking until all of the chips have been toasted. Once cooled, store in a sealed plastic bag, or other airtight container, if made ahead.

Crisp-Fried Whole Tortillas
Tostadas

Makes 12 tostadas

Tostadas are usually made with corn tortillas that are fried whole until golden brown and crisp. Flour tortillas can also be fried in the same way. They are used as edible plates for layering salads or entrées.

Vegetable oil for frying
12 (6- to 7-inch) corn or flour tortillas

In a medium skillet, heat oil to a depth of about 1 inch until the oil shimmers and a small piece of tortilla sizzles at once. Using tongs, fry the tortillas, 1 at a time, until golden brown on both sides. Drain on paper towels. When the tostadas are cool, store in sealed plastic bags in a cupboard 3 to 4 days. Tostadas are normally eaten at room temperature.

Bacon Guacamole
Guacamole con Tocino

Makes 6 appetizer servings

You just know it's good! While Classic Guacamole (page 23) is an essential part of Mexican cuisine—as a condiment and as a dip—creative variations like this one, with crisp bacon bits, abound. Serve with tortilla chips.

6 bacon slices
2 large ripe avocados (Hass variety preferred), halved, seed removed and peeled
1/4 cup finely chopped white onion
2 serrano chiles, finely chopped with seeds
2 tablespoons chopped fresh cilantro
1 tablespoon fresh lime juice
1 small tomato, seeded and chopped
Salt, to taste (optional)

1. In a large skillet, cook the bacon over medium-low heat until brown and crisp. Drain well on paper towels. When the bacon is cool, crumble it into small bits.

2. In a medium bowl, mash the avocados. Stir in the onion, serranos, cilantro, lime juice, and the reserved bacon bits. Drain off any juice from the tomato to prevent discoloring the guacamole. Gently stir the tomato into the guacamole. Add salt, if needed. (The saltiness of the bacon will determine if more salt is needed.)

Black Bean Dip
Antojito de Frijoles Negro

*Makes **4 servings***

Enjoying dips and chips with cold drinks is just about the easiest way to spend a convivial afternoon or evening with friends. This cheesy black bean dip is one of the best snacks for the occasion.

2 cups cooked black beans (Basic Pot Beans, page 461)

1/2 cup minced white onion

2 cups shredded Monterey Jack cheese

1 cup shredded cheddar cheese

2 jarred pickled jalapeño chiles (en escabeche), finely chopped

1 teaspoon jalapeño juice from the can

1/2 teaspoon ground cumin

1/4 cup sour cream

2 green onions, including 2-inches of green part, finely chopped

Prepare the beans. Reserve. Preheat the oven to 325°. Drain the beans of most of their liquid, but leave them a bit soupy. Mash half of the beans. Put all of the beans in an ovenproof serving casserole dish. Add the white onion, cheeses, jalapeños, jalapeño juice, and cumin. Mix well. Bake the bean mixture until hot and bubbling, about 15 minutes. Drizzle with sour cream and scatter the green onions on top. Serve hot with chips.

Refried Beans with Cheese
Frijoles Refritos con Queso

*Makes **4 to 6 servings***

At the Hotel Camino Real in Puerto Vallarta we ate a rich and tasty refried bean pancake studded with thin rings of serrano chile. It was perfect with icy mugs of beer. This is a good recipe to try when you have leftover cooked beans. You can use canned refried beans, but they won't taste the same.

1 tablespoon vegetable oil

3 serrano chiles, cut into very thin rounds with seeds

2 cups well-seasoned Basic Refried Beans (page 462)

1 cup coarsely shredded Monterey Jack cheese, or other good melting cheese

Corn tortilla chips

In a medium nonstick skillet, heat the oil and sauté the serrano chile rounds about 20 seconds. Add the refried beans and stir with a wooden spoon until the beans are hot and form a paste. Add the cheese and stir slowly until just melted, but still visible as swirls of cheese. Turn out onto a round serving plate and form into a fat pancake. Serve at once with tortilla chips for dipping.

Green Chiles with Cheese
Chile con Queso

Makes 4 servings

There are many versions of this popular melted cheese appetizer and most of them are very good if they are made with good quality cheese. Fresh roasted Anaheim chiles are called for in this version. They are usually fairly mild, but can be hot. Serve with tortilla chips.

3 fresh Anaheim chiles, roasted, peeled, seeded, and veins removed (page 8)
1 tablespoon unsalted butter or vegetable oil
1/2 cup finely chopped onion
1/2 teaspoon salt
1/2 teaspoon dried oregano (Mexican variety preferred), crumbled
1/4 teaspoon cumin
1/2 cup heavy cream
2 cups shredded Monterey Jack cheese

Prepare the chiles. Then, chop or dice the chiles very fine and set aside. Heat the butter or oil in a medium saucepan over medium heat and cook the onion, stirring, until softened, about 3 minutes. Add the chopped chiles, salt, oregano, cumin, and cream. Bring to a boil and cook, stirring, 1 minute. Remove the pan from the heat and stir in the cheese until melted. Serve warm.

Almond and Cheese Dip
Botana de Nuez y Queso

Makes about 1 cup

A delightful little book I purchased in Mexico, Recipes and Memories of Mexico, *by Dorothy Weeks, describes travels she took with her husband in Mexico in the 1950s and the foods they ate. I liked this simple dip and added chopped pickled jalapeño chiles to give it some heat. Serve with corn tortilla chips.*

1 cup slivered almonds
3 ounce package cream cheese, room temperature
2 to 3 tablespoons sour cream
1 to 2 jarred pickled jalapeño chiles (en escabeche), seeded and minced
Salt, to taste

In a medium dry skillet, toast the almonds, over medium heat, stirring until aromatic and golden brown, about 6 to 8 minutes. Take care not to burn the nuts or they will be bitter. Cool the nuts completely; then put them in a food processor with the cheese, sour cream and jalapeños. Blend well. If the mixture is too thick, add more sour cream to reach a dipping consistency. Taste and add salt, if needed. Transfer to a serving bowl.

Olive and Tomato Dip
Salsa de Aceituna Verde y Jitomate

Makes about 1 1/2 cups

Dips and chips are easy and well liked by almost everyone. This is a California-Mexican innovation based on ingredients commonly used in the cooking of Veracruz. For the best flavor try to use good-quality bulk olives from a delicatessen or gourmet store.

1 cup green Spanish-style pimiento-stuffed olives
1 medium tomato, seeded, and finely chopped
1 jalapeño chile, seeded, veins removed, and finely chopped
2 tablespoons chopped fresh cilantro
1 tablespoon finely chopped white onion
2 teaspoons drained capers, chopped
1 teaspoon brown sugar
Salt, to taste (optional)

Put the olives in a processor and pulse until finely chopped. Transfer to a bowl and add the remaining ingredients. Taste before adding salt, since the olives and capers are both already salty. Serve with crisp tortilla chips for dipping.

Yucatán Stuffed Cheese

Queso Relleno de Yucatán

Makes 4 servings

Manuel Arjona from Yucatán and now the chef of Maya, a Mexican restaurant in Sonoma, California contributed his recipe for this unusual cheese preparation that's very popular on the Yucatán peninsula. Imported cheese, especially whole rounds of Edam and Gouda, are less expensive there because of the free port status that exists in the state of Quintana Roo on the eastern part of the peninsula. Here, a hollowed round of Edam or Gouda is stuffed with a ground meat filling and melted cheese. This delectable filling is scooped out and eaten with tortillas or chips. It's a great party dish.

1 (2-pound) round of Edam or Gouda cheese

1/2 pound lean ground pork

1 teaspoon dried oregano (Mexican variety preferred), crumbled

1/8 teaspoon ground cayenne

1/2 teaspoon salt

1 jalapeño chile, seeded, veins removed, and minced

2 hard-cooked large eggs, peeled and chopped

11/2 tablespoons drained capers

Sauce

11/2 cups chicken stock, canned or homemade

2 tablespoons masa harina (flour for corn tortillas)

2 small Roma tomatoes, peeled, seeded, and finely chopped

2 tablespoons golden raisins

1/4 teaspoon ground cloves

1/4 teaspoon salt, or to taste

1/8 teaspoon freshly ground pepper, or to taste

1. Peel the outside wax off the cheese. Cut a 1/2-inch thick slice off the top for a lid. Hollow out the inside of the cheese to within 1/2 inch of the edge. Chop the inside cheese, reserve 1/2 cup for the sauce and store the rest. Set the cheese shell aside.

2. In a skillet, cook the pork, oregano, cayenne, and salt, stirring and breaking the pork into bits as it cooks until no longer pink, 3 to 4 minutes. Stir in the jalapeño, eggs, and capers. Spoon the mixture inside the cheese round. Replace the lid. Rub oil on the outside.

3. Wrap the stuffed cheese in cheese cloth and with the opening at the top, put in the top of a steamer with water in the bottom. Steam over medium heat 12–15 minutes, or until the cheese softens, but does not collapse (test gently with a fork).

4. Meanwhile, make the sauce. In a saucepan, stir together the chicken broth, masa harina, tomatoes, raisins, cloves, salt, and pepper. Bring to a boil, stirring, and cook until the sauce thickens slightly, 8 to 10 minutes. Add 1/2 cup of the reserved cheese and stir until melted, but do not boil. Remove from the heat.

5. To serve, remove the cloth from the cheese ball and place the cheese on a serving plate. Remove the lid. Pour the sauce over the cheese. Some will run onto the plate. Serve at once.

Mushroom Appetizer Spread
Antojito de Hongos Picadas

Makes 2 cups spread

Many varieties of wild mushrooms grow in the mountains of the states of Puebla and Tlaxcala. Mycological experts lead tours during the rainy season to search for the edible fungi found in the region. My friend, Jon Jarvis, of Mexican Mushroom Tours, contributed this appetizer recipe, using ingredients that are typical in the region's foods.

2 tablespoons olive oil
1/2 medium white onion, finely chopped
2 medium garlic cloves, finely chopped
3/4 pound fresh mushrooms, 2 to 3 kinds, including brown cremini, very finely chopped
2 poblano chiles, stemmed, seeded, veins removed, and minced
1/2 teaspoon dried oregano (Mexican variety preferred), crumbled
1/4 cup walnuts, finely chopped
1/2 teaspoon salt, or to taste
1/8 teaspoon freshly ground pepper, or to taste

Heat the oil in a large skillet and cook the onion and garlic stirring, until softened, about 3 minutes. Add the mushrooms, chiles, and oregano. Cook, stirring, until the mushroom juices are reduced and the mixture is nearly dry, 5 to 6 minutes. Add the walnuts, salt, and pepper. Taste for seasoning. Transfer to a bowl. Serve at room temperature with crisp tortilla chips or a thinly sliced baguette.

Tuna, Capers, and Jalapeños
Tostaditas con Atún, Alcaparras y Jalapeños

Makes about 1 1/2 cups

A simple mixture with plenty of spicy flavor to spread on tortilla chips, makes an easy quick appetizer. Serve with crisp corn tortilla chips.

1 (9-ounce) can white albacore tuna, packed in oil or water
1 (3-ounce) package cream cheese, at room temperature
1 tablespoon mayonnaise
2 jarred pickled jalapeño chiles (en escabeche), seeded and minced
1 green onion, including most of the green, finely chopped
1 tablespoon drained capers, chopped
1 tablespoon chopped fresh cilantro
1 teaspoon fresh lime juice or unseasoned rice vinegar
1 small tomato, seeded and finely chopped
Salt, to taste (optional)

In a medium bowl, mix very well all of the ingredients, except the tomato and salt. Gently stir in the tomato. Taste and add salt, if needed. Transfer to a decorative serving bowl.

Bean and Cheese Nachos
Nachos de Frijol y Queso

Makes 36 nachos

Nachos are a classic Mexican appetizer that also easily satisfies hungry munchers throughout the United States. A simple topping for nachos is refried beans, cheese, and a dollop of spicy red salsa.

36 Toasted Corn Tortilla Chips (page 86), or purchased
1 cup refried beans, canned or homemade
1 cup shredded Monterey Jack cheese, or other melting cheese
1/2 cup red salsa, purchased or homemade

Prepare the tortilla chips, if using homemade. Then, preheat the broiler. Spread refried beans over each tortilla chip. Top with a mound of cheese, and lay the chips in a single layer on a baking sheet. Heat under the broiler until the cheese is melted and bubbly, about 1 minute. Top each chip with a dollop of salsa. Serve at once.

Black Bean Nachos
Nachos de Frijoles Negros

Makes **36 nachos**

Crisp corn chips called tostaditas *spread with refried black beans and topped with sour cream and salsa is a favorite* botana, *or quick snack, almost everywhere.*

**36 Toasted Corn Tortilla Chips (page 86),
    or purchased**
**1 cup cooked black beans (Basic Pot Beans,
    page 461), or canned**
1 tablespoon vegetable oil or lard
2 tablespoons chopped white onion
1 medium garlic clove, finely chopped
**¹/₂ teaspoon dried oregano (Mexican variety
    preferred), crumbled**
¹/₄ teaspoon ground cumin
Salt to taste (optional)

1. Prepare the tortilla chips, if using homemade. Then, drain the beans, but do not rinse. Set aside. Heat the oil in a medium skillet over medium heat. Add the onion, garlic, oregano, and cumin. Cook, stirring, until the onion is softened, 3 to 4 minutes. Add the beans, and cook, mashing and stirring them until thick.

2. Spread a bit of the beans on the tortilla chips. Add a dollop of sour cream and salsa. Serve while the beans are warm.

Chorizo and Refried Bean Nachos
Tostaditos con Chorizo y Frijoles Refritos

Makes **24 appetizers**

Good-quality purchased ingredients can be used to make this rustic appetizer. The oven-baked tortilla chips can be made a day ahead for extra convenience.

36 Toasted Corn Tortilla Chips (page 86), or purchased
2 tablespoons vegetable oil, or more if needed
**¹/₂ pound fresh bulk chorizo, or packaged,
    with casings removed**
¹/₂ medium onion, finely chopped
2 cups canned refried beans, heated
1 cup guacamole, purchased or homemade
Red salsa, purchased or homemade

Prepare the tortilla chips, if using homemade. Then, in a medium nonstick skillet, cook the chorizo over medium heat until brown, 4 to 5 minutes. Add the onion and cook until the onion softens, about 3 minutes. To assemble, layer the chips equally with beans, chorizo, and guacamole. Put a dollop of salsa on top. Serve warm.

Cheese, Jicama, and Green Chile Nachos
Nachos de Queso, Jicama, y Chile Poblano

Makes **36 nachos**

These are great do-it-yourself party nachos. Each person assembles his or her own stacked nachos from a selection of ingredients that are arranged on a platter. It's a wonderful taste and texture combination.

36 Toasted Corn Tortilla Chips (page 86), or purchased
**1 pound Monterey Jack cheese, cut into 36
    2-inch squares**
**1 medium jicama (about 1 pound), cut into thin
    2-inch squares**
**4 large fresh green chiles, poblanos or Anaheims,
    roasted and peeled (page 8); then cut into
    2-inch squares**
1 cup lightly packed coarsely chopped fresh cilantro

Prepare the tortilla chips, if using homemade. Place them in a napkin-lined basket. On a large serving platter, arrange the cheese, jicama, chiles, and cilantro. Serve the basket of chips with the platter of ingredients next to it.

Combination Nachos
Nachos Compuestos, Las Palomas

Makes **6 to 8 servings**

Las Palomas Restaurant in Puerto Vallarta gets credit for this platter of spicy nachos. A few supermarket ingredients make these nachos easy to assemble. Serve as a finger food snack with cold beer and margaritas.

50 Toasted Corn Tortilla Chips (page 86), or purchased
1 (16-ounce) can spicy refried beans
1 cup shredded Monterey Jack cheese
1 cup shredded cheddar cheese
1 large avocado (Hass variety preferred), peeled and finely diced
6 jarred pickled jalapeño chiles (en escabeche), seeded and cut into thin strips
1 cup sour cream
1/2 cup fresh salsa, purchased or homemade

Prepare the tortilla chips, if using homemade. Then, preheat the broiler. Arrange the tortilla chips in a single layer on a cookie sheet. Spread each chip with about 1 teaspoon refried beans. Push the tortillas together, overlapping a little, into a large round. Scatter the cheeses over the surface of the tortillas. Broil until the cheese melts and bubbles, about 1 minute. Remove from the broiler, tip the pan slightly and slide onto a serving platter with the aid of a wide spatula. Arrange the avocado and jalapeños on top. Drizzle with sour cream and salsa. Serve at once.

Folded and Wrapped Tortilla Snacks

Crisp Rolled Chicken Taquitos
Taquitos de Pollo

Makes **24 appetizers**

Taquitos de pollo are a favorite snack or light meal all over Mexico, made of crisply fried filled corn tortillas. For an ideal party appetizer, cut the taquitos in half and arrange on a colorful platter, with guacamole and sour cream served in separate bowls on the side. This chicken filling is a little creamy and mildly spiced.

1 1/4 pounds skinless boneless chicken breasts
1 1/2 cups canned fat-free reduced-sodium chicken broth
8 tablespoons vegetable oil
1 medium white onion, finely chopped
2 tablespoons fresh block cream cheese
1/2 teaspoon dried oregano (Mexican variety preferred), crumbled
1/2 teaspoon salt
1/8 teaspoon freshly ground pepper, or to taste
12 (6- to 7-inch) corn tortillas

1. Place chicken breasts and broth in a medium saucepan. Bring to a boil over medium-high heat, then reduce heat to low and simmer, 12 to 15 minutes, or until the chicken is white throughout, but still moist. Set the chicken aside in the broth until cool enough to handle. With your fingers, shred the chicken into thin strips and reserve in a bowl.

2. In a medium skillet, heat 1 tablespoon of the oil over medium-high heat and cook the onions and oregano, stirring, about 2 minutes or until onions are limp. Put the onions in the bowl with the shredded chicken. Mix in the cream cheese, salt, and pepper. Reserve.

3. In a medium skillet, heat 2 tablespoons of oil over medium high heat and, using tongs, soften tortillas 1 at a time by dipping in hot oil about 2 seconds on each side or until very limp. Drain tortillas between layers of paper towels. Stack and keep covered with clean kitchen towel.

4. To fill, place 1 soft tortilla on a plate, spoon about 2 tablespoons chicken mixture in a line, across lower third of tortilla surface and roll up tightly. Secure with toothpick and lay seam side down on another plate. Repeat with remaining tortillas. Cover with plastic wrap to keep from drying out. At this point, taquitos can be held, covered and refrigerated, up to 6 hours before frying.

5. In a medium skillet, heat the remaining 2 tablespoons of oil on medium high, and fry the taquitos 2 at a time, seam side down, until lightly browned on both sides, about 2 minutes. Drain on paper towels. Repeat until all are cooked. With a sharp knife, cut each taquito in half, arrange on a plate, and serve hot.

Crisp Rolled Flautas with Chicken
Flautas de Pollo

Makes **6 flautas**

Flautas *are rolled corn tortillas with various fillings that are crisp fried and often garnished with shredded lettuce and other raw vegetables. Flautas and* taquitos *are similar, in that both are filled, rolled, and fried; however, sometimes* flautas *(meaning flutes) are made with two tortillas that are overlapped, filled, and then rolled into longer cylinders. This chicken filling is tomato based with a hint of heat.*

1¹/₂ **cups Shredded Chicken (page 271)**
1 tablespoon vegetable oil plus extra for frying tortillas
2 tablespoons finely chopped white onion
1 medium tomato, finely chopped
1 serrano chile, finely chopped with seeds
6 (6- to 7-inch) corn tortillas
1 cup finely shredded lettuce, such as romaine or iceberg
2 teaspoons fresh lime juice
6 thinly sliced radishes
¹/₂ **cup sour cream**

1. Prepare chicken. Then, in a medium skillet, heat 1 tablespoon of oil and cook the onion, stirring, until softened, 3 to 4 minutes. Stir in the tomato, serrano chile, and chicken. Set the pan aside off heat.

2. In a large skillet, heat about ¼ inch of oil until it shimmers. Dip the tortillas in the hot oil about 3 seconds, 1 at a time, until soft and limp. Drain on paper towels. Lay 1 tortilla on a working surface and put about 2 tablespoons of the chicken filling across the lower third of the tortilla. Roll tightly and secure with a toothpick. Lay seam side down on a plate and repeat with all the tortillas. Add extra oil to the skillet, if needed, and reheat until hot. Fry the flautas 2 or 3 at a time, turning, until crisp and golden brown. Drain on paper towels and remove the toothpicks.

3. Make a bed of the shredded lettuce on a plate and drizzle with the lime juice. Lay the warm flautas on top. Drizzle with sour cream. Garnish with radish slices and serve at once.

Crisp Rolled Flautas with Chorizo
Flautas con Chorizo

Makes 6 flautas

A good-quality bulk chorizo makes all the difference for these long flautas. You can also make your own chorizo (Mexican Pork Sausage, page 348). Freeze what you don't need right away.

2 teaspoons vegetable oil, plus extra for
    frying tortillas
2 tablespoons finely chopped onion
1/4 pound fresh bulk chorizo, or packaged,
    with casing removed
1 medium tomato, finely chopped
6 (6- to 7-inch) corn tortillas
1 cup very finely shredded cabbage
1 avocado (Hass variety preferred), thinly sliced
2 teaspoons fresh lime juice
1/2 cup sour cream

1. In a medium skillet, heat 2 teaspoons of oil and cook the onion, stirring, until softened, 3 to 4 minutes. Add the chorizo, breaking it into small pieces, until completely cooked, about 4 minutes. Stir in the tomato and set the pan aside off heat.

2. In a large skillet, heat about 1/4-inch of oil until it shimmers. Dip the tortillas in the hot oil, 1 at a time, until soft and limp, about 3 seconds. Drain on paper towels. Lay 1 tortilla on a working surface and put about 2 tablespoons of the chorizo filling across the lower third of the tortilla. Roll tightly and secure with a toothpick. Lay seam side down on a plate and repeat with all the tortillas. Add extra oil to the skillet, if needed, and reheat until hot. Fry the flautas 2 or 3 at a time until crisp and golden brown. Drain on paper towels and remove the toothpicks.

3. Make a bed of shredded cabbage on a plate. Lay the warm flautas on top. Arrange the sliced avocado around the flautas and sprinkle them with lime juice. Drizzle sour cream over the flautas. Serve at once.

Mushroom and Epazote Tacos
Tacos de Hongos y Epazote

Makes 4 servings

Wild mushrooms grow in the pine forests of the mountains surrounding Mexico City. During the rainy season from June to September the public markets sell a wide variety of mushrooms, and the market food stalls called fondas *offer* cazuelas *(casseroles) of hot flavorful mushrooms to eat with fresh corn tortillas. Look for fresh or dried epazote in Mexican markets.*

4 (6- to 7-inch) corn tortillas
2 tablespoons olive oil
1 medium white onion, finely chopped
1 large garlic clove, finely chopped
1 pound brown cremini mushrooms,
    cleaned and sliced
1 jalapeño chile, seeded, veins removed,
    and finely chopped
1/4 cup chopped fresh epazote leaves,
    or 1 tablespoon dried epazote
1/2 teaspoon salt, or to taste

1. In a deep skillet, heat the oil over medium heat and cook the onion and garlic until softened, about 3 minutes. Add the remaining ingredients and cook, stirring frequently, until the mushrooms are tender and most of the juices have cooked away, about 8 minutes.

2. Heat the tortillas, 1 at a time, in a hot skillet, turning once or twice, until soft and warm, about 1 minute for each tortilla. Cover with foil to prevent them from drying out. To serve, spoon about 3 tablespoons of the mushroom mixture into each tortilla and folk in half. Serve at once.

Creamy Mushroom Tacos
Tacos de Hongos

Makes 8 to 10 tacos

Taquerias (taco snack shops) abound all over Mexico, but these mushroom-filled tacos are more apt to be found in the central highlands of Mexico around Mexico City and Puebla, where a wild mushrooms grow in the mountains.

4 guajillo chiles, cut open, seeded, veins removed, and toasted (page 9)
1 large tomato, peeled and roughly chopped
1 small garlic clove, chopped
1/2 teaspoon dried oregano (Mexican variety preferred), crumbled
1/2 teaspoon ground cumin
1 1/2 tablespoons vegetable oil
1/3 cup heavy cream or half and half
1/2 teaspoon salt, or to taste
3 tablespoons vegetable oil or olive oil
About 1 1/2 pounds cremini mushrooms, halved and thinly sliced (4 cups)
1 medium white onion, finely chopped
1/4 cup finely chopped fresh epazote leaves or cilantro
1/8 teaspoon freshly ground pepper, or to taste
3/4 cup crumbled or grated cotija cheese
10 (6- to 7-inch) corn tortillas

1. Prepare the chiles. Soak them in a bowl of hot water about 20 minutes. Drain and put the chiles in a blender jar. Add the tomato, garlic, and oregano. Blend to a thick smooth paste. If too thick to grind, add water, 1 tablespoon at a time. Heat 1/2 tablespoon of the oil in a small saucepan over medium heat. Add the chile mixture and cook, stirring, until thick and pasty, 3 to 4 minutes. Stir in the cream and simmer, uncovered, until thick and smooth, about 3 minutes. Add 1/4 teaspoon of the salt, or to taste. Cover and set the sauce aside.

2. Heat the remaining oil in a large skillet over medium-high heat. Add the mushrooms and onions. Cook, stirring frequently, until the moisture has cooked away, and the mixture is nearly dry. Stir in the epazote and reserved chile sauce. Cook, stirring, 1 minute to heat through.

3. Transfer the mushrooms to a serving dish. Sprinkle with about 2 tablespoons of the cheese. Serve with soft warm tortillas. Pass the remaining cheese at the table.

Cactus Tacos
Tacos de Nopalitos

Makes about 6 tacos

Mexican tacos are generally made with small soft corn tortillas, about 4 inches in diameter. It's quick hand-to-mouth food that's meant to be eaten as soon as it's made. Although still a rarity in the United States, fresh cactus is often used in Mexican kitchens, and serving them in tacos is easy with cactus strips sold in jars. Buy the kind packed in water. Don't buy those in brine.

2 cups rinsed and drained strips of cactus (nopalitos)
1 tablespoon olive oil
1/2 large white onion, finely chopped
1/2 teaspoon salt, or to taste
Fresly ground pepper, to taste
6 (5- to 6-inch) corn tortillas
Crumbled queso fresco (fresh Mexican cheese)
Fresh salsa, purchased or homemade

1. Cut the cactus strips into 1/4-inch dice and set aside. In a medium skillet, heat the oil and cook the onion, stirring, until it starts to brown, 4 to 5 minutes. Season with salt and pepper. Stir in the reserved diced cactus and heat through completely. Set aside.

2. Heat a small nonstick skillet and warm the tortillas, 1 at a time, until soft and pliable. To assemble, put a portion of the cactus filling on half of each warm tortilla. Top with queso fresco and salsa. Fold in half and serve at once.

Tacos with Steak, Cactus, and Onions
Tacos de Bistek, Nopales, y Cebollas

*Makes **4 tacos***

When we went to view the ruins of Cacaxtla in the tiny state of Tlaxcala only a few miles from Puebla, we were invited to a home to watch amaranth candy being made. Amaranth, a plant with edible leaves and seeds, is grown in the area. The seeds are ground to use like flour, or toasted and mixed with honey for candy. While we were there, we were treated to a snack of the special regional tacos made with blue corn tortillas. The thin steaks, cactus, and onions were quickly cooked on a hot griddle and stuffed into fresh blue corn tortillas. Green salsa and cold beer accompanied the tacos. White corn tortillas can be used in place of blue corn tortillas.

Fresh Tomatillo Salsa (page 34)
2 fresh small cactus paddles, thorns cut off and trimmed (optional)
2 thin (¹/4-inch) steaks, about 8 ounces total
¹/2 medium white onion, thinly sliced
Vegetable oil
Salt, to taste
4 (6- to 7-inch) blue corn or white corn tortillas

1. Prepare the salsa if using the cactus. Then cut finger-like strips of each cactus paddle lengthwise to within 1½ inch of the edge to resemble the palm of a hand. Heat a flat griddle or large cast iron skillet until hot. Put the cactus paddles on the griddle. Cook about 1 minute.

2. Turn the cactus, and add the steaks and onion to the griddle. Brush everything with oil. Cook, turning everything, 2 to 3 times, until the meat is done and the cactus and onion are tender. Season with salt.

3. Transfer everything to a cutting board. Chop the steaks into small pieces. Cut each cactus paddle in half. Warm the tortillas on the griddle until pliable. Divide the cactus, meat, and onion among the tortillas. Fold in half and serve at once with the salsa.

Potato and Green Chile Tacos
Tacos con Papas y Rajas

*Makes **8 small tacos***

Cuernavaca, near Mexico City, is a welcome retreat for a day or overnight visit. The vast public market is not to be missed and the fondas (food stalls) turn out an incredible selection of things to eat and drink. Soft warm corn tortillas filled with potatoes, chiles, and fresh salsa especially pleased me, and they are easy to make at home.

3 small (4 ounces) red or white potatoes
3 large poblano chiles, roasted, peeled, seeded, and veins removed (page 8)
1 tablespoon vegetable oil or olive oil
¹/2 medium white onion, finely chopped
¹/2 teaspoon salt, or to taste
¹/4 teaspoon dried oregano (Mexican variety preferred), crumbled
8 (6- to 7-inch) corn tortillas
Salsa (red or green), purchased or homemade

1. Cook the potatoes in water to cover until tender, 12 to 15 minutes. Peel the potatoes and finely dice or chop them Put in a bowl. Cut the chiles into short thin strips (¼ × 1 inch). Add to the bowl of potatoes. In a large nonstick skillet, heat the oil over medium heat and cook the onion until it starts to brown, about 4 minutes. Add the potatoes, chiles, salt, and oregano. Cook, stirring, until completely heated through, about 3 to 4 minutes.

2. Heat a medium, dry skillet over medium heat and soften the tortillas, 1 at a time, turning until pliable and hot. Cover the heated tortillas with a clean kitchen towel to keep soft and hot. To assemble, spoon about 3 tablespoons of the potato mixture and 1 tablespoon of salsa on half of each tortilla. Fold in half. Serve at once.

Mashed Potato Tacos with Red Salsa
Doblados de Papas
Makes **4 snacks**

In the state of Puebla, a quick mashed potato taco is typical street food that's economical, filling, and nourishing. Add red salsa for a simple tortilla snack. My friend, Chef Ricardo Muñoz Zurita shared this tasty, easy recipe.

Fresh Salsa Mexicana (page 24), or purchased
2 medium (1/2-pound) potatoes, peeled and sliced
2 tablespoons olive oil or unsalted butter
1/2 teaspoon salt, or to taste
4 (6- to 7-inch) corn tortillas
2 teaspoons vegetable oil or lard

1. Prepare the salsa if using homemade. Then, in a saucepan, cook the potatoes in water to cover until soft, 8 to 10 minutes. Drain and mash with oil, or butter, and season with salt. Soften corn tortillas in a hot dry skillet until limp, 10 to 12 seconds. Fill each with about 3 tablespoons of mashed potatoes and fold in half.

2. Brush the outside of each taco with oil. Put in a hot skillet and cook the tacos, turning, until just starting to brown, but still pliable. Serve with fresh salsa.

Fish Tacos
Tacos de Pescado
Makes **6 tacos**

In Baja, where fresh fish is plentiful along both coasts of the peninsula, fish tacos are among the most popular quick snacks in the region. My brother-in-law, Frank Davis, lives part of each year in Baja and uses this standard procedure to make the typical fish tacos made by many food vendors in Ensenada.

4 ripe medium tomatoes, finely chopped
1 small garlic clove, finely chopped
1/4 onion, finely chopped
1 serrano chile with seeds or seeded jalapeño chile, finely chopped
2 tablespoons chopped fresh cilantro
3/4 teaspoon salt
1/4 cup mayonnaise
1/4 cup plain yogurt
6 fish fillets, about 2 inches wide by 4 inches long
1/2 cup all-purpose flour
1/8 teaspoon garlic powder
1/8 teaspoon freshly ground pepper, or to taste
1/2 cup beer, any kind
Oil for frying
6 (6- to 7-inch) corn tortillas
1/4 small head cabbage, finely shredded
Lime wedges

1. In a medium bowl, mix together the tomatoes, garlic, onion, chile, cilantro, and 1/4 teaspoon of the salt. Set the salsa aside. In another bowl, mix the mayonnaise and yogurt together. Set aside.

2. Pat the fish dry with paper towels. In a medium bowl mix the flour, garlic powder, 1/2 teaspoon of the salt and pepper. Stir in the beer and mix well. Dip the fish into the beer batter and lay on waxed paper 15 to 20 minutes. In a deep skillet, pour oil to a depth of 2 inches and heat to 375°. Fry the fish, 2 pieces at a time, turning once until crisp and golden brown outside and barely flakes inside. Drain on paper towels.

3. Heat a dry nonstick skillet and warm the tortillas, 1 at a time until soft and pliable. Stack between layers of a clean kitchen towel to keep warm. To assemble, layer on each warm tortilla 1 fish fillet, plus the amount of salsa, mayonnaise, and cabbage desired. Fold in half and serve.

Red Snapper Fish Tacos
Pescadillas

Makes 4 servings

Commercial fishing is an important industry in Acapulco where seafood restaurants and snack stands abound. Crisp rolled fish tacos called pescadillas *are a treat to try in Acapulco and some coastal villages nearby. Serve guacamole with the tacos.*

³/₄ **pound boneless red snapper, or other white fish fillets**
1 small garlic clove, finely chopped
¹/₂ **teaspoon dried oregano (Mexican variety preferred), crumbled**
¹/₄ **teaspoon salt, or to taste**
2 tablespoons vegetable oil, plus oil for frying the tacos
1 medium tomato, finely chopped
¹/₄ **cup finely chopped white onion**
1 serrano chile, minced with seeds
2 teaspoons fresh lime juice
2 tablespoons chopped fresh cilantro
8 (6- to 7-inch) corn tortillas

1. Season the fish with the garlic, oregano, and salt. Heat the oil in a medium skillet, over medium-high heat, and sauté the fish on both sides until just opaque inside, about 3 to 4 minutes on each side, depending on the thickness of the fish. Using a fork, flake the fish and put in a bowl.

2. When the fish is cool, add the tomato, onion, garlic, serrano chile, lime juice, and cilantro. Toss gently to mix.

3. Heat 1 tortilla, turning once or twice, on a hot griddle or dry skillet until soft, about 15 seconds. Put the tortilla on a plate, and spoon about ¹/₈ of the fish mixture along the lower third of the tortilla. Roll into a tight cylinder and secure with wooden toothpicks. Repeat with remaining tortillas and fish.

4. In a clean skillet, heat oil to a depth of ¼ inch in the pan. Fry 2 or 3 tacos at a time until golden brown and crisp on the outside. Drain on paper towels, remove the toothpicks, and serve hot.

Open-Faced Chicken and Cheese Quesadillas
Tortillas de Harina con Pollo y Queso

Makes 2 servings

These maverick open-faced quesadillas make a simple and eye-appealing light lunch. The flour tortillas are an edible base and can be fried crisp ahead of time.

¹/₄ **cup vegetable oil**
2 (7-inch) flour tortillas
1 skinless boneless chicken breast half
¹/₈ **teaspoon salt, or to taste**
Salt and freshly ground pepper, to taste
1 cup shredded Monterey Jack cheese
¹/₄ **cup fresh salsa, purchased or homemade**
¹/₄ **cup sour cream**
Cilantro sprigs

1. Preheat the broiler. Heat the oil in a medium skillet until hot and shimmering. Fry the tortillas, 1 at a time, until crisp and lightly browned on both sides. Drain on paper towels. Add additional oil, if needed. In the same skillet, cook the chicken breast until browned on both sides and opaque in the center, about 8 minutes total. Season with salt and pepper. Cut the chicken crosswise into thin strips. Reserve.

2. Put the tortillas on a large baking sheet and divide the cheese evenly on top. Run under the hot broiler until the cheese is melted, about 45 seconds. Remove from the oven. Arrange half of the chicken in the center of each tortilla. Top with salsa and sour cream. Garnish with a sprig of cilantro. Serve at once.

Chicken Quesadillas
Quesadillas de Pollo

Makes **4 to 6 appetizer servings**

Flour tortillas filled with chicken and cheese are crisp and golden brown on the outside with shredded chicken and melted cheese on the inside for a tantalizing light meal. This version is easy to prepare at home.

³/₄ pound chicken tenders (tenderloin pieces)
¹/₄ teaspoon salt, or to taste
1 tablespoon vegetable oil
¹/₃ cup finely chopped onion
¹/₄ cup prepared thick and chunky salsa
8 (6- or 7-inch) flour tortillas
1 cup grated Monterey Jack cheese
Additional oil for frying

1. Sprinkle the chicken tenders with salt. Heat the oil in a skillet over medium heat, and sauté the chicken, turning 2 to 3 times, until golden brown, about 3 to 4 minutes. Remove the chicken to a plate. Add the onion to the skillet, and cook 2 minutes. Remove the pan from the heat and stir in the salsa. With clean fingers, shred the chicken into strips, and mix with the onions and salsa.

2. To assemble the quesadillas, place 4 of the tortillas on a flat surface, and sprinkle each with about 2 tablespoons of the cheese. Layer with the chicken and the remaining cheese. Top with remaining tortillas. In a clean medium skillet, heat about 2 teaspoons oil over medium heat. Fry the quesadillas, 1 at a time, 1 to 2 minutes, or until lightly browned. Carefully lift the quesadilla with a wide spatula, and turn. Fry the second side until lightly browned, about 1 minute. Add additional oil to the pan, as needed, for each quesadilla. Cut into quarters and serve.

Quesadillas with Oven-Barbecued Beef
Quesadillas de Carne de Res

Makes **4 servings**

When polls are taken on where to get the best tacos, burritos, and other snacks in San Francisco, La Taqueria on Mission Street is at or near the top every time. Owner Miguel Jara's high standards for authentic Mexican snacks and service makes La Taqueria worth a visit. The beef and cheese quesadillas made with soft fresh flour tortillas are fantastic, but they must be made separately and served hot off the griddle. This is a procedure more than a recipe, but one you're bound to commit to memory. This recipe serves four, but adjust the recipe to make as many as you want.

Oven-Barbecued Beef (page 342)
1¹/₂ cups shredded Monterey Jack cheese
1 cup fresh red salsa, purchased or homemade
Vegetable oil or melted lard for frying
4 (7- to 8-inch) flour tortillas

1. Prepare the barbecued beef. Then, shred the amount of beef needed and have ready in a bowl by the stove along with separate bowls of the cheese and salsa. Put a small bowl of oil and a pastry brush near the heat source for the skillet or a flat griddle. Lay newspaper with a layer of paper towels on the counter for draining the quesadillas.

2. Heat a dry skillet or griddle over medium heat. Place 1 tortilla on a flat working surface and brush both sides with oil. Fry the tortilla in the hot pan about 5 seconds per side. Immediately remove it to the towels, and put a layer of meat, then a layer of cheese and a layer of salsa on half of the tortilla. Fold the tortilla in half and return to the pan. Fry until golden on both sides. Drain quickly on paper towels and serve at once. Repeat, making as many quesadillas as desired.

Quesadillas with Avocado
Quesdillas de Aguacate

Makes 12 snack triangles

Cheese by itself, and just about anything else—in this case, avocado—is layered inside toasted tortillas to make quesadillas. Fresh salsa may be served with these quesadillas to spoon a dollop on top of each snack.

1 ripe avocado (Hass variety preferred), peeled and mashed
1 tablespoon finely chopped onion
1 teaspoon fresh lime juice
2-to 3 dashes hot pepper sauce, such as Tabasco
1/4 teaspoon salt
6 (7-inch) flour tortillas
1 cup shredded Oaxaca or Monterey Jack cheese
Vegetable oil for frying

1. In a bowl, mix the avocado, onion, lime juice, Tabasco sauce, and salt. Lay 3 of the tortillas on a work surface. Spread each tortilla equally with the avocado mixture to within about ½-inch from the edge. Sprinkle cheese equally on top of the avocado on each tortilla. Put the remaining tortillas on top to close like a sandwich. Brush each top tortilla lightly with oil.

2. Heat a large nonstick skillet over medium heat. Invert one of the tortilla stacks and lay in the pan, oiled side down. Again brush the top tortilla with oil. Toast until light brown and crisp. With a large wide spatula turn the stack over and brown the second side. Repeat with the remaining stacks. When all are brown and crisp on both sides cut each stack into quarters. Arrange on a plate. Serve warm.

Quesadillas with Zucchini and Cheese
Quesadillas de Calabacitas y Queso

Makes 12 quesadillas

This appetizer is made by filling flour tortillas with shredded zucchini and cheese, then folding them like a turnover and finally browning them quickly in oil for a crunchy exterior. The quesadillas are cut into triangles and served as an appetizer.

1 tablespoon vegetable oil, plus extra for browning the quesadillas
6 small zucchini, coarsely shredded and moisture squeezed out
1/4 medium white onion, finely chopped
1 large garlic clove, finely chopped
1/4 teaspoon salt, or to taste
1 cup shredded Monterey Jack cheese
1 tablespoon prepared salsa
12 (6- to 7-inch) flour tortillas

1. In a large skillet, heat the oil over medium-high heat. Add the zucchini, onion, and garlic. Cook, stirring, about 1 minute. Scrape the vegetables into a medium bowl and let stand until cool. Season with salt. Stir in the cheese and the salsa.

2. To assemble the quesadillas, lay 1 tortilla on a flat surface and put about 2 tablespoons of the zucchini mixture on one half of the tortilla. Fold the other half over to create a half-moon shape. Repeat with the remaining tortillas and zucchini. Heat about 1 tablespoon of oil in a nonstick skillet, brown the quesadillas on both sides, and put on a baking sheet lined with paper towels. Keep warm in a 200° oven while cooking the remaining quesadillas. Add extra oil as needed. To serve, cut each quesadilla in half, and serve at once.

Quesadillas with Squash Blossoms
Quesadillas de Flor de Calabazas

Makes **8 quesadillas**

Golden squash blossoms are used extensively throughout Mexico as a filling for quesadillas. These beautiful blossoms are becoming more available in the United States in season at farmers' markets and in some Mexican or Italian markets. The cooked filling of chopped blossoms, onion, garlic, tomato, and epazote is tucked inside a folded tortilla and lightly fried. This version from food stalls in Puebla's public market uses ready-made corn tortillas for convenience. Most authentic quesadillas are made with uncooked masa *dough that is pressed into tortillas, filled, folded, and then fried.*

5 ounces (about 25) large squash blossoms
1 tablespoon olive oil
1/2 cup chopped white onion
1 large garlic clove, finely chopped
2 medium tomatoes, peeled and finely chopped
1 serrano chile, finely chopped with seeds
1 tablespoons chopped fresh epazote leaves
1/4 teaspoon dried oregano (Mexican variety preferred), crumbled
1/4 teaspoon salt, or to taste
1/3 cup crumbled cotija or mild feta cheese
8 (6- to 7-inch) corn tortillas
Vegetable oil for frying

1. To prepare the blossoms, cut off the stems and remove the green petals at the base of the flowers. Pinch off the stamen from inside the blossoms. Rinse gently and shake off excess water. Cut crosswise about 1/2-inch thick. Set aside.

2. In a large nonstick skillet, heat the olive oil over medium heat and cook the onion and garlic, stirring, until the onion is tender, about 4 minutes. Add the tomatoes, serrano, *epazote*, oregano, and salt. Cook, partially covered, until the blossoms cook down and juices are reduced, 6 to 8 minutes. Remove the pan from the heat. Cool 5 minutes and stir in the cheese.

3. To assemble, heat the tortillas, 1 at a time, in a hot dry skillet until pliable. Put about 3 teaspoons filling on half of the tortilla and fold over. Put on a plate and repeat with the remaining tortillas. In the same skillet, heat vegetable oil to a depth of about 1/4 inch. Fry the quesadillas, 2 at a time, until golden on both sides. Drain on paper towels and serve while still hot.

Quesadilla Stack with Onions and Cheese
Quesadillas de Cebollas y Queso

Makes **12 small appetizer wedges**

Flour tortillas are stacked with caramelized onions and cheese filling between the layers for these quesadillas. These are great to make ahead. I butter the outside of the tortilla stacks before covering and storing them. Then just before serving I toast them on a stovetop grill pan or skillet. Easy!

2 tablespoons olive oil
3/4 pound red onions, finely chopped (about 1 1/2 cups)
1 teaspoon unseasoned rice vinegar
1/2 teaspoon sugar
2 tablespoons chopped fresh oregano or 1 teaspoon dried oregano (Mexican variety preferred)
1/2 cup crumbled cotija or mild feta cheese
3 tablespoons mayonnaise
1/2 teaspoon salt
1/8 teaspoon freshly ground pepper, or to taste
6 (7-inch) flour tortillas
Unsalted butter or margarine, at room temperature

1. In a skillet, heat the oil over low heat and cook the onions, stirring frequently, until they are soft and light brown, 8 to 10 minutes. Add the vinegar, sugar, and 1 teaspoon of water. Cook, stirring, until the liquid evaporates, 2 to 3 minutes more.

Transfer the onions to a bowl and cool. When the onions are lukewarm, add the oregano, cheese, mayonnaise, salt, and pepper. Mix and set aside.

2. Lay 2 tortillas on a flat surface. Spread ¼ of the onion mixture on each tortilla. Place a second tortilla on top of the onion mixture and spread the remaining onion mixture equally on both tortillas. Lay the remaining 2 tortillas on top of each stack. Spread a thin film of butter on the top tortilla in each stack. Invert the two stacks and spread a thin film of butter on the unbuttered side. Put the two stacks on a plate with a piece of wax paper between them. If made ahead, cover and refrigerate until shortly before serving.

3. Heat a grill pan over medium high heat and lay 1 tortilla stack on the hot pan. Toast until crisp with grill marks from the pan ridges, about 1 to 2 minutes. Flip and brown the second side, 1 to 2 minutes. Repeat with the second stack. Cut each stack into 6 equal wedges. Serve warm.

Quesadillas with Chiles and Mushrooms
Quesadillas de Chile Poblano y Hongo

Makes **4 servings**

Quesadillas contain more than just melted cheese these days. Here, roasted strips of poblano chile and mushrooms make a special appetizer quesadilla that's cut into wedges. Serve with fresh or bottled salsa, if desired.

2 large poblano chiles, roasted, peeled, seeded, and veins removed (page 8)
2 teaspoons vegetable oil
8 medium white or brown button mushrooms, thinly sliced
2 green onions, thinly sliced
4 (10-inch) flour tortillas
1 cup shredded Monterey Jack or manchego cheese

1. Cut the roasted poblano chiles into ½-inch squares. Set aside. Heat the oil in a medium skillet and cook the mushrooms until they release their juices and start to brown, 3 to 4 minutes. Remove the pan from the heat and stir in the chiles and green onions.

2. Lay 2 of the tortillas on a work surface. Scatter ¼ cup of cheese on each tortilla. Top equally with the mushroom mixture. Scatter remaining cheese evenly over the tortillas. Top with the remaining tortillas.

3. Heat a large dry skillet and toast the quesadillas, 1 at a time, until light brown on both sides and the cheese is melted, 1 to 2 minutes on each side. Cut the quesadillas into wedges. Serve at once.

Goat Cheese Quesadillas
Quesadillas de Queso de Chiva

Makes **16 appetizers**

The Spanish brought cows and goats to Mexico, and cheese making followed, with much of it being made in central Mexico, in the states of Guanajuato, Michoacan, and Jalisco. Goat cheese is produced there too, and creative chefs are using it in some of their new-style dishes. The sweetness of pan-roasted onion pairs remarkably well with the tangy goat cheese. Fuerte restaurant in the charming and popular city of Tlaquepaque, a village outside of Guadalajara in Jalisco, gets credit for this simple recipe.

2 (½-inch-thick) rounds white onion
8 (6- to 7-inch) flour tortillas
6 ounces goat cheese, at room temperature
Vegetable oil for frying
Fresh red salsa, purchased or homemade

1. Lay a 6-inch square of aluminum foil in the bottom of a small dry skillet and heat the skillet over medium heat. Place the onion rounds on the foil and dry-roast until nicely browned, 6 to 8 minutes, repositioning the rounds once or twice to brown evenly. Turn and brown the second side until the onion is tender, but not soft, about 6 minutes. Remove to a cutting board and chop the onion. Lay 4 tortillas on a flat surface and spread with the goat cheese. Scatter the onion evenly on the cheese. Top with the remaining 4 tortillas.

2. In a large nonstick skillet, heat about 1 tablespoon of oil over medium heat and cook the quesadillas, 1 at a time, until golden and crisp on both sides, 1 to 2 minutes on each side. Add more oil as needed. Cut each quesadilla into quarters. Top each quarter with about 1 teaspoon of salsa. Serve at once.

Chickpea Quesadillas with Cheese
Quesadillas de Garbanzos

Makes **about 10 appetizers**

Sometimes corn tortilla dough is mixed with other ingredients. Mashed chickpeas in the dough produces a softer, moister texture inside and gives the dough a slightly different flavor. The dough is made into quesadillas and fried until crisp and brown. These appetizers, common in Tlaxcala and Puebla, should be eaten within a few minutes after frying. You can find a tortilla press in some Mexican markets.

1/2 cup plus 1 tablespoon instant masa harina
1/2 cup warm tap water
1/4 cup canned chickpeas (garbanzo beans), drained and rinsed
1 teaspoon chipotle salsa, or adobo from canned chipotles
4 (8-inch) squares of plastic wrap to line tortilla press
8 ounces Oaxaca string cheese, or other melting cheese, cut into thin strips, 1-inch long × 1/2-inch wide
Vegetable oil for frying

1. In a medium bowl, mix the masa and water to a soft smooth dough. Mash the garbanzo beans to a coarse purée and mix with the masa dough. Add the chipotle salsa. Mix to a moist soft dough that does not stick to the hands. Just until the dough comes together, and is easy to manage, about 2 minutes. If sticky, add masa flour 1 tablespoon at a time. Form the dough into balls about large walnut size. Cover the balls with plastic wrap to prevent drying out.

2. Lay 1 plastic square on the bottom of a tortilla press, and place 1 dough ball in the center of the press. Put another plastic square on top of the ball. Gently press the tortilla handle to make a 3½-inch circle. Remove the top plastic square. Put a small thin slice of cheese on half of the dough circle and lift the bottom plastic square and fold over to enclose the cheese inside the dough in a half moon shape. Seal the edges. Remove the plastic and place on a plate. Repeat pressing each dough ball between 2 plastic squares, then filling, folding, and removing the plastic square.

3. Heat oil to a depth of about ½ inch in a medium skillet. Fry each quesadilla in the hot oil until crisp and brown on both sides, about 2 to 3 minutes total. Drain on paper towels. Serve the quesadillas at once.

Yucatán Egg-Stuffed Tortillas with Pumpkin Seed Sauce
Papadzules

Makes **4 servings**

Papadzules *is a traditional Mayan dish of tortillas stuffed with hard-boiled eggs, covered with pumpkin seed sauce, and topped with tomato sauce. In the traditional way, the green oil is squeezed from the pumpkin seeds to drizzle over the top of the dish as a final flourish. This extra step is time consuming, so I left it out.*

Yucatán Tomato Sauce (page 44)
1¼ cups raw shelled pumpkin seeds
Corn oil, safflower or canola oil for frying
1 medium white onion, chopped
2 medium garlic cloves, finely chopped
10 to 12 fresh epazote leaves, or 1 teaspoon
    dried epazote
1 habanero or serrano chile, seeded and veins
    removed (wear protective gloves)
1¾ cups canned fat-free reduced-sodium
    chicken broth
4 hard-cooked large eggs, peeled and chopped
8 (6- to 7-inch) corn tortillas

1. Prepare the tomato sauce. Then, in a large dry skillet, toast the pumpkin seeds, stirring, until aromatic, starting to brown, and popping around in the pan, 3 to 4 minutes. Reserve on a plate to cool.

2. In the same pan, heat 2 tablespoons of oil over medium heat and cook the onion until softened, about 3 minutes. Add the garlic and cook 1 minute. Transfer to a blender. (Save the skillet for later use.)

3. To the blender, add the reserved pumpkin seeds, epazote, chile, and ½ cup of the broth. Process to a thick paste. Add the remaining chicken broth, a little at a time, blending after each addition to a thick smooth sauce. Transfer the sauce to a medium nonstick skillet and cook over low heat, stirring frequently, until it simmers,

3 to 4 minutes. Do not boil, or the sauce might curdle. (If it does, blend again.) Cover and reserve in the pan, off heat.

4. Reheat the tomato sauce. In a medium nonstick skillet, heat 1 tablespoon oil, and soften the tortillas, 1 at a time on both sides until warm and limp. Stack on a plate. To assemble, dip each tortilla in the pumpkin seed sauce to coat both sides. Lay the coated tortilla on a plate. Put a small portion of the chopped egg along the center of each tortilla, roll, and lay seam side down on a warm platter. Repeat until all are dipped, filled, and rolled. To serve, put 2 stuffed tortillas on each of 4 plates. Top with heated tomato sauce. Serve hot.

Bean Burritos
Burritos de Frijol

Makes **4 servings**

Burritos are soft flour tortillas that are filled with just about anything and rolled. Burritos are traditionally eaten with the hands like a sandwich. Some sit-down restaurants provide a fork and knife to eat plump burritos.

4 (9- to 10-inch) flour tortillas
2 cups refried beans, canned or homemade
1½ cups shredded Monterey Jack or cheddar
    cheese
½ cup fresh salsa, purchased or homemade

1. Soften the tortillas in a large hot dry skillet, or heat in the microwave according to microwave instruction, until soft and pliable.

2. Spread each soft warm tortilla with ¼ of the beans and top equally with shredded cheese. Fold in the sides and roll in a cylinder.

3. Heat skillet or griddle over medium-high heat, then place burrito seam-side down on the hot skillet and cook briefly, turning, until the cheese melts, about 2 minutes. Serve hot with the salsa to add while eating.

Tijuana Pork Burritos
Tijuana Burritos de Cerdo

Makes **6 servings**

Thin slices of pork are seasoned, then grilled and chopped, for this type of pork burrito typical in Tijuana. The pork is wrapped in a soft flour tortilla along with avocado salsa, and shredded lettuce. Flour tortillas are used a great deal along the border of northern Mexico. Maggi is a bottled seasoning extract that's widely used in Mexican cooking. Look for it in Mexican markets.

1 pound lean pork (such as pork loin), sliced about 1/2-inch thick
2 large garlic cloves, finely chopped
1 teaspoon Maggi seasoning extract or Worcestershire sauce
1 teaspoon Chipotle and Tomatillo Sauce (page 49) or 1 mashed canned chipotle chile en adobo
1 teaspoon vegetable oil
1 large ripe avocado (Hass variety preferred)
1 medium tomato, seeded and finely chopped
1/4 medium white onion, finely chopped
1 serrano chile, finely chopped
2 tablespoons chopped fresh cilantro
Juice of 1 fresh lime
1/4 teaspoon salt
6 (7-inch) flour tortillas
Shredded lettuce

1. Cover the pork slices with plastic wrap and pound them to an even 1/4-inch thickness with a meat mallet or rolling pin. Put the meat in a pie plate. In a small bowl combine the garlic, seasoning extract, chipotle sauce, and oil. Spoon over the meat, and turn the slices several times to coat with the marinade. Marinate the meat 25 to 30 minutes.

2. Meanwhile, in a medium bowl mash the avocado with a fork. Add the tomato, onion, serrano, cilantro, lime juice, and salt. Stir gently to mix.

3. Heat a nonstick skillet over medium-high heat. Put the seasoned meat in the pan, and cook, turning 2 to 3 times until nicely browned and cooked through, 3 to 4 minutes total. Remove the meat to a cutting board and chop into bite-size pieces. Transfer the chopped pork to a bowl.

4. Heat the tortillas, 1 at a time, on a hot griddle, comal, or in a dry skillet. Lay 1 tortilla on a working surface, and spread with 1/6 of the avocado salsa. Add 1/6 of the chopped grilled pork, and some shredded lettuce. Fold in the sides and roll the tortilla into a cylinder. Repeat with the remaining tortillas. Serve warm.

Grilled Chicken Burritos
Burritos de Pollo Asada

Makes **4 servings**

Burritos probably originated in the state of Sonora and never spread deep into Mexico, but certainly gained in fame and size when established in the United States. These grilled chicken burritos are typical of the ones made at Burritos Bol Corona in Tijuana.

4 skinless boneless chicken breast halves
1/2 teaspoon salt
1 tablespoon fresh lime juice
2 tablespoons vegetable oil
4 (11-inch) flour tortillas
1 1/2 cups heated refried beans, canned or homemade
1 cup spicy fresh salsa (red or green), purchased or homemade
1 cup very finely shredded lettuce

1. Preheat a grill, broiler, or stovetop grill pan. Sprinkle the chicken with salt and lime juice. Brush both sides with vegetable oil. Cook over hot coals, under a hot oven broiler, or in a hot grill pan until lightly browned on both sides and opaque in the center, 6 to 8 minutes total. Chop into small pieces or cut into thin strips.

2. Warm the tortillas in a large hot skillet, 1 at a time, turning, until soft and pliable, about 20 seconds per tortilla. Layer the warm tortillas with ¼ of the refried beans, salsa, chicken, and lettuce. Fold in the sides and roll. Serve at once.

Stuffed and Fried Flour Tortillas
Chimichangas Chicas de Picadillo

Makes **6 snack-size servings**

Chimichangas *are burritos that are fried after being filled and rolled. They are found mainly in the state of Sonora in northern Mexico where very large thin flour tortillas are used. My recipe is more manageable for home cooks, and features a simplified* picadillo *(chopped meat) filling for small flour tortillas to be served as a first course or light snack.*

Basic Cooked Tomato Sauce (page 42)

1 tablespoon olive oil

1 pound lean ground pork or beef

1 medium onion, finely chopped

1 cup spicy prepared thick and chunky salsa

⅓ cup raisins

1 teaspoon dried oregano (Mexican variety preferred), crumbled

½ teaspoon ground cinnamon (Mexican canela or Ceylon variety preferred)

¼ teaspoon ground allspice

½ teaspoon salt

6 (8- to 9-inch) flour tortillas

Vegetable oil for frying

½ cup sour cream

Chopped fresh cilantro

1. Prepare the tomato sauce and keep warm. Then, in a large skillet, heat olive oil over medium heat. Add the meat, and cook, breaking it up, until no longer pink, about 3 minutes. Add the onion and cook, stirring, about 3 minutes. Add the salsa, raisins, oregano, cinnamon, allspice, and salt. Cook, stirring occasionally, until mixture is nearly dry, 6 to 8 minutes. Remove from the heat and set the picadillo aside.

2. In a large dry skillet, soften the tortillas, 1 at a time, over medium heat, turning once or twice until soft and warm, about 1 minute total for each tortilla. Stack and cover with a kitchen towel to keep warm. (Or microwave the tortillas, wrapped in damp paper towels, about 1 minute on high.)

3. Preheat the oven to 200°. Put 1 warm tortilla on a plate. Put about 3 tablespoons filling in the center. Fold the bottom up over the filling, fold in the sides, and fold the top down, overlapping, envelope style. Secure with toothpicks, and put on a tray. Repeat with remaining tortillas.

4. In a large skillet, heat 2 tablespoons of oil over medium heat. Add the filled tortillas, 2 at a time, folded side down, and fry until golden brown on the bottom, about 45 seconds. Turn and brown the second side, 30 to 40 seconds. Place on a baking sheet and keep warm in the oven while frying remaining chimichangas. To serve, put the chimichangas on individual plates, ladle the warm tomato sauce on top, add a dollop of sour cream, and sprinkle with cilantro. Serve at once.

Masa Dough Snacks

Masa Shells for Sopes
Sopes

Makes **about 16 snacks**

Sopes are small corn tortillas, made a little thicker, with pinched-up edges to hold a topping. There are many versions of these masa shells, and some have different names, but they are almost all the same. This recipe provides the special technique used to form and bake sopes. There are endless possibilities for toppings and several kinds are in this book. Fresh masa from a tortilla factory or homemade tortilla dough using masa harina is the base for the sopes. Masa harina (corn flour for tortillas) is available in most supermarkets, and is not the same as cornmeal. You'll need a tortilla press to make these. Cast-iron and aluminum both work; look for them in Mexican groceries, in kitchen stores, or by mail (see page 620).

Basic Corn Tortilla Dough (page 133)

1 teaspoon vegetable oil

Tortilla press

Plastic wrap, cut into two 8-inch squares (heavy duty is best)

1. Prepare the tortilla dough. Then, form the dough into 16 equal balls and cover with plastic wrap to keep soft. Heat a large skillet over high heat and brush with a few drops of oil. Using a tortilla press, put an 8-inch square of plastic on the bottom of the tortilla press. Place 1 of the dough balls on the center and top with another piece of plastic. Lower the handle and press lightly to form a patty about 3 inches in diameter and ¼ inch thick. Pick up the sope with one hand and remove the top piece of plastic. Flip the dough onto the other hand. Remove the second piece of plastic and place the patty on the hot skillet. Cook about 1 minute. Turn and cook until light brown on the bottom. (The interior will still be soft.)

2. Remove sope from the heat, and while still hot, pinch up the pale top edge to make a small rim all around. Work fast—the sopes are hot! Put the sope on a plate, cover with plastic and repeat with the remaining sopes. Once you get the hang of it, you can press and bake the sopes quickly. Put the sopes in a sealed plastic bag and store refrigerated up to 1 day ahead. Before assembling, the sopes will be fried and filled. To complete and serve, see the recipes for Masa Shells with Chicken and Potatoes (page 108) or Ground Beef Sopes (page 109).

Masa Shells with Chicken and Potatoes
Sopes de Pollo y Papa

Makes **about 16 appetizers**

Masa *shells (called* sopes*) are served all over Mexico. They are topped with just about anything and are quite addictive!*

Masa Shells for Sopes (page 107)
2 skinless boneless chicken breast halves
Oil for frying
$1/2$ medium white onion, finely chopped
2 (4-ounce) cooked boiling potatoes, peeled and finely diced
$1/2$ teaspoon salt
$1/2$ cup green salsa, purchased or homemade
$1/2$ cup crumbled cotija or mild feta cheese
6 small radishes, thinly sliced

1. Prepare the masa shells. Then, cover and set aside. Cook the chicken breasts over medium heat in 1 cup of salted water until no longer pink in the center, about 8 minutes. Remove the pan from the heat and cool the chicken in the liquid about 10 minutes. When cool, shred the meat and reserve in a bowl.

2. In a medium nonstick skillet, heat about 1 tablespoon of oil and cook the onion, stirring, until translucent, about 3 minutes. Add the diced potatoes and salt. Cook, stirring, until the potatoes start to brown, about 5 minutes. Transfer to the bowl with the chicken. Stir in the salsa. Set aside.

3. Wipe out the skillet with paper towels. Add fresh oil to a depth of about 1 inch and cook over medium-high heat until the oil shimmers. Fry the reserved masa shells, 3 to 4 at a time, turning once until golden on both sides, about 2 minutes on each side. Drain on paper towels. Put a portion of the chicken mixture on each sope. Sprinkle each with cheese and garnish with thinly sliced radish rounds. Serve at once.

Masa Shells with Refried Beans and Chicken
Sopes de Pollo y Frijoles Refritos

Makes **about 16 appetizers**

Warm refried beans, finely diced fried potatoes, green onion, chicken, and spicy green salsa add up to one of the most popular sopes ever. The sopes and layered components can be made ahead. The final frying and filling of the sopes goes pretty fast. Make plenty, for they'll be snapped up quickly.

Pan-Roasted Tomatilla Sauce (page 35), or purchased green salsa
Masa Shells for Sopes (page 107)
Shredded Chicken (page 271)
3 teaspoons olive oil
2 medium cooked potatoes, peeled and cut into $1/4$-inch dice
2 green onions, finely chopped
$1/4$ teaspoon salt, or to taste
$1/8$ teaspoon freshly ground pepper, or to taste
Oil for frying
1 cup heated refried beans, canned or homemade
Green salsa, purchased or homemade
Sour cream
Sliced radishes (optional)

1. Prepare the salsa. Reserve. Then, prepare the masa shells. Cover and set aside. Then, prepare the shredded chicken. Cover and set aside, or if made ahead, refrigerate until ready to use. Then, in a nonstick skillet, heat the oil over medium heat and cook the potato, stirring, until lightly browned, about 5 minutes. Add the onions, salt and pepper. Cook for 1 minute. Reserve in the pan off heat.

2. In another skillet, pour oil to a depth of about 1 inch and cook over medium-high heat until the oil shimmers. Fry the masa shells, 3 or 4 at a time, turning once until golden on both sides. Drain on paper towels.

3. Spread about 1 teaspoon of warm refried beans on each shell. Add about 1 teaspoon potato and 1 tablespoon of the shredded chicken. Top with 1 teaspoon of salsa and a dollop of sour cream. Add a thin slice of radish on top of the sour cream, if desired. Serve at once.

Ground Beef Sopes
Sopes con Carne Molida

Makes about 16 appetizers

Spicy ground beef is an easy topping that almost everyone likes for rustic finger foods called sopes. Prepare all the parts ahead and keep them warm. Masa shells are fried just before being filled, and need to be served right away. For convenience, mix the ground beef with a prepared red salsa of your choice.

Masa Shells for Sopes (page 107)
2 teaspoons olive oil
1/2 medium onion, finely chopped
1/4 pound ground beef
1/2 cup prepared spicy red salsa
2 tablespoons chopped fresh cilantro
Oil for frying
1 cup heated refried beans, canned or homemade
1 cup finely shredded lettuce
Sour cream

1. Prepare the masa shells. Cover and set aside. Then, in a medium nonstick skillet, heat the oil over medium heat and cook the onion, stirring, until translucent, about 3 minutes. Add the ground beef and cook, breaking up lumps into small bits, until the meat is browned and cooked through, 6 to 8 minutes. Stir in the salsa and cilantro. Set aside off heat.

2. In another skillet, pour oil to a depth of about 1 inch and cook over medium-high heat until the oil shimmers. Fry the masa shells, 3 or 4 at a time, turning once until golden on both sides. Drain on paper towels.

3. Spread 1 teaspoon of warm refried beans on each shell. Add 1 tablespoon of the beef mixture and top with a bit of shredded lettuce. Add a dollop of sour cream. Serve at once.

Masa Cups with Spicy Meat Filling
Garnachas con Carne Molida

Makes about 16 appetizers

Fresh masa dough is formed into small cups or shells called garnachas in Yucatán. One minor difference with sopes is that these garnacha cups are deeper. The little shells are finger food and can be filled with just about anything.

Basic Corn Tortilla Dough (page 133)
All-purpose flour for dusting
Vegetable oil for frying
1 pound lean ground pork or beef
1/2 medium onion, finely chopped
2 medium garlic cloves, finely chopped
1 teaspoon dried oregano (Mexican variety preferred), crumbled
2 medium tomatoes, peeled and chopped
1 teaspoon bottled chipotle salsa
1/4 teaspoon salt, or to taste
Fresh salsa, sour cream, and chopped cilantro (optional)

1. Lightly dust a baking sheet with flour. Make the masa dough (tortilla dough) and roll into approximately golf-ball size pieces. Flatten each ball to about 2½ inches. Using thumbs and fingers, pinch up the edges all around and form into shallow bowls about ¾-inch deep. Place the formed shells on the baking sheet. Cover with plastic wrap to prevent drying out until ready to fry.

2. In a large skillet, heat 1 tablespoon of oil over medium heat. Break up the meat and add to the hot oil. Cook, stirring until no longer pink, 3 to 4

minutes. Add the onion, garlic, and oregano. Cook, stirring, for 5 minutes. Add the tomatoes and chipotle salsa. Raise the heat and cook briskly to reduce the juices. Season with salt. Remove from the heat. Keep warm while frying the shells.

3. In a heavy medium skillet, pour oil to a depth of 1½ inches. When the oil shimmers, fry the shells in batches, on both sides, until golden brown. Drain on paper towels. Fill the shells with the meat mixture while still hot. Top with a little salsa, sour cream, and a sprinkle of cilantro, if desired. Serve at once.

Masa Cups with Mushrooms and Chiles
Garnachas de Hongos y Chiles Poblanos

Makes **about 12 appetizers**

Garnachas are cup-shaped shells formed with corn tortilla dough from Yucatán. The shells are fried and filled with any number of things. Mushrooms, poblano chiles, and a spicy sauce fill these garnachas.

Basic Corn Tortilla Dough (page 133)

All-purpose flour for dusting

Mushrooms and Poblano Chiles in Guajillo Sauce (page 454)

Vegetable oil for frying

Finely chopped epazote leaves or fresh cilantro, for garnishing

1. Make the masa dough (tortilla dough) and roll into approximately golf-ball-size pieces. Flatten each ball to about 2½ inches. Using thumbs and fingers, pinch up the edges all around and form into shallow bowls about ¾ inch deep. Place the formed shells on a baking sheet, dusted with flour. Cover with plastic wrap to prevent drying out while preparing the mushroom filling.

2. In a heavy medium skillet, pour oil to a depth of 1½ inches. When the oil shimmers, fry the shells, in batches, on both sides until golden brown, about 1 to 2 minutes on each side. Drain on paper towels. Fill the shells with the mushroom mixture while still hot. Sprinkle the tops with chopped epazote leaves or cilantro, if desired, and serve at once.

Masa Dough Shells with Crab
Chalupas con Jaiba

Makes **about 16 small appetizers**

Corn tortilla dough formed into ovals shaped like canoes are called chalupas. *These chalupas are fried crisp and filled with crab and green salsa for a terrific appetizer.*

Basic Corn Tortilla Dough (page 133)

Vegetable oil for frying

Fresh Tomatillo Sauce (page 34), or purchased

½ pound fresh or frozen crab meat, picked over

1. Prepare the masa dough. Divide the dough into 8 equal balls about 2 inches in diameter, then divide each ball in half for 16 (1-inch) balls. Put the balls on a platter and cover with plastic wrap to prevent drying. Form 1 ball into an oval shape resembling a canoe. Pinch up a ⅓-inch rim all around the edge. Repeat with the remaining balls.

2. In a medium skillet, heat oil to a depth of about ½ inch. Fry the chalupa shells 2 or 3 at a time over medium-high heat until crisp and golden, about 2 minutes on each side. (If the oil gets too hot, adjust the temperature, as needed.) Drain the masa shells on paper towels.

3. Prepare tomatillo sauce. Then, fill each chalupa equally with crab and top with a dollop of green sauce. Serve at once.

Masa Cakes from Veracruz
Bocoles

Makes **12 bocoles**

Patricia Quintana, cookbook author and cooking instructor from Mexico City, has been a friend and source of information about Mexican cuisine for many years. Patricia taught me to make bocoles, *fat little* masa *cakes that are served with eggs and sausage for breakfast in the Huasteca region of Veracruz, where Patricia's family owns a ranch. Sometimes* bocoles *are stuffed with cheese or beans.*

1 cup masa harina (flour for corn tortillas)

1/2 cup lukewarm tap water

2 tablespoons plus 2 teaspoons vegetable
    shortening

1/4 teaspoon salt

1. Put the ingredients in a food processor and process until the mixture comes together to form a soft smooth dough. Remove from the processor and knead the dough by hand to test the moistness. The dough should be moist and soft, but should not stick to your hands. If too dry, moisten hands with water and work the dough until it reaches the desired consistency. Put the dough in a plastic bag and let rest for 20 to 30 minutes.

2. Heat a comal, griddle, or skillet over medium heat. Flatten egg-size balls of dough—by hand or in a tortilla press— into small cakes 2½ to 3 inches in diameter and ¼ inch thick. Cook in a large, dry pan for 3 minutes on each side or until crusty and flecked with brown in spots. Serve bocoles warm.

Note: To stuff the bocoles: When they are hot off the pan, slit an opening with a small sharp knife and slip in a small thin piece of cheese, such as Monterey Jack, Oaxaca, or asadero.

Potato Masa Cakes with Grilled Chicken
Tortitas de Papas y Masa con Pollo Asada

Makes **4 servings**

Strips of pan-grilled chicken are stacked on a crisp potato masa *cake for this modern Mexican presentation. The chicken can also be cooked on an outdoor grill, if desired.*

4 Potato Masa Cakes (page 114)

2 teaspoons plus 1 tablespoon olive oil

1/2 teaspoon salt, or to taste

4 skinless boneless chicken breast halves

3 cups fresh (from about 3 ears) or frozen
    corn kernels (thawed)

2 teaspoons unsalted butter

Fresh salsa, purchased or homemade

Sour cream

Chopped cilantro

1. Preheat the oven to 200°. Prepare the Potato Masa Cakes, and keep warm in the oven while cooking the chicken. Rub the chicken with the 2 teaspoons of oil and season with about ¼ teaspoon of the salt. Heat a stovetop grill pan over medium-high heat and cook the chicken breasts about 4 to 5 minutes per side or until browned with grill marks on the outside, firm to the touch, and no longer pink inside at the thickest part.

2. Meanwhile, in a skillet, cook the corn with the butter, stirring, until completely heated through, 3 to 4 minutes. Reserve in the pan off heat.

3. Remove the chicken to a cutting board and slice thinly crosswise. Remove the potato cakes from the oven and put 1 cake in the center of each of 4 warm plates. Arrange the chicken strips equally on top of each potato cake and top each with some salsa and a dollop of sour cream. Spoon a portion of the corn around the cakes on each plate. Scatter chopped cilantro over all.

Masa Patties Stuffed with Beans and Cheese
Gorditas de Frijoles y Queso

Makes **12 snacks**

Gordita, *or "little fat one", generally means a savory snack made with corn tortilla dough. The size and what goes on top or inside varies from region to region. Just as with similar snacks called* sopes *and* chalupas, *it's an adventure trying all different kinds when traveling in Mexico.*

This recipe is from Dona Julia's Gorditas in Zacatecas, a wonderful fast food establishment that offers a number of fillings stuffed inside the plump tortillas—all made fresh to order.

Basic Corn Tortilla Dough (page 133)
1¹/₂ cups refried beans, canned or homemade
1 cup shredded Chihuahua or Monterey Jack cheese
Jarred pickled jalapeño chiles (en escabeche), seeded and cut into strips or rings

1. Prepare the dough. Have ready a tortilla press and 2 (8-inch) squares of plastic wrap or 2 small plastic sandwich bags. Then, make 12 egg-size tortilla balls. Put on a plate; cover to keep moist.

2. Open the tortilla press. Lay 1 piece of plastic on the bottom and drape the second piece over the hinged lid. Put 1 ball of dough on the plastic on the bottom of the press and lay the other piece of plastic on top of the dough. Lower the hinged lid and press gently to form a 4-inch tortilla about ¹/₃-inch thick. Open the lid and pick up the fat tortilla. Peel off the top piece of plastic. Flip over the tortilla and carefully peel off the second piece of plastic.

3. Lay the tortilla on the hot pan. Cook until the edges look dry, about 40 seconds. With a spatula, turn and cook the second side for 1 minute. Turn again and cook for 15 seconds. (If it puffs, that's good, it will be easier to cut open for the filling.) Put the tortillas on a plate, cover to keep moist

and repeat making small fat tortillas until all are finished.

4. With a small sharp knife, cut a slit in one side of each tortilla and gently slide the knife blade back and forth to make a pocket for the filling. Stuff the pockets with about 2 tablespoons refried beans, 1 tablespoon cheese, and 2 or 3 strips of jalapeño. Brush the gorditas on both sides with oil and cook on a hot griddle or in a hot skillet, turning 2 to 3 times, until flecked with brown but still soft, about 2 minutes total. Serve at once.

Masa Patties Stuffed with Pork, Onion, and Salsa
Gorditas de Cerdo

Makes **12 snacks**

These masa *patties are stuffed with a delicious combination of pork, onion, and salsa. These* gorditas *are from Dona Julia Gorditas, a great little place in Zacatecas.*

Basic Corn Tortilla Dough (page 133)
2 teaspoons vegetable oil or olive oil
1 pound thinly sliced (¹/₄ inch) pork cut from the leg or sirloin
¹/₄ teaspoon salt, or to taste
1 medium white onion, finely chopped
2 medium garlic cloves, finely minced
¹/₂ cup thick and chunky bottled salsa

1. Proceed as described in steps 1 and 2 of Masa Patties Stuffed with Beans and Cheese (preceding recipe).

2. To make the filling, heat the oil in a large non-stick skillet over medium-high heat. Cook the pork until brown on both sides and white inside, but still juicy, 2 to 3 minutes on each side. Season with salt and transfer pork to a cutting board. Finely chop and reserve.

3. In the same skillet, cook the onion, stirring, until translucent, about 3 minutes. Add the garlic and cook 1 minute. Return the chopped pork to the pan. Add the salsa and stir to mix.

4. With a small sharp knife, cut a slit in one side of each tortilla and gently slide the knife blade back and forth to make a pocket for the filling. Stuff the pockets with about 2 to 3 tablespoons of the pork mixture. (Any leftover pork makes great tacos or burritos.)

5. Brush the gorditas on both sides with oil and cook on a hot griddle or in a hot skillet, turning 2 to 3 times, until flecked with brown, about 2 minutes total, but still soft. Serve at once.

Masa Snacks, Veracruz Style
Picadas

Makes **18 to 20 appetizers**

No wonder picadas, *the filled* masa *dough snacks similar to those called* sopes *in other parts of Mexico, are so popular in Veracruz. The typical red and green toppings are colorful, and taste great! Picadas are finger foods and should be served as soon as they are made.*

This recipe is for picadas with red sauce. (To make picadas with the green topping, make masa shells exactly as directed in this recipe, and top with Fresh Tomatillo Sauce, page 34, instead of red sauce.)

Basic Corn Tortilla Dough (page 133)

1 tablespoon vegetable oil, plus extra for frying the picadas

¹/₄ cup finely chopped onion

1 medium garlic clove, finely chopped

1 serrano chile, finely chopped with seeds

4 plum tomatoes (about 8 ounces), broil-roasted (page 8)

2 tablespoons chopped fresh cilantro

¹/₄ teaspoon salt, or to taste

¹/₂ cup crumbled cotija or mild feta cheese

1. Form the masa dough into 18-to-20 equal balls of about 1 ounce each. Using a tortilla press, place a piece of plastic on the open tortilla press, and put 1 masa ball in the center. Lay another piece of plastic on top of the ball. Lower the handle to press into a 3-inch circle.

2. Heat a small dry skillet over medium-high heat until hot. Peel the plastic off the masa patty and pan-bake 15 seconds, turn over and cook another 15 seconds. Remove from the pan and quickly pinch up the edge of the partially baked masa to form a tiny rim of about ¼ inch all around. Cover with a kitchen towel to keep moist. Repeat with the remaining balls. Reserve the shells while preparing the tomato sauce.

3. In a medium skillet, heat the oil and cook the onion, garlic, and serrano chile. In a blender, blend the roasted tomatoes and cilantro. Add to the skillet, and cook until the mixture thickens and is nearly dry. Season with salt. The topping can be made ahead and stored refrigerated up to 2 days.

4. In the same skillet used for cooking the masa patties, heat enough oil to cover the bottom of the pan. When the oil shimmers, fry the reserved picada shells on both sides until golden brown, 1 to 2 minutes. Drain on paper towels. Top each picada with about 1 tablespoon of the tomato sauce. Sprinkle ½ teaspoon of cheese on top, and serve at once while still warm.

Potato Masa Cakes
Tortitas de Papa y Masa

Makes 4 (4-inch) round cakes

Mashed potato mixed with corn tortilla dough makes a wonderful potato cake to eat alone or serve with a variety of toppings. See recipes for Potato Masa Cakes with Grilled Chicken (page 111) and Potato Masa Cakes with Vegetables page 448).

2 medium Russet potatoes (about 8 ounces), peeled and thinly sliced

1 tablespoon butter, at room temperature

¹/₂ cup masa harina (flour for corn tortillas)

¹/₄ teaspoon salt

¹/₃ cup water

1 teaspoon vegetable oil

Vegetable oil for frying

1. In a small saucepan, cook the potato in salted water to cover until very tender, about 8 minutes. Drain and mash potato with the butter while still hot. Cool until lukewarm.

2. In a mixing bowl, using clean hands, mix the masa harina, salt, and water together to make a soft dough. If too dry, add additional water 1 to 2 teaspoons at a time until the dough is moist and soft, but not sticky. Add the mashed potato and work it into the masa with your hands. Divide the dough into 4 equal pieces and form into balls.

3. Put 1 ball between 2 pieces of plastic wrap and gently press and pat lightly with your hands to make a 4-inch round cake about ¹/₃-inch thick.

4. Preheat the oven to 200°. In an 8-inch non-stick skillet, heat about 1 tablespoon of oil over medium heat. Remove the plastic and fry the cake until golden brown and crisp on both sides, about 5 minutes per side. Put on a baking sheet and keep warm in the oven while frying the remaining cakes. Serve hot.

Masa Potato and Cheese Snacks, Oaxaca Style
Molotes de Papa y Queso, estilo Qaxaca

Makes about 30 molotes

I first tasted molotes in Oaxaca as part of the traditional celebration for the Day of the Dead (Dia de Los Muertos), on November 2, that's celebrated all over Mexico. It's both a reverent and joyful time when it is believed that the dead return to earth for a night with relatives and friends. Dia de Los Muertos is a mixture of ancient traditions and Catholic beliefs brought to Mexico by Spain.

Just outside the cemetery, food vendors prepare all sorts of snacks, including these, which I liked so much I soon learned how to make them. Serve them with the salsa of your choice.

2 medium Russet potatoes (about 8 ounces), peeled and quartered

2 cups masa harina (flour for corn tortillas)

1¹/₄ cups hot water

³/₄ cup crumbled cotija or grated Parmesan cheese

¹/₂ teaspoon salt

1 pound Monterey Jack cheese, cut into 30 sticks, 2-inches long × ¹/₄-inch wide

Vegetable oil for frying

1. In a medium saucepan, boil the potatoes in water to cover until very tender, 12 to 15 minutes. Drain well, and put in a wide shallow bowl. Coarsely and gently break up the potatoes with a fork. Cool the potatoes to room temperature, and allow the steam to dissipate.

2. Meanwhile, in a medium bowl, mix the masa harina with the water. With clean hands, work the dough together until smooth and soft but not sticky. Cover with plastic wrap to prevent drying.

3. Put the cotija cheese in a food processor bowl, and pulse until finely crumbled. Add the prepared masa dough and salt. Pulse to mix. Add the potato and pulse to combine with the dough. The dough should be soft but not sticky. (Add water, 1 teaspoon at a time, if too stiff.)

4. Remove the dough to a flat working surface, and divide the dough into 1½-inch balls. Cover with plastic wrap. To form the molotes, press 1 ball of dough into a 3-inch circle and put 1 stick of the cheese across the center. Wrap the dough around to enclose the cheese. Seal the ends well, with no cheese peeking through, and gently shape the molote to resemble a torpedo. Lay the molote on a baking sheet and cover with a clean kitchen towel. Repeat with remaining dough.

5. In a medium skillet, heat 1 inch of vegetable oil until hot. Fry the molotes, 3 or 4 at a time, frequently turning them, until golden brown, about 2 minutes. Drain on paper towels. Keep warm in a 200° oven. Serve warm.

Masa White Bean Snack
Tlacloyos

Makes **about 16 snacks**

Estela Salas Silva, owner and instructor of Mexican Home Cooking in Tlaxcala, about 2 hours from Mexico City, teaches traditional regional cooking in her spacious kitchen. I loved these oval-shaped masa-*based bean snacks— somewhat like quesadillas in that they are soft inside and slightly crisp on the surface—so Estela shared her recipe. A tortilla press is needed.*

2 medium tomatoes, cored
2 serrano chiles, stemmed
¼ cup loosely packed cilantro
1 small garlic clove, chopped
¼ teaspoon salt, or to taste
Basic Corn Tortilla Dough (page 133)
2 (8-inch) squares of plastic wrap
1 cup cooked and seasoned white beans, mashed, canned or homemade
Vegetable oil or lard, for frying
½ cup grated cotija or mild feta cheese

1. In a saucepan, bring about 2 cups water to a boil. Add the tomatoes and chiles. Cook until the tomatoes and chiles are tender, about 5 minutes. Drain and transfer tomatoes and chiles to a blender. Add the cilantro, garlic, and salt. Blend well. Transfer to a bowl.

2. Prepare the masa dough; then, roll the dough into balls 1½ inch in diameter. Cover to keep from drying out. Set up tortilla press. Put 1 piece of plastic on the bottom of the tortilla press. Place 1 dough ball on the plastic covered press. Top the ball with another piece of plastic. Lower the handle and press into 3-½- to 4-inch tortilla about ⅛-inch thick. Remove the top piece of plastic. Holding the tortilla with the bottom piece of plastic attached, spread 1 tablespoon of beans on top of the tortilla. Fold tortilla in half, remove the second piece of plastic and shape the tortilla into an oval and pat to flatten. Pinch the edges to seal the beans inside. Repeat until all are filled.

3. Heat a dry nonstick skillet over medium-high heat. Cook the filled tortillas on the hot pan, 2 at a time, until light brown on the bottom, about 3 minutes. Turn and cook until lightly browned. Brush tops lightly with oil. Turn again and cook 1 minute. Brush with oil, turn and cook 1 minute more. Remove to a plate. Cover to keep warm. Repeat until all are cooked. Top each tlacloyo with the tomato sauce and sprinkle with cheese. Serve at once.

Masa Quesadillas with Cheese
Quesadillas

Makes about 16 snacks

Cheese turnovers, called quesadillas, are a favorite snack all over Mexico. Quesadillas are often made with ready-made tortillas, especially in the United States, but these authentic quesadillas are made from scratch using the uncooked masa *dough that is the same as that used for making corn tortillas.*

Basic Corn Tortilla Dough (page 133)
1/4 teaspoon salt
6 ounces Oaxaca string cheese, or other melting cheese, thinly sliced
20 fresh epazote leaves, finely shredded (optional), or substitute 1/2 cup coarsely chopped fresh cilantro
2 to 3 serrano chiles, thinly sliced with seeds
Vegetable oil, for frying

1. Prepare the dough. Then, dampen your hands with water, and mix the dough with the salt, working it very well until soft. Form the dough into 16 small balls of equal size. Using a tortilla press, put 1 piece of plastic on the open press and lay 1 ball in the center. Put a second piece of plastic on top of the dough, and lower the handle to press out a 3-1/2-to 4-inch circle. Peel off the top piece of plastic.

2. Put a small slice of cheese on 1/2 of the circle, but not too close to the edge. Add a few shreds of epazote or cilantro and about 3 thin slices of serrano on top. Lift the plastic and gently fold the dough together so that the edges meet. Press to seal the edges together, and peel off the plastic. Put the filled quesadilla on a lightly floured baking pan, and cover to prevent drying out. Repeat with the remaining dough.

3. Heat oil to a depth of 1/4 inch in a medium skillet until it shimmers. Fry the quesadillas, 2 at a time, until golden brown on both sides, about 1 to 2 minutes per side. Drain on paper towels and serve at once.

Tortilla Appetizer with Beef and Green Sauce
Picaditas de Carne y Salsa Verde

Makes 4 snacks

El Balcon is a small café in Puebla that specializes in antojitos *(snacks). Picaditas, another form of* sopes, *are typical of Puebla, and they are made with small fresh tortillas. The edges are pinched to make a rimmed cup, which can hold a variety of toppings. This snack is excellent for brunch or an informal lunch.*

Basic Corn Tortilla Dough (page 133)
1 tablespoon vegetable oil
1/2 medium white onion, very thinly sliced
8 ounces thinly sliced (1/4 inch) lean beefsteak
1/4 teaspoon salt, or to taste
1 cup green salsa, purchased or homemade
1/4 cup crumbled queso fresco (fresh Mexican cheese)

1. Prepare the tortilla dough, making 4 fresh corn tortillas, 1/4-inch thick and about 4 inches in diameter.

2. Heat a medium dry skillet or Mexican comal over medium-high heat. Put 1 tortilla on the pan. Cook until it loosens easily from the pan, about 45 seconds. (It should still be pale in color.) Turn and cook 35 seconds. Remove from the pan and pinch up a 1/3-inch edge all around. Return to the pan, flat side down. Cook 30 seconds. Transfer to a plate. Cover to keep warm. Repeat with remaining tortillas. Stack, covered, on the same plate.

3. Heat the oil in the same skillet over medium-high heat. Cook the onion, stirring, until it starts to brown, 3 to 4 minutes. Transfer to a plate. Cook the steak in the same skillet until brown on both sides and just cooked through, about 2 minutes on each side. Season with salt. Transfer the meat to a cutting board and finely chop it

4. To assemble, spread 2 tablespoons of green salsa on each picadita. Top each with about 3 tablespoons of the chopped steak and onion. Sprinkle with cheese and serve at once.

White Bean and Pumpkin Seed Masa Appetizer
Poc-Ka-Nes

Makes 8 appetizers

Manuel Arjona, originally from Yucatán, prepared these delicious crispy masa appetizers stuffed with white beans and pumpkin seeds for my cooking class, when we had a group lunch at his restaurant Maya, in Sonoma, California. Chef Arjona serves his poc-ka-nes (a Mayan word) on a bed of finely shredded Red and Green Cabbage Slaw (page 172).

Tomatillo and Chipotle Chile Sauce (page 36)
Basic Corn Tortilla Dough (page 133)
1 cup raw hulled pumpkin seeds
1 cup cooked canned white beans, drained of all liquid
1 tablespoon chopped fresh chives, or tops of green onions
1/2 teaspoon salt, or to taste
1/4 teaspoon freshly ground pepper, or to taste
Oil, for frying

1. Prepare the tomatillo salsa. Cover and reserve. Then prepare the tortilla dough. Cover with plastic wrap and let rest about 20 minutes. Meanwhile, prepare the filling. In a dry skillet, toast the pumpkin seeds until they start to brown and pop in the pan. Transfer to a plate.

2. When the pumpkin seeds are cool, grind them coarsely in a food processor and put in a bowl. Add the beans, chives, salt, and pepper. Mix well. The mixture will be thick and hold its shape on a spoon. Reserve.

3. Line a tray with plastic wrap. Prepare the tortilla dough to make 8 tortillas. Press 1 (4½-inch) tortilla. Peel off the top piece of plastic, and lay the tortilla on a flat work surface with the bottom piece of plastic still attached. Put about 1 tablespoon of the reserved bean filling on one half of the tortilla. Carefully fold the tortilla over, using the plastic as a guide, and press the edges together to form a crescent. Unfold the piece of plastic. Seal the edges of the filled crescent. Place on the tray. Repeat, pressing, filling, and folding the tortillas until all are finished.

4. In a deep skillet, pour oil to a depth of about 2 inches and heat until the oil shimmers. Fry the filled tortillas 1 or 2 at a time, until deep golden brown on both sides, about 2 minutes on each side. Drain on paper towels. Serve hot, topped with the salsa.

Sandwiches, Bread Snacks, and Turnovers

Shrimp Toasts
Pan Tostada con Camarones

Makes **about 20 appetizers**

Mexican cooks use bread as a base for appetizers, in much the same way as it is used for tapas in Spain. Here, Mexican rolls or a French baguette loaf are sliced and topped with avocado butter and shrimp for a quick appetizer.

Avocado Butter recipe (page 18), doubled
$^1/_2$ pound (14 to 16) small cooked shrimp
Salt, to taste
1 long French baguette, cut into about 20 slices or about 4 oval Mexican sandwich rolls (bolillos), sliced
2 to 3 tablespoons unsalted butter, at room temperature

1. Prepare the double quantity of avocado butter. Then, drain the shrimp and pat dry with paper towels. Chop coarsely. Set aside.

2. In a large bowl, mix the avocado butter with the shrimp. Season with salt, if desired. Set aside.

3. Preheat the broiler. Lightly butter the bread and put the slices on a baking sheet and toast lightly. Mound about 1 heaped tablespoon of the avocado and shrimp mixture on each bread slice. Serve at once.

Mushroom Toasts
Pan Tostada con Hongos

Makes **about 20 appetizers**

Mushrooms and the herb epazote *are favorite flavor partners in central Mexico and they make a rich tasty topping for toasted slices of Mexican rolls or French baguettes.*

1 tablespoon olive oil
1 teaspoon unsalted butter
1 pound medium white button mushrooms, coarsely chopped
$^1/_4$ cup Mexican crema or heavy cream
1 teaspoon chopped fresh epazote leaves (or substitute oregano)
$^1/_2$ teaspoon salt, or to taste
Freshly ground pepper, to taste
1 long French baguette, cut into about 20 slices, or 4 oval Mexican sandwich rolls (bolillos), sliced
3 to 4 tablespoons unsalted butter, at room temperature
2 to 3 jalapeño chiles, seeded, veins removed, and minced

1. Heat the oil and butter in a medium skillet and cook the mushrooms, stirring, until the juices evaporate and they start to brown, about 4 minutes. Stir in the crema, epazote, salt and pepper. Cook, stirring, 1 minute. Reserve off heat.

2. Preheat the broiler. Lightly butter the bread, put the slices on a baking sheet and toast lightly. Top the toasts with a portion of the mushrooms and garnish with a sprinkle of minced jalapeño.

Avocado and Jalapeño Snack
Botana de Aguacate y Jalapeño

Makes **about 24 appetizers**

Here's a quick and easy party appetizer made with avocado and spicy jalapeño chiles spread on toasted bolillos *(oval Mexican sandwich rolls) or French rolls and garnished with crisp radish rounds. If making these ahead, toast the bread lightly to prevent the spread from soaking through.*

2 large ripe avocados (Hass variety preferred)

2 tablespoons mayonnaise

2 teaspoons fresh lime juice

2 fresh jalapeños chiles, seeded, veins removed, and finely chopped

Salt, to taste

4 oval Mexican sandwich rolls (bolillos) or other sandwich rolls, thinly sliced crosswise

4 to 5 radishes, washed, trimmed, and thinly sliced

1/2 cup crumbled cotija or mild feta cheese

In a medium bowl, mash the avocados. Stir in the mayonnaise lime juice, and the jalapeños. Season with salt. Put about 2 teaspoons of the mashed avocado mixture on each slice. Top with 2 to 3 radish slices. Sprinkle lightly with cheese. Arrange the appetizers on a serving plate, and serve at once.

Mexican Chicken Sandwiches
Tortas de Pollo

Makes **4 servings**

Boca Chica Hotel in Acapulco made just about the best tortas *I've ever tasted. The tortas are very easy to assemble if you have some leftover refried beans (you could use canned beans in a pinch), and a couple of chicken breasts to poach and shred.*

3 skinless boneless chicken breast halves, shredded (Shredded Chicken, page 271)

4 oval Mexican sandwich rolls (bolillos) or other sandwich rolls, split lengthwise

1 cup refried beans, warmed

2 medium tomatoes, thinly sliced

1/2 cup finely shredded lettuce

1/2 large ripe avocado, mashed

3 tablespoons Chipotle Mayonnaise (page 18)

1. Prepare the shredded chicken. Then, in the bottom half of each roll, pull out a little of the soft center to make a depression, and fill each with 1/4 of the beans, and top with 1/4 of the chicken, tomatoes, and lettuce.

2. In a small bowl, mix the avocado and chipotle mayonnaise. Spread the roll tops equally with the avocado mixture, and close the sandwiches. Serve at once.

Roast Beef, Avocado, and Bean Sandwiches
Tortas de Carne Al Horno

Makes **2 servings**

Sometimes called pepitos *(Little Joes), these sandwich rolls filled with cold roast beef, avocado, beans, lettuce, and pickled jalapeños are easy to make using thinly sliced roast beef from a deli, or cold leftover roast beef.*

2 oval Mexican sandwich rolls (bolillos) or other sandwich rolls, split lengthwise

2 teaspoons Dijon or yellow mustard

4 ounces thinly sliced deli roast beef

1/2 avocado (Hass variety preferred), thinly sliced

1/2 cup finely shredded lettuce

2 jarred pickled jalapeño chiles (en escabeche), seeded and finely chopped

1 tablespoon mayonnaise

1/4 to 1/3 cup heated refried beans, canned or homemade

1. Spread 1 teaspoon of mustard on each bottom roll half. Layer each with half of the roast beef and avocado.

2. In a small bowl, mix the lettuce, jalapeños, and mayonnaise. Put half of the lettuce mixture on top of the avocado layer on each roll. Spread about 2 tablespoons beans on the top roll halves. Close the sandwiches with the top roll halves. Serve.

Pork Sandwiches with Tomato Sauce
Tortaes Ahogada

Makes 2 servings

Ahogadas, *famed "drowned" pork sandwiches, are a must when in Guadalajara. Our first ahogada was part of a private lunch at Jose Cuervo's tequilla distillery arranged by our traveling companions, Don and Donna Luria, owners of Café Terra Cotta in Tucson and Scottsdale, Arizona. The second ahogada came from a food stall in the plaza in Tlaquepaque. Both of the juicy sandwiches were delicious, with plenty of roasted pork and drenched with a thin mild tomato sauce. My version is a bit different from the two mentioned above, but equally wonderful and properly "drowned."*

Tomato Sauce for Tortas (page 44), warmed in a pan
12 ounces fresh pork stew meat, cut into
    $1/2$-inch pieces
1 teaspoon vegetable oil
$1/4$ teaspoon salt, or to taste
2 oval Mexican sandwich rolls (bolillos) or other
    sandwich rolls, split lengthwise
1 medium avocado (Hass variety preferred),
    thinly sliced
$1/2$ cup shredded cabbage or lettuce
1 tablespoon finely chopped onion (optional)
Hot pepper sauce, such as Tabasco

1. Prepare the tomato sauce, then preheat the oven to 400°. Put the pork pieces in a single layer in an ovenproof baking dish. Add the oil and salt. Toss to coat the meat with the oil. Roast, uncovered, until sizzling and light brown, about 25 minutes. Remove from the oven, stir to separate the meat pieces, and set aside.

2. Remove a small amount of the soft center of the roll to make a cavity for the filling. Heat the

rolls in the oven 3 to 4 minutes. Remove from the oven and dip the cut sides of the rolls into the warm sauce to soak well. Put half of the cooked pork on each bottom roll half. Top with avocado, cabbage or lettuce, and onion. Close the sandwiches, cut in half, and spoon 2 tablespoons of the sauce over the top of each sandwich. Serve at once with plenty of paper napkins. Bottled hot sauce is served on the side for those who like it spicy!

Turkey and Avocado Sandwiches
Tortas de Pavo y Aguacate

Makes 4 servings

Freshly cooked or leftover turkey makes wonderful sandwiches, Mexican style. Use bolillos *(oval Mexican sandwich rolls) or French sandwich rolls. Cooked chicken can be substituted for the turkey.*

1 cup (packed) shredded or chopped cooked
    deli or leftover turkey meat
3 tablespoons mayonnaise, plus extra to spread
    on the rolls
1 teaspoon fresh lime juice
$1/4$ teaspoon salt, or to taste
$1/8$ teaspoon freshly ground pepper, or to taste
4 oval Mexican sandwich rolls (bolillos) or other
    sandwich rolls, split lengthwise
1 large ripe tomato, very thinly sliced
1 large avocado (Hass variety preferred),
    peeled and thinly sliced
1 cup finely shredded lettuce

1. In a medium bowl mix together the turkey, 3 tablespoons of the mayonnaise, lime juice, salt, and pepper. Set aside.

2. Spread a little mayonnaise on each cut side. Cover each bottom roll half with $1/4$ of the turkey mixture. Top with tomato, avocado, and lettuce. Cover with the roll tops and serve.

Grilled Lamb Sandwiches
Tortas de Cordero

Makes 4 servings

Lamb steaks cut from the leg and thinly sliced, then briefly barbecued, grilled, or pan-fried, make absolutely delicious tortas. Grilled green onions, avocado, shredded lettuce, and mayonnaise complete the sandwich. Salsa is served on the side. (Ask the butcher to cut meat from the leg into thin steaks.) These tortas are terrific for a summer party. Serve with beans, Cactus Salad (page 170), and Mexican Potato Salad (page 177) for a fine meal.

1 pound thinly sliced (¹⁄₄-inch) boneless lamb steak

1 large garlic clove, finely chopped

¹⁄₂ teaspoon salt

1 teaspoon fresh lime juice

2 teaspoons olive oil

Freshly ground pepper, to taste

8 green onions

4 oval Mexican sandwich rolls (bolillos) or other
    sandwich rolls, split lengthwise

3 to 4 tablespoons mayonnaise

1 large avocado (Hass variety preferred),
    thinly sliced

Shredded lettuce, such as romaine or iceberg

Salsa of choice, purchased or homemade

1. Prepare an outdoor grill or preheat a stovetop grill pan. Trim excess fat from the lamb. Mash the garlic, salt, lime juice and oil together and rub all over the meat. Sprinkle with pepper.

2. When it is hot, put the meat and the onions on the greased grill. Cook the meat until brown on the outside and barely pink inside, about 4 minutes total. Transfer to a cutting board.

3. Add the onions to the grill, and cook, turning once or twice, until tender, about 8 minutes total. Transfer to a plate. Chop the lamb into bite-size pieces.

4. To assemble, spread mayonnaise on all the roll halves. Layer the bottom half of each roll with a portion of the meat, 2 green onions, ¹⁄₄ of the sliced avocado, and shredded lettuce. Put on the roll tops and serve with salsa to be added at the table.

Cuban Sandwiches
Tortas Cubana

Makes 4 servings

When searching for a torta (sandwich on a roll) in Oaxaca, we were advised to go straight to the Del Jardin Restaurant at the zócalo (main plaza), sit at one of the outdoor tables, and order the torta cubana and a cold beer. It's a Mexican experience, regardless of the torta's origin. To make these great sandwiches, use soft oval Mexican rolls called bolillos or French rolls for the bread. Serve with a small bowl of pickled carrots and jalapeños, which are packed in jars and are widely available in supermarkets.

4 oval Mexican sandwich rolls (bolillos) or other
    sandwich rolls, split lengthwise

2 teaspoons yellow mustard

2 teaspoons mayonnaise

¹⁄₄ pound thinly sliced deli-style baked ham

¹⁄₂ pound thinly sliced deli-roasted pork

1 large avocado (Hass variety preferred),
    thinly sliced

1 medium tomato, thinly sliced

Lay the rolls on a flat surface, cut side up. Remove a small amount of the soft center from each roll, making a shallow cavity. Spread one half of each roll with mustard, and the other half with mayonnaise. Layer the roll bottoms equally with the ham, pork, avocado and tomato. Put on the roll tops and serve.

Tuna and Jalapeño Sandwiches
Tortas de Atún
Makes **4 servings**

A tuna sandwich, Mexican style, includes the zesty taste of pickled jalapeño chiles (jalapeños en escabeche). Serve tuna tortas with crisp corn tortilla chips.

1 (6½-ounce) can solid white tuna, drained
2 tablespoons mayonnaise, plus extra to spread
   on the rolls
2 jarred pickled jalapeño chiles (en escabeche),
   seeded and finely chopped
4 oval Mexican sandwich rolls (bolillos) or other
   sandwich rolls, split lengthwise
1 cup finely shredded lettuce
2 medium tomatoes, thinly sliced

In a bowl, mix the tuna, 2 tablespoons of the mayonnaise, and the chopped jalapeños. Lay the rolls on a flat surface and spread each cut side with mayonnaise. Spread the tuna equally on half of each roll. Top equally with lettuce and tomato. Put on the roll tops.

Shrimp and Avocado Sandwiches
Tortas de Camarones
Makes **4 servings**

Small precooked shrimp from the fish market mixed with avocado and mayonnaise fill this terrific Mexican torta *(sandwich on a roll), that's easy to make. Serve with chips and salsa on the side.*

4 oval Mexican sandwich rolls (bolillos) or other
   sandwich rolls, split lengthwise
1 tablespoon unsalted butter, at room temperature
½ pound (14 to 16) small cooked shrimp
1 large avocado (Hass variety preferred),
   peeled and chopped
2 tablespoons mayonnaise
1 green onion, finely chopped
1 tablespoon chopped fresh cilantro
2 medium tomatoes, thinly sliced
¼ teaspoon salt
¾ cup finely shredded lettuce

Butter each half of the rolls and set aside. In a medium bowl, mix the shrimp, avocado, mayonnaise, onion, and cilantro. Divide the shrimp mixture equally on the bottom half of each roll. Top with sliced tomatoes. Sprinkle lightly with salt. Add lettuce, if desired. Close the sandwiches with the roll tops. Serve.

Bacon, Onion, and Tomato Sandwiches
Tortas de Tocino, Cebolla, y Tomate
Makes **4 servings**

This torta *(sandwich) can be made on a French roll, which is most like the native* bolillo *that's used for Mexican sandwiches. The bacon, onion, and tomato filling is good any time, but it's especially appropriate for brunch. For an authentic touch, serve the tortas with some pickled jalapeños on the side.*

16 bacon slices
1 medium white onion, thinly sliced
4 oval Mexican sandwich rolls (bolillos) or other
   sandwich rolls, split lengthwise
4 teaspoons Mexican crema, sour cream,
   or mayonnaise
2 medium tomatoes, thinly sliced
½ cup finely shredded lettuce, any kind
4 teaspoons prepared salsa

1. In a nonstick skillet, cook the bacon until brown and crisp. Drain on paper towels. Pour off all but 1 tablespoon of the fat from the skillet. Cook the onion in the skillet, stirring frequently, until it softens and begins to brown, about 4 minutes. Remove the onion to a plate.

2. Spread 1 teaspoon of crema on the bottom half of each roll. Put 4 slices of bacon on each roll; then layer with ¼ of the onion, tomato, and lettuce. Spoon 1 teaspoon salsa on top of each roll, and cover each torta with the top half of the roll.

Poblano Chile, Beans, and Cheese Sandwiches
Tortas de Barrio
Makes 2 servings

After a long drive through the high desert of north-central Mexico—broken occasionally by agricultural fields and surprisingly, some vineyards—my husband and I were hungry when we reached Zacatecas, a colonial gem. Right away, we set out on foot along steep cobblestone streets and found this simple but scrumptious torta *in one of the* taquerias *on our route. I've streamlined the process to make this* torta, *but all the filling ingredients are the same.*

1 poblano chile, roasted, peeled, seeded, and veins removed (page 8)
2 oval Mexican sandwich rolls (bolillos) or other sandwich rolls, split lengthwise
2 teaspoons unsalted butter at room temperature
1 cup heated refried beans, canned or homemade
1/2 cup shredded Monterey Jack cheese
Red salsa, purchased or homemade

1. Prepare the chile. Then, remove the stem from the chile, and cut in half lengthwise. Set aside. Remove some of the soft inside from the bottom half of each roll to create a hollow. Spread all 4 halves with butter.

2. Heat a large dry nonstick skillet and warm the rolls, cut side down until lightly toasted, about 2 minutes. Layer each roll bottom with ½ of the warm beans, ½ of the cheese, 1 tablespoon of salsa, and ½ of the roasted chile. Cover with the roll tops. Serve at once with more salsa on the side, if desired.

Breaded Veal Sandwiches
Cemitas Milanesa
Makes 2 servings

This sandwich with the Italian name is most common in northern Mexico, but is on menus all over the country. Cemitas *are sesame-seed rolls from the state of Puebla. The hearty version stuffed with thin fried breaded veal (or beef), avocado, cheese, and more, was my favorite. Use a good-quality large, round sesame seed roll for the bread.*

2 pieces cooked *Milanesa* (Breaded Veal Cutlet, page 372)
2 round sesame seed rolls
Olive oil
8 thin strips Oaxaca cheese, or other white melting cheese
1/2 avocado, thinly sliced
2 jarred pickled jalapeño chiles (en escabeche), seeded and cut into thin strips
1/2 cup shredded lettuce

1. Prepare half the Milanesa recipe. Keep the meat warm in a 200° oven. Then, heat a griddle, comal, or nonstick skillet over medium heat. Cut the rolls in half and brush the cut sides with olive oil. Place the rolls cut side down, on the hot griddle. Heat about 1 minute.

2. Lay the bottom roll halves on a flat surface. Top each with 1 piece of meat, cheese, avocado slices, jalapeño strips, and shredded lettuce. Drizzle the lettuce with a little more olive oil. Close the sandwiches and serve.

Mexican Sausage Turnovers
Empanadas de Chorizo

Makes 16 turnovers

Spicy chorizo is an excellent filling for substantial savory empanadas. You can make chorizo from the recipe for Mexican Pork Sausage (page 348), or purchase a good-quality chorizo. Serve the turnovers warm with crisp-cut jicama, cucumber sticks, and icy cold beer.

Savory Pastry Dough for Turnovers (page 555)
2 teaspoons vegetable oil
1/2 medium onion, finely chopped
1/2 pound fresh bulk chorizo, or packaged, with casings removed

1. Prepare the dough. Cover and refrigerate while making the filling. In a medium skillet, heat the oil over medium heat and cook the onion, stirring, until softened, about 3 minutes. Add the chorizo breaking it into small pieces and cook until brown and well done, 6 minutes. Transfer to a plate to cool completely.

2. Preheat the oven to 400°. Place half of the reserved dough on a floured board and roll it out thin. Cut into 4-inch circles. Gather the scraps and re-roll. Put 1 tablespoon of the filling on each circle and fold in half. Moisten the edges with water and crimp with a fork or fingers to seal. Place on an ungreased baking sheet. Brush the tops with beaten egg white and bake until golden brown, about 15 minutes. Cool on a rack. Repeat rolling, filling, and baking with the remaining half of the dough.

Onion, Chipotle, and Epazote Turnovers
Empanadas de Cebolla, Chipotle y Epazote

Makes 16 4-inch turnovers

These turnovers have a vegetarian filling sealed inside a rich flaky pastry. Make picnic-size 4-inch turnovers, or cut small pastry circles for cocktail appetizers.

Savory Pastry Dough for Turnovers (page 555)
1 tablespoon olive oil
1 large (8-ounce) red onion, very finely chopped
1/4 teaspoon salt, or to taste
2 canned chipotles en adobo, seeded and mashed
1 tablespoon chopped epazote leaves

1. Prepare the dough. Cover and refrigerate while making the filling. In a medium skillet, heat the oil over medium heat and cook the onion, stirring frequently until very soft and all juices have cooked away, about 10 minutes. Stir in the salt, chipotles, and epazote. Cook for 1 minute. Transfer to a plate and cool completely.

2. Preheat the oven to 400°. Place half of the reserved dough on a floured board and roll out thin. Cut into 4-inch circles. Gather the scraps and re-roll. Put 1 tablespoon of the filling on each circle and fold in half. Moisten the edges with water and crimp with a fork or fingers to seal. Place on an ungreased baking sheet. Brush the tops with beaten egg white and bake until golden brown, about 15 minutes. Cool on a rack. Repeat rolling, filling, and baking with the remaining half of the dough.

Vegetable Snacks

Fried Potato Chips with Lime and Chili
Papitas Fritas con Limón y Chili

Makes **4 to 5 servings**

If you ever get the chance to stroll through the central plaza in Tlaquepaque, keep your senses alert for the potato chip vendor. The site of his huge tub of hot oil and the aroma of crisp fried potatoes will lead you to his stall. You will receive a paper bag of freshly fried potato chips squeezed with lime juice and dusted with chili powder. If you love potatoes, you'll flip over these.

Below is the procedure for an informal party more than a recipe. I provide basic measurements but make as many as you want. It's most fun if you can set up to fry outdoors!

Oil for deep-frying
4 large white potatoes
Salt, to taste
Purchased chili powder, to taste
Fresh lime wedges

Peel and thinly slice the potatoes with a mandoline or in a food processor, using the thin slicing blade. In a deep fryer, wok, or large heavy pot, pour oil to a depth of about 4 inches, and heat over medium-high heat until the surface of the oil shimmers, and a few drops of water sizzle when flicked into the oil. Fry the sliced potatoes in batches until crisp and golden brown. Drain on paper towels. Sprinkle with salt and chili powder. Squeeze on lime juice. Serve warm on sturdy paper plates or heavy brown paper or in small brown paper bags.

Spicy Fried Onion Rings
Picanté Cebollas Fritos

Makes **6 servings**

Fried onion rings are a cocktail treat on both sides of the border. They disappear fast when served up hot and spicy. Even though they're easy to make, they have to be fried at the last minute.

3 medium yellow onions, cut into ¹/₄-inch slices
2 cups all-purpose flour
1 tablespoon purchased chili powder
2 teaspoons ground cayenne
2 teaspoons ground paprika
¹/₂ teaspoon salt, or to taste
Vegetable oil, for deep frying

1. Separate the onions into rings and set aside on a plate. In a large bowl mix the flour, chili powder, cayenne, paprika, and salt.

2. Heat oil to a depth of about 4 inches in a heavy saucepan or deep fryer until it shimmers and a few drops of water sizzle when flicked into the oil. Dredge a few onion rings at a time in the flour and fry until golden. Drain on paper towels. Repeat and fry the remaining onion rings. Serve at once.

Fried Stuffed Jalapeño Chiles
Jalapeño Poppers

Makes 8 appetizers

Several years ago these spicy deep-fried jalapeño appetizers appeared like a maverick wave in northern Baja and swept into Southern California before the craze calmed down. They remain popular and now appear on restaurant appetizer menus around the country.

8 jarred pickled jalapeño chiles (en escabeche), drained
4 ounces Monterey Jack cheese, cut into thin strips, 1-inch long × 1/4-inch wide
2 large eggs, beaten
1/2 teaspoon baking powder
1/4 cup all-purpose flour
2 tablespoons finely crushed corn flakes
Vegetable oil for frying

1. Cut a slit from the stem end to within 1/2 inch of the tip of each chile. Carefully remove the seeds. Stuff each chile with a piece of cheese.

2. In a bowl, beat together the egg, baking powder, flour, and corn flakes. Pour oil to a depth of about 1 inch into a small skillet and heat until a drop of the egg batter sizzles at once when dropped into the oil. Dip the chiles into the batter and fry 2 or 3 at a time until golden on both sides, about 1 to 2 minutes. Drain on paper towels. Serve hot.

Jicama with Red Chili and Lime
Jicama con Chili y Limón

Makes 4 to 6 servings

Street vendors all over Mexico sell jicama dusted with red chili powder and offer lime wedges to squeeze over the jicama. Generally, only one end of the jicama spear is sprinkled with chili, so the spear can be picked up by the other end without getting red chili on your fingers. Serve this popular combination as an appetizer before, or with, almost any Mexican meal.

1 medium jicama (about 12-ounces)
2 tablespoons pure ground ancho or California chile powder
1/2 teaspoon salt
2 limes, quartered

Peel the jicama, and cut into 1/2-inch-by 2-inch spears or wedges. Mix the chili powder and salt. Sprinkle one end of each jicama spear lightly with the chili powder-salt mixture. Arrange on a serving plate with the lime wedges. Serve cold.

Pickled Jalapeños and Carrots
Jalapeños y Zanahorias en Escabeche

Makes 6 to 8 appetizer servings

A bowl of pickled vegetables is brought to the table in most restaurants in Mexico. The jalapeños in this recipe are boiled briefly to tame some of the heat, making this a rather mild version. Be forewarned, however, jalapeños can be very hot, so wear protective gloves when cleaning these or other hot chiles. Serve this dish as an appetizer or a condiment.

12 large fresh jalapeño chiles
4 medium carrots, peeled
1 medium white onion, peeled and sliced
2 cups water
1 cup white wine vinegar
2 bay leaves
8 whole allspice berries
6 whole cloves
2 teaspoons sugar
2 tablespoons extra-virgin olive oil
2 tablespoons unseasoned rice vinegar
1 teaspoon ground cumin
1/2 teaspoon salt

1. Cut about ½ inch off the top of each chile leaving the stem attached. Reserve the caps. Cut the remaining chiles crosswise into rings about ⅓ inch wide. Remove the seeds with a sharp paring knife from the centers of the rings, and reserve the rings with the caps. Slice the carrots crosswise, on the bias, about ⅓ inch thick, and put the carrots with the onion.

2. In a medium nonreactive saucepan, bring to a boil the water, white wine vinegar, bay, allspice, cloves, and sugar. Add the jalapeño caps and rings and cook, uncovered, until barely tender, about 5 minutes. With a slotted spoon remove the chiles to a bowl, and drain any excess water.

3. In the same boiling solution, cook the carrots and onion until crisp-tender, 3 to 4 minutes. Drain well and put in the bowl with the chiles. Add the olive oil, rice vinegar, cumin, and salt. Toss gently to coat with the marinade. Cool, then refrigerate about 6 hours, or overnight for best flavor. To serve, arrange the chiles, carrots, and onion on a small platter. Garnish with the stemmed caps. Serve cold or at room temperature.

Cauliflower with Guacamole
Coliflor con Guacamole

Makes 8 to 10 appetizer servings

Cauliflower was brought to Mexico by way of Europe and is grown in most of the agricultural regions of the country. For this light appetizer, crunchy cauliflower is quickly cooked, then cooled and arranged on a platter and served with guacamole for dipping.

1 medium head of cauliflower (about 2 pounds)
1 teaspoon salt
1 tablespoon unseasoned rice vinegar
1 tablespoon vegetable oil
2 large ripe avocados (Hass variety preferred)
2 tablespoons finely chopped white onion
1 serrano chile, minced with seeds
2 tablespoons fresh lime juice
1 tablespoon chopped fresh cilantro

1. Trim the cauliflower and cut into 1½-inch pieces. In a large saucepan of boiling water, cook the cauliflower until barely tender, about 3 minutes. Drain and rinse under cold running water to stop the cooking. Drain again, and put the cauliflower into a medium bowl and toss with ½ teaspoon of the salt, vinegar, and oil.

2. Cut the avocados in half and remove the pits. With a large spoon, scoop avocados from the skin and place in a bowl. Mash with a fork. Stir in the onion, serrano, lime juice, cilantro, and remaining salt. Put the guacamole into a serving bowl. To serve, place guacamole in the center of a large round platter. Arrange the cauliflower pieces around the bowl. Serve at once.

Potato Patties
Gorditas de Papa

Makes about 20 patties

El Biche Pobre restaurant in Oaxaca serves plump potato patties on their special tasting platter of typical botanas (snacks). Here is my interpretation. Top the patties with fresh red or green salsa.

1 pound (about 2 medium) baking potatoes, peeled and sliced
½ cup crumbled cotija or mild feta cheese
2 tablespoons masa harina (flour for corn tortillas)
2 large eggs, beaten
¼ teaspoon salt, or to taste
⅛ teaspoon freshly ground pepper, or to taste
Vegetable oil for frying

1. In a large saucepan, boil the potatoes in water to cover until tender. Drain and mash while hot; then cool to lukewarm. Add the cheese, masa harina, egg, salt, and pepper. Mix well. Form into small round patties about 2-inches in diameter and ½-inch thick.

2. In a medium skillet, heat the oil to a depth of about ¼ inch and brown the patties, 3 or 4 at a time, on both sides until crisp and golden brown. Drain on paper towels. Serve hot with fresh salsa.

Stuffed Potato Appetizer
Botana de Papitas

Makes **4 to 6 servings (16 appetizers)**

Bite-size red potatoes are available in most of Mexico's public food markets, but small 2-ounce red potatoes are easier to find here, so that's what I used for this recipe. Each potato is cut in half, baked, and stuffed—which can be done ahead. A final finish under a hot broiler to melt the cheese takes only a few minutes. Buy potatoes that are uniform in size and shape.

8 (2-ounce) small red potatoes, scrubbed and halved crosswise
2 teaspoons olive oil plus extra to brush on potatoes
¹/₄ teaspoon salt, or to taste
¹/₃ cup finely chopped white onion
1 cup shredded manchego cheese
Finely chopped fresh parsley (optional)

1. Preheat oven to 400°. Using a small sharp knife shave a very thin slice off the bottom half of the potato pieces so they will sit flat. Brush the potatoes all over with oil and place cut side up on a baking sheet. Sprinkle lightly with salt and bake in preheated oven under tender, about 25 minutes.

2. Remove from the oven and, when cool enough to handle, scoop out the centers with a melon ball scoop to form a cup. Chop the centers very finely and set aside.

3. Heat 2 teaspoons of olive oil in a medium skillet and cook the onion over medium heat until it starts to brown, about 4 minutes. Stir in the reserved chopped potato. Cool. Mix in the cheese.

4. Fill the potato cups equally with the cheese mixture and put on a baking sheet. Shortly before serving, preheat an oven broiler and broil the stuffed potatoes until the cheese melts. Sprinkle with parsley, if desired. Serve warm.

Fried Plantain Pancakes I
Tostones

Makes **9 (5-inch) tostones**

I learned about tostones when I traveled to Tabasco with a group of dedicated cooks who were introduced to the foods of the region. We were with cooking instructor and author Diana Kennedy, and chocolate expert and historian Elaine Gonzales. Elaine guided us through cacao plantations and explained the history of chocolate, and Diana demonstrated the cooking of some regional dishes, including tostones *made from plantains* (plátanos machos). *We ate* tostones *or fried plantains in some form daily.*

I make these smashed plantain pancakes in two ways. This recipe, in which they are fried once to soften them and then a second time to make them crisp, is the more traditional way. In the second version (Fried Plantain Pancakes II, page 129) the plantains are steamed before they are flattened and fried. Both methods give good results. A tortilla press is needed to make the pancakes.

3 large firm barely-ripe plantains (with mostly green peel)
Oil for frying, such as safflower, corn, or canola oil
Salt, to taste
Tortilla press
2 (8-inch square) pieces of plastic to line the tortilla press

1. Trim both ends off the plantains and cut them crosswise in 2-inch-long pieces. Peel off the skin. (There should be 3 pieces per plantain.)

2. In a small heavy saucepan, pour oil to a depth of about 2 inches and heat until the surface shimmers. Fry 2 to 3 pieces of plantain at a time, turning with the aid of two wooden spoons, until golden brown on all sides, about 6 minutes. Drain on paper towels. Repeat until all are fried and drained. Reserve pan of oil off heat.

3. Preheat the oven to 200°. Put 1 piece of plastic on the bottom of the tortilla press and stand 1 plantain piece upright in the center of the plastic. Flatten the plantain slightly with the palm of your hand. Place the second piece of plastic on top of the plantain. Close the hinged top and press the handle gradually to flatten the plantain to a circular shape with irregular edges about 5 inches in diameter.

4. Pour about 4 tablespoons of oil from the pan of reserved oil into a large nonstick skillet and heat until the oil shimmers. Peel the top piece of plastic from the tostone. Sprinkle with salt. Flip the tostone onto your palm and carefully remove the second piece of plastic. Carefully transfer the tostone to the hot oil and fry, turning with a wide spatula, until brown on both sides. Drain on paper towels. Keep warm on a paper-lined baking sheet in the oven. Repeat the process with the other plantains until all are fried. Serve warm.

Fried Plantain Pancakes II
Tostones

Makes 9 (5-inch) tostones

Tostones *are flattened and fried plantains from the state of Tabasco. If you prefer not to double fry the tostones, try this method of steaming the plantains before pressing them flat. If you wish to try both methods to compare the results, read the instructions for Fried Plantain Pancakes I (page 128). A tortilla press is needed to make the pancakes.*

3 large firm barely-ripe plantains (with mostly green peel)
Pan with a steamer insert
Oil for frying, such as safflower, corn, or canola oil
Salt, to taste
2 (8-inch square) pieces of plastic to line the tortilla press

1. Trim both ends off the plantains and cut them crosswise in 2-inch-long pieces. Peel off the skin. (There should be 3 pieces per plantain.) Pour about 2-inches of hot tap water in the bottom of a steamer and bring to a boil. Put the plantain pieces on the steamer rack, cover with a piece of foil and put on the lid. Steam the plantains 8 minutes. Remove to a plate. Blot with paper towels and let cool 6 to 8 minutes.

2. Put 1 piece of plastic on the bottom of the tortilla press and stand 1 plantain piece upright in the center of the plastic. Flatten the plantain slightly with the palm of your hand. Put the other piece of plastic on top of the plantain and close the hinged top. Press the handle gradually to flatten the plantain to a circular shape with irregular edges about 5 inches in diameter.

3. In a large nonstick skillet, heat about 4 tablespoons of oil until the oil shimmers. Peel the top piece of plastic from the tostone. Sprinkle with salt. Flip the tostone onto your palm and carefully remove the second piece of plastic. Carefully transfer the tostone to the hot oil and fry, turning with a wide spatula, until brown on both sides. Drain on paper towels. Keep warm in a 200° oven on a paper lined baking sheet. Repeat until all are flattened and fried. Serve.

Other Snacks

Spicy Roasted Cocktail Peanuts
Cacahuates con Chile

Makes 2 cups

Peanuts are often brought to the table when the drinks are served, and if they're not you just have to ask, "Tiene Cacahuates?" ("Do you have peanuts?") to get some of these spicy nuts delivered. Raw red peanuts with skins are used in Mexico, and can be found in health food stores or some supermarkets in the United States. If you prefer, use peanuts without skins.

3 to 4 small garlic cloves, quartered lengthwise
3/4 pound raw red peanuts with skins on
2 teaspoons vegetable oil
4 whole chiles de arbol, cut crosswise 3 times
    and seeded
1/2 teaspoon salt, or to taste

Preheat oven to 300°. Put all of the ingredients in an 8-inch baking pan. Toss to coat with oil. Roast, uncovered, in preheated oven, stirring occasionally, until the nuts are crisp and brown, about 1 hour to 1 hour 15 minutes. Remove the nuts from the oven and discard the pieces of chile. (Some folks like the crisp bits of garlic, so leave them in, if you like.) Let peanuts stand until cool. Store in a covered container. Peanuts will keep crisp for 2 to 3 weeks.

Toasted Pumpkin Seeds
Botana de Pepitas

Makes 1 cup

Pumpkin seeds are used in many dishes in Mexican cooking. They taste great as a snack with cocktails and also add a nice crunch to salads. Green hulled pumpkin seeds can be found in health food stores and most Mexican markets.

2 teaspoons olive oil
1 cup green hulled pumpkin seeds
1/4 teaspoon salt, or to taste

Heat the oil in a medium nonstick skillet over medium heat. Add the pumpkin seeds and salt. Toast, stirring constantly, until the seeds pop in the pan and start to turn brown, 4 to 5 minutes. Transfer to a plate. Cool; then store in an airtight container at room temperature for 3 to 4 days.

Deviled Eggs, Mexican Style
Huevos Endiablados

Makes 4 to 6 servings

Deviled eggs are prepared for picnics and party buffets in Mexico just like here, but the seasonings may differ.

6 hard-cooked large eggs, peeled
2 tablespoons mayonnaise
1 teaspoon fresh lime juice
1/2 teaspoon ground cumin
2 teaspoons capers, chopped
1/4 teaspoon salt, or to taste
Purchased chili powder, to taste
Cilantro sprigs

Cut the eggs in half lengthwise. Remove the yolks and put them in a bowl. Mash well and mix in the mayonnaise, lime juice, cumin, capers, and salt. Fill the egg white halves equally with the yolk mixture. Sprinkle lightly with chili powder. Arrange on a serving plate. Garnish with cilantro. Serve cold.

Enchiladas, Tamales, *and* Tortilla Casseroles

Basic Dough Preparations 133

Basic Corn Tortilla Dough

Basic Corn Tortillas

Basic Tamale Dough

Masa Dumplings

White Flour Tortillas

Basic Crepes

Corn Crepes

Enchiladas and Crepes 138

Cheese Enchiladas in Red Sauce

Swiss Enchiladas

Turkey Enchiladas in Green Sauce

Seafood Enchiladas

Black Bean Enchiladas

Stacked Beef Enchiladas

Vegetable Enchiladas

Folded Tortillas in Bean Sauce

Folded Tortillas in Tomato Sauce

Folded Tortillas in Pasilla Chile Sauce

Mushroom Crepes

Crepes with Corn Mushroom

Corn Crepes with Chicken and Corn

Tamales 147

Tamales with Chicken

Tamales with Beef or Pork

Tamales with Shrimp

Fresh Corn Tamales

Tamales with Jalapeños, Cheese, and Corn

Vegetable Tamales with Black Bean Sauce

Tamales, Monterrey Style

Tamales in Banana Leaves, Oaxaca Style

Tamales Wrapped in Swiss Chard

Yucatán Tamale Pie

Tortilla Casseroles 156

Baked Aztec Chicken Casserole

Chicken and Tortilla Casserole with Green Sauce

Meatball and Tortilla Casserole

Pork and Tortilla Casserole

Cheese and Tortilla Casserole

Potato and Tortilla Casserole

Tortilla, Corn, and Zucchini Casserole

Tortilla, Bean, and Corn Casserole

Tortillas in Ancho Chile and Red Pepper Cream Sauce

*M*asa (a corn-based mixture or dough) is the element from which so much of delicious Mexican cooking evolves—tortillas and *tamales* (*masa*-coated fillings wrapped in corn husks or leaves and steamed)—are only two classic examples.

To make *masa*, dried field corn is boiled and then soaked at least six hours or overnight in slaked lime (*cal*) to remove the outer hull. The soaked corn (*nixtamal)* is then rinsed and drained before being finely ground into the mixture or dough known as *masa*.

Tortillas, the unleavened, pancake-shaped bread most commonly made from *masa*, are used in countless ways as an ingredient and an accompaniment. Eating a freshly made corn tortilla (sprinkled with a little coarse salt) can be one of life's simplest, but most pleasurable food experiences. It may instantly make you a believer in preparing them from scratch. If you're game, once you have the dough, the tortilla press, and a *comal* (Mexican griddle) or skillet, your efforts will be quickly rewarded with thin, soft tortillas to use as you please.

Prepared fresh *masa* can be purchased from a tortilla factory, or the dough can be made at home from dehydrated corn flour (*masa harina*). Recipes to make basic tortilla and tamale dough from *masa*

harina begin this chapter, and are used in the related recipes in this chapter, and in many of the *masa* snacks in the Appetizers chapter (page 62). The recipe for easy-to-make white flour tortillas is here, too. These are more commonly used in northern Mexico for burritos and other dishes.

Other recipes in this chapter are for the more substantial dishes (usually served hot) that use tortillas or crepes for main courses, such as enchiladas (rolled, filled tortillas, topped with sauce and/or cheese, then baked), *chilaquiles* (a casserole-like dish with fried tortillas layered with sauce, toppings, and cheese or cream), *tamale* pie, or casseroles. The recipes often call simply for corn tortillas; you can use store-bought for convenience but homemade will always produce the best dish. And if you can't make them yourself, buying freshly made from a tortilla factory will of course be superior to packaged store-bought.

It may be surprising to also see crepe dishes in this chapter, but they are common in Mexico due to French influence following Mexican independence from Spain in 1821, and through the 1860s, when the French Emperor Napolean III's troops occupied the country. Corn crepes, easily made and also included in this chapter, are a Mexican-American adaptation and can be used as an alternative for tortillas in certain dishes.

Basic Dough Preparations

Basic Corn Tortilla Dough
Masa para Tortillas

Makes **about 1 pound** *masa* **dough for 12 (6-inch) tortillas**

This recipe details how to prepare dough to make corn tortillas from dried corn flour called masa harina. *The dough is also used to make a number of* masa-*based snacks, such as* sopes, gorditas, *and* chalupas. *(See Appetizers and Snacks chapter, pages 62–130.)*

If there is a tortilla factory near your home, you can buy prepared wet masa instead of making your own dough. Either way, the dough will work very well. (You don't have to worry about overworking masa dough because there's no gluten that can toughen as there is in wheat flour doughs.)

2 cups masa harina (flour for corn tortillas)
1¹/₃ cups warm water
¹/₄ teaspoon salt

1. In a large bowl, mix the masa, water, and salt together with your hands until combined. Knead the dough very well until moist and smooth, but not sticky, about 3 to 5 minutes. If the dough is at all crumbly or seems too dry, moisten hands with water, and knead some more. If the dough sticks to your hands, add masa harina, 1 tablespoon at a time, to achieve a moist, smooth dough.

2. Cover the bowl with plastic wrap, and let the dough rest about 20 minutes before using, or refrigerate for up to 3 days, or wrap and freeze for up to 3 months.

Basic Corn Tortillas
Tortillas de Maiz

Makes **12 (6-inch) corn tortillas**

Here you'll find how to press corn tortillas from fresh masa *dough—or from fresh tortilla dough purchased from a tortilla factory—how to use a tortilla press, then how to bake the formed tortillas.*

Always put the dough between pieces of plastic or it will stick to the tortilla press. Stack the tortillas as they are baked to keep them warm and moist. When the tortillas are cool, put them in a plastic bag, and refrigerate up to 1 week. Reheat tortillas briefly in a hot dry skillet, or directly over a gas flame until warm and pliable, or reheat in a microwave oven.

Tortilla press
Plastic wrap
Basic Corn Tortilla Dough (see preceding recipe)

1. Form the dough into 12 equal balls, about golf ball size. Keep the dough lightly covered with plastic wrap while working, to prevent the dough from drying out. Heat a Mexican comal or medium skillet over medium-high heat.

2. Open the tortilla press, and place 1 piece of plastic on the bottom of the press. Put a ball of dough on the plastic and lay another piece of plastic on top of the dough. Lower the hinged lid quite firmly to form a round tortilla. Open the lid, and lift the tortilla with the plastic onto the palm of your hand. Carefully peel off the top piece of plastic. Pick up the tortilla from underneath, with the bottom piece of plastic still attached. Flip the tortilla over in your hand and peel off the bottom piece of plastic.

3. Lay the tortilla on the hot pan. Cook 20 to 30 seconds, or until the edges look dry. With a flexible spatula, flip the tortilla over, and cook about 1 minute. Turn again and cook 15 seconds. Put the hot tortilla between folds of a clean kitchen towel. Repeat to make 12 tortillas.

Pressing Tortillas

Making tortillas is a tradition that dates back to the Aztecs. After the *masa* dough was made, it was patted by hand into thin discs. These days, hand-pressing is still practiced by some cooks, but most people use a tortilla press. The best and most common press is about 7 inches in diameter and made of heavy cast iron with a silver finish. Lightweight presses made of aluminum are not as good because they may not remain stable as you work. In my experience, rustic wooden presses can be difficult to use, although they are beautiful to display. Tortilla presses are sold in Mexican or Latin-American markets and some cookware stores in the United States. Always line the plates of the press with plastic before pressing tortillas, or the dough will stick to the metal surface. After using it, clean the press with a damp sponge or cloth and dry well to prevent rusting.

In a pinch, it is possible to press tortillas without specialized equipment by placing the dough between pieces of plastic, then putting a completely flat object on top, and pressing firmly and evenly to form the tortilla.

Basic Tamale Dough
Masa para Tamales

Makes 14 to 16 small tamales

This basic dough is easy to work with and is used for most of the tamale recipes in this book. Vegetable shortening and butter are used instead of lard, which is more common in Mexico. If you prefer lard for more authentic flavor, substitute ½ cup Basic Fresh Lard (page 19) in place of both fats in this recipe.

To make preparing tamales easier, make the dough and filling a day ahead. Cover and refrigerate until ready to use. Also, if you live near a tortilla factory, ready-to-use fresh masa for tamales can be purchased instead of making this dough.

1½ cups masa harina (flour for corn tortillas)
1 teaspoon baking powder
1 teaspoon salt
¼ cup vegetable shortening
¼ cup unsalted butter, at room temperature
1¼ cups warm water plus extra, if needed

1. In a medium bowl, mix together the masa harina, baking powder, and salt. Set aside. In another medium bowl, using an electric mixer, beat shortening and butter until creamy. Beat in about one quarter of each of the masa mixture and water. Continue beating and adding the remaining masa and water in 3 additions. Beat until the dough is soft and fluffy, scraping down the edges of the bowl as needed, about 4 to 5 minutes.

2. To test, drop a small piece of dough into a glass of water. If it floats, the dough is ready, if not, beat some more. The dough should be soft, moist, and easy to spread, but not wet or sticky. If dough is too thick, beat in 1 tablespoon water at a time. The dough is ready to use, or cover and refrigerate for up to 3 days, or freeze up to 3 months. Bring to room temperature before using.

Masa Dumplings
Chochoyones

Makes about 16 dumplings

Tiny dumplings made with masa harina *(corn flour for tortillas) are traditionally added to yellow* mole *stews, such as Pork and Vegetables in Yellow Mole, page 357, or some soups in Oaxaca. Lard is usually mixed with the* masa *to make the dough for the dumplings, but vegetable oil is used in this version. Forming the dumplings is similar to shaping "thumbprint" cookies.*

³/₄ cup masa harina (flour for corn tortillas)
¹/₄ teaspoon salt
¹/₂ cup warm water
2 teaspoons vegetable oil

In a bowl, mix the masa harina, salt, and water to make a soft, moist dough. Add the oil and salt. Mix very well with your hands and form into small balls about the size of a large cherry. Make an indentation with your finger in each ball so that it resembles a small fat bowl. Put the dumplings on a plate and cover with plastic wrap. The dumplings are ready to use.

White Flour Tortillas
Tortillas de Harina

Makes 12 (8-inch) tortillas

The Spanish introduced cattle, sheep, and goats to Mexico along with the wheat to feed them. Wheat flour and the making of flour tortillas followed, particularly in Sonora, Baja, and much of northern Mexico. Traditional Mexican cooks mix and knead the dough by hand, but here's the modern way to make flour tortillas with a food processor.

2 cups all-purpose flour
1 teaspoon baking powder
¹/₂ teaspoon salt
¹/₄ cup vegetable shortening
¹/₂ cup plus 1 tablespoon lukewarm water

1. Put the flour, baking powder, and salt in a food processor. Pulse 3 to 4 times to blend. Add the shortening and process until well blended with a mealy texture, about 10 seconds. Add the water all at once, and process until the dough cleans the sides of the bowl, then process about 15 seconds more. Remove the dough to a lightly floured board, and cut into 12 equal pieces. Roll each piece into a ball, cover with plastic wrap and let rest about 45 minutes at room temperature.

2. With a rolling pin, on a floured board, roll each ball into a thin tortilla about 8 inches in diameter and ⅛-inch thick. Heat a medium ungreased skillet over high heat. Place 1 tortilla in the hot pan. (The tortilla should rise in spots on the top surface in about 2 seconds if the pan is hot enough.) Cook about 5 seconds, or until the underside has brown spots. Turn and cook 3 to 4 seconds on the second side, until barely spotted. Place tortilla between folds of a clean kitchen towel. Repeat rolling and pan-cooked tortillas, and stack as they are finished. Keep them covered. Serve while still warm, or cool, place in a plastic bag, and refrigerate. Flour tortillas will keep refrigerated up to 2 weeks, or frozen up to 3 months.

3. To reheat, place tortillas, 1 at a time in a hot skillet, turning every 3 to 4 seconds until soft and pliable. The tortillas may also be heated in a microwave following the manufacturer's instructions.

Basic Crepes
Crepas

Makes about 12 crepes

Crepes are used in a number of ways in Mexico, especially in restaurants serving sophisticated savory dishes or desserts. Crepes with Corn Mushroom (page 146), is probably the best-known savory crepe dish, and Mexican Caramel Crepes (page 557), is a famous dessert crepe dish.

1 cup milk
2 large eggs
³/₄ cup all-purpose flour
¹/₄ teaspoon salt
1¹/₂ tablespoons unsalted butter, melted
¹/₂ teaspoon vegetable oil

1. Put the milk, eggs, flour, and salt in a blender. Blend on high speed until completely smooth, 10 to 12 seconds. Add the melted butter and blend 10 seconds. Let the batter rest covered at room temperature about 45 minutes.

2. Lightly oil a 6- to 7-inch crepe pan or 8-inch nonstick skillet and heat over medium-high heat. When the oil is hot, give the batter a good stir to remix, then pour about ¼ cup batter into the pan and quickly tilt the pan in all directions so batter runs evenly over the entire surface. (Use a pot holder as some skillet handles get very hot.) Cook about 25 seconds, or until the surface looks dry and the edges are lightly browned.

3. With a small flexible spatula, lift and turn crepe. Cook about 10 to 15 seconds and flip crepe out onto a plate. Repeat with the rest of the batter. Oil the pan if crepes begin to stick and stir the batter frequently to keep it well mixed. Stack the cooked crepes; they are ready to use.

Note: Crepes may be cooked ahead, cooled, wrapped in plastic wrap, and refrigerated up to 3 days or frozen up to 1 month. Return crepes to room temperature before separating to prevent crepes from sticking together. Handle carefully; they are tender.

Corn Crepes
Crepas de Harina de Maíz

Makes **about 16 crepes**

Classic French crepes became firmly entrenched in the cuisine of Mexico following the French reign in the mid-nineteenth century, but it's an American idea to make a batter of cornmeal mixed with flour for another kind of crepe. These are tender and are an excellent substitute for tortillas in baked enchiladas, or instead of classic crepes in some savory dishes such as Corn Crepes with Chicken and Corn (page 146). Corn crepes, kept firm with eggs and flour, hold well when sauced ahead of time, and don't become soggy the way corn tortillas do.

2 large eggs
1 cup milk
1/2 cup all-purpose flour
1/2 cup yellow cornmeal
1/2 teaspoon salt
1/4 teaspoon sugar
2 tablespoons unsalted butter, melted
Vegetable oil, for frying

1. Put all the ingredients except the vegetable oil in a blender and blend 15 seconds. Scrape down the sides of the jar and blend 20 seconds. Transfer the batter to a deep bowl and let stand at room temperature at least 1 hour before baking (in a separate recipe). Cover and refrigerate up to overnight if made ahead.

2. Lightly oil a 6- to 7-inch crepe pan or 8-inch nonstick skillet and heat over medium-high heat. When the oil is hot, give the batter a good stir to remix, and pour about 2 tablespoons of batter into the pan and quickly tilt the pan in all directions so batter runs evenly over the entire surface. (Use a pot holder as some skillet handles get very hot.)

3. Cook about 5 seconds, or until the surface looks dry and the edges are lightly browned. With a small flexible spatula, lift and turn crepe. Cook about 5 seconds and flip crepe out onto a plate. Repeat with the rest of the batter. Oil the pan if crepes begin to stick and stir the batter frequently to keep it well mixed. Stack the cooked crepes; they are ready to use.

Note: Crepes may be cooked ahead, cooled, wrapped in plastic wrap and refrigerated up to 3 days or frozen up to 1 month. Return crepes to room temperature before separating to prevent crepes from sticking together. Handle carefully; they are tender.

Enchiladas and Crepes

Cheese Enchiladas in Red Sauce
Enchiladas Rojas de Queso

Makes **8 enchiladas**

Enchiladas with cheese fillings are made just about everywhere and serving them with spicy chile sauce is common. Often, a single cheese enchilada may be served alongside meat or chicken entrées. Or serve several together as a simple main course. The kind of cheese used varies from region to region. For example, Chihuahua cheese is used in the north and Oaxaca cheese in Oaxaca. Experiment with different cheeses to suit your taste.

5 cups (double recipe) Basic Red Chile Sauce
   (page 47)
1 cup *Crema* (page 18) or sour cream
¹/₃ cup vegetable oil
8 (6- to 7-inch) corn tortillas
3 cups shredded Monterey Jack or cheddar cheese
¹/₂ medium white onion, finely chopped
4 green onions, chopped, including 2 inches
   of green

1. Prepare sauce. Set aside and keep the sauce warm on low heat. Prepare crema, if using. Preheat the oven to 350°.

2. In a medium skillet, heat the oil over medium heat. With tongs, dip the tortillas, 1 at a time, in the hot oil until limp, about 3 seconds. Drain on paper towels. Stack the tortillas on a plate and cover with a clean kitchen towel to keep them soft and warm.

3. To assemble the enchiladas, spoon about ¼ cup of the sauce on a plate. Lay 1 tortilla on the plate and turn once to cover with sauce. Top with about ¼ cup of cheese and about 1 teaspoon chopped onion. Roll into a cylinder and place seam side down in a 9- × 13-inch baking dish. Repeat until all tortillas are filled, rolled, and placed side by side in the dish.

4. Pour about 1 cup of the remaining sauce over the enchiladas to cover completely. Cover and store remaining sauce for another use. Sprinkle the remaining cheese on top. Bake until the sauce is bubbling and the cheese is melted, about 20 minutes. Garnish with crema or sour cream and chopped green onion. Serve at once.

Swiss Enchiladas
Enchiladas Suizas

Makes **12 enchiladas**

Chicken-filled Swiss enchiladas with a rich topping of green sauce, cheese, and sour cream are popular all over Mexico. The name refers to the richness of cream and cheese for which Switzerland is so well known. I first encountered them many years ago at Sanborn's House of Tiles in Mexico City. I was lucky enough to get the recipe, and it's still my favorite.

3 cups (1¹/₂ recipe) Shredded Chicken (page 271)

4 poblano chiles, roasted, peeled, and seeded (page 8)

2 pounds tomatillos, husked, rinsed, and quartered

¹/₂ cup fresh cilantro sprigs, packed, plus 2 tablespoons chopped

2 tablespoons chopped white onion

2 serrano chiles, chopped with seeds

1 teaspoon dried oregano (Mexican variety preferred), crumbled

¹/₂ cup chicken broth (from cooking the chicken)

¹/₂ teaspoon sugar

1 teaspoon salt, or to taste

¹/₃ cup vegetable oil

12 (6- to 7-inch) corn tortillas

2 cups shredded Monterey Jack cheese

4 green onions, finely chopped, including 2 inches of green

¹/₂ cup Mexican crema or sour cream thinned with milk

1. Prepare the chicken and reserve. Then, prepare the poblano chiles and chop them coarsely. Put the chiles in a blender. Add the tomatillos, cilantro, onion, serrano chiles, oregano, chicken broth, sugar, and salt. Purée, in batches if necessary, until smooth. Transfer the green sauce to a large saucepan and cook over medium heat, partially covered, stirring often, for 12 to 15 minutes to blend flavors. Adjust seasoning, if needed. Set aside.

2. Preheat the oven to 350°. Heat the oil in a medium skillet over medium-high heat until it shimmers. With tongs, dip the tortillas, 1 at a time in the hot oil until limp, about 3 seconds. Drain on paper towels. Stack and cover to keep them soft and warm. Mix ¹/₂ cup of the cooked green sauce with the shredded chicken.

3. To assemble the enchiladas, put 1 tortilla on a plate and put about 2 tablespoons of chicken on the tortilla and roll into a cylinder. Place seam side down in a large 9- × 13-inch baking pan. Repeat until all tortillas are filled, rolled and placed side by side in the dish.

4. Pour the remaining green sauce over all. Scatter the cheese and onions on top. Bake, uncovered, about 20 minutes or until the sauce is bubbling and the cheese is melted. Drizzle crema over the top and sprinkle with chopped cilantro.

Turkey Enchiladas in Green Sauce

Enchiladas Verde de Pavo

Makes **8 enchiladas**

Bellinghausen, a Mexican restaurant with a German name, has been serving traditional Mexican dishes to a loyal following of local citizens and visitors for some 40 years in the Zona Rosa of Mexico City. In this sprawling metropolis of 20 million people, immigrants from around the world have settled and blended into the populace, adopting and sometimes adapting the local cuisine. Bellinghausen is most popular for the midday meal (comida), *when regular customers head for the pleasant courtyard in the back. I often order these enchiladas filled with chunky pieces of turkey and covered with spicy tomatillo sauce. Servings are garnished with crisp raw vegetables on baby romaine leaves.*

Basic Cooked Tomatillo Sauce (page 46)
Basic Cooked Turkey Breast (page 311)
2 teaspoons vegetable oil plus ¹/₃ cup to soften tortillas
¹/₂ cup chopped white onion
¹/₂ teaspoon dried thyme
¹/₂ teaspoon cumin
2 tablespoons cream cheese, at room temperature
8 (6- to 7-inch) corn tortillas
1 cup crumbled cotija or mild feta cheese
Raw vegetables such as 1 bunch radishes; 2 medium carrots, cut into sticks; and 1 cucumber, peeled and sliced (optional)

1. Prepare the tomatillo sauce. Cover and reserve. Prepare the cooked turkey breast and dice enough turkey to measure about 2 cups packed. Put the diced turkey into a bowl and stir in ¹/₂ cup of the tomatillo sauce. (Cover and refrigerate the remaining turkey for another use.)

2. Preheat the oven to 350°. Heat the 2 teaspoons of oil over medium heat in a small skillet and cook the onion, thyme, and cumin until the onion softens, about 3 minutes. Reduce heat to low, stir in the cream cheese until it melts. Turn off the heat add the mixture to the diced turkey. Stir to combine. Set aside.

3. Heat the remaining ¹/₃ cup of oil in a medium skillet. With tongs, dip 1 tortilla at a time in the hot oil until limp, 4 to 6 seconds. Drain on paper towels. Stack the tortillas on a plate and cover with a clean kitchen towel to keep them soft and warm.

4. To assemble the enchiladas, put 1 tortilla on a plate and spread ¹/₄ cup of turkey on the tortilla. Roll into a cylinder and place seam side down in a 9- × 13-inch baking dish. Repeat until all the tortillas are filled, rolled, and placed side by side in the dish. Pour the tomatillo sauce over the enchiladas to cover completely. Place a piece of aluminum foil loosely over the casserole, and bake until the sauce bubbles and the enchiladas are heated through, 20 to 25 minutes. Scatter crumbled cheese on top. Serve at once. Garnish each serving with the raw vegetables if desired.

Seafood Enchiladas

Enchiladas de Mariscos

Makes **12 enchiladas**

A filling with a combination of seafood varieties makes excellent enchiladas that are fancy enough for a special dinner. The sauce can be made ahead. Assemble and bake the enchiladas shortly before serving for the best texture. Seafood enchiladas are common along both coasts of Mexico.

‍⅓ cups (double recipe) Basic Cooked Tomatillo
    Sauce (page 46)
1 tablespoon olive oil
¹/₂ pound red snapper or Pacific snapper fillets,
    cut into ¹/₄-inch pieces
4 sea scallops, neatly diced (¹/₄ inch)
¹/₂ pound (36 to 40) small shrimp
8 medium button mushrooms, cleaned and chopped
6 green onions, chopped, including 2 inches of
    green part
¹/₂ red bell pepper, chopped
¹/₂ teaspoon salt, or to taste
¹/₈ teaspoon freshly ground pepper, or to taste
¹/₃ cup vegetable oil
12 (6- to 7-inch) corn tortillas
1¹/₄ cups shredded Monterey Jack cheese
12 green pimiento-stuffed olives,
    sliced crosswise

1. Prepare the tomatillo sauce. Reserve in the pan
off heat. Then, heat the olive oil in a large skillet over
medium heat and cook the fish pieces 1 minute.
Add the scallops. Toss and cook 1 minute. Stir in the
shrimp. Transfer seafood to a bowl. In the same
skillet, cook the mushrooms, onions, and pepper,
adding more oil if needed. Mix in the seafood.
Season with salt and pepper. Reserve off heat.

2. Preheat oven to 350°. Grease a 9- × 13-inch baking dish. In a clean skillet, heat about ¹/₃ cup vegetable oil. Dip the tortillas, 1 at a time, in the hot
oil until limp, about 3 seconds. Drain on paper
towels. Stack and cover to keep soft and warm.
When all tortillas are soft, place 1 on a plate. Put
about 2 tablespoons filling on the tortilla. Roll into
a cylinder and place seam side down in the baking
pan. Repeat, until all tortillas are filled, rolled, and
placed side by side in the dish.

3. Pour the green sauce over all. Sprinkle with
the cheese. Bake 25 minutes, or until cheese is
melted and sauce is bubbling. Arrange sliced
olives on top. Serve hot.

Black Bean Enchiladas
Enchiladas de Frijol Negro
Makes **8** enchiladas

*These black bean enchiladas are coated and
baked in red chile sauce. Cook the beans a day
ahead, or in a pinch, canned black beans may
be used. Prepare a double batch of the chile
sauce and freeze any that's leftover.*

5 cups (double recipe) Basic Red Chile Sauce
    (page 47)
¹/₃ cup vegetable oil
8 (6- to 7-inch) corn tortillas
2 cups Basic Refried Beans (page 462)
    with black beans
1 cup shredded Oaxaca or Monterey Jack cheese
¹/₂ cup Mexican crema or sour cream
4 green onions, chopped, including 2 inches of
    green part

1. Prepare chile sauce. Set aside and keep the
sauce warm on low heat. Preheat the oven to 350°.

2. Prepare the sauce. Then, grease a 9- × 13-inch
baking pan. In a medium skillet, heat the oil over
medium heat. With tongs, dip the tortillas, 1 at a
time, in the hot oil until limp, about 3 seconds.
Drain on paper towels. Stack the tortillas on a
plate and cover with a clean kitchen towel to keep
them soft and warm.

3. To assemble the enchiladas, spoon about
¹/₄ cup of the sauce on a plate. Lay 1 tortilla on the
plate and turn once to coat with sauce. Place the
tortilla on another plate and put about ¹/₄ cup of
beans on the tortilla. Roll into a cylinder and place
seam side down in the baking pan. Repeat, until
all tortillas are filled, rolled, and placed side by
side in the pan. Pour about 1 cup of the remaining sauce over the enchiladas to cover completely.
Sprinkle with the cheese. Bake until the sauce is
bubbling and the cheese is melted, about 20 minutes. Drizzle with crema or sour cream and scatter green onions on top. Serve at once.

Stacked Beef Enchiladas
Enchiladas de Carne de Res

Makes **6 to 8 entrée servings**

Quite a few years ago, I developed this recipe for a cooking demonstration that I presented at the California State Fair in Sacramento. I stacked the enchiladas because it was easier to offer samples to an audience of fifty or more. If you want to feed a crowd, you can double the ingredients (or more).

2¹/₂ pounds boneless beef stew meat

5 tablespoons vegetable oil plus more for frying

3 medium garlic cloves, chopped

1 bay leaf

1 teaspoon dried oregano (Mexican variety preferred), crumbled

¹/₂ teaspoon salt, or to taste

Freshly ground pepper, to taste

Ancho Chile Sauce for Enchiladas (page 48)

1 large white onion, chopped

1 (7-ounce) can diced green chiles

¹/₂ teaspoon ground cumin

2 medium tomatoes, peeled and finely chopped

12 (6- to 7-inch) corn tortillas

1 cup grated Monterey Jack cheese

3 thinly sliced green onions, green and white parts

¹/₂ cup sliced black olives

¹/₂ cup Mexican crema or sour cream

3 teaspoons fresh chopped cilantro

1. Trim the meat of fat or gristle. Cut into 1-inch pieces. Heat the oil in a large pot. Brown the meat in batches, and remove to a bowl until all pieces are browned. Return the meat to the pan, and add the garlic, bay leaf, oregano, salt, pepper, and 2½ cups water. Bring to a boil; then reduce heat to low, cover and simmer about 1½ hours, or until the meat is very tender. Remove pan from the heat and cool the meat to lukewarm in the broth. Remove the meat and shred. Cover and reserve. Save the broth for the enchilada sauce.

2. Prepare the ancho chile sauce. Then, heat the remaining oil in a large skillet and cook the onion, stirring, until it starts to brown, 4 to 5 minutes. Add the diced green chiles, cumin, and tomatoes. Bring to a boil and cook, stirring, 3 minutes. Add the shredded meat. Add salt, if desired. Remove from the heat.

3. Preheat the oven to 350°. Grease a large 11- × 16-inch baking pan, with an edge, large enough to accommodate 4 tortillas laid out flat, so that they don't overlap. Heat oil to a depth of ½ inch in a medium skillet, and soften the tortillas, 1 at a time, by passing through the hot oil, holding the edge with tongs, until limp, about 3 seconds. Drain on paper towels. Stack and cover to keep them soft and warm.

4. Ladle a thin film of the reserved enchilada sauce on the bottom of the pan. Place 4 tortillas side by side in the pan. Top each tortilla with about 4 tablespoons of the meat mixture. Place a second tortilla over the meat. Top with meat as before and place a third tortilla over the meat. Cover each stack completely with chile sauce. Sprinkle the tops of each stack with ⅓ of the grated cheese, ⅓ of the chopped onion, and ⅓ of the sliced olives. Bake, uncovered, until the cheese is melted and the sauce bubbles, 15 to 20 minutes. Remove from the oven and cut into wedges. Dollop each serving with crema or sour cream and sprinkle with cilantro.

Vegetable Enchiladas
Enchiladas de Verduras

Makes 8 enchiladas

Vegetable-filled enchiladas can make a complete vegetarian meal or they can be a side dish to serve with grilled meats.

Basic Cooked Tomatillo Sauce (page 46)

1 tablespoon olive oil

1/2 medium white onion, chopped

2 medium zucchini, coarsely shredded

1 cup corn kernels (from about 1 large ear of corn), or thawed, if frozen

1/2 red bell pepper, finely chopped

2 tablespoons Mexican crema or sour cream

2 tablespoons chopped fresh cilantro

1/2 teaspoon cumin

1/4 teaspoon salt, or to taste

Freshly ground pepper, to taste

2 to 3 tablespoons vegetable oil

8 (6- to 7-inch) corn tortillas

1 cup shredded manchego cheese

2 green onions, thinly sliced crosswise

1. Prepare the sauce. Cover and keep warm. Preheat the oven to 375°. Heat the oil in a medium skillet and cook the onion until it starts to brown, 3 to 4 minutes. Add the zucchini, corn, and red pepper. Cook, stirring frequently, until the vegetables are crisp-tender, about 5 minutes. Add the crema, cilantro, salt, and pepper. Set aside.

2. In a medium skillet, heat about 2 tablespoons vegetable oil until it shimmers. Using tongs, dip tortillas, 1 at a time, into the hot oil to soften. Drain on paper towels and stack on a plate. Cover to keep them soft and warm.

3. To assemble the enchiladas, put 1 tortilla on another plate and spoon about ¼ cup of the vegetable mixture on the lower third of the tortilla. Roll into a cylinder and place seam side down, in a 9- × 13-inch baking dish. Repeat until all the tortillas are filled, rolled, and placed side by side in the dish. Pour the cooked tomatillo sauce over the enchiladas. Sprinkle with the cheese and green onions. Bake until the cheese is melted and the enchiladas are heated through, 15 to 20 minutes. Serve at once.

Folded Tortillas in Bean Sauce
Enfrijoladas

Makes 8 tortillas

Corn tortillas dipped in puréed beans, folded, and garnished with cheese and onion, is a popular traditional snack in Oaxaca. Enfrijoladas are easy to make at home. The rich flavors really stand out in this simple dish.

Fresh epazote, *a pungent native Mexican herb with woody stems and serrated leaves about 2 inches long, imparts a subtle distinctive taste that's difficult to describe, but once smelled and tasted will be remembered. If fresh epazote is not available, just leave it out or use fresh oregano for a different flavor.*

Queso fresco, a soft crumbly cheese, is widely available in the United States. Panela, sold in flat round wheels, has a spongy texture.

2 cups Black Bean Sauce (page 55)
1 tablespoon finely chopped fresh epazote leaves, or chopped fresh oregano
¹/₃ cup vegetable oil
8 (6- to 7-inch) corn tortillas
¹/₂ cup crumbled queso fresco (Mexican fresh cheese) or grated panela cheese
¹/₄ cup finely chopped white onion

1. Prepare the black bean sauce. Then, add fresh epazote, if available. Put the bean sauce in a medium skillet and keep warm.

2. In another skillet, heat about ⅓ cup oil until hot. Using tongs, dip tortillas, 1 at a time, in the oil until pliable and hot, about 3 seconds. Stack the tortillas on paper towels.

3. When all are ready, dip each tortilla in the warm bean sauce and quickly fold in quarters to a triangular shape. Place 2 folded tortillas on each of 4 plates. Spoon a little more sauce on each serving. Sprinkle the tops evenly with cheese and onion. Serve.

Folded Tortillas in Tomato Sauce
Entomatadas

Makes 8 tortillas

Corn tortillas dipped in tomato sauce and folded (entomatadas) are a specialty of Oaxaca and are in the enchilada family along with enfrijoladas *and* enmoladas. *In each case the sauce is different, and some have fillings, while others are simply sauced and garnished with a bit of onion and cheese. Some cooks add a dash of cinnamon, allspice, and a little brown sugar for a little more complex flavor, and perhaps to balance the acidity of the tomatoes. A very thin tortilla, called a* blandita, *is used in Oaxaca. Here, you can use traditional corn tortillas.*

2 cups Tomato Sauce for Folded Tortillas (page 43)
¹/₃ cup oil
8 (6- to 7-inch) corn tortillas
¹/₂ cup crumbled queso fresco (Mexican fresh cheese) or grated panela cheese
¹/₂ medium white onion, very thinly sliced
Chopped fresh cilantro

1. Prepare the tomato sauce and keep warm in a wide saucepan. Then, in a medium skillet, heat about ⅓ cup oil and using tongs, dip tortillas, 1 at a time in the hot oil until soft and hot, about 3 seconds. Drain and stack on paper towels.

2. Dip the softened tortillas, 1 at a time, in the warm tomato sauce. Fold into quarters to a triangle shape. Place 2 sauced and folded tortillas on each of 4 plates. Spoon about 3 more tablespoons of the sauce over each serving. Sprinkle each serving with cheese and garnish with onion and cilantro. Serve at once.

Folded Tortillas in Pasilla Chile Sauce
Dobladas de Chile Pasilla

Makes **8 tortillas**

Dobladas *is one of the names for folded, sauced corn tortillas that are served as a snack, a first course, or a light meal.* Dobladas *are a kind of enchilada.*

2 cups (double recipe) Pasilla Chile Sauce (page 26)
1 tablespoon olive oil or vegetable oil
2 medium tomatoes, peeled and finely chopped
1/3 cup vegetable oil for frying
8 (6- to 7-inch) corn tortillas
4 green onions, including green tops, coarsely chopped
1 cup shredded Monterey Jack cheese

1. Prepare the chile sauce. Set aside off heat. Then, in a small skillet, heat the oil over medium heat and cook the tomatoes, stirring, until the juices bubble, 2 to 3 minutes. Stir in the chile sauce and heat through.

2. In a medium skillet, heat 1/3 cup of oil, until hot. Using tongs, dip tortillas, 1 at a time, in the oil until pliable and hot, about 3 seconds. Stack the tortillas on paper towels.

3. Dip the tortillas, one at a time, in the warm sauce just to coat both sides. Fold each into quarters to a triangle shape. Place 2 on each of 4 serving plates. Pour the remaining heated sauce over the tortillas and top each equally with the onions and cheese. Serve at once.

Mushroom Crepes
Crepas con Hongos

Makes **12 crepes**

La Cava is a wonderful restaurant in Mexico City. I often order this dish as a first course or a light entrée.

Basic Crepes (page 136)
Guajillo Chile Sauce with Cream (page 50)
1 poblano chile, roasted, peeled, and seeded (page 8)
2 tablespoons olive oil or vegetable oil
1 pound white mushrooms, finely chopped (about 2 cups)
1/2 medium white onion, finely chopped
2 tablespoons finely chopped fresh epazote leaves (or substitute 1 teaspoon dried epazote or dried oregano, crumbled)
1/2 teaspoon salt, or to taste
Freshly ground pepper, to taste
1/2 cup crumbled cotija or mild feta cheese
Finely chopped fresh flat-leaf parsley

1. Prepare the crepes and reserve on a plate. Prepare the chile sauce and reserve in the pan. (Both of these items can be prepared 1 to 2 days in advance.)

2. Prepare the chiles. Then, in a large skillet, heat the oil over medium heat and cook the mushrooms and onions, stirring frequently, until the moisture has evaporated. Chop the chile and add to the pan along with the epazote, salt, and pepper. Stir to mix. Remove from heat and let cool about 10 minutes before filling the crepes.

3. Preheat the oven to 350°. Grease an 8- × 12-inch baking dish. Put about 1/3 cup filling on each crepe. (Do not overfill or they will be difficult to roll.) Roll, burrito style—with bottom folded toward center, sides folded in over the bottom, and then rolled into a cylinder—to encase the filling. Place seam side down in prepared baking dish. Reheat the sauce and pour over all. Top with grated cheese. Bake until hot and bubbly, about 20 minutes. Place 2 crepes on each of 4 serving plates. Sprinkle with parsley. Serve at once.

Crepes with Corn Mushroom
Crepas de Cuitlacoche

Makes 12 crepes

Cuitlacoche *(also spelled* huitlacoche*) is a gray to black fungus (similar to a mushroom) that grows on corn in the rainy season. This ingredient dates back to Aztec cooking and is quite an exotic delicacy.* Crepas de Cuitlacoche *is a prized dish that's served as a separate course in many sophisticated restaurants. Look for canned cuitlacoche in Mexican markets or from mail-order sources (see page 620).*

Basic Crepes (page 136)
Guajillo Chile Sauce with Cream (page 50)
2 poblano chiles, roasted, peeled, seeded (page 8)
   and chopped or finely diced
2 tablespoons unsalted butter
1/2 medium white onion, finely chopped
1 tablespoon chopped fresh epazote or 1/2 teaspoon
   dried epazote
2 (about 9-ounce) cans cuitlacoche, chopped
1 cup shredded Oaxaca or Monterey Jack cheese

1. Prepare the crepes. Cover and reserve. Prepare the chile sauce. Reserve in the pan off heat. Prepare the chiles.

2. In a skillet, heat the butter and cook the onion, stirring, until it starts to brown, 3 to 4 minutes. Add the chiles to the onion along with the cuitlacoche and 2 teaspoons of water. Cook over medium heat, stirring, 4 to 5 minutes, until the liquid is evaporated.

3. Preheat the oven to 350°. Butter a 7- × 11-inch baking dish. Lay 1 crepe on a flat surface. Put about 1½ tablespoons filling on the crepe, roll into a cylinder and place in the baking dish, seam side down. Repeat, filling and rolling the remaining crepes and place them side by side in the dish. Pour the sauce over the crepes. Sprinkle with

cheese and bake 18 to 20 minutes, or until the crepes are completely heated through, the sauce bubbles and the cheese is melted. Place 2 crepes on each of 6 serving plates. Serve hot.

Corn Crepes with Chicken and Corn
Crepas de Elote con Pollo y Elote

Makes 8 crepes

Enchiladas become crepas *when the filling is wrapped in savory corn crepes. For a striking plate with great color, serve the corn crepes with Tomato and Avocado Salad (page 165).*

8 (1/2 recipe) Corn Crepes (page 137)
Basic Cooked Tomatillo Sauce (page 46)
Shredded Spiced Chicken (page 271)
2 teaspoons unsalted butter
1 cup cooked corn kernels, fresh, or thawed if frozen
1/4 teaspoon salt

1. Prepare the corn crepes. Set aside on a plate. Prepare the tomatillo sauce. Set aside in a bowl. Prepare the shredded chicken. Set aside in a bowl. In a small skillet, melt the butter over medium heat. Add the corn and salt. Cook, stirring, until heated through, about 2 minutes.

2. Preheat oven to 375°. In an 11- × 7-inch ovenproof baking dish, spread about ¾ cup of the tomatillo sauce on the bottom. Fill one crepe with about ¼ cup of the chicken mixture. Roll into a cylinder and place seam side down in prepared baking dish. Repeat, filling and rolling remaining crepes, and place them side by side in the dish. Cover each of the filled rolled crepes with about ¼ cup of tomatillo sauce. Bake until completely heated through, about 20 minutes. To serve, put 2 crepes on each of 4 plates. Reheat the corn and scatter the corn equally over each serving.

Tamales

Tamales with Chicken
Tamales de Pollo

Makes **about 16 small tamales**

Chicken tamales are among the easiest to make and the most popular to eat. Here, the shredded chicken is mixed with a spicy salsa verde (green chile sauce), purchased or homemade. Dried corn husks are available in Mexican markets and many supermarkets.

Basic Tamale Dough (page 134)
16 corn husks, plus extra to line the steamer
Shredded Chicken (page 271)
2 teaspoons vegetable oil
1/2 medium white onion, finely chopped
1/3 cup salsa verde, purchased or homemade

1. Soak the corn husks in hot tap water for 2 hours. Meanwhile, prepare the tamale dough and keep it at room temperature and prepare the chicken and reserve in a bowl.

2. In a small skillet, heat the vegetable oil over medium heat and cook the onion, stirring, until it starts to brown, about 4 minutes. Mix the onion with the shredded chicken. Stir in the salsa verde. Set aside.

3. Remove the corn husks from the water. Put on a plate and cover with a clean damp kitchen towel to keep moist. Put 1 husk on a work surface. Put about 2 tablespoons of dough in the center of the husk and spread into a ¼-inch thick rectangle, to within 1 inch of the wide end and about 3 inches from the pointed end. Put about 1 tablespoon of the filling in a line down the middle of the dough. Overlap the sides of the husk over the filling. Fold the pointed end toward the wide end and put on a plate folded side down. Repeat with remaining husks and filling.

4. Put about 3 inches of water into a large metal steamer and drop in a coin. (A rattling coin means there's still water in the pot.) Line the steamer rack with extra corn husks. Arrange tamales folded ends down on the husks. Cover with more corn husks or aluminum foil. Tuck a kitchen towel on top and put on the lid. Bring to a boil and steam the tamales 1 hour or until the dough is firm and the husk pulls away from the dough. Do not let the steamer boil dry. If the coin stops rattling, very cautiously add hot water. Serve the tamales hot with additional green sauce, if desired.

Tamales with Beef or Pork
Tamales de Res o Cerdo

Makes **about 16 small tamales**

Tamales are always easier to prepare if the dough and filling are made in advance. Remember also to soak the corn husks ahead of time. Tamales can be wrapped and steamed in pieces of aluminum foil if corn husks aren't available.

Basic Tamale Dough (page 134)

2 cups (¹/₂ recipe) Ancho Chile Sauce for Enchiladas (page 48)

16 corn husks, plus extra to line the steamer

2 pounds boneless beef stew meat or pork shoulder, cut into 1-inch pieces

¹/₂ medium white onion, finely chopped

2 medium garlic cloves, finely chopped

1 bay leaf

1. Prepare the tamale dough and keep it at room temperature. Prepare ancho chile sauce and reserve.

2. Soak corn husks in hot tap water for 2 hours. Meanwhile, put the meat, onion, garlic, and bay into a large saucepan. Add water to just cover. Bring to a boil; reduce heat to medium-low and simmer, until meat is tender, about 1 hour.

3. Cool the meat in the broth; then remove and tear into shreds. Put the meat in a bowl. Add ¹/₂ cup of the ancho sauce. Mix well. Strain the meat broth and save for another use.

4. Remove the corn husks from the water. Put on a plate and cover with a clean damp kitchen towel to keep moist. Put 1 husk on a work surface. Put about 2 tablespoons of dough in the center of the husk and spread into a ¹/₄-inch thick rectangle to within 1 inch of the wide end and about 3 inches from the pointed end. Put about 1 tablespoon of filling down the middle of the dough. Overlap the sides of the husk over the filling. Fold the

pointed end toward the wide end and put on a plate folded side down. Repeat with remaining husks and fillings.

5. Put about 3 inches of water and a coin into a large steamer. (A rattling coin means there's still water in the pot.) Line the steamer rack with extra corn husks. Arrange the tamales folded ends down on the husks. Cover with more corn husks or aluminum foil. Tuck a kitchen towel on top and put on the lid. Bring to a boil and steam tamales 1 hour or until the dough is firm and easily pulls away from the husk. Do not let the steamer boil dry. If the coin stops rattling, very cautiously add hot water.

6. Reheat the remaining chile sauce. Serve with the tamales. To store, keep tamales wrapped and refrigerated up to 3 days, or freeze up to 3 months. Reheat in a steamer or microwave.

Tamales with Shrimp
Tamales de Camarones

Makes **about 12 tamales**

Shrimp tamales are made along the coasts of Mexico where shrimp are abundant. This version of shrimp tamales is flavored with Basic Roasted Tomato Sauce (page 42). The salsa can be made ahead, covered, and refrigerated overnight. Remember to soak the corn husks in advance.

Basic Roasted Tomato Sauce (page 42)

Basic Tamale Dough (page 134)

12 soaked corn husks plus extra to line the steamer

24 medium shrimp, peeled, deveined, and tails removed

1. Prepare the tomato salsa. Prepare the tamale dough. Salsa and dough should be at room temperature. Soak the corn husks in hot water for 2 hours.

2. Remove the corn husks from the water. Put on a plate and cover with a clean damp kitchen towel to

Hot Tamales For Every Taste

The word *tamal* (singular for tamales) comes from the Nahuatl word *tamalli* and refers to something wrapped up. A tamal consists of a leaf as a wrapper, the *masa* (dough), and the filling. Wrapping leaves are dried or fresh corn husks, banana leaves, and sometimes chard or other native leaves. The fillings are meats, poultry, fish, vegetables, and often have a coating of *mole* or other sauce to moisten the filling.

To make tamales, the masa dough and filling are prepared separately. Dried corn husks are soaked to soften them, or green leaves are steamed or parboiled to make them pliable. When all the elements are ready, the leaf is spread with masa, topped with filling, and then folded over the fillings. Then the tamales are steamed in the top of a large metal double boiler-steamer, under a layer of more leaves to prevent excess moisture from dripping on the tamales.

Tamales are made in many sizes, from small appetizer bites to the giant *zacahuil* from the Huasteca region of Veracruz; it is so large that the masa and meats must be wrapped in layers of huge banana leaves, then secured with wire. The *zacahuil* I watched being prepared was then placed on a wooden plank and carried to the village oven to bake about eight hours. Later, the spectacular unwrapping of the huge tamal sent billows of steam and incredible aromas into the room. Masa and filling were spooned onto plates and the feast began!

Besides a great variety of savory tamales, there are also sweet tamales filled with different kinds of fruits and nuts. These are commonly eaten for breakfast with hot chocolate or as an evening treat. People are often surprised to learn of the great variety of tamales in Mexico. Travelers to Mexico are rewarded when they discover and taste some of the regional tamales such as *uchepos* (fresh corn) from Michoacan, tamales in banana leaves from Oaxaca and Yucatán, or delicate, sweet yellow *canarios* (canaries), from central Mexico. Sampling all the various tamales is a true culinary adventure, because many of these exceptional versions are seldom found outside their region.

keep moist. Put 1 corn husk on a flat surface. Put 3 tablespoons of dough in the center of the husk and spread into a ¼-inch-thick rectangle to within 1-inch of the wide end and about 3 inches from the pointed end. Place 2 shrimp on the dough and top with 1 tablespoon of the salsa. Overlap the sides of the husk over the filling. Fold the pointed end toward the wide end and put on a plate folded side down. Repeat with remaining husks and fillings.

3. Put about 3 inches of water and a coin into a large steamer. (A rattling coin means there's still water in the pot.) Line the steamer rack with extra corn husks. Arrange the tamales folded ends down on the husks. Cover with more corn husks or aluminum foil. Tuck a kitchen towel on top and put on the lid. Bring to a boil and steam tamales about 1 hour, or until the dough is firm and easily pulls away from the husk. Do not let the steamer boil dry. If the coin stops rattling, very cautiously add hot water.

4. Serve the tamales hot with remaining salsa. To store, keep tamales wrapped and refrigerated up to 1 day, or freeze up to 3 months. Reheat in a steamer directly from the refrigerator or freezer.

Fresh Corn Tamales
Uchepos

Makes about 24 tamales

Tamales made from ground fresh corn and steamed in fresh corn leaves are called uchepos. *In this recipe a little masa helps to thicken the ground corn mixture. There is no filling in* uchepos, *but they are often served with a salsa.*

6 medium ears of corn with all leaves attached
1/3 cup masa harina (flour for corn tortillas)
1/2 teaspoon baking powder
1/4 cup softened butter, lard, or solid vegetable shortening
2 teaspoons sugar
1/2 teaspoon salt

1. With a sharp heavy knife, cut around the wide end of each ear of corn to release the corn husks from the cobs. Peel off the husks without tearing. Put the husks in a large pan of warm water. Rinse then wrap them in a damp kitchen towel. Remove all silk from the corn and discard. Rinse the corn and cut the kernels off the cobs into a large bowl. With the dull side of the knife scrape the residual corn from the cobs from top to bottom into the bowl.

2. Grind the corn in a food processor to a coarse purée, pulsing about 10 to 12 times. Transfer back to the bowl. Mix in the remaining ingredients, and beat well with a wooden spoon about 30 seconds.

3. For each tamale, put about 1/4 cup filling on the inside curved part of the leaf near the wide end. Fold in the two sides, overlapping, to cover the filling. Fold the narrow end toward the wide end. Lay seam side down on a plate. Cover with a damp towel. Repeat until all are filled.

4. Put about 3 inches of water into a large steamer and drop in a coin. (A rattling coin means there's still water in the pot.) Line the steamer rack with extra corn husks. Stack the tamales, folded ends down on the husks. Cover with more corn husks or aluminum foil. Tuck a kitchen towel on top and put on the lid. Bring to a boil; then reduce heat to a medium boil. Steam the tamales 45 minutes or until the dough pulls away from the husk. Do not let the steamer boil dry. If the coin stops rattling, very cautiously add more hot water.

Tamales with Jalapeños, Cheese, and Corn
Tamales de Jalapeños, Queso, y Elote

Makes 16 small tamales

Fresh green jalapeños, cheese, and fresh corn kernels wrapped and steamed in tamale dough is a great combination. Open the steaming hot tamales and spoon fresh tomato salsa on top for a real treat. These are really easy to make.

Basic Tamale Dough (page 134)
16 corn husks, plus extra to line the steamer
1 cup cooked corn kernels, fresh or frozen
2 large jalapeño chiles, seeded, and cut into thin strips
1/2 cup crumbled cotija or mild feta cheese
2 cups fresh tomato salsa, purchased or homemade

1. Prepare the tamale dough and keep it at room temperature. Soak the corn husks in hot tap water for 2 hours.

2. Remove the corn husks from the water and put on a plate. Cover with a clean damp kitchen towel to keep moist. Put 1 husk on a flat surface. Put about 3 tablespoons dough in the center of the husk and spread into a 1/4-inch-thick rectangle to within 1 inch of the wide end and about 3 inches from the pointed end. Put about 1 teaspoon corn kernels on the dough and press them into the dough. Add 2 to 3 strips of chile, and 1 teaspoon cheese. Overlap the sides of the husk over the filling. Fold the pointed end toward the wide end and put on a plate, folded side down. Repeat with the remaining husks and filling.

3. Put about 3 inches of water into a large steamer and drop in a coin. (A rattling coin means there's still water in the pot.) Line the steamer rack with extra corn husks. Arrange the tamales folded ends down on the husks. Cover with more corn husks or aluminum foil. Tuck a kitchen towel on top and put on the lid. Bring to a boil. Steam the tamales 1 hour or until the dough is firm and the husk pulls away from the dough. Do not let the steamer boil dry. If the coin stops rattling, very cautiously add hot water. Serve the tamales with fresh tomato salsa to be added at the table.

Vegetable Tamales with Black Bean Sauce
Tamales de Verduras y Salsa de Frijol Negro

Makes 14 to 16 small tamales

Chef, cookbook author, and friend John Sedler made vegetable tamales at a cooking class I once attended. This is my adaptation of John's tamales. I serve the tamales with black bean sauce, for a first course with striking presentation.

Basic Tamale Dough (page 134)

Black Bean Sauce (page 55)

16 corn husks, plus extra to line the steamer

1 tablespoon vegetable oil

1/2 medium onion, finely chopped

4 medium button mushrooms, finely chopped

1 medium carrot, peeled and cut into 1/4-inch dice

1 medium zucchini, ends trimmed and cut into 1/4-inch dice

1/2 teaspoon dried oregano (Mexican variety preferred), crumbled

1/2 teaspoon ground cumin

1/2 teaspoon salt

1 cup cooked corn kernels

1/2 cup crumbled cotija or mild feta cheese

1/3 cup chopped fresh cilantro

1. Prepare the tamale dough and keep it at room temperature. Prepare the black bean sauce and reserve in a saucepan. Soak the corn husks in hot tap water for 2 hours.

2. Heat the oil in a medium skillet over medium heat and cook the onion until softened, 3 to 4 minutes. Add the remaining ingredients, except the corn and cheese. Cook the vegetables briefly, about 2 minutes. They will be hot but still crisp. (They will finish cooking while the tamales steam.) Transfer to a bowl and cool.

3. Remove the corn husks from the water. Put on a plate and cover to keep moist. Lay 1 husk on a flat surface. Put about 3 tablespoons of dough in the center of the husk and spread into a 1/4-inch-thick rectangle to within 1 inch of the wide end and about 3 inches from the pointed end. Put about 1 tablespoon of filling down the middle of the dough. Overlap the sides of the husk to enclose the filling. Fold the pointed end toward the wide end and put on a plate, folded side down. Repeat with remaining husks and fillings.

4. Put about 3 inches of water and a coin into a large steamer kettle. (A rattling coin means there's still water in the pot.) Line the steamer rack with extra damp corn husks. Arrange the tamales folded ends down. Cover with more corn husks or aluminum foil. Tuck a kitchen towel on top and put on the lid. Bring to a boil and steam the tamales for 1 hour or until the dough is firm and easily pulls away from the husk.

5. Reheat the sauce. For each serving, unwrap 2 tamales and place on a serving plate. Spoon about 2 tablespoons of sauce over the middle of the tamales. Scatter corn kernels and crumbled cheese over each serving. Garnish with a sprinkle of chopped cilantro.

Tamales, Monterrey Style
Tamalitos Norteños

Makes about 24 small tamales

These little tamales are a traditional evening treat for the residents of Monterrey, in the northern state of Nuevo Leon. The small, thin tamales are filled with machaca *(dried beef), or* picadillo *(minced meat sautéed with flavorings), accompanied by a hot chocolate drink known as* champurrado. *I've simplified the filling by using ground pork cooked with a few herbs and spices. Pick out 24 of the smallest dried corn husks for these small tamales or trim larger ones, if you like. Serve them hot in the husks along with cups of hot chocolate, if you want to be traditional. Some people prefer a cold beer.*

Basic Tamale Dough (page 134)
24 small corn husks, plus extra to line the steamer
1 teaspoon vegetable oil
1 pound lean ground pork
1/4 teaspoon salt, or to taste
2 tablespoons finely chopped onion
1 small garlic clove, finely chopped
1/4 cup thick and chunky bottled red salsa
1 teaspoon chili powder
1/4 teaspoon ground cinnamon (Mexican canela or Ceylon variety preferred)
1/4 teaspoon ground cumin
1/8 teaspoon ground allspice

1. Prepare the tamale dough and reserve it at room temperature. Soak the corn husks in hot tap water about 2 hours.

2. Meanwhile, heat the oil in a skillet and cook the pork, stirring and breaking it into small pieces, until no longer pink, 3 to 4 minutes. Add salt, then the onion and garlic. Cook, stirring, until the onion softens, about 3 minutes. Add the remaining ingredients. Cook 5 minutes, stirring frequently to blend flavors. Add salt if desired. Remove from heat to cool. When cool enough to handle, using fingers or a fork, break up any pork clumps to make a fine-textured mixture. Cool completely.

3. To assemble the tamales, remove corn husks from the water, pat dry and put on a plate. Cover with a damp kitchen towel to keep moist. Tear about 30 thin strips from the extra corn husks for tying around the tamales. Put 1 husk on a flat surface. Put 2 teaspoons of tamale dough in the center of the husk and spread into a thin rectangle. Put 1 teaspoon filling down the center of the dough. Fold the sides of the husk toward the center, overlapping. Fold the top and bottom toward the center and repeat with remaining husks and filling. Any extra filling can be refrigerated or frozen for another use.

4. Put about 3 inches of water in the bottom of a large steamer and drop in a coin. (A rattling coin means there's still water in the steamer.) Line the steamer rack with extra husks. Arrange tamales seam side down. Cover with more corn husks or aluminum foil. Tuck a kitchen towel on top. Put on the lid and steam about 1 hour or until the dough is firm and the husk pulls away from the dough. Do not let the steamer boil dry. If the coin stops rattling, very cautiously add hot water. Serve hot.

Tamales in Banana Leaves, Oaxaca Style
Tamales de Oaxaca

Makes about 12 tamales

My husband and I have been staying at the Misión de los Angeles hotel in Oaxaca for many years. The spacious gardens and serene setting welcomes us after a long day of driving, walking, and exploring. The typical Oaxacan tamal steamed in a banana leaf is almost always on the menu of the hotel's dining room. The tamales can also be purchased in many cafes or at the huge Abastos Mercado located across the railroad tracks from the center of the city. In the United States, banana leaves can be found in Mexican and Asian markets.

Oaxacan Red Mole (page 58) or other mole sauce
Basic Tamale Dough (page 134)
12 (10-inch) squares of banana leaf (Techniques, page 10)
12 thin strips of banana leaf
Shredded Chicken (page 271)

1. Prepare the mole sauce, tamale dough, and shredded chicken. Keep them at room temperature. Prepare banana leaves.

2. Lay 1 banana leaf square on a flat surface. Spread about 2 tablespoons dough in the center of the leaf. Top with 2 tablespoons chicken and 2 tablespoons sauce. Fold the sides of the leaf, overlapping them, to cover the filling. Fold the top and bottom toward the center to form a square package. Tie with strips of banana leaf. Repeat until all tamales are filled and wrapped.

3. Put about 3 inches of water into a large steamer and drop in a coin. (A rattling coin means there's still water in the pot.) Line a steamer with extra pieces of banana leaf. Stack the tamales, seam side down, on the steamer rack. Cover with a banana leaf or aluminum foil. Tuck a kitchen towel on top and put on the lid. Bring to a boil and steam tamales about 1 hour or until the dough comes easily away from the banana leaf when you test 1 packet. Retie, and serve packets hot.

Tamales Wrapped in Swiss Chard

Tamales de Acelgas

Makes about 12 tamales

Katherine Williams and her late husband, Al Williams, owned the once-famous Papagayo Room Mexican restaurant in San Francisco's Fairmont Hotel. Charismatic owner-host Al Williams spent part of his early life in Mexico City and later introduced Americans in San Francisco to authentic Mexican cuisine. The Papagayo Room's elegant surroundings attracted Hollywood stars such as Humphrey Bogart, Marilyn Monroe, and Woody Allen from the 1940s through the 1970s. After the restaurant closed, the Williams' operated Papagayo School of Cooking, where I was inspired and entertained during many memorable classes.

After her husband's death, Katherine Williams wrote a book based on their restaurant's recipes. Katherine's tamales wrapped in Swiss chard were new to me then, but I have since enjoyed other versions. Chard leaves are wonderful wrappers and make the whole package edible. I serve them as a separate course with cooked tomato sauce.

Basic Shredded Pork (page 346)
1/2 cup purchased thick and chunky red salsa
Ranchera Sauce (page 44)
Basic Tamale Dough (page 134)
12 large chard leaves, rinsed and thick stems removed

1. Prepare the pork. Mix the purchased red salsa with the shredded pork. Prepare the ranchera sauce. Prepare the tamale dough. If made ahead and refrigerated, bring the pork, sauce, and dough to room temperature about 1 hour before using.

2. In a large pot of boiling water, blanch the chard leaves until pliable, 40 seconds. Drain and cool. With a sharp knife, cut out about 2 inches of the thick center rib from each leaf. Cover leaves with a damp towel to keep moist.

3. Put 1 chard leaf on a flat surface. Put about 2 tablespoons of dough in the center of the leaf and spread into a 1/2-inch-thick rectangle. Put about 2 tablespoons shredded pork on the dough. Put 1 more tablespoon of dough on top of the meat, and spread to cover the meat. Fold the leaves overlapping on all sides to make a package. (The blanched leaves are tender and will cling together.) Repeat with remaining chard leaves.

4. Put about 3 inches of water and a coin in the bottom of a large steamer. (A rattling coin means there's still water in the pot.) Line the steamer rack with foil. Arrange the tamales, folded side down. Cover with foil and tuck a kitchen towel over the top. Put on the lid. Bring to a boil and steam tamales about 1 hour, or until the dough is firm and easily pulls away from the leaf. To serve, heat the sauce and spoon about 1 tablespoon of warm sauce on top of each wrapped tamal. These tamales do not freeze well, but can be refrigerated 2 to 3 days and reheated in the steamer.

Yucatán Tamale Pie
Mucbil Pollo

Makes **4 to 6 servings**

This is a richly seasoned dish of chicken, herbs, spices, and tomatoes baked inside a thick wrap of tamale dough that's covered with banana leaves to hold in the juices. My introduction to Mucbil Pollo *was in the beautiful tropical home of Perla and John Ehrenberg near Merida, where Perla demonstrated the cooking of this dish. Later, I worked out this recipe using foil to cover the dish, instead of wrapping the whole thing in banana leaves. If you wish to use banana leaves, line the casserole dish completely and fold the excess over the top, then cover the top snugly with foil.*

Basic Tamale Dough made with chicken broth (page 134)
Yucatán Red Seasoning Paste (page 23)
2 cups canned fat-free reduced-sodium chicken broth
6 skinless chicken thighs on the bone
6 plum tomatoes, cored and quartered
1 large red onion, sliced
2 tablespoons chopped fresh epazote leaves, or 1 teaspoon dried epazote
1/2 teaspoon salt
Freshly ground pepper, to taste

1. Prepare the tamale dough using chicken broth instead of water for the liquid. Cover and refrigerate. Prepare the red seasoning paste and put it into a medium bowl. Add ½ cup of water and mix until smooth, and pour into a large 4 to 6 quart saucepan. Add the chicken broth and the chicken pieces. Arrange the tomatoes and onion on top. Sprinkle with epazote, salt, and pepper. Bring to a boil, reduce heat to medium-low, cover and simmer until the chicken is tender, about 30 minutes.

2. Remove the chicken, tomatoes and onion from the broth. Return the broth to a boil and cook until reduced by half; then reserve off heat. When the chicken is cool enough to handle, remove the meat from the bones, discarding the bones, and tear the meat into bite-size pieces. Return the chicken, tomatoes, and onion to the broth. Mix and set aside.

3. Preheat oven to 400°. Grease a shallow 2½-quart casserole dish. (An earthenware casserole dish is perfect.) Spread or press about ⅓ of the tamale dough on the bottom and sides of the dish. Spoon the chicken, tomatoes, and onion mixture into the dish. Spread the remaining tamale dough over the top to enclose the filling. Cover tightly with foil. Bake 25 minutes. Remove the foil and bake until the top is barely browned, about 30 to 35 minutes more. Serve hot.

Tortilla Casseroles

Baked Aztec Chicken Casserole
Budín Azteca

Makes 4 to 6 servings

There are many versions of this classic layered tortilla and chicken casserole that is popular on both sides of the border. As far as I know, there's no specific Aztec origin; the title (literally, Aztec pudding) is just a fanciful name given by a cook, and it stuck. It's a pretty common dish and is also called Moctezuma Pie.

Basic Cooked Tomatillo Sauce (page 46)
Shredded Chicken (page 271)
4 poblano chiles, roasted, peeled and seeded (page 8)
Oil for frying the tortillas
12 (6- to 7-inch) corn tortillas
1 cup sour cream
1¹/₂ cups shredded Oaxaca or Monterey Jack cheese

1. Prepare the tomatillo sauce. Reserve in the pan off heat. Prepare the shredded chicken. Reserve in a bowl. Roast, peel, and seed the chiles. Remove the stems and cut the chiles into short thin strips. Reserve in a bowl.

2. Preheat oven to 350°. In a medium skillet, heat oil to a depth of about ½ inch until hot. Using tongs, fry the tortillas, 1 at a time, until barely stiff but not brown, about 20 seconds. Drain on paper towels.

3. Arrange 4 tortillas, overlapping, to cover the bottom of a square 8-inch baking dish. Cover with ½ of the chicken, ½ of the chile strips, ⅓ of the sour cream, ⅓ of the sauce, and ⅓ of the cheese. Top with 4 tortillas and repeat with layers of chicken, chile strips, sour cream, sauce, and cheese. Top with the 4 remaining tortillas,

remaining sour cream, sauce, and cheese. Bake until completely heated through and bubbling, about 25 minutes. Serve hot.

Chicken and Tortilla Casserole with Green Sauce
Chilaquiles de Pollo con Salsa Verde

Makes 4 servings

Crisp tortilla strips combined with shredded chicken and green tomatillo sauce, then baked, is one of the most common chilaquiles, a dish made with strips of dry tortillas mixed with other ingredients and sauce. Chilaquiles is a staple of breakfast buffets all over Mexico. It's good anytime of the day. If tortillas are fresh, spread out on a flat surface about 30 minutes to dry a bit before using.

6 (6- to 7-inch) corn tortillas, halved and cut into strips about ¹/₂ inch wide
Vegetable oil for frying
1 medium white onion, halved and thinly sliced
1 pound tomatillos, husked
2 cups canned fat-free reduced-sodium chicken broth
1 poblano chile, roasted, peeled, seeded, and chopped (page 8)
¹/₂ cup loosely packed coarsely chopped fresh cilantro
1 serrano chile, chopped with seeds
¹/₂ teaspoon ground cumin
¹/₂ teaspoon dried oregano (Mexican variety preferred), crumbled
¹/₂ teaspoon salt, or to taste
¹/₄ teaspoon sugar
2 chicken breast halves, on the bone, with or without skin
¹/₄ cup crumbled cotija or mild feta cheese

1. In a small skillet, such as cast iron, heat oil to a depth of about 1 inch until hot. Fry the tortilla strips, in batches, until golden and crisp. Drain on paper towels and set aside. Remove all but 1 tablespoon of the oil from the skillet. Add the onion, and cook, stirring, until the edges begin to brown, about 4 minutes. Reserve off heat.

2. Cook the tomatillos in boiling water to cover until barely tender, 4 to 5 minutes. Drain the tomatillos and put them in a blender jar. Add the onion, poblano, cilantro, serranos, cumin, oregano, salt, and sugar to the blender and reserve.

3. Put the chicken in a medium saucepan with the chicken broth. Bring to a boil, then reduce the heat to low, cover, and simmer the chicken until opaque throughout, about 12 minutes. Remove the chicken to a plate. When cool enough to handle, shred the chicken and reserve. Discard the bones and skin.

4. Put ½ cup of the chicken broth into the blender jar with the tomatillo mixture and purée until nearly smooth. (The sauce should have some texture.) Pour the sauce and remaining chicken broth into a large saucepan and bring to a boil. Reduce heat to low, cover, and simmer the sauce 6 to 8 minutes. Add salt, if needed.

5. Preheat the oven to 375°. To assemble the chilaquiles, put the shredded chicken, tortilla strips, and the green sauce into an 8-inch square baking dish. Stir gently to combine. Sprinkle with the cheese. Bake about 20 minutes or until completely heated through. Serve hot.

Meatball and Tortilla Casserole
Chilaquiles con Albondigas

Makes **8 servings**

During a cooking class in Puerto Vallarta I presented this dish to my tour group. It's a great crowd-pleaser. The recipe can be doubled and served in a large clay casserole dish or paella pan. It's like pasta made with tortilla with a tropical fruit salad or fruit sal. accompaniment. If tortillas are fresh, . on a flat surface about 30 minutes to a bit before using.

Basic Red Chile Sauce (page 47)
Appetizer Meatballs (page 71)
Corn oil or other vegetable oil for frying
**12 (6- to 7-inch) corn tortillas, cut into
    ¹/₂-inch-wide strips**
2 medium white onions cut into half rings
¹/₂ teaspoon salt, or to taste
1 cup grated Monterey Jack or cheddar cheese
Chopped fresh cilantro, for garnish

1. Prepare the red chile sauce. Prepare the meatballs and keep them warm in the cooking broth.

2. Pour oil to a depth of about 1 inch in a medium skillet and heat until it shimmers. Fry the tortilla strips, in batches, until golden. Drain on paper towels.

3. In a large wide saucepan, heat 2 tablespoons of the oil from the skillet over medium heat and fry the onions until they start to brown, 4 to 5 minutes. Add the prepared red chile sauce and ½ cup of the cooking broth from the meatballs. Break the fried tortilla strips in half and add to the sauce mixture. Stir to combine and heat through. If the tortillas are still dry, stir in some additional liquid. Mix in the cheese to just combine, and transfer the contents to a clay casserole dish or other attractive serving dish.

4. Arrange the heated meatballs around the outside edge of the dish. Sprinkle with cilantro. (The chilaquiles can be kept warm in a 200° oven about 20 minutes, for the best texture, after that they become soggy.)

Pork and Tortilla Casserole
Chilaquiles con Puerco

Makes **4 servings**

Corn tortillas are no longer considered fresh by Mexican standards after about 1 day, but they are never wasted. Chilaquiles *is a perfect example of how leftover tortillas are used to make something rustic and wonderful. Serve with guacamole and a green salad. If tortillas are fresh, spread out on a flat surface about 30 minutes to dry a bit before using.*

Oil for frying

6 (6- to 7-inch) corn tortillas, each cut into 8 wedges

1 medium onion, chopped

2 medium garlic cloves, chopped

3/4 pound boneless pork, cut into bite-size pieces

1 teaspoon dried oregano (Mexican variety preferred), crumbled

1/2 teaspoon ground cumin

1 bay leaf

1 1/4 cups canned fat-free reduced-sodium chicken broth

2 medium tomatoes, cored

2 guajillo chiles, cut open and seeded

12 to 14 fresh epazote leaves, or 1 tablespoon dried epazote

2 to 3 tablespoons chopped fresh cilantro

1. In a skillet, heat oil to a depth of 1 inch, and fry the tortilla wedges until crisp and light brown. Drain on paper towels. Reserve. In a 3-quart saucepan heat 2 tablespoons of the oil from frying the tortillas over medium heat, and cook the onion and garlic, stirring frequently, until lightly browned, 5 to 6 minutes. Add the pork, cumin, and bay leaf. Cook, stirring, until the meat is no longer pink, about 6 minutes. Add the chicken broth, and bring to a boil; then reduce the heat to low, cover and simmer until the pork is tender, about 25 minutes.

2. Meanwhile, preheat the oven to 400°. Put the tomatoes in a small foil-lined baking dish and roast until soft and wrinkled, about 20 minutes. Reserve.

3. In a small nonstick skillet, over medium heat, toast the chiles, turning and pressing them flat onto the pan with a spatula until they are aromatic and a bit of orange color appears on the skin, 35 to 40 seconds. (Do not burn them.) Break the chiles into pieces and put in a blender with the roasted tomatoes, epazote, and 1/4 cup of water. Blend as smooth as possible. Pour through a fine-mesh strainer into the pan with the pork. Discard the debris from the strainer.

4. Add the toasted tortilla wedges to the pork, and stir gently to mix everything together. Reheat over medium heat, scraping the bottom of the pan frequently to prevent scorching the dish. Spoon the chilaquiles onto 4 serving plates. Sprinkle with cilantro. Serve at once.

Cheese and Tortilla Casserole
Chilaquiles de Queso al Horno

Makes **4 servings**

Simple casseroles made with leftover corn tortillas are popular in Mexico. Corn tortillas are fried, combined with whatever is handy, then baked. Chilaquiles de queso can be served for a light meal, or even for breakfast with ham, sausage, or eggs. If tortillas are fresh, spread out on a flat surface about 30 minutes to dry a bit before using.

Vegetable oil for frying
8 (6- to 7-inches) corn tortillas, cut into 1-inch pieces
1/2 medium onion, chopped
3 medium tomatoes, peeled and coarsely chopped
2 garlic cloves, chopped
1 serrano chile, chopped with seeds
1/2 teaspoon dried thyme
1/2 cup Mexican crema or sour cream
1 cup shredded Monterey Jack cheese

1. Heat about 1 inch of oil in a medium heavy skillet until the oil shimmers. Fry the tortilla pieces, in batches, until golden brown, about 1 to 2 minutes. Remove with a slotted spoon. Drain on paper towels, then reserve in a large bowl. Pour off all but 1 tablespoon of the oil from the skillet, and sautée the onion, stirring, until it begins to brown, 3 to 4 minutes. Reserve off heat.

2. Preheat oven to 375°. Put the tomatoes, garlic, chile, thyme, and ¼ cup of water in a blender jar and purée until smooth. Add to the skillet with the onions, and cook 6 to 8 minutes to blend the flavors. Put the tomato mixture into the bowl with the tortilla pieces, and stir gently to combine, and transfer the mixture to an 8-inch square baking dish. Drizzle on the crema, and scatter the cheese over the top. Bake until completely heated through and the cheese is melted, about 20 minutes. Serve.

Potato and Tortilla Casserole
Chilaquiles de Papa

Makes **6 to 8 servings**

Donna Nordin, a dear friend and travel buddy, is executive chef and owner of Café Terra Cotta in Tucson and Scottsdale, Arizona. The menu features contemporary southwestern dishes and some innovative Mexican dishes, as well such as potato chilaquiles. At the restaurant, blue corn tortillas are used for this dish; but since they are pretty hard to come by, I use regular white corn tortillas.

5 New Mexico or California dried red chiles
1¹/2 teaspoons salt, or to taste
4 medium potatoes (about 1 pound), peeled and
    thinly sliced
12 (6- to 7-inch) corn tortillas, each cut into 8 wedges
2 cups heavy cream
1 cup shredded cheddar cheese

1. Remove the stems and seeds from the chiles and put the chiles in a bowl. Pour boiling water over the chiles and let stand to soak 1 hour. Reserve 1 cup of the soaking liquid, and discard remaining liquid. Put the chiles in a blender with the cup of reserved liquid and ½ teaspoon of the salt. Blend until smooth. Press through a fine-mesh strainer into a bowl, pushing and scraping to extract the pulp. Discard the debris left in the strainer. (There will be about 1 cup purée.)

2. Preheat the oven to 350°. Grease a 9- × 13-inch baking pan. Put the puréed chiles in a large bowl. Add all of the remaining ingredients and stir to combine. Transfer the mixture to the baking pan and spread to even the top. Bake, uncovered, 45 to 50 minutes, or until the potatoes are tender when pierced with the tip of a sharp knife. Cut into squares and serve.

Tortilla, Corn, and Zucchini Casserole
Chilaquiles de Elote y Calabacitas

Makes **4 servings**

Corn tortillas are cut into thin strips and fried before being mixed with the vegetables and sauce. The casserole is topped with cheese and baked in the oven. Serve as a side dish with a meat entrées, or as a light meal with salad.

6 (6- to 7-inch) corn tortillas, halved and cut into
    thin strips
Vegetable oil for frying
$^1/_2$ medium onion, chopped
1 teaspoon ground cumin
1 medium zucchini, chopped
1 cup corn kernels, fresh or frozen
2 jalapeño chiles, seeded and chopped
1 cup chopped canned tomatoes with juices
1 cup canned fat-free reduced-sodium
    chicken broth
$^1/_4$ cup loosely packed chopped fresh cilantro
$^1/_4$ teaspoon salt, or to taste
$1^1/_2$ cups grated Monterey Jack cheese

1. In a medium skillet, heat oil to a depth of about ½ inch until it simmers. Fry the tortilla strips, in batches, until golden and crisp. Drain on paper towels and set aside.

2. Preheat oven to 375°. Remove all but 1 tablespoon of the oil from the skillet. Add the onion, and cook, stirring, until the edges start to brown, about 3 to 4 minutes. Add the cumin, zucchini, corn, and chiles. Cook, stirring, until the vegetables are crisp-tender, about 4 minutes.

3. Add the tomatoes, broth, cilantro, and salt. Bring to a boil and transfer the mixture to an 8-inch square baking dish. Add the tortilla strips and half of the cheese. Stir gently to combine.

Press to level the top. Sprinkle with remaining cheese. Bake until completely heated through and the cheese melts, about 20 minutes. Serve hot.

Tortilla, Bean, and Corn Casserole
Chilaquiles de Frijoles y Elote

Makes **4 servings**

Dry or stale corn tortillas are used creatively in Mexico for dishes such as chilaquiles. *For this tasty version of chilaquiles, strips of fried tortillas are mixed with cooked black beans, corn, onions, tomatoes, and broth. The dish is topped with cheese and run under a hot broiler to melt the cheese.*

6 (6- to 7-inch) corn tortillas, each cut into
    8 wedges
Vegetable oil for frying
1 cup finely chopped onion
$^1/_2$ teaspoon dried oregano (Mexican variety
    preferred), crumbled
2 medium tomatoes, peeled and chopped
1 tablespoon ancho or pasilla chili powder
1 cup cooked black beans, canned or homemade
    (drained and rinsed, if canned)
1 cup cooked corn kernels
1 cup baby spinach leaves, washed
1 cup canned fat-free reduced-sodium
    chicken broth
2 tablespoons chopped fresh cilantro
$^1/_2$ teaspoon salt, or to taste
1 cup shredded Chihuahua or mild cheddar
    cheese

1. If the tortillas are very fresh, spread them on a counter to dry a bit—about 30 minutes. Heat oil to a depth of about ½ inch in a skillet. Fry the tortilla wedges until barely browned and almost crisp. Drain on paper towels. Reserve.

2. Preheat the oven broiler. In a deep saucepan, heat 1 tablespoon of the oil used for frying the tortillas, and cook the onion until softened, 3 to 4 minutes. Add the tomatoes, ancho powder, beans, corn, spinach, and chicken broth. Bring to a boil.

3. Stir in the reserved tortilla wedges, cilantro, and salt. Continue to stir until the tortillas start to soften, 3 to 4 minutes. Turn the mixture into a shallow ovenproof baking dish. Top with the cheese. Broil about 6 inches from the heat until the cheese melts and bubbles. Serve at once.

Tortillas in Ancho Chile and Red Pepper Cream Sauce
Chilaquiles en Chile Ancho Crema

Makes **4 servings**

One day, while testing recipes, I discovered this very pleasing combination of corn tortilla wedges in ancho chile cream sauce, that is similar to pasta in a sauce. Serve this easy informal dish for lunch with a salad, or top with a fried egg and crisp, crumbled bacon for brunch.

1¹/₂ cups (1¹/₂ recipe) Ancho Chile and Red Pepper Cream Sauce (page 48)

6 (6- to 7-inch) corn tortillas, each cut into 8 wedges

¹/₂ cup crumbled queso fresco (fresh Mexican cheese)

2 tablespoons chopped fresh cilantro

1. Prepare ancho cream sauce. Reserve in the pan off heat. Then, spread the tortilla wedges, overlapping, in a large nonstick skillet. Pour the sauce over the tortillas to coat them. Heat the tortillas and sauce over medium heat, moving the wedges around as the sauce starts to boil. Cook until completely heated through, 3 to 4 minutes. (The tortillas will become limp and absorb some of the sauce, and some may break, but that's okay.)

2. With a wide spatula, divide the tortillas and sauce among 4 shallow soup plates. Sprinkle with cheese and cilantro. Serve hot.

Salads

A Mexican meal might be considered incomplete without raw and cold cooked vegetables preceding or garnishing the main course. Traditional dishes served as first courses, such as seafood cocktails, marinated cold fish, fruit salads, hearts of palm salads, Cactus Salad (page 170), and avocado and tomato salads, are among the traditional salad-type dishes that have been eaten for centuries.

With the advent of *nueva cocina* (the new cuisine), which really took off in the 1990s, the salads and starters picture is changing, led by chefs serving creative new dishes that incorporate native and typical Mexican ingredients, including composed vegetable salads and special main-dish salads of meats or fish with vegetables. It's a popular enough trend that Mexican cooking magazines also feature photos and recipes for contemporary salads, and home cooks are following their creative lead.

Although there has long been a concern about the safety of the water in Mexico, and, as a result, an unwillingness of many people to eat uncooked produce, many Mexican cooks and chefs have made efforts to use treated water to clean raw vegetables and fruits. Slowly, the sight, aroma, and taste of these delicious salads, and the safety assurances, are winning people over. (If you visit Mexico, however, it does still pay to be cautious, especially in rural areas.)

Very often, some vegetables for salads are cooked first, then marinated and served cold, making salads that are flavorful—and safe.

In the United States, we can include all kinds of wonderful salads and inventive first courses when planning a Mexican meal. This chapter offers plenty of choices, whether you want to be traditional or try something from the emerging new style of Mexican cooking.

Vegetable Salads

Tomato and Avocado Salad
Ensalada de Jitomate y Aguacate

Makes **4 servings**

Vine-ripened tomatoes are key to this beautifully composed salad. The combination of tomatoes, avocados, and onions with lime and jalapeños appears all over Mexico.

1 large jalapeño chile, seeded, veins removed
    and minced

1 tablespoon fresh lime juice

2 teaspoons unseasoned rice vinegar

$1/2$ cup extra-virgin olive oil

$1/2$ teaspoon salt, or to taste

3 large ripe tomatoes, cut into wedges

1 small white onion, peeled and thinly sliced

2 medium avocados (Hass variety preferred),
    peeled and sliced

Freshly ground pepper, to taste

$1/4$ cup chopped fresh cilantro

1. In a medium bowl, whisk together the chile, lime juice, vinegar, and oil. Season with salt. On a large serving platter, arrange the tomatoes, onion, and avocado in overlapping rows.

2. Whisk the dressing again to recombine, and spoon all over the salad. Sprinkle with more salt, if desired, pepper, and cilantro and serve.

Avocado, Tomato, and Jicama Salad
Ensalada de Aguacate, Tomate, y Jicama

Makes **4 to 6 servings**

Mexicans are masters of artfully arranging platters of foods. Beautiful hand-crafted pottery pieces help to make the compositions visually appealing. The components for this salad can be sliced and arranged separately on a serving platter for a buffet, or cut into uniform-size pieces and tossed together in a bowl. Either way, it's good eating!

3 tablespoons olive oil

1 tablespoon white wine vinegar

$1/2$ teaspoon salt, or to taste

$1/8$ teaspoon freshly ground pepper, or to taste

2 large ripe tomatoes, sliced, or cut into
    $1/2$-inch pieces

2 avocados (Hass variety preferred), peeled
    and sliced or diced

1 medium jicama, peeled and sliced or diced

10 to 12 radishes (1 bunch), left whole,
    or thinly sliced

2 to 3 jalapeños, seeded, veins removed,
    and cut into thin slivers

In a small bowl, whisk the oil, vinegar, salt, and pepper together. Set aside. Serve the salad on a platter, arrange the tomatoes, avocados, jicama, radishes, and jalapeños in rows. For a mixed salad, put all of the ingredients in a bowl. Drizzle the dressing over the salad on the platter, or toss with the vegetables for the mixed salad.

Tomato and Red Onion Salad
Ensalada de Jitomate y Cebollas Rojas

Makes **4 servings**

A great variety of tomatoes of different colors and sizes have come to the world from Mexico. What could be easier or more striking than a platter of vine-ripened tomatoes with a tangle of marinated red onions to serve as a summer salad?

1 medium red onion (6 ounces), peeled and
    thinly sliced
2 tablespoons red wine vinegar
2 tablespoons water
$^1/_2$ teaspoon salt
$^1/_4$ teaspoon sugar
4 medium ripe tomatoes ($1^1/_2$ pounds), sliced
1 tablespoon finely chopped fresh cilantro
    or fresh oregano

1. In a small saucepan, bring about 2 cups of water to a boil. Remove the pan from the heat and add the sliced onion. Soak the onion for 1 minute. Drain and transfer the onion to a small bowl. Add the vinegar, 2 tablespoons water, salt, and sugar. Stir and let stand for 20 to 30 minutes.

2. Meanwhile, arrange the sliced tomatoes on a serving plate. Drain the onions and scatter over the tomatoes. Sprinkle with cilantro or oregano.

Green Salad with Tomato and Green Chile Strips
Ensalade Verde con Jitomate y Rajas

Makes **4 servings**

A pile of lightly dressed greens topped with diced tomatoes, thin strips of roasted poblano chile, and a sprinkle of cotija cheese is a very appealing modern salad.

2 poblano chiles, roasted, peeled, seeded, and
    veins removed (page 8)
2 tablespoons olive oil
2 teaspoons unseasoned rice vinegar
$^1/_4$ teaspoon salt, or to taste
6 cups torn lettuce greens
$^1/_8$ teaspoon freshly ground pepper, or to taste
2 medium tomatoes, seeded and finely diced
$^1/_4$ cup crumbled cotija cheese, or grated
    Parmesan

1. Prepare the chiles. Remove the stems and cut into short, very thin strips.

2. In a small bowl, whisk together the oil, vinegar, and salt. Put the lettuce in a large bowl. Add the dressing and toss lightly to coat. Add the black pepper and toss. Divide the salad among 4 serving plates. Top with the reserved chile strips and the tomatoes. Sprinkle equally with cheese. Serve at once.

Caesar Salad
Ensalada de Caesar

Makes **4 servings**

Caesar Salad was invented in the 1920s in Tijuana, Mexico, by Alexander and his brother Ceasar Cardini, owners of a popular local restaurant. The story goes that late one evening near closing time, Alex welcomed some late diners and, with only a few ingredients to work with after a busy day, Ceasar, the chef, whipped up the first Caesar Salad.

Now, there are so many versions of the salad that the origins are often forgotten, but Tijuana still claims Caesar Salad as its own. This updated version does not contain raw egg in the dressing.

1/2 cup olive oil

2 tablespoons red wine vinegar

1 tablespoon fresh lemon juice

4 anchovy fillets, chopped

2 large cloves garlic, chopped

1 teaspoon Dijon mustard

1/4 cup freshly grated Parmesan cheese

1/8 teaspoon freshly ground pepper, or to taste

1 large head romaine lettuce, washed, dried, and
    torn into pieces

1 cup croutons

1. In a blender, thoroughly combine the oil, vinegar, lemon juice, anchovies, garlic, and mustard. Add the Parmesan and black pepper. Blend until creamy and smooth. Transfer to a small bowl and reserve, or, if made ahead, cover and refrigerate up to 3 days. Whisk thoroughly before using.

2. Put the lettuce and croutons in a large salad bowl. Add the dressing and toss well.

Mixed Vegetable Salad
Ensalada Mixta

Makes 4 servings

Maria Marquez Merrill, of San Miguel de Allende, was tour guide, interpreter, and cooking teacher for several tours that I led to the region. Maria prepared this salad during one of our cooking classes. We cooked the vegetables in the morning, and assembled the salad just before serving.

4 small new potatoes (about 9 ounces), unpeeled

2 medium carrots, peeled and cut into 3/4-inch pieces

1/4 of a medium cauliflower, cut into small florets

1/4 pound fresh green beans, cut into 1-inch lengths

1/2 teaspoon salt, or to taste

2 tablespoons olive oil

2 medium tomatoes, coarsely chopped or cubed

6 to 8 inner romaine lettuce leaves

1/2 cup Basic Vinaigrette (page 210)

1. In a medium pan of boiling water to cover, cook the potatoes until tender, but not soft, 12 to 16 minutes, depending on the size of the potatoes. Cool under running water, peel, and cut into 3/4-inch cubes. Put into a large bowl and set aside.

2. Cook the carrots, cauliflower, and green beans, each separately, uncovered, until crisp-tender. The carrots take about 4 minutes, cauliflower about 3 minutes, and the green beans about 6 minutes. Rinse each vegetable through a sieve under cold running water to stop the cooking. Shake excess water. Put the cooked vegetables in the bowl with the potatoes. Add the salt and olive oil, and toss gently. Cover and refrigerate until the vegetables are cold, at least 1 hour.

3. Remove the vegetables from the refrigerator shortly before serving and add the tomatoes. Toss the salad with sufficient vinaigrette to coat generously. Line a shallow bowl or serving platter with the romaine leaves. Mound the vegetables on the lettuce. Serve cold.

Romaine and Zucchini Salad
Ensalada de Lechuga y Zucchini

Makes 4 servings

Raw zucchini contributes a pleasing crunch and mild taste to this easy salad. Mexican fresh cheese, queso fresco, *can be found in most supermarkets or Latin-American food stores.*

4 cups shredded romaine lettuce

2 small zucchini, cut crosswise into thin rounds

1 large tomato, chopped

1 tablespoon chopped flat-leaf parsley

2 tablespoons olive oil

2 teaspoons white wine vinegar

1/2 teaspoon salt, or to taste

1/8 teaspoon freshly ground pepper, or to taste

2 to 3 tablespoons crumbled queso fresco
    (fresh Mexican cheese)

In a large salad bowl, combine romaine, zucchini, tomato, and parsley. In a small bowl whisk together the oil, vinegar, salt, and pepper. Pour over the salad and toss gently to coat. Serve on individual salad plates with crumbled cheese on top.

Watercress Salad
Ensalada de Berros

Makes 4 servings

Watercress is a member of the mustard family and is gathered in many areas of Mexico where it grows along the banks of cold water streams in certain climates, just like in the United States. The crisp leaves with a peppery pungent flavor adds a snap to this salad, that's a good companion for grilled meats or poultry.

1 bunch watercress, sprigs only, with thick stems removed, washed and spun dry

4 cups washed and torn lettuce of choice, spun dry

1 medium tomato, seeded and finely chopped

2 tablespoons finely chopped white onion

2 tablespoons chopped fresh cilantro

$1/2$ to 1 serrano or jalapeño chile, minced

3 tablespoons olive oil

1 tablespoon unseasoned rice vinegar

1 teaspoon fresh lime juice

$1/2$ teaspoon salt, or to taste

In a large nonreactive bowl place the watercress, lettuce, tomato, onion, cilantro, and chile. Stir gently to mix. Add the olive oil, vinegar, lime juice, and salt. Toss to coat with the dressing. Serve cold.

Marinated Zucchini Salad with Fresh Oregano
Ensalada de Calabacitas con Oregano

Makes 4 servings

Zucchini in a light marinade with fresh oregano makes a colorful and appetizing single-ingredient salad presented in the nueva cocina style—with the slices decoratively overlapping on a serving plate. Of course, if you're in a hurry, this can be a fabulously fast and delicious dish to make; just put the cooked slices in a bowl and mix with the dressing. It may not look as striking, but the flavors are still wonderful. Fresh oregano is key here, so reserve this recipe for when you can find it, instead of substituting dried oregano. If cotija cheese is not available, mild feta can be used.

4 medium (about 1 pound) zucchini of uniform size

2 tablespoons olive oil

1 tablespoon white wine vinegar

$1/4$ teaspoon salt

$1/8$ teaspoon freshly ground pepper, or to taste

2 tablespoons finely chopped fresh oregano leaves

2 tablespoons crumbled cotija cheese

Trim the zucchini, then cut it crosswise on the bias into ¼-inch thick slices. Heat 1 tablespoon of the oil in a large nonstick skillet. Cook the zucchini in a single layer, in batches, turning once, until crisp tender with bright green edges, about 2 to 3 minutes. Remove to a bowl, and cool 10 minutes. To the bowl add the remaining oil, and the vinegar, salt, pepper, and oregano. Mix gently to coat the zucchini. On a serving plate, arrange the zucchini in an overlapping pattern. Top with the crumbled cheese. Serve at room temperature.

Zucchini Boats with Guacamole
Barcas de Calabacitas con Guacamole

Makes **4 servings**

No Name Restaurant is a well-known eatery in charming Tlaquepaque, a suburb of Guadalajara. If you go, it's a cinch to find by asking any merchant along the pedestrian-only main street of shops and restaurants in this restored colonial town. Legend has it that the original owners were selling liquor illegally and didn't want a sign out front, so people were directed to "that place behind the high wall over there without a name." When alcohol became legal the name stuck, and now a very small sign is posted on the exterior wall. The food at No Name is creative, with some unusual selections. I liked the zucchini boat salad and here it is, my way.

4 medium zucchini
2 teaspoons olive oil
¹/₄ teaspoon salt, or to taste
Classic Guacamole (page 23)
2 large ripe tomatoes, seeded and diced
2 tablespoons crumbled cotija cheese or queso fresco (fresh Mexican cheese)

1. Slice the zucchini in half lengthwise. Scoop out the centers with a melon ball scoop, leaving a ½-inch edge. (Save the centers for another use.) Brush the zucchini on both sides with olive oil and sprinkle lightly with salt.

2. Heat a large nonstick skillet over medium heat and cook the zucchini, cut side down, for about 2 minutes. Turn and cook 2 to 3 more minutes. The zucchini will still be slightly crisp and bright green. Remove to a plate. Cool.

3. Prepare the guacamole. Then, when the zucchini are completely cool, fill the centers with guacamole. (Reserve extra guacamole.) Put 2 halves in the center of each of 4 serving plates. Surround with diced tomato. Sprinkle crumbled cheese over all. Serve at room temperature.

Carrot and Zucchini Salad
Ensalada de Zanahorias y Calabacitas

Makes **4 servings**

Salads of cooked vegetables are everyday fare in Mexico, and are often part of the entrée. This duo goes well with saucy dishes such as Grilled Chicken Breasts with Ancho Chile Sauce (page 274).

4 medium carrots, peeled and trimmed
3 medium zucchini, washed and trimmed
1 tablespoon olive oil
1 to 2 tablespoons fresh lime juice
1 tablespoon minced fresh mint
¹/₂ teaspoon salt, or to taste
¹/₈ teaspoon freshly ground pepper, or to taste

1. Cut the carrots and zucchini on the bias into oval slices about ¼ inch thick. Cut each oval in half lengthwise. Bring to a boil 1 cup of water in a medium nonstick skillet, and cook the carrots, covered, until barely tender, about 2 minutes. With a slotted spoon, remove the carrots to a large bowl and set aside.

2. In the same skillet, cook the zucchini, uncovered until crisp-tender, about 1 minute. Drain and add to the bowl of carrots. Cool about 5 minutes. Stir in the oil, lime juice, mint, salt, and pepper. Serve at room temperature.

Emerald Salad
Ensalada Esmeralda

Makes 4 servings

Elena Zelayeta, author or Elena's Secrets of Mexican Cooking, *was born in Mexico, but spent most of her life in San Francisco where she became known for her wonderful Mexican food. Her recipe for this beautiful salad made of mostly green ingredients was my inspiration. I've been making my version of her salad for more than thirty years. I omit raw onion, use fresh green chiles instead of canned, and use my own vinaigrette.*

Basic Vinaigrette (page 210)

2 tablespoons olive oil

4 medium (1 pound) zucchini, thinly sliced

2 poblano or Anaheim chiles, roasted, peeled (page 8) and cut into thin strips or squares

1 large avocado (Hass variety preferred), peeled and cubed

8 pimiento-stuffed green olives, sliced crosswise

Salt and freshly ground pepper, to taste

Romaine lettuce, shredded or chopped

1/3 cup crumbled queso fresco (fresh Mexican cheese)

Prepare the vinaigrette, then heat the oil in a large nonstick skillet and sauté the zucchini, until crisp-tender and still bright green, about 2 minutes. Transfer to a large bowl. Refrigerate about 15 minutes, then add to the bowl the chile strips, avocado, and pimientos. Add the pepper and about 2 tablespoons vinaigrette. Toss to coat the salad. Add salt, if needed. Make a bed of lettuce on a serving platter. Mound the salad on the lettuce. Sprinkle crumbled cheese on top.

Cactus Salad
Ensalada de Nopalitos

Makes 4 servings

Cactus, with a taste and texture similar to green beans, is commonly used in many parts of Mexico for salads and other preparations, and is slowly being adopted in the United States. Packaged cactus can be found in the supermarket with chilled foods or in the produce section, cut into ready-to-use squares. Cactus is also packed in jars. If using the bottled product, look for the cactus packed only in water and salt. Either fresh or jarred cactus can be used for this recipe.

2 cups packaged fresh cactus squares, or bottled cactus, drained, rinsed, and cut into squares

2 medium tomatoes, cut into wedges

2 tablespoons chopped white onion

1 to 2 serrano chiles, finely chopped with seeds

2 tablespoons chopped fresh cilantro

2 tablespoons olive oil

2 teaspoons white wine vinegar

1/2 teaspoon salt, or to taste

6 romaine lettuce leaves, coarsely shredded

2 tablespoons crumbled queso fresco (fresh Mexican cheese) or mild feta cheese

1. If using fresh cactus squares, cook quickly in a pan of boiling water to cover, 1 to 2 minutes, to retain the color and crispness and to remove some of the slippery coating. Drain well in cold running water. If using bottled cactus, simply drain through a strainer and rinse very well in cold running water and cut into ½-inch squares.

2. In a large bowl, mix the cooked cactus, tomatoes, onion, serrano chiles, and cilantro. Add the oil, vinegar, and salt. Toss to mix. Arrange the lettuce on a platter. Mound the salad on the lettuce, and scatter the cheese on top.

Handling and Preparing Cactus (*Nopales*)

The whole oval paddles of the prickly pear cactus are called *nopales* and *nopalitos* when cut into strips or squares. They are used extensively in many parts of Mexico, especially in the north and central regions. Cactus is often boiled, sautéed, or grilled and used in salads, with eggs, or as a taco filling. Cactus has a mild pleasant flavor and texture somewhat like green beans.

The common cactus sold in outdoor markets has thin paddles with spines or thorns attached. Look for small paddles that are firm and not limp or wrinkled. Wear thick protective gloves when handling fresh cactus, even with the species cultivated to have fewer spines, for there will still be some almost hair-like spines to scrape off.

Before cooking, put on gloves, then cut off the blunt end and trim about one-quarter inch off the outside edge of the paddle. Shave off the thorns with a vegetable peeler, or thin sharp knife. The paddles will keep fresh in the refrigerator, sealed in a plastic bag up to 3 days, or cut into squares or strips and use as needed.

Cabbage Salad
Ensalada de Col

Makes **4 servings**

In a small cooking school in Leon, Mexico, north of Mexico City, I learned the rudiments of Mexican cooking 25 years ago. Daily hands-on lessons from native instructors were intensive and thorough. The school no longer exists, but I still teach and use many of the recipes, including this simple cabbage salad.

4 cups finely shredded cabbage
2 medium carrots, peeled and shredded
1/2 cup cooked thawed frozen or fresh peas
1 to 2 serrano chiles, minced with seeds
**1 large avocado (Hass variety preferred), peeled
    and cut into 1/4-inch dice**
3 tablespoons fresh lime juice
2 tablespoons mayonnaise
1/2 teaspoon salt, or to taste
1/4 teaspoon freshly ground pepper, or to taste

In a medium bowl, toss the cabbage, carrots, peas, and serrano chiles together. In a small bowl, gently mix the avocado, lime juice, mayonnaise, salt, and pepper. Add to the cabbage mixture, and stir thoroughly to combine. Refrigerate for at least an hour. Serve cold.

Cabbage and Cheese Salad with Tortillas
Ensalada de Col y Queso con Migas

Makes 4 servings

Bits of fried tortillas, called migas, *and grated cheese appear in this unique cabbage salad that I created for a cooking class—and it was a huge success. Oaxaca cheese is now available in many supermarkets or Mexican markets. If you can't find it, substitute mozzarella.*

Vegetable oil for frying
3 (6- to 7-inch) corn tortillas, cut into 1/2-inch squares
1/2 large head cabbage, finely shredded
1 cup coarsely shredded Oaxaca cheese
1/4 cup lightly packed chopped fresh cilantro
1 large ripe tomato, chopped
2 green onions, finely chopped
1 jarred pickled jalapeño chile (en escabeche), seeded, veins removed, and finely chopped
2 tablespoons olive oil
1 tablespoon unseasoned rice vinegar
1/2 teaspoon salt, or to taste
1/8 teaspoon freshly ground pepper, or to taste

1. In a small skillet pour oil to a depth of about ½ inch and heat over medium heat until it shimmers. Fry the tortilla squares in batches until crisp and golden brown. Remove with a slotted spoon and drain on paper towels. Set aside.

2. Put all of the remaining ingredients in a large bowl. Add the fried tortillas and toss everything together. Serve at once.

Red and Green Cabbage Slaw
Ensalada de Col Rojo y Verde

Makes 4 servings

Many Mexican chefs in the United States have brought the spirit of innovation to Mexican cooking traditions with great success. Near the historic square in Sonoma, California, is Maya, a lively contemporary Mexican restaurant notable for both its traditional and imaginative Mexican dishes. This simple cabbage slaw is the creation of Chef Manual Arjona from Yucatán, a state at the tip of southern Mexico. The salad is topped with Pan-Roasted Tomatillo Sauce (page 35).

Pan-Roasted Tomatillo Sauce (page 35)
1/4 medium red cabbage, very thinly shredded
1/4 green cabbage, very thinly shredded
1 tablespoon olive oil
1 1/2 teaspoons unseasoned rice vinegar
1/4 teaspoon salt, or to taste
1/8 teaspoon freshly ground pepper

Prepare the sauce. Then, in a medium bowl toss all of the ingredients together. Add salt, if needed. Transfer to 4 serving plates, stacking each salad in a pile. Crown each salad with about 2 tablespoons salsa on top.

Jicama Salad Bowl
Taza de Jicama

Makes 2 to 3 servings

During a recent visit to Mexico, while walking through the busy market fondas *(food stalls) in the historical colonial city of Guanajuato in central Mexico, my husband and I noticed a carefully peeled jicama with the center scooped out and filled with a crisp salad of orange, avocado, and radish pieces. My husband was so intrigued that he couldn't wait to create a jicama salad bowl as soon as we got home.*

One salad can be shared by 2 to 3 people in the same way as a table salsa is shared, to be eaten along with the entrée. When the filling is eaten, slice up the jicama bowl and eat it, too! Look for pale-skinned, uniformly round and unblemished, medium-size jicamas for the best-looking and best-tasting jicama bowls. Serve with fish or chicken entrées.

1 pale-skinned round jicama (about 1¼ pounds)

1 orange, peeled and cut into small pieces

1 avocado (Hass variety preferred), peeled, seeded, and cut into small pieces

4 to 5 radishes, quartered

1 jalapeño chile, seeded, veins removed, and finely diced

1 teaspoon olive oil

1 teaspoon fresh lime juice

¼ teaspoon salt, or to taste

1 seedless cucumber, sliced into ¼-inch rounds

1. Cut a ¼-inch slice off the bottom of the jicama so it will sit flat. Cut a 1-inch slice off the top. Peel the jicama as neatly as possible. Using a melon ball tool carefully scoop out the center, leaving a ¾-inch shell all around. Set aside.

2. Put the orange, avocado, radishes, and jalapeño in a medium mixing bowl. Cut some of the scooped out center into small pieces and add to the bowl. Add the oil, lime juice, and salt. Toss to mix. Spoon the salad into the jicama shell. (Any extra salad can be added to the bowl later, or served separately.) Place the jicama shell on a round serving plate. Arrange the cucumber slices around the jicama. The salad can be made ahead and refrigerated for up to 2 hours before serving.

Hearts of Palm and Tomato Salad
Ensalada de Palmitos y Jitomates

Makes 4 to 6 servings

Hearts of palm come from the center portion of a tropical palm tree called the cabbage palm. Most canned hearts of palm come from Brazil, but the palm also grows in Mexico and Florida and is eaten fresh in some areas along the Caribbean coast. It is often used in salads and occasionally soups in Mexico. Sliced hearts of palm and cherry tomatoes with tossed greens makes an excellent salad.

1 (14-ounce) can hearts of palm, drained and rinsed

1 cup ripe cherry tomatoes, rinsed and halved

5 cups chopped romaine lettuce

2 tablespoons chopped fresh flat-leaf parsley

¼ cup extra-virgin olive oil

1 to 2 tablespoons white wine vinegar

½ teaspoon salt

3 tablespoons crumbled cotija or mild feta cheese

Freshly ground pepper, to taste

Soak the hearts of palm in warm water for 10 minutes to minimize any "tinny" flavor. Drain the hearts of palm, then cut them crosswise into 1-inch pieces and put them into a large salad bowl. Add the tomatoes, lettuce, and parsley. In a small bowl, whisk together the oil, vinegar, and salt. Pour over the salad and toss gently. Add the cheese and pepper. Toss again. Serve cold.

Cauliflower Salad
Ensalada de Coliflor

Makes **4 servings**

Cold cauliflower with a piquant creamy dressing can be served as a salad or as a side dish to accompany grilled fish or chicken. For contrasting color, I surround the salad with crisp-cooked carrot coins.

2 medium carrots, peeled and thinly sliced
1 medium head of cauliflower
1 tablespoon mayonnaise
1 tablespoon sour cream
1 teaspoon Dijon mustard
1 teaspoon fresh lime juice
1/4 teaspoon salt
1/8 teaspoon freshly ground pepper, or to taste
1 tablespoon minced fresh flat-leaf parsley

1. In a large pan of boiling salted water cook the carrots until barely tender, 2 to 3 minutes. Remove the carrots with a slotted spoon, reserving the water, and rinse under cold running water to stop the cooking. Reserve in a bowl. Separate the cauliflower into small florets.

2. Bring the same pan of water to a boil, adding more water if needed, and cook the cauliflower, uncovered, until crisp-tender, about 3 minutes. Drain and rinse under cold running water to stop the cooking. Drain again and put into a large bowl.

3. In a small bowl mix the mayonnaise, sour cream, mustard, lime juice, salt, and pepper. Add to the cauliflower and stir gently to mix. Arrange the cauliflower on a round serving platter. Sprinkle with parsley. Arrange the carrots around the cauliflower. Serve cold or at room temperature.

Chayote Salad
Ensalada de Chayote

Makes **6 servings**

Chayote *is a pale green pear-shaped member of the squash family that is used all over Mexico, and also in the southern United States, where it is called mirliton. Chayote is prepared in much the same way as any summer squash.*

This salad comes from El Naranjo, a wonderful restaurant in a restored colonial building in Oaxaca. The owner-chef, Iliana de la Vega, prepares both traditional and very creative new-style Oaxacan cuisine. Fresh oregano is important for the right flavor of the salad.

2 chayote squash, halved lengthwise
3 tablespoons extra-virgin olive oil
2 teaspoons white wine vinegar
1/2 teaspoon salt, or to taste
1 tablespoon vegetable oil
1 medium red onion, peeled and thinly sliced
1 tablespoon red wine vinegar
1/2 teaspoon sugar
Freshly ground pepper, to taste
1 tablespoon finely chopped fresh flat-leaf parsley
1 tablespoon finely chopped fresh oregano
1/4 cup finely crumbled cotija or mild feta cheese

1. In a large pan of boiling water, cook the chayote until crisp-tender, about 20 minutes. Drain and cool under running water. Peel the chayote and cut crosswise into thin slices. Put the slices in a shallow bowl. Whisk together oil, vinegar, and salt. Spoon over the chayote, and let marinate, at room temperature, 25 to 30 minutes.

2. Meanwhile, in a medium skillet, heat the vegetable oil over medium heat, and cook the onion, stirring, 2 minutes. Add the vinegar and sugar.

Stir until the sugar is dissolved, about 20 seconds. Transfer the onions to a bowl. Season with salt and freshly ground black pepper. Let cool to room temperature.

3. To assemble the salad, arrange the chayote slices, overlapping, on the outside edges of a serving plate. Place the onions in the center of the arrangement. Sprinkle the parsley, oregano, and cheese over all. Serve the salad cold.

Chopped Radish Salad
Ensalada de Rábanos

Makes **4 servings**

Radishes are a common garnish on plates all over Mexico. Their crunchiness and sharpness makes them a favorite Mexican nibble. This salad features crisp and bright radishes mixed with other chopped vegetables.

1¹/₂ **cups coarsely chopped or diced radishes**
1 **cup chopped iceberg lettuce**
1 **cup chopped or diced jicama**
¹/₂ **medium cucumber, peeled, seeded, and chopped**
2 **chopped green onions, including the green part**
2 **tablespoons chopped fresh cilantro or parsley**
1 **jalapeño chile, seeded, veins removed, and finely chopped**
1 **tablespoon olive oil**
2 **teaspoons fresh lime juice**
1 **teaspoon unseasoned rice vinegar**
¹/₄ **teaspoon salt, or to taste**

In a large bowl mix the first seven ingredients (the vegetables) together. Add the oil, lime juice, vinegar, and salt. Toss well to coat the vegetables. Refrigerate for at least an hour. Serve cold.

Green Bean Salad
Ensalada de Ejotes

Makes **4 servings**

Young and tender green beans are best for this salad. Cook them until crisp-tender and still bright green. The salad is presented on a platter, but it can also be arranged on individual salad plates. Serve with sauced meats or poultry.

¹/₂ **white onion, thinly sliced**
1 **pound fresh green beans, trimmed**
3 **tablespoons vegetable oil or olive oil**
2 **teaspoons white wine vinegar**
¹/₂ **small garlic clove, mashed**
¹/₂ **teaspoon salt, or to taste**
2 **medium tomatoes, cut into wedges**
2 **tablespoons chopped fresh cilantro**

1. In a large deep skillet, or wide saucepan, bring about 1 quart of water to a boil. Add the onion, and blanch 20 seconds. With a slotted spoon, remove the onions, and put into a bowl of cold water to stop the cooking; then drain well. In the same boiling water, cook the green beans, uncovered, until the beans are just a bit limp, but still bright green and crisp-tender, 5 to 6 minutes. Drain immediately, and rinse under cold running water to stop the cooking.

2. Put the well-drained onions and green beans in a large bowl. Add the oil, vinegar, garlic, and salt. Toss well to coat, and put the vegetables on a serving platter. Arrange the tomatoes around the beans, and sprinkle the cilantro over all.

Green Bean and Egg Salad
Ensalada de Ejotes y Huevo

Makes **4 servings**

Mexican salads are often made of cooked vegetables. Young green beans, cooked whole and dressed with vinaigrette are as wholesome as they are pretty, especially when garnished with colorful white and yellow bands of grated hard-cooked eggs. This salad was served as part of a midday buffet at San Angel Inn, a lovely restaurant in Mexico City. To preserve the bright green color of the beans do not add the dressing until shortly before serving, or the vinaigrette will cause the beans to fade.

1 pound small fresh green beans (uniform in size)
$1/2$ garlic clove, minced
$1/2$ teaspoon salt
1 tablespoon olive oil
2 teaspoons unseasoned rice vinegar
1 tablespoon finely chopped fresh oregano
$1/2$ teaspoon mustard
1 hard-cooked egg, peeled

1. Trim the ends of the beans. In a medium skillet, bring to a boil about 2 cups of water. Add the beans and cook, uncovered, until crisp-tender and still bright green, 5 to 7 minutes. Drain off the water, leaving the beans in the pan. Stir in the garlic and ¼ teaspoon of the salt into the beans while still hot. Set aside to cool.

2. In a small bowl, whisk together the oil, vinegar, oregano, mustard, and the remaining ¼ teaspoon of salt. Set aside.

3. Separate the white from the yolk of the egg. Finely shred the egg white onto a small plate. Grate the egg yolk on another small plate. Shortly before serving, toss the cooked green beans with the vinaigrette and arrange the beans in an even line on a serving plate. Sprinkle the shredded egg white over the top center of the beans and sprinkle the egg yolk over the white.

Green Bean, Jicama, and Pomegranate Salad
Ensalada de Ejotes, Jicama, y Granada

Makes **4 servings**

Scatter vibrant red pomegranate seeds over green beans, jicama, and shredded cabbage for a beautiful first course salad. Pomegranates are grown in many parts of central and northern Mexico and are used to brighten a number of traditional dishes, especially in fall and winter. The pinkish to red-skinned fruits are about the size of an orange and have jewel-like seeds packed solid in compartments that are separated with thin white membranes. Each tiny seed has a juicy, bright red coating that's sweet-tart and quite wonderful. The seeds are best separated by cutting the fruit in half, then breaking open the seed sacs under a bowl of cold water in the sink, to minimize splattering juices. Separate the seeds and place them in a bowl. The seeds can be kept frozen in plastic bags for about three months.

For this salad, young, thin green beans are best since they are more tender and only need a short cooking time.

1 tablespoon fresh lime juice
1 teaspoon unseasoned rice vinegar
$1/2$ teaspoon salt
1 tablespoon olive oil
$1/2$ pound thin green beans ($2^1/2$ to 3 inches long)
1 small jicama (about 12 ounces), peeled and cut into thin sticks, ¼-inch thick and 2-inches long
1 cup finely shredded cabbage
2 tablespoons chopped Italian flat-leaf parsley
$1/8$ teaspoon freshly ground pepper, or to taste
$1/2$ cup pomegranate seeds

1. In a small bowl whisk together the lime juice, vinegar, salt, and olive oil.

2. In a saucepan of boiling salted water cook the green beans, uncovered, until crisp-tender and still bright green, about 4 minutes. Drain under cold running water to stop the cooking. Blot moisture with paper towels and put in a large bowl. Add the jicama, cabbage, and parsley. Toss to combine.

3. Add the dressing, and toss to coat the salad with the dressing. Add the pepper and toss gently. Divide the salad among 4 serving plates. Scatter pomegranate seeds equally over the salads.

Mexican Potato Salad
Ensalada de Papas Mexicana
Makes **4 servings**

Taxco is filled with silver shops—and tourists. But, there's more there than just good shopping. At this memorable stop on the road between Mexico City and Acapulco you can enjoy the magnificent eighteenth century cathedral of Santa Prisca, steep winding cobblestone streets, a fascinating public market, mining history, and of course, great food. It was at lunch many years ago, at the Hotel De La Borda, that I had a potato salad like this for the first time. This recipe was one souvenir worth taking home.

Herbed Vinaigrette (page 210)
2 medium red potatoes, peeled and cut into
    1/2-inch cubes
2 medium carrots, peeled and cut into 1/2-inch cubes
1 cup peas, fresh or frozen
2 tablespoons finely chopped white onion
1 tablespoon finely chopped fresh mint
1/2 teaspoon salt, or to taste

1. Prepare the vinaigrette. Then, cook the potatoes in a medium pan of boiling water until tender, about 5 minutes. With a slotted spoon, remove the potatoes to a bowl and set aside. Add the carrots to the same pan and cook until just tender, about 3 minutes. Remove and put in the bowl with the potatoes. Cook the peas in the same water for about 30 seconds. Drain and rinse under cold running water. Add to the bowl with potatoes and carrots.

2. Add the onion, mint, and 2 to 3 tablespoons of the vinaigrette. Toss to mix. Serve chilled or at room temperature.

Corn, Potato, and Poblano Chile Salad
Ensalada de Elote, Papa, y Chile Poblano
Makes **6 servings**

Mexican cooks use corn, potatoes, and chiles, ingredients native to Central and South America, in a variety of dishes. Serve this salad at room temperature with grilled meats or chicken.

3 large ears fresh yellow corn, husked
2 poblano chiles
2 medium new potatoes, cooked, peeled, and
    cut into 1/2-inch dice
2 medium tomatoes, chopped
2 green onions, finely chopped
1 jalapeño chile, finely chopped
2 tablespoons chopped fresh cilantro
1 teaspoon ground cumin
3 tablespoons vegetable oil or olive oil
2 tablespoons white wine vinegar
1 teaspoon salt
1/2 teaspoon freshly ground pepper, or to taste

1. In a pot of boiling water, cook the corn about 3 minutes or until just tender. Do not overcook. Remove the corn and rinse under cold running water to stop the cooking. With a sharp knife, cut the kernels off the cobs. Put the corn into a large bowl.

2. Roast the poblanos over a flame, or under a broiler until charred all over. Steam in a plastic bag about 8 minutes. Rub off the skins, seed, and cut into 1/2-inch dice. Add to the corn along with the tomatoes, onions, jalapeños, cilantro, and cumin. Mix. Add the remaining ingredients. Toss gently to coat the salad with the dressing.

Poblano Chile and Corn Salad
Ensalada de Poblano y Elote

Makes **4 servings**

For this salad, poblano chile strips are marinated then tossed with corn. It's a classic combination that can be spicy depending on the poblanos. After the chiles are roasted and cut open, a small taste will reveal if they are hot or not. Serve with grilled meats or poultry.

4 poblano chiles, roasted, seeded, veins removed, and peeled (page 8)

2 tablespoons chopped white onion

2 tablespoons unseasoned rice vinegar

3 ears of corn, with kernels cut off the cobs

1/4 cup olive oil

2 teaspoons finely chopped fresh oregano or 1/2 teaspoon dried oregano (Mexican variety preferred)

1/4 teaspoon ground cumin

1/4 teaspoon salt, or to taste

Prepare the chiles. Cut them into thin strips and put them in a medium bowl. Add the onion and vinegar. Marinate about 1 hour. In a medium skillet, cook the corn kernels in boiling water to cover about 3 minutes. Drain and cool under running water. Mix with the poblano strips. Add the oil, oregano, cumin, and salt. Toss and serve.

Mushroom and Poblano Chile Salad
Ensalada de Hongos y Chile Poblano

Makes **4 servings**

Street vendors in Puebla, Mexico City, and other central Mexican cities, often mix mushrooms and chiles to fold up inside a tortilla. Combining them in a salad with a Caesar salad-like dressing (which originated in Tijuana), makes this a lively mushroom salad.

1/2 pound fresh white mushrooms, trimmed and thinly sliced

2 poblano chiles, roasted, peeled, seeded, veins removed, and cut into thin strips (page 8)

6 radishes, washed, trimmed, and thinly sliced

2 cups shredded romaine lettuce

1/4 cup olive oil

1 tablespoon white wine vinegar

2 oil-packed anchovy fillets, finely chopped

1/4 teaspoon salt, or to taste

1/8 teaspoon freshly ground pepper, or to taste

Cotija or mild feta cheese, crumbled

Put the mushrooms, poblano strips, radishes, and lettuce in a large salad bowl. In a small bowl, whisk together the oil, vinegar, anchovies, salt, and pepper. Pour over the salad and toss to mix well. Serve the salad with crumbled cheese on top.

Mushroom and Avocado Salad
Ensalada de Hongos y Aguacate

Makes **4 servings**

White mushrooms and avocado with baby spinach leaves and shredded cabbage is an inventive mixed salad that's really wonderful dressed with a salsa vinaigrette.

1/2 recipe Salsa Vinaigrette (page 211)

12 medium white mushrooms, cleaned and thinly sliced

1 avocado (Hass variety preferred), peeled and cut into 1/2-inch pieces

4 cups rinsed and dried baby spinach leaves

3/4 cup finely shredded cabbage

2 tablespoons chopped flat-leaf parsley

2 tablespoons crumbled cotija or mild feta cheese

Prepare the vinaigrette. In a bowl, gently mix the mushrooms and avocado with about 1/4 cup of the vinaigrette. In another bowl toss the spinach, cabbage, and parsley with about 2 tablespoons of the vinaigrette and divide the spinach mixture among 4 serving plates. Top each equally with the mushrooms and avocado. Sprinkle the salads with the cheese.

Artichoke Salad with Sunflower Seed Dressing
Ensalada de Alcachofas con Pepitas

Makes **4 servings**

Fresh artichokes are not a traditional part of the Mexican kitchen, but canned artichokes are popular in urban areas and are often marinated or added to salads.

1 (9-ounce) package frozen artichoke hearts or 1 (14-ounce) can
1/3 cup packed fresh flat-leaf parsley
1 medium garlic clove, chopped
1 serrano chile, chopped with seeds
2 tablespoons salted dry-roasted sunflower seeds
2 tablespoons fresh lime juice
1/4 cup olive oil
1 head iceberg lettuce, torn into bite-size pieces
1 medium tomato, coarsely chopped

1. Cook the artichoke hearts according to the package directions, or use rinsed and drained canned artichoke hearts. Quarter the artichokes and set aside.

2. Put the parsley, garlic, serrano, sunflower seeds, lime juice, and olive oil in a blender and purée until nearly smooth with some texture. Reserve in the blender. Put the lettuce, tomato, and artichoke hearts in a large bowl. Add the dressing and toss gently to coat with the dressing. Refrigerate for at least an hour. Serve cold.

Asparagus Salad with Fresh Salsa Mexicana
Ensalada de Espárragos con Salsa Fresca

Makes **4 servings**

Many Mexican dishes reflect the colors of the nation's flag, as does this fresh green asparagus salad with red tomato salsa and a scattering of fresh white cheese (queso fresco) that's widely available in United States supermarkets.

Fresh Salsa Mexicana (page 24)
1 pound fresh asparagus (thin spears preferred)
1 tablespoon olive oil
1/2 teaspoon salt, or to taste
1/2 cup crumbled queso fresco (fresh Mexican cheese)

1. Prepare the salsa. Then, cut off the tough ends of the asparagus spears. Bring a large pan of water to a boil. Add the asparagus and cook, uncovered, until crisp-tender, about 4 to 6 minutes, depending on the size of the asparagus spears. Drain under cold running water to stop the cooking.

2. Lay the spears on a clean kitchen towel and blot excess water. Arrange the asparagus side by side on a serving platter. Drizzle with olive oil and sprinkle with salt. Turn the asparagus to coat with the oil and salt. Spoon a ribbon of fresh salsa across the center of the asparagus spears. Sprinkle the cheese over all. Serve cold.

Vegetables in Chipotle Vinaigrette
Verduras en Vinagreta de Chipotle

Makes **4 to 6 servings**

I tried this cold vegetable plate years ago at the Hotel Colonial in Puebla and have been serving it ever since. Serve with a basket of thinly sliced baguette.

2 canned chipotle chiles en adobo, rinsed, seeded, and chopped
1 teaspoon adobo sauce from the can of chiles
2 tablespoons unseasoned rice vinegar
1 teaspoon dark brown sugar, or to taste
1/2 teaspoon Worcestershire sauce
3 tablespoons olive oil
1/2 teaspoon salt
2 medium white potatoes, scrubbed and thinly sliced
2 medium carrots, peeled and thinly sliced diagonally
1 cucumber, peeled and thinly sliced
2 medium tomatoes, cut into wedges
Cilantro or parsley sprigs

1. In a blender, blend the chiles, adobo sauce, vinegar, sugar, oil, and salt until smooth. Reserve in a bowl.

2. Cook the potatoes and carrots in two separate pots of boiling salted water to cover until tender, about 8 minutes for the potatoes, and 4 minutes for the carrots. Drain and cool under cold running water to stop the cooking. Drain again and blot excess water with paper towels. Put in a large bowl. Add about half of the reserved dressing. Toss gently to coat the vegetables. Let marinate at room temperature about 30 minutes.

3. To serve, arrange the potatoes, carrots, and cucumber in overlapping rows on a large platter. Add the tomato wedges. Drizzle the remaining dressing over all. Garnish with cilantro.

Cold Vegetables in Vinaigrette
Verduras Frio en Vinagreta

Makes **4 to 6 servings**

Cold marinated vegetables are a traditional part of Mexican cuisine to be served with enchiladas and other tortilla dishes, or with a platter of assorted cold meats. Cook each vegetable separately to prevent overcooking.

Basic Vinaigrette (page 210)
4 medium white or red boiling potatoes (of equal size)
3 medium carrots, peeled and thinly sliced
3/4 pound fresh small green beans, ends trimmed
2 to 3 medium zucchini, thinly sliced

1. Prepare the vinaigrette. Reserve. Cook the potatoes in boiling salted water to cover until tender, but not soft, 15 to 18 minutes. Using a large slotted spoon, transfer the potatoes to a strainer and cool under running water, peel, and thinly slice. Put in a large bowl.

2. Continue to cook each kind of vegetable in the same boiling salted water, separately, to prevent overcooking. Transfer and cool them in the same manner for each kind, and put them in the bowl with the potatoes. Cook the carrots about 3 minutes, the green beans 5 to 6 minutes, depending on the size, and the zucchini about 1 minute.

3. Add the vinaigrette to the bowl and toss gently to coat. Add salt, if needed. Put the vegetables in the refrigerator until cold, about 20 to 30 minutes, or up to overnight. Serve as a tossed salad or spoon each vegetable separately into rows on a serving platter. Serve cold.

Fruit and Vegetable Salads

Romaine, Orange, and Pomegranate Salad
Ensalada de Lechuga, Naranja, y Granada

Makes **4 servings**

Little red jewels of pomegranate seeds often brighten holiday dishes. The tart-sweet seeds add a special flavor and texture to this easy salad.

1 head romaine lettuce, washed and spun dry
1 orange, peeled and cut into bite-size pieces
1 apple, quartered, cored, and thinly sliced
1 pomegranate, red seeds only (see Note)
2 tablespoons chopped fresh cilantro or parsley
2 tablespoons olive oil
1 teaspoon red wine vinegar
1/4 teaspoon salt, or to taste
1/8 teaspoon freshly ground pepper, or to taste

Tear the romaine leaves into bite-size pieces and put them in a large bowl. Add the remaining ingredients and toss well. Serve cold.

Note: To prepare the pomegranate, cut it in half with a large sharp knife and then break the fruit apart in a bowl of cold water in the sink (to minimize splattering juices) to expose the seeds. Separate the seeds, one by one, and place them in a bowl. Discard all the connecting white membrane and skin.

Greens with Grapefruit
Ensalada Verde con Toronja

Makes **4 servings**

Finely shredded romaine lettuce, pale green cabbage, and cilantro, mixed with a mild vinaigrette and garnished with segments of pink grapefruit is a combination I really like. The idea for the salad comes from one prepared by American chef Billy Cross at his cooking school in Ensenada, Baja, Mexico. That salad was adorned with fresh lobster from Ensenada's fish market, but this version can be prepared for everyday eating. It's so simple, pretty, and very refreshing. For peak freshness, assemble just before serving.

2 tablespoons olive oil
2 teaspoons unseasoned rice vinegar
1/2 teaspoon salt
4 cups finely shredded romaine lettuce
2 cups finely shredded cabbage
1/2 cup coarsely chopped fresh cilantro
2 pink grapefruit, peeled with no white pith remaining, and cut into segments between the membranes

In a small bowl, whisk together the oil, vinegar, and salt. In a large bowl toss the romaine, cabbage, and cilantro together. Add the dressing and toss to coat the greens. Arrange the grapefruit segments equally on each salad. Serve cold.

Greens with Mango and Sunflower Seeds
Ensalada Verde de Mango y Pepitas

Makes 4 servings

Dry-roasted sunflower seeds top this refreshing chopped salad of romaine, cabbage, mango, and radishes, made with typical ingredients commonly found in outdoor markets through-out Mexico.

2 tablespoons fresh lime juice
1 tablespoon honey
2 teaspoons white wine vinegar
1/4 teaspoon salt, or to taste
2 tablespoons olive oil
**1 mango, peeled, pitted, and diced or
    coarsely chopped**
2 cups coarsely shredded romaine lettuce
1 cup chopped cabbage
6 to 8 radishes, thinly sliced
1/2 cup dry-roasted sunflower seeds

In a small bowl, whisk together the lime juice, honey, vinegar, salt, and oil. Set aside. Put all of the remaining ingredients, except the sunflower seeds, in a large bowl. Toss with the dressing. Sprinkle with sunflower seeds. Serve at once.

Mixed Greens and Strawberry Salad
Ensalada Mixta con Fresas

Makes 4 servings

A salad of delicate sweet strawberries mixed with salad greens may be a surprise written in any language. The idea for this nueva salad came from La Capilla Restaurant in the lovely colonial city of San Miguel de Allende. It pairs well with spicy or rich dishes.

2 tablespoons vegetable oil
2 teaspoons fresh lime juice
1/4 teaspoon sugar
1/4 teaspoon salt
4 cups torn lettuce of your choice
1 cup shredded cabbage
10 to 12 ripe strawberries, sliced lengthwise
1/4 cup chopped pecans
Mint sprigs

In a small bowl, whisk together the oil, lime juice, sugar, and salt. In a large bowl, toss together the lettuce, cabbage, and strawberries with the dressing. Mound the salad equally on each of 4 serving plates. Scatter the pecans equally over the salads. Garnish with mint sprigs.

Spinach, Jicama, and Mango Salad
Ensalada de Espinaca, Jicama, y Mango

Makes 4 servings

Iliana de la Vega, owner-chef of El Naranjo restaurant in Oaxaca, always impresses me with her creative salads. Iliana uses local and native ingredients, successfully combining the old with the new.

2 tablespoons sliced almonds
4 cups baby spinach, washed and dried
**1/2 medium jicama, peeled and cut into thin
    matchsticks**
**1 ripe mango, peeled, cut off the pit, and
    thinly sliced**
2 teaspoons red wine vinegar
1/4 teaspoon salt
2 tablespoons olive oil
**2 tablespoons crumbled cotija or
    mild feta cheese**

1. In a small dry skillet, toast the almonds, stirring, until aromatic and lightly browned, about 2 minutes. Set aside. In a large bowl place the spinach, jicama, and mango.

2. In a small bowl, whisk together the vinegar, salt, and oil. Add the dressing to the salad and toss. Add the nuts to the salad and toss to mix. Divide the salad among 4 serving plates. Sprinkle with cheese.

Spinach Salad with Oranges and Jalapeños
Ensalada Espinaca con Naranjas y Jalapeños

Makes **4 servings**

Iliana de la Vega is the gracious and creative chef-owner of El Naranjo Restaurant in Oaxaca. Her menu always features some creative new dishes along with excellent traditional fare. This imaginative spinach salad is based on one of Iliana's offerings that I enjoyed one evening during a recent visit. Mexican panela cheese, a mild fresh cheese with tender spongy texture, is available here in many supermarkets or Mexican markets, or substitute ricotta cheese, if necessary.

Basic Vinaigrette (page 210)

5 cups fresh spinach leaves, washed and spun dry

2 oranges, peeled, white pith removed, and cut into bite-size pieces

1/2 medium jicama, peeled and cut into thin matchsticks

2 jarred pickled jalapeño chiles (en escabeche), seeded and cut lengthwise into thin strips

8 (1/4-inch-thick) slices of panela cheese

8 to 12 radishes, washed with some leaves attached

Prepare the vinaigrette. Then, in a large mixing bowl toss the spinach, oranges, and jicama with enough dressing to coat lightly. Garnish with jalapeño strips, overlapped cheese slices, and radishes.

Cabbage and Orange Salad
Ensalada de Col y Naranja

Makes **4 servings**

This refreshing salad of crunchy cabbage with juicy oranges is a natural to accompany spicy dishes.

3 tablespoons olive oil or vegetable oil

1 tablespoon white wine vinegar

1/2 teaspoon salt, or to taste

1/8 teaspoon freshly ground pepper, or to taste

4 cups finely shredded cabbage

2 medium navel oranges

2 green onions, including 2 inches of the green, finely chopped

2 tablespoons chopped fresh cilantro

1 large avocado (Hass variety preferred), peeled and diced

In a small bowl, whisk together the oil, vinegar, salt, and pepper. Put the cabbage in a large bowl. With a sharp knife, cut both ends off the oranges, and cut away the rind and the white pith. Cut the oranges into bite-size pieces and put in the bowl with the cabbage along with the onions, cilantro, and avocado. Add the dressing and toss gently to coat the salad. Serve cold.

Pineapple, Cabbage, and Romaine Salad
Ensalada de Piña, Col, y Romaine

Makes 4 servings

Just imagine how pretty and refreshing a chopped salad made of sweet fresh pineapple, crunchy cabbage, and crisp romaine lettuce would be served with a saucy spicy entrée. Try it with Chicken in Oaxacan Red Mole (page 301) or with Shrimp in Red Chile Sauce (page 406).

3 teaspoons olive oil
2 teaspoons unseasoned rice vinegar
¹/₄ teaspoon salt, or to taste
¹/₂ fresh pineapple, peeled and cut into
    small pieces
¹/₄ medium head of cabbage, finely chopped
2 cups coarsely chopped romaine lettuce leaves
2 tablespoons chopped fresh flat-leaf parsley

In a small bowl, whisk together the oil, vinegar, and salt. Put the remaining ingredients in a large bowl. Add the dressing and toss to mix. Refrigerate for at least an hour. Serve cold.

Pineapple, Corn, and Pomegranate Salad
Ensalada de Piña, Elote, y Granada

Makes 4 servings

The town of Guanajuato tumbles along a deep gorge in the rugged mountains of central Mexico that once supplied precious minerals. Now this lovely little colonial city in central Mexico is known for its music festivals. The small plaza, Jardin de la Union, shares a pleasant flat area with a few sidewalk cafes, hotels, and shops. From every direction, steep winding streets descend into the plaza.

In a charming sidewalk café I had this salad with its unusual combination of ingredients. It was served with a sweet mayonnaise dressing, but I prefer a vinaigrette. For convenience or a different flavor, you can substitute raisins for the pomegranate seeds.

1 small pineapple, husked and cut into bite-size pieces
1 cup cooked fresh corn kernels, or thawed, if frozen
¹/₂ cup pomegranate seeds (about 1 pomegranate)
2 tablespoons vegetable oil
1 tablespoon fresh lime juice
¹/₄ teaspoon salt, or to taste
Shredded lettuce, such as romaine or iceberg

In a large bowl toss together all of the ingredients except the lettuce. Refrigerate for at least an hour. To serve, line each of 4 serving plates with lettuce and divide the salad among the plates. Serve cold.

Citrus, Jicama, and Watercress Salad
Ensalada de Naranjas y Berros

Makes 4 servings

A bed of peppery watercress, topped with a mixture of juicy citrus fruits, crisp jicama, and radishes mingle for a fresh-tasting salad that goes very well with simply prepared fish such as Sautéed Fish Fillets with Golden Garlic and Lime (page 394).

2 tablespoons vegetable oil
3 teaspoons unseasoned rice vinegar
¹/₄ teaspoon salt, or to taste
1 bunch watercress, thick stems removed,
    washed and spun dry
2 navel oranges
1 large or 2 small grapefruits
1 cup peeled finely diced jicama (from about
    one 1-pound jicama)
8 radishes, thinly sliced

In a small bowl, whisk together the oil, vinegar, and salt. In a medium bowl toss the watercress with half of the dressing and toss to mix. Place on a large serving plate.

. Peel the oranges and grapefruit and remove all the white pith. Cut into bite-size pieces and put in a medium bowl. In the same bowl, add the jicama and radishes to the citrus fruits, then with the remaining dressing. Mound the salad on the bed of watercress. Refrigerate for at least an hour. Serve cold.

Grapefruit, Orange, and Avocado Salad
Ensalada de Toronja, Naranja, y Aguacate

Makes **6 servings**

The tartness of citrus fruits and the creaminess of avocado work ideally together. I like adding crunchy cabbage and dark green romaine lettuce to create this refreshing salad.

4 cups shredded romaine lettuce

1/4 medium head of cabbage, finely shredded

1/4 cup lightly packed chopped fresh cilantro

1 ruby grapefruit

2 navel oranges

2 avocados (Hass variety preferred), peeled and diced (1/2 inch)

1/2 medium red onion, very thinly sliced

2 tablespoons olive oil

1 teaspoon unseasoned rice vinegar

1/2 teaspoon salt, or to taste

1/8 teaspoon freshly ground pepper, or to taste

Put the cabbage, lettuce, and cilantro in a large bowl. Cover and refrigerate. Peel the grapefruit and the oranges and remove all the white pith. Cut into bite-size pieces and put in a medium bowl. Add the avocados, onion, olive oil, vinegar, salt, and pepper. Combine and let marinate for about 10 minutes. Add to the lettuce mixture and toss gently to mix. Serve.

Avocado and Melon Salad
Ensalada de Aguacate y Melón

Makes **6 to 8 servings**

Here's a typical salad combination that's found all over Mexico. Mound this fresh chunky salad on an oval platter or in a shallow bowl to show off the colors and textures. The salad goes with almost everything, but I especially like it with grilled chicken breasts or grilled shrimp.

1 ripe cantaloupe, peeled and cut into bite-size pieces

1 medium cucumber, peeled, halved lengthwise, seeded, and sliced

1 large jalapeño chile, seeded, veins removed, and finely chopped

Juice of 2 limes

1/2 teaspoon salt

2 large avocados (Hass variety preferred), peeled and cut into bite-size pieces

2 tablespoons chopped cilantro

In a large bowl, toss together the melon, cucumber, jalapeño, lime juice, and salt. Gently stir in the avocado and cilantro. Refrigerate for at least an hour. Serve cold.

Cantaloupe and Cucumber Salad
Ensalada de Melón y Pepina

Makes 4 to 6 servings

Juicy sweet chunks of cold cantaloupe makes a grand summer salad made with common ingredients found in Mexican markets everywhere. Serve it with steak or any kind of seafood.

1 medium cantaloupe, peeled and cut into bite-size pieces
1/2 medium cucumber, peeled and seeded
1/4 red bell pepper, cut into thin strips
1/4 teaspoon salt, or to taste
1/8 teaspoon freshly ground pepper, or to taste
3 teaspoons olive oil
2 teaspoons white wine vinegar
1 tablespoon finely slivered fresh mint (optional)

Put the cantaloupe in a large bowl. Cut the cucumber in quarters lengthwise and cut crosswise into ½-inch pieces. Add to the bowl along with the remaining ingredients. Toss to coat with the oil and vinegar. Refrigerate for at least an hour. Serve cold.

Jicama, Melon, Cucumber, and Tomato Salad
Ensalada de Jicama, Melón, Pepino, y Jitomate

Makes 8 servings

Bright combinations of fruits and vegetables with a light dressing are common all over Mexico. For a variation, substitute another melon for the cantaloupe, such as honeydew or Crenshaw.

1 medium jicama, peeled and cut into thin strips
1 medium cantaloupe, peeled and cut into bite-size pieces
1/2 large cucumber, peeled, halved, and thinly sliced
1 (1-pint) basket cherry tomatoes, rinsed and halved
1/4 cup coarsely chopped fresh cilantro
2 tablespoons fresh orange juice
2 tablespoons fresh lime juice
2 teaspoons white wine vinegar
3 to 4 drops hot pepper sauce (such as Tabasco)
1/2 teaspoon salt, or to taste
2 tablespoons olive oil or vegetable oil
1/4 cup crumbled cotija or mild feta cheese

In a shallow bowl, toss together the jicama, cantaloupe, cucumber, and tomatoes. In a small bowl, whisk together the orange juice, lime juice, vinegar, hot pepper sauce, salt, and oil. Pour the dressing over the salad and toss to mix. Sprinkle the cheese over the top of the salad. Refrigerate at least an hour. Serve cold.

Three Melon Salad
Ensalada de Tres Melónes

Makes 6 to 8 servings

Mexican melons are among the sweetest, most flavorful melons anywhere. This stunning combination of three melons is perfectly complimented with red or purple seedless grapes and slivers of red onion all pulled together with lime vinaigrette.

¹/₃ cup vegetable oil

2 tablespoons lime juice

1 teaspoon unseasoned rice vinegar

¹/₄ teaspoon salt, or to taste

¹/₂ ripe cantaloupe, peeled and cut into
   ³/₄-inch pieces

¹/₂ ripe honeydew melon, peeled and cut into
   ³/₄-inch pieces

2 cups ³/₄-inch pieces watermelon, seeded

1 cup seedless red or purple grapes

¹/₄ red onion, cut into very thin slivers

Lettuce leaves or shredded lettuce of choice

In a small bowl, whisk together the oil, lime juice, vinegar, and salt. In a large bowl, place the 3 melons, grapes, and onion. Add the dressing and mix gently. Refrigerate at least an hour. To serve, line 6 to 8 serving plates with lettuce. Divide the salad among the plates. Serve cold.

Jicama, Carrot, and Pineapple Salad
Ensalada de Jicama, Zanahoria, y Piña

Makes 4 servings

Thin matchsticks of jicama and shredded carrot combined with pineapple is a refreshing salad that's very easy to make if you use precut pineapple. Serve with grilled halibut, swordfish, or chicken breast.

1 medium jicama, peeled and cut into thin sticks

2 medium carrots, peeled and coarsely grated

1¹/₂ cups fresh or canned pineapple chunks, well
   drained and cut in half (see Note)

1 jalapeño chile, seeded, veins removed, and
   finely chopped

2 tablespoons fresh lime juice

2 tablespoons olive oil

¹/₂ teaspoon salt, or to taste

In a large bowl, mix the jicama, carrots, pineapple, and jalapeño. In a small bowl, whisk together the lime juice, oil, and salt. Pour over the salad and toss to coat. Refrigerate at least an hour. Serve cold.

Note: To prevent too much juice from accumulating in the salad, add the pineapple just before serving.

Christmas Eve Salad
Ensalada de Noche Buena

Makes **6 servings**

This is a stunning traditional salad that's usually served as part of a joyful meal after mass on Christmas. The salad is also on tables at parties after posadas—re-enactments of Mary and Joseph seeking shelter in Bethlehem for the birth of the baby Jesus—or for any special occasion meal during the Christmas season.

Some versions of the salad also include sugar cane sticks, peeled and cut into chunks or chopped to garnish the salad. The bright combination of fruits and vegetables are most spectacular when artfully arranged on a large platter. Pair with Spanish-Style Salt Cod (page 399), which is often eaten in Mexico during the holiday season.

4 small fresh beets (about 1 pound)
1/2 medium jicama, peeled and finely diced
1/2 fresh pineapple, peeled and cut into
    3/4-inch pieces
2 medium oranges, peeled and cut into
    3/4-inch pieces
1 medium banana, peeled and cut into
    3/4-inch pieces
6 large romaine lettuce leaves, finely shredded
2 medium red apples, halved, cored and thinly sliced
1/2 cup pomegranate seeds
1/3 cup chopped dry-roasted peanuts
1/4 cup olive oil or vegetable oil
1 tablespoon fresh lime juice
2 teaspoons unseasoned rice vinegar
1/2 teaspoon sugar
1/4 teaspoon salt

1. Put the beets in a medium saucepan. Add water to cover and bring to a boil over medium heat. Cook, covered, until tender when pierced with the tip of a sharp knife, about 30 minutes.

Drain and rinse under cold water to cool. Peel and slice the beets about 1/4-inch thick. The beets can be cooked ahead, covered, and refrigerated until you are ready to assemble the salad.

2. In a large bowl gently mix the jicama, pineapple, oranges, and banana. On a large serving platter, arrange a bed of lettuce. Mound the jicama and fruit salad in the center of the platter. Make a ring of overlapping apple slices around the salad. Make a ring of overlapping beet slices around the apples. The shredded lettuce should be visible as the outside ring around the edge of the plate. Sprinkle peanuts and pomegranate seeds over all.

3. In a small bowl, whisk together the oil, lime juice, vinegar, sugar, and salt. Drizzle over the entire salad and serve.

Mango and Poblano Salad with Toasted Pecans
Ensalada de Mango y Chile Poblano con Nuez

Makes **4 servings**

Traditional ingredients joined in a new combination make this a colorful and refreshing salad. Pecans are native to North America and grow in temperate climates of northern and central Mexico as well as the United States.

1/4 cup pecans, coarsely chopped
3 tablespoons white wine vinegar
1/8 teaspoon salt
1/4 cup extra-virgin olive oil
1/4 teaspoon salt
4 cups salad greens washed, spun dry, and
    torn into pieces
1/4 cup loosely packed fresh cilantro leaves
1 large ripe, but firm, mango, peeled and cut into
    thin strips
2 poblano chiles, roasted and cut into thin strips
    (page 8)

1. Put the pecans in a single layer in a small skillet and toast over medium-low heat, stirring until lightly browned and fragant, 7 to 10 minutes.

2. In a small bowl, whisk together the vinegar, salt, and olive oil. Set aside.

3. In a large bowl toss the lettuce, cilantro, mango, and poblanos with just enough dressing to coat. Divide the salad among 4 serving plates. Scatter the nuts equally over each serving. Serve cold.

Papaya Salad
Ensalada de Papaya

Makes **4 servings**

Mexican papayas have juicy flesh that is deep pink to red inside, and these large wonderful fruits, shaped somewhat like a flat football with yellowish skin, frequently show up in many United States markets. Try them as part of a fruit salad.

2 cups (1-inch) papaya pieces

1 cup (1-inch) pineapple pieces

1 ripe banana, peeled and cut into 1/2-inch pieces

1 red apple, unpeeled, cut into 1/2-inch pieces

1/2 cup seedless green grapes

1 tablespoon finely chopped fresh mint

1 teaspoon fresh lime juice

1/4 teaspoon salt

4 mint sprigs

In a large bowl gently mix the ingredients together. Divide the salad among 4 glass serving bowls. Garnish each bowl with a sprig of mint.

Hearts of Palm, Avocado, and Orange Salad
Ensalada de Palmitos, Aguacate, y Naranja

Makes **4 servings**

In the center of small palm trees, there are white edible layers called palmitos *(hearts of palm) that are eaten in salads, soups, and other dishes. Although fresh heart of palm is found in Mexico and in Florida where it also grows, canned is more available for the home cook in the United States. Be sure to rinse them well, and then soak them in warm water for a few minutes to remove any "tinny" taste. Hearts of palm with creamy avocado and juicy oranges make a stylish modern salad.*

1 (14 1/2-ounce) can hearts of palm, drained and thoroughly rinsed

4 cups torn lettuce of choice

1 large orange, peeled with all white pith removed

1 ripe avocado (Hass variety preferred), pitted and peeled

1/4 cup mayonnaise

2 teaspoons unseasoned rice vinegar

1 teaspoon fresh lime juice

1/4 teaspoon salt, or to taste

1/8 teaspoon freshly ground pepper, or to taste

1. Soak the drained hearts of palm in a medium bowl of warm water to cover for about 10 minutes. Drain well. Cut the spears into rounds about 3/4-inch thick. Set aside.

2. Put the lettuce in a large salad bowl. Add the palm to the salad. Cut the orange into bite-size pieces and add to the bowl along with any juices. Cut the avocado into 1-inch pieces and add to the bowl.

3. Add the mayonnaise, vinegar, lime juice, salt, and pepper. Toss the salad gently to combine the ingredients. Serve.

Hearts of Palm Salad with Oranges and Radishes
Ensalada de Palmitos, Naranjas, y Rábanos

Makes **4 servings**

Fresh hearts of palm, grown in Mexico and other countries, are seldom available for home cooks in the United States, but they occasionally appear on upscale restaurant menus here. I order them every chance I get. Canned hearts of palm are easier to find and are a suitable replacement. The canned ones should be rinsed well and then soaked in warm water for a few minutes to wash away any "tinny" taste. Palm hearts are creamy white and tender with a mild taste. In this salad, juicy sweet oranges and crisp radishes team up with the hearts of palm with great results.

1 (14½-ounce) can hearts of palm, drained and thoroughly rinsed

4 cups finely shredded romaine lettuce

2 medium navel oranges, peeled, pith removed, and sliced into half rounds

10 to 12 radishes, washed, trimmed, and sliced into rounds

¼ cup olive oil

2 tablespoons unseasoned rice vinegar

1 tablespoon fresh orange juice

½ teaspoon salt

⅛ teaspoon freshly ground pepper, or to taste

2 tablespoons finely chopped flat-leaf parsley

1. Soak the drained hearts of palm in a medium bowl of warm water to cover for about 10 minutes. Drain well. Cut the spears into rounds about ¾-inch thick. Set aside.

2. Divide the lettuce among 4 serving plates. Arrange the hearts of palm, oranges, and radishes on the lettuce. In a small bowl, whisk together the oil, vinegar, orange juice, salt and pepper. Drizzle the dressing equally over the salads. Sprinkle with parsley and serve.

Yucatán Fruit Salad
Xek

Makes **6 servings**

Marilyn Tausend's Culinary Adventures to Mexico have been great fun and a valuable part of my continued travels and study. Marilyn seeks out wonderful culinary spots to visit and she arranges for excellent instructors to teach in every location. This cooling salad was presented to our group by Perla Ehrenberg, one of the instructors, who was living in a village near Merida in Yucatán where the year-round tropical climate produces an abundance of fruits. The amount of each fruit can be flexible. Also try adding some mango, if you like.

2 tangerines, peeled and cut into bite-size pieces

2 oranges, peeled and cut into bite-size pieces

1 grapefruit, peeled and cut into bite-size pieces

2 cups fresh pineapple chunks

½ medium jicama, peeled and cut into bite-size squares

¼ cup packed chopped fresh cilantro

1 tablespoon Bitter Orange Juice Substitute (page 17), or 2 teaspoons orange juice and 2 teaspoons grapefruit juice

1 chile piquin, crumbled, or ⅛ teaspoon crushed red pepper

Mix all of the ingredients in a large bowl. Refrigerate for at least an hour. Serve cold.

Salads with Meat, Poultry, or Fish

Roast Beef Salad
Ensalada de Carne de Res

Makes **4 servings**

Mexicans buy cold thinly sliced roast beef at full-service delicatessens just as we do in the United States. Roast beef salad is found on some upscale restaurant menus or fancy buffets in Mexico's major cities. The salad makes an excellent light meal served with good crusty bread.

1 pound thinly sliced cold roast beef
Basic Vinaigrette (page 210)
5 cups shredded lettuce
1 medium cucumber, peeled, seeded and
    thinly sliced
1 large ripe avocado (Hass variety preferred),
    peeled and diced
1/2 medium red onion, very thinly sliced
2 medium tomatoes, cut into thin wedges
Cilantro sprigs

1. Cut the roast beef slices crosswise into pieces about 2 inches wide. Roll into cylinders and reserve.

2. Prepare the vinaigrette. Then, in a large bowl mix the lettuce, cucumber, avocado, and onion. Add enough vinaigrette to moisten the salad. Toss to mix. Mound the salad evenly among 4 serving plates. Arrange the rolled beef equally on top of each salad. Place tomato wedges around the outside edge of each plate. Garnish with cilantro. Refrigerate for at least an hour. Serve cold.

Watercress and Bacon Salad
Ensalada de Berros y Tocino

Makes **4 servings**

All kinds of wild greens are gathered by cooks in Mexico, including watercress. As a child, I gathered watercress with my grandmother from the banks of a small spring-fed stream on my grandparents' farm in southern Idaho, so I was taken by this salad that appeared in a Mexican cooking magazine. I usually arrange the salad on a platter for self-service.

1 bunch watercress, well rinsed
8 large green romaine leaves, rinsed
8 bacon strips
1 medium tomato, chopped
2 tablespoons unseasoned rice vinegar
1/4 teaspoon salt
3 tablespoons extra-virgin olive oil
1/4 cup crumbled cotija or mild feta cheese

1. Trim the large stems off the watercress. Tear the romaine leaves into bite-size pieces. Dry the greens in a lettuce spinner, and put them into a bowl. Cover and refrigerate.

2. In a medium skillet, over medium heat, cook the bacon until brown and crisp. Drain on paper towels, break into small pieces, and reserve.

3. Add the tomato to the bowl of greens. In a small bowl, whisk together the vinegar, salt and oil. Add the dressing to the salad and toss to coat. Mound the salad on a serving platter. Sprinkle the top with the cheese and the bacon. Serve.

Green Salad with Bacon and Potatoes
Ensalada Verde con Tocino y Papas

Makes **4 servings**

Here's a terrific modern salad from Mexico City made with popular everyday ingredients. A food processor slicing blade can be used to slice the potatoes really thin.

¹/₃ **cup pine nuts**

6 bacon slices, cut crosswise into 1-inch pieces

2 small white potatoes, sliced very thin (about ¹/₁₆ inch)

6 cups chopped lettuce, such as romaine or iceberg

¹/₄ **cup coarsely chopped fresh cilantro**

1 medium tomato, finely chopped

3 tablespoons olive oil

1 tablespoon white wine vinegar

1 tablespoon crumbled cotija or mild feta cheese

¹/₄ **teaspoon salt, or to taste**

1. In a medium dry skillet, toast the pine nuts, stirring, until lightly browned, about 2 minutes. Reserve on a plate. In the same skillet, cook the bacon over medium heat until crisp and brown on both sides. Drain on paper towels, break into small pieces, and reserve.

2. Remove all but about 2 teaspoons of the fat from the skillet. Place the potato slices in a single layer in the same hot skillet and cook, turning 3 to 4 times, until tender and lightly browned, about 4 to 5 minutes. Reserve on a plate.

3. Put the lettuce, cilantro, and tomato in a large bowl. Add the olive oil, vinegar, cheese, and salt. Toss well to coat the lettuce. Divide the salad equally among 4 salad plates. Arrange the potato slices in a single overlapping line across the center of each salad. Scatter the bacon pieces on each side of the potatoes. Sprinkle the pine nuts on top. Serve at once.

Spinach Salad with Pork Rinds
Ensalada de Espinaca con Chicharrónes

Makes **6 servings**

I discovered this dish at the home of Roldolfo Morales, a well-known Mexican painter. He opened his restored historic mansion in Ocotlan, for a culinary trip I led to nearby Oaxaca City. We had a wonderful lunch, prepared by the resident cook. Everything was presented on beautiful Mexican pottery, including this salad, which everyone really liked. Chicharrón, a very popular snack and topping in Mexico, can be purchased in many supermarkets or Mexican markets in this country.

8 cups spinach leaves, rinsed and spun dry

3 tablespoons olive oil

1 tablespoon unseasoned rice vinegar

¹/₂ **teaspoon salt**

¹/₈ **teaspoon freshly ground pepper, or to taste**

4 large ripe tomatoes, sliced crosswise

2 large avocados (Hass variety preferred), peeled and cut into ¹/₂-inch cubes

3 tablespoons fresh lime juice

3 tablespoons coarsely chopped fresh cilantro

1 cup crumbled chicharrón (fried pork rinds)

In a large bowl, toss the spinach with the olive oil, vinegar, salt, and pepper. Make a bed of spinach on a large platter. Arrange the tomatoes in overlapping rows on the spinach. Scatter the avocado cubes on top. Drizzle with lime juice, and sprinkle with cilantro. Scatter the chicharrón bits over all.

Chicharrón, a National Snack

Chicharrón is crisp-fried pork skin that is a favorite *antojito* (snack) all over Mexico. Throughout the country, big golden brown sheets of *chicharrón* are displayed in large baskets by street vendors, in nearly every marketplace, and served as appetizers in many Mexican restaurants. After the skin is removed from the pig and air-dried outdoors for about twelve hours, the skin is placed in a large vessel of boiling lard. When it starts to brown, it is removed from the first vat and put into a second vat of boiling lard that is hotter than the first. This double boiling causes the skin to get puffy, porous, and very crisp.

In the United States, *chicharrónes* are sold in small packages, like potato chips, and the large sheets have been broken into small irregular 2- to 3-inch pieces. I select packages with the darker brown *chicharrónes* because they are crisper and less greasy.

Of course, crisp-fried pork skin is not a health food, but since only a small amount is eaten, it's no worse than other deep-fried, calorie-laden foods that we love.

Chicharrón is also cooked in sauce for some traditional dishes. When cooked, it softens and becomes chewy with a texture that I don't enjoy, but I do like crisp *chicharrónes* crumbled over a salad, or a few pieces dipped into guacamole, or sprinkled with chili powder and lime juice. *Chicharrón* is worth trying, for those who enjoy authentic food experiences.

Corn and Zucchini Salad with Pork Rinds
Ensalada de Elote y Calabacitas con Chicharrónes

Makes **4 servings**

Fresh summer corn with zucchini and crunchy bits of chicharrón *makes a delightful salad that goes well with chicken enchiladas.*

3 large fresh ears of corn
2 medium zucchini, trimmed and finely diced
1 medium tomato, finely diced
2 green onions, thinly sliced crosswise
1 jalapeño chile, seeded, veins removed, and finely chopped
2 tablespoons chopped fresh cilantro
1 tablespoon white wine vinegar
$1/4$ teaspoon salt, or to taste
$1/4$ teaspoon ground cumin
2 tablespoons olive oil
$1/8$ teaspoon freshly ground pepper, or to taste
$3/4$ cup crumbled chicharrón (fried pork rinds)

1. In a large pot of boiling water, cook the corn until crisp-tender, 3 to 4 minutes. Using tongs, remove the corn from the water, and reserve the water. Rinse the corn under cold running water and cut the kernels off the cobs, discarding the cobs. Put the corn kernels in a large bowl.

2. In the same boiling water, blanch the diced zucchini for about 20 seconds. Drain and rinse under cold running water to stop the cooking. Shake off excess water, then add zucchini to the bowl with the corn. Add the remaining ingredients, except the chicharrón. Toss to coat with the dressing. Add the chicharrón and toss again. Adjust seasoning. Serve at once.

Purslane and Bacon Salad
Ensalada de Verdolagas y Tocino

Makes **4 servings**

Purslane, called verdolagas, *is a succulent plant with small fleshy leaves that grows wild almost everywhere. Although it is considered a weed by many gardeners in this country, it's used a lot in Mexico, often cooked, teamed with pork, or eaten raw as in this salad. This little green has been gaining some recognition by cooks here, and is seasonally available in some farmers' markets.*

6 slices bacon

4 cups shredded lettuce, such as romaine

2 cups purslane, rinsed and snipped into
    small pieces

6 small white mushrooms, thinly sliced

2 green onions, finely chopped

2 tablespoons honey

1 tablespoon ketchup

2 teaspoons red wine vinegar

1/2 teaspoon Worcestershire sauce

1/4 teaspoon salt, or to taste

1. In a skillet, cook the bacon until crisp and brown. Drain on paper towels. When cool, crumble coarsely. Reserve.

2. Put the lettuce, purslane, mushrooms, and onions in a large bowl. In a small bowl put the remaining ingredients, and whisk well to mix. Pour the dressing over the salad and toss to mix. Serve the salad at once sprinkled with the bacon.

Chicken and Tortilla Salad
Ensalada de Pollo y Tortillas

Makes **4 servings**

Grilled chicken and crisp tortilla strips are arranged on a bed of greens tossed with tomato and avocado for a modern salad from Mexico City.

1/2 cup corn oil or canola oil

4 (6- to 7-inch) corn tortillas, cut into 1/4-inch-thick
    strips

4 skinless boneless chicken breast halves

1/2 teaspoon salt, or to taste

Freshly ground pepper, to taste

8 cups washed and dried torn salad greens,
    such as romaine, red or green leaf, or a mix

1/4 cup loosely packed chopped fresh cilantro

1 tablespoon finely chopped fresh oregano or
    1/2 teaspoon dried oregano (Mexican variety
    preferred)

1 tablespoon unseasoned rice vinegar

3 tablespoons olive oil

1 large tomato, cut into 1/2-inch dice

1 large avocado (Hass variety preferred),
    cut into 1/2-inch dice

2 jarred pickled jalapeño chiles (en escabeche),
    seeded, veins removed, and cut into very
    thin strips

1. In a skillet, heat the oil over medium-high heat and fry the tortilla strips, in batches, until crisp and golden brown. Drain on paper towels. Reserve.

2. Pour out all but about 2 tablespoons of the oil used to fry the tortillas. In the same skillet, fry the chicken breasts until golden brown on both sides and cooked through, about 8 minutes total. Season with salt and pepper. Transfer the chicken to a cutting board and let stand for about 5 minutes. Cut the cooled chicken into thin strips.

3. Put the greens, cilantro, and oregano in a large bowl. Add the vinegar, oil, and salt, or to taste.

oss to coat the greens. Add the tomato, avocado
nd jalapeño strips. Toss gently to mix. Transfer
he salad to a platter and scatter the chicken and
ortilla strips over the salad.

. Divide the salad among 4 large plates. Slice the
hicken breasts across the grain and arrange
 sliced breast on each of the salads. Scatter the
ortilla strips on top of each salad. Serve.

Chicken, Ham, and Cheese Salad
Ensalada de Pollo, Jamón, y Queso Cazadores

Makes **4 servings**

*On the menu at Restaurant Cazadores in the
colonial city of Zacatecas this Chef's Salad was the
house specialty. It was attractively arranged and
certainly large enough for a whole meal. At home I
arrange the salad on a large platter for self-service.*

Basic Vinaigrette (page 210)

4 cups shredded or chopped lettuce, such as
    romaine, red or green leaf, or a mix

1 cup shredded cabbage

2 jarred pickled jalapeño chiles (en escabeche),
    seeded, veins removed, and finely chopped

2 medium tomatoes, seeded and diced

1 cup cooked diced deli-style smoked ham

1 cup cooked diced chicken

$1/2$ cup shredded yellow cheese, such as cheddar

$1/2$ cup shredded white cheese, such as
    Monterey Jack

$1/2$ medium white onion, very thinly sliced

Prepare the vinaigrette. In a large bowl toss the lettuce, cabbage, and chopped chiles with just enough
dressing to lightly coat the greens. Mound on a
serving platter. Arrange the remaining ingredients, except the cheeses and onion, on the platter.
Drizzle the remaining dressing over the top and
scatter the cheeses and onion over all. Serve cold.

Chicken Salad with Cucumber and Mint
Ensalada de Pollo con Pepino y Yerbabuena

Makes **4 servings**

*Mexican home cooks like easy luncheon or light
meal salads just as we do. This one is adapted
from a Mexican magazine in Mexico City.
The chipotle chile adds a spicy punch to the
salad dressing.*

2 tablespoons vegetable oil

4 skinless boneless chicken breast halves

$1/2$ teaspoon salt, or to taste

4 cups finely shredded lettuce, such as romaine
    or green leaf

1 medium cucumber, peeled, seeded, and diced
    (about $1/2$ inch)

2 tablespoons finely chopped fresh mint

1 tablespoon finely chopped fresh parsley

3 tablespoons mayonnaise

3 teaspoons fresh lime juice

1 mashed canned chipotle chile en adobo

2 hard-cooked eggs, peeled and quartered
    lengthwise

8 radishes, sliced into rounds

1. In a large nonstick skillet, heat the oil over
medium heat. Season the chicken breasts with
salt and cook until lightly browned on both
sides and white inside, but still juicy, about
8 minutes. Remove to a cutting board. When cool
enough to handle, cut lengthwise into thin strips.
Reserve.

2. Put all the remaining ingredients, except the
eggs and radishes, in a large bowl. Add the
chicken strips. Toss gently to mix well. Adjust salt.
Mound the salad equally on 4 serving plates.
Garnish with egg wedges and radish rounds.
Serve at once.

Chicken and Vegetable Salad with Chipotle Vinaigrette
Salpicón de Pollo

Makes 3 to 4 servings

When I travel with Marilyn Tausend on her Culinary Adventures trips through Mexico, our days are filled with eating pleasures such as this pretty and tasty salad from Teresita's Restaurant in Puebla.

Shredded Chicken (page 271)
2 canned chipotle chile en adobo, rinsed and seeded
1/2 teaspoon adobo sauce from the can
3 teaspoons unseasoned rice vinegar
1 1/2 teaspoons dark brown sugar
1 tablespoon olive oil
1/2 teaspoon salt, or to taste
1 medium potato, peeled and finely diced (about 1/2 inch)
1 medium carrot, peeled and finely diced (about 1/2 inch)
1/2 cup cooked fresh or frozen peas
1 medium tomato, finely chopped
1/4 medium white onion, very thinly sliced

1. Prepare the chicken, then cover and refrigerate. Cut the rinsed and seeded chipotle chiles into matchstick-thin strips. Reserve.

2. In a small bowl, whisk together the adobo sauce, vinegar, sugar, olive oil and 1/4 teaspoon of the salt.

3. Bring about 2 cups of water to a boil in a medium saucepan. Add the potato and carrot. Cook until tender, 3 to 4 minutes. Drain through a sieve and rinse under cold running water. Put in a large bowl. Add the cooked peas, tomato, chicken, and remaining 1/4 teaspoon of salt. Add

about 1/2 of the chipotle dressing and toss to mix. Mound the salad on a serving platter. Garnish with sliced onion and chile strips. Drizzle with the remaining dressing.

Turkey Salad with Chipotle Mayonnaise
Ensalada de Pavo con Mayonesa Chipotle

Makes 4 servings

There are so many wonderful dishes to make with Mexico's large native bird. Here is a contemporary turkey salad to serve as a light meal or as part of a buffet.

3 cups diced Basic Cooked Turkey Breast (page 311)
1/2 cup Chipotle Mayonnaise (page 18)
1 large avocado (Hass variety preferred), peeled and diced
1/2 medium cucumber, peeled, seeded, and thinly sliced
1 cup diced jicama
2 tablespoons chopped fresh cilantro
1 teaspoon fresh lime juice
3 ripe medium tomatoes cut into wedges
2 1/2 cups shredded lettuce, such as iceberg or romaine

1. Prepare the turkey breast, then put it in a large bowl. Prepare the mayonnaise.

2. Mix the remaining salad ingredients, except the tomatoes and lettuce, with the turkey. Add the dressing and toss to coat. Arrange a layer of shredded lettuce on a serving platter. Mound the salad on the lettuce and surround with tomato wedges.

Shrimp and Avocado Salad
Ensalada de Camarónes y Aguacate

Makes **4 servings**

For this modern nueva cocina *salad the ingredients are very finely diced and mixed with a little mayonnaise and lime juice to hold everything together. For a special presentation, the salad is packed into a ramekin and inverted onto a bed of lettuce, but you can serve it as you please. Whole shrimp decorate the top of the salads.*

3/4 **pound (50 to 60) small shrimp, peeled and cooked, tails removed**
3 **tablespoons finely diced jicama**
1 **plum tomato, seeded and very finely diced or minced**
1 **tablespoon finely chopped fresh parsley**
1/2 **jarred pickled jalapeño chile (en escabeche), seeded and minced**
1 **teaspoon mayonnaise**
1 **teaspoon fresh lime juice**
1/4 **teaspoon salt, or to taste**
1 **avocado (Hass variety preferred), peeled and mashed**
8 **butter or red leaf lettuce leaves**

1. Rinse and drain the cooked shrimp. Reserve 8 whole shrimp. Chop the remaining shrimp into 1/4-inch pieces and put in a bowl. If made ahead, add all of the remaining ingredients except the avocado to prevent it from turning brown. Refrigerate the shrimp mixture.

2. About one hour before serving, mix the avocado into the shrimp salad and refrigerate again until ready to serve. To serve, place 2 lettuce leaves on each of 4 serving plates. Tightly pack about 1/2 cup of the shrimp salad into a 1/2 cup ramekin or flat-bottomed measuring cup. Invert onto a serving plate. Repeat with remaining plates. Place 2 of the reserved whole shrimp on top of each salad. Serve at once.

Yucatán Shrimp Salad
Camarónes Yucatán

Makes **4 servings**

This Yucatán-style shrimp starter or salad is marinated in a vinegar mixture or escabeche, *as it's called in Yucatán, while the shrimp are still hot from cooking. It's a common method of preparing shrimp and other seafood. This dish has long been a favorite among my cooking students.*

1 **pound (16 to 20) large shrimp, peeled and deveined**
2 **tablespoons red wine vinegar**
1/4 **cup olive oil**
1 **to 2 serrano chiles, minced with seeds**
1/2 **medium white onion, halved crosswise and very thinly sliced**
1/2 **teaspoon dried oregano (Mexican variety preferred), crumbled**
1/4 **teaspoon salt, or to taste**
1 **large tomato, cut into small dice**
1/4 **cup fresh lime juice**
1/4 **cup chopped fresh cilantro**
4 **cups shredded lettuce, such as romaine or iceberg**
Radishes and lime wedges

1. In a medium saucepan of boiling water, cook the shrimp until pink and curled, 3 to 4 minutes. Drain the shrimp and put them in a glass or ceramic bowl. While the shrimp are still hot, stir in vinegar, oil, serrano chile, onion, oregano and salt. Cover and marinate in the refrigerator, tossing 2 to 3 times, until cold, at least 2 hours and up to 6 hours.

2. Remove the shrimp from the refrigerator. Add the tomato, lime juice, and cilantro to the bowl with the shrimp. Stir to combine. Divide the lettuce among 4 salad plates, and pile the shrimp mixture equally on top of the lettuce. Garnish each plate with radishes and lime wedges. Serve cold.

Chiles Stuffed with Rice and Shrimp Salad
Chiles Rellenos con Ensalada de Arroz y Camarónes

Makes 4 servings

Poblano chiles, roasted, peeled, and chilled are stuffed with cold rice and shrimp for this stunning salad. Provide a knife and fork so the chiles can be cut and eaten with the filling. All the parts can be made ahead and even plated and refrigerated for a couple of hours before serving. The idea for this fabulous stuffed chile comes from Chapulin restaurant in Oaxaca.

4 large poblano chiles, roasted and peeled (page 8)

Rice Salad (page 209) without the garnishes

36 medium raw shrimp, peeled, tails removed, and deveined

3 teaspoons olive oil

¹/₄ teaspoon crushed red pepper

2 teaspoons Worcestershire sauce

¹/₄ teaspoon salt, or to taste

3 medium plum tomatoes, cored, seeded, and finely diced

¹/₃ cup sour cream, diluted with 2 teaspoons milk

1. Prepare chiles. Then, using a small sharp knife, cut a slit lengthwise from the stem end to within 1 inch of the tip of each chile. Keep the stems intact. Make a short crosswise cut at the top of the lengthwise cut, to form a "T" and carefully cut out the seed pod. Rinse the chiles under running water to wash out the remaining seeds. Pat the chiles dry with paper towels. Cover and refrigerate.

2. Prepare the rice salad, but do not include the radishes, olives, or lettuce. Cover the salad and refrigerate.

3. Put the shrimp into a large bowl. Add the oil, red pepper, Worcestershire, and salt. Let stand about 20 minutes. Heat a large nonstick skillet over medium heat and cook the shrimp, turning, until curled and cooked through, 5 to 6 minutes. Transfer the shrimp to a bowl. When cool enough to handle, set aside 12 whole shrimp for the final presentation. Cut the rest of the shrimp into ¹/₂-inch pieces. Mix the small shrimp pieces with the rice salad.

4. To assemble, stuff each chile with about ¹/₂ cup of the rice and shrimp salad. Reshape the chiles to their original form with the opening on top showing some of the filling. Place the stuffed chiles in the center of 4 serving plates. Spoon the remaining rice along one side of each chile, but do not cover any of the green. Garnish each plate with the diced tomatoes. Drizzle the tops of the chiles with sour cream. Place 3 of the reserved whole shrimp on top of each stuffed chile. Serve cold.

Shrimp and Grapefruit Salad
Ensalada de Camarónes y Toronja

Makes **4 servings**

Mixed greens topped with segments of pink grapefruit, sliced avocado, and cooked bay shrimp make a lovely luncheon salad that's adapted from a recipe by Patricia Quintana, a cookbook author and cooking instructor from Mexico City. Patricia used grapefruit juice or sour Seville orange juice in her dressing. I include segments of the grapefruit as well as the juice, and I also use small cooked shrimp in place of large shrimp.

2 pink grapefruit, peeled and white pith cut away (juices reserved)

5 cups mixed baby greens or salad greens of choice

1 tablespoon slivered fresh mint

2 tablespoons olive oil

2 teaspoons unseasoned rice vinegar

2 teaspoons grapefruit juice (from cutting the grapefruit)

$^1/_2$ teaspoon salt, or to taste

1 large avocado (Hass variety preferred), peeled and thinly sliced

$^1/_2$ pound (36 to 40) cooked small shrimp

8 to 12 whole radishes, washed with some leaves attached

Cut the grapefruit from between the membranes into segments (over a bowl to catch juices). Reserve the segments on a plate. In a large bowl, toss together the greens, mint, oil, vinegar, the two teaspoons grapefruit juice, and the salt. Divide the greens among 4 plates. Arrange the grapefruit, avocado, and shrimp on top. Garnish each plate with radishes. Serve at once.

Shrimp and Vegetable Salad
Ensalada de Camarónes y Verduras

Makes **4 servings**

Serve this versatile salad as part of any Mexican party, or pile it on crisp fried tortillas to make tostadas.

3 tablespoons fresh lime juice

1 teaspoon white wine vinegar

1 teaspoon ground cumin

$^1/_4$ teaspoon salt, or to taste

Freshly ground pepper, to taste

$^1/_4$ cup olive oil

2 medium tomatoes, seeded and chopped

1 cup cooked corn kernels, fresh or frozen

1 cup cooked black beans, canned or homemade, drained and rinsed

1 avocado (Hass variety preferred), peeled and cut into $^1/_2$-inch pieces

$^1/_2$ medium cucumber, peeled, seeded, and finely diced

3 green onions, finely chopped

2 jalapeño chiles, seeded, veins removed, and finely chopped

$^3/_4$ pound (50 to 60) cooked small shrimp

$^1/_2$ cup sour cream, diluted with milk

$^1/_4$ cup chopped fresh cilantro, lightly packed

In a small bowl, whisk together the lime juice, vinegar, cumin, salt, and pepper. Gradually whisk in the oil. Set aside. In a large bowl gently mix the tomatoes, corn, beans, avocado, cucumber, onion, jalapeños, and shrimp. Add the dressing and toss to combine. Adjust salt. Mound the salad on a serving platter or in a shallow bowl. Drizzle sour cream over the top and sprinkle with cilantro.

Shrimp, Jicama, and Tomato Salad

Ensalada de Camarónes, Jicama, y Jitomate

Makes 4 servings

Shrimp are used in abundance all along both coasts of Mexico. This salad features shrimp in a typical seafood cocktail sauce piled on top of the tossed salad. It is a terrific first course salad.

1 pound (18 to 22) medium shrimp, peeled and deveined

¹/₂ cup bottled cocktail sauce, or more to taste

4 cups torn romaine lettuce

1 cup very thin strips of peeled jicama

1 large ripe tomato, coarsely chopped

2 green onions, cut crosswise into thin rounds

3 tablespoons olive oil

2 teaspoons white wine vinegar

¹/₂ teaspoon salt, or to taste

¹/₈ teaspoon freshly ground pepper, or to taste

Lime wedges

Cilantro sprigs

1. In a pot of boiling water, cook the shrimp until pink, 3 to 5 minutes. Drain and cool under cold running water. Put the shrimp into a bowl, toss with the cocktail sauce, and refrigerate.

2. Put the lettuce, jicama, tomato, and onions in a large salad bowl. In a small bowl, whisk together the oil, vinegar, salt, and pepper. Pour over the salad and toss to coat the vegetables with the dressing. Divide the salad among 4 serving plates. Pile the shrimp equally on top of each salad. Garnish with lime wedges and cilantro sprigs. Serve at once.

Hearts of Palm and Shrimp Salad

Ensalada de Palmitos y Camarónes

Makes 4 servings

Hearts of palm are slender and ivory colored and come from the inner core of a species of palm tree that grows in many tropical regions of Mexico. The flavor is mild and pleasant, somewhat like artichoke hearts. Fresh hearts of palm are a rarity, but canned ones are very good, especially if they are rinsed and soaked well to lessen any "tinny taste". Hearts of palm and tiny pink shrimp are an elegant combination to serve as a first course in this contemporary presentation.

1 (14-ounce) can hearts of palm, drained and rinsed

¹/₂ pound (36 to 40) cooked small shrimp, cut in half crosswise

1 serrano chile, minced with seeds (wear protective gloves)

2 tablespoons mayonnaise

¹/₄ teaspoon salt, or to taste

2 medium tomatoes, each cut into 8 wedges

Parsley sprigs

In a medium bowl of warm tap water, soak the hearts of palm for 10 minutes to remove any "tinny" taste. Drain very well and chop coarsely. Add the shrimp, serrano chile, mayonnaise, and salt. Mix well. Pack ¹/₂ cup in a flat-bottomed measuring cup or ramekin and invert to unmold onto an individual serving plate. Place 4 tomato wedges around the shrimp. Repeat to make 4 servings. Garnish each plate with parsley.

Papaya and Melon Salad with Shrimp
Ensalada de Papaya y Melón con Camarónes

Makes 4 servings

Pale green honeydew melon and Mexican papaya—larger than Hawaiian with a flat football shape, and a color range of sunset pink to reddish orange—are really striking served together. La Cava restaurant in Mexico City served a lovely salad like this with tiny bay shrimp.

¹/₂ ripe honeydew melon
¹/₂ medium Mexican papaya or whole Hawaiian papaya
2 tablespoons fresh lime juice
2 teaspoons vegetable oil
¹/₂ teaspoon sugar
¹/₄ teaspoon salt, or to taste
¹/₂ pound (36 to 40) cooked small shrimp
Parsley sprigs

1. Scoop out the melon seeds. Peel the melon and halve lengthwise. Slice the melon crosswise ½-inch thick and put in a large shallow bowl or pie plate. Discard papaya seeds and peel. Slice the papaya crosswise ½-inch thick, and put in the bowl with the melon.

2. In a small bowl, whisk together the lime juice, oil, sugar, and salt. Spoon over the fruit and turn gently to coat with the dressing. Let stand about 10 minutes. Arrange the melon and papaya equally among 4 serving plates. Scatter the shrimp equally over the fruit. Garnish the salads with parsley sprigs. Serve cold.

Spicy Crab Salad on Tortillas
Tostadas de Jaiba

Makes 4 servings

Corn tortillas fried until crisp and golden brown are the base for tostadas *that are piled high with almost anything. These* tostadas *are topped with a spicy crab salad. The oceans along Mexico's long coastline provide several species of crab; use whatever fresh crab is available in your area.*

Vegetable oil for frying
¹/₂ cup Chipotle Mayonnaise (page 18) or sour cream
4 (6- to 7-inch) corn tortillas
2 medium tomatoes, finely chopped
1 ripe avocado (Hass variety preferred), peeled and cut into ¹/₂-inch cubes
¹/₄ white onion, finely chopped
1 serrano chile, finely chopped with seeds
2 tablespoons chopped cilantro
¹/₄ cup fresh lime juice
2 cups cooked fresh crabmeat, coarsely shredded
¹/₂ teaspoon salt, or to taste
1 cup finely shredded romaine lettuce

1. Prepare mayonnaise, if using. Then, in a medium skillet, heat vegetable oil to a depth of about ½ inch. Fry the tortillas, 1 at a time, turning, until crisp and golden brown on both sides. Drain on paper towels. (This can be done ahead.)

2. In a large bowl, stir together the tomato, avocado, onion, serrano chile, cilantro, and lime juice. Add the crabmeat and salt. Toss gently to combine. To assemble, put 1 crisp tostada on each of 4 plates, and divide the lettuce equally among the tostadas. Spoon the crab mixture equally on top. Add a dollop of chipotle mayonnaise and serve at once.

Cactus Salad with Tuna
Ensalada de Nopalitos con Atún

Makes 4 servings

Nopales *are the tender young paddles of the cactus plant, with a flavor somewhat like green beans. Fresh cactus can be found in Mexican markets, and more recently, in many supermarkets. Often, fresh cactus is de-thorned, and cut into pieces ready to use. Cut cactus is sold canned or in jars. I don't recommend the canned, because they are soft and lack flavor, but cactus packed in jars is convenient and works well for salads. Use cactus strips packed in jars with only water and salt.*

1 (6-ounce) can all-white albacore tuna, drained

2 cups cactus strips, drained, rinsed, and diced

2 medium tomatoes, diced or coarsely chopped

4 cups torn iceberg lettuce

2 tablespoons chopped fresh cilantro or parsley

3 tablespoons olive oil

1 tablespoon white wine vinegar

1/2 teaspoon salt, or to taste

1/8 teaspoon freshly ground pepper, or to taste

2 hard-cooked eggs, peeled and quartered lengthwise

1/4 cup crumbled cotija or mild feta cheese

In a large bowl, put all of the ingredients, except the eggs and cheese. Toss well to mix. Taste for salt. Divide the salad among 4 serving plates. Garnish each salad equally with the egg wedges, and sprinkle with cheese. Serve cold.

Tuna and Chickpea Salad
Ensalada de Atún y Garbanzos

Makes 4 servings

Garbanzo beans (chickpeas) and tuna join to make a versatile salad that can be piled on a tostada *for a light meal, served in a bowl at a buffet, or plated as a first course salad with mixed greens.*

2 (6-ounce) cans solid white tuna, drained

1 (15-ounce) can chickpeas (garbanzo beans), drained and rinsed

2 green onions, finely chopped, including 3 inches of green

2 jarred pickled jalapeño chiles (en escabeche), seeded and chopped

2 medium tomatoes, seeded and finely chopped

1/4 cup lightly packed chopped cilantro or parsley

3 tablespoons olive oil

1 1/2 tablespoons unseasoned rice vinegar

2 teaspoons fresh lime juice

1 teaspoon Dijon mustard

1/4 teaspoon salt, or to taste

In a large bowl, break up the tuna into small pieces with a fork. Add all of the remaining ingredients and toss to mix. The salad can be covered and refrigerated up to 4 hours for best flavor. Serve cold.

Tuna-Stuffed Tomato Salad
Ensalada de Tomato Relleno con Atún

Makes 4 servings

To really enjoy this salad, choose the best vine-ripened tomatoes, and serve the salad for lunch or a light evening meal on a hot day. You can just mound the tuna on thick slices of deep red tomatoes, as is often done in Mexico, but I like to cut the tomatoes in a petal design and put the filling in the center.

4 large vine-ripened red tomatoes, rinsed

2 (6-ounce) cans all-white albacore tuna, drained

1/3 cup mayonnaise, or more, to taste

2 tablespoons drained capers

1 to 2 jarred pickled jalapeño chiles (en escabeche), seeded and minced

4 cups finely shredded, washed, and dried fresh spinach

2 teaspoons olive oil

1 teaspoon unseasoned rice vinegar

1/4 teaspoon salt

1 tablespoon finely chopped parsley

1. Cut the core out of the tomatoes. Stand 1 tomato, cored side up, on a flat surface. With a sharp knife, cut from the top straight down to within 1 inch of the bottom into evenly spaced 4 segments or into 8, if desired. Gently spread open like petals. Repeat until all are cut. Set aside.

2. In a bowl, mix the tuna, mayonnaise, capers, and chiles. In another bowl, toss the spinach, oil, vinegar, and salt together. To assemble the salads, divide the spinach evenly among 4 serving plates. Place 1 tomato in the center of each plate on the bed of spinach. Spoon the tuna mixture equally inside each tomato cavity. Sprinkle with chopped parsley. Serve at once.

Pickled Ancho Chiles Stuffed with Tuna
Rellenos de Chiles Anchos en Escabeche con Atún

Makes **4 servings**

It was with enthusiastic amazement that I ate stuffed ancho chiles for the first time in a restaurant in the 1970s, when I ordered chiles rellenos and the dish arrived made with dried anchos instead of fresh green chiles. That day I learned a whole new way to use these dried red chiles. Several years later, I enjoyed them again in another classic dish as prepared by Chef Miguel Ravego of Austin, Texas. This recipe follows his technique. Serve as a first course salad.

4 large blemish-free ancho chiles of equal size

1 cup red wine vinegar

1 cup water

2 tablespoons dark brown sugar

2 bay leaves

1/2 teaspoon allspice berries

4 whole cloves

1/2 teaspoon dried oregano (Mexican variety preferred)

2 (about 3-inch-long) fresh mint sprigs

2 tablespoons olive oil

1 (9-ounce) can solid white tuna, drained

3 tablespoons mayonnaise

1 teaspoon fresh lime juice

Small lettuce leaves, such as red leaf or butter lettuce

1/4 cup crumbled queso fresco (fresh Mexican cheese)

Chopped fresh cilantro

1. Wipe the chiles with a damp paper towel to remove dust. In a hot dry skillet warm the chiles briefly until they soften and are pliable. Slit the chiles down 1 side, seed, and devein, leaving the stems intact. Reserve. In a medium saucepan, bring to a boil the vinegar, water, brown sugar, bay leaf, allspice berries, and oregano. Remove the pan from the heat. Add the reserved chiles, fresh mint, and olive oil. Cover and marinate at room temperature, turning gently once or twice, 6 to 8 hours.

2. About 1 hour before serving, mix the tuna, mayonnaise, and lime juice in a medium bowl. Drain the chiles and discard the marinade. Stuff the chiles equally with the tuna. The marinated chiles are fragile, so handle very gently to prevent tearing them. Place 1 stuffed chile on each of 4 serving plates. Garnish with lettuce leaves. Sprinkle with crumbled cheese and chopped cilantro. Serve at once.

Scallops and Avocado in Red Pepper Sauce
Callos y Aguacate en Salsa de Chile Rojo Dulce

Makes **4 servings**

Along the Malecon (seaside walkway) in Mazatlán, there are a number of restaurants serving ocean-fresh seafood of all kinds. Eating scallop ceviche with avocado prompted me to create this version. I present the dish in an elegant new style.

Red Bell Pepper Sauce (page 61)
1 large vine-ripened tomato, peeled and chopped
1 serrano chile, chopped with seeds
1 tablespoon olive oil
8 sea scallops, cut horizontally into 3 slices
1/2 teaspoon salt, or to taste
3 tablespoons fresh lime juice
2 ripe avocados (Hass variety preferred), peeled and sliced lengthwise
Cilantro sprigs

1. Prepare the bell pepper sauce, adding the tomato and the serrano chile to the blender when puréeing the sauce. Strain the sauce as directed in the recipe. Adjust salt. Cover and refrigerate the sauce until cold.

2. In a large nonstick skillet, heat the oil over medium heat and cook the scallops, turning once, just until firm, (but do not brown), about 1 minute. Transfer to a plate to cool. Add salt and drizzle with half of the lime juice, turning to coat. Drizzle the remaining lime juice on the avocado slices.

3. To serve, pour about ⅓ cup of the red pepper sauce in the center of each of 4 salad plates. Tilt the plates to pool the sauce. Arrange the avocado slices equally on the sauce, in a fan shape, among the plates. Arrange the scallops equally on top. Garnish each plate with a sprig of cilantro. Serve cold.

Scallop, Orange, and Avocado Salad
Ensalada de Callos, Naranja y Aguacate

Makes **4 servings**

This pretty scallop salad is typical of specialties found along the Mexican seacoast.

3/4 pound (about 80) tiny bay scallops
1 tablespoon plus 2 teaspoons fresh lime juice
4 cups finely shredded romaine lettuce
1 large avocado (Hass variety preferred), peeled and cut into 1/2-inch dice
1 orange, peeled and cut into 1/2-inch pieces
1 serrano chile, stemmed and finely chopped with seeds
2 tablespoons chopped fresh cilantro
3 teaspoons light olive oil or vegetable oil
1 teaspoon white wine vinegar
1/2 teaspoon salt, or to taste

1. In a medium saucepan, bring about 1 quart of water to a boil. Add the scallops, reduce the heat to low, and cook the scallops until just opaque throughout, 45 to 50 seconds. (Do not overcook.) Cool under running water. Drain well, and put in a bowl. Stir in 1 tablespoon of the lime juice. Set aside.

2. In a large bowl, put the lettuce, avocado, orange, serrano, cilantro, and the reserved scallops. Add the remaining 2 teaspoons of lime juice, oil, vinegar, and salt. Toss gently to coat the salad with the dressing. Serve at once.

Lobster Salad

Ensalada de Langosta

Makes 4 servings

Using fresh lobster is best, but frozen uncooked lobster tails work very well in this simple appetizer salad that allows the lobster to stand out. The idea for the salad comes from El Rey Sol restaurant in Ensenada.

2 teaspoons Dijon mustard

2 tablespoons unseasoned rice vinegar

2 tablespoons fresh orange juice

3 tablespoons olive oil

1/2 teaspoon salt, or to taste

4 spiny or Pacific uncooked lobster tails (thawed, if frozen)

4 cups finely shredded romaine lettuce

1 ripe avocado (Hass variety preferred), peeled and cut into 3/4-inch dice

Tomato wedges or cherry tomatoes

1. In a small bowl, whisk together the mustard, vinegar, and orange juice. Gradually whisk in the oil. Season with salt and pepper. Reserve.

2. Bring a large pot of salted water to a boil. Add the lobster tails and cook 8 minutes. Cool in cold water. Drain; then cut the shells open and remove the meat. Cut the lobster meat crosswise and put into a bowl. Mix lobster with 1½ tablespoons of the reserved dressing and set aside. In another bowl, mix the greens and avocado with the remaining dressing. Adjust salt. Divide the salad among 4 serving plates. Arrange the lobster meat evenly on top of each salad. Garnish with tomato wedges. Serve.

Octopus Salad

Ensalada de Pulpo

Makes 4 servings

For years I watched others enjoy octopus in salads and seafood cocktails, until I finally tasted an octopus salad in Merida, and I enjoyed its mild and pleasant flavor.

Specialty fish markets often carry cleaned fresh or frozen octopus. Young, small octopus, about 1½ to 2 pounds, is the most tender and desirable. Small whole octopus should cook slowly for about one hour for the best texture.

1 (1½- to 2-pound) octopus, cleaned

1 teaspoon salt, or to taste

2 tablespoons olive oil

1 tablespoon fresh lime juice

2 teaspoons unseasoned rice vinegar

1/8 teaspoon freshly ground pepper, or to taste

2 medium tomatoes, chopped

1/4 medium white onion, finely chopped

1 to 2 jalapeño chiles, seeded, veins removed, and finely chopped

1 to 2 medium garlic cloves, minced

1/4 cup lightly packed chopped fresh cilantro

3 cups shredded lettuce, such as romaine or iceberg

1 large avocado (Hass variety preferred), peeled and diced

1. In a large saucepan, bring about 2 quarts water to a boil. Add the octopus and ½ teaspoon of the salt. Cover, and simmer over medium-low heat until tender, about 45 minutes to 1 hour. Drain and cool the octopus; then cut into ¾-inch pieces and put into a large bowl.

2. Add the oil, lime juice, vinegar, the remaining ½ teaspoon of salt, and pepper. Stir to mix. Cover and refrigerate at least 1 hour and up to 6 hours. Shortly before serving add the tomatoes, onion, jalapeños, garlic, cilantro, and avocado. Toss gently. Make a bed of lettuce on a platter. Mound the salad on the lettuce. Serve at once.

Fish Fillet Salad with Avocado-Tomatillo Dressing
Salpicón de Pescado con Salsa de Aguacate y Tomatillo
Makes **4 small servings**

Cold fish salad called salpicón *is quite typical along the Veracruz seacoast. The fish is cooked, shredded, and combined with vegetables and a salsa or dressing. Any firm white fish may be used for this delicious* salpicón. *Serve as a first course with crusty rolls.*

Avocado and Tomatillo Sauce (page 24)
1 pound boneless fish fillets, such as halibut or sea bass
¹/₄ white onion, sliced
2 garlic cloves, peeled and thinly sliced
2 sprigs parsley
¹/₂ teaspoon salt
1 medium carrot, peeled, finely diced, and boiled for 2 minutes
1 medium tomato, cored, seeded, and diced
1 to 2 jarred pickled jalapeño chiles (en escabeche), seeded, veins removed, and very thinly sliced
2 tablespoons chopped fresh cilantro

1. Prepare the avocado-tomatillo sauce. Cover and reserve in a bowl. Pour 1½ cups water in a skillet large enough to hold the fish in one layer. Add the onion, garlic, parsley, and salt. Bring to a boil over medium heat and cook 3 minutes. Add the fish and cook, turning after 5 minutes. Continue cooking 3 to 5 minutes more or until the fish is opaque in the thickest part. Remove the fish and cool completely; then break the fish apart by hand into small pieces, and put in a bowl.

2. Add the cooked carrot and about ½ cup of the avocado salsa to the bowl. Toss gently to mix. Adjust salt. Mound the fish on a round serving plate. Scatter the tomato, jalapeños, and cilantro over the top. Serve cold; pass the remaining avocado salsa at the table.

Bean and Grain Salads

Marinated Black Bean Salad
Ensalada de Frijoles Negro
Makes **8 servings**

Although beans have been part of Mexican meals for centuries—usually served hot with or after a meal—only recently have they been used to make delectable salads. Black beans are an excellent salad choice.

To help the beans hold their shape while cooking, I use a cook-soak method allowing the starches to expand slowly, keeping the skins intact. If you pay attention to the cooking, the beans should be whole and tender when finished.

1 pound dried black beans
2 bay leaves
1 teaspoon dried oregano (Mexican variety preferred), crumbled
2 medium tomatoes, seeded and chopped
3 finely chopped green onions
2 to 3 serrano chiles, finely chopped with seeds
¹/₄ cup olive oil
2 to 3 tablespoons white wine vinegar
2 tablespoons chopped fresh cilantro
1 teaspoon ground cumin
¹/₂ teaspoon salt, or to taste
¹/₄ teaspoon freshly ground pepper, or to taste

1. Sort the beans. Remove any dirt, straw, pebbles, etc. Put the beans in a fine-mesh strainer and rinse well, then put them into a large pot with water to cover by about 3 inches. Add the bay leaves and oregano. Bring to a boil, uncovered. Lower the heat and simmer, uncovered, 10 minutes. Turn off the heat. Cover and soak 30 minutes.

2. Bring to a boil again, and simmer slowly, partially covered, until the beans are tender, but not too soft, about 1 hour to 1 hour and 20 minutes.

1. Drain off the bean broth and save for soup, if desired, or discard. Put the beans into a large mixing bowl. Cool to room temperature. Add the remaining ingredients and mix gently. Cover and refrigerate at least 1 hour. Adjust seasoning.

Lupe's Bean Salad
Lupe's Ensalada de Frijoles

Makes **4 servings**

Lupe Fregoso, a friend all through my school days, invited me to have lunch in her home when we were about nine years old. It may have been my first taste of Mexican food. Although I have long forgotten what else we had, I vividly remember the bean salad, and soft, warm, corn tortillas that we ate with the salad as you would a piece of bread. The Fregoso family was from the state of Jalisco, near Guadalajara, and the salad probably reflected what native ingredients were available to her family in our northern California home. Although authentic Mexican ingredients are now more readily available, this simple salad, based on memory, is good even today, especially with the warm tortillas.

4 cups chopped or torn lettuce, such as iceberg or romaine

1 cup cooked and drained red kidney beans, canned or homemade

1 medium tomato, chopped

2 green onions, finely chopped

1/2 teaspoon ground cumin

1/4 teaspoon salt, or to taste

1/8 teaspoon freshly ground pepper, or to taste

1 tablespoon mayonnaise

2 to 3 jarred pickled jalapeño chiles (en escabeche), seeded, veins removed, and cut into thin strips

Put all of the ingredients in a large bowl, except the mayonnaise and chiles. Gently mix in the mayonnaise. Add the chiles to the salad, or put the strips of jalapeños on a small plate to be eaten at the table, if desired.

Chickpea and Roasted Green Chile Salad
Ensalada de Garbanzo y Chiles Verdes

Makes **6 servings**

Mexican home cooks appreciate the convenience of canned chickpeas just as we do. This was inspired by a recipe in Cocina Rapida, *a Mexican food magazine. I lightened the salad by changing the creamy dressy to a vinaigrette.*

4 fresh Anaheim chiles, roasted, peeled, seeded, and veins removed (page 8)

2 (15-ounce) cans chickpeas (garbanzo beans), drained and rinsed

2 medium tomatoes, cored and finely chopped

1/2 cup loosely packed chopped fresh cilantro

2 tablespoons finely chopped red or white onion

3 tablespoons olive oil

2 tablespoons fresh lime juice

1 tablespoon unseasoned rice vinegar

1 teaspoon Dijon mustard

1 teaspoon ground cumin

1/2 teaspoon salt, or to taste

1/8 teaspoon freshly ground pepper, or to taste

Prepare the chiles. Cut the roasted chiles into 1/2-inch squares and put them into a large bowl. Add all the remaining ingredients and toss to mix. Adjust seasoning. Serve cold.

Chickpea, Tomato, and Pickled Red Onion Salad
Ensalada de Garbanzo, Jitomate y Cebollas en Escabeche

Makes **4 servings**

Chickpeas (garbanzos in Spanish) are widely used throughout Mexico in soups, stews, salads, and even in sweet cakes. Canned chickpeas are fine for this salad, but vine-ripened tomatoes are important for the best flavor. Queso fresco (fresh Mexican cheese) is available in many supermarkets.

1 red onion, pickled (Pickled Red Onions, page 19)
1 (15-ounce) can chickpeas, drained and rinsed
3 medium tomatoes, seeded and finely diced
2 teaspoons red wine vinegar
¹/₂ teaspoon salt, or to taste
1 tablespoon olive oil
Freshly ground black pepper, to taste
¹/₄ cup crumbled queso fresco (fresh Mexican cheese)

Prepare the pickled red onion and let marinate at least 1 hour. Reserve in a small bowl. In a large bowl combine the chickpeas, tomatoes, vinegar, salt, olive oil, and pepper. Drain the onions and add to the salad along with the crumbled cheese. Toss gently to mix. Serve cold or at room temperature.

Fresh Fava Bean Salad
Ensalada de Fabas

Makes **4 servings**

Years ago, during a visit in late Spring to Guadalajara when fresh fava beans were in season, I was fascinated by the baskets and boxes brimming with fresh fabas (broad beans or fava beans) for sale in the public market.

At that time, fresh fava beans were a novelty to me, but now many supermarkets and farmer's markets in the United States feature them when in season. Fresh fava beans must be shelled, just like peas, and then boiled for a few minutes. The thin outer skin is then removed to reveal the bright green, mild-tasting bean inside. Modern chefs love to use them in salads or as a garnish on artistically presented plates. For this salad the beans are marinated and served cold.

1³/₄ pounds unshelled fresh fava beans
1 red jalapeño chile, seeded, veins removed, and finely chopped, or ¹/₄ finely chopped red bell pepper (or both, if you wish)
1 finely chopped green onion
2 teaspoons fresh mint, finely chopped
1 tablespoon chopped fresh cilantro
¹/₂ teaspoon ground cumin
3 teaspoons white wine vinegar
2 tablespoons extra-virgin olive oil
Salt and freshly ground pepper, to taste
2 cups finely shredded iceberg lettuce

1. In a pot of boiling salted water, cook the shelled fava beans until crisp-tender, 12 to 15 minutes. Drain and rinse under cold running water. Remove the thin outer skin by pinching the beans. The skins usually slip off quite easily. Put the peeled beans in a large bowl.

2. Add all of the remaining ingredients, except the lettuce. Toss to mix. Adjust the seasoning. Add the lettuce and toss again. Divide among 4 serving plates. Serve cold.

Rice Salad
Ensalada de Arroz

Makes **6 servings**

Rice salad, dressed very simply in vinaigrette and a few capers can be served with Yucatán Cold Spiced Turkey (page 317). It also goes well with grilled or sautéed fish. Rice salad is a good traveler to pack for a picnic.

¹/₃ cup olive oil
1 cup long grain white rice
¹/₄ cup fresh orange juice
2 tablespoons unseasoned rice vinegar
¹/₂ teaspoon salt, or to taste
¹/₄ teaspoon freshly ground pepper, or to taste
4 green onions, finely chopped
¹/₄ cup loosely packed chopped fresh cilantro
2 tablespoons capers, drained but not rinsed
Radishes
Pimiento-stuffed green olives
Romaine lettuce leaves (small inner leaves)

1. In a wide 2-quart saucepan, heat 1 tablespoon of the oil over medium heat and cook the rice, stirring, until aromatic, about 3 minutes. Add 2 cups warm tap water and bring to a boil. Stir to settle the rice and bring to a boil again. Reduce the heat to low, cover, and cook until the liquid is absorbed and the rice is tender, about 20 minutes. Fluff with a fork and let the rice stand 10 minutes. Transfer to a large bowl and cool to room temperature, about 20 minutes.

2. Meanwhile, in a bowl, combine the remaining oil with the orange juice, vinegar, salt, and pepper. Whisk to blend well. When the rice is cool, add the onions, cilantro, capers, and dressing. Toss to mix. Adjust seasoning. Mound the salad on a serving plate. Garnish with radishes, olives, and small lettuce leaves. Serve at room temperature. The salad can be made ahead and refrigerated for 4 to 6 hours.

Rice and Corn Mushrooms with Avocado and Shrimp
Arroz y Cuitlacoche con Aguacate y Camarónes

Makes **4 servings**

El Sacromonte in Guadalajara is an elegant restaurant that serves inventive and gorgeously presented nueva cocina *(new-style cooking) dishes. We were really impressed with this fancy first course, formed in a ring with a crown of shrimp on top, and wanted to reproduce it at home. Donna Nordin, my good friend, traveling partner, and the owner-chef of Café Terra Cotta in Arizona, developed this recipe. It's as good as we remembered.*

Cuitlacoche, *a kind of mushroom that grows on corn in the rainy season, is available in cans in some Mexican markets. Adelita or Herdez brands are both good. For the ring, use an empty 6-ounce tuna fish can, opened on both ends and thoroughly washed.*

2 teaspoons olive oil, plus more to coat ring
12 large shrimp, peeled and deveined
¹/₂ can (about 4 ounces) cuitlacoche
2 cups canned fat-free reduced-sodium chicken broth
1 cup long-grain white rice
¹/₂ teaspoon salt
2 large ripe avocados (Hass variety preferred), peeled
2 teaspoons fresh lime juice
Salt and freshly ground pepper, to taste
Cilantro sprigs
3 medium tomatoes, seeded and neatly diced (¹/₄ inch)

1. Rub a film of oil on the inside of the "ring" to form the layers of rice and avocado. Reserve. Preheat oven broiler. Brush each shrimp with oil and place the shrimp on a baking sheet. Sprinkle lightly with salt. Broil the shrimp until pink and curled, 2 to 3 minutes. Reserve refrigerated.

2. Coarsely chop the cuitlacoche in a food processor and scrape into a bowl. Put the chicken broth, rice, salt, and about 2 tablespoons of the cuitlacoche in a saucepan and bring to a boil. Reduce the heat to low, cover, and simmer for 20 minutes, or until the liquid has evaporated and the rice is tender. Remove the pan from the heat and stir in the remaining cuitlacoche. Cool to room temperature.

3. Meanwhile, mash the avocados with the lime juice. Season with salt and pepper. Set aside.

4. To serve, place the ring in the center of a serving plate. Hold the ring in place with one hand and spoon in rice to ¾ full, pressing down with the back of the spoon. Spoon avocado on top of the rice to fill the ring, spreading it flat. Slide the ring straight up to remove. Crown the top with 3 shrimp. Place a long sprig of cilantro in the center. Carefully spoon the diced tomato around the rice. Wipe out the ring, and rub with oil. Repeat for the other 3 servings. Serve at once.

Dressings

Basic Vinaigrette
Vinagreta

Makes **about 1 cup**

A basic vinaigrette in Mexican cuisine is a simple oil, vinegar, salt, and pepper combination. It brightens the flavors of all kinds of salads and cold vegetables. The olive oil adds richer flavor.

¾ cup extra-virgin olive oil
¼ cup white or red wine vinegar
¼ to ½ teaspoon salt, or to taste
⅛ teaspoon freshly ground pepper, or to taste

Whisk all of the ingredients together in a bowl, or put all of the ingredients in a half-pint jar and shake vigorously. If the dressing separates before using, shake again. Dressing keeps refrigerated for 2 to 3 weeks.

Herbed Vinaigrette
Vinagreta por Ensalada

Makes **about ½ cup**

When fresh herbs are in season or readily available, use them to make a flavorful, wonderfully refreshing salad dressing.

2 tablespoons white wine vinegar
½ teaspoon Dijon mustard
2 tablespoons coarsely chopped fresh cilantro
1 tablespoon fresh oregano leaves, or ½ teaspoon dried oregano (Mexican variety preferred)
½ teaspoon ground cumin
¼ teaspoon salt, or to taste
⅓ cup extra-virgin olive oil

Put all of the ingredients in a blender and purée until smooth. Adjust seasoning. Dressing keeps 3 to 5 days refrigerated.

Mango Vinaigrette
Vinagreta de Mango

Makes about 1 cup

Nueva cocina has changed the menus of many modern restaurants. Consequently, salads have become more popular, inspiring creative dressings. Spoon the mango dressing over cold, crisp leafy greens or on grilled chicken breasts or fish fillets. Mexican vinegars, often made from pineapple, are light and not very sour. Unseasoned rice vinegar is the substitute I prefer.

1/2 cup chopped ripe fresh mango
2 tablespoons fresh lime juice
1 tablespoon unseasoned rice vinegar
1 teaspoon sugar
1/8 teaspoon ground cinnamon (Mexican canela or Ceylon variety preferred)
Pinch salt
3 tablespoons vegetable oil or olive oil

Put all of the ingredients in a blender and blend until smooth. Transfer to a bowl. Adjust seasoning. Use within one day.

Salsa Vinaigrette
Vinagreta de Salsa

Makes about 1 cup

Vinaigrette made with the ingredients typical to a salsa makes a lively dressing. Try it with tossed greens or even with one of my favorites, Mushroom and Avocado Salad (page 178).

1 large vine-ripened tomato, peeled, seeded, and chopped
2 tablespoons chopped white onion
1 serrano chile chopped with seeds
2 tablespoons fresh lime juice
1 tablespoon chopped fresh cilantro
1/4 teaspoon salt, or to taste
1/4 cup olive oil or vegetable oil

Put all of the ingredients, except the oil, in a blender. Blend until smooth. With the motor running, pour the oil through the lid opening and blend until emulsified. Adjust salt. Transfer to a jar. Cover and refrigerate up to 2 days.

Orange-Chipotle Vinaigrette
Vinaigrette de Naranja-Chipotle

Makes about 1/3 cup

Chipotle chile enlivens the taste of this dressing that's wonderful with tossed greens or drizzled over grilled or fried fish fillets.

2 tablespoons fresh orange juice
1 teaspoon orange zest
2 teaspoons unseasoned rice vinegar
1/2 teaspoon mashed canned chipotle en adobo
1/4 teaspoon salt
2 tablespoons olive oil

In a small bowl whisk together the orange juice, zest, vinegar, chipotle, and salt. Whisk in the oil until thoroughly mixed. Use fresh or store in the refrigerator up to 2 days.

Soups

exican soups are among the world's best, and they are a very important part of the cuisine. The Mexican kitchen has created a delicious variety of soups that fit almost any menu. Mexican soups are often categorized as *caldo* (a meat-, chicken-, or fish-broth soup with vegetables, herbs, and spices*); sopa* (soup or chowder); *crema* (puréed soup of vegetables which is usually, but not always, enriched with cream); *pozole* (hearty soup of dried corn [hominy], and pork or chicken, with fresh garnishes of lettuce or cabbage, radishes, and often avocado).

This chapter offers a sampler of both classic and innovative Mexican recipes. Tortilla soups, which include strips of crisp tortillas plus other savory ingredients, are very popular, and there are several here, including versions with chicken, the classic, as well as with shrimp, and with pork and vegetables. Other classics, such as Black Bean Soup (page 248) and Cream of Fresh Corn and Poblano Chile Soup

(page 253) are also delicious starters. Another favorite is Pork and Red Chile Hominy Soup (page 224), a rich and spicy broth with hominy and pork that's great to serve to a crowd. Fava Bean Soup (page 247), Winter Squash Soup (page 262), and Cauliflower and Pecan Soup (page 257) are special comfort soups while cold soups like Mexican Gazpacho (page 265) and Avocado Soup (page 266) are welcome and cooling on a hot day.

Eating soup in Mexico is not just about what fills the bowl, but also what it's served with. Fresh garnishes like avocado, tomato, shredded lettuce or cabbage, chopped onion, or chiles, and a refreshing dash of fresh lime juice, add layers of flavor and texture that each person can tailor to her or his taste.

Most of the soups in this chapter are really easy to make and many taste even better if made ahead, so when you plan a Mexican meal, do include soup.

Basic Broths

Basic Chicken Stock
Caldo de Pollo

Makes **about 2 quarts**

This stock is a terrific base for soups or stews, and the cooked chicken meat is shredded to use for enchiladas, tacos, tortas, soups, and in many other ways. I sometimes enhance my stock by adding a 14-ounce can of fat-free reduced-sodium chicken broth, for a more pronounced flavor.

1 (3-pound) chicken, cut into pieces
1 medium white onion, sliced
1 large carrot, scrubbed and sliced (do not peel)
1 celery rib, sliced
3 medium garlic cloves, peeled
2 bay leaves
2 parsley sprigs
8 black peppercorns, cracked
1/2 teaspoon salt

1. Put the chicken in a large pot with 2½ quarts of water. Bring to a boil; then reduce the heat, and simmer, skimming any foam that rises to the surface.

2. Add all of the remaining ingredients, reduce the heat, and simmer, partially covered, 1 hour. Remove the chicken pieces to a platter.

3. When cool, remove the meat from the bones. Discard the bones and shred the meat. Cover and refrigerate. Strain the stock through a strainer, and discard the solids. When the stock is cool, skim the fat from the top. Cover and refrigerate for up to 3 days, or freeze for up to 3 months.

Basic Fish Stock
Caldo de Pescado

Makes **about 2 quarts**

Fish stock is quite easy to make and will improve the flavor of fine fish soups and stews. Chicken broth can be used instead and it's quite satisfactory (without distorting the desired fish flavor). I'm not wild about bottled clam juice and never use it in place of fish stock or chicken broth.

An all-purpose fish stock is made with the bones and heads of mild-flavored white fish. Salmon, for example, makes a much stronger flavored stock that is fine if making a soup or other dish containing salmon; otherwise the general rule is to use the bones and heads of white fish. Buy fish stock bones from a reliable fishmonger. Remove the red gills from the heads, or ask the fishmonger to do it for you. The gills give an undesirable flavor to the stock.

3 pounds white fish heads, frames or bones, skinned and fins and gills removed
2 tablespoons olive oil
1 large white onion, coarsely chopped
2 green onions, chopped including the green part
1 medium carrot, scrubbed and sliced
1 cup dry white wine
2 bay leaves
2 parsley sprigs
1 teaspoon dried oregano (Mexican variety preferred), crumbled
6 cups water

1. Heat the oil in a large pot. Add the onions and carrot. Cook, stirring, 3 minutes. Add the fish bones and all the remaining ingredients. Bring to a simmer over medium-low heat, skimming the foam that comes to the surface. Partially cover and simmer 30 minutes.

2. Strain the stock through a strainer into a bowl, pressing to recover the juices. Discard all the debris from the strainer. Cool the stock. Refrigerate in a covered container, for 3 days, or freeze for 3 months.

Cheese in Tomato Broth
Quesilla

Makes 4 servings

*Marilyn Tausend, owner of Culinary Adventures,
introduced me to El Bajio in Mexico City. This
delightful restaurant, owned and operated by
Chef Carmen Ramirez Degollado and her
daughter Maria Carmen Degollado, serves excellent authentic Mexican food. During a recent
visit, our group enjoyed a magnificent brunch
of several courses. A fresh tomato broth topped
with fat strips of panela, a fresh tender cheese,
was served with soft corn tortillas. It was
unusual and delicious. Fresh epazote leaves
garnished the broth and imparted their distinctive taste and a touch of green. If epazote is not
available, add fresh cilantro leaves instead. The
flavor is different, but still good.*

4 vine-ripened medium tomatoes, cored and
    cut into chunks
1/4 red bell pepper, coarsely chopped
2 tablespoons chopped white onion
1 serrano chile, chopped with seeds
2 medium garlic cloves, sliced
1/4 teaspoon salt, or to taste
8 fat strips (about 2-inches long × 1/2-inch wide)
    panela cheese, or substitute queso fresco
    (fresh Mexican cheese)
8 epazote leaves, or substitute cilantro leaves
Corn tortillas

1. In a blender, purée the tomatoes, red pepper,
onion, serrano, garlic, and 1/4 cup water until
smooth. Transfer to a saucepan. Bring to a boil,
reduce the heat to low, and simmer, covered,
20 minutes to cook the ingredients and blend
the flavors. Season with salt. Cool the mixture
10 minutes and return to the blender. Blend until
very smooth.

2. Pour the broth through a fine-mesh strainer
back into the saucepan, pressing to extract the
pulp and juices. Discard the bits of skin and seeds
in the strainer. Bring the broth to a boil, reduce
the heat to low, and simmer 5 minutes. Adjust
seasoning. Divide the broth among 4 small shallow serving bowls. Place 2 strips of cheese side by
side in each bowl. Place 1 epazote leaf on each
piece of cheese. Serve hot.

Note: If cheese is so tender that it cracks or falls apart, just
arrange chunks in the center of the bowls and top with epazote.

Chicken and Turkey Soups

Tortilla Soup
Sopa de Tortilla

Makes **8 servings**

Tortilla soup is a classic and there are many versions. Sometimes the soup contains shredded chicken and sometimes not. It depends on the whim of the cook or whether the poached chicken that creates the flavorful broth is needed for enchiladas or some other dish. After the chicken is cooked to make the broth, the decision is yours. The soup is delicious either way.

8 (6- to 7-inch) corn tortillas, cut into strips
    (Fried Corn Tortilla Chips and Strips, page 85)

2 quarts Basic Chicken Stock (page 215)

2 ancho chiles, seeded and veins removed

3 medium tomatoes, peeled and chopped

2 tablespoons vegetable oil

1 medium white onion, thinly sliced

3 medium garlic cloves, finely chopped

1 teaspoon dried oregano (Mexican variety
    preferred), crumbled

1 teaspoon ground cumin

1 medium carrot, thinly sliced

$1/2$ teaspoon salt, or to taste

3 tablespoons chopped fresh cilantro

1 large avocado (Hass variety preferred),
    peeled and diced

1 cup cubed Monterey Jack cheese

2 limes, each cut into 4 wedges

1. Prepare the tortilla strips and set aside. Prepare the chicken stock and set aside. Soak the chiles in hot water for about 20 minutes. Purée the soaked chiles and tomatoes in a blender. Reserve in the blender.

2. In a large pot heat the oil and fry the onion until softened, 3 to 4 minutes. Add the garlic, oregano, cumin, and the reserved puréed chiles and tomatoes. Cook, stirring, until the mixture thickens, about 5 minutes. Add the chicken stock, carrot, and salt. Bring the soup to a boil, then reduce the heat to low, cover and simmer until the carrot is tender and the flavors marry, about 20 minutes.

3. To serve, divide tortilla strips among soup bowls. Ladle hot soup over the tortillas. Sprinkle each serving with cilantro. Pass the avocado, cheese, and lime wedges separately for each person to add at the table.

Note: If you wish, shred about 1 cup of cooked chicken (from poaching the chicken), and stir into the soup at the time you add the carrot.

Yucatán Lime Soup
Sopa de Lima

Makes **4 servings**

Sour limes called limas agrias *are traditionally used in this terrific Yucatán soup, but any fresh lime will give the soup its distinctive tart flavor.* Sopa de Lima *is the Yucatán version of tortilla soup. Crisp fried strips of corn tortillas are added to the soup just before serving.*

4 (6- to 7-inch) corn tortillas, several days old, cut into thin strips and fried (Fried Corn Tortilla Chips and Strips, page 85)

2 skinless chicken breast halves, on the bone

2 (14¹/₂-ounce) cans fat-free reduced-sodium chicken broth

4 medium garlic cloves, thinly sliced

2 parsley sprigs

1 medium white onion, chopped

2 medium tomatoes, peeled and chopped

1 jalapeño chile, seeded, veins removed, and chopped

1 teaspoon dried oregano (Mexican variety preferred), crumbled

1 teaspoon salt

¹/₃ cup fresh lime juice

¹/₄ cup lightly packed coarsely chopped fresh cilantro

1 large avocado (Hass variety preferred), peeled and thinly sliced

1. Fry the tortilla strips in batches until crisp and golden brown, about 30 seconds for each batch. Drain on paper towels.

2. Put the chicken breasts, chicken broth, garlic, and parsley in a medium saucepan. Bring to a boil; then reduce the heat and simmer until the chicken is white throughout, about 15 minutes. Cool the chicken in the broth 20 minutes; pull the meat off the bone and shred coarsely. Reserve on a plate. Discard the bones. Strain the chicken broth through a strainer into a medium bowl and reserve.

3. In a large soup pot, heat 1 tablespoon of the oil from frying the tortillas and cook the onion until softened, about 3 minutes. Add the tomatoes, jalapeño, and oregano. Cook, stirring, until the juices reduce and the mixture is nearly dry, about 5 minutes. Add the reserved chicken broth, shredded chicken, salt, lime juice, and cilantro. Bring to a boil; then reduce the heat and simmer 5 minutes. To serve, divide the tortilla strips among 4 soup bowls. Ladle the soup over the tortillas. Divide the avocado slices among the bowls. Serve hot.

Turkey Tortilla Soup
Sopa de Tortilla con Pavo

Makes **4 servings**

Have leftover turkey? Make turkey soup with vegetables and crisp strips of fried tortillas. It's a meal in a bowl.

4 (6- to 7-inch) corn tortillas, cut into thin strips ¹/₄ inch wide and fried (Fried Corn Tortilla Chips and Strips, page 85)

¹/₂ medium white onion, chopped

2 medium garlic cloves, finely chopped

¹/₂ teaspoon dried oregano (Mexican variety preferred), crumbled

¹/₄ teaspoon dried marjoram

4 cups turkey broth (from Basic Cooked Turkey Breast, page 311)

1 tablespoon tomato paste

1 to 2 teaspoons pasilla or ancho chili powder

¹/₄ pound thin green beans, cut into 1-inch pieces

2 medium carrots, peeled and thinly sliced crosswise

1 cup shredded or diced turkey meat

¹/₄ teaspoon salt, or to taste

2 tablespoons chopped fresh cilantro

1 lime, cut into wedges

. Fry the tortilla strips until crisp and light brown. Drain on paper towels. Add 1 tablespoon of the frying oil to a large saucepan and cook the onion and garlic until they begin to brown, 3 to 4 minutes. Add the oregano, marjoram, broth, tomato paste, and ground chile. Bring to a boil over medium-high heat.

2. Add the beans and carrots. Cook, over medium heat, until the vegetables are tender, about 12 minutes. Add the turkey and salt. Cook until the soup is completely heated through, 4 to 5 minutes.

3. Divide the tortilla strips among 4 soup bowls. Ladle the hot soup into the bowls. Garnish with cilantro. Serve with lime wedges.

Chicken and Rice Soup
Sopa Xochitl

Makes **4 servings**

I've enjoyed many variations of this classic soup, but Chef Joaquim Castillo of Casa Vieja restaurant in Tlaquepaque, located just outside Guadalajara, gets my vote for this light and spicy version.

1 cup cooked Rice with Carrots (page 473)

2 chicken breast halves on the bone

4 cups canned fat-free reduced-sodium chicken broth

1/4 cup finely diced celery

1/2 teaspoon dried oregano (Mexican variety preferred)

1/4 medium white onion, finely chopped

1 medium tomato, seeded and finely chopped

1 tablespoon chopped fresh cilantro

1 to 2 serrano chiles, thinly sliced crosswise with seeds

1 teaspoon fresh lime juice

1/4 teaspoon salt, or to taste

1 avocado (Hass variety preferred), sliced crosswise

1. Prepare rice then reserve 1 cup for the soup. Cover and refrigerate remaining rice for later use. Remove the chicken skin and discard. Put the chicken in a large saucepan. Add the chicken broth, celery, and oregano. Bring to a boil, skimming the foam as needed, then reduce the heat, cover, and simmer until the chicken is cooked through, about 20 minutes. Remove the pan from the heat and let chicken sit in the broth about 10 minutes.

2. Meanwhile, mix together in a medium bowl the onion, tomato, cilantro, serrano chile, lime juice and salt. Set aside. Remove the chicken from the broth, and when cool enough to handle, pull the meat off the bone and shred coarsely. Discard the bones and return the shredded meat to the broth in the pan. Add the reserved cooked rice and the tomato mixture. Bring the soup to a boil. Reduce the heat and simmer the soup, uncovered, 5 minutes. Divide hot soup among 4 bowls. Top with avocado slices and serve.

Corn and Chicken Soup
Sopa de Elote y Pollo

Makes 4 servings

This chile-flavored broth, brimming with corn, tomato, onion, and shredded chicken, is substantial enough for a light meal.

2 tablespoons olive oil or vegetable oil

1/2 large white onion, chopped

2 medium garlic cloves, thinly sliced

2 teaspoons pure ancho or pasilla chili powder

1 teaspoon ground cumin

1 teaspoon dried oregano (Mexican variety preferred), crumbled

4 plum tomatoes, peeled and finely diced

4 cups canned fat-free reduced-sodium chicken broth

1/2 teaspoon salt, or to taste

2 small skinless boneless chicken breast halves

1 cup fresh corn (from about 1 ear) or frozen corn kernels

2 green onions, sliced crosswise

Chopped fresh cilantro

1 lime, cut into wedges

1. Heat the oil in a large heavy pot. Add the onion and cook, stirring, until the edges start to brown, 3 to 4 minutes. Add the garlic, chili powder, cumin, oregano, and tomatoes. Cook, stirring frequently, until the tomato juices have evaporated and the mixture is almost dry, 3 to 4 minutes. Add the broth and salt. Bring to a boil. Add the chicken. Cover the pan, reduce the heat to low, and simmer until the chicken is cooked through, about 10 minutes.

2. Using tongs, remove the chicken breasts, cool, then shred the meat. Add the corn and green onions. Cook 3 minutes. Return the chicken to the pan and cook 3 more minutes. Serve hot, garnished with chopped cilantro and lime wedges.

Chicken and Vegetable Soup
Sopa de Pollo y Verduras

Makes 4 servings

In this soup, some of the vegetables are puréed for extra body and some are shredded and added later along with the shredded chicken, for texture and color. The result is lush and satisfying.

2 skinless boneless chicken breast halves

4 cups canned fat-free reduced-sodium chicken broth

1 tablespoon olive oil

1 medium onion, chopped

2 large garlic cloves, chopped

1/2 teaspoon dried oregano (Mexican variety preferred), crumbled

1 medium (8-ounce) russet potato, peeled and thinly sliced

1/8 teaspoon crushed red pepper

2 medium zucchini, ends trimmed and coarsely shredded

1 medium carrot, peeled and coarsely shredded

1/2 red bell pepper, cut into short 1/4-inch strips

1/2 teaspoon salt, or to taste

2 tablespoons chopped fresh cilantro

1. Cut the chicken breasts into 2-inch pieces and put them in a medium saucepan. Add 2 cups of the chicken broth. Bring to a boil over medium heat. Reduce heat to low, cover, and simmer until the meat is no longer pink, about 5 minutes. Reserve the chicken in the broth off heat.

2. In a large saucepan, heat the oil over medium heat and cook the onion, garlic, and oregano, stirring, until the onion is softened, 3 to 4 minutes. Add the potato, crushed red pepper, and 2 remaining cups of the chicken broth. Bring to a boil, reduce heat to medium-low, cover and cook until the potato is very tender, 12 to 15 minutes.

3. Transfer the soup to a blender and purée until smooth. Return the puréed soup to the pan. Shred the reserved chicken and set aside.

. Add the broth from cooking the chicken to
he puréed soup along with the zucchini, carrot,
ell pepper, and salt. Cook over medium heat,
tirring frequently, until the vegetables are
ender, 5 to 6 minutes. Add the shredded chicken.
Ieat through completely. Serve hot, sprinkled
vith cilantro.

Chicken and Avocado Soup
Caldo de Pollo y Aguacate

Makes **4 servings**

*Iomemade chicken stock delivers the best flavor
or this light soup, which includes shredded
hicken and sliced avocado. A whole chipotle
hile adds a touch of spicy heat. Serve as a first
ourse before a special meal, such as Beef
Tenderloin, Huasteca Style (page 341) or Pork
Roast with Plantains and Tangerines (page 353).*

 cups Basic Chicken Stock (page 215)
 **cup coarsely shredded cooked chicken breast
    (from cooking the chicken for the stock)**
 **whole canned chipotle chiles en adobo,
    rinsed and seeded**
 **large avocado (Hass variety preferred),
    thinly sliced**
alt, to taste
Cilantro sprigs
Lime wedges

*Prepare the chicken stock and store in the refrig-
rator if made more than a few hours ahead.
Then, measure out 4 cups and store the remaining
tock for another use. Put the 4 cups of stock into
 saucepan. Add the chicken and the chipotle
hile. Bring to a boil, then reduce the heat to low
nd add the avocado. Heat 1 minute. Remove the
hipotle. Add salt. Divide the soup among
 soup bowls. Place 1 cilantro sprig on top of each
erving. Serve with lime wedges.*

Chicken Broth with Chickpeas
Caldo de Pollo con Garbanzos

Makes **4 to 6 servings**

*This simple soup was served at a special dinner I
attended, arranged by Chef Ricardo Muñoz as a
finale for a group tour. It was one of the most
unusual and enjoyable parties I've ever attended.
A caravan of boats took a leisurely path along the
historic canals of Xochimilco in Mexico City. We
rode in the main boat, which also contained a
long, festively decorated table. Then came the second boat, where musicians played, followed by a
third boat, which contained a kitchen.*

*When it was time for dinner, the kitchen boat
pulled up alongside us and the team of cooks came
aboard our boat to serve a truly memorable meal,
including this wonderful rich chicken broth in hand-
made brown clay pottery mugs. A small bowl of
condiments was passed around the table, for garnishing the soup. We followed the traditional method,
and drank the broth first, then scooped out the
chickpeas with a spoon. It is a wonderful soup, and
you will love it too—for a fiesta or a simple meal.*

6 cups Basic Chicken Stock (page 215)
**1 cup canned chickpeas (garbanzo beans),
    drained and rinsed**
Salt, to taste
**2 to 3 serrano chiles, seeded, veins removed,
    and minced**
2 tablespoons minced white onion
1/4 cup chopped fresh cilantro
Lime wedges

Prepare chicken stock. Strain and put 6 cups into a
clean saucepan. Bring to a boil. Add the chickpeas
and bring to a boil again; then reduce heat to low
and simmer 1 minute. Add salt, if desired. Serve in
heated mugs. Put the minced chiles, onion, and
cilantro in small bowls. Put the lime wedges on a
small plate. Pass the garnishes at the table.

Chicken in Red Chile-Tomato Broth
Chilpachole de Pollo y Chayote

Makes **4 to 6 servings**

This soup of rich red chile broth with generous chunks of chicken and chayote (a pear-shaped squash that is used similarly to summer squash), can make a meal when eaten with warm corn tortillas, to dip into the flavorful soup. Fresh lime juice is always added just before eating.

6 cups canned fat-free reduced-sodium chicken broth

6 skinless boneless chicken thighs

1 medium chayote, peeled and cut into 1-inch cubes

4 large garlic cloves, thinly sliced

1 teaspoon salt, or to taste

8 guajillo chiles, toasted and seeded (page 9)

4 ancho chiles, toasted and seeded (page 9)

1 tablespoon olive oil or vegetable oil

1 (6- to 7-inch) corn tortilla, quartered

1/2 medium white onion, chopped

4 plum tomatoes, halved lengthwise

1 tablespoon chopped epazote leaves, or 1 teaspoon dried epazote

1/2 teaspoon dried oregano (Mexican variety preferred), crumbled

Lime wedges

1. Put the chicken broth in a large saucepan. Trim excess fat from the chicken, and cut into 1-inch pieces. Add the chicken and the chayote to the broth. Add half of the garlic and ½ teaspoon of the salt. Bring to a boil; then reduce heat to low, cover and simmer until the chicken and chayote are tender, about 20 minutes. Reserve in the pan off heat.

2. Meanwhile prepare the chiles. Then, soak them in a bowl of hot water, 20 minutes. While the chiles soak, heat the oil in a large nonstick skillet and fry the tortilla quarters until crisp and lightly browned on both sides. Transfer to a blender.

3. In the same skillet, fry the onion stirring, 1 minute. Add the remaining garlic, stirring, until onions and garlic start to brown about 3 minutes. Add the remaining salt. Transfer to the blender. In the same skillet, cook the tomatoes on both sides until soft and the skins are charred in spots, about 5 minutes. Transfer to the blender.

4. Drain the chiles, discarding the water, and add the chiles to the blender. Add 1 cup of the chicken broth from cooking the chicken. Blend as smoothly as possible. (Blend in batches, if necessary.)

5. Pour the chile purée through a strainer into the pan with the broth and chicken, pressing to extract most of the solids and juices. Discard the debris. Add the epazote and oregano to the broth. Bring to a boil; then reduce heat to low, cover and simmer 15 minutes to blend the flavors. Adjust seasoning. Serve hot with lime wedges.

Red Chile Broth with Chicken and Epazote
Mole Epazote

Makes **4 servings**

Teresita's Restaurant in Puebla City, about 90 miles southeast of Mexico City, served this excellent soupy type of mole in deep earthenware soup bowls. The mole followed appetizers of quesadillas and soft tacos. Be sure to add small chunks of avocado and a squirt of lime juice to the soup at the table to heighten the flavor. If you can't find fresh epazote, use dried epazote that's found in most Mexican grocery stores.

2 skinless chicken breast halves, on the bone

4 cups canned fat-free reduced-sodium chicken broth

4 small guajillo chiles, toasted and seeded (page 9)

1/4 medium white onion, coarsely chopped

1 medium garlic clove, sliced

2 plum tomatoes, quartered

8 epazote leaves, chopped, or 1 teaspoon dried epazote

1/2 teaspoon dried oregano (Mexican variety preferred), crumbled

1/2 teaspoon salt, or to taste

large avocado (Hass variety preferred), peeled and diced

ime wedges

. Put the chicken breasts in a pan with the hicken broth. Bring to a boil, reduce the heat to ow and simmer until the chicken is cooked hrough, about 20 minutes. Remove the chicken rom the broth to cool. Cover to keep moist.

. Meanwhile, prepare the chiles. Put in a bowl vith hot water to cover. Soak 20 minutes. ransfer the soaked chiles to a blender and disard the soaking water.

. Add the onion, garlic, tomato, epazote, regano, and 1 cup of the chicken broth from ooking the chicken to the blender. Blend as moothly as possible. Pour the puréed chile mixure through a strainer into the pan with the emaining broth, pressing to extract all the juices. Discard the seeds and pulp left in the strainer.

. Bring the chile broth to a boil, then reduce the eat to low, cover, and simmer 10 minutes to ook the onion and tomato and blend the flavors.

. Coarsely shred the chicken and discard the ones. Add the shredded chicken to the chile roth, and season with salt. Heat through and erve hot. Pass diced avocado and fresh lime vedges at the table.

Chicken and Tomato Broth with Vermicelli Pasta
Sopa de Fideos

Makes 4 servings

Sopa de fideos, *is a much-loved home-style soup made with thin coils of vermicelli that are browned in oil, and then added to the broth. Crumbled* queso cotija *is often sprinkled over the soup at the table.* Cotija *cheese is now available in some supermarkets, or Latin American markets. Parmesan cheese may be substituted.*

4 tablespoons vegetable oil

2 ounces dry coils of vermicelli (fideos), broken into pieces

1/2 medium white onion, finely chopped

2 medium garlic cloves, minced

4 plum tomatoes, roasted, peeled, and chopped (page 8)

2 jalapeño chiles, seeded, ribs removed, and chopped

4 cups canned fat-free reduced-sodium chicken broth

2 tablespoons coarsely chopped fresh cilantro

1/2 teaspoon salt, or to taste

Grated cotija cheese (optional)

1. Heat 3 tablespoons of the oil in a medium skillet. Add the broken pieces of vermicelli, and stir-fry until golden brown, about 3 minutes. Work quickly to prevent burning. Remove with a slotted spoon to paper towels to drain.

2. In a medium saucepan, heat the remaining oil, and cook the onion and garlic until softened, about 3 minutes. Add the tomatoes and jalapeños. Cook, stirring, until the tomato juices have cooked away. Add the broth and cilantro. Simmer the soup, partly covered, about 12 minutes. Season with salt, then sprinkle with cotija, if using.

Pork and Beef Soups

Tortilla Soup with Pork and Vegetables
Sopa de Tortilla de Cerdo y Verduras

Makes **4 servings**

A confetti of diced vegetables and bits of pork in a flavorful broth make a delightful soup that's as healthful as it is pretty. Crisp tortilla strips, creamy avocado, salty cheese, and tart lime juice garnish the soup to complete the nuance of taste so important in many Mexican soups.

4 (6- to 7-inch) corn tortillas, cut into thin strips (¹/₄-inch wide) (Fried Corn Tortilla Chips and Strips, page 85)

Vegetable oil for frying tortillas, plus extra to fry pork

¹/₂ pound pork stew meat (from the sirloin or shoulder), cut into ¹/₂-inch pieces

¹/₂ medium white onion, finely diced

1 medium garlic clove, finely chopped

¹/₂ teaspoon dried oregano (Mexican variety preferred), crumbled

¹/₂ teaspoon ground cumin

¹/₈ teaspoon crushed red pepper

3 cups canned fat-free reduced-sodium chicken broth

¹/₃ cup canned tomato sauce

1 medium carrot, peeled and finely diced

1 medium zucchini, ends trimmed, and finely diced

1 cup corn kernels, fresh (from about 1 ear) or frozen

¹/₂ cup finely diced celery

¹/₂ cup finely diced red bell pepper

1 avocado (Hass variety preferred), peeled and cut into squares

2 tablespoons crumbled cotija cheese

Lime wedges

1. Fry the tortilla strips until crisp and light brown. Drain on paper towels and reserve. This can be done up to 3 days ahead. Store the strips in a sealed plastic bag.

2. In a large heavy saucepan, heat about 2 tablespoons oil over medium heat. Add the pork and sauté, stirring, until lightly browned, about 3 to 4 minutes. Using a slotted spoon, remove the pork to a bowl.

3. Add the onion, garlic, oregano, cumin, and crushed red pepper to the pan and cook, stirring, scraping up all the brown bits on the pan bottom, until the onion is limp, 3 to 4 minutes. Add the broth, tomato sauce, carrot, zucchini, corn, celery, and red pepper. Bring to a boil, then reduce the heat to low, cover, and simmer until the vegetables are tender, about 10 minutes.

4. Return the pork to the soup, and simmer 5 minutes. Ladle the hot soup into bowls. Top with tortilla strips, avocado, and cheese. Serve with lime wedges to squeeze the juice over the soup.

Pork and Red Chile Hominy Soup
Pozole Rojo de Puerco

Makes **8 servings**

Pozole is a hearty rich main dish soup, that originated in the state of Jalisco. The main ingredient is hominy—dried white or yellow corn kernels that have been boiled and soaked in slaked lime to remove the hull, and then drained, rinsed, and cooked for about 2 hours. Pozole also contains onions, garlic, and chiles and is often made with pork—or sometimes chicken and its broth—and is always served with fresh toppings, such as cabbage or lettuce, radishes, cilantro, and fresh lime juice.

*This version is easy to prepare at home, using
canned hominy as a convenience and even
though it doesn't contain the traditional whole
pig's head or pig's feet, it's delicious and wholesome. I use meaty, country-style pork ribs from
the loin section. Country-style pork ribs are sold
boneless or on the bone. It's quite simple to cut
the meat away from the bone, or ask the butcher
to cut bone-in meat into two-inch pieces.*

*The ground chile (which can be quite hot, so add
with caution) can be found in the Mexican section
of supermarkets, or in Latin-American food stores.
Masa harina adds body and extra flavor to the
pozole. It can be purchased in the flour section of
most supermarkets. Oval Mexican sandwich rolls,
called bolillos, are usually served with the soup.*

boneless country-style pork ribs, trimmed of
    excess fat, and cut into 1-inch pieces or 2-inch
    pieces for bone-in meat

(14¹/₂-ounce) cans reduced-sodium chicken broth

tablespoons vegetable oil

large white onion, chopped

large garlic cloves, chopped

medium carrots, peeled and thinly sliced

to 3 tablespoons pure ground pasilla or ancho chile

to 2 tablespoons seasoned chili powder,
    such as Crown Colony

¹/₂ tablespoons dried oregano (Mexican variety
    preferred), crumbled

tablespoon ground cumin

teaspoon dried thyme

teaspoon salt

15-ounce) cans white hominy, drained
    and rinsed

14¹/₂-ounce) cans peeled and diced tomatoes

cup, loosely packed chopped fresh cilantro

2 tablespoons masa harina (flour for corn
    tortillas)

ely shredded cabbage

ed avocado

sh lime wedges

1. Put the pork pieces in a medium heavy pan.
Add 1 can of the chicken broth and 1 cup of
water. Bring to a boil over medium heat. Reduce
heat to low, cover, and cook the meat until tender,
about 40 minutes. Reserve the meat in the broth,
off heat. If the pork is on the bone, you may
remove the meat from the bone, if desired, when
it's cool enough to handle. Reserve the meat and
discard the bones.

2. In a heavy large pot, heat the oil and fry the
onion 2 minutes. Add the garlic and cook stirring, until onions and garlic are softened, 2 to 3
minutes. Add the carrots, ground chile, seasoned
chili powder, oregano, cumin, thyme, and salt.
Cook, stirring, 30 seconds.

3. Add the remaining chicken broth, hominy,
tomatoes, cilantro, masa harina, and the reserved
pork with its broth. Bring to a boil, and cook
over medium-low heat, covered, 25 minutes to
blend the flavors. Adjust salt, if needed. Serve the
pozole in shallow soup plates garnished with
shredded cabbage and avocado. Pass the lime
wedges at the table.

Pork Sparerib Soup
Caldo de Puerco

Makes **4 servings**

This rustic dish is a meaty soup-stew that's often made with spareribs, but for easier eating, I use boneless country ribs. With Whole-Wheat Rolls (page 523), this is satisfying enough to be a meal.

2 tablespoons olive oil or vegetable oil

1 pound boneless country-style pork ribs, cut into 1-inch pieces

1/2 teaspoon salt, or to taste

1/8 teaspoon freshly ground pepper, or to taste

2 cups canned fat-free reduced-sodium chicken broth

2 teaspoons chopped fresh epazote leaves, or 1/2 teaspoon dried epazote

1 teaspoon ground cumin

1/4 teaspoon crushed red pepper

1 large white onion, chopped

3 medium garlic cloves, thinly sliced

2 medium carrots, peeled and sliced

1 turnip, peeled and cut into 1/2-inch pieces

2 small zucchini, trimmed and sliced

2 cups finely shredded cabbage

Lime wedges

Fresh red tomato salsa (Fresh Salsa Mexicana, page 24), or purchased

1. In a large saucepan, heat the oil over medium heat and sauté the pork, stirring, until lightly browned. Season with salt and pepper. Add the chicken broth, 2 cups of water, epazote, cumin, crushed pepper, onion, and garlic. Bring to a boil, then reduce the heat to low, cover and simmer until the meat is very tender, about 45 minutes.

2. Add the carrots and turnip. Cook until tender, about 15 minutes. Add the zucchini and cabbage. Cook until these are tender, 6 to 8 minutes. Adjust seasoning. Serve with lime wedges and salsa.

Meatball Soup
Sopa de Albondigas

Makes **4 servings**

Small, well-seasoned meatballs with a touch of fresh mint are simmered in this traditional soup which is often found in the state of Jalisco and in northern Mexico. Sometimes the meatball mixture contains rice. A squirt of fresh lime juice is the key to the finished flavor.

1/2 pound lean ground beef

2 tablespoons finely ground dried bread crumbs

1 tablespoon minced onion plus 1/2 medium onion, sliced

1 medium garlic clove, minced

1 tablespoon finely chopped fresh mint

1 teaspoon ground ancho or pasilla chili powder

1/2 teaspoon ground cumin

1/4 teaspoon salt, or to taste

1 large egg

2 tablespoons olive oil or vegetable oil

1 (14 1/2-ounce) can beef broth

1 1/2 cups canned fat-free reduced-sodium chicken broth

1 cup canned peeled diced tomatoes with juices

1/2 teaspoon dried oregano (Mexican variety preferred), crumbled

1 medium carrot, peeled and thinly sliced

1 celery rib, thinly sliced crosswise

2 tablespoons coarsely chopped fresh cilantro

Lime wedges

1. In a large bowl, mix together the ground beef, bread crumbs, onion, garlic, mint, chili powder, cumin, salt, and egg. Form the meat into small meatballs.

2. Heat 1 tablespoon of the oil in a large nonstick skillet over medium heat and cook the meatballs, turning frequently, until lightly browned, about 6 minutes. Reserve off heat.

. Heat the remaining tablespoon of oil in a large
saucepan over medium heat and cook the sliced
onion until limp, about 3 minutes. Add the
remaining ingredients except the lime wedges.
Add the reserved meatballs. Bring the soup to a
boil, then reduce the heat to medium-low and
simmer until the vegetables are tender, 15 to 20
minutes. Serve with lime wedges.

Shredded Beef Soup
Sopa de Carne de Res Deschebrado

Makes **4 servings**

*A delicious broth results from cooking chunks of beef
for this beef soup from Sonora that's often made
with oxtails. I like this boneless version because it's
easier to eat. A few vegetables, herbs, and spices
are added to the broth. A little chopped onion and
cilantro goes on top and fresh lime juice is squeezed
into the soup as a final touch. Serve with* bolillos
(oval Mexican sandwich rolls) or crusty French rolls.

1 tablespoon plus 2 teaspoons vegetable oil
1 pound beef stew meat, cut into 2-inch pieces
1 (14¹/₂-ounce) can beef broth
1 bay leaf
1 medium onion, thinly sliced
2 medium garlic cloves, thinly sliced
2 medium tomatoes, peeled, seeded, and chopped
1 teaspoon dried oregano (Mexican variety
    preferred), crumbled
1 teaspoon dried thyme
1 cup corn kernels, fresh (from about 1 ear) or frozen
1 small zucchini, cut into ¹/₂-inch cubes
1 medium carrot, peeled and cut into ¹/₂-inch cubes
1 jalapeño chile, seeded, ribs removed, and
    finely chopped
1 teaspoon salt, or to taste
1 teaspoon freshly ground pepper, or to taste
Finely chopped white onion
Chopped fresh cilantro
Lime wedges

1. In a large pot, heat the tablespoon of oil over
medium-high heat. Cook the meat in batches,
turning frequently, until browned. When all is
browned, add the beef broth, 1½ cups of water,
and the bay leaf. Bring to a boil, uncovered,
skimming the foam that rises to the top. Reduce
the heat to low, cover, and simmer until the
beef is tender, about 1 hour. With a slotted
spoon, remove the beef from the broth. When
cool enough to handle, shred the meat and return
to the broth.

2. Meanwhile, in a skillet, heat the remaining
2 teaspoons of oil and cook the onion, stirring,
until limp, about 2 minutes. Add the garlic, tomatoes, oregano, and thyme. Bring to a boil and
cook, stirring, until the tomato juices reduce and
the mixture is nearly dry, 3 to 4 minutes.

3. Transfer the tomato mixture to the beef broth
along with the corn, zucchini, carrot, jalapeño,
salt, and pepper. Bring to a boil, then reduce the
heat to low, cover and simmer until the vegetables are tender, about 15 minutes. Remove the
bay leaf. Top each serving with chopped onion
and cilantro. Serve hot with lime wedges.

Tripe Soup
Menudo

Makes 4 servings

This legendary soup is said to remedy hangovers. True or not, it's popularity rises on Saturday and Sunday mornings, and especially on New Year's Day. Mexican restaurants and markets post signs declaring its availability, to cater to the demand. Menudo *is the common name given to Mexican tripe soups, which are made from the lining of beef stomach, but the soup is also called* pancita *(little stomach) in some parts of Mexico. Tripe is easy to find in most meat markets, and honeycomb tripe is the most tender and flavorful. This soup really does taste better than it sounds if you are unfamiliar with tripe—so don't wait until you have a hangover to try it!*

1 pound beef honeycomb tripe, rinsed well
    and drained
2 tablespoons pure ancho or pasilla chili powder
1¹/₂ teaspoons salt
2 teaspoons dried oregano (Mexican variety
    preferred), crumbled
8 medium garlic cloves, chopped
1 pound meaty country-style pork ribs
1 (14-ounce) can white or yellow hominy,
    rinsed and drained
¹/₂ medium white onion, chopped
¹/₈ teaspoon crushed red pepper
2 green onions, including 2 inches of green, chopped
1 tablespoon chopped fresh cilantro
Lime wedges

1. Cut the drained tripe into ½-inch squares, and put in a medium pan with water to cover. Bring to a boil; then reduce heat and simmer 10 minutes. Drain through a colander and rinse with cold water. Return the tripe to the pan.

2. Add 8 cups of water, the chili powder, salt, oregano, and garlic. Bring to a boil; then reduce the heat and simmer, partially covered, 1 hour. Add the pork to the soup. Cook until the pork is very tender, about 1½ hours.

3. Remove the meat to a plate. When cool enough to handle, shred the meat, and discard fat and bones. Return the shredded meat to the soup. Add the hominy, onion, and crushed pepper. Cook about 15 minutes to blend the flavors. Serve hot, sprinkled with green onion and cilantro. Pass lime wedges at the table.

Fish Soups

Shrimp Tortilla Soup
Sopa de Tortilla con Camarónes

Makes **4 to 6 servings**

In the state of Veracruz on the east coast of Mexico, I enjoyed so many seafood dishes that I was constantly taking notes on things to try at home, like this shrimp soup. The soup is lowfat but satisfying enough to make a meal. The crisp tortilla strips are pushed into the soup as it's eaten.

(6- to 7-inch) corn tortillas, cut into thin strips, about 1/4 inch wide

poblano chiles, roasted and peeled (page 8)

3/4 pound (12 to 15) large shrimp

scallions, cut into 1-inch pieces

parsley sprig

teaspoon dried oregano (Mexican variety preferred), crumbled

1/2 cup dry white wine

teaspoon salt

2 teaspoons olive oil

1 medium white onion, quartered lengthwise and thinly sliced

4 medium garlic cloves, finely chopped

2 large tomatoes, peeled and finely chopped, or 1 cup canned

1 (14 1/2-ounce) can fat-free reduced-sodium chicken broth

1 cup fresh (from about 1 ear) or frozen corn kernels

Lime wedges

1. Preheat oven to 350°. Put the tortilla strips on a large baking sheet in one layer. Toast until light brown and crisp, 10 to 12 minutes. Reserve.

2. Prepare the chiles. Then cut them into strips and reserve. Peel the shrimp, and put the shells in a medium nonreactive saucepan. Devein the shrimp and cut each one crosswise into thirds. Cover and refrigerate.

3. To the pan with the shrimp shells, add scallions, parsley, oregano, wine, salt, and 2 cups of water. Bring to a boil, uncovered, over high heat. Reduce heat to low, cover, and simmer the shells 15 minutes. Pour the broth through a strainer into a bowl, pressing on the solids to extract the juices. Discard solids. Set broth aside.

4. In a large saucepan, heat olive oil over medium heat. Cook the onion and garlic, stirring, until softened, 3 to 4 minutes. Add the tomatoes, raise heat to high and cook, stirring, until the mixture is nearly dry, about 4 minutes.

5. Add the reserved shrimp broth, chicken broth, chile strips, corn, and the shrimp. Bring the soup to a boil, then reduce the heat and simmer until the shrimp are pink, about 3 minutes. Divide the soup among 4 soup bowls, and place a generous stack of tortilla strips on top of each serving. Pass lime wedges at the table. Serve at once.

Shrimp and Hominy Soup
Pozole de Camarón

Makes **4 servings**

The creative dishes I've tasted at Chapuline Restaurant in Oaxaca are a continuing inspiration. I especially like the chef's flavorful shrimp soup that is a blending of old and new: pozole, or dried corn with the hull removed, and shrimp are cooked in a lighter broth than in the usual stew-like pozoles (a dish named after the main ingredient). Fresh epazote can be difficult to find, so substitute cilantro for fresh herb flavor, even though the taste is different.

2 cups Basic Chicken Stock (page 215)
    or canned broth

³/₄ pound (14 to 17) medium shrimp, in the shell

1 cup water

2 ancho chiles, stemmed, seeded, veins removed,
    and cut into pieces

1 tablespoon olive oil

¹/₂ medium white onion, chopped

2 medium garlic cloves, finely chopped

2 medium tomatoes, peeled and finely chopped

1 teaspoon dried oregano (Mexican variety
    preferred), crumbled

¹/₂ teaspoon cumin

1 tablespoon chopped fresh epazote leaves,
    or fresh chopped cilantro

1 (15-ounce) can white or yellow hominy,
    drained and rinsed

¹/₂ teaspoon salt, or to taste

1 large avocado (Hass variety preferred),
    thinly sliced

Lime wedges

1. Prepare the chicken stock, if using homemade. Then, peel the shrimp and devein. Reserve the shrimp in a bowl and put the shrimp shells in a medium saucepan with the chicken broth, water, and ancho chiles. Bring to a boil; then reduce the heat to low, cover and simmer 5 minutes. Remove from the heat and reserve the broth in the pan.

2. Heat the oil over medium heat in a large saucepan and cook the onion until softened, about 3 minutes. Add the garlic and cook 1 more minute. Add the tomatoes, oregano, and cumin. Cook until the juices are reduced and the mixture is nearly dry. Pour the reserved broth through a mesh strainer directly into the soup pot, pushing to extract all the juices. Discard the solids.

3. Add the reserved shrimp, epazote, hominy, and salt to the pot. Bring to a boil; then reduce the heat and simmer the soup until the shrimp are cooked, about 8 minutes. Divide the soup among 4 soup bowls. Add sliced avocado to each bowl. Serve hot, with lime wedges on the side.

Shrimp in Green Broth
Huatape de Camarón

Makes **4 to 6 servings**

Huatape *is a basic soup from the Gulf coast state of Tamaulipas, where the long coastline provides an abundance of shellfish and a great variety of fish.*

The traditional broth for huatape *is red, made from ancho chiles and tomatoes. The delicious green broth for this modern version is made from blending tomatillos, lettuce leaves, epazote, onion, garlic, corn tortillas, and green chiles. Water is often used to dilute the broth, but I prefer to use half chicken broth and half water. The corn tortillas dissolve to add body and extra flavor to the broth. After the broth simmers to a rich brew, the shrimp is cooked in the broth. Serve the soup with crusty rolls to dip into the broth.*

reen Chile Strips (page 428)

3 pound tomatillos, husked, rinsed, and quartered

romaine lettuce leaves (large green outside leaves), rinsed and torn into pieces

2 fresh epazote leaves (if unavailable, just leave out)

'2 cup lightly packed fresh cilantro sprigs

'2 medium white onion, coarsely chopped

serrano chiles, sliced crosswise with seeds

'2 teaspoon dried oregano (Mexican variety preferred), crumbled

(6- to 7-inch) corn tortillas, torn into small pieces

(14¹/2-ounce) can fat-free reduced-sodium chicken broth

tablespoons olive oil

cups water

/2 teaspoon salt, or to taste

pound (18 to 22) medium shrimp, peeled and deveined

1. Prepare the chile strips. Reserve. Then, put the tomatillos, lettuce, epazote, cilantro, onion, chiles, oregano, tortilla, and ½ cup of the chicken broth into a blender and purée as finely as possible, about 1 minute.

2. In a large saucepan, heat the oil over medium heat, and pour in the puréed mixture. Bring to a boil, then cover, and cook, stirring frequently, until the mixture thickens, about 10 minutes.

3. Add the remaining chicken broth, water, and salt. Bring to a boil, stirring, then cover, and cook over medium-low heat 10 to 15 minutes until the ingredients are well cooked and the flavors are blended. Add the shrimp and cook, uncovered, until the shrimp are pink and curled, 4 to 5 minutes. Add the green chile strips. Cook 1 minute. Adjust salt. Serve hot in soup bowls.

Shrimp in Red Chile Broth
Chilpachole de Camarón

Makes **4 servings**

Lake Catemaco, south of Veracruz on the Gulf coast, was our destination with our bird expert friends, Dix and Didi Boring. We were visiting the Tropical Ecological Zone (Los Tuxlas), to view toucans, parrots, and other jungle wonders.

The nature preserve is well off the beaten path, so after a wonderful day and two trips along muddy, rutted roads in the back of a pick-up truck, I was revived and rewarded with this most delicious and messy soup (with unpeeled shrimp), at La Luna, a simple restaurant bordering the lake. The soup is also found all along the coast of Veracruz. My version of the soup calls for peeling the shrimp before serving, for more delicate eating. The lime juice adds a refreshing, tangy touch to finish the soup.

1 pound (16 to 20) large raw shrimp in the shell

4 thick slices white onion

4 large garlic cloves, sliced

1 teaspoon salt, or to taste

8 guajillo chiles, toasted and seeded, veins removed (page 9)

4 ancho chiles, toasted and seeded, veins removed (page 9)

1 tablespoon vegetable oil

1 (6- to 7-inch) corn tortilla, quartered

4 plum tomatoes, halved lengthwise

2 cups canned fat-free reduced-sodium chicken broth

1 tablespoon chopped epazote leaves, or substitute 1 teaspoon dried oregano (Mexican variety preferred), crumbled

Lime wedges

1. Put the shrimp in a large saucepan with 4 cups water, 2 slices of the onion, 2 of the garlic cloves, and ½ teaspoon of the salt. Bring to a boil, lower the heat, cover and simmer until the shrimp are pink and curled, 5 to 6 minutes.

2. With a slotted spoon, remove the shrimp and save the stock. Cool the shrimp under cold running water. Remove the shells and put the shells back into the stock. Devein the shrimp and refrigerate in a covered bowl. Boil the shrimp stock 10 minutes, uncovered, to reduce and intensify the flavor. Pour the stock through a strainer, pressing on the solids to extract all the liquid. Discard the pulp and shells. Reserve the stock in the pan.

3. Soak the toasted and seeded chiles in a bowl of hot water 20 minutes. Heat the oil in a large nonstick skillet and fry the tortilla quarters until crisp and golden brown on both sides. Transfer to a blender.

4. In the same skillet, cook the remaining onion slices until translucent, about 3 minutes. Add the rest of the garlic and cook, stirring, one more minute. Transfer to the blender.

5. In the same skillet, cook the tomatoes on both sides until soft and the skins are charred with black spots. Transfer to the blender. Drain the chiles and add them to the blender. Add 1 cup of the chicken broth. Blend as smoothly as possible.

6. Pour the mixture through a strainer into the reserved shrimp stock. Add the remaining chicken broth and epazote. Bring to a boil. Reduce the heat to low and simmer 10 minutes to blend the flavors. Add the reserved shrimp. Simmer 5 minutes. Adjust seasoning. Serve hot with lime wedges.

Coastal Seafood Soup
Caldo de Mariscos

Makes **8 servings**

Seafood soups are popular all along Mexico's extensive coastlines, and they contain whatever fish comes from the region. This tasty soup is from Acapulco. Maggi is a popular and common seasoning concentrate frequently used by Mexican cooks throughout the country. It is widely available in supermarkets in the United States. Or you can substitute Worcestershire, which Mexicans call English sauce.

3/4 pound (14 to 17) medium shrimp in the shell
3 green onions, cleaned and cut into 1-inch pieces
1 celery rib, cut into 1-inch pieces
1 medium carrot, cut into 1-inch pieces
1 sprig parsley
1 teaspoon dried oregano (Mexican variety preferred), crumbled
1 bay leaf
1/2 cup dry white wine
1/2 teaspoon salt
3 tablespoons olive oil
1 large white onion, chopped
6 medium garlic cloves, thinly sliced
4 medium tomatoes, peeled, seeded, and finely chopped
1 teaspoon Maggi seasoning extract or Worcestershire sauce
2 small new potatoes, peeled and cut into 1/2-inch dice
1 jalapeño chile, seeded, veins removed, and finely chopped
2 (141/2-ounce) cans reduced-sodium chicken broth
1 pound white fish fillets, such as cod, snapper, or sea bass, cut into 1-inch pieces
1/2 teaspoon salt, or to taste
1/4 teaspoon freshly ground pepper, or to taste
Chopped fresh cilantro
2 fresh limes, cut into wedges

Peel the shrimp and reserve the shells in a medium nonreactive saucepan. Devein the shrimp, and cut each shrimp crosswise into thirds. Put the cleaned shrimp into a bowl, cover and refrigerate. To the pan with the shrimp shells, add the scallions, celery, carrot, parsley, oregano, bay leaf, wine, salt, and 2½ cups of water. Bring to a boil, uncovered, over high heat. Reduce the heat to low, and simmer, covered, 10 minutes. Pour the broth through a strainer placed over a medium bowl, pressing on solids to extract all the juices. Discard the solids. Set the broth aside.

In a large saucepan, heat the oil over medium heat. Add the onion and garlic. Cook, over medium heat, stirring, until the onion begins to brown, 3 to 4 minutes. Add the tomatoes and Maggi. Cook, stirring frequently, until the tomato juices have cooked away, 4 to 5 minutes.

Add the potatoes, jalapeño, chicken broth, and the reserved shrimp broth. Partially cover, and cook over medium-low until the potatoes are tender, 6 to 8 minutes. Add the fish and shrimp. Cook until the fish is opaque, and the shrimp are pink and curled, 3 to 4 minutes. Add the salt and pepper. Serve the soup sprinkled with cilantro. Pass lime wedges at the table.

Seven Seas Soup
Caldo de Siete Mares

Makes **6 to 8 servings**

Two to three times each year, Dorothy and Frank Davis, my sister and her husband, drive from their home in northern California to their second home on Mexico's Baja peninsula. They have favorite food stops along the way in Mexico, often eating Seven Seas Soup, and gave me this version from Ensenada's port-side restaurants, where it appears on most menus.

The kind of fresh seafood varies according to what's available, as long as the total is seven

(but who's counting?). Home cooks can make their own fish stock or use chicken broth as a base for the soup. Serve as a main dish with crusty rolls and squeeze the fresh lime juice into the soup just before eating.

8 cups Basic Fish Stock (page 215) or canned chicken broth

¼ cup olive oil

1 large white onion, chopped

4 large garlic cloves, finely chopped

1 (16-ounce) can diced tomatoes, puréed in a blender

1 cup dry white wine

1½ teaspoons dried oregano (Mexican variety preferred), crumbled

1 teaspoon ground cumin

1 teaspoon salt, or to taste

½ teaspoon crushed red pepper

24 small clams, scrubbed and rinsed

¾ pound (12 to 15) large shrimp, peeled and deveined

1 pound skinless boneless fish fillets (4 different kinds—such as halibut, snapper, cod, mahimahi—cut into 1-inch pieces)

8 sea scallops, cut into quarters

½ cup loosely packed chopped fresh cilantro

Lime wedges

1. Prepare the fish stock, if making homemade. Then, in a large pot, heat the oil over medium heat and cook the onion, partially covered, stirring frequently, until tender, about 6 to 8 minutes. Add the garlic, broth, tomatoes, wine, oregano, cumin, salt, and crushed pepper. Bring to a boil, reduce the heat to low, cover and simmer 20 minutes to blend the flavors.

2. Add the clams to the soup. Cover the pot and cook until the shells open, about 8 minutes. Discard any that do not open. Add the shrimp, fish pieces, and scallops. Simmer until the seafood is just cooked through, 4 to 5 minutes. Stir in the cilantro. Adjust seasoning. Serve with lime wedges.

Concepción Bay Scallop Chowder
Sopa de Callos

Makes 4 servings

Peggy Higgenbotham, an avid cook, American friend, and seasonal neighbor of my sister in Mulege, Mexico, on the Baja peninsula, contributed this recipe that she created. The beautiful Concepción Bay nearby provides plenty of bay scallops for her culinary inspiration.

3 small potatoes, peeled and finely diced
1 carrot, peeled and chopped
1 medium white onion, chopped
2¹/₂ cups canned chicken broth
1 bay leaf
¹/₄ teaspoon freshly ground pepper, or to taste
¹/₄ teaspoon dried thyme
1 tablespoon unsalted butter
¹/₂ pound white mushrooms, thinly sliced
¹/₂ pound (about 50) tiny bay scallops
¹/₂ cup dry white wine
1 cup heavy cream
2 tablespoons chopped fresh parsley

1. Put the potatoes, carrot, onion, broth, bay leaf, pepper, and thyme in a large pot and bring to a boil. Reduce the heat to low and simmer, covered, until the vegetables are very tender, about 20 minutes. Remove the bay leaf and transfer the mixture to a blender. Blend until smooth. Return to the cooking pot.

2. While the vegetables cook, heat the butter in a large skillet and cook the mushrooms, stirring, until they release their juices, 3 to 4 minutes. Add the scallops and wine. Bring to a boil, and cook 1 minute. Stir in the cream and add to the vegetable mixture. Heat through completely. Serve hot sprinkled with parsley.

Oyster Soup
Sopa de Ostiones

Makes 4 servings

A bowl of rich, steaming oyster soup is made in many seafood specialty restaurants along both coasts of Mexico.

2 tablespoons unsalted butter
1 medium white onion, finely chopped
1 rib celery, finely chopped
1 medium garlic clove, minced
1 (14¹/₂-ounce) can fat-free reduced-sodium chicken broth
¹/₂ teaspoon salt
¹/₈ teaspoon crushed red pepper
2 cups heavy cream or half and half
1 (8-ounce) jar fresh shucked small oysters
1 tablespoon chopped fresh cilantro or flat-leaf parsley

In a 3-quart saucepan, melt the butter and cook the onion, celery, and garlic over medium-low heat, covered, stirring frequently, until the vegetables are softened, about 5 minutes. Add the broth, salt, and red pepper. Bring to a boil. Cover, reduce heat and simmer 8 minutes. Add the cream and oysters with the liquid. Heat until hot and steaming, but do not boil. Stir in the cilantro. Serve hot.

Catfish Soup
Caldo Michi

Makes **4 servings**

Catfish is harvested from the rivers and lakes in the state of Jalisco. Much of it goes into catfish soup, offered at almost every market food stall and at restaurants throughout the region. This version comes from Guadalajara. I use fresh, farm-raised catfish, available in most United States fish markets.

- tablespoon olive oil or vegetable oil
- large white onion, chopped
- large garlic cloves, thinly sliced
- medium tomatoes, peeled and chopped
- cups canned fat-free reduced-sodium chicken broth
- medium carrots, peeled and thinly sliced
- rib celery, thinly sliced
- serrano chiles, halved lengthwise with seeds
- bay leaves
- teaspoon dried oregano (Mexican variety preferred), crumbled
- /2 teaspoon ground cumin
- /4 teaspoon dried thyme leaves
- /4 to 1 pound catfish fillets, cut into 1-inch pieces
- tablespoons chopped fresh cilantro
- /2 teaspoon salt, or to taste
- Lime wedges

1. In a large pot, heat the oil over medium heat and cook the onion, stirring frequently, until it begins to brown, about 4 minutes. Add the garlic and tomatoes. Cook, stirring, until the tomato juices are reduced, 4 to 5 minutes. Add the broth, carrots, celery, serrano chiles, bay leaves, oregano, and thyme. Bring to a boil, then reduce the heat to low, cover and simmer until the vegetables are tender, 12 to 14 minutes.

2. Remove the serrano chiles and bay leaves from the soup. Add the fish, cilantro, and salt. Cook until the fish is opaque inside, 6 to 8 minutes. Serve the soup hot with lime wedges.

Vegetable and Bean Soups

Corn, Onion, and Jalapeño Soup
Sopa de Elote, Cebolla, y Jalapeño

Makes **4 servings**

Quick to make and soul-restoring soups are just right for busy days. A small unassuming restaurant in the city of Puebla served a simple light soup very much like this one. It proves that just a few ingredients are all you need to produce something wonderful.

- 2 tablespoons unsalted butter or vegetable oil, or a combination
- 1 small white onion, coarsely chopped
- 2 (14¹/₂-ounce) cans fat-free reduced-sodium chicken broth
- 1¹/₂ cups fresh (from about 2 medium ears) or frozen corn kernels
- 3 large fresh jalapeño chiles, seeded, veins removed, and cut into small squares or thin strips
- ¹/₂ teaspoon ground cumin
- ¹/₄ teaspoon salt, or to taste

In a medium saucepan, heat the butter or oil, and cook the onion, stirring until the onion begins to brown, 4 to 5 minutes. Add the remaining ingredients except the salt, and cook 4 to 5 minutes. Add salt and serve hot.

Zucchini, Corn, and Green Chile Soup
Sopa de Calabacitas, Elote, y Chile Verde

Makes **4 servings**

This light and simple soup calls for canned, peeled, and diced green chiles, which are often used by home cooks in Mexico. They are readily available in supermarkets in the United States, too.

3 cups Basic Chicken Stock (page 215) or canned fat-free reduced-sodium chicken broth

1 tablespoon unsalted butter or olive oil

1/2 cup chopped white onion

3 medium zucchini (3/4 pound), cut into 1/2-inch dice

1 cup fresh corn kernels (from one large ear)

1 (4-ounce) can peeled and diced green chiles

1/2 teaspoon ground cumin

1/2 teaspoon salt, or to taste

Lime wedges

Prepare the chicken stock, if using homemade. Melt the butter in a 2-quart saucepan, and cook the onion over medium heat until softened, about 3 minutes. Add the broth, zucchini, corn, chopped chiles, cumin, and salt. Bring to a boil, then reduce the heat, cover, and simmer until the zucchini is tender, about to 6 to 8 minutes. Serve with lime wedges.

Corn, Squash Blossom, and Zucchini Soup
Sopa de Elote, Flor de Calabasa, y Calabacitas

Makes **4 servings**

Daily markets in Mexico, with beautiful produce piled high and beckoning, are truly inspirational. With Mexico's long growing season, this garden-fresh soup made with some of the stars of the market, can be made just about anytime there, but for us in the United States it is usually just a summer delight, so make the most of seasonal bounty. For a final sparkle, add a squeeze of fresh lime juice at the table.

1 tablespoon vegetable oil

1/2 medium white onion, thinly sliced

2 medium garlic cloves, finely chopped

1/2 teaspoon cumin

4 cups chicken broth, canned or homemade

2 small zucchini, cut into 1/2-inch pieces

2 small ears of corn, cut crosswise into 1 1/2-inch wheels

4 fresh squash blossoms, stemmed and coarsely chopped

2 tablespoons fresh cilantro

1/2 teaspoon salt, or to taste

Lime wedges

In a large saucepan, heat the oil over medium heat and cook the onion and garlic until softened, about 3 minutes. Add the remaining ingredients, except the lime wedges, and cook until the vegetables are tender, 6 to 8 minutes. Serve hot with lime wedges.

Squash Blossom Soup
Sopa de Flor de Calabaza

Makes **4 servings**

Squash blossoms are used a great deal in Mexican cooking. The delicate blossoms are stuffed and fried, chopped and added to quesadillas and omelets, and featured in this light popular soup. In the United States, squash blossoms, in season, can be found in farmers' markets or specialty produce markets.

4 cups Basic Chicken Stock (page 215) or canned chicken broth
1 pound (about 20) squash blossoms
1 tablespoon olive oil
1 teaspoon unsalted butter
1 medium white onion, chopped
1 small zucchini, neatly diced (about $1/4$ inch)
2 medium garlic cloves, minced
$1/4$ teaspoon salt
$1/8$ teaspoon pepper
$1/4$ teaspoon dried thyme
1 cup cooked shredded chicken (from making the stock)
2 tablespoons chopped fresh cilantro

1. Prepare chicken stock, if using homemade. Then, remove the stems and pistils from the squash blossoms. Rinse blossoms and shake off excess water. Coarsely chop the blossoms and reserve.

2. In a large saucepan, heat the oil and butter. Add the onion and cook, stirring, until softened, 3 to 4 minutes. Add the zucchini, garlic, salt, pepper, and thyme. Cook, stirring, until the zucchini is crisp-tender, about 4 minutes. Add the remaining ingredients, including the chicken stock, and heat through completely, 3 to 4 minutes. Serve hot.

Mixed Vegetable Soup
Sopa de Verduras

Makes **4 servings**

Maria M. Merrill, a cooking instructor in San Miguel de Allende, made this soup for our last comida (mid-day meal) from the vegetables left from a week of cooking classes. The recipe evolved as she cooked the soup. If you don't have all the ingredients, follow Maria's lead and make use of the vegetables on hand.

1 tablespoon vegetable oil or olive oil
1 medium white onion, coarsely chopped
1 rib celery, cut crosswise in $1/2$-inch pieces
2 medium carrots, peeled and cut in $1/2$-inch pieces
$1/4$ head of cabbage, coarsely chopped
1 tablespoon coarsely chopped flat-leaf parsley
$1/4$ cup canned tomato sauce
1 ($14^{1}/_2$-ounce) can fat-free reduced-sodium chicken broth
2 medium zucchini, cut in $1/2$-inch pieces
$1/4$ teaspoon salt, or to taste

Heat the oil in a medium saucepan, and cook the onion and celery over medium heat until barely softened, about 4 minutes. Add all of the remaining ingredients except the zucchini and salt. Bring the soup to a boil, then reduce the heat to medium-low, cover, and simmer 8 minutes. Add the zucchini and cook, partially covered, until the zucchini is tender, but not mushy, 6 to 8 minutes. Add salt. Serve hot.

Poblano, Carrot, and Cauliflower Soup
Sopa de Poblano, Zanahoria, y Coliflor

Makes **4 servings**

A few years ago, while my husband and I were in the colonial city of Morelia, capital of the state of Michoacan, we enjoyed a leisurely comida *(midday meal) in the courtyard of Los Comansales restaurant. The soup served with our meal was wonderful and worth recreating at home. Dark green poblano chiles, bright orange carrots, and white cauliflower lend wonderful texture, intriguing flavor, and splendid color to the soup.*

2 large poblano chiles
2 tablespoons olive oil or vegetable oil
**1 medium white onion, halved lengthwise and
    sliced crosswise**
1 medium tomato, peeled, seeded, and chopped
1 medium garlic clove, finely chopped
**$1/2$ teaspoon dried oregano (Mexican variety
    preferred), crumbled**
$1/4$ teaspoon dried thyme
4 cups canned fat-free reduced-sodium chicken broth
2 medium carrots, peeled and thinly sliced crosswise
$1 1/2$ cups bite-size cauliflower florets
$1/2$ teaspoon salt, or to taste
$1/8$ teaspoon freshly ground pepper, or to taste
$1/4$ cup lightly packed chopped fresh cilantro

1. Roast the poblano chiles over a direct flame or under an oven broiler, turning frequently, until charred all over, about 8 to 10 minutes. If using a broiler, check often to see that they don't get too black or shriveled. Put the chiles in a plastic or paper bag and let steam 6 to 8 minutes. Rub off the skins. Remove and discard the stems and seeds. Rinse the chiles and pat dry with a paper towel. Cut into short ¼-inch-thick strips. Set aside.

2. In a large pot, heat the oil over medium heat and cook the onion, stirring, until softened, 3 to 4 minutes. Add the tomato, garlic, oregano, and thyme. Cook, stirring, until the mixture is nearly dry, about 4 minutes. Add the broth and carrots. Bring to a boil, reduce heat to low, cover, and simmer until the carrots are tender, 6 to 8 minutes. Add the cauliflower, reserved poblano strips, salt, and pepper. Cook until the cauliflower is tender, about 4 minutes. Stir in the cilantro. Serve hot.

Potato, Cactus, and Carrot Soup
Sopa de Papa, Nopalitos, y Zanahoria

Makes **4 servings**

Mexican soups often include nopalitos *(cactus strips) with other vegetables. Cactus packed in jars can be found in the United States in Mexican markets or many supermarkets. (Choose water-packed, not brine-packed jarred cactus.) This savory soup is a fine starter course for dinner, or for lunch with quesadillas or tacos.*

1 tablespoon olive oil or vegetable oil
1 medium white onion, chopped
3 medium plum tomatoes, peeled and finely chopped
2 large garlic cloves, finely chopped
**$1/2$ teaspoon dried oregano (Mexican variety
    preferred), crumbled**
$1/2$ teaspoon ground cumin
4 cups canned fat-free reduced-sodium chicken broth
2 medium potatoes, peeled and cut into $1/2$-inch dice
2 medium carrots, peeled and cut into $1/2$-inch dice
$3/4$ cup rinsed and diced bottled cactus
**$1/4$ cup coarsely chopped parsley, flat-leaf
    preferred**
$1/2$ teaspoon salt, or to taste
$1/8$ teaspoon freshly ground pepper, or to taste

1. Heat the oil in a large saucepan over medium heat and cook the onion, stirring, until softened, 3 to 4 minutes. Add the tomatoes, garlic, oregano, and cumin. Cook until tomato juices reduce and the mixture thickens, about 3 minutes. Add the broth, potatoes, and carrots. Bring to a boil, then duce heat to low, cover and cook until the vegables are tender, 15 to 20 minutes.

Add the cactus, parsley, salt, and pepper. mmer the soup until completely heated through d the flavors blend, about 5 minutes. Serve hot.

weet Potato Soup
opa de Camote
lakes **4 servings**

weet potatoes are native to the Americas and re used in all sorts of dishes in Mexico. There re several varieties, and some are mistakenly abeled yams. For this soup, use the dark-kinned variety with orange flesh.

} orange-fleshed sweet potatoes (about 1 pound)

2 tablespoons olive oil or vegetable oil

1/2 medium white onion, finely chopped

4 cups canned fat-free reduced-sodium chicken broth

1 guajillo chile, stem, veins, and seeds removed

1/2 teaspoon cumin

1 cup fresh (from about 1 large ear) or frozen corn kernels

2 green onions, sliced, including 3 inches of green tops

1/2 teaspoon salt, or to taste

1/3 cup Mexican crema or sour cream (optional)

1. Scrub and peel the potatoes. Cut into neat 1/2-inch pieces. Reserve 2 1/2 cups in a bowl. Cover with cold water to prevent flesh from turning brown. (Store any extra sweet potato for another use.)

2. In a large saucepan, heat the oil over medium heat and cook the onion, stirring, until soft, about 4 minutes. Drain the potatoes, add them to the pan along with the broth, chile, and cumin. Bring to a boil, then reduce heat to low, cover, and simmer until the potatoes are tender, but still intact, 6 to 8 minutes.

3. Add corn, green onions, and salt. Cook 5 minutes. Remove the chile and discard. Divide the soup among 4 bowls. Garnish with a swirl of crema or sour cream, if desired.

Mushroom and Onion Soup, Puebla Style
Sopa de Hongos y Cebollas
Makes **4 servings**

Edible wild mushrooms are highly prized in Mexico, and many kinds are gathered during the rainy season from June to September. Some restaurants in the city of Puebla feature soups similar to this one when wild mushrooms are abundant. Use an assortment of mushrooms that you like or that are available, but include a few of the most flavorful, such as porcini, shiitake, or portobello. Top it off with a fresh splash of lime.

2 tablespoons vegetable oil

2 tablespoons unsalted butter

1/2 medium white onion, coarsely chopped

2 medium tomatoes, peeled, seeded, and chopped

2 medium garlic cloves, finely chopped

1/2 teaspoon dried oregano (Mexican variety preferred), crumbled

3/4 pound mixed mushrooms, cleaned and thickly sliced

1/4 cup coarsely chopped fresh cilantro

3 cups chicken stock or canned fat-free reduced-sodium chicken broth

1 cup canned beef broth

1/2 teaspoon salt, or to taste

1/8 teaspoon freshly ground pepper, or to taste

Lime wedges

1. In a large pot, heat the oil and butter over medium heat until the butter foams, and cook the onion over medium-low heat, stirring frequently, until golden, about 8 minutes.

2. Add the tomatoes, garlic, and oregano. Cook, stirring, until the mixture is nearly dry, about 4 minutes. Add the mushrooms and cilantro. Cook until the mushrooms release some of their juices, 4 to 5 minutes. Add the chicken and beef broths, salt, and pepper. Simmer 10 minutes. Pass the limes at the table.

Mushroom and Tomatillo Soup
Sopa de Hongo y Tomatillo

Makes **4 servings**

Queretaro is a pretty colonial city in central Mexico. It has a rich history, beginning with the Otomi Indians, whose descendants still live in the region. In the 1500s it came under Spanish influence, which is still seen in the picturesque plazas, churches, and open-air restaurants. In past years, whenever my husband and I drove from Mexico City to San Miguel de Allende, we made a point to have a meal at a lovely restaurant in Queretaro, La Fonda del Refugio. This soup was one of my favorite dishes on the menu.

1/2 **pound tomatillos, husks removed and rinsed**

4 **whole medium garlic cloves, unpeeled**

1/4 **cup lightly packed coarsely chopped cilantro**

1 **teaspoon dried oregano (Mexican variety preferred), crumbled**

4 **cups canned fat-free reduced-sodium chicken broth**

1/4 **cup long grain white rice**

2 **tablespoons olive oil**

1/2 **medium white onion, thinly sliced**

12 **medium brown cremini mushrooms, sliced**

4 **shiitake mushrooms, stemmed and sliced**

1/2 **teaspoon salt, or to taste**

1. Heat a medium dry skillet over medium heat and pan roast the tomatillos and garlic, turning occasionally until the vegetables are softened and lightly browned in spots. Transfer the roasted garlic and tomatillos, as they are ready, to a blender. Add the cilantro, oregano, and 1 cup of the chicken broth. Blend until smooth. Transfer to a large saucepan.

2. Add the remaining broth and rice. Bring to a boil. Reduce the heat and simmer until the rice is tender, about 15 minutes.

3. Meanwhile, in a medium skillet, heat the oil over medium heat and cook the onion until translucent, about 4 minutes. Add the mushrooms and cook, stirring, until they start to brown, 5 to 6 minutes. Transfer to the soup pot. Add the salt. Simmer the soup for 5 minutes, covered, to blend the flavors.

pinach Soup Cuauhtemoc
ɔpa Cuauhtemoc

akes **4 servings**

uauhtemoc was a legendary chief in Mexico ho is honored by a monument along the Paseo ? la Reforma, a major avenue in Mexico City. his recipe is adapted from one by Maria de arbia of Mexico City, in her book, Mexico hrough My Kitchen Window. *Greens of all inds are used in Mexican soups and stews.*

2 **cup vegetable oil**
(6- to 7-inch) corn tortillas, cut into 3/4-inch squares
2 medium white onion, finely chopped
large garlic cloves, finely chopped
medium tomatoes, peeled, seeded, and chopped
quart chicken stock or canned chicken broth
cups lightly packed coarsely chopped fresh spinach leaves
/4 cup chopped fresh cilantro
/8 teaspoon crushed red pepper
/2 teaspoon salt, or to taste
1/8 teaspoon freshly ground pepper, or to taste

1. In a small skillet, heat the oil until it shimmers. Fry the tortilla squares in the hot oil over medium-high heat golden brown and crisp, about 1 minute. Drain on paper towels, and set aside.

2. Spoon about 2 tablespoons of the same hot oil into a 2-quart saucepan. Add the onion and garlic. Cook over medium heat until softened, about 3 minutes. Add the tomatoes, and cook, stirring, until the mixture is nearly dry, 2 to 3 minutes.

3. Add the broth and bring to a boil. Add the spinach, cilantro, red pepper, salt, and black pepper. Reduce the heat to medium-low and simmer until the spinach is tender and the flavors blend, about 10 minutes. Divide the crisp tortilla squares among 4 soup bowls and ladle the hot soup into the bowls. Serve at once.

Spinach and Macaroni Soup
Sopa de Espinaca

Makes **4 servings**

Small elbow macaroni adds body to this appealing spinach soup. The cheese adds richness, and fresh lime juice—added just before eating—tops off the authentic flavor. Mexican home cooks in urban areas use macaroni and other pastas in a number of dishes, and this simple soup reflects everyday cooking in Mexico City, Guadalajara, Monterrey, or other modern Mexican cities.

1/2 cup small dried elbow macaroni
1 tablespoon olive oil
1/4 medium white onion, chopped
2 medium garlic cloves, minced
1 cup canned puréed tomatoes
3 cups canned fat-free reduced-sodium chicken broth
2 cups coarsely chopped fresh spinach
1/2 teaspoon salt, or to taste
1/4 teaspoon crushed red pepper
1/4 cup crumbled cotija cheese, or substitute Parmesan cheese
1 fresh lime, quartered

1. In a pot of salted boiling water, cook the macaroni until tender, about 5 to 6 minutes. Drain in cold running water. Set aside.

2. In a large saucepan, heat oil over medium heat, and cook the onion and garlic until softened, 3 to 4 minutes. Add the tomatoes, and cook, stirring frequently, until reduced and thickened, about 5 minutes. Add the broth, and bring to a boil. Stir in the spinach, salt, red pepper, and macaroni. Simmer, uncovered, 5 minutes. Divide the soup among 4 soup bowls, and sprinkle with cheese. Serve at once with lime wedges.

Onion and Cheese Soup
Sopa de Cebolla y Queso

Makes **4 servings**

My good friends Carol and Bob Puccinelli spend a part of each winter in Puerto Vallarta. They really liked this soup, prepared by the cook of their seaside villa, so we worked out the recipe from the cook's list of ingredients. It's no surprise that chicken bouillon is called for, since the product is widely used in Mexican kitchens to enhance soups, stews, and some sauces. The croutons make it a truly satisfying dish.

4 (1/2-inch-thick) slices oval Mexican sandwich rolls (bolillos) or other sandwich rolls
2 tablespoons unsalted butter, at room temperature
1 tablespoon olive oil or vegetable oil
1 medium white onion, halved lengthwise and thinly sliced crosswise
4 cups canned fat-free reduced-sodium chicken broth
1 teaspoons granulated chicken-flavor bouillon
1/4 cup finely crumbled cotija or mild feta cheese
Chopped fresh cilantro (optional)

1. To prepare the croutons, butter the bread on both sides and fry in a hot skillet 1 to 2 minutes per side until crisp and toasted, or alternatively, toast under an oven broiler until crisp and brown, about 1 minute per side. Set aside.

2. In a large saucepan, heat the oil over medium-low heat and cook the onion, covered, stirring frequently, until limp and tender, but not browned, about 10 minutes. Add the chicken broth and bouillon. Bring to a boil, then reduce heat to low and simmer the soup, covered, 10 minutes.

3. To serve, ladle the soup into 4 soup bowls. Sprinkle with cheese. Put 1 crouton on top of each serving. Garnish with cilantro, if desired. Serve hot.

White Onion Soup
Sopa de Cebolla Blanca

Makes **6 servings**

Bellinghausen Restaurant in Mexico City, with a German name and Mexican ownership, has been in business for more than forty years, and serves many Mexican specialties. About the only German touch is draft beer—not unusual, since German biermeisters played a role in teaching Mexico to make beer. Bellinghausen is one of my favorite places for lunch and people watching. Our favorite spot is the garden patio in the back, and I almost always order the wonderful onion soup made with white onions. This is my version of the soup.

6 cups Basic Chicken Stock (page 215) or canned chicken broth
3 tablespoons unsalted butter
3 large white onions (about 1 3/4 pounds), thinly sliced
1 teaspoon salt
1/4 teaspoon freshly ground pepper, or to taste
4 ounces Monterey Jack cheese, cut into 1/2-inch dice
3 tablespoons chopped fresh cilantro

1. Prepare the chicken stock, if using homemade. Then, in a large saucepan, melt the butter over medium-low heat, and cook the onions, partially covered, stirring occasionally, until very tender and fragrant, but not brown, about 15 minutes.

2. Stir in the salt, pepper, and chicken stock. Bring the soup to a boil, and cook 4 to 5 minutes to blend the flavors. Serve the soup hot. Pass the cheese, cilantro, and limes to add at the table.

eek and Rice Soup
ɔpa de Porro y Arroz

akes **4 servings**

ɛks are available in many of the major public
arkets in Mexico. The small amount of rice
ves a bit of body to this quick brothy and
ealthful soup.

tablespoon olive oil

large leeks, white and pale green parts only,
    washed and thinly sliced crosswise
    (about 2 cups)

medium garlic cloves, finely chopped

medium carrot, peeled and neatly diced,
    about 1/4 inch

/2 teaspoon ground cumin

/8 teaspoon crushed red pepper

/2 teaspoon salt, or to taste

cups canned fat-free reduced-sodium
    chicken broth

1/4 cup long-grain white rice

2 tablespoons chopped fresh cilantro,
    or flat-leaf parsley

In a large pot, heat the oil over medium-low heat.
Add the leeks, garlic, and 1 tablespoon of water.
Cook, covered, stirring frequently, until limp
and tender, 6 to 8 minutes. Add the remaining
ingredients and bring to a boil. Reduce the heat,
cover, and simmer until the vegetables and rice
are tender, about 15 minutes. Adjust seasoning.
Serve at once.

Juan's Garlic and Cactus Soup
Juan's Sopa de Ajo y Nopalitos

Makes **4 to 6 servings**

*Juan Jose Lozano of Leon, Mexico, shared this
soup recipe at a cooking class I attended.
Cooking makes the garlic mild, mellow, and
soft. The cactus adds a slight tartness, and the
swirls of egg add richness, while the broth and
beer balance the whole for an intriguing and
satisfying soup.*

    *Juan added an unusual, hard-to-find sour
cactus called* xoconoxtle. *I use bottled cactus
packed in water for this soup. It's readily available in many supermarkets or Mexican food
markets in the United States.*

2 tablespoons unsalted butter

12 large garlic cloves, very thinly sliced

4 cups chicken stock or canned fat-free
    reduced-sodium chicken broth

1/2 cup canned beef broth

1/2 cup beer, any kind

1 cup rinsed water-packed jarred cactus strips
    (nopalitos)

1/2 teaspoon salt, or to taste

2 large eggs

1. In a large saucepan, melt the butter over
medium-low heat and cook the garlic, stirring,
until fragrant but not brown, about 2 minutes.
Add the remaining ingredients except the eggs.
Raise the heat and bring the soup to a boil, then
reduce heat to low, partially cover, and simmer
until the garlic is soft, 8 to 10 minutes.

2. In a small bowl beat the eggs until frothy.
Bring soup to a boil over medium-high heat. Stir
the soup briskly with a fork while pouring the
eggs into the soup. Cook 1 minute. Serve hot.

Sonoran Cheese Soup
Sopa de Queso

Makes 4 servings

There are many versions of this rich cheese soup with potatoes and tomatoes in the Sonoran region of northern Mexico. Using nonfat chicken broth and cream are not a contradiction here. I prefer the thickness, flavor, and richness this combination develops. (A lighter milk product might curdle the soup during cooking, too.)

1 tablespoon unsalted butter
1 tablespoon vegetable oil
6 green onions, chopped
2 large garlic cloves, chopped
2 medium (about 12 ounces) white or red
   boiling potatoes, peeled and diced
2 medium tomatoes, peeled, seeded, and chopped
1 (14¹/2-ounce) can fat-free reduced-sodium
   chicken broth
1 cup heavy cream
¹/2 teaspoon salt, or to taste
¹/8 teaspoon crushed red pepper
4 ounces Monterey Jack cheese, cut into
   ¹/2-inch dice

1. In a large saucepan, heat the butter and oil over medium heat. Cook the green onions and garlic until softened, about 2 minutes. Add the potatoes and tomatoes, and cook, stirring, until the tomato juices evaporate, 4 to 5 minutes.

2. Add the chicken broth, cream, salt, and crushed pepper. Bring to a boil, reduce the heat to medium-low and simmer until the potatoes are very tender, 15 to 20 minutes. Divide the cheese among 4 soup bowls. Ladle the hot soup over the cheese and serve at once.

Alphabet Soup for Children
Sopa de Letras para Niños

Makes 2 to 3 servings

Mexican children, like children around the world, are fascinated by miniature letters of the alphabet, in pasta form, floating in their soup. They take delight in naming the letters that appear in their spoons before popping them into their mouths. The small amount of cumin adds a subtle, special flavor but won't startle young taste buds. Alphabet pasta should be available in most grocery stores.

2 teaspoons vegetable oil
2 tablespoons minced white onion
¹/2 teaspoon cumin
2 plum tomatoes, peeled, seeded, and
   finely chopped
2 cups canned fat-free reduced-sodium
   chicken broth
¹/4 cup small alphabet pasta
¹/4 teaspoon salt, or to taste

In a medium saucepan, heat the oil over medium heat and cook the onion and cumin until the onion softens, about 3 minutes. Add the tomatoes, and cook, stirring, until the juices are absorbed and the mixture is nearly dry. Add the chicken broth and bring to a boil. Add the pasta and salt to the boiling broth and cook, uncovered, stirring to prevent sticking, until the pasta is tender, about 8 minutes. Serve hot.

Vegetarian Pinto Bean Soup
Sopa de Frijol

Makes **4 servings**

Beans of all kinds bubble away in clay pots throughout Mexico and just about everybody consumes a bowl of soupy beans every day. This homey pinto bean soup from northern Mexico is satisfying and warming on a cold day, and doesn't contain meat or meat broth, so it's a great soup for vegetarians, or if you don't have meat in the house. Ground chili powder can be found in cellophane packages in the Mexican section of most supermarkets or in Mexican markets. For best flavor make this a day before serving.

½ **pound dried pinto beans**
1 bay leaf
1 teaspoon dried oregano (Mexican variety preferred), crumbled
½ **teaspoon ground cumin**
1 tablespoon vegetable oil
1 medium onion, finely chopped
2 medium garlic cloves, finely chopped
2 plum tomatoes, peeled and finely chopped
2 teaspoons ground ancho or pasilla chili powder
1 teaspoon salt

1. Pick over the beans carefully and remove any foreign particles. Put the beans in a strainer and rinse under cold running water. Put the beans, bay leaf, oregano, and cumin in a large saucepan with water to cover by about 2 inches. Bring to a boil over medium high heat, then reduce heat to medium-low, cover and cook until the beans are tender and the liquid thickens, 1½ to 2 hours. Do not let the beans boil dry. Check the water level during cooking and add hot water, when needed, about ¼ cup at a time. There should always be about ½ inch of water above the level of the beans.

2. Meanwhile, heat the oil over medium heat in a medium skillet and cook the onion, stirring, until it browns, about 5 minutes. Add the garlic, tomatoes, and ground chili. Cook, stirring, until the tomato juices evaporate, 2 to 3 minutes. When the beans are tender, add the onion mixture to the beans. Add salt, and continue cooking for about 20 minutes to blend flavors. Remove the bay leaf, and serve hot.

Chickpea and Corn Soup
Sopa de Garbanzo y Elote

Makes **4 servings**

For a number of years I rented villas in Puerto Vallarta and led winter cooking trips to the area. I supplied a number of recipes for the group to prepare, but we always experimented and came up with new ideas. We went to the public market to purchase ingredients, and the participants cooked in teams to prepare a complete meal. This soup was created during one of those culinary holidays.

Maggi seasoning extract is a flavor enhancer and is found in most supermarkets. Our in-house cook showed us how to prepare Baked Fish Fillets with Almonds (page 380) to pair with the soup.

1 tablespoon olive oil or vegetable oil
1/2 medium white onion, finely chopped
3 medium garlic cloves, finely chopped
1/2 teaspoon dried oregano (Mexican variety preferred), crumbled
1/2 teaspoon ground cumin
1/4 teaspoon dried thyme
3 medium tomatoes, peeled and finely chopped
1 (15-ounce) can chickpeas (garbanzo beans), drained and rinsed
1 cup corn kernels (from about 1 large ear of corn)
4 cups chicken broth, canned or homemade
1/2 teaspoon Maggi seasoning extract or Worcestershire sauce
1/2 teaspoon salt, or to taste
1/4 teaspoon crushed red pepper
1 avocado (Hass variety preferred), peeled and diced
Chopped fresh cilantro
Lime wedges

1. In a large pot, heat the oil over medium heat. Cook the onion until translucent, 3 to 4 minutes. Add the garlic, oregano, cumin, thyme, and tomatoes. Cook, stirring, until the tomato juices reduce and the mixture is nearly dry, 4 to 5 minutes.

2. Add the chickpeas, corn, broth, Maggi, salt, and red pepper. Bring to a boil, then reduce the heat, cover and simmer until the corn is tender and the flavors blend, 8 to 10 minutes. Divide among 4 soup bowls. Top each serving with avocado and cilantro. Serve hot with lime wedges.

Chickpea, Potato, and Tomato Soup
Sopa de Garbanzo, Papa, y Jitomate

Makes **4 servings**

Only fresh ripe tomatoes provide the right flavor for this fine soup, so plan to make it when tomatoes are at their peak.

1 tablespoon vegetable oil
1/2 medium white onion, finely chopped (about 3/4 cup)
2 large garlic cloves, finely chopped
1/2 teaspoon ground cumin
1/2 teaspoon dried oregano (Mexican variety preferred), crumbled
1/8 teaspoon crushed red pepper
2 large vine-ripened tomatoes, peeled and finely chopped
1 tablespoon tomato paste
4 cups canned fat-free reduced-sodium chicken broth
2 medium potatoes (12 ounces), peeled and finely diced
1 1/2 cups cooked chickpeas (garbanzo beans), canned or homemade
1/4 cup coarsely chopped fresh cilantro
1/2 teaspoon salt, or to taste

1. Heat the oil in a large pot and cook the onion, stirring frequently, until softened, 3 to 4 minutes. Add the garlic, cumin, oregano, and crushed red pepper. Cook, stirring, 1 minute. Add the tomatoes and tomato paste. Cook until the juices reduce and the mixture is nearly dry, about 3 minutes.

Add the broth, potatoes, and chickpeas. Bring
a boil, reduce the heat, cover and simmer until
e potatoes are tender, 12 to 15 minutes. Stir in
e cilantro and salt. Adjust seasoning. Serve hot.

hickpea and Cabbage Soup
ith Sausage
opa de Garbanzo y Col con Longaniza

akes **4 servings**

*inborn's is a very old and respected restaurant,
w a chain, that originated in Mexico City
ore than fifty years ago, in an historic build-
g dated 1735. It was in a branch of Sanborn's
at I enjoyed this excellent soup.*

*Mexican cooks remove the outer skins from
e chickpeas (for better texture), by rubbing
e cooked chickpeas between their fingers or in
e palms of their hands. It's easy to do, but not
tirely necessary. Longaniza is a highly sea-
ed cured sausage. Use linguica or kielbasa,
substitutes.*

ablespoons vegetable oil

pound longaniza sausage, cut into rounds
   1/4-inch thick

medium white onion, chopped

arge garlic clove, minced

arge Roma tomatoes, peeled and chopped

:ups coarsely chopped cabbage

cup lightly packed fresh parsley leaves

14 1/2-ounce) cans fat-free reduced-sodium
   chicken broth

:up canned chickpeas (garbanzo beans), drained;
   outer skins rubbed off (optional)

teaspoon salt, or to taste

In a 4-quart pot, heat oil over medium heat.
ld the sausage rounds and cook, turning, until
ght brown about 4 to 5 minutes. Remove the
usage to a plate. In the same oil, cook the onion
id garlic, stirring, until softened, about 2 minutes.

2. Add the tomatoes, and cook, stirring, until the
tomato juices have cooked away, 2 to 3 minutes.
Add the cabbage and parsley, and cook, stirring,
until wilted, 3 to 4 minutes.

3. Stir in the broth, chickpeas, salt, and the
reserved sausage. Bring to a boil, then reduce the
heat, cover and simmer the soup 10 minutes to
blend the flavors. Serve hot.

Fava Bean Soup
Sopa de Haba

Makes **4 servings**

*Lots of fava beans are grown in Mexico. This
slow-cooking, nourishing soup calls for dried,
peeled yellow fava beans sold in packages or in
bulk but not always easy to find in the United
States. I buy the fava beans in Latin-American
markets, imported from Mexico or Peru. If dried
fava beans can't be found, small dried lima
beans could be substituted. The flavor will be
somewhat different though.*

2 cups dried peeled yellow fava beans

3 cups water

1 cup canned fat-free reduced-sodium chicken broth

1 tablespoon vegetable oil

1/2 medium white onion, finely chopped

3 medium garlic cloves, finely chopped

**1/2 teaspoon dried oregano (Mexican variety
   preferred), crumbled**

1/2 teaspoon ground cumin

1/4 teaspoon dried thyme

1/2 teaspoon salt, or to taste

1/4 teaspoon freshly ground pepper, or to taste

1. In a 2-quart saucepan, soak the fava beans in
the 3 cups of water 1 hour. Put the pan over
medium-high heat, add the chicken broth and
bring to a boil. Reduce the heat to low, cover and
simmer until some of the beans are tender, about
45 minutes.

2. Meanwhile, heat the oil in a skillet, and cook the onion, garlic, oregano, cumin, and thyme stirring, until the onion is softened, 3 to 4 minutes. Scrape the skillet contents into the soup pan. Cover and cook until the soup thickens, and the fava beans are soft and falling apart, about 1 hour more. If the soup is too thick, add a bit more broth to achieve the desired consistency. The soup should have some texture. Season with salt and pepper. Serve hot.

Fava Bean and Cactus Soup
Sopa de Habas y Nopalitos

Makes 4 servings

Estela Salas Silva shared this recipe from her family collection. Cooks from everywhere travel to attend Señora Silva's cooking classes in her home just outside Tlaxcala near Puebla. Dried peeled fava beans and nopalitos (cactus strips) can be found in Latin-American food markets in the United States. Buy cactus strips packed in water, not brine, and be sure to rinse them thoroughly.

1 cup dried peeled fava beans, rinsed

1/2 teaspoon salt, or to taste

3 medium tomatoes, peeled and chopped

1/2 cup drained, rinsed, and diced jarred cactus (nopales)

2 tablespoons olive oil

1 sprig fresh thyme, or 1/2 teaspoon dried

1/8 teaspoon freshly ground pepper, or to taste

Chopped fresh cilantro

Put the fava beans in a large saucepan. Add 4½ cups water and the salt. Bring to a boil, then reduce heat to low, cover and simmer, stirring frequently, until the beans are soft and falling apart, about 1 hour. When the beans are tender, add the tomatoes, cactus, oil, thyme, and pepper. Cook, uncovered, 10 minutes. Adjust seasoning. Serve sprinkled with cilantro.

Puréed Soups

Black Bean Soup
Sopa de Frijol Negro

Makes 8 servings

More than twenty years ago, I prepared this black bean soup for a class, and the majority of the twenty or so students attending had never before seen black beans. How times have changed, and now we know what the Mexicans have known for centuries—black beans are delicious!

For the best flavor, cook the beans a day ahead. Pequin chiles are tiny red dried chiles that are quite fiery. Sherry imparts a lovely flavor and shows Spanish influence. Amontillado-style sherry is aged, for a richer, mellower flavor.

Basic Pot Beans (page 461) for black beans

2 tablespoons vegetable oil

2 medium white onion, chopped

3 medium garlic cloves, chopped

2 pequin chiles, crumbled, or 1/4 teaspoon crushed red pepper

1 (14-ounce) can stewed tomatoes

1 1/2 teaspoons dried oregano (Mexican variety preferred), crumbled

1/2 teaspoon ground cumin

1/2 teaspoon dried marjoram

1 teaspoon salt, or to taste

1/3 cup sherry, amontillado preferred

Lime wedges

1. Prepare the black beans. Then, heat the oil in a large skillet and cook the onion over medium heat until it begins to brown, about 5 minutes. Add the remaining ingredients, except the sherry, and cook, stirring, 5 minutes.

2. Add the mixture to the beans and simmer 20 minutes to blend the flavors. Purée the soup in

:hes in a blender or food processor. Return soup to the pan and bring to a boil, stirring [fre]quently. Adjust salt. Shortly before serving, stir [t]he sherry. Serve hot with the lime wedges.

[Be]an and Tomato Soup
[So]pa de Frijol y Jitomate

[Mak]es **4 servings**

[Thi]s mild bean soup is an excellent starter
[cou]rse when a spicy dish follows. Try to cook the
[bea]ns one day ahead; the beans will taste better,
[mak]ing for a more flavorful soup. Another way
[of ser]ving the soup is to offer crisp tortilla
[chip]s to be crumbled into the soup at the
[table f]or crunch and extra flavor.

[] **dried small pinto beans**
[] **s water**
[teas]**poon dried oregano (Mexican variety**
  preferred), crumbled
[tea]**spoon ground cumin**
[tab]**lespoon olive oil or vegetable oil**
[la]**rge white onion, chopped**
[me]**dium garlic cloves, thinly sliced**
[(1]**4-ounce) can diced tomatoes**
[te]**aspoon salt, or to taste**
[t]**easpoon freshly ground pepper, or to taste**
[c]**up loosely packed coarsely chopped**
  fresh cilantro
[gr]**een onions, finely chopped**
[t]**o 1/3 cup Mexican crema or sour cream**
[lim]**e wedges**

1. Sort the beans and remove any small pebbles or other debris. Put the beans in a strainer and rinse well. Put the beans, water, oregano, and cumin into a 2-quart saucepan, and bring to a boil, uncovered. Reduce the heat to low, cover, and simmer the beans until tender and the broth thickens, about 2 hours.

2. Heat the oil in a medium skillet, and cook the onion and garlic, stirring frequently, until they begin to brown, 4 to 5 minutes. Scrape the skillet contents into a blender jar or food processor. Add the cooked beans, tomatoes, salt, and pepper. Blend until smooth.

3. Return the puréed soup to the same pan. Add the cilantro and green onions. Bring the soup to a boil over medium-low heat, then reduce the heat to low, and cook about 5 minutes to blend the flavors. Stir the soup often, scraping the bottom of the pan to prevent sticking or scorching. Serve the soup hot with a dab or decorative drizzle of the crema on top. Pass the lime wedges at the table.

Tarascan Bean Soup

Sopa Tarasca

Makes 8 servings

*This creamy smooth bean soup is named for the
Tarascan Indians who live in the mountains of
the Patzcuaro region of Mexico in the state of
Michoacan. The major town, Patzcuaro, on the
shores of Lake Patzcuaro, is well known for its
Festival of the Dead* (Dia de los Muertos), *celebrated primarily on November 2. Tourists from
everywhere visit Patzcuaro, and the tiny island
of Janitizio in the lake, to view the celebration.*

*There are two typical Tarascan Soups. This
version is a puréed mixture of beans, tomatoes,
chiles, herbs, and spices, and topped with crisp
tortilla strips, chiles, and cheese. I learned how
to make it by watching the cook in a restaurant
in Patzcuaro. Dried pink or pinto beans can be
used for the soup, based on preference and
availability. Another soup, with the name
Tarascan Soup, is based on chicken broth and is
very much like Tortilla Soup (page 217).*

1/2 **pound dried pink, or pinto beans**
2 **teaspoons dried oregano (Mexican variety
preferred), crumbled**
2 **bay leaves**
1 1/2 **teaspoons salt**
3 **medium tomatoes, rinsed and cored**
3 **ancho chiles, seeded and veins removed**
1 **tablespoon vegetable oil**
1 **large white onion, coarsely chopped**
6 **large garlic cloves, peeled and thinly sliced**
1 **(14 1/2-ounce) can chicken broth**

Garnish

Vegetable oil
4 **(6- to 7-inch) corn tortillas, cut into thin strips**
4 **pasilla or ancho chiles, seeded, veins removed,
and cut into 1/2-inch pieces**
1 **cup cubed panela or mild feta cheese**

1. Sort the beans and remove any debris. Rinse in
a strainer and put the beans into a large saucepan
with the oregano and bay leaves. Add water to
about 2 inches above the level of the beans. Bring
to a boil, uncovered, then reduce heat, cover, and
simmer until the beans are tender and the broth
thickens, about 1 1/2 to 2 hours. Stir the beans
occasionally, and add more water if needed.
When the beans are tender, add 1 teaspoon of the
salt. Reserve off heat.

2. Preheat the oven to 450°. Put the tomatoes in
a foil-lined pie plate and roast in the oven until
the skins are lightly charred and the tomatoes are
soft and wrinkled, 25 to 30 minutes. Meanwhile,
soak the chiles in hot water 30 minutes.

3. While the tomatoes roast and the chiles soak,
heat the oil in a medium skillet over medium
heat. Add the onion, garlic, and the remaining
1/2 teaspoon of salt. Cook, stirring, 3 minutes.
Reduce the heat to low, cover, and cook the onion
and garlic until golden.

4. Drain the chiles and discard the water. In a
blender, purée the cooked beans, tomatoes,
chiles, onions, and garlic, in batches until
smooth. Return the purée to the saucepan, and
stir in the chicken broth. Bring the soup to a boil,
uncovered, over medium heat, and cook, stirring
frequently, about 5 minutes. Adjust seasoning.

5. Prepare the garnish: Heat 1 inch of oil in a
small skillet. Fry tortillas until crisp; transfer
them to a plate, then fry chiles 3 to 4 seconds.
Serve the soup topped with crisp tortilla strips,
fried chile strips, and the cheese.

nato and Red Bean
tilla Soup
a de Tortilla de Jitomate
ijol Rojo

s 6 to 8 servings

is one of many soups that benefit from the tion of crisp tortillas. This fine bean soup is fying enough to serve on a blustery winter north of the border. Swiss Enchiladas (page would be a good choice to follow the soup.

to 7-inch) corn tortillas, cut into thin strips and fried (Fried Corn Tortilla Chips and Strips, page 85)

s dried small red beans, sorted and rinsed

ps water

y leaves

teaspoons dried oregano (Mexican variety preferred), crumbled

spoon ground cumin

blespoon vegetable oil

dium onion, chopped

dium garlic cloves, thinly sliced

sh jalapeño chiles, seeded, veins removed, and chopped

-ounce) can stewed tomatoes

ounce) can tomato sauce

spoon salt, or to taste

aspoon freshly ground pepper, or to taste

ped fresh cilantro

wedges

1. Prepare the tortilla strips and reserve. Then, put the beans, water, bay leaves, oregano, and cumin in a large pot and cook, covered, about 2 hours, or until very tender. Stir occasionally and add hot tap water to 1 inch above the beans if the beans show above the water level.

2. While the beans cook, heat the oil in a medium skillet and cook the onion, garlic, and jalapeños until softened, about 4 minutes. Add the mixture to the tender cooked beans along with the tomatoes, tomato sauce, salt, and pepper. Discard the bay leaves.

3. Blend the bean mixture in batches in a blender or food processor until smooth. Return the puréed soup to the pot and bring to a boil over medium heat, uncovered. Reduce heat to low and simmer 15 minutes, stirring frequently to blend the flavors. If the soup is too thick, add a little broth or water. To serve, divide the tortilla strips among individual soup bowls and ladle the hot soup into the bowls. Sprinkle with cilantro and pass the lime wedges at the table. The soup freezes well for 3 months.

Richard Sandoval's Tortilla Soup
Sopa de Tortilla de Richard Sandoval

Makes 4 servings

Executive Chef Richard Sandoval, owner of the Maya Restaurants in New York and San Francisco, contributed his special recipe for tortilla soup. The creamy texture of the soup is achieved by puréeing and straining the ingredients and then presenting the soup with a garnish of crisp tortilla squares, diced avocado, and fresh cheese.

The two dried chiles, guajillo and ancho, are often teamed in Mexican cooking for a more complex chile flavor with medium heat. Both kinds can be found in most Mexican markets and in specialty grocery stores. Keep in mind when choosing chiles that the guajillo is generally hotter, but as with all chiles, there are surprises. Experiment to see what works for your desire for fire.

6 (6- to 7-inch) corn tortillas
Vegetable oil for frying
1 guajillo chile, stemmed, seeded, veins removed, and cut into pieces
1 ancho chile, stemmed, seeded, veins removed, and cut into pieces
¼ large Spanish onion, chopped
1 medium garlic clove, chopped
6 plum tomatoes (about 12 ounces) quartered
3½ cups chicken stock, canned or homemade
1 (about 6-inch) sprig fresh epazote
1 teaspoon salt, or to taste
2 teaspoons fresh lime juice
1 teaspoon honey
½ avocado (Hass variety preferred), finely diced (½ inch)
3 ounces finely diced queso fresco (fresh Mexican cheese)
¼ cup Mexican crema or sour cream

1. Cut 2 of the tortillas into ½-inch squares (like confetti). Reserve. In a medium skillet, pour oil to a depth of about 1 inch and heat until the oil shimmers. Fry the 4 whole tortillas, 1 at a time, turning with tongs, until crisp and golden brown on both sides. Drain on paper towels. In the same hot oil, fry the tortilla squares until golden brown. With a slotted spoon remove the squares and drain on paper towels. Reserve in a bowl.

2. In a large saucepan, heat 1 tablespoon of oil and fry the chiles, onion, and garlic, stirring, until the onion and garlic start to brown, about 3 minutes. Add the tomatoes, and cook, stirring, until the juices are bubbling, about 3 minutes.

3. Break the fried whole tortillas into spoon-size pieces and add to the tomato mixture along with the chicken stock and epazote. Bring to a boil; reduce heat to low, cover, and simmer 25 minutes. Remove the epazote and transfer the mixture to a blender or food processor. Purée until smooth. Pour the soup through a strainer into a large bowl. Discard the debris.

4. Rinse the pan and return the soup to the pan. Bring to a boil over medium-low heat, uncovered, stirring frequently to prevent sticking. Season with salt, lime juice, and honey. The soup should be the consistency of heavy cream. If too thick, add hot chicken broth or water to reach the desired consistency. To serve, place a portion of the tortilla squares, avocado, and cheese in the center of 4 shallow soup bowls. Ladle in the hot soup. Top with a dollop of crema.

White Bean Soup
Sopa de Frijol Blanco

Makes 4 servings

Beans of every color are grown and marketed in Mexico. For this soup, I use small white beans and cook the beans a day ahead for best flavor. Canned white beans may be substituted, but home-cooked taste better.

ps cooked small white beans (Basic Pot Beans,
  page 461)
blespoon olive oil
nedium white onion, chopped
·ge garlic cloves, chopped
edium carrot, peeled and thinly sliced
easpoon dried oregano (Mexican variety
  preferred), crumbled
easpoon dried thyme
easpoon crushed red pepper
1¹/₂ cups canned fat-free reduced-sodium
  chicken broth
blespoons chopped fresh flat-leaf parsley
easpoon salt, or to taste

epare the beans. Then, in a large saucepan, heat
oil over medium heat and cook the onion,
red, stirring occasionally until softened, about
nutes. Add the garlic, carrot, oregano, thyme,
ed pepper, and ¹/₂ cup of the chicken broth.
; to a boil, then reduce the heat to low, cover, and
er until the carrots are tender, 10 to 12 minutes.
ansfer the mixture to a blender or food
essor. Add the cooked beans. Purée until
th. Return the soup mixture to the sauce-
Stir in enough of the remaining broth to
: the soup the consistency of thin gravy. Add
arsley and salt. Bring to a boil over medium
then reduce the heat to low and simmer the
  uncovered, stirring frequently, about 10
tes, to blend the flavors. Serve hot.

C am of Fresh Corn and
P lano Chile Soup
C na de Elote y Poblano

N ; 8 servings

C   with poblano *chiles is one of my absolute*
f   *te combinations of the Mexican kitchen,*
a   *often crave this wonderful soup. A blender*
w   *best to purée the vegetables for this soup.*

4 poblano chiles
8 medium ears yellow corn
2 cups water
1 cup canned fat-free reduced-sodium
  chicken broth
1 medium white onion, sliced
2 tablespoons unsalted butter
¹/₂ teaspoon salt, or to taste
2 cups heavy cream
4 ounces Monterey Jack cheese, cut into
  ¹/₄-inch cubes

1. Roast the chiles directly over a gas flame, or
under a preheated broiler, turning frequently
with tongs, until charred all over, about 3 to
4 minutes. Watch carefully to prevent charring
too much, or the chiles will get too soft. Put the
chiles into a plastic bag, and let steam about
5 minutes. Wearing rubber gloves, peel, seed, and
chop the chiles. Set aside.

2. Cut the corn kernels from the cobs over a
large bowl, and scrape the cobs to get the remaining pulp.

3. In a large soup pot, bring the water and
chicken broth to a boil. Add the corn kernels,
corn pulp, onion, butter, and salt. Cook 5 to
6 minutes. Remove the pan from the heat.

4. In a blender jar, purée the corn mixture and
the reserved chopped chiles, in batches if necessary, until smooth. Add 1 cup of the cream, and
blend again, about 30 seconds.

5. Pour the blended soup back into the same
soup pot, and bring to a boil, over medium
heat, stirring frequently. Reduce heat to low,
and stir in the remaining 1 cup of cream and
cook, uncovered, stirring frequently, until steaming hot, 3 to 4 minutes. Adjust seasoning. Put
2 tablespoons of diced cheese into the bottom
of each soup bowl, and ladle the hot soup into
the bowls.

Cream of Poblano Chile and Potato Soup
Crema de Sopa Poblano

Makes **4 servings**

In the colonial city of Puebla, the chef at the Maria Bonita restaurant prepared this rich and wonderful soup and shared the recipe. It is important to buy firm and shiny dark green chiles that are really fresh. Avoid chiles that are wrinkled and beginning to soften.

4 large poblano chiles
1 tablespoon unsalted butter
1 tablespoon vegetable oil
1 medium white onion, chopped
2 large garlic cloves, chopped
1 medium (6-ounce) Russet potato, peeled and thinly sliced
3/4 cup water
1/4 cup chopped fresh flat-leaf parsley, plus more for garnish
1 cup chicken stock or canned fat-free reduced-sodium chicken broth
1/2 cup corn kernels, fresh (from about 1/2 ear) or thawed if frozen
1/2 cup heavy cream
1/2 teaspoon salt, or to taste

1. Roast the chiles directly over a gas flame or under a preheated broiler, turning frequently with tongs, until charred all over, about 3 to 4 minutes. Watch carefully to prevent charring too much or the chiles may get too soft. Place in a plastic bag and steam about 5 minutes. Wearing rubber gloves, rub or scrape off the charred skin. Cut the chiles open, remove the seeds and veins. Chop coarsely and reserve.

2. In a large heavy saucepan, heat the butter and oil over medium heat. Cook the onion and garlic, stirring frequently, until softened, 3 to 4 minutes. Add the potato, water, parsley, and chicken stock. Bring to a boil, then reduce the heat to medium-low and cook until the potato is very tender, about 15 minutes.

3. Meanwhile, bring a small pot of water to a boil and cook the corn until just tender, about 3 minutes. Drain and reserve.

4. When the potato is done, transfer the contents of the saucepan to a blender or food processor. Add the reserved chiles, cream, and salt. Purée until smooth. Return the soup to the saucepan, and bring to a boil over medium-low heat, stirring frequently, to prevent scorching. Divide the soup among 4 soup bowls. Garnish each serving with about 2 tablespoons of corn, and sprinkle with parsley.

tato, Garlic, and
ipotle Soup
ɔa de Papa, Ajo, y Chile Chipotle

es **4 servings**

to soup with aromatic roasted garlic and spiced
smoky chipotle chile has great flavor and ele-
smoothness. Maggi, the seasoning extract
h used in Mexico to enhance flavor, can be
d in most supermarkets. Worcestershire sauce
be substituted, if desired, or just leave it out.

1   ɪd garlic
1   lespoon olive oil
1   lespoon unsalted butter
1   ɔn, chopped
3   dium potatoes (1 pound), peeled and
     hinly sliced
3   s canned fat-free reduced-sodium chicken broth
1   ɪed chipotle chile en adobo, seeded and
     hopped
¹⁄   ɪspoon Maggi seasoning extract or
     Vorcestershire sauce
¹⁄   ɪspoon salt, or to taste
C∣   ɪed fresh cilantro

1. :heat the oven to 350°. Slice the top off the
gɑ   head, and put the garlic, cut side up, in a
sn   ovenproof bowl. Drizzle with the olive oil,
cc   with foil and bake 40 minutes, or until soft.
W   cool enough to handle squeeze the garlic
oι   the skins and reserve.

2. lt the butter in a large saucepan over
m∣   m heat and cook the onion, covered, stir-
riɪ   equently, until limp, about 4 minutes. Add
th   ɔtatoes, broth, chipotle chile, and the
res   d roasted garlic. Cook until the potatoes are
soɪ   ɔout 20 minutes. Transfer the mixture to a
ble   r or food processor and blend until smooth.
Re   the soup to the pan and bring to a boil,
un   red, stirring frequently over medium-low
heɑ   dd salt. Serve hot, sprinkled with cilantro.

Creamed Onion Soup
Crema de Cebolla

Makes **4 servings**

*Cooking the onions slowly for this soup releases
all their natural sweetness. Follow the soup
course with a spicy dish, such as Sautéed Sea
Bass with Pasilla Chile Sauce (page 390) or a
simple Chicken Tostada (page 69). This soup
is based on one my husband, Bill, and I had
on a trip to Copper Canyon in the state of
Chihuahua, in northern Mexico.*

2 tablespoons unsalted butter
3 medium onions (about 1 pound), thinly sliced
¹⁄₈ teaspoon crushed red pepper
¹⁄₂ teaspoon salt, or to taste
1¹⁄₂ cups canned fat-free reduced-sodium
   chicken broth
1 cup whole milk
1 small (3 ounce) white potato, peeled and
   finely chopped
1 tablespoon chopped fresh cilantro

1. Melt the butter in a large soup pot and cook
the onion, covered, over medium-low heat, stirring occasionally, until limp and tender, about
15 minutes. Add the red pepper, salt, chicken
broth, milk, and potato. Bring to a boil over
medium heat, then reduce the heat to low and
simmer, partially covered, stirring occasionally,
until the potato is tender, 8 to 10 minutes.

2. Pour the soup into a blender and pulse a few
times on low speed until just blended with
some texture. Return the soup to the pan and
bring to a boil over medium-low heat, uncovered, stirring frequently, until steaming hot. Serve
hot, sprinkled with cilantro.

Creamy Onion and Meatball Soup
Crema de Cebolla con Albondigas

Makes 4 to 6 servings

There is no cream in this unique puréed soup adapted from a cookbook, The Food and Drink of Mexico *by George C. Booth. He wrote that the soup originated in the city of Puebla and was called* Sopa de Crema. *My version is slightly different, in that I sauté the onions before boiling them to enhance the flavor, I use a mixture of ground beef and pork for the meatballs, and add* masa harina *to thicken the broth. The soup is unusual and quite delicious.*

1 slice white bread

1 tablespoon milk

1 large egg, beaten

1/2 pound lean ground beef or pork, or a mixture of the two

1/4 teaspoon dried oregano (Mexican variety preferred), crumbled

1/2 teaspoon salt

1/4 teaspoon freshly ground pepper, or to taste

2 tablespoons unsalted butter

2 large white onions, finely chopped

1 tablespoon masa harina (flour for corn tortillas)

4 cups chicken broth, canned or homemade

2 tablespoons chopped fresh flat-leaf parsley or cilantro

4 teaspoons sherry

1. In a small bowl soak the bread in the milk and mash with a fork. Mix in the beaten egg. With clean hands, mix in the meat, oregano, salt, and pepper. Form into small (about 1-inch) meatballs. Reserve on a plate.

2. In a large saucepan, melt the butter over medium heat. Add the onions and cook, stirring, 2 minutes. Add 1 cup of water, cover, reduce heat to low, and simmer until the onions are very tender, about 15 minutes.

3. Transfer the onion mixture to a blender or a processor. Add the masa harina and 2 cups of the chicken broth. Purée until smooth.

4. Return the soup to the saucepan. Add the remaining 2 cups of chicken broth. Bring to a boil. Drop in the meatballs and parsley. Cook, partially covered, stirring occasionally, until the meatballs are completely cooked through, 18 to 20 minutes. Adjust seasoning. Stir in the sherry. Serve hot.

Cauliflower and Onion Soup
Sopa de Coliflor y Cebolla

Makes 6 servings

This lowfat but satisfying soup from south of the border is just right for cold weather meals north of the border.

1 tablespoon vegetable oil or olive oil

1 medium white onion, chopped

2 (14 1/2-ounce) cans fat-free reduced-sodium chicken broth

1 cup lowfat milk

1 medium (about 8-ounce) baking potato, peeled and sliced

1 medium (about 2-pound) cauliflower, separated into florets

4 green onions, chopped, including most of the green tops

1 teaspoon ground cumin

1 teaspoon salt, or to taste

1/2 teaspoon freshly ground pepper, or to taste

1 tablespoon minced red jalapeño chile, or red bell pepper

1. In a large saucepan, heat the oil over medium heat, and cook the onion, stirring frequently, until softened, about 4 minutes. Add the broth, milk, potato, cauliflower, green onions, cumin, and salt. Bring to a boil over high heat, then reduce the heat, cover, and simmer until the vegetables are very soft, about 20 minutes.

Transfer the soup to a blender or food proces-
and purée until smooth. Return the soup to
pan, and stir in the pepper. Bring to a boil,
overed, over medium-low heat, stirring fre-
ntly, until steaming hot, 3 to 4 minutes. Serve
with a sprinkle of the minced red pepper.

uliflower and Pecan Soup
ma de Coliflor y Pacana

es **4 servings**

liflower and toasted pecans are blended
eate this enchanting creamy soup from
ral Mexico.

ispoons olive oil

ispoons unsalted butter

iedium white onion, chopped

ip pecan pieces

¹/2-ounce) cans fat-free reduced-sodium
chicken broth

ip whole milk

iedium (about 1-pound) cauliflower,
separated into florets

aspoon salt, or to taste

aspoon freshly ground pepper, or to taste

lapeño chile, seeded, veins removed, and
finely minced

a large saucepan, heat the oil and butter
medium heat and cook the onion until
ned, 3 to 4 minutes. Add the pecans, and
, stirring, 45 seconds, being careful not to
h them. Add the broth, milk, cauliflower,
salt. Bring to a boil, then reduce the heat to
cover, and simmer until the cauliflower is
tender, about 15 minutes.

ansfer the soup to a blender or food proces-
nd purée until smooth. Return the soup to
an and stir in the pepper. Bring to a boil,
vered, over medium-low heat, stirring fre-
tly, until steaming hot, 3 to 4 minutes. Serve
ith minced chile sprinkled on top.

Carrot Soup
Sopa de Zanahoria

Makes **4 servings**

*Cumin and a touch of crushed hot red pepper
add flavor, and the potato gives a creamy quality to this smooth and simple carrot soup from
Chihuahua in northern Mexico, the state of the
incredible Copper Canyon and home of the
Tarahumara Indians. The soup is special
enough for entertaining.*

1 tablespoon vegetable oil or olive oil

¹/2 medium white onion, chopped (about ³/4 cup)

1 teaspoon cumin seeds

¹/4 teaspoon crushed red pepper

**4 medium (about 1 pound) carrots, peeled and
thinly sliced**

**1 medium (about 4-ounce) potato, peeled and
thinly sliced**

4 cups chicken broth, canned or homemade

¹/2 teaspoon salt

2 tablespoons Mexican crema or sour cream

1 tablespoon chopped fresh cilantro

1. Heat the oil in a large soup pot over medium
heat. Add the onion, and cook, stirring, until
softened, about 3 minutes. Add the cumin seeds
and red pepper. Cook, stirring, 1 minute. Add
the carrots, potato, chicken broth, and salt.
Bring to a boil, then reduce the heat, cover, and
simmer until the carrots are very tender, about
18 minutes.

2. Transfer the soup to a blender or food processor and purée until smooth. Return the soup to
the pan and bring to a boil, uncovered, stirring
frequently, until steaming hot, 3 to 4 minutes.
Serve hot, garnishing each serving with a swirl of
crema and a sprinkle of cilantro.

Carrot, Chickpea, and Tomato Soup

Sopa de Zanahoria, Garbanzo, y Jitomate

Makes **4 servings**

Fondas, *the small food stalls in Mexico's public markets, always post their specialties to tempt passersby. It's a sensory treat and inspiring to wander through the* fondas *and see what's cooking. A stroll through the market in Guanajuato in central Mexico led to the idea for this simple, tasty soup.*

2 tablespoons olive oil or vegetable oil

$1/2$ medium onion, chopped

2 medium garlic cloves, chopped

2 medium carrots, thinly sliced

2 cups cooked chickpeas (garbanzo beans), canned or homemade

1 large ripe tomato, peeled and chopped

1 tablespoon coarsely chopped fresh flat-leaf parsley

1 ($15^1/2$-ounce) can fat-free reduced-sodium chicken broth

$1/2$ teaspoon salt, or to taste

$1/8$ teaspoon freshly ground pepper, or to taste

1. In a large soup pot, heat the oil over medium heat and cook the onion and garlic, stirring, until softened, 3 to 4 minutes. Add the remaining ingredients and bring to a boil; then reduce the heat, cover and simmer until the carrots are very tender, 15 to 18 minutes.

2. Transfer to a blender or food processor and purée on low speed until smooth. Return the soup to the pan and bring to a boil, uncovered, over medium-low heat, stirring frequently, until steaming hot, 3 to 4 minutes. Adjust seasoning. Serve hot.

Purée of Chickpea Soup

Crema de Garbanzo

Makes **4 to 6 servings**

Mexicans uses chickpeas, which they call garbanzos, in a variety of dishes. This flavorful soup is like one my husband and I had in Oaxaca. Make the soup with canned beans, or with cooked dried beans (see Basic Chickpeas, page 470). Mexican cooks rub the thin skins off the cooked beans to make the texture of the soup creamier. I have found it to be quite easy to do; but if you are short on time or prefer the health benefit of extra fiber from the skins, leave them on.

2 tablespoons unsalted butter

1 medium onion, chopped

1 medium carrot, chopped

2 large garlic cloves, chopped

$1/2$ teaspoon ground cumin

$1/2$ teaspoon salt, or to taste

$1/8$ teaspoon crushed red pepper

3 cups cooked chickpeas (garbanzo beans), canned or homemade, drained

1 ($14^1/2$-ounce) can reduced-sodium chicken broth

1 tablespoon chopped fresh cilantro

1. In a medium saucepan, melt the butter over medium heat, and cook the onion, carrot, and garlic, stirring often, 5 minutes. Add the cumin, salt, and crushed pepper. Cook 1 minute. Add the drained chickpeas and the chicken broth and cook 1 minute.

2. Transfer the soup mixture to a blender or food processor and purée until smooth.

3. Return the soup to the pan, and bring to a boil, partially covered, over medium-low heat. Reduce the heat to low, cover, and simmer, stirring frequently, 8 to 10 minutes to blend the flavors. Serve the soup hot, sprinkled with cilantro.

paragus Soup
ɔa de Esparragos

'es **4 servings**

*h asparagus is often served in upscale
:ican restaurants in urban areas such as
:ico City. Although not native to the region,
iragus is grown in Mexico and even imported
the United States during part of the year, so
iot surprising that Mexicans enjoy it just as
lo. To make this soup, asparagus is cooked in
ken broth until very tender, then blended
oth. For a bright touch, garnish the soup
strips of canned pimiento, or finely diced,
red bell pepper, if you wish.*

und fresh asparagus spears

:lespoons unsalted butter

iedium white onion, chopped

ɔs canned fat-free reduced-sodium
   chicken broth

to 7-inch) corn tortilla, torn into small pieces

ɪp cream or half and half

iaspoon salt, or to taste

iaspoon freshly ground pepper, or to taste

ed pimiento strips

ut or break off the tough ends of the aspara-
Chop the remaining asparagus spears into
ch pieces.

elt the butter in a large saucepan, and cook
nion, covered, stirring frequently, until limp,
t 3 minutes. Add the chicken broth and
agus. Bring to a boil, then reduce the heat,
, and cook until the asparagus is very tender,
t 15 minutes. Stir in the tortilla pieces and
n.

our the soup contents into a blender or food
ssor and purée until smooth. (Do this in
es, if necessary.)

4. Return the blended soup to the pan. Season
with salt and pepper. Bring to a boil over medium-
low heat, stirring frequently, until steaming hot,
3 to 4 minutes. Ladle into individual bowls and
top each serving with a few strips of pimiento.

Cream of Spinach Soup
Crema de Espinaca

Makes **4 servings**

*The Mexican kitchen offers a seemingly endless
variety of soups. Greens of all kinds are incorporated into soups to give color, texture, and flavor. Spinach blended with potatoes and onion is
especially pleasing.*

2 teaspoons olive oil

1/2 medium white onion, chopped

2 small potatoes (about 8 ounces), peeled and
   thinly sliced

4 cups washed spinach, trimmed of coarse stems
   and chopped

4 cups canned fat-free reduced-sodium
   chicken broth

1/2 cup cream or half and half

1 teaspoon salt, or to taste

1/8 teaspoon freshly ground pepper, or to taste

2 tablespoons finely chopped green onions

1. Heat the oil in a large pot, and cook the onion
until softened, 3 to 4 minutes. Add the potatoes,
spinach, and chicken broth. Bring to a boil, then
reduce the heat to low, cover and simmer until
the potatoes are tender, 12 to 15 minutes.

2. Transfer to a blender or food processor and
purée until smooth. Return the soup to the pot.
Stir in the cream, salt, and pepper. Bring to a boil,
uncovered, over medium-low heat, stirring frequently, until steaming hot, about 5 minutes.
Adjust seasoning. Serve hot, sprinkling each serving with the green onion.

Puréed Pea Soup
Crema de Guisante

Makes 4 servings

Women in Mexico's public markets can often be seen sitting surrounded by a pile of fresh pea pods, efficiently, almost rhythmically, releasing bright green peas from pod after pod.

In the Yucatán region of Mexico, peas are scattered as a garnish over a number of typical dishes. In Mexico City, peas show up in creamy smooth soups like this one.

This soup is best made with fresh peas, although still tasty made with frozen. The red pepper sauce is an optional garnish but adds a lively touch of color and flavor.

1/4 cup Red Bell Pepper Sauce (page 61), optional
1 tablespoon vegetable oil
1/2 medium white onion, finely chopped
1 medium garlic clove, thinly sliced
1 small (3-ounce) white potato, peeled, quartered, and sliced
2 cups fresh or frozen peas
2 cups chicken broth, canned or homemade
1/4 teaspoon crushed red pepper
1/2 teaspoon salt, or to taste

1. Prepare the red pepper sauce, if using. Then, in a medium saucepan, heat the oil over medium heat. Add the onion and garlic. Cook, stirring, until the onion is softened, about 3 minutes. Add the potato, peas, broth, crushed red pepper, and salt. Bring to a boil, cover, and reduce the heat and simmer until the potatoes are tender, 8 to 10 minutes.

2. Transfer the soup to a blender or food processor and purée until smooth. Return the soup to the pan and bring to a boil, uncovered, over medium-low heat, stirring frequently until steaming hot, 3 to 4 minutes. Serve hot, drizzled with red pepper sauce, if desired.

Green Chile and Tomatillo Soup
Sopa de Chile Poblano y Tomatillos

Makes 4 servings

Traditional ingredients are presented in an unusual way in this scrumptious contemporary soup that's my own innovation.

1 tablespoon vegetable oil
1/2 medium white onion, chopped
1 medium garlic clove, chopped
1/2 teaspoon dried oregano (Mexican variety preferred), crumbled
2 large poblano chiles, roasted and peeled (page 8)
3/4 pound (about 12) tomatillos, husked and quartered
1/2 cup loosely packed chopped fresh cilantro
3 cups canned fat-free reduced-sodium chicken broth
1 tablespoon masa harina (corn flour for tortillas)
1/2 teaspoon salt, or to taste
1/8 teaspoon freshly ground pepper, or to taste
1/3 cup Mexican crema or sour cream

1. In a large saucepan, heat the oil over medium heat. Add the onion, garlic, and oregano. Stir to coat with oil. Cover and cook on low heat 5 minutes. Add the chopped chiles, tomatillos, cilantro, and chicken broth.

2. In a small bowl mix the masa harina with about 2 tablespoons broth and stir into the soup pot. Bring the soup to a boil; then reduce the heat and simmer, partially covered, until the tomatillos are soft, 12 to 15 minutes. Season with salt and pepper.

3. Transfer the soup to a blender or food processor and purée until smooth. Return the soup to the pan and bring to a boil, over medium-low heat, stirring frequently, until steaming hot, 3 to 4 minutes. Serve hot, drizzled with crema.

ayote Soup
)a de Chayote

es **4 servings**

green pear-shaped chayote, indigenous to
ico, is a type of squash that's now available
)st everywhere in the United States. It's often
| in the same way as summer squash. The
ate flavor of the chayote takes well to a bit of
' seasoning, as in this soup.

ge chayote, cut in half lengthwise

lespoon olive oil

ispoon unsalted butter

hite onion, finely chopped

ge garlic cloves, thinly sliced

ispoon dried oregano (Mexican variety
preferred), crumbled

 crushed red pepper

is canned fat-free reduced-sodium
chicken broth

dium zucchini, thinly sliced

peño chile, seeded, veins removed, and chopped

ip lightly packed chopped fresh cilantro

lespoon masa harina (corn flour for tortillas)

spoon salt, or to taste

ip Mexican crema or sour cream

1)ok the chayote in a pan of boiling salted
: to cover, until tender, 30 to 40 minutes. Cool
r cold running water. Peel and discard the
outer skin. Slice the chayotes crosswise, and
ve in a blender or food processor.

2 a large saucepan, heat the oil and butter
medium heat and cook the onion until soft-
3 to 4 minutes. Add the oregano, red pepper,
ı, zucchini, jalapeño, cilantro, and masa
a. Bring to a boil, reduce the heat to low,
and simmer until the zucchini is tender,
t 10 minutes.

3 ınsfer the soup to a the blender or food
issor with the chayote and purée until

smooth. Return the soup to the pan and bring to
a boil, over medium-low heat, stirring frequently,
and cook 3 to 4 minutes. Season with salt. Serve
hot with a swirl of crema on top.

Hearts of Palm Soup
Crema de Palmito

Makes **4 servings**

La Cava restaurant in Mexico City gets credit for
this elegant soup which gets a spark of spicy heat
from chipotle chiles. I remember it well, for the
night we dined at La Cava a fairly strong earth-
quake shook the capital city. After some moments
of hesitation, dining resumed, and I finished this
delicious rich soup. Fresh hearts of palm are rare
and hard to find in the United States, but canned
are available in most supermarkets.

1 tablespoon unsalted butter or olive oil

1/2 medium white onion, finely chopped

2 cups canned fat-free reduced-sodium chicken broth

3/4 cup heavy cream or half and half

**1 (14-ounce) can hearts of palm, drained, rinsed,
and chopped**

**1 to 2 canned chipotle chiles en adobo, seeded
and chopped**

1/2 teaspoon salt, or to taste

2 teaspoons finely chopped fresh parsley

1. In a large wide saucepan, melt the butter over
medium-low heat and cook the onion, covered,
stirring frequently until the onion is tender, about
5 minutes. Add the remaining ingredients except
the parsley, and bring to a boil. Reduce the heat to
low, partially cover and simmer 5 minutes.

2. Transfer the soup to a blender or food processor
and purée until smooth. (There will be some texture
from tiny bits of the palm hearts.) Return the soup
to the pan and bring to a boil over medium-low
heat, stirring frequently, and cook 3 to 4 minutes.
Adjust seasoning. Serve hot, sprinkled with parsley.

Zucchini and Onion Soup
Sopa de Calabacitas

Makes **4 servings**

Make use of a bumper crop of zucchini by adding this typical Mexican soup to your recipe file. Use small to medium zucchini for the soup, since they are mild, sweet, and have fewer seeds than overgrown squash. The soup can be served hot or cold.

2 tablespoons unsalted butter
1 medium white onion, chopped
1¼ pounds (about 6 small) zucchini, sliced
1 teaspoon salt, or to taste
¼ teaspoon freshly ground pepper, or to taste
1 cup water
4 green onions, including 2 inches of the green, chopped
½ cup chicken broth, canned or homemade
½ cup cream
2 tablespoons chopped fresh cilantro

1. In a medium saucepan, melt the butter over medium heat. Add the onion and cook, stirring, until softened, 3 to 4 minutes. Add the zucchini, salt, pepper, and water. Cover, and cook over medium heat until the zucchini are very soft, 12 to 15 minutes. Add the green onions, broth, and cream. Cook, uncovered, 5 minutes.

2. Transfer soup to a blender or food processor and purée until smooth. Return to the pan— if serving hot—and reheat over medium heat, stirring frequently, until steaming hot, 3 to 4 minutes. If serving cold, chill in the refrigerator at least 2 hours before serving. Garnish with cilantro.

Winter Squash Soup
Sopa de Calabaza

Makes **4 servings**

Large baking squash and pumpkins are native to Mexico, and are seen in markets throughout the country. Use whatever winter squash you like for this soup. I like butternut squash because of its smooth texture, bright color, and sweet buttery flavor.

1 butternut squash, about 2 pounds, or other baking squash
2 tablespoons olive oil
½ medium onion, chopped
3 medium garlic cloves, chopped
1 medium carrot, peeled and thinly sliced
1 teaspoon ground cumin
½ teaspoon salt, or to taste
⅛ teaspoon freshly ground pepper, or to taste
⅛ teaspoon crushed red pepper
1 (14½-ounce) can fat-free reduced-sodium chicken broth
Mexican crema, sour cream, or plain yogurt
Chopped fresh cilantro

1. Carefully cut squash in half with a cleaver or large heavy chef's knife, and scoop out the seeds. Cut away the peel and cut the orange flesh into 1-inch pieces. In a large saucepan, heat the oil over medium heat, and cook the onion and garlic, stirring, until they begin to brown, 4 to 5 minutes. Add the squash and all the remaining ingredients, except the sour cream and cilantro. Bring the soup to a boil, then reduce the heat to medium-low and simmer, covered, 15 to 20 minutes, or until the vegetables are very tender.

2. Transfer the soup to a blender or food processor and purée the soup in batches until smooth. If the soup is too thick, add additional hot broth a little at a time.

Return the soup to the pan and bring to a boil
r medium-low heat, stirring frequently to pre-
t scorching. Serve hot, garnished with a swirl
rema, and a sprinkle of cilantro.

lery and Corn Soup
ma de Apio y Elote

es **4 servings**

*ppetizing photograph of cream soup with
y and corn caught my eye as I was browsing
ugh Kena, a Mexican food magazine. The soup
nice contrast of textures, achieved by puréeing
of the vegetables and mixing the smooth
e with the remaining unpuréed vegetables. I
ened the soup by replacing most of the cream
chicken broth, and added potato for a
nier finish, and a little red pepper for color.*

2   spoons olive oil
1   spoon unsalted butter
1/ edium onion, finely chopped
1   ll (4-ounce) potato, peeled and finely diced
    1/4 inch)
1   finely diced celery (1/4 inch)
1   corn kernels, fresh (from about 1 ear)
    r thawed, if frozen
1/ dium red bell pepper, finely diced (1/4 inch)
2   s canned fat-free reduced-sodium
    hicken broth
1/ spoon ground cumin
1/ heavy cream
1/ spoon salt, or to taste
1/ spoon freshly ground pepper, or to taste

1. a large saucepan, heat the oil and butter
ov medium heat and cook the onion until
tra cent, 3 to 4 minutes. Add 1/2 cup of the cel-
er d 1/2 cup of the corn. Bring to a boil, reduce
th at, cover, and cook until the vegetables are
ve nder, about 12 to 15 minutes. When done,
tra r the vegetables to a blender or food

processor and purée until smooth. Return the
puréed mixture to the pan.

2. While the vegetables are cooking, put the
remaining 1/2 cup celery, 1/2 cup corn, red bell pepper, and 1/2 cup water into a small saucepan. Bring
to a boil and cook until tender, 3 to 4 minutes. Add
these as they are to the puréed soup mixture in the
pan. Stir in the cream, salt, and pepper. Bring to a
boil, uncovered, over medium-low heat, stirring
frequently, and cook 3 to 4 minutes. Serve hot.

Leek Soup
Crema de Porro

Makes **4 servings**

*Leeks puréed with potato for smoothness and
poblano chile for extra flavor, make a delightful
creamy soup that's very low in fat.*

1 large poblano chile, roasted and peeled
3 large leeks
1 tablespoon unsalted butter
1 (4-ounce) potato, peeled and thinly sliced
2 cups canned fat-free reduced-sodium chicken broth
3/4 cup milk
1/4 teaspoon salt, or to taste
1 tablespoon very finely chopped fresh flat-leaf
    parsley

1. Prepare the chile. Then remove the stem and
cut out and discard the seeds. Coarsely chop the
chile and set aside.

2. Wash the leeks then trim off the root end and
discard the dark green leaves. Cut the leeks in half
lengthwise and rinse well to rid them of any dirt or
sand between the layers of leaves. Chop the leeks,
using only the white and tender pale green part.

3. Melt the butter in a medium saucepan. Add the
leeks and cook, covered, stirring frequently, until
softened, about 5 minutes. Add the chile to the pan
along with the potato and chicken broth. Bring to a

boil, then reduce the heat, cover, and simmer until the potatoes are very tender, about 15 minutes.

4. Transfer the soup to a blender or food processor and purée until smooth. Add the milk and salt. Blend again. Return the soup to the pan, and bring it to a boil, uncovered, over medium-low heat, stirring frequently. Cook 3 to 4 minutes. Adjust seasoning. Serve hot, garnished with a sprinkle of parsley.

Lentil Soup
Sopa de Lentejas

Makes 4 servings

Dried lentils of several hues are available in Mexican markets throughout the country. I use red lentils, which can be found in most health food stores in the United States, for this delicately colored soup. Brown or green lentils can be used and will still taste good, but the color of the soup will be quite different.

1 cup red lentils
2 tablespoons olive oil or vegetable oil
3 medium garlic cloves, chopped
1 teaspoon ground cumin
1 medium carrot, peeled and coarsely chopped
1 (14¹/₂-ounce) can fat-free reduced-sodium chicken broth
1 (14-ounce) can diced tomatoes
1 cup water
¹/₈ teaspoon crushed red pepper
¹/₂ teaspoon salt, or to taste
Cilantro sprigs

1. Pick over the lentils, and remove any small pebbles or debris. Place the lentils in a strainer and rinse thoroughly. Drain and set aside.

2. In a large pan, heat the oil over medium heat, and cook the onion, garlic, and cumin, stirring, until the onion begins to brown, 3 to 4 minutes. Add the carrot, broth, tomatoes, water, crushed pepper, salt, and the reserved lentils. Bring to a boil,

then reduce the heat to low, cover and simmer until the lentils are tender, about 15 to 20 minutes.

3. Transfer soup to a blender or food processor, and purée, in batches if necessary. Return the blended soup to the pan, and bring to a boil, uncovered, over medium-low heat, stirring frequently, and cook 3 to 4 minutes. Serve hot, topped with a sprig of cilantro in each bowl.

Sweet Potato and Red Pepper Soup
Crema de Camote y Chile Dulce Rojo

Makes 4 servings

Bright orange sweet potatoes, often called yams, and roasted red bell pepper, puréed with broth and wine, make this new-wave (nueva cocina) Mexican soup beautiful and delicious.

1 large red bell pepper
1 tablespoon olive oil
¹/₂ cup chopped white onion
3¹/₂ cups canned fat-free reduced-sodium chicken broth
¹/₂ cup dry white wine
1 (12-ounce) orange-fleshed sweet potato, peeled, quartered lengthwise, and thinly sliced
¹/₂ teaspoon salt, or to taste
¹/₈ teaspoon freshly ground pepper, or to taste
2 tablespoons finely crumbled cotija or mild feta cheese

1. Preheat the oven broiler. Cut the red pepper in half lengthwise. Discard the stem and seeds. Put the pepper, skin side up, on a foil-lined pie plate and press with palm to flatten. Roast under the broiler until charred and blistered, about 4 to 5 minutes. Transfer to a plastic bag and steam 10 to 12 minutes. Remove the skin. Coarsely chop the pepper and place near the stove.

2. In a large saucepan, heat the oil over medium heat and cook the onion, stirring, until softened, 3 to 4 minutes. Add the broth, wine, potato, salt, and coarsely chopped red pepper. Bring to a boil, then reduce

heat to low, cover and simmer until the pota-
[...] and pepper are very tender, 18 to 20 minutes.
[T]ransfer the soup to a blender or food processor
[...] purée until smooth. Return the soup to the
[...] and bring to a boil over medium-low heat, stir-
[...] frequently, and cook 3 to 4 minutes. Stir in the
[...]per. Adjust seasoning. Divide among 4 soup
[...]ls. Scatter the crumbled cheese and reserved
[...]d red pepper equally over each bowl. Serve hot.

[W]alnut Soup
[Sop]a de Nuez

[Mak]es **4 servings**

*[It is] a common practice in the Mexican kitchen
[to u]se nuts and seeds to thicken and add flavor
[to a]ll kinds of dishes. This lovely first course
[soup] comes from the colonial city of Puebla,
[sout]heast of Mexico City.*

[1 tab]lespoon unsalted butter
[1 tab]lespoon vegetable oil
[1 cu]p chopped white onion
[1 t]easpoon dried oregano (Mexican variety
   preferred), crumbled
[3 cu]p chopped walnuts, finely ground in a processor
[2] cups chicken broth, canned or homemade
[1 t]easpoon crushed red pepper
[1 cu]p heavy cream
[1 t]easpoon salt, or to taste
[1 tab]lespoon finely chopped flat-leaf parsley

[1] [In] a large saucepan, melt the butter with the oil
[over] medium heat. Add the onion and oregano.
[Stir] and cook, stirring frequently, until the onion
[soft]ens, about 4 minutes. Add the walnuts, broth,
[and] crushed red pepper. Bring to a boil, then reduce
[the h]eat to low, cover and simmer 15 minutes.

[2] [Tr]ansfer the soup to a blender or food proces-
[sor a]nd purée until smooth. Add the cream and
[salt.] Blend smooth. Return to the pan. Bring to a
[boil] over medium heat. Cook, stirring, 1 minute.
[Serve] hot, garnished with parsley.

Cold Soups

Mexican Gazpacho
Gazpacho Mexicano

Makes **4 servings**

*Gazpacho, the classic Spanish cold tomato soup,
has found a home in the Mexican kitchen,
except it is spiced up with chiles and garnished
with cilantro and fresh lime juice.*

2 pounds vine-ripened fresh tomatoes,
   peeled and chopped
1/2 medium cucumber, peeled, seeded,
   and chopped
1 celery rib, chopped
2 tablespoons chopped onion
1 medium garlic clove, chopped
1 to 2 large jalapeño chiles, seeded, veins removed,
   and chopped
1 tablespoon red wine vinegar
1 (12-ounce) can spicy tomato juice,
   such as Snappy Tom
1/4 cup extra-virgin olive oil
1/2 teaspoon salt, or to taste
2 tablespoons chopped fresh cilantro
2 limes, quartered

In a blender or food processor, blend all of the
ingredients except the cilantro and limes. Transfer
to a large bowl. Cover and refrigerate until very
cold, 3 to 4 hours. Serve with a sprinkle of
cilantro. Pass lime wedges at the table.

Maria's Tomato Gazpacho
Maria's Sopa de Gazpacho

Makes 4 servings

Casa Celeste, on the Gold Coast of Puerto Vallarta, was the beautiful seaside home we stayed in when I escorted two groups on cooking holidays in the area. Our cook, Maria, prepared her mild, tomato-rich gazpacho soup for dinner one evening. Everyone liked it, and this is her recipe.

4 slices white bread, cut into 1/2-inch cubes

Vegetable oil for frying the bread

4 cups canned tomato juice

1 green bell pepper, washed, seeded, and finely chopped

1 medium cucumber, peeled and finely chopped

2 large ripe tomatoes, peeled and finely chopped

1/2 white onion, finely chopped

1/2 teaspoon salt, or to taste

Freshly ground pepper, to taste

1 ripe avocado (Hass variety preferred)

1. Preheat the oven to 400°. Put the bread cubes on a baking sheet and toast in the oven until dry and beginning to brown about 5 minutes. Remove from the oven. Heat the oil in a skillet until shimmering and fry the toast until crisp and brown. Drain on paper towels and put into a small condiment bowl to serve with the soup.

2. Put half of the chopped green pepper, half of the cucumber and half of the tomatoes in a blender. Put the remaining chopped vegetables into separate small condiment bowls. Put all of the chopped onion in a small condiment bowl. Set the condiment bowls aside until you serve the soup.

3. Add 1 cup of the tomato juice to the blender and purée the vegetables as smoothly as possible.

Pour the purée into the bowl with the remaining tomato juice. Add salt and pepper. Cover and refrigerate at least 1 hour, or up to 6 hours. The soup is best served the day it's made.

4. Shortly before serving, peel and dice the avocado and put it into a small condiment bowl. Arrange all the condiment bowls on the table for each person to add to the soup. Ladle the cold soup into individual bowls and serve.

Avocado Soup
Crema de Aguacate

Makes 4 servings

Cold avocado soup is among the more sophisticated soups of Mexico, which I discovered in the capital city. Elegant restaurants in Mexico City often serve it from a glass bowl nestled in an ice-filled heavy silver goblet. It's refreshing and delicious, however you present it.

2 large ripe avocados (Hass variety preferred), peeled and mashed

1 serrano chile, chopped with seeds

2 (14 1/2-ounce) cans fat-free reduced-sodium chicken broth

1/4 cup fresh lime juice

1/4 teaspoon salt, or to taste

1/4 cup Mexican crema or sour cream

2 tablespoons chopped fresh flat-leaf parsley

Dry sherry

In a blender or food processor, purée all the ingredients except the sherry until smooth. Refrigerate the soup (at least 3 hours) until shortly before serving. Divide the soup among 4 cold soup bowls. Pass a small pitcher of sherry at the table for each person to add about 1 teaspoon to the soup, if desired.

...ld Chayote Soup
...pa Fria de Chayote

...es **6 servings**

...erto Santibanez Cervantes, now in Austin, *...as, was among the first young chefs in Mexico* *...egin experimenting and developing Mexican* *...es in the new way called* nueva cocina. *This* *...le cold soup is one of Roberto's innovations.* *...yote is a pale green pear-shaped member of* *...squash family.*

...blespoon unsalted butter

...all leek, white part only, washed and thinly sliced

...up chopped white onion

...edium garlic clove, chopped

...errano chile, finely chopped with seeds

...ayotes, peeled, seeded, and diced in $1/4$-inch pieces

...ps chicken stock or canned fat-free reduced-sodium chicken broth

...easpoon salt, or to taste

...mall bunch of cilantro (washed and tied together in a bouquet)

...up heavy cream

...old golden delicious apple, peeled and diced in $1/4$-inch pieces just before serving (see Note)

...n a heavy saucepan, heat the butter over medium ... Add the leek, onion, garlic, and chile. Cover and ... slowly at medium-low heat 3 minutes. Add ...chayote and cook, stirring frequently, 5 minutes. ... the stock or broth and the salt. Bring to a boil. ... the cilantro bouquet, reduce heat to low, and ...ner until the chayote is tender, about 15 minutes. ...ard the cilantro. Cool the soup to lukewarm.

...ransfer the soup to a blender or food processor ...purée until smooth. Return the soup to the ...and bring to a boil. Add the cream and sim-...uncovered, 5 minutes, stirring with a wooden ...n. Adjust seasoning, remembering that the ...ning's impact will decrease once the soup ...s. Refrigerate until the soup is very cold, at least

4 hours. Serve in bowls placed on crushed ice, if possible. Garnish with freshly peeled diced apple.

Note: Peel and dice the cold apple at the very last minute. Do not rub with lemon or lime juice, and don't soak in water, or the apple will lose flavor and crisp texture.

Chilled Zucchini-Cilantro Soup
Sopa Fria de Calabacitas y Cilantro

Makes **4 servings**

Fuerte restaurant in Tlaquepaque reflects nueva cocina *in its varied menu. Instead of blending the zucchini with rich cream, I substitute chicken broth to lighten the soup.*

2 teaspoons olive oil

1 medium white onion, chopped

1 teaspoon ground cumin

$1/2$ teaspoon dried oregano (Mexican variety preferred), crumbled

$1^1/2$ pounds small zucchini, thinly sliced

2 ($14^1/2$-ounce) cans fat-free reduced-sodium chicken broth

$1/4$ cup lightly packed fresh cilantro

$1/2$ teaspoon salt, or to taste

Freshly ground pepper, to taste

Mexican crema, sour cream, or yogurt

1. In a large saucepan, heat the oil over medium heat and cook the onion, stirring, until translucent, about 4 minutes. Stir in the cumin and oregano. Cook 30 seconds. Add the zucchini and broth. Bring to a boil, and cook until the zucchini is very tender, about 20 minutes. Cool for about 10 minutes. Stir in the cilantro.

2. Transfer the soup to a blender or food processor and purée, in batches if necessary, until smooth. Transfer to a bowl. Season with salt and pepper. Cover and refrigerate until cold, about 3 hours. Soup can be made 1 day ahead. To serve, ladle soup into bowls. Garnish with a swirl of crema, sour cream, or yogurt.

Poultry

Basic Chicken Dishes 271

Shredded Chicken

Shredded Spiced Chicken

Shredded Chicken in Green Sauce

Minced Spicy Chicken

Grilled Chicken Skewers

Sautéed Chicken Livers with Green Onions

Chicken with Chile or Nut Sauces 274

Grilled Chicken Breasts with Ancho Chile Sauce

Grilled Chicken in Red Chili Sauce with Zucchini and Corn

Baked Chicken with Mushrooms and Ancho Chile

Chicken with Chipotle Chiles and Tequila

Sautéed Chicken with Chipotle Chile Sauce

Grilled Chicken with Red Chile and Orange Sauce

Sautéed Chicken with Pasilla Chile Sauce

Chicken with Poblano Cream Sauce

Baked Chicken with Serrano Chile Cream Sauce

Sautéed Chicken with Almond Sauce

Baked Chicken with Pecans

Chicken with White Nut Sauce

Other Fried, Grilled, and Baked Chicken Dishes 283

Chicken with Black Bean and Avocado Salsa

Chicken and Corn with Fiery Cilantro-Mint Sauce

Chicken with Poblano Chiles, Sour Cream, and Cheese

Chicken in Roasted Tomato Sauce

Chicken with Portobello Mushrooms

Grilled Chicken with Cactus

Chicken Thighs with Onions and Nutmeg

Chicken Mazatlán

Chicken Tampico with Mayonnaise and Olives

Chicken, Ticul Style

Fried Chicken, Sonora Style

Plaza Chicken from Morelia

Lime Chicken

Chicken in Tangerine Sauce

Chicken with Tamarind

Braised Chicken with Prunes

Chicken for a King

Chicken in Its Own Juice

"Drunken" Chicken

Chicken Breasts with Yucatán Green Seasoning Paste

Chicken Breasts with Pumpkin Seed Crust

Rolled Chicken Breasts with Spinach

Rolled Chicken Breasts with Poblano Chiles and Goat Cheese

Stuffed Chicken Breasts with Black Bean Sauce

Chicken with Red Chile Steamed in Foil

Chicken, Pibil Style

Chicken Moles and Stews 300

Chicken in Mole Sauce
from Puebla

cken in Oaxacan Red Mole

hicken in Oaxacan Green
Mole with White Beans

Chicken Breasts with
Yellow Mole

ride's Mole with Chicken

apantla-Style Mole Sauce
with Chicken

ken and Green Chile Stew

hicken, Mushrooms, and
Red Pepper Stew

icken Stew, Chiapas Style

hicken Stew with Chiles
and Spices

Chicken Tinga

xacan Toasted Corn Stew
with Chicken and Pork

ken, Aguascalientes Style

Turkey 311

Basic Cooked Turkey Breast

Turkey Cutlets with
Almond Crust

Yucatán Spiced Turkey Cutlets

Turkey with Mushrooms
and Tomatillos

Turkey with Creamy Green
Pumpkin Seed Sauce

Turkey in Spiced Vinegar Sauce

Turkey Stew

Turkey and Hominy Stew

Turkey Meat Loaf

Yucatán Cold Spiced Turkey

Yucatán Stuffed Turkey Breast
with White Sauce

(Variation) Roasted Whole
Turkey with White Sauce

Duck, Game Hens, and Quail 320

Braised Duck for Tacos

Duck Breasts with
Blackberry Sauce

Duck Breasts with
Poblano Chiles

Duck in Green Pumpkin
Seed Sauce

Cornish Hens Roasted
with Chili Rub

Cornish Hens with
Fiery Cilantro-Mint Sauce

Quail with Corn and
Cucumber and Jalapeño Salsa

Quail with White Beans

The turkey is Mexico's indigenous bird, but chickens were brought to Mexico during colonization in the 1500s, and today chicken is the preferred poultry in Mexican cooking. However, turkey is still widely used for celebration and holiday dishes when it's served with traditional *moles*, and in other regional specialties, such as Yucatán Stuffed Turkey in White Sauce (page 318). Wild ducks, quail, and other game birds have also been eaten in Mexico for centuries, and hunting game birds is still practiced in some areas during hunting seasons. Domesticated ducks and quail are eaten in contemporary cooking, but are mainly found on restaurant menus.

Poultry is most often served with classic sauces, such as Chicken in Oaxacan Red Mole (page 301). Moles are sauces with a heritage dating back to the Aztecs, which can be described but never truly appreciated until tasted. One of the most delicious and well-known moles is a "newer" one—Mole Sauce from Puebla (*Mole Poblano*), on page 56—which was developed after Mexico came under Spanish rule in the 1500s. The rich, complex-flavored sauces are made with a variety of ingredients including chiles (which often reflect the color in the name), garlic, herbs, spices, and sometimes chocolate. Although now moles are served with a variety of foods, they pair best with poultry.

Chicken is particularly favored for simpler dishes, in which it is grilled, sautéed, or baked, and served with a variety of sauces or accompaniments. It's a natural for tacos and quesadillas, and main dishes with basic sauces including Lime Chicken (page 290), Sautéed Chicken with Chipotle Chile Sauce (page 277), and Chicken in Roasted Tomato Sauce (page 284).

The current trend in Mexico toward innovative dishes—combining the old and the new—is producing inspiring recipes such as Chicken and Corn with Fiery Cilantro-Mint Sauce (page 283), Duck Breasts with Poblano Chiles (page 321), and Quail with White Beans (page 325).

You'll find lots of ways in this chapter to add both traditional and *nuevo* Mexican cooking to weeknight dinners and very special occasions.

asic Chicken Dishes

redded Chicken
lo Deshebrado

es **about 2 cups**

ked chicken is shredded for all kinds of
:ks, soups, salads, enchiladas, and other
es. A whole chicken is often poached
shredded, but for a small amount of
dded chicken, this method is quicker and
e convenient.

icken breast halves on the bone with skin

ick slices medium white onion

:dium garlic cloves

ps canned fat-free reduced-sodium chicken broth

ut the chicken breasts, onion, and garlic in a
ium pan. Add the chicken broth. Bring to a
, uncovered, then reduce the heat to low,
r, and simmer until the meat is tender, about
ninutes. Cool the chicken in the broth about
ninutes.

ake the chicken out of the broth. Remove the
and bones and discard, reserving the meat.
g your fingers, tear the meat into thin or
se shreds. The shredded chicken is ready to
Strain the broth and store, covered and
gerated, for another use.

Shredded Spiced Chicken
Pollo Deshebrado Picante

Makes **about 3 cups**

Instead of poaching chicken breasts, I often braise them with onions, herbs, and spices before shredding. The chicken has great flavor cooked this way. Use to fill enchiladas, crepes, tacos, sandwiches, or as a topping for tostadas.

3 skinless boneless chicken breast halves

1 tablespoon olive oil or vegetable oil

2 tablespoons chopped onion

1 teaspoon pure ground ancho chili powder (not a chili blend)

$1/2$ teaspoon dried oregano (Mexican variety preferred), crumbled

$1/8$ teaspoon ground allspice

$1/4$ teaspoon salt, or to taste

1. Trim the chicken of all visible fat, and cut each breast crosswise into 3 equal pieces. Heat the oil in a nonstick skillet over medium-high heat and cook the chicken about 2 minutes per side, or until lightly browned on the outside. Add all of the remaining ingredients. Stir to combine, reduce the heat to low, and add 1 tablespoon of water. Cover and simmer until the chicken is no longer pink inside at the thickest part, 4 to 5 minutes.

2. Remove the chicken pieces and when cool enough to handle, shred the chicken and return it to the pan. Stir to mix. Adjust seasoning. The chicken is ready to use, or cover and refrigerate up to overnight.

- Add Habenero sauce & onion powder

Shredded Chicken in Green Sauce
Pollo Deshebrado en Salsa Verde

Makes **about 4 cups**

Shredded chicken with spicy tomatillo sauce is a favorite filling for burritos or tacos. Burritos are a northern Mexico preparation, especially in the state of Sonora. Burritos are often made of large, thin flour tortillas. Chicken, beef and pork are the most common fillings. Shredded or chopped meats are layered with beans, salsa, lettuce, and whatever else strikes the fancy, then rolled into a cylinder and eaten at once. This shredded chicken can also be used as a filling for tamales.

4 skinless boneless chicken breast halves
2 cups canned chicken broth
1 tablespoon vegetable oil
1 small onion, chopped
2 medium garlic cloves
6 medium tomatillos, husked and quartered
2 serrano chiles
¹/₂ cup loosely packed cilantro sprigs
1 teaspoon dried oregano (Mexican variety preferred), crumbled
¹/₂ teaspoon ground cumin
¹/₂ teaspoon sugar
¹/₂ teaspoon salt, or to taste
¹/₈ teaspoon pepper, or to taste

1. In a medium saucepan, simmer the chicken with the chicken broth, over medium-low heat until the chicken is no longer pink inside, about 12 minutes. Remove the chicken to a bowl, cover and let stand while making the sauce. Reserve the broth.

2. In a skillet, heat the oil and cook the onion and garlic until softened, 3 to 4 minutes. Scrape the mixture into a blender or food processor. Add the tomatillos, serranos, cilantro, oregano, cumin,

sugar, and ¼ cup of the chicken broth. Purée until smooth.

3. Transfer the mixture to a saucepan and cook about 8 minutes, stirring, to reduce the liquid and blend the flavors. Add salt and pepper. Shred the cooled chicken and mix with the sauce. Use as a filling for burritos or tacos. Store the remaining chicken broth for another use.

Minced Spicy Chicken
Picadillo de Pollo

Makes **4 cups**

A mixture of minced cooked chicken with onions, tomatoes, chiles, spices, raisins, and olives is used as a filling for such things as Stuffed Chiles with Shredded Spiced Chicken (page 422), or as a topping for masa *dough snacks called sopes (Masa Shells for Sopes, page 107). Chicken picadillo is also a delicious filling for tamales, empanadas, tacos, and more.*

2 chicken breasts half on the bone with skin
2 cups canned chicken broth
1 tablespoon olive oil
¹/₂ medium onion, finely chopped
2 large garlic cloves, finely chopped
2 medium tomatoes, peeled and finely chopped
2 jarred pickled jalapeño chiles (en escabeche), seeded and finely chopped
¹/₃ cup raisins
8 pimiento-stuffed green olives, chopped
¹/₂ teaspoon ground cinnamon (Mexican canela or Ceylon variety preferred)
¹/₄ teaspoon ground allspice
¹/₂ teaspoon salt, or to taste
Freshly ground pepper, to taste

1. Put the chicken, skin side down, and chicken broth in a medium saucepan. Bring to a boil over medium heat, then reduce heat to low and simmer 12 minutes. Turn the chicken over and simmer

ninutes. Cool the chicken in the pan off heat.
en the chicken is cool enough to handle, sepa-
the meat from the skin and bones and finely
it into small bits. Discard the skins and bones.

eat the olive oil in a large skillet over medium
and cook the onion and garlic, stirring, until
ned, 3 to 4 minutes. Add the remaining
edients, except the reserved chicken, and
, stirring, until the juices have evaporated
the mixture is nearly dry, 6 to 8 minutes.

ix in the reserved chicken. Transfer to a bowl.
chicken picadillo is ready to use as directed
ur recipe. If made ahead, cool to room tem-
ture, cover and refrigerate up to 3 days, or
e up to 3 months.

lled Chicken Skewers
ambres de Pollo

es **4 servings**

r touring the blue agave *fields and viewing the
ila-making operation in the town of Tequila,
Guadalajara, we were guests for lunch at the
Cuervo distillery's entertaining center. The
dish was grilled chicken and vegetables clev-
skewered on spears from the* agave *plant, but
wooden skewers work just as well. Horsemen's
s (page 464) accompanied the skewered
ken. If serving with the beans, cook them
ahead and reheat shortly before serving.*

4 skinless boneless chicken breast halves
2 tablespoons vegetable oil or olive oil
2 large garlic cloves, mashed
1 tablespoon fresh lime juice
1/4 teaspoon salt, or to taste
1/4 teaspoon freshly ground pepper, or to taste
1 red bell pepper, seeded and cut into 1 1/2-inch
    squares
1/2 pound (1/4-inch-thick) fully cooked deli-baked
    ham, cut into 1 1/2-inch squares
1/2 large onion, separated into 1 1/2-inch pieces
2 poblano chiles, seeded, veins removed,
    and cut into 1 1/2-inch squares
4 thick wooden skewers soaked in water about
    1 hour

1. Cut the chicken into 1½-inch pieces and put
in a bowl. Add the oil, garlic, lime juice, salt, and
pepper. Toss to coat the chicken with the marinade. Cover and refrigerate 1 hour.

2. Prepare an outdoor grill (and grease the rack)
or preheat the broiler. Thread the ingredients
on the skewers in the following order: 1 piece red
pepper, 1 piece chicken, 1 piece ham, 1 piece
onion, 1 piece chicken, 1 piece ham, 1 piece onion,
and 1 piece poblano chile. Repeat until 4 skewers
have been threaded.

3. Cook the skewers on the grill or in the broiler,
turning 2 to 3 times, until the ingredients are
lightly charred and the chicken is no longer pink
inside, about 6 to 8 minutes. Serve hot.

Sautéed Chicken Livers with Green Onions
Higaditos con Cebollitos

Makes **4 servings**

Here, sautéed chicken livers are cooked with a bit of Worcestershire, which Mexicans sometimes call English sauce. In this recipe, the livers are topped with small green onions for an easy, economical way to prepare often-neglected chicken livers. Serve them with Rice with Mixed Vegetables (page 477) or another Mexican rice dish.

³/₄ pound chicken livers

1 tablespoon vegetable oil

2 teaspoons Worcestershire sauce

¹/₈ teaspoon freshly ground pepper, or to taste

8 green onions, including about 2 inches of the green

1. Trim the connective tissue from the livers and cut them into 1-inch pieces. Heat the oil in a nonstick skillet. Add the livers and cook, turning, until firm, about 1 minute. Add the Worcestershire and pepper. Cook, stirring, until browned on the outside and barely pink inside, about 3 minutes more. Transfer to a plate.

2. Cook the green onions in the same pan, stirring frequently, until limp and crisp-tender, about 4 minutes. Put the onions on the plate with the liver. Serve hot.

Chicken with Chile or Nut Sauces

Grilled Chicken Breasts with Ancho Chile Sauce
Pechugas de Pollo con Salsa de Chile Ancho

Makes **4 servings**

Ancho chiles make a rich red sauce that ranges from mild to quite hot. The savory sauce served with smoky-tasting barbecued chicken breasts is a winning combination. If possible, grill the chicken over white-hot coals of mesquite charcoal for authentic flavor. Serve with Mexican-style beans and salad.

Ancho Chile Sauce for Enchiladas (page 48)

4 skinless boneless chicken breast halves

1 small garlic clove, mashed

¹/₂ teaspoon salt

2 teaspoons olive oil or vegetable oil

¹/₈ teaspoon freshly ground pepper, or to taste

1 tablespoon chopped fresh cilantro

1. Prepare the chile sauce and reserve. Then, make a hot fire in an outdoor grill or, alternatively, preheat an oven broiler or stovetop grill pan.

2. Lay the chicken breasts on a platter. In a small bowl, mash the garlic, salt, oil, and pepper together to make a paste. Rub the mixture all over the chicken.

3. When the outdoor grill fire, broiler, or grill pan is hot, grill the chicken, turning once or twice, about 4 to 5 minutes per side, or until well marked from the grill and no longer pink inside at the thickest part. To serve, reheat the sauce, spoon over the grilled chicken, and sprinkle with the chopped cilantro.

illed Chicken in Red Chili
uce with Zucchini and Corn
:hugas de Pollo en Salsa de Chili
lida con Calabacitas y Elote

es **4 servings**

's a recipe that uses ground ancho *or*
lla *chili powder (called* chili molida*),*
ad of whole dried chiles, to make the sauce
he chicken. This contemporary dish is
htened with bits of zucchini, corn, and red
pepper. Maggi seasoning extract is a popu-
roduct in Mexico that's widely available in
supermarkets here. Worcestershire sauce is
cceptable substitute.

3 lespoons vegetable oil

1/ edium white onion, peeled and finely
:hopped

1 ablespoons pure ground ancho or pasilla
:hili powder

1 easpoons masa harina (flour for corn tortillas)

1 lespoon tomato paste

1 spoon ground cumin

1/ aspoon dried oregano (Mexican variety
referred), crumbled

1/ aspoon brown sugar

1/ aspoon Maggi seasoning extract or
Worcestershire sauce

1 canned beef broth

4 less boneless chicken breast halves

1/: aspoon salt

1 espoon unsalted butter

1 lium zucchini, cut into 1/4-inch dice

1 e ear of corn, kernels cut off

1/: dium red bell pepper, cut into 1/4 inch dice

2 espoons chopped fresh cilantro

1. In a heavy medium saucepan, heat 2 table-spoons of the oil over medium heat. Add the onion, and cook, stirring frequently, until the onion begins to brown, 3 to 4 minutes. Add the ground chili, masa, tomato paste, cumin, oregano, brown sugar, Maggi, and beef broth. Stir to combine. Bring to a boil, then reduce the heat and simmer the sauce, partially covered, stirring frequently to prevent sticking, until thickened, 8 to 10 minutes. Reserve in the pan, off heat. (Sauce can be made ahead to this point. Cover and refrigerate up to 2 days.)

2. Prepare a hot fire in an outdoor grill, or heat an oven broiler or stovetop grill pan. Brush the chicken with the remaining tablespoon of oil, and season with 1/4 teaspoon of the salt. Grill the chicken turning frequently once or twice, about 4 to 5 minutes per side or until no longer pink inside at the thickest part and firm to the touch.

3. Meanwhile, in a medium skillet, heat the butter over medium heat. Add the zucchini, corn, red pepper, and remaining salt. Cook, tossing, until sizzling and heated through, about 2 minutes. Reheat the sauce.

4. To serve, put a chicken breast in the center of each of 4 plates. Spoon the chili sauce over the chicken, and let it pool onto the plate. Scatter the heated vegetables over the top. Sprinkle with cilantro.

Baked Chicken with Mushrooms and Ancho Chile

Pollo con Hongos y Chile Ancho

Makes 4 servings

San Miguel de Allende is a city of steep hills and beautiful colonial buildings in the state of Guanajuato in central Mexico. It has a large permanent American population attracted to its beauty, climate, arts, and crafts. During one of my stays, when I was escorting a culinary group, I had this chicken dish at El Patio restaurant. The dish was prepared with a small half chicken covered with the mushrooms and sauce. I prefer to use whole chicken legs with thighs attached. The herb epazote *is important to the flavor, but if unavailable, use cilantro. It won't taste quite the same, but it will still be very good.*

2 large ancho chiles, cut open and seeded,
    veins removed

2 tablespoons vegetable oil

4 whole chicken legs with thighs attached

³/₄ pound brown crimini mushrooms, thinly sliced

2 medium tomatoes, peeled and chopped

¹/₂ cup chicken broth, canned or homemade

¹/₂ medium white onion, coarsely chopped

1 medium garlic clove, chopped

2 sprigs of epazote, leaves only (or substitute
    ¹/₄ cup fresh cilantro)

¹/₂ teaspoon salt, or to taste

¹/₈ teaspoon freshly ground pepper, or to taste

1. In a small dry skillet, toast the chiles over medium heat, turning, until aromatic, about 1 minute. Soak in a bowl of hot water 20 minutes, then drain.

2. Meanwhile, in a large nonstick skillet, heat the oil over medium heat and brown the chicken on both sides, 2 to 3 minutes per side. Remove to an ovenproof casserole dish.

3. In the same skillet, cook the mushrooms, stirring, about 3 minutes. Add to the casserole dish with the chicken. Reserve the skillet.

4. Preheat the oven to 350°. Put the tomatoes, chicken broth, onion, garlic, epazote leaves, salt, pepper, and the reserved chiles in a blender or food processor and blend until smooth. Reheat the skillet, and pour in the sauce. Cook, stirring, 3 to 4 minutes. Pour over the chicken and mushrooms. Cover and bake until the chicken is tender, 40 to 45 minutes. Divide the chicken and sauce equally among 4 serving plates. Serve hot.

icken with Chipotle Chiles
d Tequila
lo Guisado con Chipotle y Tequila

es **4 servings**

a Viejo is a very special place in the Polanco
rict of Mexico City. The restaurant is on the
floor of a small luxurious hotel with the
e name. Traditional dishes, such as this
sed chicken dish, are skillfully executed.
icans often add a bit of tequila to some of
· dishes in the same way as wine or brandy
it be used in other cultures. Tequila imparts
btle peppery flavor to help balance and bring
iatural flavors. Tequila also tends to mellow
hiles. You can leave it out if you wish.

2 lespoons olive oil
4 iless boneless chicken breast halves
1/ aspoon salt, or to taste
1/ edium white onion, thinly sliced
2 dium garlic cloves, thinly sliced
6 n tomatoes, peeled and quartered
1 ned chipotle chile en adobo, seeded and
hopped
8 ll (1 pound) red potatoes, scrubbed and halved
1 canned fat-free reduced-sodium
hicken broth
1/. o tequila
6 in onions, sliced crosswise into 1-inch pieces

1. heat the oven to 450°. Heat 1½ tablespoons
of e oil in a large ovenproof skillet over
m im-high heat and cook the chicken until
br ied on both sides and firm to the touch, 4 to
5 i utes per side. Season with salt. Transfer the
ch in to a plate.

2. the skillet add the onion and garlic. Cook,
sti g, until softened, about 3 minutes. Add the
rei iing ingredients, except the green onions.
Cc 5 minutes. Return the chicken to the pan.
Br to a boil, stirring to mix the chicken with

the vegetables. Transfer the pan to the oven and
cook, uncovered, until the chicken and potatoes
are tender, about 20 minutes.

3. Meanwhile, toss the green onions with the
remaining oil and cook in a nonstick skillet
over medium heat until starting to brown, but
barely tender, 1 to 2 minutes. Serve the chicken,
potatoes, and sauce with green onions scattered
on top.

Sautéed Chicken with Chipotle Chile Sauce
Pechugas de Pollo con Salsa de Chipotle

Makes **4 servings**

*Tomatillo and Chipotle Chile Sauce is so great with
chicken that I have a container of it in my refrigerator almost all the time. The sauce should be at
room temperature for this dish. Serve the chicken
with a savory Zucchini Pudding (page 436), a
moist baked dish that's called* budín *in Spanish,
and black beans for a winning combination.*

Tomatillo and Chipotle Chile Sauce (page 36)
1 tablespoon olive oil
2 teaspoons fresh lime juice
1 medium garlic clove, mashed
1/2 teaspoon salt
4 skinless boneless chicken breast halves

1. Prepare the chipotle sauce. Reserve. Then mix
together half of the olive oil, with the lime juice,
garlic, and salt. Coat the chicken pieces with the
mixture.

2. Heat the remaining oil in a medium skillet and
cook the chicken about 4 to 5 minutes per side or
until golden brown on the outside, firm to the
touch, and no longer pink inside at the thickest
part. To serve, spoon some of the chipotle sauce
over each chicken breast.

Grilled Chicken with Red Chile and Orange Sauce

Pechugas de Pollo con Salsa Roja y Naranja

Makes 6 servings

Dark red ancho chiles have a rich dried fruit flavor that pairs well with the sweet-tart flavor of orange juice. Grill the chicken on a stovetop grill pan or over hot coals on an outdoor grill. Either way, it's quick and easy, because the sauce can be prepared ahead, leaving only the chicken to cook at the last minute.

4 ancho chiles

2 tablespoons vegetable oil, plus extra to brush on the chicken

¼ medium white onion, chopped

2 medium garlic cloves, thinly sliced

1 teaspoon dried oregano (Mexican variety preferred), crumbled

1 cup canned chicken broth

3 tablespoons undiluted frozen orange juice concentrate, thawed

2 tablespoons tomato paste

1 tablespoon unseasoned rice vinegar

1 tablespoon dark brown sugar

1 teaspoon salt

6 skinless boneless chicken breast halves

Cilantro sprigs

1. Wipe the chiles with a damp paper towel. Cut the chiles open, and remove the stems and seeds. Heat a skillet over medium heat, and toast the chiles, turning, until they are aromatic. (Do not burn or chiles will be bitter.) Put the chiles in a bowl of hot water and soak to soften, about 20 minutes.

2. In a heavy medium saucepan, heat 2 tablespoons of the oil over medium heat. Add the onion, garlic, and oregano. Cook, stirring, until beginning to brown, 2 to 3 minutes. Stir in the broth and orange juice. Add the tomato paste, vinegar, sugar, and ½ teaspoon of the salt. Bring to a boil, then reduce the heat to low, and simmer, stirring frequently, 5 minutes.

3. Put the saucepan contents into a blender or food processor. Lift and drain the chiles from the soaking liquid, and add to the blender. Purée until smooth. (The sauce should be about as thick as ketchup.) Return the sauce to the saucepan, and bring to a boil, then reduce heat to low, and cook, stirring frequently, about 8 minutes, to blend the flavors. Remove the sauce from the heat, cover and reserve. (Sauce can be made ahead to this point. Refrigerate to store. Reheat before serving.)

4. Make a hot fire in an outdoor grill, or preheat a stovetop grill pan. Brush the chicken breasts with the remaining oil, and season with the remaining ½ teaspoon of salt. Cook the chicken about 4 to 5 minutes per side, or until lightly browned on the outside, firm to the touch, and no longer pink inside at the thickest part. To serve, reheat the sauce and spoon a pool of sauce on each serving plate and place a chicken breast on each plate, or. Cut each chicken breast crosswise into ½-inch strips and fan out over the sauce. Garnish with cilantro.

[S]utéed Chicken with [...]silla Chile Sauce

[Pe]chugas de Pollo con Salsa de Chile [...]silla

[Mak]es 4 servings

[...]st of chicken goes very well with dark spicy
[...]lla chile sauce. I like to serve Chayote and
[...]rots (page 431) with the chicken.

[...]la Chile Sauce (page 26)
[...] [t]aspoons olive oil
[...] [sk]nless boneless chicken breast halves
[...] [t]easpoon salt, or to taste
[...] [ta]spoons sesame seeds, toasted

[Prep]are the chile sauce. Then, heat the oil in a large
[n]r[ons]tick skillet and cook the chicken about 4 min-
[...] [t]u per side or until it is browned on the outside,
[f...] to the touch, and no longer pink inside at the
[t...] [thick]est part. Season with salt. Serve each chicken
[b...] [breas]t with a little of chile sauce spooned on top.
[S...] [Sprin]kle each serving with the sesame seeds.

[Chi]cken with Poblano Cream [Sau]ce

[Pe]chugas de Pollo con Crema Poblano

[Make]s 4 servings

[...]s a contemporary dish of chicken breasts topped
[w...] a lovely green sauce of poblano chiles, onions,
[ch...en] broth, and cream, that's similar to a dish
[I...] in Tlaquepaque, a suburb of Guadalajara.
[Fi...] corn is perfect with the chicken.

3 large poblano chiles, roasted and peeled
(page 8)

2 tablespoons olive oil

1/2 medium white onion, chopped

2 large garlic cloves, thinly sliced

3/4 cup canned fat-free reduced-sodium
chicken broth

1/4 cup heavy cream

1/2 teaspoon salt, or to taste

4 skinless boneless chicken breast halves

1. Prepare the chiles. Then, remove the stems
and seeds. Cut one of the roasted chiles into short
thin strips and reserve. Chop the remaining
2 chiles and put them in a blender.

2. In a medium saucepan, heat 1 tablespoon of
the oil over medium-low heat and cook the
onion and garlic, covered, until the onion is
translucent, about 4 minutes. Transfer to the
blender with the chiles. Add the chicken broth
and blend until smooth. Return the blended mixture to the same saucepan. Stir in the cream and
1/4 teaspoon of the salt. Bring to a boil, then
reduce the heat and simmer, stirring, 4 to 5 minutes to blend the flavors. Adjust seasoning and
reserve off heat.

3. In a large nonstick skillet, heat the remaining tablespoon of oil and cook the chicken
breasts 4 to 5 minutes per side, or until lightly
browned on the outside, firm to the touch,
and no longer pink inside at the thickest part.
Season with the remaining 1/4 teaspoon of salt.
Reheat the sauce. Serve with the heated sauce
spooned over the chicken. Scatter the reserved
chile strips on top.

Baked Chicken with Serrano Chile Cream Sauce
Pechugas de Pollo con Salsa de Crema de Chile Serrano

Makes **4 servings**

In this recipe that I developed for a cooking class, both the creamy serrano sauce and the method of cooking the chicken in the oven are modern innovations. It's quite an elegant dish and looks very inviting when served with slender carrot and jicama sticks.

Serrano Chile Cream Sauce (page 51)
Carrot and Jicama Sticks (page 438)
4 boneless chicken breast halves with skin on
1/4 teaspoon salt
2 teaspoons vegetable oil
2 tablespoons finely chopped fresh parsley

1. Prepare the serrano cream sauce. Cover and set aside, or if made ahead store covered in the refrigerator for up to 2 days. Reheat before serving. Prepare the carrots and jicama.

2. Preheat the oven to 400°. Trim excess fat or flabby skin from the chicken breasts. Season with salt and brush all over with oil. Place on a foil-lined baking sheet, skin side up, and bake until the skin is golden brown, about 15 minutes.

3. While the chicken cooks, reheat the sauce and the vegetables, if necessary. To serve, place 1 chicken breast on each of 4 serving plates. Arrange the carrots and jicama on each plate. Spoon some of the sauce over each chicken breast and sprinkle with parsley. Pass the remaining sauce at the table.

Sautéed Chicken with Almond Sauce
Pechugas de Pollo con Salsa Almendra

Makes **4 servings**

This is a wonderful dish for a special dinner. You can make the almond sauce ahead and cook the chicken shortly before serving. Serve with rice and Pineapple Salsa (page 41).

1 cup Almond Sauce (page 52)
4 skinless boneless chicken breast halves
1 tablespoon vegetable oil or olive oil
1/4 teaspoon salt, or to taste
1 tablespoon chopped fresh cilantro

1. Prepare the almond sauce. Then, preheat the oven to 200°. Put the sauce in an ovenproof bowl. Cover and keep warm in the oven.

2. Trim the chicken of any visible fat. Place each breast between 2 sheets of plastic wrap and pound it with the flat side of a meat mallet or with a rolling pin to an even 1/4-inch thickness.

3. In a large skillet, heat the oil over medium heat. Season the chicken with salt and cook about 3 to 4 minutes per side or until lightly browned on the outside and no longer pink in the thickest part. Serve hot with some of the sauce spooned over each breast. Sprinkle with cilantro. Pass the rest of the sauce at the table.

ked Chicken with Pecans
:hugas de Pollo con Pacanas

:es **4 servings**

his dish, chicken breasts are baked with a
k sauce made of pecans, tomatoes, and
es. Serve the chicken with rice. For a
:ial meal, start with Hearts of Palm Soup
ge 261).

rge poblano chile, roasted and peeled
(page 8)

:inless boneless chicken breast halves

:easpoon salt, or to taste

:easpoon freshly ground pepper, or to taste

:easpoon dried oregano (Mexican variety
preferred), crumbled

iblespoons fresh lime juice

iblespoon unsalted butter

:aspoons olive oil

/2-inch thick) slices baguette bread

:up pecan pieces

pound plum tomatoes, cored and quartered

teaspoon ground cumin

teaspoon ground allspice

teaspoon ground cloves

cup chicken broth, canned or homemade

Prepare the chile and reserve. Then, season
chicken with salt, pepper, and oregano. Rub
over. Put on a plate and drizzle evenly with
lime juice. Turn to coat. Let marinate about
minutes.

2. Meanwhile, preheat the oven to 350°. In a skillet heat the butter and olive oil over medium
heat. Fry the bread until golden brown on both
sides. Transfer to a blender. In the same skillet,
fry the pecan pieces, stirring, until slightly
toasted, about 1 minute. (Do not let them burn.)
Transfer to the blender along with the remaining
ingredients. Purée until nearly smooth, but with
some texture.

3. Spread about 3 tablespoons of the purée in the
bottom of a shallow greased casserole dish large
enough to hold the chicken in one layer. Put the
chicken on the sauce. Spread the remaining sauce
evenly over the chicken. Bake 30 to 35 minutes, or
until the chicken is no longer pink inside at the
thickest part.

4. While the chicken bakes, remove the stem and
seeds from the chile and cut into thin strips.
Serve the chicken with the sauce spooned on top.
Garnish with the chile strips.

Chicken with White Nut Sauce
Pollo en Pipian Blanco

Makes **4 servings**

Roberto Santibanez Cervantes of Mexico City and now executive chef of Fonda San Miguel in Austin, Texas, shared this recipe that he created. The cloak of creamy pipian *sauce on the chicken is made of lightly toasted almonds and sesame seeds along with other herbs and spices. Serve the chicken with fresh salsa and black beans.*

4 skinless chicken breast halves on the bone
**1 medium carrot, scrubbed and thickly sliced
    (do not peel)**
$1/2$ medium onion, thickly sliced
4 large garlic cloves, sliced
1 small celery rib, thickly sliced
1 parsley sprig
1 bay leaf
1 teaspoon salt or to taste
$3/4$ cup slivered almonds
$1/4$ cup sesame seeds
2 allspice berries, or $1/8$ teaspoon ground allspice
1 whole clove
8 fresh mint leaves
**1 jalapeño chile, seeded, veins removed, and
    coarsely chopped**
1 tablespoon olive oil or vegetable oil
**1 to 2 jarred pickled jalapeño chiles (en escabeche),
    seeded and finely diced**
6 to 8 pitted green olives, thinly sliced
1 tablespoon drained capers

1. In a large saucepan, put the chicken, carrot, onion, half of the garlic, celery, parsley, bay leaf, and ½ teaspoon of the salt. Add water to cover and bring to a boil. Reduce the heat to medium-low, partially cover, and simmer 20 minutes. Reserve off heat in the broth.

2. Meanwhile, in a medium dry skillet, over medium heat, lightly toast the almonds, stirring constantly, until fragrant and just beginning to brown, about 2 minutes. Transfer to a blender or food processor. In the same skillet toast the sesame seeds in the same way. Add to the blender with the almonds. Add the remaining garlic, allspice, clove, mint, and fresh jalapeño. Pour in 1 cup of the reserved chicken broth. Blend to a smooth purée.

3. Heat the oil in a large saucepan over medium heat. Slowly add the sauce (so it doesn't splatter), cover and cook, stirring frequently, about 8 minutes to blend flavors. The sauce will thicken as it cooks, so stir in about 2 more cups (strained) chicken broth, a little at a time, to reach a consistency that coats the back of a wooden spoon. Stir in the olives, capers, and pickled jalapeños.

4. Meanwhile, de-bone the chicken breasts and stir chicken pieces into the sauce. Serve hot.

Other Fried, Grilled, and Baked Chicken Dishes

Chicken with Black Bean and Avocado Salsa
Pechugas de Pollo con Salsa de Frijol Negro y Aguacate

Makes **4 servings**

Captivating black beans and creamy avocados work their magic in so many dishes, and chicken breasts are a constant in most kitchens on both sides of the border, so the three together are a natural combination. The chicken can be pan-fried or grilled. Mexican Rice (page 472) is a perfect accompaniment for this dish.

Black Bean and Avocado Salsa (page 25)
1 tablespoon olive oil
1 medium garlic clove, mashed
1 teaspoon dried oregano (Mexican variety preferred), crumbled
1 teaspoon salt
1 teaspoon freshly ground pepper
4 skinless boneless chicken breast halves

Prepare the salsa. Reserve in a bowl. Then, mix together half of the oil, garlic, oregano, salt, and pepper. Rub the mixture all over the chicken breasts. Heat the remaining oil in a large non-stick skillet, or prepare an outdoor grill, if grilling the chicken.

Cook the chicken 4 to 5 minutes per side or until golden brown on the outside, firm to the touch, and no longer pink inside at the thickest part. Serve the chicken with about 2 tablespoons of the salsa spooned on top. Pass any remaining salsa at the table.

Chicken and Corn with Fiery Cilantro-Mint Sauce
Pollo y Elote con Salsa de Cilantro-Yerbabuena

Makes **4 servings**

Here's a new-wave Mexican chicken dish with fresh corn and a bright salsa of cilantro and mint that's special enough for company.

Fiery Cilantro-Mint Sauce (page 30)
2 tablespoons unsalted butter
1/4 medium white onion, finely chopped
4 cups corn kernels (from about 4 medium ears)
1/2 teaspoon salt, or to taste
1/4 teaspoon ground cumin
1 tablespoon olive oil or vegetable oil
4 skinless boneless chicken breast halves

1. Prepare the cilantro-mint sauce. Cover and refrigerate. Melt the butter in a large nonstick skillet, over medium heat, until it foams. Cook the onion, stirring, until softened, about 3 minutes. Add the corn and cook until tender, about 5 minutes. Season with 1/4 teaspoon of the salt and cumin. Set aside off heat.

2. In another large skillet, heat the oil over medium heat until it shimmers and cook the chicken 4 to 5 minutes per side, or until browned on the outside, firm to the touch, and no longer pink inside in the thickest part. To serve, place 1 chicken breast in the center of each of 4 plates. Top each breast with some of the sauce. Spoon the corn equally around the chicken on each plate. Pass the remaining sauce at the table.

Chicken with Poblano Chiles, Sour Cream, and Cheese
Pollo con Rajas, Crema, y Queso

Makes 4 servings

This is a typical combination, throughout Mexico, of shredded chicken with sour cream and cheese that's rich and delicious. I serve it with rice or with black beans, or with both. Soft, warm tortillas also usually accompany the dish. Add a crisp salad for a complete meal. Cotija cheese, also called añejo, is an aged cheese with a flavor similar to mild feta or Parmesan. It's now available in many places in the United States.

2 large poblano chiles, roasted and peeled (page 8)

4 boneless chicken breast halves with skin on

2 cups canned fat-free reduced-sodium chicken broth

2 tablespoons olive oil

1 large white onion, halved lengthwise and sliced crosswise

1/2 teaspoon dried oregano (Mexican variety preferred), crumbled

1/2 teaspoon ground cumin

1/4 teaspoon salt, or to taste

1/8 teaspoon freshly ground pepper, or to taste

1 cup Mexican crema or sour cream

1/3 cup crumbled cotija or mild feta cheese

1. Prepare the chiles. Stem and seed the roasted chiles, and cut the chiles into thin strips. Reserve. Put the chicken breasts in a saucepan. Add the broth and bring to a boil, uncovered, then reduce the heat to low, cover and simmer until the meat is tender, 15 to 18 minutes. Cool the chicken in the broth 15 minutes. Remove the chicken from the broth, then remove and discard the skin. Coarsely shred the meat, cover and reserve. Strain the broth, cover, and refrigerate the broth for another use.

2. In a skillet, heat the oil over medium heat and cook the onion, stirring, 3 minutes. Add the reserved chile strips, oregano, cumin, salt, and pepper. Cook, stirring, 1 minute. Reduce the heat to low and gently stir in the reserved chicken and crema. Heat through completely, but do not boil. Mound the chicken mixture on a serving platter and sprinkle the cheese on top. Serve at once.

Chicken in Roasted Tomato Sauce
Pollo en Salsa de Jitomate Casera

Makes 4 servings

A whole cut-up chicken can be used for this home-style dish, but I prefer the leg-thigh quarters, braising them slowly in the sauce until the meat is succulent and tender. Serve with steamed rice and Grapefruit, Orange, and Avocado Salad (page 185).

Basic Roasted Tomato Sauce (page 42)

4 chicken leg-thigh quarters, on the bone

1 tablespoon fresh lime juice

1 teaspoon salt

2 tablespoons olive oil

2 tablespoons chopped fresh cilantro

1. Prepare the tomato sauce and reserve in the pan. Then, preheat the oven to 350°. Trim excess fat from the chicken and rub all over with the lime juice and season with the salt.

2. Heat the oil in a large nonstick skillet over medium heat. Add the chicken and cook, turning 2 to 3 times until golden brown, 8 to 10 minutes. Transfer the chicken to an ovenproof casserole dish. Pour the tomato sauce over the chicken. Cover and bake until the meat is very tender when pierced with a fork, 45 to 50 minutes. Sprinkle with cilantro. Serve at once.

icken with Portobello
ıshrooms
lo con Hongos

es **4 servings**

*ana Trilling, a cookbook author, owns a
king school located in the countryside near
aca City. On one tour I escorted to Oaxaca,
ana told us about the delicious wild mush-
ms that are brought to the Oaxacan markets
n the surrounding mountains during the
ıy season. We used one of the earthy, rich-
ing mushrooms, nanacates, in a dish similar
his wonderful recipe. Portobello mushrooms
be substituted.*

hole portobello mushrooms, about 5 inches
  in diameter

ıblespoons olive oil

teaspoon salt, or to taste

teaspoon freshly ground pepper, or to taste

ıedium garlic cloves, minced

cup canned fat-free reduced-sodium
  chicken broth

ablespoons dry white wine

ıpe plum tomatoes, peeled and chopped

errano chile, stemmed and finely chopped
  with seeds

teaspoon dried oregano (Mexican variety
  preferred), crumbled

kinless boneless chicken breast halves

ablespoons chopped fresh cilantro

Remove and discard the stems from the mush-
ɔms. With a melon-baller, scrape and discard
ɘ black gills from the mushrooms. Wipe the
ushrooms clean with paper towels.

2. In a large nonstick skillet, heat 2 tablespoons
of the oil over medium heat. Place the whole
mushrooms, top side down, in the skillet.
Sprinkle with half of the salt, the pepper, and the
garlic. Cook, turning the mushrooms 2 to 3 times
until the juices appear, about 4 minutes. Add the
chicken broth and wine. Cover, reduce the heat to
low, and simmer, turning once, until the mushrooms are tender when pierced with the tip of a
sharp knife, about 5 to 7 minutes. Remove the
mushrooms to a cutting board and reserve.

3. To the juices in the same skillet, add the tomato,
serrano, and oregano. Cook stirring, 3 minutes.
Cut the cooled mushrooms into thin slices about
¼ inch wide and return the mushrooms to the
pan. Turn off the heat, cover, and reserve.

4. In another skillet, heat the remaining tablespoon of oil over medium heat. Season the
chicken with the remaining salt and cook about
4 to 5 minutes per side, or until lightly browned
on the outside, firm to the touch, and no longer
pink inside at the thickest part.

5. To serve, reheat the mushroom mixture. Cut
the chicken breasts crosswise into ½-inch wide
strips. Divide the mushrooms and sauce among
4 serving plates. Arrange the chicken breast strips
equally on top of each serving. Sprinkle cilantro
over all.

Grilled Chicken with Cactus
Pechugas de Pollo con Nopalitos

Makes 4 servings

Traditional ingredients presented in new ways makes dining in upscale Mexican restaurants quite an adventure these days. This dish is a striking plate of pan-grilled chicken in a classic cooked tomato sauce, presented on a bed of diced cactus. The idea for the dish came from Adobe Restaurant in Tlaquepaque, a suburb of Guadalajara, where I have spent many pleasurable days wandering through the craft shops housed in restored colonial buildings, and enjoying the local cuisine.

Basic Cooked Tomato Sauce (page 42)
2 cups water-packed jarred cactus strips (nopalitos), drained
2 tablespoons olive oil
1/2 medium white onion, finely chopped
1 medium garlic clove, finely chopped
1 teaspoon salt, or to taste
4 skinless boneless chicken breast halves
Freshly ground pepper, to taste
Crumbled queso fresco (fresh Mexican cheese), or mild feta cheese

1. Prepare the tomato sauce. Reserve in the pan off heat. Cut the cactus strips into ½-inch pieces. Rinse well.

2. In a medium skillet, heat 1 tablespoon of the olive oil and cook the onion, stirring, until it starts to brown, about 4 minutes. Add the garlic, reserved cactus and ¼ teaspoon of the salt. Cook, stirring, 2 minutes. Reserve off heat.

3. Brush the chicken with the remaining olive oil and season with the remaining salt and pepper. Heat a stove top grill pan over medium-high heat and cook the chicken about 4 to 5 minutes per side or until well marked from the grill, firm to

the touch, and no longer pink inside at the thickest part.

4. To serve, reheat the tomato sauce and cactus. Divide the cactus evenly among 4 serving plates and place 1 chicken breast on top of each serving. Spoon some of the heated tomato sauce over each chicken breast. Sprinkle with cheese. Serve hot. Pass remaining sauce at the table.

Chicken Thighs with Onions and Nutmeg
Pollo con Cebollas y Nuez Moscada

Makes 4 servings

Chicken thighs or legs become tender and succulent by cooking slowly in this rich sauce lightly infused with nutmeg. Nutmeg came to Mexico via sailing vessels from Asia to Acapulco in the late 1500s and was distributed throughout most of the country. Mexican home cooks usually go for the whole chicken, which they cut up themselves; I buy chicken thighs or legs for convenience.

2 tablespoons vegetable oil
1 teaspoon salt
8 chicken thighs or legs on the bone; skinned, if desired
2 large white onions, coarsely chopped
1 teaspoon grated nutmeg
1 teaspoon dried thyme
3 tablespoons coarsely chopped fresh cilantro
1/8 teaspoon freshly ground pepper
1/2 cup water

1. Preheat the oven to 325°. Heat the oil in a heavy skillet over medium-high heat. Add the chicken to the hot oil, and season with ½ teaspoon of the salt. Cook the chicken until browned on the outside, about 5 minutes; then put the chicken in an ovenproof casserole dish.

n the same pan, cook the onions over
dium-low heat, stirring frequently, until they
n golden brown, 15 to 20 minutes. Add the
meg, thyme, cilantro, pepper, and the remain-
salt. Stir to mix with the onions. Stir in the
er, and bring to a boil.

Pour the skillet contents over the chicken in
casserole dish. Cover and bake until the meat
ery tender and easily pierced with a fork in the
kest part, about 45 minutes. Serve hot.

icken Mazatlán

llo Mazatlán

es **4 servings**

*zatlán, a popular Pacific coast vacation
tination, is the home of this platter of fried
ken and potatoes presented on a layer of
ked vegetables and shredded lettuce. It's a
t meal! In Mazatlán the chicken is poached
ore frying, but I prefer to brown the chicken
t and finish it in the oven.*

nall red potatoes, unpeeled

edium zucchini, diced

ound small green beans

blespoons vegetable oil

eces of chicken, 4 half-breasts on the bone
and 4 legs

aspoon salt, plus extra for the vegetables

aspoon dried oregano (Mexican variety
preferred), crumbled

blespoon olive oil

aspoons unseasoned rice vinegar

ips shredded lettuce, such as romaine or
iceberg

rge avocado (Hass variety preferred), peeled,
seeded, and sliced

10 radishes, trimmed and washed

sh salsa, purchased or homemade

- to 7-inch) corn tortillas

1. Put the potatoes in a pot of salted water and
bring to a boil. Cook over medium heat until the
potatoes are tender, about 20 to 40 minutes,
depending on size. Peel as soon as the potatoes
are cool enough to handle.

2. Steam the diced zucchini on a steaming rack
over boiling water in a medium saucepan until
crisp tender, about 4 minutes. Reserve in a bowl.
Remove the steaming rack from the pan and cook
the green beans in boiling water to cover until
crisp-tender, about 6 minutes. Drain and rinse
under cold tap water to stop the cooking. Reserve
in a bowl.

3. Preheat oven to 350°. Trim all excess fat from
the chicken and pat dry with paper towels. Heat
oil in a large nonstick skillet. Fry the chicken,
in batches if necessary, about 4 to 5 minutes per
side until lightly browned on the outside. Season
with ½ teaspoon of the salt and ½ teaspoon of
the oregano.

4. Transfer the chicken to a baking dish and bake
until tender and cooked through, 30 to 35 minutes. Cut the cooked potatoes into quarters and
fry in the same pan until lightly browned. Season
with the remaining salt and remaining oregano.
Add more oil if needed. Put the potatoes in the
baking dish with the chicken to keep warm.

5. Heat a nonstick skillet over medium heat, then
warm the tortillas, one at a time, until limp and
hot to the touch. Stack and wrap in a clean cloth
napkin or foil, then reserve in a basket.

6. To assemble, line a large serving platter with
shredded lettuce. Put the zucchini and green
beans on the lettuce. Season with salt. Drizzle
with the olive oil and vinegar. Arrange the hot
chicken and potatoes over the top. Garnish the
edges of the platter with avocado and radishes.
Spoon a little fresh salsa over everything. Pass a
bowl of salsa at the table. Accompany with soft,
warm corn tortillas.

Chicken Tampico with Mayonnaise and Olives
Pollo con Mayonesa y Aceitunas

Makes 4 servings

The contrast of pan-grilled chicken, hot from the pan, spread with a blend of cold mayonnaise, Mexican crema, and olives—in the style of Tampico, on the Gulf of Mexico—makes a delightful lunch or light supper. Mexican crema is widely available in most supermarkets or in Mexican markets. Sour cream is an acceptable substitute. Serve with bolillos *(oval Mexican sandwich rolls) or other crusty bread.*

¹/₂ cup mayonnaise

2 tablespoons Mexican crema, or sour cream

¹/₂ cup coarsely chopped pitted green Spanish olives or other Mediterranean olives

1 serrano chile, minced with seeds

1 tablespoon finely chopped fresh flat-leaf parsley

4 skinless boneless chicken breast halves

2 teaspoons fresh lime juice

1 tablespoon olive oil

Salt and pepper, to taste

1. In a small bowl, mix the mayonnaise, crema, olives, chile, and parsley. Cover and refrigerate.

2. Rub the chicken breasts all over with lime juice, oil, salt, and pepper. Heat a stovetop grill pan over medium heat, and cook the chicken 4 to 5 minutes per side or until it is well marked from the grill, it is firm to the touch, and it is no longer pink inside.

3. Transfer the chicken to a platter or individual plates. Spread the mayonnaise mixture equally on top of each fillet. Serve while the chicken is still hot.

Chicken, Ticul Style
Pollo Ticul

Makes 4 servings

This colorful Yucatán dish, similar to one served in the village of Ticul, near Merida, is a complete meal. I first encountered the dish in the dining room of the Panamericana Hotel in Merida and have presented it many times in cooking classes. This recipe calls for preparing several parts before assembling the whole, and much of the cooking can be done ahead. Fried plantain, radishes, and lettuce garnish the plate. Pickled onions and fresh salsa accompany the dish.

2 cups cooked and mashed black beans (Basic Pot Beans, page 461)

Yucatán Tomato Sauce (page 44)

Pickled Red Onions (page 19)

Yucatán Habanero Sauce (page 31)

Fried Plantains (page 456)

4 Crisp-Fried Whole Tortillas (page 86)

1 tablespoon olive oil or vegetable oil

4 skinless boneless chicken breast halves

¹/₂ teaspoon salt

¹/₄ cup grated cotija or mild feta cheese

Radishes and shredded lettuce, for garnish

1. Prepare the black beans, then the tomato sauce. Prepare the pickled onions, salsa, plantains (keep warm in 200° oven), and the tortillas.

2. In a large nonstick skillet, heat the oil over medium heat and cook the chicken 4 to 5 minutes per side or until lightly browned on the outside, firm to the touch, and no longer pink inside at the thickest part. Season with salt.

3. To assemble the dish, place 1 tortilla on each of 4 plates. Spread each with ¹/₂ cup of warm beans. Place a chicken breast on the beans. Top each breast with about ¹/₄ cup of heated tomato sauce.

nkle each serving equally with grated cheese.
nish each plate with warm plantains, lettuce,
 radishes. Pass the pickled onions and salsa at
table.

ied Chicken, Sonora Style
llo Frito, Estilo Sonora

es **4 servings**

*hole chicken cut into serving pieces would
ically be used for this recipe in Mexico, but I
fer just chicken breasts. The accompanying
ked and raw vegetables contribute to the fla-
and color of this attractive dish.*
Pure ancho or pasilla chili powders (chili
lida) are called pure because they contain
other seasonings. They can be found in the
xican section of most supermarkets. American
li powder can be substituted, but the flavor
l be different because they contain other sea-
ings, such as oregano and cumin.*

edium potatoes, peeled and cut into
 1/2-inch cubes

edium zucchini, trimmed and cut into
 1/2-inch cubes

ablespoons olive oil

kinless boneless chicken breast halves

easpoon salt, or to taste

teaspoon freshly ground pepper, or to taste

teaspoon dried oregano (Mexican variety
 preferred), crumbled

ablespoons unseasoned rice vinegar

ablespoon pure ground ancho or
 pasilla chili powder

o 8 small romaine lettuce leaves

nedium tomatoes, sliced

rred pickled jalapeño chiles (en escabeche),
 cut into strips

1. In a medium saucepan of boiling water, cook
the diced potatoes until barely tender, 4 to 5 minutes. With a slotted spoon transfer the potatoes
to a colander and rinse under cold running water
to stop the cooking. Reserve in a bowl. In the
same pan of boiling water cook the zucchini
until barely tender, about 40 seconds. Drain
and cool under running water. Reserve in a separate bowl.

2. Preheat the oven to 200°. In a large nonstick
skillet, heat 1 tablespoon of the oil over medium-
high heat and cook the chicken, 4 to 5 minutes
per side or until golden brown on the outside,
firm to the touch, and no longer pink inside at
the thickest part. Season with 1/2 teaspoon of the
salt, pepper, and oregano. Transfer to a platter,
cover, and keep warm in the oven.

3. In the same skillet, add the remaining oil and
the reserved potatoes, vinegar, chili powder, and
the remaining 1/2 teaspoon of salt. Cook, stirring
frequently, until the potatoes start to brown, 6 to
8 minutes. Add the zucchini and cook, stirring,
until completely heated through, 3 to 4 minutes.
Adjust seasoning. Arrange the vegetables around
the chicken on the platter. Garnish with the lettuce leaves and tomatoes. Scatter the jalapeños
over the chicken.

Plaza Chicken from Morelia
Pollo de Plaza

Makes **4 servings**

Plaza chicken is an institution in Morelia, the capital of the state of Michoacan. Every evening in the central plaza, food vendors set up portable cooking stations to prepare this full meal composition of chile-sauced, fried chicken, carrots, potatoes, onions, and cheese enchiladas. It's quite dramatic to watch being made and very satisfying to eat. The dish is manageable for home cooks by cooking some of the parts ahead. Serve with radishes and a green salad.

Basic Red Chile Sauce (page 47)

4 leg-thigh chicken quarters

1 teaspoon salt, or to taste

Vegetable oil for frying

2 large garlic cloves, minced

1 teaspoon dried oregano (Mexican variety preferred), crumbled

4 small potatoes, peeled and cut into 1/2-inch pieces

4 medium carrots, peeled and cut into 1/2-inch pieces

1 medium white onion, chopped

2 teaspoons cider vinegar

4 (6- to 7-inch) corn tortillas

1 cup shredded Oaxaca or Monterey Jack cheese

1. Prepare the red chile sauce. Reserve in the pan off heat. Then, preheat the oven to 250°. Season the chicken with 1/2 teaspoon of the salt. Heat 2 tablespoons oil in a large nonstick skillet over medium-high heat and cook the chicken about 4 to 5 minutes per side, or until lightly browned on the outside, but not cooked through. Add the garlic, oregano, and 1/2 cup of the chile sauce.

Turn to coat the chicken with sauce. Cover, reduce the heat to low and cook the chicken until tender and cooked through, 20 to 25 minutes. Reserve in a pan in the oven.

2. Bring to a boil 6 cups of water in a large saucepan and cook the potatoes and carrots until crisp-tender, about 8 minutes. Drain, leaving the vegetables in the pan.

3. Return the pan to medium-low heat. Add 1 tablespoon of oil, onion, vinegar, and the remaining salt. Cover and cook, stirring frequently, until the vegetables are tender, 8 to 10 minutes. Add 1/4 cup of the chile sauce. Stir gently to coat with the sauce. Put the pan of vegetables in the oven with the chicken to keep warm.

4. In a medium skillet, heat 1 tablespoon oil. Dip the tortillas, one at a time, in the hot oil, turning once, until limp and hot, about 8 seconds. Drain and stack on paper towels. To serve, put 1/4 cup of cheese on each tortilla. Roll and put 1 on each of 4 serving plates. Coat each tortilla with some of the remaining chile sauce. Put 1 piece of chicken on each of the 4 plates. Add a portion of the vegetables. Serve hot.

Lime Chicken
Pollo con Limón

Makes **4 servings**

Carlos O'Brien's in the Zona Rosa section of Mexico City is a lively place to dine and is one of Carlos Anderson's many popular restaurants throughout Mexico. The area has long had elegant restaurants and hotels, and this menu offers some innovative and interesting Mexican dishes, including Pollo con Limón, *which I recreated at home. The chicken goes well with black beans and just about any fruit salsa.*

blespoons olive oil

edium onion, quartered and thinly sliced

edium garlic cloves, minced

:inless boneless chicken breast halves

:easpoon Maggi seasoning extract or
  Worcestershire sauce

teaspoon salt, or to taste

teaspoon freshly ground pepper, or to taste

cup fresh lime juice

cup coarsely chopped fresh cilantro

In a large nonstick skillet, heat the oil over
·dium-high heat. Cook the onion and garlic,
·ring frequently, until they begin to brown,
:o 5 minutes. Remove the onion and garlic
a bowl.

Add the chicken to the same skillet, season
th the salt and pepper, and cook about 4 to
minutes per side or until lightly browned on
e outside, firm to the touch, and no longer
nk inside at the thickest part. Sprinkle the
aggi on the chicken, and distribute the onion
ι top. Add the lime juice and cilantro. Cook
minute. Serve the chicken hot with the onion
ιd the pan juices.

hicken in Tangerine Sauce

ollo en Salsa de Naranja Tangerina

Iakes **4 servings**

*licia Franyuti de Cornish, owner of Hacienda
e las Flores in San Miguel de Allende, has
rranged special dinners for my culinary groups
ι the dining room of her hotel. During a visit
ɔ San Miguel, Alicia gave me this recipe that is
Mexican with French influence. It's elegant and
lelicate enough for non-spicy eaters. You can
ubstitute mandarins if you like. Serve on a bed
ɔf steamed spinach.*

4 to 6 tangerines

1 tablespoon olive oil

2 teaspoons unsalted butter

4 skinless boneless chicken breast halves

$1/2$ teaspoon salt, or to taste

$1/8$ teaspoon freshly ground pepper

$1/2$ medium white onion, finely chopped

1 medium garlic clove, minced

$1/2$ cup dry white wine

1 bay leaf

$1/4$ teaspoon dried marjoram

$1/4$ teaspoon dried thyme

4 crisp cooked bacon slices, drained and broken
  into small pieces

2 teaspoons chopped fresh parsley

1 teaspoon cornstarch mixed with 2 teaspoons
  water or juice

1. Peel 2 of the tangerines, and separate into segments. Gently remove any seeds and pith with a
small sharp knife. Reserve the segments on a
plate. Squeeze the juice from the remaining tangerines. Pour the juice through a fine-mesh
strainer into a bowl and discard the pulp.
Measure out ½ cup and reserve for the sauce.

2. Preheat the oven to 350°. In a large nonstick
skillet, heat the oil and butter over medium heat.
Cook the chicken about 3 minutes per side, but
not cooked through. Season with salt and pepper.
Remove to an ovenproof casserole dish.

3. To the skillet, add the onion, garlic, reserved
tangerine juice, wine, bay leaf, marjoram, and
thyme. Bring to a boil and cook, stirring, 2 minutes. Reduce the heat to low, and add the bacon,
parsley, and cornstarch. Cook, stirring, until the
sauce thickens and clears, about 1 minute. Adjust
seasoning, and remove the bay leaf.

4. Pour the sauce over the chicken, cover, and bake
until the chicken is cooked through, 15 to 20 minutes. Add the tangerine segments and heat through,
about 1 minute. Serve hot with the sauce spooned
on top, and garnish with the tangerine segments.

Chicken with Tamarind
Pollo con Tamarind

Makes 4 servings

Tamarind paste adds a note of tartness to the flavors of this chicken dish. Although tamarind is native to Asia and northern Africa, it is a very popular ingredient in Mexico, especially in a refreshing beverage called fresca de tamarindo *(Tamarind Cooler, page 596). In the later 1500s, Spanish galleons from Asia landed in Acapulco and brought tamarind, and many other products, such as nutmeg, cinnamon, cloves, and tea to the area and other parts of the country.*

I prefer to use the whole leg-thigh chicken pieces for this dish, since the legs become very tender and the flavors are enhanced by a longer cooking time. Chicken breasts can be cooked this way, too, but the roasting time should be shorter or the meat will be dry. Mango Salsa (page 39) and rice are good accompaniments for the chicken.

Tamarind Paste (page 21)
1 ancho chile, stemmed and seeded,
    veins removed
2 small plum tomatoes, cored and coarsely
    chopped
2 tablespoons ketchup
2 teaspoons olive oil
1/2 teaspoon ground cinnamon (Mexican canela
    or Ceylon variety preferred)
1/4 teaspoon ground allspice
1/8 teaspoon freshly ground pepper, or to taste
4 chicken leg-thigh pieces, attached
1/2 teaspoon salt, or to taste

1. Prepare the tamarind paste. Then, measure out 3 tablespoons and put in a blender. Cover and store the remaining paste for another use. Put the chile in a bowl of hot water and soak 20 minutes. Add the chile to the blender and discard the water. Add the tomatoes, ketchup, oil, cinnamon, allspice, and pepper. Blend to a thick smooth purée with the consistency of ketchup. If too thick, add just enough water to achieve the right consistency. Transfer the sauce to a bowl and reserve.

2. Preheat the oven to 300°. Season the chicken with salt. Line a large shallow baking pan with foil and grease the foil to prevent sticking. Arrange the chicken skin side up in a single layer in the pan. Roast, uncovered, 30 minutes. Raise the oven temperature to 375° and brush the chicken with the reserved tamarind mixture. Cook, turning and brushing the chicken with additional tamarind glaze about every 10 minutes until the chicken is dark brown and tender, about 35 to 40 more minutes. Serve hot.

Braised Chicken with Prunes
Pollo con Ciruelas

Makes 4 servings

When my husband and I first traveled to San Cristobal de Las Casas in the highlands of Chiapas in southern Mexico in 1974, we stayed at the Molina de la Alborada, a lovely hillside inn. This mild chicken stew with strong Spanish roots was one of the regional specialties that I especially enjoyed. Whole cut-up chicken was originally used for the dish, but I use boneless chicken breasts.

blespoons olive oil or vegetable oil

ɔneless chicken breasts with skin on

edium white onion, thinly sliced

rge garlic cloves, very thinly sliced

rge carrots, peeled and cut into $^1/_2$-inch rounds

aspoon salt, or to taste

aspoon dried oregano (Mexican variety
preferred), crumbled

teaspoon dried thyme

teaspoon ground cinnamon (Mexican canela
or Ceylon variety preferred)

teaspoon ground allspice

cup canned fat-free reduced-sodium
chicken broth

cup dry white wine

aspoons cider vinegar

edium zucchini, cut into $^1/_2$-inch rounds

pitted dried prunes

teaspoon freshly ground pepper, or to taste

rred pickled jalapeño chiles (en escabeche),
seeded and sliced

Preheat oven to 350°. In a large, flameproof
serole dish, heat the oil over medium heat. Add
chicken and cook about 3 minutes per side, or
til lightly browned on both sides but not
ɔked through. Remove the chicken to a plate.

In the same skillet, cook the onion, garlic, carts, salt, oregano, thyme, cinnamon, and all-
ice, stirring, for 2 minutes. Add the chicken
ɔth, wine, and vinegar. Bring to a boil, cover,
luce heat to medium-low and cook until the
rrots are crisp-tender, about 10 minutes. Add
e zucchini, prunes, and reserved chicken.

Cover the casserole dish, then bake 25 to 30
inutes or until the vegetables are tender. Stir in
e pepper, then adjust seasoning. Serve hot,
rnished with strips of pickled jalapeños.

Chicken for a King
Pollo de Rey

Makes **4 servings**

*I have been cooking this recipe for many years and
have yet to serve it to a king, but my husband, family, and friends all love it. The recipe came from the
late Elena Zelayeta, a cookbook author from San
Francisco. I have made some changes to reduce the
amount of fat in the sauce. For a striking contrast
of colors, serve with Tomatillo Cilantro Rice (page
474) or Green Rice (page 474). Mexico produces
some fine brandies, such as Pedro Domecq, a well-
known label on both sides of the border. Most of the
grapes for brandy are grown in Baja and Sonora.*

1 large red bell pepper, roasted and peeled
(page 8)

4 skinless boneless chicken breast halves

1 teaspoon salt

$^1/_8$ teaspoon freshly ground pepper

3 teaspoons olive oil

$^1/_4$ cup heavy cream

$^1/_4$ cup canned fat-free reduced-sodium chicken broth

1 tablespoon Mexican brandy, or other brandy

4 to 6 dashes hot pepper sauce, such as Tabasco

$^1/_2$ cup packed shredded manchego or Swiss cheese

1. Prepare the pepper. Reserve. Then, trim the
chicken of any excess fat. Place each breast
between 2 pieces of plastic and pound with the
flat side of a meat mallet or rolling pin to an even
$^1/_4$-inch thickness. Season with $^1/_2$ teaspoon of the
salt and the pepper.

2. Heat the oil in a large nonstick skillet and cook
the chicken about 3 minutes per side, or until
lightly browned on the outside but not cooked
through. Place in a single layer in a large baking
dish. Set aside. Reserve the skillet for the sauce.

3. Preheat oven to 350°. Coarsely chop the roasted
peppers and put in a blender. Add the cream,

chicken broth, and brandy. Blend until smooth. Pour the sauce into the reserved skillet and bring to a boil. Add the remaining salt and hot pepper sauce. Cook until the sauce reduces and thickens, about 3 minutes. Pour over the chicken. Sprinkle each breast equally with the shredded cheese. Place in the oven and bake until the cheese melts and the sauce is bubbling around the edges, 8 to 10 minutes. Serve hot.

Chicken in Its Own Juice
Pollo en su Jugo

Makes 4 servings

Just the name of this popular dish from Guadalajara made me want to try it. For the best flavor, use all the chicken parts for this simple stovetop dish. Serve with good bread or tortillas to sop up the wonderful juices. Mexican Rice (page 472) or Corn and Cabbage (page 418) go well with the chicken. A bottle of hot sauce or a small bowl of red or green salsa is usually on the table to add to the chicken.

1 (3- to 4-pound) chicken, cut into serving pieces
2 tablespoons vegetable oil or olive oil
1/2 teaspoon salt, or to taste
1/8 teaspoon freshly ground pepper, or to taste
2 large white onions, halved lengthwise and
    sliced crosswise
3/4 cup canned fat-free reduced-sodium
    chicken broth
2 tablespoons white wine vinegar
1/2 teaspoon dried thyme
1/2 teaspoon ground cumin

1. Wash the chicken and pat dry with paper towels. Trim excess fat and any excess skin. Season with salt and pepper. Heat the oil in a large deep skillet and cook the chicken about 3 minutes per side, or until lightly browned on the outside but not cooked through. Remove the chicken to a bowl.

2. Fry the onions in the same oil until limp, about 4 minutes. Return the chicken to the pan. Add the broth, vinegar, thyme, and cumin. Bring to a boil; reduce heat to low, cover and simmer until the chicken is tender, 25 to 30 minutes. (If desired, for easier eating, pull the meat off the bones in large pieces and return the meat to the broth. Discard the bones.) Serve the meat and juices in shallow soup plates.

"Drunken" Chicken
Pollo Borracho

Makes 4 servings

When a dish contains some kind of alcohol, it's often called "drunken." Sherry is the spirit in this braised chicken dish with strong Spanish influences, which began after Spain established communities in Mexico in the mid-1500s. They brought with them familiar European ingredients. Soon the Indian and European cultures began to blend cooking ingredients from Europe with native ingredients of the New World. Because much of the early trade came through the port at Veracruz, that region and other Gulf coast areas still maintain a great deal of Spanish influence in regional dishes.

2 tablespoons vegetable oil or olive oil
4 chicken leg-thigh quarters
1/2 teaspoon salt, or to taste
1/2 medium white onion, sliced in half rings
1 large garlic clove, finely chopped
1 teaspoon dried oregano (Mexican variety
    preferred), crumbled
1 large tomato, peeled and finely chopped
1/2 cup chicken broth, canned or homemade
1/4 cup dry sherry
1/4 teaspoon ground cinnamon (Mexican canela
    or Ceylon variety preferred)
1/8 teaspoon ground allspice
1/8 teaspoon crushed red pepper
1 tablespoon chopped fresh parsley

Preheat the oven to 350°. In a large nonstick [skill]et, heat the oil over medium heat, and cook the [chic]ken about 5 minutes per side, or until golden [bro]wn on the outside but not cooked through. [Sea]son with salt, and transfer the chicken to an [ove]nproof casserole dish.

[I]n the same skillet, cook the onion, garlic, and [ore]gano 1 minute. Add the tomato and cook until [the] juices are reduced and the mixture is nearly [dry]. Stir in the broth, sherry, cinnamon, allspice, [cru]shed pepper, and parsley. Bring to a boil and [pou]r over the chicken in the casserole dish. Cover [and] bake the chicken 35 to 40 minutes, or until [ver]y tender. Serve hot.

[Ch]icken Breasts with Yucatán [Gr]een Seasoning Paste
[Pe]chugas de Pollo al Recado Bistek

[Ma]kes **4 servings**

[Th]is dish highlights one of Yucatán's most intrigu-[ing] seasoning pastes called recado bistek, *which is [ma]de by grinding together toasted garlic, onion, [lot]s of black pepper, oregano, cloves, cinnamon, [cum]in, and dried chiles. The paste is moistened [wi]th orange juice and slathered all over boneless [ch]icken breasts before grilling to produce chicken [wi]th flavor that really wakes up your taste buds. [Th]e chicken can be grilled over hot coals or [ind]oors a stovetop grill pan. Serve with Yucatán [Ca]bbage Salsa (page 38) and black beans or rice.*

[1 t]ablespoon Yucatán Green Seasoning Paste
   (page 22)
[2 t]easpoons fresh orange juice
[1 t]easpoon olive oil
[4 s]kinless boneless chicken breast halves

Prepare the seasoning paste. Then, in a small [bo]wl, mix the tablespoon of paste, orange juice, [an]d olive oil. With a sharp knife cut 3 slits, ½ inch [de]ep, on the smooth side of each chicken breast

and put the breasts on a platter. Brush all over with the marinade. Cover and refrigerate about 2 hours.

2. Remove the chicken from the refrigerator about 30 minutes before cooking. Prepare an outdoor grill (and grease the rack), or preheat a stovetop grill pan. Grill the chicken about 4 to 5 minutes per side until well marked from the grill, and it is no longer pink inside at the thickest part. Serve hot.

Chicken Breasts with Pumpkin Seed Crust
Pechugas de Pollo con Migas de Pepitas

Makes **4 servings**

Native pumpkin seeds are used in a new way to give chicken breast a nutty-flavored crust. I like to serve the chicken with black beans and Grapefruit, Orange, and Avocado Salad (page 185).

³/₄ cup raw hulled green pumpkin seeds
¹/₂ teaspoon ground cumin
4 skinless boneless chicken breast halves
¹/₂ teaspoon salt, or to taste
¹/₈ teaspoon freshly ground pepper, or to taste
2¹/₂ tablespoons vegetable oil

1. Toast the pumpkin seeds in a dry skillet over medium heat, tossing and stirring, until they have a wonderful toasty smell, start to brown, and pop around in the pan, about 2 to 3 minutes. When the seeds are completely cool, put them in a food processor and pulse until chopped into small pieces, or put them in a plastic bag, and pound them lightly with a rolling pin. Put the chopped pumpkin seeds in a pie plate. Add the cumin, mix, and reserve.

2. Put each chicken breast between 2 sheets of plastic wrap and pound them with the flat side of a meat mallet or a rolling pin, one at a time, to an even ¼-inch thickness. Season the chicken with the salt and pepper, and rub about ½ teaspoon of oil over each breast. Coat the smooth side of each chicken breast with the chopped pumpkin seeds, and place seed side up on a plate. Press the seeds firmly with the palm of your hand to help them adhere to the chicken.

3. Heat the remaining oil in a large nonstick skillet, over medium heat, and cook the chicken breasts, seed sides down, until the meat appears white all around the outside edges, about 4 minutes. Turn the chicken carefully with a spatula and cook until no longer pink in the thickest part, 2 to 3 minutes more. Serve hot.

Rolled Chicken Breasts with Spinach
Pollo Relleno con Espinaca

Makes 4 servings

Leonardo Espinosa Retana of El Campanario restaurant in San Miguel de Allende shared this contemporary recipe. The stuffed chicken breast is served with finely diced cooked vegetables.

4 skinless boneless chicken breast halves

¼ teaspoon salt

4 to 5 tablespoons queso fresco (fresh Mexican cheese)

1 jalapeño chile, seeded, veins removed, and minced

2 teaspoons finely chopped fresh oregano

1 bunch spinach leaves, washed, dried, and stems removed

1 large egg white, well beaten

½ cup dry bread crumbs

Zucchini and Carrots with Tomato (page 435)

3 tablespoons olive oil

1. Trim chicken breasts of any visible fat. Place each breast between two sheets of plastic wrap and pound them, one at a time, with flat side of a meat mallet or a rolling pin, to an even ⅛-inch thickness. Sprinkle lightly with salt. Set aside.

2. In a small bowl work together the cheese, chile, and oregano. Lay out the flattened chicken breasts. Using your fingers, spread the breasts equally with the cheese to within ½ inch of the edge. Cover each with 2 layers of spinach leaves. (Store remaining spinach for another use.) Fold in the ragged edges to meet in the center, and roll lengthwise into cylinders. Secure with toothpicks.

3. Put the egg white in a shallow bowl and put the bread crumbs on a plate. Brush the rolled breasts all over with egg white and roll in the crumbs. Put the chicken rolls on a plate and refrigerate about 25 minutes. Meanwhile, prepare the vegetables and reserve in the pan.

4. Preheat the oven to 400°. Line a baking sheet with foil. Heat the oil in a large nonstick skillet over medium-high heat and brown the chicken rolls, turning, 3 to 4 minutes. Place seam side down on the baking sheet and bake 15 to 20 minutes, or until crisp on the outside and cooked through. Reheat the vegetables. To serve, cut each roll on an angle in half. Arrange on serving plates to show the filling. Spoon the zucchini, corn, and tomatoes around the chicken.

Rolled Chicken Breasts with Poblano Chiles and Goat Cheese
Relleno de Pechugas con Chile Poblano y Queso de Chiva

Makes 4 servings

My husband and I had breakfast one morning with Chef Ricardo Muñoz of Mexico City, a historian of Mexican cuisine, but also innovative in his cooking. Ricardo described this stuffed chicken breast dish and suggested that I try it. I did and I loved the delicious intermingling of flavors. Goat cheese is made as a cottage industry in

...xico and it pairs well with poblano chiles and ...ken. I like to serve the chicken rolls on a bed ...ice with Pine Nuts (page 475). Pineapple ...a (page 41) is also good with the chicken.

... ge poblano chiles
... inless boneless chicken breast halves
... easpoon salt, or to taste
... blespoons soft goat cheese, such as
   montrachet or California chevre
... aspoons drained capers, chopped
... ge egg white, well beaten
... up dry bread crumbs
... blespoons olive oil or vegetable oil

1 ...oast the chiles over a direct flame until ...red all over, or place on a baking sheet and ...t under a broiler, turning, until charred on all ...s, about 5 minutes. Put the roasted chiles in a ...tic or paper bag and steam 8 to 10 minutes. ... the chiles. Cut the chiles in equal halves, ...stem end to the tip. Discard the stems and ...s. There should be 4 equal pieces. Rinse and ...dry with paper towels. Set aside.

2 ...rim the chicken of any visible fat. Place the ...sts between two sheets of plastic wrap and ...d with the flat side of a meat mallet or a ...ng pin to an even ⅛-inch thickness. Sprinkle ...salt. Set aside.

3 ...a small bowl, work together the goat cheese ...capers. Lay out the flattened chicken breasts, ...oth side down, and spread the goat cheese ...lly on each breast, to within ½ inch of the ... Put 1 piece of reserved roasted chile on ...heese. Fold in the ragged edges and roll the ...sts into cylinders. Secure with toothpicks. ...h the rolls all over with the beaten egg white ...roll in the crumbs. Put the rolls on a plate ...refrigerate about 30 minutes.

4 ...eheat the oven to 400°. Line a baking sheet ...foil. Heat the oil in a large nonstick skillet

over medium-high heat and brown the rolls, turning, 3 to 4 minutes. Place the rolls, seam side down, on a baking sheet. Bake 15 to 20 minutes or until the rolls are crisp on the outside and the meat is white throughout. To serve, cut each roll crosswise into 4 rounds. Overlap the slices on serving plates to show the filling.

Stuffed Chicken Breasts with Black Bean Sauce
Pechugas Rellenas con Salsa de Frijol Negro

Makes 4 servings

These chicken breasts are stuffed with cheese and herbs, then quickly browned on an oven-proof grill pan or skillet and finished in a hot oven. The chicken is served with a smooth, spicy black bean sauce. Stuffed chicken breasts are fairly common in Mexican restaurants. These contain both a melting cheese and a drier grated cheese for a more complex flavor. Poblano Chile Strips with Fried Onions (page 429) or Fried Plantains (page 456) go well with the chicken.

Black Bean Sauce (page 55)
4 skinless boneless chicken breast halves
½ cup grated Oaxaca or Monterey Jack cheese
¼ cup crumbled or grated cotija or mild feta cheese
2 green onions, finely chopped
1 jalapeño chile, seeded, veins removed, and finely chopped
1 tablespoon finely chopped fresh oregano
1 tablespoon chopped cilantro, plus extra for garnish
½ teaspoon salt, or to taste
Freshly ground pepper, to taste
2 teaspoons vegetable oil or olive oil

1. Prepare the black bean sauce. Reserve in the pan off heat. Preheat oven to 450°. Trim excess fat from the chicken breasts. Using a sharp knife, cut each breast lengthwise making a pocket for stuffing as large as possible without cutting through the edges on the other sides. Set aside on a plate.

2. In a medium bowl, mix together the cheeses, onion, chile, oregano, and cilantro. Fill each chicken breast pocket equally with the mixture. Season the chicken with salt and pepper. Brush both sides with oil.

3. Heat a stovetop grill pan or large skillet over medium heat. (If using a skillet, pour in about 1 tablespoon cooking oil. Do not oil a grill pan.) Cook the stuffed breasts until lightly browned on both sides, 3 to 4 minutes per side.

4. Transfer the pan with the chicken to the oven and roast until the meat is white throughout, about 15 minutes. To serve, reheat the sauce and spoon some of the sauce on each of 4 serving plates and top with a chicken breast. Sprinkle each serving with cilantro.

Chicken with Red Chile Steamed in Foil
Mixiotes de Pollo en Guajillo

Makes 4 servings

Maguey *is the common name of a species of the plant* agave *that is classified with aloes, amaryllis, and lilies. More than one hundred species have been recorded by botanists in the Americas. Tequila, mezcal, and pulque are all alcoholic beverages made from certain species of agave.* Maguey *is also the source for* mixiote, *a thin papery layer stripped away from maguey leaves and traditionally used as a wrapping for cooking. This traditional item is rarely obtainable, even for most Mexicans. Stripping the outer layer of the maguey leaves to get the* mixiote *kills the entire plant, and this practice has caused great damage to fields of maguey. When I visited the states of Tlaxcala and Puebla, it was explained that parchment paper or aluminum foil is often used for wrapping foods nowadays; however, the traditional dishes are still called* mixiotes.

This recipe was given to me by Estela Salas Silva, owner of and teacher at a culinary school, Mexican Home Cooking, in Tlaxcala, near the city of Puebla. Serve the chicken with Pan-Roasted Potatoes and Carrots (page 445) or any rice dish.

Guajillo chiles are medium-hot, dark-red dried chiles with a smooth, shiny skin. Guajillos, along with ancho chiles, are among the most popular dried chiles to use for cooked sauces. You can use bay leaves or epazote leaves for flavor in this dish, but if using bay, discard the leaves before serving. Epazote leaves are often found in Mexican markets. They are edible and can be left in the dish.

3 guajillo chiles, stemmed and seeded, veins removed
1 teaspoon ground cumin
3 whole cloves
1 large garlic clove, peeled and thinly sliced
1 teaspoon cider vinegar
1/2 teaspoon salt, or to taste
4 skinless boneless chicken breast halves
4 bay leaves or fresh epazote leaves

1. Put the guajillos in a small pan of hot water and bring to a boil. Turn off the heat, cover, and soak 30 minutes. Drain and rinse the chiles. Put the chiles in a blender along with the cumin, cloves, garlic, vinegar, and salt. Blend until

oth. If too thick to blend, add 1 tablespoon of
er at a time to free the blades. Blend to a thick
ée. Pour the sauce through a strainer into a
l, pressing with a wooden spoon to extract
pulp. Discard the debris.

Put the chicken in a glass pie plate. Spread the
e purée all over the chicken. Cover, refriger-
and marinate about 6 hours or overnight.

Prepare 4 (12-inch) squares of aluminum foil.
one piece of chicken and a little marinade on
ece of foil. Put 1 bay leaf or epazote leaf on
Fold the foil to wrap the chicken and make a
t seal. Repeat with the remaining chicken and
es of foil. Place the packages on a steamer
Add water to the bottom of a 2- to 2½-quart
mer pot and bring to a boil. Cover and steam
r simmering water 18 to 20 minutes. To test
doneness, open one packet. The chicken
uld be white in side at the thickest part. If not,
rap and cook a few more minutes. If done,
e the packets to be opened at the table.

icken, Pibil Style
lo Pibil

es **4 servings**

*s is one of the classic dishes of the state of
atán. Cooking meats over coals in pits dug
he ground is an ancient Mayan method
se result is nowadays often simulated by
baking. Banana leaves are available in
e Asian and Latin-American markets. Serve
delectable chicken with warm corn tortillas
oak up the juices. Accompany with plain
med rice. This recipe requires advance
aration, so begin one day ahead.*

¹/₃ cup Yucatán Red Seasoning Paste (page 23)
¹/₄ cup Bitter Orange Juice Substitute (page 17),
   or fresh Seville orange juice if available
4 skinless chicken breast halves, on the bone
4 skinless chicken thighs, on the bone
¹/₂ teaspoon salt
1 tablespoon vegetable oil
Banana leaves (page 10 for preparation
   instructions)
1 white onion, thinly sliced
1 medium tomato, sliced
2 *guëro* (yellow) chiles, stemmed, seeded,
   veins removed, and cut into thin strips

1. Prepare paste and juice and set aside. Then,
with the tip of a sharp knife, pierce the chicken
pieces in 4 or 5 places. Season with salt. Put the
chicken in a large bowl. In another bowl, firmly
mix the seasoning paste, orange juice, and half of
the oil. Pour the mixture over the chicken and
turn the pieces over to coat. Cover and refrigerate
about 6 hours or overnight.

2. Preheat the oven to 350°. Line a large baking
pan or clay casserole dish with aluminum foil
pieces that are long enough to fold back over the
top of the pan. Cut the banana leaves to line the
pan, on top of the foil. Put the chicken breasts in
the pan on the banana leaves; then add the thighs
and all of the marinade, overlapping the chicken
pieces, if necessary.

3. In a medium skillet, heat the remaining oil
and fry the onion until it begins to brown, about
4 minutes. Put the onion, tomato and chiles on
top of the chicken. Fold the banana leaves completely over the chicken and then fold the foil
over all, crimping the edges to make a tight seal.
Bake 1½ hours. Remove the chicken from the
banana leaves and serve hot with the sauce.

Chicken Moles and Stews

Chicken in Mole Sauce from Puebla
Mole Poblano de Pollo

Makes 8 servings

Mole poblano *refers to the special dark reddish-brown mole (meaning "sauce") from the city of Puebla. One story that's often told is that mole poblano was first made in the Santa Rosa Convent by the Sister Superior as a special dish to honor a visiting archbishop. This famous kitchen, founded in 1740, features brick walls inlaid with beautiful hand-painted Talavera tiles. It is now a museum filled with magnificent cazuelas (large clay cooking vessels for making mole).*

Mole poblano, is probably the most well-known mole outside Mexico, and is traditionally served with chicken or turkey.

Make the sauce at least one day ahead; it can even be made and frozen. Then the mole is ready to reheat and serve on short notice over fried or braised poultry. This stellar dish is served by itself with warm tortillas to dip into the sauce.

Mole Sauce from Puebla (page 56)
8 chicken quarters (either breast-wing or leg-thigh)
Salt, to taste
Freshly ground pepper, to taste
Oil for frying
1/4 cup sesame seeds, toasted

1. Prepare the mole poblano at least one day ahead. Cover and refrigerate. About 1 hour before serving, bring the sauce to room temperature.

2. Preheat oven to 350°. Line a baking sheet with foil. Trim all excess fat and skin from the chicken. Season lightly with salt and pepper. Heat about 3 tablespoons oil in a large nonstick skillet over medium heat. Cook the chicken, in batches, about 3 minutes per side or until lightly browned on the outside, but not cooked through. As each browns, put it on the baking sheet in a single layer.

3. When all the chicken is done, cover the baking sheet with foil and bake until the chicken is tender and cooked completely through, about 35 to 45 minutes.

4. Meanwhile, in a small skillet, over medium heat, toast the sesame seeds, stirring, until aromatic and just starting to brown, 2 to 3 minutes. Reserve.

5. About 20 minutes before the chicken is done, bring the mole sauce to a boil over medium heat, then reduce the heat to low, cover and simmer, stirring frequently to prevent scorching, until ready to serve. If the sauce is too thick, thin with hot chicken broth to the consistency of gravy.

6. To assemble, put 1 chicken quarter on each of 4 dinner plates. Pour the sauce equally over each serving, letting it pool onto the plate. Sprinkle with toasted sesame seeds. Serve hot.

icken in Oaxacan Red Mole

llo Coloradito

tes **4 servings**

Mexican cuisine, it's said that "often the
ce is the dish." Such is the case with Mole
oradito (red mole sauce), one of Oaxaca's
ven moles" that's generally served in a rather
in fashion, as most moles are, with just a
ked chicken quarter on the center of the plate
othered in mole *and sprinkled with sesame*
ds. This typical presentation might also have
mall mound of rice and a sprig of cilantro on
plate. It's a classic presentation focusing
ention on the complex sauce. A side dish of
ked vegetables might be served with the
cken. Warm corn tortillas are served to dip
o the sauce. The sauce is best if made a day
more ahead.

xacan Red Mole (page 58)

about 2-pound) chicken, quartered

ablespoons olive oil or vegetable oil

easpoon dried oregano (Mexican variety
    preferred), finely crumbled

teaspoon salt, or to taste

ablespoon sesame seeds

antro sprigs

rm corn tortillas

1. Prepare the mole several hours or a day ahead, for best flavor. Then trim excess fat and loose skin from the chicken. Heat the oil in a large frying pan over medium heat until it shimmers. Rub the chicken with oregano and season with salt. Place the chicken, skin-side down, and cook until golden brown, 5 to 6 minutes. Turn and cook the second side minutes until golden brown, about 6 minutes. Cover the pan, reduce the heat to low and cook the chicken until no longer pink inside, about 20 minutes.

2. Reheat the mole sauce until simmering. Place 1 chicken quarter on each of 4 plates. Cover each serving equally with sauce letting it pool onto the plate. Sprinkle sesame seeds on top and garnish with a sprig of cilantro. Serve with tortillas.

Moles with Poultry

The word mole (pronounced MOH-lay) comes from the Nahuatl word *molli* meaning sauce. Moles are complex sauces made with an amazing number of ingredients, up to 20 or even more. Moles come in a variety of colors—red, green, yellow, brown, black, and shades in between. The ingredients include dried and fresh chiles; toasted nuts, seeds, bread, tortillas, herbs, and spices; tomatoes, tomatillos, onion, garlic, plantains, pineapple, and dried fruits such as raisins and prunes; and occasionally, chocolate, to add extra depth and sweetness to the sauce.

Regional moles abound, and cooks are proud of their own regional version that is passed down through family generations. Mole Poblano from Puebla, is the best known, but examples from other regions, such as from Oaxaca—called the "land of seven moles"—include Yellow Mole, Red Mole, Green Mole, Black Mole, Coloradito, Manchamanteles (meaning table-cloth stainer), and Chichilo. Moles are considered celebrations dishes made for very special occasions, and most often are served with chicken and turkey (Mexico's indigenous bird).

Chicken in Oaxacan Green Mole with White Beans
Pollo en Mole Verde de Oaxaca y Frijoles Blancos

Makes 4 servings

Mole Verde, Oaxaca style, is different than the green moles of other regions. The state of Oaxaca is often called, "the land of the seven moles"

although there could be dozens more. This mole features the distinctive and important flavors of the green herbs epazote *and* hoja santa. *(See page 620 for mail-order sources. There's really no substitute for them, but if necessary, substitute dried epazote for fresh and cilantro for the hoja santa.) Cooked white beans are added shortly before serving. It's a great dish!*

2 cups cooked small white beans (Basic Pot Beans, page 461)

4 skinless chicken legs with thighs attached, on the bone

1 (14 1/2-ounce) can reduced-sodium chicken broth

1 medium (about 6 ounces) white onion, cut into chunks

6 large garlic cloves, peeled

1 carrot, scrubbed and cut into chunks

1/4 teaspoon crushed red pepper

1/2 pound fresh tomatillos, husked, rinsed, and quartered

3 large jalapeño chiles (3 ounces), seeded, veins removed, and chopped

1 teaspoon ground cumin

1/2 teaspoon ground allspice

1/8 teaspoon ground cloves

1 tablespoon vegetable oil

3/4 cup loosely packed flat-leaf parsley

3 (6-inch) sprigs epazote, leaves only, or 1 teaspoon dried epazote

2 medium size hoja santa leaves, torn into pieces (or 1/2 cup loosely packed fresh cilantro sprigs)

2 tablespoons masa harina (flour for corn tortillas)

1/2 teaspoon salt, or to taste

1/4 teaspoon freshly ground pepper, or to taste

1/2 teaspoon sugar, or more if sauce is too tart

1. Prepare the beans and reserve. Put the chicken into a large saucepan. Add the broth, 1 cup of water, half of the onion, half of the garlic, the carrot, and the crushed red pepper. Bring to a boil, then reduce the heat and simmer the chicken, covered, until

er, 30 to 35 minutes. Remove the chicken
es to a bowl and cover to keep moist. Pour the
ked broth through a strainer into a bowl and
rve for the sauce. Discard the debris.

n a blender or food processor, blend the tomatil-
jalapeños, cumin, allspice, cloves, the remaining
of the onion, and the remaining garlic. Add
p of the chicken broth, and blend until smooth.

n a large saucepan, heat the oil until it shimmers.
wly pour in the tomatillo mixture (so it won't
tter), and cook, stirring frequently, 5 minutes.

n the same blender jar, blend the parsley, epa-
e, hoja santa, masa, salt, pepper, and sugar with
up of the cooked chicken broth. Purée the mix-
e until smooth, and pour into the pan with the
ce. Cook over low heat, stirring frequently to
vent sticking, 20 minutes. Add the cooked
cken and the white beans. Simmer, partially
ered, 10 to 15 minutes to heat through and
nd flavors. Adjust seasoning. Serve hot.

hicken Breasts with
ellow Mole
echugas de Pollo con Mole Amarillo

akes **4 servings**

*llow mole is one of the classic seven mole
uces of Oaxaca. Mole Amarillo isn't actually
llow, but pale in color. The Oaxacan chiles for
llow mole, chilhuacle and chilcosle, are diffi-
lt to find in the United States, so I have used
her chiles to create this version.*

*In this modern interpretation, the mole is
rved as a thick sauce over cooked chicken breasts,
ith green beans and potatoes on the side. In the
nore classic yellow mole the sauce is thinned
ith broth and served as a soupy stew with meat
r chicken, green beans, potatoes, and chayote all
ooked together. In my recipe, the potatoes are
ven-roasted instead of boiled, and the green*

*beans and yellow bell pepper add a fresh and
bright contemporary note to the dish. The sauce
tastes best if it's made ahead and reheated.*

Yellow Mole (page 60)
8 small red potatoes, scrubbed and quartered
1 tablespoon olive oil
1 teaspoon fresh lime juice
1 medium garlic clove, minced
4 skinless boneless chicken breast halves
Salt, to taste
³/₄ pound small fresh green beans, trimmed and halved
¹/₂ yellow bell pepper, cut into ¹/₂-inch-wide strips

1. Prepare the yellow mole. Reserve off heat in the
pan. Preheat the oven to 350°. In a saucepan of
boiling salted water, cook the potatoes 5 minutes.
Drain and return to the pan. Add 2 teaspoons oil
and toss to coat. Transfer the potatoes to an ovenproof baking dish and roast, uncovered, until
tender and lightly browned, 40 to 45 minutes.

2. Meanwhile, in a small bowl, mix the remaining
oil, lime juice, and garlic. Rub all over the chicken
breasts and let stand about 15 minutes.

3. In a saucepan of boiling salted water, cook the
green beans and yellow pepper until crisp-tender,
6 to 8 minutes. Drain. Transfer to an ovenproof
bowl and set aside. When the potatoes are tender,
turn the oven temperature down to 200° and put
the green beans and pepper in the oven to keep
warm while cooking the chicken.

4. Reheat the sauce over low heat. Heat a stove
top grill pan or large nonstick skillet over
medium heat and cook the chicken about 4 to
5 minutes per side or until golden brown on the
outside, firm to the touch, and no longer pink
inside at the thickest part. Add salt.

5. To serve, place 1 chicken breast on each of 4
plates. Arrange the potatoes and vegetables equally
on each plate. Spoon some of the heated sauce over
each chicken breast. Garnish with cilantro sprigs, if
desired. Pass the remaining sauce at the table.

Bride's Mole with Chicken
Mole de Novia con Pollo

Makes **6 servings**

A delectable mole dish was made for a Mexican party I once attended in California's Napa Valley. The caterer was from the state of Jalisco in Mexico. It's a custom to serve special moles for wedding celebrations throughout Mexico. This is my interpretation of the dish. Mexican chocolate, which contains sugar and cinnamon, is widely available in the United States, packed in round cardboard containers in the Mexican section of most supermarkets. The commonly found brands in this country are Ibarra and Abuelita. Serve with rice.

6 skinless boneless chicken breast halves

4 cups canned fat-free reduced-sodium chicken broth

8 guajillo chiles, toasted (page 9)

2 tablespoons sesame seeds, toasted

4 prunes, cut into small pieces

¼ cup fresh orange juice

¼ teaspoon crushed red pepper

¼ teaspoon ground allspice

2 tablespoons vegetable oil

½ medium onion, chopped

2 large garlic cloves, thinly sliced

1 (6- to 7-inch) corn tortilla, quartered

½ teaspoon dried oregano (Mexican variety preferred), crumbled

¼ cup red wine

1 ounce Mexican chocolate (such as Ibarra)

1. Cut each chicken breast crosswise into 3 pieces and put in a large saucepan. Add the broth, and cook, covered, over medium heat until tender, about 10 minutes. Let the chicken cool in the broth.

2. Meanwhile, toast the chiles; then soak them in hot tap water 25 minutes. Toast the sesame seeds.

Drain the chiles and discard the water. Put the chiles, sesame seeds, prunes, orange juice, crushed pepper, and allspice in a blender. Reserve.

3. In a small skillet, heat 1 tablespoon of the oil over medium heat and fry the onion, garlic, tortilla, and oregano, stirring, until they start to brown, 3 to 4 minutes.

4. Transfer onion mixture to the blender. Add the wine and 1½ cups of the chicken broth from cooking the chicken. Blend as smoothly as possible, then pour through a fine-mesh strainer into a large bowl, pressing with a wooden spoon to extract the soft pulp and juice. Discard the debris.

5. In a large saucepan, heat the remaining tablespoon of oil over medium heat until it shimmers. Gently add the chile mixture (to minimize splattering). Cook, stirring, 1 minute. (If the sauce is too thick, add hot chicken broth to reach the desired consistency.) Add the chocolate. Reduce the heat to low, cover and simmer, stirring frequently, until the chocolate melts and the flavors blend, about 15 minutes. Add the chicken. Bring to a simmer and cook 3 to 4 minutes. Serve hot.

Papantla-Style Mole Sauce with Chicken
Mole Papantla con Pollo

Makes **8 servings**

This is adapted from a recipe by Carmen Degollado, owner-chef of El Bajío Restaurant in Mexico City. Carmen also teaches and made this delicious and unusual mole in a cooking class I attended. It's definitely worth the time spent to prepare it. Papantla is a region in the state of Veracruz near the Gulf coast.

A ripe plantain should be used in this recipe, because it will be sweeter, softer, and much less starchy than hard green plantains. Piloncillo is unrefined sugar that's pressed into hard cones or s. It's available in Mexican markets and in *Mexican section of some supermarkets.* *wn sugar is a good substitute for* piloncillo. *cooking or baking,* piloncillo *is often dis-* *ed in broth or water. It can also be pulver-* *l in a food processor, or grated by hand.* *ve the chicken with rice.*

- nicken thighs on the bone
- nicken breast halves, on the bone
- ups canned chicken broth
- ncho chiles, seeded, veins removed, and toasted (page 9)
- ablespoons olive oil
- ounces (about 5 to 6) Roma tomatoes, cored
- 5- to 7-inch) corn tortilla, torn into pieces
- lice of sweet baguette (½-inch thick)
- ipe plantain (skin a bit yellow, but mostly dark in color and slightly soft when lightly pressed), peeled and cut into 1-inch pieces
- whole cloves
- innamon stick (Mexican canela or Ceylon variety preferred), broken into pieces
- anned chipotle chiles en adobo, seeded, or 1 tablespoon chipotle salsa, purchased or homemade
- ounces piloncillo (Mexican raw sugar cones sold by weight), or dark brown sugar
- teaspoon salt, or to taste
- opped fresh cilantro
- ne wedges

Cook all the chicken pieces in the chicken roth in a large pot until cooked through and nder. Cook the breasts 20 minutes; then remove em to a bowl and cover, to prevent overcook- ig. Remove the thighs about 10 minutes later (or) minutes total), and put them in the bowl with ie chicken breasts. Keep the broth warm over w heat until added to the sauce.

In a medium skillet, toast the anchos until aro- natic and slightly blistered. Do not burn. Put the anchos in a medium bowl and cover with hot water. Soak about 20 minutes.

3. Preheat the oven to 325°. In the same skillet used for toasting the anchos, heat the oil over medium-high heat. Add the tomatoes, tortillas, bread, plantain, cloves, and canela. Cook, stir- ring, frequently, until the tomatoes soften and the skins blister and char lightly.

4. Transfer the skillet ingredients to a blender. Add 2 cups of the reserved chicken broth, the soaked anchos, and the chipotles. Blend until very smooth. Transfer the blended sauce to a large heavy ovenproof pan or casserole dish.

5. Cook, stirring, until the sauce comes to a boil, about 3 minutes. Add the piloncillo and 1 cup of the reserved broth. Cook, stirring, over low heat, until the sugar melts, about 5 minutes. The sauce should have the consistency of heavy cream. If too thick, add additional hot broth. Add salt. Add the cooked pieces of chicken to the pan, and transfer to the oven and cook until the chicken is no longer pink inside, and the sauce is simmer- ing, about 20 to 25 minutes. Serve hot.

Chicken and Green Chile Stew
Guisado de Pollo y Chile Poblano

Makes 4 servings

Home-style stewed chicken is a favorite every-day kind of dish that's prepared all year round, with regional variations throughout Mexico. It's particularly wonderful as a cold-weather meal served with warm tortillas or good crusty bread to dip into the tasty sauce. The lime juice added just before eating is a classic touch and adds a refreshing brightness to the stew.

1 tablespoon olive oil or vegetable oil

1 large white onion, halved lengthwise and sliced

4 skinless boneless chicken thighs, cut in 1-inch pieces

3 skinless boneless chicken breast halves, cut in 1-inch pieces

1 celery rib, sliced crosswise

6 medium garlic cloves, thinly sliced

1 teaspoon dried oregano (Mexican variety preferred), crumbled

1/2 teaspoon ground cumin

1 large ripe tomato, peeled, seeded, and coarsely chopped

2 1/2 cups canned fat-free reduced-sodium chicken broth

4 poblano chiles, roasted, peeled, and seeded (page 8)

1/2 teaspoon salt, or to taste

1/8 teaspoon freshly ground pepper, or to taste

Lime wedges

1. Heat the oil in a large saucepan over medium-high heat and cook the onion, stirring until it begins to brown, about 4 minutes. Add the chicken pieces, celery, garlic, oregano, cumin, tomato, and chicken broth. Bring to a boil; then reduce the heat to low, cover and simmer until the chicken is very tender, about 25 minutes.

2. Cut the chiles into 1-inch pieces and add to the stew. Season with salt and pepper. Cook 8 to 10 minutes to blend the flavors. Serve hot with lime wedges.

Chicken, Mushrooms, and Red Pepper Stew
Guisado de Pollo, Hongos, y Chile Rojo

Makes 4 servings

Boneless chicken thighs, mushrooms, and sweet red peppers simmer together in a sauce thickened with masa harina *(corn tortilla flour) and seasoned with traditional herbs and aromatics for this stew from northern Mexico. De arbol chile adds a punch of spicy heat to the stew. Serve with rice or soft, warm tortillas.*

2 pounds skinless boneless chicken thighs

4 medium garlic cloves, sliced

2 bay leaves

1 1/2 teaspoons dried oregano (Mexican variety preferred), crumbled

1/2 teaspoon dried thyme leaves

1/2 teaspoon salt, or to taste

1 tablespoon olive oil

1/2 medium white onion, chopped

6 ounces brown mushrooms, sliced

1 medium red bell pepper, cut into 1/2-inch squares

1 de arbol chile, toasted, seeded, and broken into pieces

1/2 cup lightly packed coarsely chopped fresh cilantro

1 tablespoon masa harina (flour for corn tortillas)

1. Trim the chicken thighs of excess fat and cut into 1-inch pieces. Put the chicken, garlic, oregano, thyme, and salt into a 2-quart saucepan. Add water to barely cover the chicken. Bring to a boil, then reduce the heat to low, cover and simmer until the chicken is tender, 30 to 35 minutes. Reserve in the pan off heat.

When the chicken is tender, heat the oil in a
medium skillet, and cook the onion until it starts
to brown, about 4 minutes. Add the mushrooms,
pepper, and ¼ cup of the broth from cooking
the chicken. Cook, stirring, until the liquid completely boils away, to concentrate the flavors,
about 3 minutes. Stir the skillet contents into the
pan with the chicken.

In a small, hot, dry skillet, toast the de arbol
chile until it releases its aroma and starts to
color, about 10 seconds. Wearing protective
gloves, cut the chile open and discard the seeds.
Break or cut the chile into small bits (⅛ inch) and
add to the stew.

In a small bowl, mix the masa harina with
tablespoons of water, and stir into the stew,
mixing well to blend. Bring the stew to a boil over
medium-high heat; then reduce the heat to low
and simmer, stirring, until the broth thickens,
to 4 minutes. Adjust seasoning. Serve hot.

Chicken Stew, Chiapas Style
Estofado de Pollo Estilo Chiapas

Makes **4 to 6 servings**

*San Cristobal de las Casas is a colonial
city in the southern state of Chiapas only
100 miles from Guatemala. The rich Indian
culture still thrives as seen in the locally made
crafts and hand-woven fabrics. My husband
and I were there long before political upris-
ings put Chiapas in the international news.
We stayed at the Molina de la Alborada hotel
just outside the city. One evening, the cook
prepared a tasty regional chicken stew deli-
ciously accented with green olives and chopped
pickled jalapeños. We were welcomed into the
kitchen, so I took notes and later concocted
this recipe at home. The ingredient list is long,
but the stew is easy to prepare. Serve with
good crusty bread.*

4 skinless chicken thighs, on the bone
4 skinless chicken breast halves, on the bone
1 (14½-ounce) can fat-free reduced-sodium
   chicken broth
2 bay leaves
2 teaspoons salt
1 tablespoon olive oil
½ medium white onion, chopped
5 medium garlic cloves, peeled and thinly sliced
2 medium tomatoes, cored and chopped
1 teaspoon dried oregano (Mexican variety
   preferred), crumbled
½ teaspoon dried thyme
½ teaspoon ground cinnamon (Mexican canela
   or Ceylon variety preferred)
¼ teaspoon ground cloves
⅛ teaspoon freshly ground pepper
2 small red or white potatoes, scrubbed and diced
   (½ inch)
2 medium carrots, peeled and cut in ½-inch pieces
1 medium zucchini, cut in ½-inch pieces
8 pimiento stuffed olives, sliced crosswise
4 jarred pickled jalapeños, seeded and finely chopped

1. Put the chicken in a large pot. Add the broth,
1 cup of water, bay leaves, and 1 teaspoon of the salt.
Bring to a boil, then reduce the heat to low and simmer until the chicken is tender, about 25 minutes.

2. Meanwhile, heat the oil in a large skillet, and
cook the onion until softened, 3 to 4 minutes.
Add the garlic, tomatoes, oregano, thyme, cinnamon, cloves, and pepper. Bring to a boil, then
reduce the heat to medium-low and cook, stirring,
5 minutes. Transfer to a blender and purée.
Reserve in the blender.

3. When the chicken is tender, remove the bay
leaves. Add the purée to the broth and bring to a
boil. Add the potatoes, carrots, zucchini, and the
remaining teaspoon of salt to the stew. Cover and
cook over moderate heat until the vegetables are
tender, 20 to 25 minutes.

4. Serve in shallow soup plates. Top each serving
equally with olives. Pass jalapeños at the table.

Chicken Stew with Chiles and Spices
Estofado de Pollo

Makes 4 servings

I enjoyed a rich chicken stew similar to this at a roadside restaurant near Villahermosa in the state of Tabasco. I use boneless chicken thighs in my version of the stew, which is now a family favorite. The toasted corn tortilla adds flavor and acts as a thickener for the blended sauce. Serve with Rice with Plantains (page 476).

6 skinless boneless chicken thighs, cut into 1-inch pieces

1 (15¹/₂-ounce) can fat-free reduced-sodium chicken broth

3 ancho chiles (about 2 ounces), cut open and seeded, veins removed

4 ripe plum tomatoes (about ³/₄ pound), rinsed and cored

1¹/₂ tablespoons vegetable oil

1 medium white onion, chopped

4 large garlic cloves, peeled and thinly sliced

1 teaspoon dried oregano (Mexican variety preferred), crumbled

2 (6- to 7-inch) corn tortillas, quartered

¹/₄ cup sliced almonds

³/₄ teaspoon salt, or to taste

¹/₂ teaspoon ground cinnamon (Mexican canela or Ceylon variety preferred)

¹/₄ teaspoon allspice

1. Put the chicken and the broth in a saucepan. Bring to a boil, uncovered, then reduce the heat to low, cover, and simmer until the chicken is tender, 20 to 25 minutes. Reserve, in the pan off heat.

2. In a dry skillet, over medium heat, toast the anchos, turning 2 to 3 times, until aromatic, 10 to 15 seconds. Put the chiles in a bowl of hot water to cover. Soak about 20 minutes.

3. Place rack in upper third of the oven. Preheat oven broiler. Put the tomatoes in foil-lined pie plate and broil until skins are lightly charred all over, 8 to 10 minutes. Remove from the oven and put the tomatoes, with skins, and all the collected juices into a blender and reserve.

4. Meanwhile, heat the oil in a medium skillet, over medium heat. Cook the onion, garlic, and oregano, stirring, until the onion softens, 3 to 4 minutes. Transfer to the blender with the tomatoes. In the same skillet, toast the tortilla pieces on both sides until stiff and light brown. Put in the blender. In the same skillet, toast the almonds, stirring, until barely brown, and put in the blender.

5. To the blender, add the soaked chiles, 2 tablespoons of the soaking water, salt, cinnamon, allspice, and 1 cup of broth from cooking the chicken. Blend until very smooth. Pour the blended sauce into the pan with the chicken and remaining broth. Stir to mix. Bring to a boil. Reduce the heat to low, and cook, partially covered, stirring frequently, 10 to 12 minutes to blend the flavors. Serve hot.

Chicken Tinga
Tinga de Pollo

Makes 4 servings

A tinga is a special kind of stew from Puebla that's most often made with pork, but is also made with other meats. This version is made with boneless chicken thighs. The cooked chicken is shredded and wrapped in soft warm tortillas for wonderful juicy tacos. Canned chipotle chiles in adobo sauce are readily available in the Mexican section of most supermarkets. If you can get it, good quality chorizo, made in bulk by some meat markets, is better than the packaged variety. Accompany the tinga with black beans.

pounds boneless skinless chicken thigh meat,
    cut into 2-inch pieces

cup canned fat-free reduced-sodium
    chicken broth

pound fresh bulk chorizo, or packaged,
    with casings removed

medium white onion, chopped

edium garlic cloves, chopped

teaspoon dried oregano (Mexican variety
    preferred), crumbled

edium tomatoes, peeled, seeded, and chopped

anned chipotle chiles en adobo, seeded
    and minced

ablespoons chopped fresh cilantro

t, to taste

rge ripe avocado (Hass variety preferred),
    peeled and thinly sliced

up finely shredded lettuce, romaine or iceberg

Put the chicken and the broth in a large pan
d bring to a boil over medium heat. Reduce the
t to low, cover and simmer until the chicken is
y tender, about 30 minutes.

Meanwhile, in a large skillet, cook the chorizo
er medium heat, stirring to break up the
mps, until it starts to brown, 3 to 4 minutes. If
orizo is quite fatty, drain off all but 1 table-
oon of the fat. Add the onion, garlic, and
egano. Cook, stirring, until the onion is limp,
out 3 minutes. Add the tomatoes, chipotles and
antro. Cook, uncovered, to reduce the juices,
o 4 minutes.

Lift the cooked chicken pieces from the broth
d shred coarsely. Add the chicken to the tomato
ixture along with ¼ cup of the broth. Bring to
boil. Add salt, if needed. Serve hot, to stuff
side warm tortillas with avocado and lettuce.

Oaxacan Toasted Corn Stew with Chicken and Pork
Segueza Nueva

Makes **8 servings**

*This recipe is adapted from a dish I learned at
Susana Trilling's cooking school in Oaxaca. It is
based on a Zapotec dried corn stew. The Zapotecs
are one of the native groups in the state of Oaxaca
that continue to practice their ancient traditions.
Many of them are master weavers and are known
for their fine rugs. In the past, they created
impressive and important ceremonial centers that
flourished for a period of about 400 years, from
AD 350 to AD 750. These remarkable archeologi-
cal sites can still be seen in the Valley of Oaxaca.*

*For a different interpretation of the stew, I
use fresh corn in place of dried. Hoja Santa
leaves can be mail-ordered (see page 620), or,
if impossible to find, use fresh cilantro instead.
The flavor will be different, but still very good.
Serve with rice.*

4 cups canned chicken broth
4 boneless country-style pork ribs, cut into
    1-inch pieces
8 skinless, boneless chicken thighs, trimmed of
    excess fat, and cut into 1-inch pieces
1 large white onion, peeled and quartered
1 teaspoon dried oregano (Mexican variety
    preferred), crumbled
8 guajillo chiles, stemmed and seeded, veins removed
2 large tomatoes, peeled and chopped
4 tomatillos, husks removed and rinsed
6 medium garlic cloves, peeled
2 whole cloves
6 peppercorns
1 tablespoon vegetable oil
4 large ears yellow corn, kernels cut off
2 hoja santa leaves, or 2 sprigs epazote
1 teaspoon salt, or to taste
Chopped fresh cilantro

1. In a large pot, bring 4 cups chicken broth to a boil. Add the pork pieces. Cover and simmer 30 minutes. Add the chicken, onion, and oregano. Cook until the chicken is very tender, about 25 minutes. Set aside.

2. Boil 2 cups of water in a medium saucepan. In a hot dry skillet, toast the chiles over medium heat, until they are aromatic and the skins blister. Put the chiles in the pan of boiling water, remove the pan from the heat and soak the chiles about 20 minutes to soften.

3. Put the tomatoes into a blender jar and reserve. In a dry skillet, toast tomatillos, garlic, cloves, and peppercorns. Add to the blender jar. Place corn kernels in the same skillet, and toast, stirring constantly, until flecked with brown. Scrape the skillet bottom to incorporate the brown bits, and to prevent burning. Set aside off heat.

4. Lift the onion from the broth and the chiles from the soaking liquid and put into the blender jar with the tomatoes, tomatillos, garlic, cloves, and peppercorns. Blend until smooth.

5. Pour the mixture through a strainer into a bowl, pressing it to extract the purée. Discard seedy pulp. Heat the oil in a medium saucepan over medium heat. Add the blended chile mixture and cook, stirring frequently, until thickened, about 10 minutes.

6. Put the chile mixture in the pan with the pork and chicken. Add the corn and the hoja santa (or epazote) to the pan. Cover and cook, stirring frequently, 10 to 12 minutes to blend flavors. Remove the hoja santa or epazote. Add salt. Serve the stew in shallow bowls, garnished with chopped cilantro.

Chicken, Aguascalientes Style
Pollo Aguascalientes

Makes 4 servings

Aguascalientes, the capitol of the state of Aguascalientes, located north of Guadalajara, is named for the many hot springs nearby. One of the oldest festivals in the country, the annual agricultural fair called Feria de San Marcos *is celebrated in late April and early May in honor of the city's patron saint. This regional chicken dish is one of the popular dishes prepared during the fair. Instead of frying the accompanying potatoes, as customary, I like to oven-roast them separately.*

6 small potatoes (each about 3 ounces), scrubbed and quartered

1 teaspoon salt, or to taste

1/8 teaspoon freshly ground pepper, or to taste

3 tablespoons olive oil

1 (3- to 4-pound) chicken, cut up, or chicken parts of choice

1 large white onion, sliced

1/2 pound fresh bulk chorizo, or packaged, with casings removed

2 medium garlic cloves, chopped

3 medium tomatoes, peeled and finely chopped

1 tablespoon fresh lime juice

1 teaspoon dried oregano (Mexican variety preferred), crumbled

1/2 teaspoon sugar

1/4 teaspoon ground cinnamon (Mexican canela or Ceylon variety preferred)

1/8 teaspoon ground cloves

1/2 cup canned fat-free reduced-sodium chicken broth

3 jarred pickled jalapeño chiles (en escabeche), seeded, and sliced

Preheat the oven to 425°. In a medium bowl, [toss] the potatoes with about 1 tablespoon of the [olive] oil and put in an ovenproof baking dish. [Spr]inkle with ½ teaspoon of the salt and pepper. [Ro]ast until golden brown and tender, 40 to [50] minutes.

[T]rim excess fat from the chicken. Add the re[ma]ining salt or more, as desired. Heat the remain[ing] oil in a large skillet and cook the chicken about [3 m]inutes per side, or until lightly browned on [bo]th sides but not cooked through. Remove the [chi]cken to a plate.

[A]dd the onion to the skillet and cook, stirring [un]til limp, about 3 minutes. Add the chorizo and [coo]k, breaking up into small pieces, until lightly [br]owned. Add the garlic, tomatoes, lime juice, [or]egano, sugar, cinnamon, and cloves. Cook, stir[rin]g, until the juices reduce, 4 to 5 minutes.

[R]eturn the chicken to the pan and add the [ch]icken broth. Stir to coat the chicken with the [sa]uce. Bring to a boil, reduce the heat to low, [co]ver and simmer until the chicken is very ten[de]r, 30 to 35 minutes. To serve, arrange the [ch]icken on a large platter. Spoon the sauce over [th]e chicken and scatter the jalapeños on top. [Su]rround the chicken with the roasted potatoes. [Se]rve hot.

Turkey

Basic Cooked Turkey Breast
Pechuga de Pavo Cocido

Makes **about 4 cups shredded or diced meat and 4 cups broth**

Turkey parts are very convenient and practical when preparing enchiladas, sandwiches, salads, and saucy turkey dishes. This is the way to cook a small amount of fresh turkey at home instead of buying cooked turkey from a deli. There is also the bonus of the turkey broth to use for soup.

1 (2- to 3-pound) boneless turkey breast half, with or without skin
6 cups water
1 medium onion, peeled and quartered
1 large carrot, washed and cut into chunks
3 sprigs parsley
3 medium garlic cloves, peeled and sliced
1 bay leaf
2 teaspoons salt

1. Put the turkey in a large pot and add the water. Add the remaining ingredients and bring to a boil, uncovered, skimming the surface as needed. Reduce heat to low, cover and simmer until the meat is white in the center, 35 to 40 minutes. Cool the turkey, uncovered, in the broth.

2. When the turkey is cool enough to handle, proceed with your recipe. Or, transfer to a separate container, cover and refrigerate up to 2 days. (Turkey can be frozen, but it's much better when freshly cooked.) Strain and store the turkey cooking broth, refrigerated or frozen, to use in soups or sauces.

Turkey Cutlets with Almond Crust
Pavo Almendra

Makes **4 servings**

Mexico's native bird is easier than ever for us to prepare in the United States, since fresh turkey parts are sold everywhere. Turkey cutlets stay moist with a crisp, chopped-almond crust in this innovative modern dish.

4 (1¹/₂ pounds) turkey cutlets

2 tablespoons fresh lime juice

1 medium garlic clove, pressed

¹/₂ cup slivered blanched almonds, finely chopped

¹/₄ teaspoon ground cumin

1 teaspoon salt, or to taste

2 medium tomatoes, cored and neatly diced, about ¹/₂ inch

1 avocado (Hass variety preferred), peeled and cut into ¹/₂-inch dice

1 tablespoon finely chopped white onion

1 serrano chile, stemmed and minced with seeds

1 tablespoon olive oil

1 tablespoon unsalted butter

Coarsely chopped fresh cilantro

1. Put the turkey on a plate and rub all over with 1 tablespoon of the lime juice and the garlic. On another plate, mix the chopped nuts, cumin, and ¹/₂ teaspoon of the salt. Coat the turkey pieces, one at a time, on one side with the nut mixture, pressing with palm of your hand to help the nuts adhere to the meat. Let stand, nut side up, about 10 minutes.

2. Meanwhile, in a medium bowl, gently stir together the tomatoes, avocado, onion, serrano, remaining lime juice, and remaining salt. Adjust seasoning. Set aside.

3. In a large nonstick skillet, heat the oil and butter over medium heat. Cook the cutlets, nut side down, until golden brown on the bottom, about 4 minutes. Using a wide spatula, carefully turn the cutlets and cook the second side until browned and no longer pink inside, 3 to 4 minutes. Place 1 cutlet, nut side up on each of 4 plates. Spoon the tomato-avocado mixture equally on the side of each serving. Sprinkle cilantro over all.

Yucatán Spiced Turkey Cutlets
Pavo en Xak

Makes **4 servings**

The turkey is indigenous to the Yucatán region. It was eaten centuries ago by the Mayans and is still enjoyed today. Today, the popularity of turkey is reflected on the menus of regional restaurants. Since we no longer have to purchase a whole bird every time we wish to enjoy turkey, I find turkey cutlets are ideal to use with a delicious easy-to-prepare Yucatán spice rub called Xak. Cook the turkey cutlets on a stovetop grill pan, or a nonstick skillet. A fresh salsa should accompany the turkey.

1 tablespoon Yucatán Dry Spice Rub (page 21)

4 (about 1¹/₂ pounds) turkey cutlets

1 medium garlic clove, mashed

1 tablespoon fresh lime juice

¹/₄ teaspoon salt, or to taste

1 tablespoon plus 2 teaspoons olive oil

Mango-Avocado Salsa (page 39) (optional)

1. Prepare the spice rub. Measure out 1 tablespoon and set aside. Store the remaining spice rub for future use. Place the turkey cutlets on a plate. In a small bowl, mix the garlic, lime juice, salt, and 1 tablespoon of the oil. Spoon marinade over the turkey and turn to coat. Sprinkle the spice mixture evenly over both sides of the turkey. Cover and marinate, turning once or twice, about 1 hour.

2. Prepare the salsa, if using. Then, heat a stovetop grill pan over medium heat. (If using a skillet, heat 1 tablespoon of oil in the pan.) Place the cutlets on the hot pan. Cook 2 to 3 minutes per

...or until the cutlets are marked well by thew
...l and the meat is no longer pink inside at the
...kest part. Serve hot with the salsa, if using.

...rkey with Mushrooms
...d Tomatillos
...vo con Hongos y Tomatillos

...kes **4 servings**

*...easy to add healthful turkey to menus year-
...nd by using fresh turkey parts. Here, turkey
...lets are presented with an innovative vegetable
...ping in this contemporary Mexican entrée.*

...ablespoon olive oil or vegetable oil
...medium onion, coarsely chopped
...red bell pepper, cut in ³/₄-inch squares
...errano chile, seeded, veins removed, and
    finely chopped
...pound medium white mushrooms, quartered
...pound medium tomatillos, husked, rinsed,
    and quartered
...teaspoon ground cumin
...teaspoon dried oregano (Mexican variety
    preferred), crumbled
...cup canned chicken broth
...cup loosely packed chopped fresh cilantro
...ablespoon unsalted butter
...(about 1¹/₂ pounds) turkey cutlets
...teaspoon salt, or to taste
...teaspoon freshly ground pepper, or to taste

In a large skillet, heat the oil over medium heat
...d cook the onion until translucent, about 3 min-
...tes. Add the pepper, chile, and mushrooms. Cook,
...irring, until the mushrooms give up their juices
...d start to brown, about 4 minutes. Add the
...matillos, cumin, and oregano. Cook, stirring,
...minutes. Add the broth and cilantro. Bring to a
...oil; then remove from heat and reserve in the pan.

In another large nonstick skillet, heat the but-
...er over medium heat. Season the turkey with salt

and pepper and cook about 2 to 3 minutes per
side or until browned on the outside, firm to the
touch, and no longer pink inside at the thickest
part. Overlap the turkey slices on a serving platter. Reheat the sauce, adjust seasoning, and spoon
over the turkey.

Turkey with Creamy Green Pumpkin Seed Sauce
Pavo en Pipian Verde con Crema

Makes **4 servings**

*Pumpkin seed sauce with turkey is an ancient
combination that's special enough for entertaining. The sauce enriched with cream can
be prepared ahead and reheated. Serve with
roasted sweet potatoes or rice.*

Green Pumpkin Seed Sauce (page 54)
¹/₂ **cup heavy cream**
¹/₂ **teaspoon salt, or to taste**
4 **(about 1¹/₂ pounds) turkey cutlets**
2 **teaspoons olive oil**
1 **teaspoon unsalted butter**
Chopped fresh cilantro

1. Prepare the pumpkin seed sauce. Remove
1 cup of the sauce to a medium pan and keep it
warm. Store remaining sauce in a covered container and freeze up to 3 months. Add the cream
to the sauce and bring to a boil. Add salt, if
needed. (The pumpkin seed sauce will contain
salt, but after adding cream, it may need a bit
more.) Reserve in the pan off heat.

2. Season the turkey with ½ teaspoon salt. Heat
the olive oil and butter in a large nonstick skillet
over medium heat until the butter sizzles. Add the
turkey and cook 2 to 3 minutes per side, or until
lightly browned on the outside and no longer pink
on the inside, but still moist. Serve the heated
sauce over the turkey. Garnish with cilantro.

Turkey in Spiced Vinegar Sauce
Pavo en Escabeche Oriental

Makes 4 servings

The cuisine of Yucatán is based on Mayan cooking traditions, with Spanish and even Lebanese, influences. A great number of Lebanese settled in Merida several generations ago and the ingredients from that cuisine mingled with Mayan and Spanish ingredients to create many of today's Yucatecan dishes. I first sampled this dish of spiced turkey and onions in broth at Los Almendros Restaurant in Merida, known for traditional regional cuisine. My husband and I were invited to the kitchen and the cooks urged us to taste some of the special dishes. The finished dish is a juicy stew, so serve it with crusty bread.

1/3 cup Yucatán Green Seasoning Paste (page 22)

1 (2¹/₂ pound) turkey thigh

1 (14¹/₂-ounce) can fat-free reduced-sodium chicken broth

2 medium garlic cloves, thinly sliced

1 teaspoon dried oregano (Mexican variety preferred), crumbled

4 allspice berries, or ¹/₄ teaspoon ground allspice

2 tablespoons olive oil or vegetable oil

1 large white onion, halved lengthwise and sliced crosswise

2 tablespoons vegetable oil

¹/₄ cup unseasoned rice vinegar

¹/₂ teaspoon salt, or to taste

1. Prepare the seasoning paste. Cover and reserve. Then put the turkey in a large pot. Add the broth and 4 cups of water. Bring to a boil over medium heat, skimming off the foam that rises to the top, and cook about 5 minutes. Add the garlic, oregano, and allspice berries. Partially cover, and simmer over low heat about 1 hour, or until the turkey is tender. Cool in the broth.

2. When lukewarm, remove the turkey. Pull off the skin and discard. Strain the broth into a bowl and reserve. Rub half of the reserved seasoning paste all over the turkey thigh and let stand 20 minutes.

3. Meanwhile, heat 1 tablespoon of the oil in a skillet and cook the onion, stirring, 1 minute. Transfer to a bowl. Stir in the vinegar, ¹/₄ teaspoon of the salt, and 2 tablespoons of water. Let marinate at room temperature.

4. Preheat the oven broiler. Place an oven rack about 5 inches from the broiler. Brush the turkey with the remaining tablespoon of oil and place on a baking sheet or on the broiler pan. Broil the turkey 3 to 4 minutes per side, or until the meat browns. (Take care not to let it burn.)

5. Remove the turkey and when cool enough to handle, separate the meat from the bone. Tear or cut the meat into bite-size pieces. Discard the bone and sinews. Reheat 4 cups of the reserved broth in a saucepan. Add the turkey meat, reserved onions, 2 tablespoons of the remaining seasoning paste, and the remaining salt. Bring to a boil, then reduce the heat to low and simmer about 5 minutes, or until completely heated through. Adjust salt, if needed. Divide the stew among 4 shallow soup bowls.

rkey Stew

isado de Pavo

kes **4 to 6 servings**

*ok fresh turkey or use leftover turkey for this
arty whole-meal stew. A splash of lime in the
w just before eating is a refreshing touch.
ve with tortillas or crusty rolls, such as the
hole-Wheat Rolls (page 523).*

ic Cooked Turkey Breast (page 311)
ablespoons olive oil
medium white onion, coarsely chopped
arge garlic cloves, thinly sliced
easpoon dried oregano (Mexican variety
    preferred), crumbled
easpoon ground cumin
medium tomatoes, peeled and chopped
ups turkey stock from cooking the turkey,
    or canned chicken broth
medium carrots, peeled and cut into
    1/2-inch pieces
medium zucchini, trimmed and cut into
    1/2-inch pieces
teaspoon salt, or to taste
teaspoon freshly ground pepper, or to taste
cup loosely packed chopped fresh cilantro
arge avocado (Hass variety preferred),
    peeled and diced
ne wedges

1. Prepare the turkey breast. Cut the cooked turkey into ½-inch cubes. Cover and reserve (there will be about 4 cups). Measure out 4 cups of turkey stock. If more broth is needed, add canned chicken broth to make 4 cups. Set the broth aside.

2. In a large saucepan, heat the oil and cook the onion until translucent, 3 to 4 minutes. Add the garlic, oregano, cumin, and tomatoes. Bring to a boil and cook until the mixture thickens, about 5 minutes. Add the reserved turkey broth, carrots, and zucchini. Bring to a boil, then reduce the heat to medium-low and simmer until the vegetables are tender, about 15 minutes.

3. Add the turkey, salt, pepper, and cilantro. Simmer the stew until completely heated through, about 5 minutes. Adjust seasoning. Serve garnished with avocado and lime wedges.

Turkey and Hominy Stew
Pozole de Pavo

Makes **4 to 6 servings**

Here is a rustic stew of braised turkey thigh meat, hominy, green chiles, herbs, and spices. Hominy is dried white or yellow corn kernels with the hull removed. When cooked, it expands and softens to a slightly chewy texture. For convenience, canned hominy is used here. Ancho or pasilla chili (chili molida) powder can be found in the Mexican section of many supermarkets. Serve with warm corn tortillas.

1 (1¹/₂- to 2-pound) turkey thigh, skin removed
1 tablespoon ancho or pasilla chili powder
1 teaspoon dried oregano (Mexican variety preferred), crumbled
1 teaspoon ground cumin
1 teaspoon salt
1 tablespoon olive oil or vegetable oil
1 medium onion, chopped
2 large garlic cloves, thinly sliced
6 plum tomatoes, peeled and chopped
2 poblano chiles, roasted, peeled, and seeded (page 8)
¹/₄ cup lightly packed chopped fresh cilantro
1¹/₂ tablespoons masa harina (flour for corn tortillas)
2 (15-ounce) cans white or yellow hominy, drained and rinsed
1 large avocado (Hass variety preferred), neatly diced, about ¹/₂ inch

1. Put 2 quarts of water and the turkey thigh in a large pot. Bring to a boil, skimming as needed. Add the chili powder, oregano, cumin, and salt. Reduce the heat, cover and simmer until the turkey is very tender, about 1 hour.

2. Meanwhile, in a large skillet, heat the oil over medium heat and cook the onion until it starts to brown, about 4 minutes. Add the garlic and tomatoes. Cook until the tomato juices are reduced, and the mixture is nearly dry, 4 to 5 minutes. Reserve off heat.

3. When the turkey is tender, remove from the liquid. When cool enough to handle, separate the meat from the bones, discarding the bone, and return the meat to the broth. Add the tomato mixture from the skillet. Cut the roasted chiles into 1-inch squares and add to the turkey pot along with the masa harina, cilantro and hominy. Bring the stew to a boil, then reduce heat and simmer 10 minutes. Adjust seasoning. Top each serving with diced avocado.

Turkey Meat Loaf
Albondigón de Pavo

Makes **4 servings**

Turkey is very important in Mexican cuisine, but ground turkey meat isn't used as much as ground pork or beef. Perhaps its versatility has not been realized, but it makes a fine Mexican-flavored meat loaf.

1¹/₂ pounds ground turkey meat
¹/₄ cup finely chopped onion
2 tablespoons prepared thick and chunky salsa
1 tablespoon canned tomato sauce
¹/₃ cup bread crumbs
1 tablespoon chopped fresh parsley
¹/₄ teaspoon salt, or to taste
Freshly ground pepper, to taste

1. Preheat the oven to 350°. Grease a 9- × 5-inch loaf pan. Put all of the ingredients into a large mixing bowl and mix thoroughly. Form into a loaf and transfer to the pan.

2. Bake until brown on top and completely cooked through, 45 to 50 minutes. Let stand 8 to 10 minutes; then slice and serve.

...catán Cold Spiced Turkey

...vo en Frio

Makes **6 to 8 servings**

...more practical to poach a turkey breast for ...s classic Yucatán dish than to tackle a whole ...key. The turkey breast is flavored with typical ...atán seasonings. The poached turkey is ...led, sliced, and served as a cold entrée or light ...ch. You may be surprised how good it is. Rice ...ad (page 209) often accompanies the turkey.

- ...B- to 4-pound) turkey breast with skin and some bone
- ...unces smoked deli-style ham, cut into thin strips
- ...easpoons olive oil
- ...nedium garlic cloves, pressed
- ...2 teaspoons ground cinnamon (Mexican canela or Ceylon variety preferred)
- ...2 teaspoons ground allspice
- ...2 teaspoons ground nutmeg
- ...easpoon ground cloves
- ...easpoon freshly ground pepper, or to taste
- ...mall onion, quartered
- ...ay leaves
- ...up dry white wine
- ...cup unseasoned rice vinegar
- ...whole orange, peeled and coarsely chopped
- ...easpoon salt, or to taste
- ...sic Vinaigrette (page 210)

1. With a sharp knife, make 3 diagonal cuts about 2 inches deep into the turkey. Tuck in the ham strips. Make a paste of the oil, garlic, cinnamon, allspice, nutmeg, cloves, and pepper. Rub it all over the turkey and into the cuts. Wrap the turkey securely with cheesecloth. Place the turkey in a large pot. Add the remaining ingredients and enough water to barely cover the turkey. Bring to a boil, reduce heat to low, cover and simmer until the turkey is tender, about 1 hour. Remove the turkey from the pot, transfer to a large platter and let stand to cool, 25 to 30 minutes.

2. Meanwhile, strain the cooking liquid, discarding the solids. Cool the stock and remove about ½ cup to moisten the turkey. Cover and refrigerate remaining stock for soup or some other use.

3. Remove the cheesecloth. Remove the meat and discard the skin and bones. Slice the turkey and arrange on a platter. Moisten with the ½ cup reserved stock. Cover and refrigerate until shortly before serving. Prepare vinaigrette. Serve the turkey cold with the vinaigrette.

Yucatán Stuffed Turkey Breast with White Sauce
Pavo en Relleno Blanco

Makes 8 servings

Instead of roasting a whole turkey for this traditional dish of the Yucatán, I prefer to roast a whole turkey breast. (If you wish to roast a whole turkey, see the box that follows.) The wonderful ground pork stuffing is mounded snugly underneath. Serve with Yucatán White Sauce (page 45) or White Sauce with Tomatoes (page 45). The sauce of choice can be made ahead or prepared while the turkey roasts.

2 cups Yucatán White Sauce (page 45),
   or 3 cups White Sauce with Tomatoes
   (page 45)
1 whole turkey breast on the bone
   (about 5 pounds)
2 large garlic cloves, mashed
1¹⁄₂ teaspoons salt, or to taste
¹⁄₂ teaspoon white pepper
1 tablespoon white wine vinegar

Stuffing

¹⁄₂ pound fresh ground pork
¹⁄₂ teaspoon dried oregano (Mexican variety
   preferred), crumbled
¹⁄₂ cup chopped pimiento-stuffed green olives
¹⁄₂ cup currants
¹⁄₄ cup chopped slivered almonds
2 tablespoons drained capers
4 cups day-old baguette bread (¹⁄₂-inch cubes)
1 cup chicken or turkey broth
1 tablespoon vegetable oil

1. Prepare the preferred sauce for the turkey. Cover and refrigerate if made ahead. Trim excess fat from the turkey. Make a paste of the garlic, 1 teaspoon of the salt, pepper, and vinegar. Rub the mixture over the turkey and under the skin. Set aside.

2. Preheat the oven to 350°. Line a large roasting pan with aluminum foil. Set aside. To prepare the stuffing, in a medium skillet over medium heat, cook the pork and oregano, stirring to break up the lumps, until no longer pink, about 3 minutes.

3. Transfer to a large mixing bowl. Add the olives, currants, almonds, capers, bread, and remaining ¹⁄₂ teaspoon of salt. Mix well. Add the broth and gently toss together until moist. Mound the stuffing mixture in the center of the prepared baking pan. Place the turkey on top of the stuffing and brush with oil. Fold the foil around the outer edges of the stuffing to prevent over browning. Cover the pan completely with another sheet of aluminum foil.

4. Place in the oven and roast 1 hour. Remove the foil cover, reduce oven heat to 325° and roast about 45 minutes, or until golden brown and an instant-read thermometer registers 165° to 170° and juices run clear when the meat is pierced with the tip of a knife.

5. Transfer turkey to a cutting board. Reheat the reserved sauce. Put the stuffing on a large platter. Slice the turkey and arrange overlapping on the stuffing. Spoon about ¹⁄₂ cup of sauce on top of the sliced turkey. Pass remaining sauce at the table.

(Variation) Roasted Whole Turkey with White Sauce

stuff a whole turkey, you will need to
rease the stuffing and the sauce recipes by
-and-one-half times the amount listed in
recipes.

For a special but uncomplicated meal, I like
tart with a Shrimp Tortilla Soup (page 229),
serve cooked vegetables such as Carrot and
ma Sticks (page 438) or Grilled Zucchini
ge 433) with the turkey.

2- to 14-pound) turkey

rge garlic cloves, mashed

aspoons salt

teaspoon ground white pepper

blespoons white wine vinegar

times quantities of ingredients for stuffing
in main recipe (page 318)

ps Yucatán White Sauce (page 45),
or 4¹/₂ cups White Sauce with Tomatoes
(page 45)

1. Trim excess fat from the turkey. Make a paste with the garlic, salt, pepper, and vinegar. Rub the paste all over the turkey and under the skin. Set aside.

2. Preheat oven to 450°. Prepare the stuffing as instructed in Steps 2 and 3 in the main recipe.

3. Stuff the turkey and place on a roasting rack, breast side up. Place in the oven and immediately reduce the oven temperature to 350°. Roast, basting the turkey occasionally with the pan drippings, about 3½ to 4 hours, until the interior temperature of the thickest part reaches 165° to 170° on an instant-read thermometer and the thigh juices run clear when pierced with the tip of a knife. Remove from the oven and let the turkey stand about 10 minutes before carving.

4. While the turkey is roasting, prepare the sauce. To serve, remove the stuffing and place in a bowl. Reheat the sauce. Carve the turkey and pour about 1 cup of the sauce over the sliced turkey. Pass remaining sauce at the table.

Duck, Game Hens, and Quail

Braised Duck for Tacos
Pato para Tacos

*Makes 4 servings as an entrée,
or about 2¹/₂ cups meat*

Tender boneless duck meat makes dynamite tacos, enchiladas, or burritos. When I buy whole ducks and use the breasts only, I save the legs and wings just for braising. The meat is so tender that it falls right off the bones. Many of the sauces or salsas in this book will go well with the duck, such as Avocado and Tomatillo Sauce (page 24), Fresh Tomatillo Salsa (page 34), or Pineapple Salsa (page 41). Tomatillo-Cilantro Rice (page 474) or Green Rice (page 474) are good with the duck.

4 duck legs and thighs

4 duck wings

1 teaspoon salt, or to taste

¹/₂ teaspoon freshly ground pepper, or to taste

1 teaspoon dried oregano (Mexican variety preferred), crumbled

¹/₄ teaspoon dried thyme

2 medium onions, sliced

1¹/₂ cups canned tomatoes with juices

1 cup chicken broth, canned or homemade

1 tablespoon red wine vinegar

1. Trim all the excess fat from the duck legs and thighs. Trim the excess skin, leaving a small portion along the center of the meat. Trim wings of excess skin and fat. Season the duck with salt, pepper, oregano, and thyme.

2. Preheat oven to 350°. Heat a large nonstick skillet over medium heat. Cook the duck pieces, skin side down, 8 to 10 minutes, or until well browned. Turn and cook until lightly browned, 4 to 6 minutes. Transfer to an ovenproof casserole dish.

3. Pour all but 1 tablespoon of the fat from the skillet. Add the onions and cook, stirring frequently, until limp and light brown, 6 to 8 minutes. Add the tomatoes, broth, and vinegar. Bring to a boil; then pour the skillet contents over the duck in the casserole dish. Cover and braise in the oven 1½ hours, or until the duck is very tender and easily comes off the bone. Remove from the oven.

4. When cool enough to handle, pull the meat off the bones, discarding the bones. Serve the duck meat and cooking juices as an entrée with rice, or use the duck as a filling for tacos, enchiladas, or burritos.

Duck Breasts with Blackberry Sauce
Pechugas de Pato con Salsa de Zarzamora

Makes 4 servings

Hacienda de los Morales, in Mexico City, once a magnificent colonial mansion, is now a renowned restaurant surrounded by beautiful gardens. This restaurant is in the upscale Polanco zone of the city where many new-style restaurants are located. The ambiance and service are top-notch, and the food has drawn my husband and me back on many occasions for more than twenty years. One of the Mexican specialties is roast duck, and I base my recipe on a wonderful dish served with tart-sweet blackberry sauce. Wild blackberries grow in Mexico, and farm-raised berries are also grown now. Maggi seasoning extract is popular in Mexico and is also widely available in supermarkets here.

blespoons finely chopped white onion

edium garlic clove, thinly sliced

cup unseasoned rice vinegar

cup thawed frozen unsweetened blackberries

up canned fat-free reduced-sodium
   chicken broth

easpoon Worcestershire sauce

teaspoon Maggi seasoning extract or
   more Worcestershire sauce

cup seedless blackberry jam

teaspoon cornstarch dissolved in
   1 teaspoon broth

teaspoon salt, or to taste

teaspoon freshly ground pepper, or to taste

oneless duck breast halves, skin on

In a medium saucepan, put the onion, garlic, d vinegar. Bring to a boil over medium-h heat and boil until reduced by half, about ninutes.

Add the blackberries, broth, Worcestershire, d Maggi. Boil, stirring frequently, until the ace is reduced to about ½ cup, about 10 to minutes. Pour the sauce through a strainer to a bowl, pressing to extract all the juices. scard the debris in the strainer. Return the uce to the pan. Add the jam and stir until e jam melts. Add the cornstarch, salt, and pep-r. Cook, stirring, until slightly thickened, 2 to minutes. Reserve off heat.

Heat a large heavy skillet over medium heat. rrange the duck breasts skin side down in the y pan. Season with the remaining salt. Cook ithout turning until the skin is nicely browned, to 10 minutes. (Fat renders as the duck cooks, d the skin becomes a bit crisp. Take care not blacken the skin.) Turn and cook the second de until medium rare, 4 to 5 minutes or iedium, 6 minutes. Transfer to a plate and let st 5 minutes.

4. Reheat the sauce over low heat. Add to the sauce the juices that collected on the plate with the duck. Thinly slice each duck breast crosswise on a diagonal. Spoon a portion of the sauce on each of 4 serving plates. Fan the duck breasts on top of the sauce on each plate.

Duck Breasts with Poblano Chiles
Pechugas de Pato con Rajas

Makes **4 servings**

Although wild ducks have been a part of the Mexican diet for centuries, duck breasts from domesticated birds are not common; but, they are offered on menus in some upscale restaurants in Mexico's larger cities and in the United States, which makes it easier to reinvent traditional Mexican dishes. Corn with Cheese (page 418) is wonderful with the duck.

2 poblano chiles, roasted and peeled (page 8)
2 tablespoons olive oil
1 medium white onion, finely chopped
$1/2$ teaspoon dried oregano (Mexican variety preferred), crumbled
2 tablespoons finely chopped fresh parsley
1 medium tomato, seeded and neatly diced
4 boneless duck breast halves with skin
$1/4$ teaspoon salt
Freshly ground pepper, to taste

1. Prepare the chiles. Then remove the stem and the seeds. Cut the chiles into short, thin strips. Set aside.

2. In a medium skillet, heat oil over medium heat and cook the onion until it starts to brown, 3 to 4 minutes. Add the oregano, parsley, and chile strips. Cook, stirring, 1 minute. Remove from the heat and stir in the tomato.

3. Heat a large heavy dry skillet over medium heat. Arrange the duck breasts skin side down in the dry pan. Cook without turning until the skin is nicely browned, about 10 minutes. (The fat will render as the duck cooks, and the skin will become crisp. Take care not to blacken the skin.) Turn and cook the second side until medium rare, 4 to 5 minutes, or medium, 6 minutes. Transfer to a plate and let rest 5 minutes.

4. Meanwhile, reheat the sauce. Slice each duck breast crosswise on a diagonal and arrange overlapping on each of 4 plates. Spoon a line of the heated sauce across each serving.

Duck in Green Pumpkin Seed Sauce
Pato en Pipian Verde

Makes 6 servings

Cooked pumpkin seed sauce (pipian), *is one of the classic Mexican sauces. The green version is* pipian verde *and the red version is* pipian rojo. *This is a very special dish that's worth the time and effort. The method of cooking the legs separately from the breasts is a technique that makes the legs tender and prevents overcooking the breast. The legs and thighs are oven-braised to succulent tenderness. The breasts are sautéed and thinly sliced. To make the dish easier to manage, ask the butcher to cut up the ducks. Serve the duck with Pineapple Salsa (page 41) and rice or beans.*

Green Pumpkin Seed Sauce (page 54)
2 (5-pound) ducks
1/2 teaspoon salt, or to taste
1/4 teaspoon freshly ground pepper, or to taste
2 tablespoons olive oil or vegetable oil
1 medium white onion, peeled and quartered
1/3 cup vermouth or dry sherry

1. Prepare the sauce. Then, if you are cutting up the ducks yourself, rinse the ducks and pat dry. With a boning knife, cut the leg and thigh away from the body in one piece. Repeat for all leg-thigh pieces. Cut all of the breast halves away from the carcass, leaving the skin attached. (Use carcasses for stock, if desired, or discard.) Trim excess fat from all the duck pieces. Season with salt and pepper.

2. Preheat the oven to 350°. In a large skillet, heat the oil over medium heat and cook the leg-thigh pieces, turning frequently, until browned on both sides, 6 to 8 minutes. Transfer to an ovenproof casserole dish.

3. In the same skillet, cook the onion 3 to 4 minutes. Put in the casserole dish with the duck. Cover and bake in preheated oven about 1½ hours, or until the duck is very tender. If cooked ahead, cover and refrigerate up to 1 day.

4. About 30 minutes before serving, reheat the legs in a 250° oven. Reheat the pumpkin seed sauce and keep warm. Heat a large heavy skillet over medium heat. Place the duck breasts skin side down in the dry hot pan. Cook, without turning, until the skin is nicely browned and crisp, about 10 minutes. (Fat renders as the meat cooks. Take care not to let the skin blacken.) Turn and cook the second side 4 to 5 minutes for medium-rare, about 6 minutes for medium.

5. Transfer to a plate and let rest 4 to 5 minutes. Slice the duck breasts and arrange on a serving platter along with the cooked legs. Spoon some of the sauce over the duck. Pass remaining sauce at the table.

Cornish Hens Roasted with Chili Rub
Gallinitas al Horno de Chili

Makes **4 servings**

Cornish hens are just the right size for a single serving. Chili Rub gives the little birds a great Mexican flavor. Serve with any number of salsas, such as Tomato and Corn Salsa (page [?], Pineapple Salsa (page 41), or Mango Salsa (page 39). Add rice or beans to complete the plate.

3 tablespoons Chili Rub (page 20)

2 medium garlic cloves, pressed

1 teaspoon salt, or to taste

1 tablespoon fresh lime juice

2 tablespoons olive oil

4 Cornish hens (about 1 pound each), rinsed, excess fat removed from cavities, and patted dry

Prepare the chili rub and remove 3 tablespoons for seasoning the hens. (Store remaining rub for future use in a sealed plastic bag.) In a small bowl, mix the chili rub, garlic, salt, lime juice, and oil. Rub the mixture all over the hens. Place the hens breast up on a large rack in a roasting pan. Let stand at room temperature for 30 minutes.

Preheat the oven to 375°. Roast the hens 15 minutes; then turn the hens over and roast until golden, about 10 minutes. Once again turn the hens, breast up, and roast 12 to 15 minutes, or until the juices run clear when a thigh is pierced with the tip of a small sharp knife. Serve 1 hen per person.

Cornish Hens with Fiery Cilantro-Mint Sauce
Gallinitas con Salsa de Cilantro-Yerbabuena

Makes **4 servings**

Cornish hens, split, seasoned, and roasted are excellent served with a blended sauce of pumpkin seeds, cilantro, and mint. In this recipe, half a hen makes a single serving. For big appetites, split and roast four hens instead of two and double the rest of the ingredients. The sauce is best served shortly after it's made.

2 Cornish game hens (about 1¼ pounds each) cut in half, rinsed, excess fat removed from cavities and patted dry

2 medium garlic cloves, pressed

1 teaspoon salt

½ teaspoon dried oregano (Mexican variety preferred), crumbled

¼ teaspoon freshly ground pepper, or to taste

1 tablespoon olive oil

Fiery Cilantro-Mint Sauce (page 30)

1. Rinse the hens and pat dry with paper towels. Place skin side up on a work surface. In a small bowl, mix the garlic, salt, oregano, pepper, and olive oil to make a paste. Rub the mixture all over the hens. Let stand about 20 minutes.

2. Preheat the oven to 400°. Line a baking sheet with foil. Place the hens, skin side up, on the baking sheet. Roast in the middle of the oven 35 minutes, or until the skin is lightly browned and juices run clear when thigh is pierced at the thickest point. Prepare the sauce while the hens are roasting. Serve each hen with an equal portion of the sauce.

Quail with Corn and Cucumber and Jalapeño Salsa

Codornices con Elote y Salsa de Pepino y Jalapeño

Makes 4 servings

Quail are highly regarded in Mexico, and these elegant little game birds are now farm-raised in the United States. Partially boned frozen quail are available in gourmet food markets and some butcher shops.

8 (about 4-ounce) partially boned quail, thawed, if frozen

1 tablespoon plus 2 teaspoons olive oil

2 teaspoons fresh lime juice

1 teaspoon brown sugar

1 large garlic clove, pressed

1 teaspoon salt

Cucumber and Jalapeño Salsa (page 29)

2 poblano chiles, roasted and peeled (page 8)

1/4 medium white onion, finely chopped

2 large ears fresh corn, kernels cut off

1/4 teaspoon dried oregano (Mexican variety preferred), crumbled

1 small tomato, seeded and finely diced

1/2 teaspoon ground cumin

1/8 teaspoon freshly ground pepper, or to taste

1. Put the quail in a medium bowl. Add 1 tablespoon of the oil, lime juice, brown sugar, garlic, and salt. Turn the quail to coat with the marinade. Cover and refrigerate for 3 to 4 hours. Remove from the marinade about 30 minutes before cooking.

2. Meanwhile, prepare the salsa. Then, remove and discard the stem and seeds from the chiles. Cut the chiles into strips then dice them into 1/4-inch pieces.

3. Heat the remaining 2 teaspoons of oil in a nonstick skillet. Add the onion, and cook until translucent, 3 to 4 minutes. Add the diced chiles, corn, and oregano. Cook covered, stirring frequently, until the corn is crisp-tender, about 5 minutes. Add the tomato, cumin, remaining 1/2 teaspoon salt, and pepper. Cook until the mixture comes to a boil, about 1 minute. Set aside off heat.

4. Preheat the broiler. Place the quail breast side down on a baking sheet. Broil 3 to 4 minutes. Turn over and cook until the skin is brown and crisp, about 3 to 4 minutes and the meat is no longer pink inside. Remove from the oven. Reheat the corn mixture, and divide among 4 serving plates. Place 2 quail on top of the corn on each plate. Spoon about 1 tablespoon of the salsa on each quail. Pass remaining salsa at the table.

Quail with White Beans
Codorneces con Frijoles Blanco

Makes **4 servings**

This easy recipe is based upon a quail dish from Sacramonte Restaurant in Guadalajara. Simply roasted quail was served on a bed of puréed white beans. Frozen, partially boned quail is found in most upscale gourmet markets in the United States. Fresh farm-raised quail is sometimes marketed in gourmet meat markets. Serve Fresh Salsa Mexicana (page 24) with the quail and beans.

White Beans with Roasted Garlic (page 469)
8 (about 4-ounce) partially boned quail, thawed, if frozen
1 tablespoon olive oil
1 large garlic clove, pressed
½ teaspoon salt

1. Prepare the white beans. Cover and reserve. The beans can be made a day ahead and refrigerated. Reheat before serving.

2. Put the quail on a foil-lined baking sheet, breast side down. Rub all over with oil, garlic, and salt. Let stand about 20 minutes.

3. Preheat oven to 475°. Roast the quail in the middle of the oven 5 minutes. Turn the quail over and roast until the skin is golden and the meat is no longer pink inside, 5 to 6 minutes. Remove from the oven. Reheat the beans. Spoon a portion of the beans in the middle of 4 serving plates. Put 2 quail on each plate.

Meats

Beef 329

Basic Shredded Beef

Shredded Beef with
Onion and Tomatoes

Mexican Dried Beef

Tequila-Lime Flank Steak
with Pickled Red Onions

Flank Steak with Mushrooms
and Green Chile Strips

Flank Steak with Tomatillo
and Sweet Pepper Salsa

Skirt Steak, Guadalajara Style

Chuck Steak with
Chihuahua Chile Salsa

Pan-Broiled Steak with
Onions and Chipotle

Beef Tenderloin Steaks,
Yucatán Style

Beef Fillet Strips in
Onion Sauce

Beef Fillet Strips
with Tomatoes, Peppers,
and Onions

Beef and Cheese Volcano

Grilled Beef, Sonoran Style,
with Onions and Chile Strips

Beef Steaks with Red Chile
and Wine Sauce

Steak with Avocado Butter
and Mango Salsa

Steak with Tomato and
Chili Sauce

Steak with Cascabel Chile
and Lime

Rib Steaks with
Ancho Chile–Red Pepper
Cream Sauce

Steak with Red Chiles

Steak, Yucatán Style,
with Green Seasoning Paste

Beef Tenderloin, Huasteca Style

Oven-Barbecued Beef

Beef Short Ribs

Boiled Rump Roast

Beef, Vegetable,
and Red Chile Stew

Durango Beef Stew

Mexican Meatloaf with
Ranchera Sauce

Pork 346

Basic Shredded Pork

Crisp Shredded Pork

Minced Spicy Pork

Ground Pork Patties

Mexican Pork Sausage

Pork Chops with Lime Butter

Pork Chops with
Poblano Chile Sauce

Yucatán Grilled Pork Steak

Barbecued Pork Steak
Marinated in Red Chile Paste

Baby Back Ribs with Tamarind

Crisp Pork Tidbits

Grilled or Spit-Roasted Pork

Pork in Guajillo Chile Sauce
with Avocado

Pork Loin Roast with
Red Onion Sauce

Pork Roast with Plantains
and Tangerines

Pork Roast with Peanut Mole

Pork Shank, Yucatán Style

Pork Tenderloin with
Red Sesame Seed Sauce

Pork Tenderloin with
errano Chile Cream Sauce

Pork Stew from Puebla

Pork and Vegetables in
Yellow Mole with
Masa Dumplings

Pork and Green Chiles

Pork in Tomatillo Sauce

Pork Stew with
Poblano Chiles and Corn

Pork "Tablecloth Stainer"

Pork, Vegetable, and
Chile Stew

Pork with Black Beans
and Chipotle Chiles

Pork Stew with Pineapple

Wedding Pork in
Red Chile Sauce

Pork in Tomato Sauce with
Diced Zucchini

Purslane with Pork

Lamb 365

Lamb Steaks with Chili Rub

Lamb Stew, Yucatán Style

Leg of Lamb in Chile Sauce

Butterflied Leg of Lamb with
Fiery Cilantro-Mint Sauce

Oven-Roasted Lamb,
Monterrey Style

Lamb Shanks in Ancho Chile
and Red Wine Sauce

Lamb in Chile Broth

Lamb in Red Chile Stew

Lamb in Red Chile with
Potatoes and Zucchini

Veal 372

Breaded Veal Cutlet

Veal in Sweet Red Pepper
Sauce

Veal Stew in Red Pumpkin
Seed Sauce

Organ Meats 374

Liver with Onions, Raisins,
and Jalapeños

Beef or Veal Tongue
in Vinaigrette

Beef or Veal Tongue
with Almond Sauce

Mexicans are unabashed meat-eaters and prepare meats in creative and enticing ways, including marinated steaks, sizzling fajitas, flavor-packed burritos, and tacos stuffed with meats cooked over mesquite coals. There are paper-thin slices of pork, beef, and lamb marinated in adobo (red chile marinade), rich meaty stews, succulent ribs and roasts, spicy sausages, meats wrapped and cooked in banana leaves, and many more ways to experience the variety of meats cooked Mexican style.

The method of cutting meat is different in Mexico than in the United States. Most of the meats are cut with the grain and are much thinner; consequently the meat cooks in less time. Meats are also often coated with traditional regional seasoning pastes for extra flavor.

Cattle, pigs, sheep, and goats were introduced to Mexico from Spain in the 1500s, and the meat from these domesticated animals broadened the Mexican diet considerably. Cattle ranching flourished in the north, where range lands of native grasses provided a suitable environment for raising stock. Wheat also became an important crop in Mexico to feed the stock. Northern Mexico is known for its superior, better-tasting beef. Beef from other areas of Mexico is generally tough and stringy since most of the cattle is not finished in feed lots or fed corn or grain. Tougher cuts of beef are well suited for thinly sliced steaks used in *fajitas*, for Mexico's popular charcoal-grilled steak dishes, and for meat used for slow-cooked stews with spicy sauces.

In Mexico, pork rivals chicken as the most-popular meat. It is excellent for roasts and stews, and for the versatile chorizo sausage, which is used with eggs at breakfast, and to flavor sandwiches, soups, sopes (masa dough cups) toppings, and tortilla fillings. Lard, a byproduct of pork, is still widely used for traditional tamales and a number of other dishes, because there's no substitute for the flavor and texture it brings to a dish. *Chicarrónes,* or fried pork rinds, are a popular snack and ingredient in many traditional dishes. Even in *nueva cocina*— the new style of modern creative cooking in Mexico—they are not left behind, for they are sometimes used as a topping in soups or in salads instead of croutons.

Barbecued lamb and goat are favorites for fiestas and other special occasions. Lamb stews are also an important part of meat cookery in many regions.

Although organ meats are not commonly eaten in the United States, they are cooked all over Mexico, so I've included a few recipes for you to try.

Many of the dishes in this chapter are easy and fast to make, and others that need a longer time to cook can often be made ahead and require little attention from the cook while they simmer or roast. You'll find plenty of reasons to include Mexican meat dishes in everyday meals or on special-occasion menus.

eef

asic Shredded Beef
arne de Res Deschebrada

akes **about 2 cups shredded meat (about 1/3 cup r portion for most recipes calling for shredded at)**

oked beef is used in pieces or shredded for chiladas, tacos, burritos, tostadas, soups, ws, and more.

/2 pounds boneless stew beef

medium white onion, sliced

nedium garlic cloves, peeled

bay leaf

teaspoon salt

Cut the beef into 1-inch pieces and put into a rge saucepan with the onion, garlic, bay leaf, d salt. Cover with cold water and bring to a il, uncovered, skimming the surface as needed. educe the heat, cover and simmer until the meat very tender, about 1 hour and 15 minutes.

Remove from the heat and cool the meat in e broth until cool enough to handle, about 5 to 30 minutes. When cool, drain the broth into container to save. Shred the meat with your fingers. Remove and discard any fat or gristle. The roth and meat are ready to use. Store the broth nd meat in the refrigerator in separate covered ontainers for 3 days, or freeze for 3 months.

Shredded Beef with Onion and Tomatoes
Ropa Vieja

Makes **4 servings**

Ropa vieja *meaning "old clothes", is the whimsical name for a very common Mexican dish. Sometimes ropa vieja is made from left-over cooked meats and other times from boiled beef that is shredded after cooking then mixed with fried onion and tomatoes. There are many versions of this well-seasoned shredded meat dish that is commonly used as a filling for tortillas to make tacos and burritos. Accompany the* ropa vieja *with guacamole and beans.*

1 pound lean beef stew meat or flank steak
1 teaspoon salt
3 tablespoons vegetable oil
1 medium white onion, finely chopped
2 large garlic cloves, finely chopped
2 serrano chiles, minced with seeds
2 medium tomatoes, peeled and chopped
8 (6- to 7-inch) corn or flour tortillas

1. Cut the meat into 1-inch pieces, and put in a medium saucepan with water to barely cover. Add ½ teaspoon of the salt. Bring to a boil, then reduce the heat, cover the pan, and cook the meat until very tender, about 1 hour. Cool the meat in its broth, 25 to 30 minutes.

2. When the meat is cool enough to handle, strain off the broth (save the broth for another use), and shred the meat with your fingers. Reserve.

3. In a medium skillet, heat 1 tablespoon of the oil, and cook the onion and garlic until just beginning to brown, 3 to 4 minutes. Add the garlic, serrano chiles, tomatoes, and the remaining ½ teaspoon of salt. Cook, stirring frequently, until most of the tomato juices have cooked away, about 5 minutes. Add the shredded meat, and cook until completely heated through, about 3 minutes. Serve with tortillas.

Mexican Dried Beef

Machaca

Makes **about 2 cups**

Mexican sun-dried beef, called machaca *or carne seca, is made in the dry desert regions of northern Mexico, especially in the state of Sonora. It's not practical or safe for most home cooks to dry meat in the sun, so here is a very good oven-made substitute to use for tacos, burritos, with eggs or potatoes, in salads, and more. It's even good just to nibble on with chips and guacamole.*

Basic Shredded Beef (page 329)
2 large garlic cloves, mashed
1 tablespoon fresh lime juice

Prepare the shredded beef. Preheat the oven to 325°. In a bowl stir together the beef, garlic, and lime juice. Spread the meat on a baking sheet and bake, stirring occasionally, until the meat is nearly dry and stiff, 15 to 20 minutes. Cool. Store in a sealed plastic bag and refrigerate up to 3 days or freeze up to 3 months.

Tequila-Lime Flank Steak with Pickled Red Onions

Carne Asada con Cebollas Rojos en Escabeche

Makes **6 servings**

The word asada *refers to meat that is grilled over coals or on a griddle, or is broiled. However prepared, it is a very popular way Mexicans eat meat. In this recipe, a tequila marinade gives a lively flavor to the grilled steak. Maggi seasoning extract, used to enhance flavor in the same way as Worcestershire, is available in most supermarkets. Topping it off with red pickled onions adds to the festive appearance. If the weather isn't right for outdoor grilling, the steak can be cooked indoors on a stovetop grill pan.*

Pickled Red Onions (page 19)
2 beef flank steaks (each about 1¹/₂ pounds)
3 medium garlic cloves, minced
¹/₂ teaspoon freshly ground pepper
¹/₃ cup tequila
3 tablespoons fresh lime juice
1 tablespoon honey
¹/₂ teaspoon bottled Maggi seasoning extract or Worcestershire sauce
3 tablespoons vegetable oil plus extra for the grill
¹/₂ teaspoon salt, or to taste

1. Prepare the onions. Then, trim the steaks of excess fat and silver skin. Score the steaks by making cuts about ½ inch deep and 2 inches apart, diagonally across the meat in two directions to make a diamond pattern on both sides. Rub the meat all over with garlic and pepper. Place the steaks in a large shallow glass baking dish.

2. In a bowl, whisk together the tequila, lime juice, honey, Maggi, and oil. Drizzle 2 tablespoons of the marinade on each steak, and turn the steaks to coat. Reserve the remaining marinade. Cover and refrigerate the meat about 2 hours or up to 8 hours.

3. Remove the meat from the refrigerator about 1 hour before cooking. Have ready a hot outdoor grill or heat a stovetop grill pan over medium-high heat. Pat the meat dry with paper towels, and season with salt just before grilling. Brush lightly with oil.

4. Grill the steaks on a hot greased grill over high heat or in the grill pan on medium-high heat, turning to brown the meat on both sides, 8 to 12 minutes total for medium-rare, depending on the thickness of the meat. (Adjust cook time for desired doneness.) Brush the steaks with the reserved marinade the last 3 minutes of cooking.

5. Remove the steaks to a cutting board and let stand 5 minutes. Cut across the grain into thin slices. Serve with pickled red onions scattered over the meat.

Flank Steak with Mushrooms and Green Chile Strips
Carne Asada con Hongos y Rajas

Makes **4 to 6 servings**

Cook the steak on an outdoor grill or on a stove-top grill pan and slice thinly. Top with pan-fried mushrooms, and strips of roasted poblano chiles. Serve with tortillas, guacamole, and fresh tomato salsa for a classic Mexican steak meal.

beef flank steaks (each about 1¹/₂ pounds)
medium garlic clove, pressed or minced
tablespoons fresh lime juice
tablespoons olive oil or vegetable oil
poblano chiles, roasted and peeled (page 8)
pound small cremini or white button mushrooms, sliced
teaspoon dried oregano (Mexican variety preferred), crumbled
teaspoon dried thyme
Salt and freshly ground pepper, to taste

Trim the steaks of excess fat and silver skin. Rub with garlic, lime juice, and 1 tablespoon of the oil. Set aside about 30 minutes at room temperature.

. Meanwhile, prepare the chiles. Then, remove the stem, cut open the peppers and remove the seeds. Cut the peppers into thin strips. Reserve.

. In a skillet, heat the remaining oil over medium heat. Add the mushrooms, oregano, and thyme. Cook, stirring until the mushrooms give up their juices and start to brown, 4 to 5 minutes. Add the reserved chile strips. Season with salt and pepper. Reserve in the pan off heat.

4. Prepare a hot outdoor grill fire, or heat a stovetop grill pan on medium-high heat. Place the steak on the hot, greased outdoor grill or grill pan. Season with salt and pepper. Cook the steak, turning once, until browned on both sides and still pink and juicy inside about 5 to 6 minutes

per side for medium rate, or adjust time for desired doneness. Transfer meat to a cutting board and let stand 5 minutes.

5. Reheat the mushrooms and chiles. Carve the meat across the grain into thin slices. Arrange on a serving platter. Spoon the mushroom mixture on top.

Flank Steak with Tomatillo and Sweet Pepper Salsa
Carne Asada con Salsa de Tomatillo y Chiles Dulce

Makes **4 servings**

Flavorful and economical flank steak is a mainstay in the cooking of northern Mexico. It's commonly seared on a griddle or grilled over coals and thinly sliced to serve with salsas, tortillas, and other condiments. Here, the steak is dressed up with a bright fresh salsa that's fancy enough for company. I serve refried black beans with the steak.

Mild Tomatillo and Sweet Pepper Sauce (page 37)
1 (1¹/₂- to 2-pound) beef flank steak
2 teaspoons olive oil plus extra for the grill
¹/₄ teaspoon salt, or to taste
¹/₈ teaspoon freshly ground pepper, or to taste

1. Prepare the tomatillo salsa. Then, trim the steak of excess fat and silver skin. Season with salt and pepper. Heat the oil in a large heavy skillet until almost smoking. Put the steak in the pan and cook 5 to 6 minutes per side over medium-high heat until well seared on the outside and still pink and juicy inside for medium rate, or adjust time for desired doneness.

2. Transfer to a cutting board and let stand 5 minutes. Carve across the grain into thin slices. Serve with the salsa.

Skirt Steak, Guadalajara Style
Arrachera

Makes 4 servings

Thin pieces of grilled skirt steak, called arrachera, *are listed on nearly every menu in and around Guadalajara. It's even advertised on restaurant billboards along the road. I had a very tender* arrachera *at El Viejo restaurant in Tlaquepaque, a suburb of Guadalajara. It was served on an oval plate with slices of fried white onion, spicy green salsa, and soft corn tortillas.*

Skirt steaks are beef diaphragm muscles with a long grain. This cut is often used to make fajitas in Mexican restaurants in the United States, and the cut is widely available in meat markets. Accompany the steak with Mexican-style beans, if desired, such as Ranch Beans with Bacon (page 463).

You can also use a stovetop grill pan for cooking the meat.

1¹/₂ pounds skirt steak, cut into 4 pieces
2 teaspoons fresh lime juice
¹/₂ teaspoon salt, or to taste
¹/₄ teaspoon freshly ground pepper, or to taste
Oil to brush on the meat and onion
1 medium white onion, halved and sliced
Tomatillo and Arbol Chile Salsa (page 35), or purchased green salsa
8 (6- to 7-inch) corn tortillas

1. Trim the steaks of excess fat and the tough silver skin. Rub the meat all over with lime juice. Season with salt and pepper. Let the meat stand at room temperature while preparing a hot barbecue fire. When the coals are hot, brush the steaks with oil and grill over hot coals, about 2 to 3 minutes per side or until well marked on the outside and still pink and juicy inside for medium rate, or adjust time for desired doneness. Let the meat stand 5 minutes before serving.

2. Meanwhile, put the onion on a large piece of aluminum foil, drizzle with a little oil, wrap the foil around the onion, and cook until crisp tender, 6 to 8 minutes, on the outside edge of the grill, turning the foil packet once or twice while the onion cooks. Wrap the tortillas in foil and warm on the grill, turning 2 to 3 times, while the meat cooks. To serve, scatter the onions equally on top of each steak. Serve with green salsa and tortillas on the side.

Chuck Steak with Chihuahua Chile Salsa
Bistec con Salsa de Chihuahua

Makes 4 servings

Thinly pounded chuck steak, grilled until well done and a bit charred, is a northern Mexico specialty, particularly in Chihuahua, one of the Mexican states that borders Texas. The meat takes on a smoky taste that's simply terrific with spicy salsa. Serve with fried potatoes and any kind of beans.

1¹/₂ cups Chihuahua Chile Salsa (page 32)
3 pounds boneless chuck steak, cut about ¹/₂-inch thick
1 tablespoon fresh lime juice
¹/₂ teaspoon salt, or to taste
¹/₈ teaspoon freshly ground pepper, or to taste

1. Prepare the chile salsa. Cover and set aside. Cover the meat with 2 pieces of plastic and pound it to an even ¼-inch thickness with the flat side of a meat mallet or with a rolling pin. Rub with lime juice and sprinkle lightly with salt and pepper. Let stand at room temperature while preparing the barbecue fire.

2. When the coals are hot, grill the meat, turning 2 to 3 times, until it is well done, but not dry, 12 to 15 minutes total. Cut the steaks into serving size pieces and discard bone. Serve hot with chile salsa on the side.

Pan-Broiled Steak with Onions and Chipotle

Bistec con Cebollas y Chipotle

Makes **4 servings**

Steaks with onions are served sizzling on iron plat-ters in parts of northern Mexico. This recipe from the northern state of Sonora, adds a spicy tomato and chipotle sauce for a real mouthful of flavor.

4 medium tomatoes, peeled and quartered

2 canned chipotle chiles, cut into 3 or 4 pieces

1 tablespoon vegetable oil

1 large white onion, thinly sliced

4 (6- to 7-ounce) sirloin or New York steaks, about 3/4-inch thick, trimmed of all fat

1 teaspoon salt, or to taste

1. Put the tomatoes and chipotle chiles in a blender and blend to a coarse purée. Reserve in the blender. Heat the oil in a heavy skillet over medium heat and cook the onions, stirring, until beginning to brown, about 4 to 5 minutes. Transfer the onions to a bowl.

2. Cook the steaks in the same hot skillet about 4 to 5 minutes per side or until well seared on the outside but still pink and juicy inside, for medium rare. Season with salt. Put the steaks on a platter.

3. Add the reserved tomato-chipotle sauce to the same hot skillet, and cook, scraping up the browned bits from the pan, 2 minutes. Stir in reserved onions and cook 2 minutes Pile the onion mixture on the steaks and serve at once.

Beef Tenderloin Steaks, Yucatán Style

Carne a la Parilla, estilo Yucatán

Makes **4 servings**

Manuel Arjona, of Maya in Sonoma, California, a restaurant that features traditional Yucatán dishes, shared this spicy, flavorful dish. Serve the steaks with a wonderful tropical salsa that's almost like a fruit salad. Serve black beans and rice with the steak, if desired.

2 1/2 cups Mango, Papaya, and Poblano Chile Salsa (page 39)

4 (7- to 8-ounce) tenderloin fillet steaks

2 tablespoons achiote paste

2 tablespoons ground ancho or pasilla chili powder

1/2 cup fresh lime juice

1/2 medium red onion, sliced

1/2 cup chopped fresh cilantro

1 1/2 tablespoons olive oil

1/2 teaspoon salt, or to taste

1/8 teaspoon freshly ground pepper, or to taste

1. Prepare the salsa. Reserve in the bowl. Prepare a barbecue fire or preheat the broiler. Put the steaks in a pie plate or shallow bowl.

2. In a medium bowl, mix the achiote paste, chili powder, and lime juice. Stir in the onion and cilantro. Pour the mixture over the steaks, and turn to coat. Marinate the meat 20 minutes.

3. Remove from the marinade, discarding the marinade, and brush the steaks on both sides with oil. Season with salt and pepper. Grill the steaks over hot coals or under a hot broiler, 3 to 4 minutes per side until browned on the outside and still pink and juicy inside, for medium-rare, or adjust time for desired doneness. Let the meat stand 5 minutes. Serve with the salsa.

Beef Fillet Strips in Onion Sauce

Puntas de Filet Arriero

Makes 2 servings

Guanajuato, a colonial city in the state of the same name in central Mexico, is known for its Festival International Cervantino *in October, in honor of the author, Miguel Cervantes. The city comes alive with drama, music, dancing, and visitors from all over the world. Guanajuato is also the birthplace of Diego Rivera, one of Mexico's most famous artists.*

During a recent visit, my husband and I stayed at the historic Posada Santa Fe, a perfect location beside the leafy Jardin Union in the center of the city. The hotel's outdoor café borders the walkways of the plaza providing diners with a constant parade of sights.

My husband and I relished the setting on a balmy late February evening where I also relished my entrée of arriero. *My beautifully presented plate of bite-size strips of beef smothered in a bold onion sauce, fresh tomatillo salsa, a fan of sliced avocado, and strips of panela cheese, elevated this dish to a sophisticated level while keeping the traditional name and terrific flavor.*

The green tomatillo can be prepared ahead. Maggi seasoning extract is available in supermarkets almost everywhere in the United States.

1 cup Basic Cooked Tomatillo Sauce (page 46)

2 teaspoons olive oil

1 teaspoon unsalted butter

3/4 pound tenderloin fillet or New York steak, cut into strips about 1/2-inch wide and 11/2-inch long

1/4 teaspoon salt, or to taste

1/8 teaspoon freshly ground pepper, or to taste

1 large white onion, halved lengthwise and sliced crosswise

1 large garlic clove, finely chopped

1/2 teaspoon dried oregano (Mexican variety preferred), crumbled

1/4 teaspoon ground allspice

1/4 cup canned beef broth or chicken broth

2 teaspoons Worcestershire (or 3 teaspoons, if not using Maggi)

1 teaspoon Maggi seasoning extract

2 teaspoons fresh lime juice

1 ripe avocado (Hass variety preferred), peeled, halved, and thinly sliced

4 (3/4-inch × 2-inch) strips of panela cheese, or substitute another mild white cheese

1. Prepare the salsa. Then, in a heavy skillet, heat the oil and butter over medium-high heat. Cook the meat, in batches, until lightly browned and still pink inside, about 2 to 3 minutes. Season with salt and pepper. Remove to a plate.

2. Add the onion, garlic, oregano, and allspice to the same pan. Reduce the heat to medium-low, cover and cook, stirring frequently, until the onion starts to brown, about 5 minutes. Add the broth, Worcestershire, Maggi, and lime juice. Bring to a boil. Reduce heat to low, cover and cook, stirring frequently, 4 minutes.

3. Return the meat and any juices to the pan. Bring to a simmer, uncovered, and cook until completely heated through, about 2 minutes. Divide between 2 serving plates. Arrange the green salsa, avocado, and cheese around the meat.

?ef Fillet Strips with
ˌmatoes, Peppers, and Onions
ˌntas de Filete a la Mexicana

ˌkes **4 servings**

ˌu can easily please steak fans with this quick
cook dish. *Puntas de Filete a la Mexicana*
ˌpears on restaurant menus all over Mexico,
ˌt it's most common in the north, where the
ˌst beef cattle are raised. The dish is usually
ˌrved with refried beans and soft, warm tor-
ˌllas. To avoid "chile burn", wear rubber gloves
ˌhen chopping or peeling chiles, and don't
ˌuch your face.

¹/₂ **pounds boneless lean beef, such as beef
    sirloin, tri-tip, or top round**
tablespoons olive oil or vegetable oil
**teaspoon Maggi seasoning extract or
    Worcestershire sauce**
medium garlic clove, minced
large white onion, coarsely chopped
**medium tomatoes, peeled and coarsely
    chopped, or 1 (14-ounce) can diced tomatoes,
    drained**
**3 Anaheim or poblano chiles, roasted and peeled
    (page 8)**
1 serrano chile, finely chopped with seeds
¹/₂ teaspoon dried thyme
¹/₂ teaspoon salt, or to taste
¹/₄ teaspoon freshly ground pepper, or to taste
¹/₄ cup loosely packed chopped fresh cilantro

1. Prepare the chiles. Then, cut out the stem and
cut open the chiles to remove the seeds and ribs.
Cut the chiles into strips, then into ¾-inch pieces.
Reserve. Trim the meat of fat, and cut the meat
into thin slices, then into 1-inch pieces. Put the
meat into a bowl, and toss with half of the oil, the
Maggi, and garlic. Let stand about 20 minutes.

2. In a large skillet, heat the remaining oil until
hot. Add half of the beef, in a single layer, and
stir-fry until browned, 3 to 4 minutes. (Don't
overcook, or the beef will be tough.) Remove the
meat to a bowl, and brown the remaining meat.
Add to the first batch of meat and set aside.

3. In the same skillet, cook the onion over
medium-low heat until it begins to brown, about
5 minutes. Add the tomatoes, chiles, thyme, and
2 tablespoons of water. Raise heat to medium and
cook, stirring frequently, until the tomatoes
soften 4 to 5 minutes. Add the meat and the juices
from the bowl. Season with salt and pepper.
When the meat is heated through, stir in the
cilantro and serve.

Beef and Cheese Volcano
Volcán con Carne

Makes **4 servings**

*Mexico City might be called the restaurant
"capital" of the country, with foods from every
region of Mexico and many foreign countries
represented. This activity on the restaurant
scene has brought an increased focus on quality
foods and special presentations. El Farolito is a
restaurant with several lively locations in the
capital city, and I especially liked its modern
twist on a beef tostada (served on a fried tortilla) made to suggest an erupting volcano.*

Oil for frying
4 (6- to 7-inch) corn tortillas
Salsa of choice, purchased or homemade
Classic Guacamole (page 23), or purchased
**4 (6-ounce) beef tenderloin fillet steaks or
    New York strip steaks, ³/₄-inch thick**
1 teaspoon salt, or to taste
Freshly ground pepper, to taste
**1 large white onion, halved lengthwise and
    thinly sliced**
**1 cup shredded manchego or Monterey Jack
    cheese**
6 to 8 cilantro or parsley sprigs

1. Preheat oven to 400°. In a heavy skillet, heat oil to a depth of about ½ inch until the oil shimmers. Fry the tortillas, 1 at a time, until crisp and light brown on both sides. Drain on paper towels. (The tostadas can be fried up to 2 days ahead. Cool, then store in a cupboard in a sealed plastic bag.)

2. Prepare the salsa and guacamole, if using homemade. Then, pour off all but about 1 tablespoon of the tortilla-frying oil in the skillet, and heat until hot. Fry the steaks about 4 minutes per side or until browned on the outside and still pink and juicy inside, for medium-rare, or adjust time for desired doneness. Season with ½ teaspoon of the salt and a bit of pepper. Remove to a cutting board and let stand 5 minutes.

3. In the same skillet, cook the onion, stirring, until limp but not soft, 4 to 5 minutes. Season with the remaining salt. Reserve in the pan. Cut the steaks into bite size pieces. Toss with the onion.

4. Place the crisp tortillas on a large baking sheet. Mound the steak and onion equally in the center of each tortilla, and put ¼ of the cheese on top of each mound. Put in preheated oven until the cheese is melted, 3 to 5 minutes. Using a large wide spatula, transfer each tostada to the center of each of 4 large serving plates. Surround the tostadas with a few snipped sprigs of cilantro or parsley. Put a tiny bit of red salsa on the top of each tostada. Serve at once, accompanied by condiment bowls of salsa and guacamole to be added at the table.

Grilled Beef, Sonoran Style, with Onions and Chile Strips
Carne Asada con Cebollas Fritas y Rajas
Makes 6 servings

Carne asada *is meat cooked over coals or on a griddle. In Sonora, in northern Mexico, beef tenderloin is often used. In this recipe the whole tenderloin is trimmed of all fat and thinly sliced lengthwise, in the traditional Mexican way, with the grain.*

Poblano Chile Strips with Fried Onions (page 429) are served with the meat. Other traditional accompaniments include refried beans, fresh salsa, guacamole, and soft tortillas.

2 pounds whole trimmed beef tenderloin
4 medium garlic cloves, peeled and pressed
¹/₂ teaspoon freshly ground pepper, or to taste
¹/₂ teaspoon ground cumin
2 tablespoons olive oil
¹/₂ teaspoon salt, or to taste
Juice of 1 to 2 limes
Poblano Chile Strips with Fried Onions (page 429)

1. Trim the tenderloin of all fat, and cut it in half crosswise. Cut each half lengthwise into thin slices (about ⅓ inch) with the grain. Put the meat on a platter.

2. In a small bowl, mix the garlic, pepper, and cumin. Add the olive oil and work into a paste. Spread the paste all over the meat. Cover with plastic wrap and marinate in the refrigerator 3 hours or overnight.

3. Prepare the poblanos with onions. About one hour before cooking the meat, prepare an outdoor grill fire. When the coals are ready, grill the meat over a very hot fire about 2 minutes per side or until browned on the outside and pink and juicy on the inside, or to desired doneness. Season the meat with salt and sprinkle with lime juice. Serve the meat with the fried onions and poblano chiles.

Beef Steaks with Red Chile and Wine Sauce

Bistec con Salsa de Chile Rojo y Vino

Makes **4 servings**

A special chile and wine sauce tops some excellent steaks at Tequila, a restaurant in Cabo San Lucas, an area of popular resorts at the tip of Baja, Mexico. This is tourist country, but here the chef has a creative touch and turns out good classic Mexican dishes as well. Serve the steaks with roasted potatoes and a green vegetable.

ancho chiles, toasted and seeded (page 9)

plum tomatoes, cut in half lengthwise

medium garlic cloves, peeled

teaspoon crushed red pepper

cup canned fat-free reduced-sodium
    chicken broth

tablespoons olive oil

cup dry red wine

tablespoon unsalted butter

teaspoon salt, or to taste

freshly ground pepper, to taste

(6-ounce) beef tenderloin fillet steaks or
    New York strip steaks, ³/₄ inch thick

1. Prepare the ancho chiles, then cut them into pieces and soak in hot water to soften, 15 minutes. Meanwhile put the tomatoes and garlic cloves in a small, dry nonstick skillet and pan-toast them, turning occasionally with tongs, until the garlic is slightly soft with some brown spots, about 5 minutes. Transfer to a blender. Continue to cook the tomatoes another 2 to 3 minutes, or until they are charred a bit on both sides. Add to the blender with the garlic. Add the soaked ancho chiles, the crushed red pepper, and ½ cup of the chicken broth. Blend until very smooth. Reserve in the blender.

2. In a medium saucepan, heat 1 tablespoon of the oil over medium heat. Add the puréed mixture gently to the pan (so it won't splatter) and cook, stirring, 1 minute. Add the wine and the remaining chicken broth. Bring to a boil, then reduce the heat to medium-low and simmer, stirring frequently to prevent sticking, until reduced and thickened, about 10 minutes. Stir in the butter and ½ teaspoon of the salt. Reserve off heat.

3. Heat the remaining oil in a large nonstick skillet over medium-high heat. Season the steaks with salt and pepper. Cook the steaks 3 to 4 minutes per side or until browned on the outside and pink and juicy inside, or adjust time for desired doneness. Reheat the sauce. Serve the steaks with a portion of the sauce spooned on top. Pass any remaining sauce at the table.

Steak with Avocado Butter and Mango Salsa

Bistec con Mantequilla de Aguacate y Salsa de Mango

Makes **4 servings**

There is great appeal to this classy new dish for the simple and elegant way the ingredients are presented. An innovative crop of Mexican chefs have emerged, especially in Mexico City, where stylish restaurants like Villa Maria are showcasing Mexican cuisine in exciting new ways. Here, a succulent tenderloin steak is grilled, then topped with creamy avocado butter and garnished with cold mango salsa. Black beans would be a good choice to complete the plate.

Mango Salsa (page 39)
Avocado Butter (page 18)
4 (6-ounce) tenderloin fillet steaks, about 1-inch thick
1/2 teaspoon salt, or to taste
Freshly ground pepper (optional)
1 tablespoon vegetable oil

1. Prepare the mango salsa and the avocado butter. Cover and reserve. Prepare an outdoor grill, or, preheat a stovetop grill pan or oven broiler. Season steaks with salt. Add pepper, if desired. Brush the steaks with vegetable oil.

2. When the coals are hot, or broiler or stovetop pan is hot, cook the steaks about 4 minutes per side, or until browned on the outside and pink and juicy inside for medium rare, or adjust time for desired doneness. Put 1 steak on each of 4 plates. Top each steak with about 1 tablespoon of avocado butter. Spoon mango salsa on the side. Pass extra avocado butter and salsa at the table.

Steak with Tomato and Chili Sauce

Bistec con Jitomate y Chili en Polvo

Makes **4 servings**

The more traditional method for making this sauce is by soaking and then grinding dried chiles, but a delicious sauce can also be made with prepared ground ancho or pasilla chili powder. I developed this sauce after being asked by students in my classes how to use Mexican chili powders in place of whole dried chilies. The general rule is to use one tablespoon of pure chili powder for each dried chile, but it's always safer to start with less, and then taste. More can always be added, but not taken out if the sauce is too hot. Pure ground chili, with no seasonings added, can be found in cellophane packages in the Mexican section of most supermarkets or in Mexican markets.

3 teaspoons vegetable oil
1 (6- to 7-inch) corn tortilla, cut in quarters
1 large white onion, halved and thinly sliced
2 medium tomatoes, cored and chopped
2/3 cup canned beef broth
1 medium garlic clove, peeled and thinly sliced
2 teaspoons pure ground ancho or pasilla chili powder
1/2 teaspoon dried oregano (Mexican variety preferred), crumbled
1 teaspoon salt
1 tablespoon olive oil
4 (6-ounce) boneless New York strip steaks, 3/4-inch thick
3 jalapeño chiles, seeded, veins removed, and cut in thin strips
3 tablespoons chopped fresh cilantro

1. In a medium skillet, heat the oil until shimmering and fry the tortilla pieces, turning, until crisp and golden brown on both sides. Drain on paper towels and reserve. In the same skillet cook the onion, stirring, until softened, 3 to 4 minutes.

th tongs, remove about ¾ of the onion and
erve in a bowl.

Transfer the remaining onions to a blender,
d add the tomatoes, broth, garlic, ground chili,
gano, and ½ teaspoon of the salt. Blend as
ooth as possible. Transfer the sauce to a
cepan and bring to a boil. Reduce heat to low,
er and simmer 8 to 10 minutes, stirring fre-
ently, until the sauce thickens and the flavors
nd. Keep warm.

In a large skillet, heat the olive oil over medium-
h heat and cook the steaks 3 to 4 minutes per
e or until browned on the outside and pink
d juicy inside for medium rate, or adjust time
· desired doneness. Season with the remaining
t. Transfer the meat to a warm platter.

To the skillet, add the reserved onions. Add the
apeño chile strips. Cook, stirring about 2 min-
s or until completely heated through. The
ile strips will still be crisp and bright green. To
ve, pour a portion of the heated sauce in the
ter of each of 4 plates. Put 1 steak on the sauce
d top with the onion and chile strips. Sprinkle
h serving with cilantro.

teak with Cascabel Chile
d Lime

stec con Chile Cascabel y Limón

ikes **4 servings**

iscabel *chiles are small, dried dark red
iles that are round like a ball and range
m moderately hot to very hot. They are
med* cascabel, *which means "rattle" because,
en shaken, the chile seeds make a rattling
und. Cascabels are often used for table sauces
central Mexico. For this recipe, a chile paste
ade from the cascabels is slathered on the
ak as it cooks, giving the meat an intense
icy flavor balanced by lime juice that's
ueezed over the cooked steak.*

10 to 12 (about 3 ounces) cascabel chiles
2 tablespoons vegetable oil
2 tablespoons chopped white onion
1 medium garlic clove, thinly sliced
Salt, to taste
Freshly ground pepper, to taste
Lime wedges
4 (6-ounce) beef sirloin steaks, 1/2-inch thick

1. Pull firmly, but gradually, on the chile stems to
release the seed pod and stems. Shake out remaining
seeds. In a small dry skillet over medium heat toast
the chiles, pressing with a spatula and turning, until
aromatic and slightly softened, 10 to 15 seconds. Put
the chiles in a bowl and barely cover with hot water.
Cover the bowl and soak the chiles about 30 minutes.

2. Meanwhile, heat 1 teaspoon of the oil in the
same skillet and cook the onion and garlic over
medium-low heat until softened, about 4 minutes.
Transfer to a blender. Taste the chile-soaking
water, and if it's not bitter, save it for the sauce.
Lift the chiles from the water and add them to the
blender. Add 3 tablespoons chile water and 2 tablespoons tap water (or 5 tablespoons water). Purée
smooth, scraping down the sides of the blender.

3. Scrape the paste into a fine-mesh strainer
placed over a bowl. Press with the back of a
wooden spoon to release the pulp. Stir ¼ teaspoon
of the salt into the paste.

4. Put the remaining oil on a plate and coat the
steaks, 1 at a time, on both sides with oil. Season
with salt and pepper. Heat a large nonstick skillet
over medium-high heat. Lay 2 of the steaks in the
hot pan. Spread about 1 teaspoon of chile paste on
top of each steak. Cook until the steaks are
browned on the bottom, about 5 minutes. Turn
the meat and spread 1 teaspoon of chile paste on
the cooked side. Cook until the steaks are done to
your taste, about 3 more minutes for medium
rare. Transfer to a plate and cover to keep warm.
Wipe pan. Repeat with the remaining 2 steaks.
Serve hot with lime wedges.

Rib Steaks with Ancho Chile-Red Pepper Cream Sauce
Bistec con Crema de Chile Ancho y Pimientas Dulce

Makes 4 servings

Ancho chile, puréed with red bell pepper, cream, and broth makes a rich sauce that's excellent with tender beefsteak. Grill the steak on an out-door barbecue or on a stove-top grill pan. Start the meal with Caesar Salad (page 166) (which originated in Tijuana) and serve Yellow Rice with Peas (page 475) with the meat.

Ancho Chile and Red Pepper Cream Sauce (page 48)
4 (7- to 8-ounce) boneless rib-eye steaks, about ²/₃-inch thick
Salt, to taste
Freshly ground pepper, to taste
1 tablespoons olive oil or vegetable oil

Prepare the sauce. Reserve off heat in the pan. Trim the steaks of excess fat. Season with salt and pepper. Rub the steaks all over with oil. Prepare a barbecue fire, or heat a stove top grill pan over medium high heat. Cook the steaks about 4 minutes per side or until well marked from the grill or pan, but still pink and juicy inside, or to desired doneness. Let the meat stand 5 minutes. Meanwhile, reheat the cream sauce. Serve hot with the sauce.

Steak with Red Chiles
Bistec con Chiles Rojos

Makes 4 servings

Anaheim chiles turn a glorious red when fully ripe. Green Anaheim chiles are more widely available in the United States; the bright ripe red stage of the same chile is much less available due to a shorter harvest time. In a typical dish from Chihuahua, in northern Mexico, red Anaheims are served with pan-grilled steaks. Since I seldom find red Anaheims for this dish, I substitute red bell peppers for the Anaheims, along with strips of ripe red jalapeño for spicy heat. Add refried beans and a salad for a complete meal.

2 red bell peppers, halved lengthwise and seeded
1 tablespoon unsalted butter
2 red jalapeño chiles, seeded and very thinly sliced
2 green onions, thinly sliced crosswise
¹/₂ teaspoon salt, or to taste
4 (6- to 7-ounce) boneless New York or rib-eye steaks
2 teaspoons olive oil
¹/₄ teaspoon freshly ground pepper, or to taste

1. Roast the bell peppers, skin side up, under a preheated broiler until the skin is charred, about 5 to 7 minutes. Put the peppers in a plastic bag to steam, about 10 minutes. Remove the skins and cut the peppers into thin strips, ¼ inch × 2 inches.

2. Heat the butter in a medium skillet, and sauté the bell peppers, jalapeños, and onions, stirring, until tender, 6 to 7 minutes. Add ¼ teaspoon of the salt. Reserve off heat.

3. Trim the steaks of excess fat and brush on both sides with the oil. Season with the remaining salt and pepper. Heat a stovetop grill pan or heavy skillet over medium-high heat. Cook the steaks about 4 to 5 minutes per side or until nicely seared on the outside and still pink and juicy inside, or to desired doneness. Reheat the peppers. Top the steaks equally with the peppers and serve.

Steak, Yucatán Style, with Green Seasoning Paste

Bistec de Recado de Bistek

Makes 4 servings

Tender steak coated with Yucatán's recado de bistek (green seasoning paste) cooks to flavorful perfection over hot coals on an outdoor grill. These steaks have bold flavors that I really like. Sliced tomatoes, avocados, and crunchy lettuce are the only accompaniments necessary.

3 teaspoons Yucatán Green Seasoning Paste (page 22)

2 teaspoons fresh lime juice

1 teaspoon olive oil plus extra to oil the grill

1 teaspoon salt

4 (6- to 7-ounce) New York or rib-eye steaks, ³/₄-inch thick

In a small bowl, mix the seasoning paste, lime juice, olive oil, salt, and pepper. Trim the fat from the steaks and spread both sides with a thin coat of the seasoning paste. Put the steaks on a plate and let season about 1 hour.

Meanwhile, prepare an outdoor grill and brush the grill with oil. When the coals are hot, brush a little more oil on the steaks to prevent sticking, and place the steaks on the grill. Cook about 4 to 5 minutes per side, or until browned on the outside and still pink and juicy inside for medium rare or adjust time for desired doneness. Serve at once.

Beef Tenderloin, Huasteca Style

Carne de Res Huasteca

Makes 6 servings

The seasoning paste for this beef roast is typical of the ingredients used in the gulf coast state of Veracruz. Huasteca refers to an ancient civilization whose descendants still inhabit the region. This recipe is an adaptation of a dish prepared by Patricia Quintana, one of Mexico's premier cookbook authors, when I visited her family's ranch in the region.

Guacamole, salsa, and grilled or pan-fried onions are excellent with the roast. Any leftovers make terrific tacos or tortas (Mexican sandwiches).

1 (3- to 4-pound) beef tenderloin

3 large garlic cloves, pressed

1 tablespoon fresh orange juice

1 teaspoon salt

1 teaspoon unseasoned rice vinegar

3 tablespoons olive oil

1¹/₂ teaspoons dried oregano (Mexican variety preferred), crumbled

1 teaspoon cumin seeds

2 whole cloves

2 teaspoons dark brown sugar

¹/₂ teaspoon freshly ground pepper, or to taste

¹/₄ teaspoon ground allspice

¹/₄ teaspoon ground cinnamon (Mexican canela or Ceylon variety preferred)

1. Trim the tenderloin of excess fat and silver skin. Then place the tenderloin on a large piece of plastic wrap and set aside. Make a paste by mashing the garlic with the orange juice, salt, vinegar and olive oil. Rub the mixture all over the meat. Wrap the meat in the plastic wrap and let stand while preparing the seasoning rub.

2. In a small dry skillet, toast the oregano, cumin, and cloves over medium heat, stirring, until aromatic, about 2 minutes. Immediately transfer to a saucer and let cool; then grind very fine in a spice grinder. (I use a coffee grinder reserved for spices.)

3. Put the spices in a bowl and mix in the sugar, pepper, allspice, and cinnamon. Unwrap the meat and coat all over with the seasoning rub. Place the meat on a rack in a baking pan and let stand about 20 minutes.

4. Preheat the oven to 425°. Roast the beef, uncovered, 40 to 45 minutes for medium-rare, 150° on a meat thermometer or adjust time for desired doneness. For tender, juicy meat, do not overcook. Remove the meat from the oven and let rest about 10 minutes before slicing.

Oven-Barbecued Beef
Barbacoa de Carne al Horno

Makes 6 to 8 servings

Mexican barbacoa is traditionally cooked in a pit, but these days we aren't likely to dig a pit when we can emulate the flavor and tenderness of barbacoa by roasting the meat slowly in a home oven. Beef chuck roast is a good cut for this cooking method. The meat can be shredded for great tacos and burritos, or served in chunks with beans and rice. Don't forget the guacamole and fresh salsa.

1 (3-pound) boneless beef chuck roast
1/2 cup canned fat-free reduced-sodium
    chicken broth
1 large white onion, coarsely chopped
4 plum tomatoes, cored and chopped
6 medium garlic cloves, peeled and thinly sliced
2 bay leaves
2 teaspoons dried oregano (Mexican variety
    preferred), crumbled
2 teaspoons dried thyme
1 teaspoon ground cumin
1 teaspoon salt
1 tablespoon cider vinegar
1/4 teaspoon crushed red pepper

1. Put the meat in a large ovenproof casserole dish or Dutch oven. Add the remaining ingredients to the dish. Turn the meat 2 to 3 times to distribute the ingredients. Seal tightly with aluminum foil and refrigerate at least 2 hours or up to overnight. Remove the meat from the refrigerator about 1 hour before cooking.

2. Preheat the oven to 300°. Then, roast the meat, covered, until falling-apart tender, about 4 hours. Transfer the meat to a large platter. Pour the juices into a strainer over a large saucepan, pressing on the solids to extract the juices. (There will

be about 1½ to 2 cups of liquid.) Discard the debris. Bring the broth to a boil over high heat and cook until reduced to about 1 cup.

3. When meat is cool enough to handle, separate into chunks or shred it. Discard fat and connective tissue. Put the meat into the reduced pan juices. Add salt, if needed. Serve hot.

Beef Short Ribs
Costillas de Res

Makes 4 servings

Slow-cooked beef short ribs are typical of the rustic cooking style of northern Mexico's cattle country. Look for lean, meaty well-trimmed ribs in specialty meat markets, and ask the butcher to cut the ribs into 3-inch pieces. Short ribs are pretty tough, but have great flavor if cooked long enough to get really tender. Serve with soupy beans (Basic Pot Beans, page 461) and Fresh Salsa Mexicana (page 24).

2 ancho chiles, cut open, stemmed, and seeded,
    veins removed
2 teaspoons dried oregano (Mexican variety
    preferred), crumbled
1 teaspoon ground cumin
2 medium garlic cloves, chopped
1/4 cup canned tomato sauce
2 teaspoons red wine vinegar
1 teaspoon honey
1 teaspoon salt, or to taste
1 tablespoon vegetable oil
4 pounds beef short ribs, cut in 3-inch sections
1/8 teaspoon freshly ground pepper, or to taste
1 large white onion, sliced
1/4 cup lightly packed chopped fresh cilantro

1. In a medium dry skillet, over medium heat, toast the chiles on both sides until they release their aromas and blister in a few places. (Do not

rn, or they will be bitter.) Put the toasted chiles
a bowl of hot water and soak about 20 minutes.
t the soaked chiles in a blender, and discard the
king water. Add the oregano, cumin, garlic,
nato sauce, vinegar, honey, and ½ teaspoon of
salt to the blender and purée until smooth. If
mixture is too thick to blend, add water, about
ablespoon at a time, to release the blades.
ape the chile purée into a bowl and reserve.

Preheat the oven to 350°. In a heavy ovenproof
, heat the oil over medium heat and brown the
f on all sides. Season with the remaining salt
l the pepper. Transfer to the oven, cover, and
e 40 minutes. Spoon chile puree equally over
ribs and bake 20 more minutes. Add the
ons and cilantro. Cover and bake 35 to 45 more
utes, or until the meat is falling-apart tender.
tal cooking time, about 1 hour, 40 minutes, or
ger.) Serve the ribs with the onions and sauce.

iled Rump Roast

te

Makes 6 servings

*In iration for this recipe came from Dolores L.
L rre's fascinating and informative book,
C king and Curing with Mexican Herbs.
T recipe comes from the state of Coahuila in
n hern Mexico. I use rump roast instead of the
e) of-round in the original recipe and made a
fe hanges in the marinade and cooking broth
to hieve a flavor that I prefer. The meat can be
se d with vegetables as a pot roast, and it's
gr for tacos, tostadas, and sandwiches.*

1 (2½- to 3-pound) rump roast
1 medium white onion, halved and thinly sliced
6 medium garlic cloves, thinly sliced
½ cup cider vinegar
1½ teaspoons salt, or to taste
¼ teaspoon freshly ground pepper, or to taste
2 tablespoons vegetable oil
1 large carrot, peeled and sliced
2 bay leaves
2 teaspoons dried oregano (Mexican variety
    preferred), crumbled
1 (12-ounce) bottle of beer

1. Put the roast in a large sealable heavy-duty
plastic bag. Add ½ of the onion, ½ of the garlic,
vinegar, 1 teaspoon of the salt, and ½ cup water.
Close the bag and turn several times to distribute
the ingredients. Refrigerate, turning once or
twice, and let marinate about 4 hours.

2. Drain the meat and discard the marinade.
Pat the meat dry with paper towels and season
with the remaining salt and pepper. In a large
Dutch oven or heavy heatproof casserole dish
heat the oil over medium heat. Put the meat in
the pot and brown lightly on all sides, about
10 minutes.

3. Add the carrot, bay leaf, oregano, the remaining onion, and remaining garlic. Pour in the beer
and ½ cup of water. Bring to a boil; then reduce
heat to low, cover and cook about 2 hours or until
the meat is tender. Remove the meat from the
liquid. Cover and let rest 10 minutes before
slicing. Strain the broth and refrigerate for later
use in soup or stew, if desired.

Beef, Vegetable, and Red Chile Stew
Mole de Olla

Makes 4 servings

Mole de Olla is a classic Mexican beef stew from central Mexico around Mexico City, requiring long, slow cooking so that the flavors mingle and the beef becomes meltingly tender. This is my version of the stew. Squeezing lime juice into the stew just before eating is a classic and tasty touch. Serve bolillos *(oval Mexican sandwich rolls) or French bread to sop up the delicious juices.*

1 pound beef chuck with bones, cut into
    2-inch pieces
1/2 pound boneless beef stew meat, cut into
    1 1/2-inch pieces
1 medium white onion, chopped
4 medium garlic cloves, thinly sliced
2 bay leaves
1 teaspoon salt
1 teaspoon dried oregano (Mexican variety
    preferred), crumbled
1/2 teaspoon ground cumin
2 ancho chiles, cut open and seeded,
    veins removed
2 guajillo chiles, cut open and seeded,
    veins removed
3 medium tomatoes, cored and coarsely chopped
10 large epazote leaves, or 1/4 cup chopped cilantro
3 medium carrots (6 ounces), peeled and sliced
    1-inch thick
1 small turnip (4 ounces), peeled and cut into
    1-inch pieces
2 small zucchini (6 ounces), sliced 1-inch thick
2 ears of corn, cut crosswise in 2-inch pieces
4 to 5 ounces young slender green beans, cut in half
2 limes, quartered

1. Put the meat in a large pot with 2 quarts of water and bring to a boil. Reduce the heat to medium-low, and skim the foam that rises to the top as it boils. After 10 minutes, add the onion, garlic, bay leaves, salt, oregano, and cumin. Cover and simmer 1 hour and 30 minutes.

2. Meanwhile, heat a medium dry skillet over medium heat, and toast the chiles, pressing them flat with a spatula, until aromatic, about 5 seconds on each side. (Do not burn, or the chiles will be bitter.) Cool the chiles; then tear into pieces, and put into a blender. Process as fine as possible. Add the tomatoes and epazote. Purée. Strain, pushing the puree with a wooden spoon, through a fine-mesh strainer into the soup pot. Cover and simmer 30 minutes.

3. Add the carrots and turnips, and cook 15 minutes. Add the zucchini, corn, and green beans. Cook until the vegetables are tender, about 12 to 15 more minutes. Taste and add salt, if needed. Serve in soup bowls. Pass the lime wedges at the table.

Durango Beef Stew
Caldillo Durangueño

Makes 4 servings

This stew is a special dish from the state of Durango in Northern Mexico, and is sometimes made with dried venison or beef, but fresh beef is frequently used, too, as in this recipe. During the 1950s and until about 1980, Durango was a popular setting for Hollywood westerns and other films. John Wayne and Burt Lancaster both spent time filming in Durango, and I'll bet they ate Caldillo Durangueño!

Serve the hearty stew, splashed with lime juice just before eating, with fresh tortillas or crusty bread and a salad such as Tomato and Avocado Salad (page 165).

ncho chiles

ablespoons safflower, corn, or olive oil

ound lean beef, cut into ¹/₂-inch pieces

edium white onion, finely chopped

edium garlic cloves, finely chopped

edium tomatoes, peeled and finely chopped

¹/₂ teaspoon dried oregano (Mexican variety preferred), crumbled

¹/₄ teaspoon dried thyme

1 (14¹/₂-ounce) can beef broth

Salt and freshly ground pepper, to taste

Lime wedges

1. Cut the chiles in half lengthwise. Remove the stems, seeds and ribs and discard. In a dry skillet, over medium heat, toast the chiles, turning and pressing with a spatula, until aromatic, 1 to 2 minutes. Put the chiles in a bowl and cover with hot tap water and soak 20 to 25 minutes.

2. Meanwhile, heat the oil over medium heat in a large heavy saucepan. Add the beef, and cook, stirring, until lightly browned, 8 to 10 minutes. Transfer the meat to a bowl. In the same pan, cook the onion, stirring, until softened, 3 to 4 minutes. Add the garlic, and cook 1 minute. Add the tomatoes, oregano, and thyme. Cook until the tomato juices reduce and the mixture thickens, 4 to 5 minutes. Return the beef to the pan. Reduce the heat to low, cover, and cook slowly while puréeing the chiles.

3. Put the soaked chiles in a blender, discarding the soaking water. Add ¹/₂ cup of the beef broth and blend as smooth as possible. Add the puree to the beef along with the remaining beef broth. Bring to a boil, then reduce the heat to medium-low, cover and simmer, stirring occasionally, until the beef is tender, about 1 hour. Serve hot with lime wedges.

Mexican Meatloaf with Ranchera Sauce
Albondigón Ranchera

Makes **4 servings**

Mexican families like meatloaves just as we do. Sometimes the meat is formed around a stuffing and then it's called Albondigón Relleno *or stuffed meatloaf. This south-of-the-border meatloaf gets a flavor boost from the spicy ranchera sauce that's spooned on top. Ranchera sauce is best known as the sauce for* Huevos Rancheras, *Mexico's most famous egg dish, but the sauce goes well with many other dishes, too.*

1¹/₂ **pounds lean ground beef**

¹/₂ **cup dry bread crumbs**

2 **tablespoons minced onion**

1 **large egg, beaten**

¹/₂ **teaspoon ground cumin**

¹/₄ **teaspoon dried thyme leaves**

¹/₄ **cup canned tomato sauce**

1 **teaspoon red wine vinegar**

¹/₂ **teaspoon salt, or to taste**

¹/₈ **teaspoon freshly ground pepper, or to taste**

Ranchera Sauce (page 44)

1. Preheat the oven to 350°. In a large bowl thoroughly mix all the ingredients, except the ranchera sauce. Form the meat into a loaf and place in a shallow baking pan. Bake until nicely browned and completely cooked through, about 1 hour.

2. Meanwhile, make the ranchera sauce. Slice and serve the meatloaf with heated ranchera sauce spooned on top.

Pork

Basic Shredded Pork
Puerco Deschebrada

Makes **about 2 cups shredded meat**

This is an easy recipe for cooking pork for stews or shredded meat recipes. It is a basic preparation that is used in many ways for tacos, enchiladas, tostadas, burritos, and more.

1¹/₂ pounds boneless pork meat, cut from the sirloin or shoulder
¹/₂ medium onion, sliced
2 medium garlic cloves, peeled
1 bay leaf
¹/₂ teaspoon salt

1. Cut the meat into 1-inch cubes. Put into a large pot with the onion, garlic, bay leaf, and salt. Add water to cover by about 1-inch. Bring to a boil, skimming the surface as needed. Reduce the heat, cover and simmer until tender, about 45 minutes.

2. Remove from the heat, uncover, and cool the meat in the broth. When the meat is cool, pour the broth through a strainer into a container and save. (Discard the debris.) Shred the meat with your fingers, removing any excess fat or gristle. The meat and broth are ready to use.

Crisp Shredded Pork
Mochomos

Makes **6 servings**

This is a flavorful pork preparation from the state of Chihuahua in northern Mexico that's perfect to wrap in a tortilla or serve with Mexican rice and beans for a simple hearty supper. For moist and tender meat, select boneless pork that has some fat. The fat can be separated from the meat after cooking. Soft, warm tortillas, guacamole and pickled jalapeños should accompany this dish.

2 pounds pork butt, or boneless country-style pork ribs
1 medium white onion, quartered
2 medium garlic cloves, peeled and thinly sliced
1 teaspoon dried oregano (Mexican variety preferred)
2 tablespoons vegetable oil or lard
¹/₄ teaspoon salt, or to taste
¹/₈ teaspoon freshly ground pepper, to taste

1. Cut the pork into 2-inch chunks. Put the meat in a large saucepan. Add the onion, garlic, and oregano. Add 2 cups of water, and bring to a boil. Reduce the heat to medium-low, cover, and cook the meat until very tender, and the water has evaporated, about 1 hour. Remove the meat, and shred it very fine with your fingers. Discard excess fat.

2. Shortly before serving, heat the oil in a medium skillet, and fry the shredded pork, stirring frequently, until brown and crisp, about 8 to 10 minutes. Season with salt and pepper. Mound the meat on a platter and serve.

Minced Spicy Pork
Picadillo

Makes about 4 cups

Picadillo *is a classic and very tasty meat mix-*
ture that's used in many regions, especially
central Mexico, as a filling for chiles rellenos,
empanadas, crepes, or tortillas. Picadillo is
made here with pork but can also be made
with beef or chicken. It can be made ahead and
it freezes well.

2 tablespoons olive oil or vegetable oil
1 medium white onion, finely chopped
2 medium garlic cloves, finely chopped
1¹/2 pounds ground pork
4 plum tomatoes, peeled and finely chopped
¹/2 medium apple, peeled and finely chopped
2 jarred pickled jalapeño chiles (en escabeche),
  seeded and minced
¹/3 cup raisins
¹/4 finely chopped slivered blanched almonds
6 pitted pimiento-stuffed green olives, chopped
¹/2 teaspoon ground cinnamon (Mexican canela
  or Ceylon variety preferred)
¹/4 teaspoon ground allspice
¹/2 teaspoon salt, or to taste

1. Heat the oil in a large skillet over medium heat
and cook the onion, stirring, until translucent,
3 to 4 minutes. Add the garlic and cook 1 minute.
Add the ground meat in small pieces and cook,
stirring, until no longer pink, about 4 minutes.

2. Add the remaining ingredients and cook, stirring frequently, until the juices have evaporated
and the mixture is nearly dry, 6 to 8 minutes.
Transfer to a bowl. The picadillo is ready to use or
store, covered, in the refrigerator up to 3 days or
freeze up to 3 months.

Ground Pork Patties
Tortitas de Cerdo

Makes 8 patties

Ground pork seasoned somewhat like the green
chorizo *made in the city of Toluca, and formed*
into patties, makes terrific tortas *(sandwiches)*
paired with guacamole. The patties are also good
for an informal dinner with beans and a salad,
or for breakfast with scrambled eggs or pancakes.

1 pound ground pork
1 medium garlic clove, pressed
1 serrano chile, finely chopped with seeds
¹/2 teaspoon dried oregano (Mexican variety
  preferred), crumbled
¹/4 teaspoon dried thyme
¹/4 teaspoon ground cumin
¹/4 teaspoon ground allspice
2 tablespoons chopped fresh cilantro
1 teaspoon unseasoned rice vinegar
¹/2 teaspoon salt, or to taste
¹/8 teaspoon freshly ground pepper, or to taste
2 teaspoons vegetable oil or olive oil

1. Put all of the ingredients, except the oil, into a
mixing bowl. Mix very well with clean hands.
Cover and refrigerate, to season, at least 2 hours,
or up to overnight. Form into 8 patties.

2. Heat the oil in a large nonstick skillet, and
cook the patties about 4 minutes per side or until
browned on the outside and no longer pink
inside. Serve hot.

Mexican Pork Sausage
Chorizo

Makes **1 pound**

Commercial chorizo is often very greasy. It's easy to make flavorful chorizo with less fat at home and freeze it in portions to be used as needed. This is the pork sausage preparation that I use in recipes calling for chorizo. No casings are required since the chorizo will be cooked in your recipe like any other ground meat.

1 pound fresh ground pork
2¹/₂ tablespoons ancho or pasilla chili powder
1 teaspoon dried oregano (Mexican variety preferred), crumbled
1 teaspoon ground cumin
¹/₂ teaspoon ground coriander
¹/₄ teaspoon dried thyme
¹/₄ teaspoon crushed red pepper
¹/₈ teaspoon ground allspice
¹/₂ teaspoon salt, or to taste
¹/₄ teaspoon freshly ground pepper, or to taste
2 medium garlic cloves, pressed
1 tablespoon unseasoned rice vinegar

Put all of the ingredients into a mixing bowl. Mix very well with clean hands. Cover and refrigerate at least overnight before using, or refrigerate up to 4 days. To store longer, freeze up to 3 months. The chorizo is ready to use.

Pork Chops with Lime Butter
Costillas de Cerdo con Mantequilla de Lima

Makes **4 servings**

Mexican pork chops are cut about ¼-inch thick, thinner than we are accustomed to in this country. I prefer boneless, center-cut pork loin chops about ½- to ¾-inch thick for pan grilling or

frying in this recipe. Try Tomatillo and Pumpkin Seed Sauce (page 36) with the pork.

4 (6-ounce) boneless center-cut loin chops, ¹/₂-inch thick
2¹/₂ teaspoons fresh lime juice
¹/₂ teaspoon salt, or to taste
Freshly ground pepper, to taste
2 teaspoons unsalted butter, at room temperature

1. Trim all the fat from the pork. Rub ½ teaspoon lime juice and ½ teaspoon olive oil on both sides of the pork and sprinkle lightly with salt. Season with black pepper on one side of each chop. Using your palm or back of a wooden spoon, press the pepper onto the surface of the meat. Reserve on a plate about 20 minutes.

2. Mix the remaining ½ teaspoon lime juice with the soft butter and reserve. Heat a stove top grill pan or nonstick skillet over medium-high heat until a drop of water sizzles immediately on the pan. Cook the pork, peppered side down, until deeply browned, about 5 minutes. Turn the meat, reduce heat to medium-low and cook about 3 minutes or until the meat is no longer pink inside, but still juicy. Put a portion of the lime butter on top of the dark side of each chop and serve at once.

Pork Chops with Poblano Chile Sauce
Costillas de Cerdo con Salsa de Chile Poblano

Makes **4 servings**

An intriguing green sauce of roasted, peeled, and blended poblano chiles perfectly compliments grilled pork chops. The chops can be grilled outdoors on a barbecue grill or indoors on a stove top grill pan. Serve with Pan-Roasted Potatoes and Carrots (page 445).

2 large poblano chiles, roasted, peeled, and
    seeded, veins removed (page 8)

2 tablespoons olive oil

$1/4$ medium white onion, chopped

2 large garlic cloves, thinly sliced

$1/2$ teaspoon dried oregano (Mexican variety
    preferred), crumbled

$1/2$ (6- to 7-inch) corn tortilla, cut into 2-inch pieces

$3/4$ cup canned fat-free reduced-sodium
    chicken broth

$3/4$ teaspoon salt, or to taste

4 (6-ounce) boneless center-cut pork loin chops,
    $3/4$-inch thick

1 medium tomato, seeded and finely diced

1. Chop the roasted chiles and put them in a
blender. Reserve. In a medium saucepan, heat
1 tablespoon of the oil over medium-low heat
and cook the onion, garlic, and oregano, covered,
stirring frequently, until the onion is tender, but
not brown, about 5 minutes. Transfer to the
blender with the chiles. Add the tortilla and
chicken broth. Blend until very smooth.

2. Return the blended mixture to the same
saucepan. Add $1/4$ teaspoon of the salt. Bring to
a boil and cook, stirring, 4 to 5 minutes to
blend the flavors. Add salt, if needed, and reserve
off heat.

3. Trim all the fat from the pork. Brush the
chops with the remaining oil and season with
salt. Heat a large stovetop grill pan, or prepare
an outdoor grill (and grease the rack). Cook
the pork until well marked from the grill,
about 5 minutes. Turn the meat; reduce the heat
to medium-low, and cook about 3 minutes or
until the meat is no longer pink inside, but still
juicy. Reheat the sauce. Serve the meat with
the heated sauce spooned on top. Garnish with
diced tomato.

Yucatán Grilled Pork Steak
Poc Chuc

Makes **4 servings**

*Grilled, thinly sliced marinated pork steak
(poc chuc) is a Yucatán specialty with all the
trimmings. Be sure to cook the accompanying
black beans ahead. Grilled red onions, cabbage
salsa, sliced avocado and tomato, and corn tortillas complete the meal.*

Yucatán Puréed Black Beans (page 468)
Yucatán Cabbage Salsa (page 38)
4 thin ($1/4$-inch) pork steaks, sirloin or leg
2 tablespoons fresh orange juice
2 tablespoons fresh lime juice
$1/2$ teaspoon salt, or to taste
Vegetable oil for brushing on the onions and meat
2 large red or white onions, sliced $1/2$-inch thick
Avocado (Hass variety preferred) and tomato slices

1. Prepare the black beans one day ahead. Reheat
shortly before serving. Prepare the cabbage salsa
about 2 hours before serving and have it ready in
a serving bowl.

2. Prepare an outdoor grill. Put the pork on a
plate. Mix the orange juice, lime juice, and salt.
Pour over the meat. Cover and set aside.

3. When the coals are hot, brush the onions with
oil and lay them on a sheet of aluminum foil.
Place on the outside edge of the grill and cook,
turning once or twice, until charred, but not
burned, 15 to 18 minutes. Remove from the grill,
cover to keep warm and set aside.

4. Brush the pork with oil, and put on the hottest
part of the grill. Grill about 2 minutes per side or
until browned on the outside and no longer pink
inside. Transfer the steaks to a serving platter.
Coarsely chop the grilled onions and scatter over
the meat. Arrange avocado and tomato slices
around the edge of the platter. Serve with the black
beans, cabbage salsa, and soft, warm corn tortillas.

Barbecued Pork Steak Marinated in Red Chile Paste
Cerdo en Adobo

Makes 4 servings

Meats marinated in adobo are seen in markets all over Mexico. It does take time to make the adobo at home, but the marinade can be used for meats, poultry, fish, and even vegetables, so it's worth the effort. Allow the steaks to marinate overnight, if possible. Classic Guacamole (page 23) and Basic Pot Beans (page 461) are excellent with the steaks.

4 tablespoons Red Chile Paste (page 20)
4 (8-ounce) pork shoulder steaks

1. Prepare the chile paste. Remove 3 to 4 tablespoons of the chile paste from the container, and store the remaining paste for future use. Spread a thin coat of chile paste on both sides of the steaks. Put the steaks in a large plastic sealable storage bag and refrigerate about 6 hours, or overnight.

2. Prepare an outdoor grill. Scrape excess adobo off the meat, and put the steaks on an oiled grill rack about 6 inches from the fire, and cook, turning frequently, until the meat is cooked through, about 8 to 10 minutes total. (Don't overcook or the meat will be dry.)

Baby Back Ribs with Tamarind
Costillitas de Cerdo

Makes 4 servings

Small slabs of browned baby back pork ribs with crispy edges and the flavor of tamarind are so succulent, they're irresistible. Slow roasting at a low temperature until the ribs are tender, then raising the oven temperature and basting with the sauce during the last minutes of cooking works best. I developed this recipe after eating the ribs at the spectacular contemporary restaurant Santa Coyote in Guadalajara. Serve the ribs with Cactus Salad (page 170) or Corn, Potato, and Poblano Chile Salad (page 177).

3 tablespoons Tamarind Paste (page 21)
1 ancho chile, stemmed, seeded, veins removed, and roasted (page 8)
1/2 teaspoon dark brown sugar
1/8 teaspoon freshly ground pepper, or to taste
4 (1-pound) slabs baby back pork ribs
1/2 teaspoon salt, or to taste

1. Prepare the tamarind paste, then measure out 3 tablespoons and put in a blender. Reserve. (Store the remaining paste for another use. It keeps indefinitely.) Put the roasted chile in a small bowl of hot water and soak 20 minutes. Add the chile and 1 tablespoon of the soaking water to the blender. Add the sugar and black pepper. Blend to a thick smooth purée with the consistency of ketchup. If too thick, add just enough soaking water to achieve the right consistency. Transfer the sauce to a bowl and reserve. Discard remaining soaking water.

2. Preheat the oven to 300°. Season the pork ribs with salt. Arrange in a single layer in a baking pan. Roast slowly, uncovered, 45 minutes. Pour off fat. Turn the ribs and roast 30 minutes. Raise the heat to 400° and baste the ribs with the reserved tamarind sauce and turn over every 15 minutes, basting each time, about 1 hour or until the ribs are dark brown and tender. If darker brown, crispier ribs are preferred, finish under the broiler a few minutes, watching carefully to prevent burning. Serve each slab whole, or cut in 2-rib portions, if desired.

Crisp Pork Tidbits
Carnitas

Makes **4 to 6 servings**

Small bits of crisp browned pork are served all over Mexico. Most of the typical carnitas *(little meats) are still prepared in huge pots of boiling lard, but excellent* carnitas *can be made at home in a simpler way using much less fat. (Although for crisp* carnitas, *it's important for the pork to have some fat.) Serve with tortillas and some trimmings to make tacos or burritos, such as guacamole, red or green salsa, and shredded lettuce or cabbage.*

2 pounds boneless pork shoulder or pork butt
1 teaspoon dried oregano (Mexican variety preferred), crumbled
4 large garlic cloves
1/2 teaspoon salt
Cooking oil or lard (about 2 tablespoons), if needed

1. Cut the pork into ¾- to 1-inch pieces. Put the pork in a large deep heavy skillet or wide heavy pan. Add oregano, garlic, and salt. Add water to nearly cover the meat with some showing above the surface. Bring to a boil.

2. Reduce heat to medium-low and cook, uncovered, at a simmer, about 45 minutes, or until all the liquid has evaporated. If the meat is still not tender, add a little more water and continue to cook until it is tender. The pork will then start to brown in the fat that has rendered during cooking. (If the meat is quite lean, there may not be enough rendered fat for the meat to brown properly, so add some cooking oil or lard.) Fry the meat, stirring frequently, until the pork bits are evenly browned and crisp. The meat is ready to use.

Grilled or Spit-Roasted Pork
Cerdo Al Pastor

Makes **about 1½ cups filling for about 4 large burritos, 4 tortas, or 6 tacos**

In small restaurants all over Mexico, vertical spits slowly roast marinated pork to perfection. A small peeled pineapple is often positioned on top of the spit, to allow the juices to drip down and flavor the meat as it cooks. Thin bits of cooked pineapple are later served with the meat.

Since most home kitchens lack a vertical spit, here's a way to season and cook pork at home for tacos, burritos, and tortas, that's truly mouth-watering. Start the recipe one day ahead, as the meat needs to marinate overnight. The dried red chiles called for in the recipe are quite common and can be found in Mexican markets and sometimes in the Mexican section of supermarkets. Each kind of chile adds its own flavor and spiciness to the marinade. The small chile de arbol is the hottest of the listed chiles.

1½ pounds boneless pork leg, or boneless country-style ribs
2 guajillo or New Mexico chiles, stemmed and seeded, veins removed
2 ancho or pasilla chiles, stemmed and seeded
2 chiles de arbol, stemmed and seeded
2 teaspoons dried oregano (Mexican variety preferred), crumbled
2 whole cloves
1 teaspoon cumin seeds
1 teaspoon salt
1/2 teaspoon freshly ground pepper, or to taste
1/2 cup white vinegar
1/2 cup water
5 large or 8 small garlic cloves, peeled and sliced
3 tablespoons vegetable oil
2 peeled pineapple rings (optional)

1. Cut the pork into slices about ⅓ inch thick and put into a glass baking dish or in a glass pie plate.

2. In a medium pan, over medium heat, cook the chiles, oregano, cloves, cumin, salt, pepper, vinegar, and water, until the chiles are soft, about 10 minutes. Cool about 5 minutes, then pour the mixture into a blender. Add the garlic and purée to a paste.

3. In the same pan, heat the oil and cook the mixture, over medium-low heat, about 5 minutes. Cool completely and spread over the meat. Cover the meat and refrigerate overnight. Remove the meat from the marinade, and scrape off the excess. Cook the meat, on a hot grill pan or in a nonstick skillet until no longer pink inside, 2 to 3 minutes on each side. Pan grill the pineapple on the edge of the pan. Chop and serve with the meat. Chop the meat into small pieces, and use to fill burritos, tacos, or tortas.

Pork in Guajillo Chile Sauce with Avocado
Cerdo en Salsa de Chile Guajillo con Aguacate

Makes 4 servings

Patricia Quintana prepared this excellent dish in her Mexico City cooking school some years ago. Fresh avocado leaves covered the pork to add a mild anise flavor to the meat as it cooked. Fresh avocado leaves are hard to find, so I substitute anise seeds in the sauce for a similar flavor. Roasted potatoes and sliced avocados are presented with the saucy pork.

Guajillo Chile Sauce (page 50)
¹/₄ teaspoon anise seeds
8 small red or white potatoes, scrubbed and quartered
2 (1-pound) pork tenderloins
3 tablespoons olive oil
Salt, as needed
Freshly ground pepper, to taste
2 large avocados (Hass variety preferred), peeled and sliced crosswise

1. Prepare the guajillo sauce, adding the anise seeds when blending the sauce. Reserve sauce.

2. Preheat the oven to 450°. Put the potatoes in an ovenproof casserole dish. Drizzle with about 1 tablespoon olive oil and toss the potatoes to coat with oil. Cover with foil and have the potatoes ready to go in the oven 25 minutes before the meat.

3. Meanwhile, trim the pork tenderloins of all silver skin. Rub the meat all over with olive oil. Season with salt and pepper. Line a heavy baking sheet with foil. Arrange the meat on the pan. Crimp the foil into a rim around the outside of the tenderloins. Let stand at room temperature 25 minutes. Put the potatoes in the oven.

4. Put the pork in the oven, and remove the foil from the potatoes. Continue to roast the potatoes 20 to 25 more minutes, and roast the pork 20 to 25 minutes or until no longer pink inside (155° to 160° on a meat thermometer). To serve, reheat the sauce. Slice the pork thinly and arrange on a serving platter. Stir any meat juices from the pan into the chile sauce. Spoon the sauce over the meat. Surround with the roasted potatoes and sliced avocados.

Pork Loin Roast with Red Onion Sauce
Lomo de Cerdo con Salsa de Cebollas Rojas

Makes 6 servings

A cooked tangy red onion sauce spooned over roasted pork is a modern adaptation for this Mexican-style dish that's been a favorite among my cooking students.

1 (3¹/₂- to 4- pound) boneless pork loin roast
1 teaspoon dried oregano (Mexican variety preferred), crumbled
1 large garlic clove, pressed
³/₄ teaspoon salt, or to taste
¹/₈ teaspoon freshly ground pepper, or to taste
Red Onion Sauce (page 61)

1. Preheat oven to 350°. Trim excess fat from the roast. Season all over with the oregano, garlic, salt, and pepper. Place the roast in a roasting pan on a rack and roast, uncovered, until browned and no longer pink inside, about 1 hour 10 minutes, or until a meat thermometer reads 160°.

2. Meanwhile, prepare the onion sauce. When the roast is done, remove it from the oven and let it rest about 5 minutes. Reheat the sauce. Slice the meat and arrange on a platter or individual serving plates with a portion of the onion sauce spooned on top. Serve hot.

Pork Roast with Plantains and Tangerines
Cerdo al Horno con Plátanos y Tangerinas

Makes **4 to 6 servings**

Boneless pork loin is my favorite meat to roast, and citrus is often teamed with pork in Mexican dishes. In this recipe, tangerines and plantains flavor the dish. Black beans are my first choice to accompany the roast.

1 teaspoon salt

1/2 teaspoon freshly ground pepper

2 teaspoons sugar

1 medium garlic clove, minced

1 (3- to 4-pound) boneless pork loin roast

1/2 cup canned fat-free reduced-sodium chicken broth, plus 1/2 cup more if needed for sauce

1/2 cup dry white wine

4 tangerines

1 teaspoon cornstarch

1 (8 to 10 ounce) ripe plantain, slightly soft with dark splotches, peeled and sliced crosswise, 1/4 inch thick

2 tablespoons chopped fresh cilantro

1. Preheat the oven to 450°. In a small bowl, mix the salt, pepper, sugar, and garlic. Rub all over the meat. Put the meat on a rack in a roasting pan and roast in the oven 30 minutes. In a cup, mix the broth and wine. After 30 minutes, open the oven and pour 1/2 cup of the liquid over the roast. Reduce the oven temperature to 325° and continue roasting 45 minutes, basting the meat every 15 minutes with the remaining 1/2 cup broth-wine mixture and the pan juices. Cook the meat until lightly browned, about 1 hour, and an instant-read thermometer registers 155° to 160°. Remove the roast to a warmed platter.

2. Meanwhile, squeeze the juice from 2 tangerines to make 1/2 cup juice. Remove the peel from the remaining 2 tangerines, separate the segments, and gently remove any seeds. Reserve the juice and fruit.

3. When the roast is done, remove it to a warmed platter. Put the roasting pan on a stove burner. (If the pan is dry, add 1/2 cup chicken broth.) Mix the cornstarch with the tangerine juice, and stir it into the pan juices. Add the plantains. Bring to a boil, stirring. Reduce the heat to low, and simmer 5 to 6 minutes, or until the plantains are tender and the sauce thickens. Add the tangerines. Heat through, about 2 minutes. Stir in the cilantro. Slice the roast and serve with the sauce spooned on top. Garnish with plantains slices and tangerine segments.

Pork Roast with Peanut Mole
Cerdo con Mole de Cacahuate

Makes **4 servings**

Moles are sauced-based dishes usually made for celebrations in Mexico. The sauces contain a long list of ingredients and are time-consuming to make but the resulting flavors are spectacular. Mole de Cacahuate, from central Mexico, a thick orange-colored sauce thickened and flavored with roasted peanuts, chiles, herbs, and spices goes very well with pork.

The sauce can be made 3 to 4 days in advance and tastes even better when reheated. A mole tends to thicken as it stands, so it may be necessary to thin it with some chicken broth when it's reheated. If you can't find boneless roast, ask the butcher to bone the roast, or, cook with the bone, but a longer cooking time will be needed.

2 cups Peanut Mole (page 59)
1 large garlic clove, mashed
1/2 teaspoon dried oregano (Mexican variety preferred), crumbled
1/2 teaspoon salt, or to taste
1/4 teaspoon freshly ground pepper, or to taste
1 tablespoon vegetable oil
1 (3- to 4-pound) boneless pork loin roast
Cilantro or parsley sprigs

1. Prepare the peanut mole. Reserve in the pan off heat. (If made ahead, cover and refrigerate up to 3 days.) Make a paste of the mashed garlic, oregano, salt, pepper, and oil. Rub the paste all over the pork roast and let the meat stand at room temperature about 30 minutes.

2. Preheat the oven to 350°. Place the meat in a roasting pan and roast, uncovered, about 1 hour and 15 minutes, or until a meat thermometer registers 155° to 160°. Remove the roast from the oven and let rest 8 to 10 minutes. Reheat the sauce. If too thick, thin with chicken broth. Thinly slice the roast and serve with the sauce spooned on top. Garnish with sprigs of cilantro or parsley.

Pork Shank, Yucatán Style
Chamorro Pibil

Makes **2 servings**

Chef Joaquim Ocampo Castillo shared this very special recipe. He's a native of Yucatán, and is now with Casa Vieja restaurant in Tlaquepaque, a suburb of Guadalajara. Fresh pork shank is seasoned with Yucatán spices, wrapped in banana leaves and steam-baked until very tender. Fresh pork shank, also called fresh pork hock (but not ham hock, which is smoked, not fresh), may need to be special ordered. If unavailable, use lamb shank instead.

Banana leaves, usually frozen in one-pound packages, can be found in Mexican and Asian markets. The leaves are about 30 to 40 inches long, and are cut to the size needed to wrap the meat. Achiote seasoning paste is found in Mexican markets. Serve with black beans and fresh salsa.

4 tablespoons Yucatán Red Seasoning Paste (page 23)
2 pork shanks (about 1 pound each)
2 banana leaves, thawed if frozen
2 plum tomatoes, thinly sliced crosswise
2 teaspoons chopped fresh epazote or cilantro
1/2 red bell pepper, thinly sliced
2 teaspoons unseasoned rice vinegar
1/2 teaspoon salt

1. Prepare the seasoning paste. Then, cut the tough outside layer of skin off the shank. Cover the pork all over with the seasoning paste. Cover and refrigerate at least 4 hours or overnight.

2. Preheat oven to 350°. Put 1 sheet of foil large enough to completely wrap 1 pork shank onto a flat surface, and cut the banana leaf to about the same size. Put the banana leaf on top of the foil. Lay the pork shank in the center of the banana leaf. Top the meat with half of the tomatoes, half the epazote, and half the pepper slices. Sprinkle with half the vinegar and salt. Wrap the pork completely in the banana leaf. Then fold the foil around the outside to make a tight seal.

3. Put the package on a large baking sheet. Repeat with the other shank. Cook in the oven 2 hours or until the meat is very tender when pierced with a fork. Open one package to test tenderness and drain off excess fat. Serve the shanks while hot, on the plate with the cooked tomatoes and peppers.

Pork Tenderloin with Red Sesame Seed Sauce
Cerdo al Horno con Pipian Rojo de Ajonjoli

Makes **4 servings**

Pork tenderloin is perfectly complemented with Red Sesame Seed Sauce (page 54). A good starter is Cabbage and Cheese Salad with Tortillas (page 172).

Red Sesame Seed Sauce (page 54)

3 pork tenderloins (about 3/4 pound each), silver skin removed

1/2 teaspoon salt, or to taste

1/4 teaspoon freshly ground pepper, or to taste

1 teaspoon dried oregano (Mexican variety preferred), crumbled

1 tablespoon olive oil or vegetable oil

1 tablespoon toasted sesame seeds (optional)

Cilantro sprigs

1. Prepare the red sesame seed sauce. Reserve in the pan off heat.

2. Preheat oven to 450°. Rub the pork with salt, pepper, and oregano. Heat the oil in a large non-stick skillet over medium-high heat. Brown the pork on both sides, about 5 minutes total. Transfer to a baking pan and roast until no longer pink inside, 18 to 20 minutes (155° to 160° on a meat thermometer). Remove from the oven and let stand 6 to 8 minutes. Reheat the sauce. Slice the pork and serve with a portion of the sauce spooned over the meat. Sprinkle with sesame seeds, if using, and garnish with cilantro. Pass remaining sauce at the table.

Pork Tenderloin with Serrano Chile Cream Sauce
Cerdo con Salsa de Crema de Chile Serrano

Makes **4 servings**

Pork tenderloin is one of the easiest cuts of pork to prepare. It becomes tender and succulent when cooked. Here, the fiery serrano chile imparts its tingling heat to the creamy white sauce. Accompany the pork with Yellow Rice with Peas (page 475).

Serrano Chile Cream Sauce (page 51)

2 pork tenderloins (about 1 pound each)

1 tablespoon vegetable oil or olive oil

1 teaspoon dried oregano (Mexican variety preferred), crumbled

1 teaspoon salt

1 tablespoon finely chopped fresh parsley

1. Prepare the serrano cream sauce. Cover and set aside, or if made ahead, refrigerate up to 2 days. Preheat the oven to 450°. Line a 9- × 12-inch baking pan with foil. Trim the tough silver skin from the pork. Brush the tenderloins all over with oil. Season with oregano and salt.

2. Heat a large nonstick skillet over medium-high heat. Add the pork and cook, turning to brown on all sides, about 5 minutes. Transfer to the roasting pan and cook until no longer pink inside, but still juicy, about 18 to 20 minutes (155° to 160° on a meat thermometer). Reheat the sauce. Thinly slice the pork and serve with the sauce spooned on top. Sprinkle with parsley.

Pork Stew from Puebla
Tinga Poblana de Cerdo

Makes 4 servings

There are many versions of this special stew from Puebla. If asked, each cook will extol the virtues of her or his family recipe. The stew can be made with pork, beef, or chicken, but chorizo is nearly always included. The stew is topped with sliced avocado and should be accompanied by warm tortillas.

2 pounds boneless pork, shoulder or sirloin, cut into 1-inch pieces

1 bay leaf

1/2 teaspoon salt

1/2 pound fresh bulk chorizo, or packaged, with casings removed

1 large white onion, thinly sliced

1 large garlic clove, minced

1 pound medium tomatoes, peeled and chopped

1/2 teaspoon dried oregano (Mexican variety preferred), crumbled

2 canned chipotle chiles en adobo, seeded and chopped

1 teaspoon adobo sauce from the can of chiles

8 small cooked red potatoes, peeled and quartered

1 large avocado (Hass variety preferred), peeled and sliced

1. Put the pork pieces and bay leaf in a saucepan. Add water just to the surface of the meat. Add the salt. Bring to a boil, then lower the heat and simmer until the meat is very tender, 45 to 50 minutes. Turn off the heat and reserve the pork in the broth.

2. In a large skillet, cook the chorizo, breaking it up into small pieces as it cooks, until it renders its fat and starts to brown, about 5 minutes. Remove the chorizo to a bowl and reserve.

3. Drain off all but 1 tablespoon of fat from the skillet. Add the onion and cook until limp, stirring and scraping the pan bottom, 2 to 3 minutes. Add the garlic, tomatoes, oregano, chiles, and adobo sauce. Cook, stirring, until the juices reduce and the mixture starts to thicken, about 3 to 4 minutes.

4. Transfer the tomato mixture to the pan with the pork. Add the reserved cooked chorizo and the cooked potatoes. Bring the stew to a boil. Reduce the heat to low and simmer, uncovered, 15 minutes to blend the flavors. Serve topped with sliced avocado.

Pork and Vegetables in Yellow Mole with Masa Dumplings
Mole Amarillo de Verduras y Chochoyones

Makes 4 servings

This is a classic stew of meat, vegetables, and tiny masa dumplings in a thin yellow mole from Oaxaca. If you make the amarillo *(yellow mole) and the dumpling dough ahead of time, the dish is quite easy. The herb* hoja santa, *or* hierba santa, *is not readily available in many locations, but can be ordered (see Mail-Order Sources for Ingredients, page 620). It has a special flavor, somewhat like sassafras with peppery and anise-like undertones. The leaves freeze well, and even though they turn dark, the special flavor remains. In this recipe, cilantro can be substituted if hoja santa can't be found. The flavor will be different, but still very good.*

Yellow Mole (page 60)
Masa Dumplings (page 135)
1¹⁄₂ **pounds boneless pork, cut into 1-inch pieces**
2 **large garlic cloves, thinly sliced**
1 **hoja santa leaf, finely chopped, or** ¹⁄₂ **cup
    chopped cilantro**
¹⁄₂ **teaspoon salt**
4 **medium red or white potatoes, scrubbed
    and cut into** ¹⁄₈**-inch pieces**
³⁄₄ **pound green beans, trimmed and cut into
    1-inch pieces**
¹⁄₂ **finely chopped white onion**
2 **tablespoons fresh lime juice**

1. Prepare the yellow mole. Reserve in the pan off heat. Make the masa dumplings. Reserve, covered on a plate.

2. Put the pork in a large saucepan with the garlic, hoja santa, or cilantro, and salt. Add 3 cups of water and bring to a boil. Reduce the heat to low, cover and simmer until the meat is tender, about 35 to 40 minutes.

3. While the meat is cooking, bring to a boil a pot of salted water and cook the potatoes until crisp-tender, about 10 minutes. With a large slotted spoon, scoop the potatoes out of the water and reserve in a bowl. In the same water, cook the beans until crisp-tender, 5 to 6 minutes. Drain and reserve the beans with the potatoes.

4. When the pork is tender, pour the reserved yellow mole into the pan with the pork. Add the reserved potatoes and beans. Bring the stew to a boil, then reduce the heat to low, cover, and simmer 5 minutes. Add the reserved masa dumplings and cook until the vegetables are tender and the dumplings are cooked through, 12 to 15 minutes. In a small bowl mix the onion and lime juice. Serve the stew hot in shallow bowls with the onion mixture spooned on top.

Pork and Green Chiles
Chile Verde

Makes **4 servings**

Chile verde *is popular on both sides of the border and is typical of the green chile dishes that are eaten in northern Mexico, Texas, and New Mexico—the region where Anaheim and New Mexico chiles are grown in abundance on both sides of the border. For the best flavor make the stew ahead and reheat before serving. Look for masa harina (the flour with which tortillas are made) in Mexican or Latin-American markets. A bottle of hot sauce is often served for those who want to spice up the stew. Chile verde is served over rice or wrapped in large flour tortillas to make burritos.*

2 tablespoons vegetable oil
1³/₄ pounds boneless pork, cut into ¹/₂-inch pieces
1 medium white onion, chopped
4 medium garlic cloves, chopped
1 teaspoon dried oregano (Mexican variety preferred), crumbled
1 teaspoon ground cumin
¹/₂ teaspoon salt, or to taste
6 fresh Anaheim or poblano chiles, roasted and peeled (page 8)
1¹/₂ tablespoons masa harina (flour for corn tortillas)

1. In a large saucepan, heat the oil over medium-high heat and brown the meat in batches. Transfer the meat to a bowl.

2. In the same pan, put the onion, garlic, oregano, cumin, and salt, and cook, stirring frequently, until the onion starts to brown, about 4 minutes. Return the meat to the pan and add 1½ cups water. Stir well to combine. Bring to a boil, reduce heat to low, cover and simmer until the meat is tender, about 45 minutes.

3. Meanwhile, prepare the chiles. Then, remove the stem and seeds. Coarsely chop the chiles and add them to the pan.

4. In a small bowl mix the masa with 3 tablespoons of water until smooth and stir the mixture into the stew. Cook, uncovered, until the chile verde thickens. Adjust seasoning. Serve hot.

Pork in Tomatillo Sauce
Cerdo en Salsa de Tomatillo

Makes **6 servings**

Pork simmered in a classic tomatillo sauce is a traditional dish that's found throughout Mexico. Serve the pork with rice and soft warm tortillas.

1¹/₂ pounds fresh tomatillos, husked and rinsed
1 medium white onion, peeled and coarsely chopped
4 medium garlic cloves
2 serrano chiles, stemmed and coarsely chopped
1 teaspoon dried oregano (Mexican variety preferred), crumbled
1 teaspoon ground cumin
¹/₂ teaspoon sugar
1 teaspoon salt
¹/₂ cup roughly chopped fresh cilantro
3 pounds boneless pork loin, cut into 2-inch chunks
3 tablespoons flour
¹/₂ teaspoon freshly ground pepper, or to taste
3 tablespoons vegetable oil

1. In a medium saucepan, bring to a boil about 1 quart of water. Add the tomatillos, onion, garlic, and serranos. Cook, uncovered, over medium heat until the tomatillos are barely soft, about 5 minutes. Drain and transfer the contents of the pan to a blender or food processor. Add the oregano, cumin, sugar, ½ teaspoon of the salt, and the cilantro. Blend to a coarse purée, and reserve.

2. Preheat the oven to 350°. Dust the pork lightly with the flour, and season with the remaining salt and pepper. In a large flameproof casserole dish, or saucepan, heat the oil, and brown the pork, in batches. Reserved browned pieces in a bowl. Return the browned meat and any collected juices to the pan; then add ⅓ cup of water, and stir well to incorporate the brown bits from the bottom of the pan. Stir in the reserved tomatillo sauce. Cover the pan, and cook in the oven until the pork is very tender, about 1 hour. Serve hot.

Pork Stew with Poblano Chiles and Corn
Guisado de Cerdo con Chile Poblanos y Elote

Makes **4 servings**

When you want a whole meal in a pot, try this pork stew from central Mexico. It's loaded with flavor, texture, and contrasting colors. Sometimes the ears of corn are simply cut crosswise into two-inch sections to cook in the stew, but the stew is much easier to eat if the kernels are cut off the cob, as in this recipe.

Epazote adds a distinct flavor to the dish but substitute fresh cilantro if epazote is not available, even though the flavor will not be quite the same.

Avocado and Melon Salad (page 185) or Cabbage and Orange Salad (page 183) go well with the stew. Soft warm tortillas should be served, too.

2 tablespoons vegetable oil
1³/₄ pounds boneless pork, shoulder or sirloin, cut into 1-inch chunks
Salt, to taste
1 large white onion, quartered lengthwise and sliced
6 medium garlic cloves, chopped
1 teaspoon dried oregano (Mexican variety preferred), crumbled
1 teaspoon ground cumin
4 plum tomatoes, peeled and chopped
2¹/₂ cups canned fat-free reduced-sodium chicken broth
1 tablespoon chopped epazote leaves or 1 teaspoon dried epazote
4 poblano chiles, roasted and peeled (page 8)
2 ears fresh corn, kernels cut off
Freshly ground pepper, to taste
Lime wedges

1. In a large pot heat the oil over medium heat and lightly brown the pork in batches. Season each batch lightly with salt. Transfer the browned pork to a bowl as it browns.

2. Put the onion, garlic, oregano, and cumin into the pot and cook, stirring, until they begin to color, 3 to 4 minutes. Return the meat to the pot and add the tomatoes, broth, and epazote. Bring to a boil, then reduce the heat to medium-low, cover and cook until the pork is very tender, about 1 hour.

3. Meanwhile, remove the stem and seeds from the chiles. Dice the chiles into ¾-inch pieces and stir into the stew along with the corn. Add freshly ground pepper and additional salt, if needed. Cook until the corn is tender, about 5 to 6 minutes. Serve the stew hot with lime wedges to squeeze over the stew.

Pork "Tablecloth Stainer"
Manchamanteles de Cerdo

Makes 4 servings

Manchamanteles, *one of the seven moles of Oaxaca and also made in central Mexico, is a unique combination of pork or chicken with vegetables, fruits, and chiles. The name for this popular stew meaning "tablecloth stainer" refers to the delicious red chile broth that, if spilled, will stain the tablecloth. My pork version is adapted from the dish served at Fonda El Refugio restaurant in Mexico City.*

5 large ancho chiles, stemmed and seeded, veins removed
¹/₄ cup vegetable oil
1 large plantain, peeled and sliced crosswise
¹/₄ cup slivered almonds
¹/₂ medium white onion, chopped
4 large garlic cloves, chopped
2 medium tomatoes, peeled and chopped
1 teaspoon dried oregano (Mexican variety preferred), crumbled
¹/₂ teaspoon ground cinnamon (Mexican canela or Ceylon variety preferred)
¹/₂ teaspoon ground allspice
2 pounds boneless pork, shoulder or sirloin, cut into 1-inch pieces
1 teaspoon salt
¹/₂ teaspoon freshly ground pepper
1 medium sweet potato, peeled and cut into bite-size pieces
1 cup pineapple chunks, fresh or canned

1. Cut the chiles into about 4 pieces and toast in a medium skillet, over medium heat, pressing with a spatula until they are aromatic and change color, 10 to 15 seconds. Submerge them in a bowl of hot water and soak 20 to 25 minutes.

2. Meanwhile, in the same skillet, heat 1 tablespoon of the oil. Add the plantain and cook, turning once, until golden brown, about 1 minute per side. Remove to a plate and reserve. In the same skillet, toast the almonds, stirring, until light brown, 2 to 3 minutes. Transfer to a blender. Add the onion and garlic to the same skillet, and cook until the onion softens, about 3 minutes.

3. Add the tomatoes, oregano, cinnamon, and allspice. Cook until the tomatoes soften, 3 to 4 minutes. Put in the blender with the almonds. Add the soaked chiles and ¹/₄ cup of the chile water, or tap water. Blend very well until thick and smooth. Reserve.

4. In a large saucepan, heat the remaining 2 tablespoons of oil over medium-high heat and cook the meat, turning, until no longer pink on the outside, 6 to 8 minutes. Season with salt and pepper. Add 1¹/₂ cups of water. Bring to a boil. Cover, reduce heat, and simmer until tender, about 45 minutes. Add the sweet potato and reserved sauce. Cook until the potato is tender, 20 to 25 minutes. Add the pineapple and reserved plantain. Cook until hot and bubbling, 6 to 8 minutes. Serve hot.

Pork, Vegetable, and Chile Stew
Estofado de Cerdo

Makes **4 servings**

Anaheim chiles are teamed with pork and vegetables in this simple stew from Nogales, on the Arizona-Mexico border. Anaheims usually rank mild on the heat scale of chiles, but an occasional hot one can surprise you, so if you're sensitive, wear protective gloves when working with the chiles. Fresh New Mexico chiles look almost the same, and they tend to be hotter. Serve with warm corn or flour tortillas.

4 large (about 8 ounces) fresh Anaheim chiles

2 tablespoons vegetable oil

1 large white onion, coarsely chopped

3 large garlic cloves, finely chopped

1 1/2 pounds boneless pork, shoulder or sirloin,
  cut into 1/2-inch pieces

1 teaspoon dried oregano (Mexican variety
  preferred), crumbled

1/2 teaspoon dried marjoram

1/2 teaspoon ground cumin

1/2 teaspoon salt, or to taste

1/4 teaspoon freshly ground pepper

2 cups canned fat-free reduced-sodium
  chicken broth

1 teaspoon Maggi seasoning extract or
  Worcestershire sauce

3 medium carrots (about 8 ounces), peeled and
  finely diced

1 medium potato (about 4 ounces), peeled and
  finely diced

2 tablespoons chopped fresh cilantro

1. Preheat oven broiler, and roast the chiles on a baking sheet placed on the top shelf of the oven under the broiler. With tongs, turn the chiles until lightly charred all over, 6 to 7 minutes. Put the roasted chiles in a plastic bag to steam 5 to 6 minutes; then rinse under cold running water, 1 at a time, and rub or peel off the skins. Cut the chiles open, remove the seeds, and cut into 1/2-inch dice. Set aside.

2. In a large saucepan, heat the oil over medium heat, and stir-fry the onion and garlic, 4 to 5 minutes, until starting to brown. Remove to a bowl. Add the meat, and stir-fry until no longer pink on the surface, 4 to 5 minutes. Return the onion and garlic to the pan. Add the oregano, marjoram, cumin, salt, and pepper. Stir in the broth and the Maggi. Bring to a boil, then reduce the heat, cover, and simmer until the meat is tender, about 25 minutes.

3. Add the carrots, potato, and cilantro. Cook until the vegetables are tender, 15 to 20 minutes. Stir in the reserved chiles. Heat through about 5 minutes and serve.

Pork with Black Beans and Chipotle Chiles
Cerdo con Frijol Negro y Chiles Chipotle

Makes **4 to 6 servings**

This is a thick pork and black bean stew with chipotle chiles that I developed for one of my cooking classes. It's a great crowd pleaser! The flavor of the dish improves if made ahead and reheated.

1 cup dry black beans, picked over and rinsed

Salt to taste

1 tablespoon olive oil or vegetable oil

2 pounds boneless pork, cut into 1-inch pieces

1 large white onion, coarsely chopped

1/2 pound medium tomatillos, husked, rinsed,
  and quartered

4 green onions, chopped

2 canned chipotle chiles en adobo, seeded and
  coarsely chopped

2 medium garlic cloves, peeled and thinly sliced

1/2 cup loosely packed snipped cilantro sprigs

2 teaspoons ground cumin

1 teaspoon dried oregano (Mexican variety
  preferred), crumbled

1 teaspoon sugar

1 cup canned fat-free reduced-sodium
  chicken broth

1. Place the sorted and rinsed black beans in a saucepan and add 4 cups of water. Bring to a boil, then reduce heat to low, cover and simmer for 5 minutes. Turn off the heat and let soak 30 minutes. Return the beans to a boil again, then reduce the heat to low, cover, and simmer until the beans are tender and the broth thickens, about 1 hour and 20 minutes. When the beans are tender, season with salt.

2. Meanwhile, heat the oil in a wide deep skillet over medium-high heat and brown the pork in batches. Transfer the meat to a bowl as the pieces are browned. In the same skillet, cook the onion with 2 tablespoons of water, stirring to scrape up the browned bits from the pan bottom, until softened, 3 to 4 minutes. Return the meat to the pan, including any collected juices from the bowl. Add the salt and mix to combine. Turn off the heat and reserve in the pan.

3. Put all of the remaining ingredients in a blender, except the reserved beans, and blend until smooth. Stir the purée into the pork mixture and bring to a boil, then reduce the heat to low, cover, and simmer until the sauce thickens and the meat is tender, about 45 minutes. Drain off the broth from the beans into a container and save for another use.

4. Add the drained beans to the pork. Cook slowly, over low heat, about minutes, to blend for flavors. Adjust seasoning. Serve in shallow bowls.

Pork Stew with Pineapple
Cerdo con Piña

Makes **4 servings**

During one of our early trips to Mexico City about 25 years ago, when the Hotel Majestic was still grand and before a devastating earthquake damaged so much of the historical center around the city's cathedral, the Majestic's rooftop dining room featured a lavish Mexican buffet. My husband and I worked our way through most of the dishes when we dined there. This is my interpretation of the pork with pineapple dish that lingers in my memory. Serve with white rice.

1 tablespoon vegetable oil or olive oil

2¹/₂ pounds boneless country-style pork, cut in 1-inch pieces

1 teaspoon salt, or to taste

¹/₄ teaspoon freshly ground pepper, or to taste

2 medium onions, sliced in wedges from top to root end

1 teaspoon dried oregano (Mexican variety preferred), crumbled

1 cup canned fat-free reduced-sodium chicken broth

³/₄ cup drained pineapple chunks, fresh or canned

¹/₄ cup of pineapple juice from draining the pineapple

1 tablespoon Worcestershire sauce

1 tablespoon ground ancho or pasilla chili powder

¹/₄ teaspoon ground cinnamon (Mexican canela or Ceylon variety preferred)

1. Preheat oven to 350°. Heat the oil in a large ovenproof pan over medium-high heat. Brown the meat, in batches, and season with ½ teaspoon of the salt and pepper. Remove the browned meat to a bowl as it browns.

2. Add the onions, oregano, and remaining salt to the pan and cook, partially covered, stirring frequently to scrape up browned bits from the pan bottom, about 2 minutes. Add the remaining ingredients and return the meat and collected juices to the pan. Stir to combine. Bring to a boil. Cover and place in the oven and cook 45 to 50 minutes or until the meat is very tender. Add salt, if needed. Serve hot.

Wedding Pork in Red Chile Sauce
Asado de Boda

Makes **4 servings**

Zacatecas is a lovely colonial city in north-central Mexico that sits in a ravine at 8,100 feet, where vast silver deposits were discovered during the Spanish reign of Mexico. During a late-winter visit, my husband and I explored much of the town on foot, pausing frequently to catch our breath at the high altitude, and to marvel at the elaborate restored buildings and cleanliness of the city. One evening, we selected La Cantera Musical restaurant for dinner. My entrée of asado de boda *was delicious.* Boda *means nuptials or wedding.*

This dish is a type of mole and is typically served for weddings or anniversary celebrations. Mexican chocolate is often used in mole dishes and is available in Mexican grocery stores and many supermarkets. The chocolate also contains cinnamon, ground almonds, sugar, and vanilla and is formed into round tablets that are packaged in cylinder shaped boxes. Ibarra or Abuelita are the most common imports. Serve with Mexican Rice (page 472).

2 pounds pork shoulder or sirloin, cut into ³/₄-inch pieces

1 teaspoon salt, or to taste

5 ancho chiles

1 tablespoon vegetable oil or lard

¹/₄ medium white onion, chopped

2 large garlic cloves, thinly sliced

3 (6 ounces) plum tomatoes, cored and chopped

1 teaspoon dried oregano (Mexican variety preferred), crumbled

¹/₂ teaspoon dried marjoram

¹/₂ teaspoon ground cinnamon (Mexican canela or Ceylon variety preferred)

3 whole cloves

³/₄ cup pork broth (from cooking the pork)

¹/₂ cup pineapple juice

2 teaspoons apple cider vinegar

1 teaspoon dark brown sugar

1 ounce Mexican chocolate (such as Ibarra brand)

1. Put the meat in a large saucepan and barely cover with water. Add ½ teaspoon of the salt. Bring to a boil, skimming the foam as needed; then reduce heat to low and simmer until tender, about 45 minutes. Drain the broth into a container and reserve. Reserve the meat off heat, covered, in the pan.

2. Meanwhile, in a dry skillet over medium heat, toast the chiles, turning and pressing with a spatula, until fragrant, about 20 seconds. Cut the chiles open and remove the seeds. Put the chiles in a bowl of hot water and soak for 20 to 25 minutes.

3. Meanwhile, heat the oil in a large nonstick skillet. Add the onion and cook, stirring, until it starts to brown, about 5 minutes. Add the garlic, tomatoes, oregano, marjoram, cinnamon, cloves, and the remaining salt. Cook, stirring, until the tomatoes are bubbling, 3 to 4 minutes. Transfer to a blender.

4. Drain the chiles and add to the blender. Discard the liquid. To the blender, add ¾ cup of reserved pork broth, pineapple juice and vinegar. Purée until very smooth.

5. Add the sauce to the pork and stir. Bring to a boil, stirring, then reduce the heat to low. Add the brown sugar and chocolate. Cook, stirring, until the chocolate melts, about 5 minutes. Cover and simmer the stew, stirring frequently to prevent sticking on the bottom, 20 minutes to blend the flavors. Adjust seasoning. The sauce should be thick enough to coat the meat. If too thick, add a little more of the pork broth. (Leftover broth can be frozen.) Serve the pork and sauce hot on serving plates with rice.

Pork in Tomato Sauce with Diced Zucchini
Cerdo con Salsa de Jitomate con Colache

Makes 4 servings

Sinaloa, on the northwest coast of Mexico, is a rich agricultural state with eleven major rivers running to the sea from the mountains to the west.

Tomatoes, squash, chickpeas, potatoes, and a great variety of other vegetables and tropical fruits are cultivated in the state. My husband and I traveled through some of this region, and this recipe comes from a dish of braised pork cooked in a simple fresh tomato sauce that's typical of the region. If yellow zucchini is not available, use all green zucchini. Tortillas or crusty oval Mexican sandwich rolls (bolillos) are a must to sop up the juicy and tasty tomato sauce.

3 pounds meaty country-style ribs, on or off the bone, cut into 3- to 4-inch pieces

1 tablespoon vegetable oil

Salt and pepper, to taste

1 medium onion, halved and thinly sliced, plus 2 tablespoons finely chopped onion

4 medium garlic cloves, chopped

1 teaspoon dried oregano (Mexican variety preferred), crumbled

1/2 teaspoon ground cumin

1/4 teaspoon dried thyme

6 plum tomatoes, peeled and chopped

1 to 2 fresh serrano chiles, stemmed and cut in half lengthwise with seeds

2 teaspoons unsalted butter

2 medium green zucchini, cut into 1/2-inch cubes

2 medium yellow zucchini, cut into 1/2-inch cubes

Salt and freshly ground pepper, to taste

1. Preheat the oven to 350°. Trim excess fat from the pork. Heat the oil in a large nonstick skillet over medium heat and cook the pork, turning, 2 to 3 times, until lightly browned, about 6 to 8 minutes. Remove the browned meat to a wide 3-quart ovenproof casserole dish.

2. In the same skillet, cook the onion, stirring, until softened, about 3 minutes. Add the garlic, oregano, cumin, and thyme. Cook, stirring, 1 minute. Add the tomatoes and 1/4 cup of water. Bring to a boil. Pour the tomatoes over the meat. Add the serrano chile. Cover and place in the oven. Immediately reduce the oven temperature to 325° and cook 1 hour or until falling-apart tender. Adjust the seasoning. Leave the meat in the oven, turned off, while cooking the squash.

3. When the meat is tender, melt the butter in a medium nonstick skillet over medium heat until it sizzles. Add the 2 tablespoons of chopped onion and cook, stirring, until softened, about 3 to 4 minutes. Add the squash and 2 tablespoons of water. Cover and cook, stirring frequently, until the squash is crisp-tender, about 4 to 5 minutes. Add salt and pepper. Adjust seasoning.

4. Serve the meat hot with the sauce spooned over the top and the squash on the side.

Purslane with Pork
Verdolagas con Cerdo

Makes 4 servings

Purslane is a common wild plant called verdolagas *that's eaten all over Mexico and is occasionally becoming available in farmer's markets in this country. The plant has small round fleshy leaves, somewhat like succulents, and a slightly tart taste. Purslane is often cooked with bits of braised pork, and it's a wonderful combination. Serve with white rice and Tomato and Red Onion Salad (page 166).*

If epazote is not available, substitute fresh cilantro, even though the taste will be different.

2 tablespoons vegetable oil
1 medium onion, chopped
³/₄ pound boneless country-style pork ribs,
    cut in ¹/₂-inch pieces
2 medium garlic cloves, chopped
2 teaspoons fresh chopped fresh epazote,
    or 1 tablespoon dried epazote
1 teaspoon dried oregano (Mexican variety
    preferred), crumbled
¹/₂ teaspoon salt, or to taste
¹/₄ teaspoon freshly ground pepper, or to taste
1 cup water
3 cups (12 ounces) purslane, thick stems removed
1 jalapeño chile, stemmed, seeded,
    veins removed, and chopped

Heat the oil in a medium nonstick skillet and cook the onion until it begins to brown, about 4 minutes. Add the pork, garlic, epazote, oregano, salt, pepper, and water. Bring to a boil; then reduce the heat to low, cover, and simmer until the pork is tender, about 20 minutes. Add the purslane and jalapeño chile. Simmer, covered, until tender, 10 to 12 minutes. Serve hot.

Lamb

Lamb Steaks with Chili Rub
Chuletas de Cordero con Especias

Makes 4 servings

A mix of dried herbs, spices, and ground red chili is rubbed all over thin lamb steaks before being grilled, giving the meat a spicy, slightly smoky flavor that's nothing short of terrific. This dish is typical of the states of Chihuahua and Sonora. The meat is grilled on an outdoor barbecue, or indoors on a ridged stove top grill pan. Serve the lamb with beans and tortillas. Jicama, Melon, Cucumber, and Tomato Salad (page 186) goes well with the steaks.

2 tablespoons Chili Rub (page 20)
4 (6-ounce) round bone lamb steaks
2 teaspoons olive oil
1 large garlic clove, mashed

1. Prepare the chili rub and measure out 2 tablespoons. Store the remaining chili rub in a sealable plastic bag for future use. Trim excess fat from the lamb, and remove the bone.

2. Cut the bone out of the lamb steaks. Then place the steaks between 2 pieces of plastic wrap and pound with the flat side of a meat mallet or with a rolling pin to an even thickness of about ¼-inch. Rub oil and garlic all over the steaks and season equally with the chili rub.

3. Prepare an outdoor grill, or heat a stovetop grill pan until hot. Cook the steaks 2 to 3 minutes per side, or until barely pink inside. Serve at once.

Lamb Stew, Yucatán Style
Cordero estilo Yucatán

Makes 4 servings

This dish of boneless lamb coated with Yucatán seasonings and cooked with onions, tomatoes, and chiles is typical of the stews served in market food stalls and some restaurants.

Small white beans, ibis, are grown in the Yucatán, so I accompany the stew with White Beans with Roasted Garlic (page 469).

Yucatán Red Seasoning Paste (page 23)

1 tablespoon unseasoned rice vinegar

1¹/₂ pounds boneless lamb, cut into 1-inch pieces

1 tablespoon olive oil

¹/₂ cup chopped white onion

2 large garlic cloves, chopped

¹/₂ medium red bell pepper, coarsely chopped or diced

1 fresh habanero chile, stemmed, seeded, ribs removed, and chopped (wear protective gloves)

2 large tomatoes, peeled and chopped

¹/₄ cup lightly packed chopped cilantro

1 cup canned fat-free reduced-sodium chicken broth

Salt, to taste

1. Prepare the seasoning paste. Mix 2 tablespoons of the paste with the vinegar and rub all over the meat. Cover and refrigerate 2 to 4 hours. Store the remaining paste for later use.

2. In a large saucepan, heat the oil over medium heat and cook the onion until softened, about 3 minutes. Add the remaining ingredients and the seasoned meat. Bring to a boil, reduce the heat to low, cover and simmer until the meat is tender, 45 to 50 minutes. Remove the cover and cook 8 to 10 minutes more to thicken a bit and reduce some of the liquid. Add salt, if needed. Serve with white beans or steamed rice.

Leg of Lamb in Chile Sauce
Pierna de Cordero Enchilada

Makes 6 servings

Slow-cooked meats braised in chile sauce is a traditional Mexican method of cooking to make meat so tender that it falls off the bone. You will need a large ovenproof casserole dish or roasting pan with a lid to hold the lamb rather snugly. Serve this with soft tortillas to soak up the juices. For a wonderful side dish with the lamb, serve Hominy, Corn, and Poblano Chiles (page 419).

4 ancho chiles,

2 medium tomatoes, cored and chopped

¹/₂ medium white onion, chopped

3 large garlic cloves, thinly sliced

12 fresh epazote leaves, or ¹/₂ teaspoon dried epazote

1 teaspoon dried oregano (Mexican variety preferred), crumbled

¹/₄ teaspoon dried thyme

2 cups canned fat-free reduced-sodium chicken broth

2 teaspoons olive oil

1 (3- to 4-pound) leg of lamb

¹/₂ teaspoon salt, to taste

Freshly ground pepper, to taste

1. In a dry skillet toast the chiles, turning until fragrant, about 20 seconds. Cut open the chiles and remove the seeds. Cut the chiles into pieces and put in a bowl of hot water and soak for 20 minutes. Drain and discard the water.

2. Transfer chiles to a blender. Add the tomatoes, onion, garlic, epazote, oregano, thyme, and 1 cup of the chicken broth. Blend as smooth as possible. In a medium saucepan, heat the oil over medium heat and add the chile mixture along with the remaining cup of broth. Cook the sauce, stirring, frequently, 5 minutes. Reserve in the pan off heat.

3. Heat the oven to 325°. Trim all excess fat from the lamb. Season with salt and pepper. Put the meat into a large casserole dish or roasting pan. Pour the sauce over the meat. Cover the pan tightly with aluminum foil and put on the lid. Braise in the oven 2½ to 3 hours, or until the meat is falling-apart tender, and easily pulls away from the bone. Serve chunks of meat and the sauce in shallow soup bowls.

Butterflied Leg of Lamb with Fiery Cilantro-Mint Sauce
Cordero con Salsa de Cilantro y Yerbabuena
Makes **6 servings**

Grill or broil the lamb until it's nice and brown with a bit of charring on the outside and barely pink inside, for mouth-watering meat that's absolutely wonderful with a nueva *sauce made of cilantro, mint, and pumpkin seeds. It's a delicious example of blending the old and the new in Mexican cooking. Serve the lamb with Baked Potatoes Stuffed with Corn (page 446).*

1 (3- to 4-pound) butterflied leg of lamb

1 tablespoon olive oil

2 large garlic cloves, minced

1 teaspoon dried oregano (Mexican variety preferred), crumbled

¹/₂ teaspoon dried thyme

³/₄ teaspoon salt, or to taste

¹/₄ teaspoon freshly ground pepper, or to taste

Fiery Cilantro-Mint Sauce (page 30)

1. Trim the lamb of excess fat. In a small bowl, mix the oil, garlic, oregano, thyme, salt, and pepper. Rub the mixture all over the meat. Let stand about 45 minutes. Prepare an outdoor grill or heat an oven broiler. Grill the lamb over hot coals or broil under a hot oven broiler, turning 3 to 4 times, until browned on the outside, and the internal temperature is 130° for medium-rare on a meat thermometer, about 25 to 30 minutes total.

2. Prepare the sauce. Let the meat rest 5 minutes before slicing. Fan a portion of the sliced lamb on individual serving plates and spoon a portion of sauce over each serving. Serve and pass remaining sauce at the table.

Oven-Roasted Lamb, Monterrey Style
Barbacoa de Cordero al Horno
Makes **6 servings**

Traditional barbacoa *is a whole lamb, goat, or pig that's seasoned and maybe marinated as in this version, then wrapped in leaves of one kind or another, and roasted in a pit. Then: a fiesta!*

It isn't necessary to dig a pit and roast meat underground to entertain your guests with succulent lamb barbacoa *anymore though. Preparing* barbacoa *in the oven is the simple contemporary way to cook lamb or baby goat in the thriving city of Monterrey, capitol of the state of Nuevo Leon, in northern Mexico. In this region, flour tortillas are always served with goat or lamb* barbacoa *along with beans, salsa, guacamole, and plenty of cold beer from the breweries of Monterrey. The meat can also be eaten as an entrée with beans, rice, and tomatoes.*

4 pounds boneless leg of lamb

¹/₂ cup fresh orange juice and 3 (2-inch) orange rind strips

¹/₂ medium white onion, coarsely chopped

4 large garlic cloves, pressed

1 medium tomato, cored and coarsely chopped

2 teaspoons dried oregano (Mexican variety preferred), crumbled

1 teaspoon ground cumin

1 teaspoon salt

¹/₄ teaspoon crushed red pepper

2 tablespoons tequila (optional)

1. Put the meat in a large ovenproof casserole dish or Dutch oven. Add the remaining ingredients. Turn the meat 2 to 3 times to distribute the ingredients. Seal tightly with aluminum foil and refrigerate 2 hours or overnight. Bring to room temperature about 1 hour before cooking.

2. Preheat the oven to 325°. Bake the meat covered with foil, until falling-apart tender, 2½ to 3 hours. Transfer the meat to a large platter.

3. Pour the juices through a fine-mesh strainer over a saucepan, pressing to extract the pulp and juices. Discard the debris. Bring the juices to a boil over high heat and cook until reduced to about 1 cup. When the meat is cool enough to handle, separate into chunks or shred. Discard fat and connective tissue. Serve the meat, sliced, with the pan juices, if desired, or the broth may be refrigerated for later use. (Remove the congealed fat on top of the juice before using.)

Lamb Shanks in Ancho Chile and Red Wine Sauce

Cordero en Salsa de Chile Ancho y Vino Rojo

Makes 4 servings

In the village of Tequila, near Guadalajara, we were served huge delicious beef shanks, called chamorro, *by our hosts at the Herradura Tequila distillery. My version uses lamb shanks since they are easier to handle and almost everyone likes them. Serve with Mexican Rice (page 472) and crusty rolls. This is a great dish for entertaining.*

Ancho Chile and Red Wine Sauce (page 49)
3 tablespoons all-purpose flour
1 teaspoon salt, or to taste
¹/₂ teaspoon freshly ground pepper, or to taste
¹/₂ teaspoon dried thyme
4 lamb shanks, trimmed of excess fat
2 tablespoons olive oil
1 medium white onion, chopped
4 medium carrots, peeled and cut into
    1-inch pieces
6 large garlic cloves, peeled and halved lengthwise

1. Prepare the sauce. Reserve off heat in the pan. In a pie plate, mix the flour, salt, pepper, and thyme. Dust the shanks all over with the flour mixture. In a large heavy deep skillet, heat the oil over medium heat and brown the shanks, turning, until all are well browned, about 10 minutes.

2. Preheat the oven to 350°. Transfer the shanks to a large ovenproof casserole dish or Dutch oven. Pour ½ cup of water over the shanks, and add the onion, carrots, garlic, and the reserved chile sauce. Turn the shanks to coat with the sauce. Cover and cook in the oven, turning the meat once or twice, until very tender, about 1½ to 2 hours. Serve the shanks with the sauce and vegetables.

Lamb in Chile Broth
Birria

Makes **4 servings**

When I'm in Guadalajara, it's a must to visit the immense Mercado Libertad. *It's an amazing place with everything for sale from fresh produce and foods of all kinds to clothing, handicrafts, and jewelry. At one of the numerous* fondas *(food stalls) is where I first ate birria, a rustic stew and one of the great specialties of the state of Jalisco. The soupy broth and shredded stewed lamb or other meat is served with lime wedges, salsa, and warm tortillas. The condiments are essential to authentic flavor of the dish. This recipe is a modern adaptation of the original pit-cooked meat. The meat needs to marinate overnight, so start one day ahead. Reheating the stew makes it taste even better.*

4 meaty lamb shanks, about 3 pounds, trimmed of all excess fat

4 ancho chiles

4 guajillo chiles

4 large garlic cloves, peeled

4 medium plum tomatoes

1¹/₂ teaspoon dried oregano (Mexican variety preferred), crumbled

³/₄ teaspoon cumin seeds

2 whole cloves

¹/₂ teaspoon ground allspice

2 tablespoons cider vinegar

2 tablespoons tequila

1 teaspoon salt

2¹/₂ cups canned fat-free reduced-sodium chicken broth

2 limes, cut into wedges

Fresh Salsa Mexicana (page 24), or purchased salsa

8 (6- to 7-inch) corn or flour tortillas

1. Put the lamb shanks in a large oven casserole dish or roasting pan with a lid. Set aside.

2. In a dry skillet, over medium heat, toast the chiles, turning, until fragrant, about 20 seconds. Cut the chiles open and remove the seeds. Cut or tear the chiles into pieces and put in a bowl. Cover with hot water and soak for about 20 to 25 minutes.

3. Meanwhile, on a large nonstick skillet, over medium heat, pan-roast the garlic and tomatoes, turning, until slightly soft and charred in spots, 8 to 10 minutes. Transfer to a blender. In the same skillet, toast the oregano and cumin seeds until aromatic, about 20 seconds. Add to the blender. Add the soaked chiles to the blender, discarding the liquid. Add the cloves, allspice, vinegar, tequila, salt, and ¹/₂ cup of water. Blend as smoothly as possible.

4. Pour the marinade through a fine-mesh strainer into the pan with the meat. Discard debris left in the strainer. Turn the meat to coat with the marinade. Cover and refrigerate 24 hours.

5. Bring the meat (in the dish) to room temperature about 1 hour before cooking. Add the chicken broth. Preheat the oven to 350°. Cover the baking dish tightly with aluminum foil. Put on the lid. Bake the meat 2 hours, or until the meat is falling-apart tender.

6. Remove the meat from the broth and let stand about 20 minutes. When cool enough to handle, separate the meat into thick shreds. Discard the bones. (If done ahead, cover and refrigerate the meat and broth separately. Then remove the congealed fat on top of the broth before finishing the dish, or the broth can be poured into a fat skimmer to remove the fat.)

7. To serve, reheat the broth. Add the meat to the broth and heat through completely. Serve in soup bowls with lime wedges, salsa, and tortillas.

Lamb in Red Chile Stew

Chile Colorado de Cordero

Makes 4 servings

Lamb simmered in a boldly seasoned red chile sauce is a typical stew dish in northern Mexico. It's spicy! Accompany the stew with warm tortillas or good crusty bread. For even more kick, bottled hot sauce is also usually on the table.

2 ounces (about 8 whole) dried guajillo chiles

2 tablespoons olive oil or vegetable oil

1 large onion, chopped

4 medium garlic cloves, finely chopped

2¹/₂ pounds boneless lamb stew meat,
    cut in 1-inch pieces

¹/₄ cup all-purpose flour

¹/₂ teaspoon salt

1 teaspoon dried oregano (Mexican variety
    preferred), crumbled

1 teaspoon dried thyme

1 teaspoon ground cumin

¹/₂ teaspoon ground allspice

¹/₂ teaspoon ground cinnamon (Mexican canela
    or Ceylon variety preferred)

1 (28-ounce) can diced tomatoes with the juice

¹/₄ cup lightly packed chopped cilantro

1 cup canned fat-free reduced-sodium
    chicken broth

Chopped green onions and lime wedges

1. Wipe chiles with damp paper towels. Cut open and discard stems, seeds and veins. Cut the chiles into pieces and put in a small saucepan with 1½ cups hot tap water. Bring to a boil, then cover and soak off heat 20 minutes. Put the chiles and the soaking water into a blender and blend as smooth as possible. Strain, pressing the purée to get all the pulp through a strainer into a bowl. Discard the residue. Set the purée aside.

2. Heat the oil in a 3- to 4-quart saucepan over medium heat and cook the onion until it starts to brown, 3 to 4 minutes. Add the garlic and cook 1 minute. Dust the meat with flour and add to the pan. Cook, stirring, until the meat is no longer pink outside, about 3 minutes.

3. Add the salt, the chile purée and all of the remaining ingredients. Stir to mix. Bring to a boil, then reduce the heat to low, partially cover with the lid askew and simmer, stirring frequently, until the meat is very tender, about 1 hour. Serve with finely chopped green onion on top and lime wedges.

Lamb in Red Chile with Potatoes and Zucchini
Cordero en Adobo con Papas y Calabacitas

Makes **4 servings**

Slow-simmered lamb stews similar to this are made in fondas (market food stalls) and by home cooks, too. The robust flavor of the stew comes from red chile paste called adobo. *I add boiled potatoes and zucchini to the stew and put a customary bowl of Pickled Jalapeños and Carrots (page 126) on the table. Accompany with soft warm tortillas, oval Mexican sandwich rolls (bolillos), or other sandwich rolls.*

¹/₂ cup Red Chile Paste (page 20)

1 tablespoon vegetable oil or olive oil

1¹/₂ pounds boneless lamb stew meat,
    cut into ¹/₂-inch pieces

¹/₂ teaspoon salt, or to taste

1 medium white onion, sliced

4 medium garlic cloves, thinly sliced

1 medium tomato, peeled and chopped

1 cup canned fat-free reduced-sodium
    chicken broth

1 tablespoon chopped fresh epazote,
    or 1 teaspoon dried epazote

¹/₄ cup coarsely chopped fresh cilantro

6 small (about 1¹/₂ pounds) whole red potatoes,
    boiled until tender

2 medium zucchini, sliced ³/₄-inch thick

1. Prepare the red chile paste. Reserve ½ cup for the stew and store the remaining for another use. In a large heavy pot, heat the oil over medium heat. Add the meat, season with salt, and brown in batches, 4 to 5 minutes per batch. Remove the meat to a bowl as it browns and reserve.

2. Add the onion and garlic to the pan and cook, scraping up any brown bits from the pan bottom, about 3 minutes. Stir in the tomato, the ½ cup of red chile paste, broth, and epazote. Bring to a boil.

3. Return the lamb to the pot. Reduce the heat to medium-low, cover, and simmer until the meat is tender, about 1 hour.

4. Meanwhile, peel the cooked potatoes and cut into 1-inch pieces. About 15 minutes before serving, stir the potatoes, zucchini, and cilantro into the stew. Simmer over low heat 15 minutes. Add salt, if needed. Serve hot in shallow soup bowls.

Veal

Breaded Veal Cutlet
Milanesa

Makes 4 servings

Milanesa is an Italian import that's been widely adopted in Mexico and is so popular that it's listed on many restaurant menus throughout the country. The meat will probably be beef steak pounded thin, but veal works well here. Lime is squeezed over the meat and it is served with refried beans, salsa, guacamole, and spicy pickled jalapeños. Milanesa is also a favorite filling for tortas (Breaded Veal Sandwiches, page 123).

1 large egg
¹/₂ cup all-purpose flour
¹/₄ teaspoon salt, or to taste
¹/₈ teaspoon freshly ground pepper, or to taste
¹/₂ cup fine bread crumbs
4 thin veal steaks, or baby beef, pounded thin (¹/₄ inch)
Vegetable oil for frying
1 lime, quartered
Basic Refried Beans (page 462), or purchased refried beans
Classic Guacamole (page 23)
Fresh Salsa Mexicana (page 24), or purchased salsa
4 jarred pickled jalapeño chiles (en escabeche), seeded and thinly sliced

1. In a shallow soup plate, beat the egg very well. In a second soup plate mix the flour, salt, and pepper. Put the bread crumbs in a third soup plate. Line up the bowls in this order: flour, egg, and crumbs.

2. In a large nonstick skillet, heat oil to a depth of about ¼ inch. Dust the meat lightly with flour, dip into the beaten egg, and coat with bread crumbs. Put the coated meat on a plate lined with wax paper and refrigerate about 1 hour. Fry the meat until brown and crisp, 2 to 3 minutes on each side. Squeeze lime juice over each piece of meat. Serve on individual plates with beans, guacamole, salsa, and pickled jalapeños.

Veal in Sweet Red Pepper Sauce
Ternera en Salsa de Pimienta Dulce

Makes 4 servings

Roasted, peeled, and puréed red bell peppers (pimientas dulce) make a rich smooth sauce that blankets thin strips of sautéed veal. This is a rather sophisticated dish since veal is expensive. Rice with Corn (page 473) is a good accompaniment to go with the saucy meat.

2 medium red bell peppers, roasted, seeded, and peeled (page 8)
¹/₂ teaspoon ground cumin
¹/₂ cup canned fat-free reduced-sodium chicken broth
¹/₄ cup heavy cream
¹/₈ teaspoon crushed red pepper
¹/₂ teaspoon salt, or to taste
1 pound boneless veal scallopini, ¹/₄-inch thick
3 teaspoons olive oil
¹/₂ large white onion, thinly sliced
2 tablespoons chopped fresh cilantro

1. Roast, seed, and peel the red peppers. Coarsely chop and put in a blender. Add the cumin, chicken broth, cream, crushed pepper, and ¼ teaspoon of the salt. Blend until smooth. Pour the sauce into a bowl and reserve.

2. Cut the veal into short thin strips, about ½ inch × 2 inches. In a large nonstick skillet, heat the oil over medium heat. Cook the veal strips, stirring, until lightly browned, 3 to 4 minutes. Season with the remaining salt. Transfer to a plate.

3. Add the onion to the skillet and cook, stirring, until softened and limp, about 4 minutes. Return the meat to the pan. Add the reserved red pepper sauce and cook, stirring, until the sauce reduces and thickens to the consistency of heavy cream, 3 to 4 minutes. Stir in the cilantro. Adjust salt. Serve.

Veal Stew in Red Pumpkin Seed Sauce
Ternera en Pipian Rojo de Pepitas

Makes 6 servings

Mexican veal, or baby beef, makes tasty home-style stews for special meals, since baby beef is less available and more expensive than mature beef. This is an excellent dish when entertaining guests. It can be made ahead and reheated, which makes it even better. Serve with one of the cabbage salads in the salad chapter. Pineapple Salsa (page 41) goes very well, too.

Red Pumpkin Seed Sauce (page 53)
2 pounds boneless veal stew, cut into 1-inch pieces
¹/₂ teaspoon salt, or to taste
2 bay leaves
1 teaspoon dried oregano (Mexican variety preferred), crumbled
1 tablespoon olive oil
2 medium white onions, thinly sliced
12 baby red potatoes, scrubbed
3 medium carrots, peeled and sliced
1 cup peas, fresh or thawed if frozen
¹/₄ cup loosely packed chopped fresh cilantro

1. Prepare the pumpkin seed sauce. Cover and reserve. Put the veal into a large saucepan and barely cover with water. Add the salt, bay, and oregano. Bring to a boil, skimming as needed. Reduce the heat to low, cover and simmer until the meat is tender, about 1 hour. Remove the bay leaves and reserve meat in the pan off heat.

2. Heat the oil in a skillet over medium heat, and cook the onion, stirring, until it starts to brown, 4 to 5 minutes. Add to the veal along with the potatoes and carrots. Bring the meat and vegetables to a boil; then reduce heat to low, cover and simmer until the vegetables are tender, about 30 minutes.

3. With a ladle, remove all but about ½ cup of the liquid from the pan. Reserve for later use, if needed. Add the reserved pumpkin seed sauce to the stew. Bring to a boil; then reduce heat to low and simmer, uncovered, 5 minutes. Thin the sauce with reserved broth, if needed. Add the peas and cilantro. Cook 10 more minutes, stirring frequently. Adjust salt. Serve in shallow bowls.

Organ Meats

Liver with Onions, Raisins, and Jalapeños
Higado con Cebollas, Pasas, y Jalapeños

Makes 4 servings

Tender young calf's liver with sautéed onions, raisins, and pickled jalapeños is a fine combination from Veracruz for those who enjoy liver.

¹/₄ cup raisins

2 tablespoons olive oil

12 ounces calf's liver, thinly sliced

¹/₂ teaspoon salt, or to taste

Freshly ground pepper, to taste

1 large onion, thinly sliced

2 to 3 jarred pickled jalapeño chiles (en escabeche), seeded and thinly sliced

1. Put the raisins in a small bowl and cover with warm water to soften 10 minutes. Heat the oil in a large skillet over medium-high heat. Cook the liver until brown on both sides, but still pink inside, about 1 minute per side. Transfer the liver to a plate.

2. Reduce heat to medium and cook the onion in the same skillet until soft and brown, 8 to 10 minutes. Drain the raisins and add to the skillet along with the sliced chiles. Return the liver to the pan and heat through completely, about 2 minutes. Divide the liver among 4 plates. Spoon the onion mixture equally over the top. Serve at once.

Beef or Veal Tongue in Vinaigrette
Lengua en Fiambre

Makes 3 to 4 servings

A classic way beef or veal tongue is prepared throughout Mexico is cooked, cooled, then eaten in a sandwich or served on a cold meat plate called fiambre. *Usually tongue is served with marinated cooked vegetables. Other cold meats, such as sliced roast beef, are often added. I also like mustard and mayonnaise with tongue. Add whatever condiments you like.*

1 small garlic clove, mashed

1 teaspoon salt, or to taste

2 tablespoons white wine vinegar

¹/₄ cup olive oil

1 beef or veal tongue (about 1¹/₂ to 2 pounds)

¹/₂ small onion, cut in chunks

2 bay leaves

1 celery rib, sliced crosswise

1 teaspoon black peppercorns

Cold Vegetables in Vinaigrette (page 180) (optional)

Oval Mexican sandwich rolls (bolillos), or other sandwich rolls

1. In a small bowl, whisk together the garlic, ¹/₂ teaspoon of the salt, vinegar, and oil. Set aside.

2. Put the tongue, onion, bay leaf, celery, peppercorns, and remaining ¹/₂ teaspoon of salt in a large saucepan. Cover with water and bring to a boil. Reduce the heat to low, partially cover, and simmer until tender, about 1 hour for veal and 2 hours for beef. Drain and let cool.

3. When the tongue is completely cool, cut off all fat and gristle. Peel off the tough outer skin. Cut into thin slices and put in a shallow bowl. Add the vinaigrette and toss to coat. Drain the tongue, discarding the vinaigrette, and arrange on a serving platter, along with the cold vegetables, if desired. Serve with rolls.

Beef or Veal Tongue with Almond Sauce
Lengua Almendrada

Makes **4 to 6 servings**

Nowadays, tongue has become more acceptable in the United States than in the recent past. This is a classic Mexican way to serve tongue as an entrée.

1 beef or veal tongue (about 1¹/₂ to 2 pounds)

3 green onions, cut crosswise into 2-inch pieces

1 medium carrot, peeled and sliced

6 medium garlic cloves, sliced

1¹/₂ teaspoons salt

2 teaspoons vegetable oil

¹/₃ cup slivered blanched almonds

2 tablespoons finely chopped onion

1 medium tomato, cored and chopped

¹/₂ teaspoon ground cumin

¹/₄ teaspoon ground allspice

Pinch ground cloves

¹/₈ teaspoon crushed red pepper

1 cup canned fat-free reduced-sodium chicken broth

2 tablespoons bread crumbs

1 tablespoon cider vinegar

Parsley sprigs

1. In a large saucepan, place the tongue, onions, carrot, garlic, and 1 teaspoon of the salt. Add water to cover by about 1 inch. Bring to a boil over medium-high heat. Reduce heat to low, cover and simmer until tender, about 1 hour for veal and 2 hours for beef. Remove from the heat and let the tongue sit in the cooking liquid until cool enough to handle, about 20 minutes.

2. Meanwhile, heat the oil in a skillet and fry the almonds, stirring, until golden, 2 to 3 minutes. Take care not to burn. Transfer the nuts to a blender. In the same skillet, cook the onion, stirring, until it starts to brown, about 3 to 4 minutes. Add the tomato, cumin, allspice, cloves, pepper flakes, and the remaining ¹/₂ teaspoon of salt. Bring to a boil and cook, stirring, 1 minute. Transfer to the blender. Add the broth, bread crumbs, and vinegar. Blend until smooth. (There should still be a little texture.)

3. Transfer the sauce to a pan and bring to a boil. Reduce the heat to low, cover, and simmer 8 to 10 minutes to blend the flavors. Reserve in the pan off heat.

4. Preheat oven to 250°. Remove the tongue from the cooking liquid. Trim off all fat and gristle. Peel off the tough outer skin. Thinly slice the tongue and arrange, overlapping, on an oven-proof platter and place in 250° oven to keep warm. Reheat the sauce and spoon the sauce over the meat. Garnish with parsley and serve.

Fish *and* Shellfish

Baked Whole Fish and Fillets 379

Roasted Sea Bass Smothered in Onions and Tomatoes

Baked Fish Fillets with Almonds

Baked Fish Fillets with Citrus-Tequila Sauce

Baked Fish Fillets with Green Chiles

Fish Fillets Baked in Banana Leaves

Fish Fillets Baked Fisherman Style

Snapper Fillets in Packages

Fish, Shrimp, and Oysters Baked in Packages

Whole Trout Baked in Foil

Baked Whole Snapper

Sautéed, Fried, and Grilled Whole Fish and Fillets 386

Red Snapper Veracruzana

Sautéed Red Snapper with Mushrooms

Sautéed Snapper Fillets in Tomato and Mushroom Sauce

Sautéed Snapper Fillets with Banana Salsa

Sautéed Snapper with Lime Cream Sauce

Grilled Sea Bass in Red Chile Marinade

Sautéed Sea Bass with Pasilla Chile Sauce

Sautéed Sea Bass with Corn Mushroom

Seared Tuna Steaks with Roasted Tomato Sauce

Seared Tuna Steaks with Yellow Chile Salsa

Seared Tuna with Oregano and Garlic

Grilled Spiced Tuna Steaks with Red Peppers and Jicama

Grilled Swordfish with Tomato and Caper Sauce

Grilled Swordfish with Tomato-Orange Salsa

Sautéed Fish Fillets with Golden Garlic and Lime

Sautéed Fish Fillets with Avocado and Tomatillo Sauce

Sautéed Fish Fillets with Orange Butter Sauce

Sautéed Fish Fillets with
Poblano Chile Sauce

Sautéed Fish Fillets
with Olive Salsa

Sautéed Fish Fillets
with Plantains

Fried Fish in a Fluffy Egg Coat

Ensenada Fried Fish Fillets
with Lime Vinaigrette

Fried Whole Fish

Sautéed Halibut with
Orange and Mint Sauce

Spanish-Style Salt Cod

Sautéed Shark with
Fiery Cilantro-Mint Sauce

Sautéed Skate with Fresh Salsa

Sautéed Squid with Almonds

Grilled Salmon with
Mango-Avocado Salsa

Sautéed Salmon with
Creamy Corn Sauce
and Toasted Pumpkin Seeds

Pan-Fried Trout with
"Drunken" Sauce

Pan-Fried Trout
with Guacamole

Batter-Fried Catfish with
Chopped Radish Salad

Shellfish 404

Shrimp in Garlic Sauce I

Shrimp in Garlic Sauce II

Shrimp in Pumpkin Seed Sauce

Shrimp in Red Chile Sauce

Grilled Shrimp Skewers

Shrimp with Peppers
and Cheese

Shrimp with Tomatoes
and Cheese

Crab and Scallop Cakes

Blue Crabs with Salsa and
Chipotle Mayonnaise

Broiled Oysters, Guaymas Style

Grilled Lobster Tails

Scallops with
Chipotle Tomato Sauce

Scallops with Corn, Zucchini,
and Tomatoes

Scallops with Melon Salsa

Broiled Scallops with Spinach

Mixed Seafood,
Campeche Style

The waters along Mexico's more than 6,000 miles of coastline contain a wide variety of fish and shellfish that have enriched Mexican cooking for centuries.

Historians relate that fish were so treasured by the great Aztec leader, Moctezuma, that he had relays of runners carry fresh fish from Veracruz, on the east coast to the Valley of Mexico, the present site of Mexico City, to satisfy his cravings. They made the 250-mile trip in two to three days, keeping the fish fresh by packing them in snow brought down from the high peak, Orizaba, which was halfway along the trail.

Today, wonderful seafood dishes abound from the riches in the Gulf of Mexico on the east coast, in the Caribbean Sea along the coast of the southern tip state of Quintana Roo, and in the Sea of Cortez and the Pacific Ocean on the Baja Peninsula and along the west coast of Mexico. Among the great variety found along the Caribbean and Gulf Coast of Mexico are shellfish such as shrimp, soft-shell crab, lobster, and oysters, as well as squid, red snapper, tuna, and shark. Along the Pacific Coast and the Sea of Cortez there are swordfish, tuna, snapper, grouper, flounder, sea bass, crabs, and lobster, again, to mention some of many.

There are also many lakes, rivers, and streams within Mexico that provide fresh-water varieties of fish and shellfish, such as trout and catfish, fresh water prawns, and crayfish. The delicate native white fish of Lake Patzcuaro in the southwestern state of Michoacan has become rather scarce and expensive, but remains a favorite. And the fishermen can still be seen catching these and other kinds of fish with expansive "butterfly" nets, although it is no longer the main method of fishing.

The recipes for fish and shellfish in this chapter present authentic dishes and preparations found in Mexican homes and restaurants, but take into account that freshness ranks above using a certain kind of fish, so you can be flexible. The dishes you make will still be representative of the cuisine, and quite delicious if the fish is fresh and carefully prepared and accompanied by an authentic sauce or salsa.

Different regions of Mexico are known for recipes that have stood the test of time. Examples are: Red Snapper Veracruzana from Veracruz, on the Gulf coast (page 386); Fish Fillets Baked Fisherman Style from Yucatán, on the Caribbean coast (page 382); and Fish Tacos from Ensenada and Baja on the Pacific coast (page 97, in the Appetizers and Snacks chapter). There are also recipes here for dishes that are popular and common throughout the country, such as Shrimp in Garlic Sauce (pages 404–405), Fried Whole Fish (page 398), and Grilled Lobster Tails (page 410).

You'll also find recipes shared or inspired by today's Mexican chefs and restaurants that are known for creative *nueva cocina*, or cooking in the new style, like Sautéed Sea Bass with Corn Mushroom (page 390), Crab and Scallop Cakes (page 408), Sautéed Snapper with Lime Cream Sauce (page 389), and Grilled Salmon with Mango-Avocado Salsa (page 401).

Plain, or with wonderful sauces—baked, fried, or grilled—fish cooked Mexican-style is quick and delicious anytime.

Baked Whole Fish and Fillets

Roasted Sea Bass Smothered in Onions and Tomatoes
Robalo al Horno de Cebollas y Jitomates

Makes **4 servings**

Sea bass fillets baked under a flavorful cloak of sautéed onions and vine-ripened tomatoes is delicious fish, Veracruz-style.

3 tablespoons olive oil

2 medium white onions, thinly sliced

1/2 cup finely chopped flat-leaf parsley

3 tablespoons capers, drained but not rinsed

3 large garlic cloves, minced

1 canned chipotle chile en adobo, seeded and mashed

6 medium plum tomatoes, cored, seeded, and finely chopped

1/2 cup dry white wine

4 (6- to 7-ounce) sea bass fillets, each about 1-inch thick

1/2 teaspoon salt, or to taste

1. Preheat the oven to 500°. Heat the oil in a large skillet over medium-high heat. Add the onions and cook, stirring, until the onions soften, about 5 minutes. Then stir in half the parsley, and the capers, garlic, and chipotle, and cook 1 minute. Stir in the tomatoes and wine. Reduce heat to low and simmer 5 minutes.

2. Sprinkle the fish fillets with salt and arrange in an ovenproof baking dish just large enough to accommodate them in a single layer. Spoon the tomato mixture over the fish. (Reserve the skillet to reduce the sauce.) Cover the dish with aluminum foil and bake until the fish is opaque but still moist inside and just barely flakes when tested with a fork, about 12 minutes.

3. Transfer the fish to 4 dinner plates. Return the sauce to the reserved skillet and bring to a boil over high heat and cook until reduced slightly, about 3 minutes. Stir in the remaining parsley. Season with salt. Spoon the sauce equally over the fish on each plate. Serve at once.

Baked Fish Fillets with Almonds
Pescado con Almendras al Horno

Makes **4 servings**

A long time ago, in Puerto Vallarta, I ate small whole pink snapper prepared this way and was hooked, but since I'm seldom able to buy beautiful whole fish like those in the United States, I prepare the dish with fillets of Pacific snapper or rock cod. Accompany the fish with Mexican Rice with Carrots (page 473).

³/4 cup whole almonds with skins

4 (6- to 7-ounce) white fish fillets, each about ³/4-inch thick

¹/2 teaspoon salt

¹/4 teaspoon freshly ground pepper, or to taste

6 scallions, including about 3 inches of the green, thinly sliced into rounds

³/4 cup loosely packed coarsely chopped fresh cilantro

4 tablespoons unsalted butter

2 medium garlic cloves, finely chopped

1 to 2 serrano chiles, finely chopped with seeds

¹/4 cup fresh lime juice

1. In a small dry skillet, toast the almonds over medium heat, stirring frequently, until aromatic, about 5 minutes. (Take care not to let them burn.) Transfer to a plate. When the nuts are cool, finely chop them. Reserve.

2. Place the fish fillets in a greased baking dish just large enough to accommodate them in a single layer. Season with salt and pepper. Scatter the onions, cilantro, and reserved toasted almonds on top.

3. Preheat oven to 350°. In a small skillet, melt the butter. Add the garlic and chiles. Cook, stirring, about 20 seconds. Add the lime juice. Stir and immediately pour the mixture over the fish. Cover with foil and bake until the fish is opaque but still moist inside and just barely flakes when tested with a fork, about 20 minutes. Serve the fish hot with the sauce spooned over the top.

Baked Fish Fillets with Citrus-Tequila Sauce
Pescado al Horno con Salsa Limón y Tequila

Makes **4 servings**

On a steamy evening in Puerto Angel on the Pacific coast, my friends and I gathered to eat in a simple thatched-roof restaurant just steps from the beach. I ordered an ice cold cerveza (beer) and the "catch of the day"—in this case, baked fillets of red snapper. A simple sauce of citrus and tequila was spooned over the fish. Tequila adds a sweet and subtle fruitiness of the agave—from which it's made and mellows the tartness of the lime juice. The fish was served with a huge pile of French fries. This recipe was inspired by that meal; make it with your favorite "catch of the day."

3 large garlic cloves, minced

2 tablespoons olive oil

¹/2 teaspoon salt

4 (6- to 7-ounce) white fish fillets, each about ³/4-inch thick

2 tablespoons fresh orange juice

1 tablespoon fresh lime juice

1 tablespoon tequila

2 tablespoons finely chopped flat-leaf parsley

1. Preheat the oven to 400°. Mix half of the garlic with 1 tablespoon of the olive oil and the salt. Rub all over the fish, and place in a single layer on a baking dish and let the fish stand at room temperature about 20 minutes. Bake the fish, uncovered, 12 to 15 minutes, or until the fish is opaque but still moist inside and just barely flakes when tested with a fork.

2. While the fish bakes, heat the remaining tablespoon of oil in a medium skillet, and cook the remaining garlic until it starts to brown, 45 seconds. Add the orange juice, lime juice, and tequila. Bring to a boil, and immediately stir in the parsley. Remove the pan from the heat. Place the cooked fish on individual serving plates. Stir the fish juices from the baking pan into the sauce. Spoon the sauce over the fish. Serve at once.

Baked Fish Fillets with Green Chiles
Pescado al Horno con Chiles Verdes

Makes **4 servings**

Here is a showy dish with great flavor that has a topping of green chiles, sunflower seeds, and capers. The inspiration came from El Sacramonte restaurant in Guadalajara. Serve with Fresh Corn Salsa (page 25) or Tomato and Corn Salsa (page 26).

4 fresh Anaheim or California chiles

2 tablespoons dry-roasted and salted sunflower seeds

1 medium garlic clove, pressed

¹/₄ teaspoon freshly ground pepper, or to taste

2 tablespoons extra-virgin olive oil

2 tablespoons capers, drained and chopped

4 (6- to 7-ounce) rock cod or halibut fillets, each about ³/₄-inch thick

¹/₂ teaspoon salt, or to taste

Cherry or grape tomatoes

Lime wedges

1. Preheat the oven broiler. Roast the chiles on the top oven shelf until charred and blistered all over, about 5 minutes. Transfer to a plastic bag and let steam 6 to 8 minutes.

2. Lower the oven temperature to 400°. Peel the chiles and remove the stems. Discard the seeds. Rinse the chiles and cut into ¹/₂-inch pieces. Put in a bowl.

3. With a mortar and pestle, in a small bowl with a heavy wooden spoon or (briefly) in a food processor, crush the sunflower seeds, garlic, and pepper together. Put in the bowl with the chiles. Add the olive oil and capers.

4. Put the fish on a foil-lined baking sheet. Season lightly with salt. Spread the chile mixture evenly on top of each fillet. Bake the fish without turning, 10 to 12 minutes, or until the flesh is opaque but still moist inside and just barely flakes when tested with a fork. Garnish with cherry tomatoes and lime wedges.

Fish Fillets Baked in Banana Leaves

Pescado al Horno Empapelado

Makes **4 servings**

The flavors and traditions of Yucatán are the inspiration behind this dish. Firm white fish fillets lightly seasoned with garlic, lime, and allspice, are wrapped in banana leaves and baked to succulence with a wonderful subtle flavor. Rock cod, snapper, or mahimahi are good fillet choices. Roasted Potatoes and Onions, Yucatán Style (page 448) and Banana Salsa (page 40) go well with the fish. Banana leaves can be found in Latin-American and Asian grocery stores, or use two layers of foil instead of one as the wrapper.

4 (6- to 7-ounce) firm fish fillets, each about ³/₄-inch thick

2 medium garlic cloves, pressed

2 tablespoons fresh lime juice

¹/₈ teaspoon ground allspice

¹/₂ teaspoon salt, or to taste

¹/₄ teaspoon freshly ground pepper, or to taste

2 teaspoons olive oil

2 tablespoons coarsely chopped fresh cilantro

2 banana leaves, cut into 15-inch squares

1. Preheat oven to 375°. Put the fish fillets on a plate. In a small bowl, make a paste of the garlic, lime juice, allspice, salt, pepper, and oil. Rub the mixture all over the fish.

2. Lay 1 12-inch-long piece of foil on a flat surface and lay 1 banana leaf on top of the foil. Put 2 fish fillets in the center of the banana leaf. Put half of the cilantro on the fish. Fold the banana leaf to enclose the fish in a package. Then fold the foil around both sides of the banana package to seal tightly so no steam escapes. Place folded side up on a baking sheet. Repeat with a second 12-inch square of foil, and the remaining banana leaf and fish.

3. Bake 15 to 20 minutes, or until the fish is opaque but still moist inside and just barely flakes when tested with a fork. (Test one package for doneness.) To serve, open the packages and transfer 1 fish fillet to each of 4 serving plates. Spoon the juices over the fish. Serve hot.

Fish Fillets Baked Fisherman Style

Tikinxic

Makes **4 servings**

Red snapper, grouper, or mahimahi are good choices for this typical Yucatán dish. Each serving is wrapped in banana leaves and foil. The sealed packages containing the fish and other ingredients are often cooked over coals on the beach in Yucatán in the traditional style of the local fishermen. In this recipe the fish is baked in a conventional oven with very good results. Making your own Yucatán Red Seasoning Paste (recado rojo) gives the fish the most authentic flavor, but purchased achiote paste, available in Mexican markets, can be substituted in a pinch.

2 tablespoons Yucatán Red Seasoning Paste (page 23) or purchased achiote paste

4 (6- to 7-ounce) firm fish fillets, each about ³/₄-inch thick

¹/₂ teaspoon salt

2 large garlic cloves, thinly sliced

2 tablespoons fresh orange juice

2 tablespoons fresh lime juice

¹/₂ teaspoon dried oregano (Mexican variety preferred), crumbled

¹/₂ teaspoon ground cumin

4 (12-inch) banana leaf squares

2 medium tomatoes, sliced

1 medium red or white onion, thinly sliced

4 *güero* (yellow) chiles, seeded and thinly sliced

12 pitted green olives, sliced

2 tablespoons unsalted butter

1. Prepare the seasoning paste, if using home-made. Then, sprinkle the fish lightly with salt. Set aside on a plate. In a blender, purée the garlic, seasoning paste, orange and lime juices, oregano, and cumin. Rub the marinade all over the fish. Cover and refrigerate for about 1 hour.

2. Preheat the oven to 350°. To assemble the fish packages, lay four 12-inch-long pieces of foil on a flat surface. Lay a banana leaf on top of each piece of foil. Put 1 fish fillet in the center of each banana leaf. Layer the tomato, onion, chile, olives, and butter equally on top of each fillet. Fold the banana leaf, overlapping, to completely enfold the fish. Then fold the foil completely around the banana package. Seal tightly so no steam escapes.

3. Lay the packages on a baking sheet. Bake 25 minutes, or until the fish is opaque but still moist inside and just barely flakes when tested with a fork. (Test one for doneness. Reclose to serve.) Serve the fish in the packages, to be opened at the table.

Snapper Fillets in Packages
Huachinango Empapelado

Makes 4 servings

Sealing food in packages is an easy way to lock in flavors and keep food moist and is an age-old method of cooking in different regions of Mexico. This recipe for fish baked in a package comes from the beautiful San Angel Inn in Mexico City. Serve with Mexican Rice (page 472). Green Beans with Mushrooms (page 453) also go well with the fish.

2 teaspoons unsalted butter

2 medium tomatoes, chopped

1 small white onion, very thinly sliced

2 serrano chiles, minced with seeds

1/4 cup lightly packed chopped fresh cilantro

4 (6- to 7-ounce) red snapper or rock cod fillets, each about 3/4-inch thick

1/2 teaspoon salt, or to taste

Freshly ground pepper, to taste

2 teaspoons olive oil

2 teaspoons dry white wine

1. Preheat the oven to 450°. Lay 4 (12-inch-long) pieces of aluminum foil on a flat surface. Rub about 1/2 teaspoon of butter in the center of each piece. On 1/2 of each piece, evenly distribute the tomatoes, onion, serranos, and cilantro. Lay 1 fish fillet on top of the vegetables. Season with salt and pepper. Drizzle each fillet with 1/4 teaspoon of olive oil and 1/4 teaspoon of wine. Fold over the foil and crimp the edges to make a tight seal.

2. Place the packages on a large baking sheet and bake 20 minutes or until fish is opaque but still moist inside and just barely flakes when tested with a fork. (Test one for doneness. Reclose to serve.) Lay a closed package on each of 4 serving plates to be opened at the table. Serve hot.

Fish, Shrimp, and Oysters Baked in Packages
Pez Torre

Makes **4 servings**

Chef Joaquim Ocampo Castillo, of Casa Vieja in Tlaquepaque on the outskirts of Guadalajara, shared this wonderful recipe. We made our first visit to the region more than thirty years ago, and we still join the throngs of visitors who enjoy the locally made folk art, modern art, ceramics, jewelry, and crafts of all kinds. Many shops and restaurants are conveniently located along the pedestrian-only street through the center of town, so rest and sustenance in a number of good restaurants are only steps away. Casa Vieja is one of our favorites.

4 teaspoons unsalted butter

4 plum tomatoes, thinly sliced (about 6 slices each)

1 small white onion, halved and thinly sliced

4 (6- to 7-ounce) white fish fillets, each about 3/4-inch thick

12 medium shrimp, peeled and deveined

8 medium oysters

2 tablespoons chopped fresh cilantro

1 tablespoon chopped fresh parsley

Salt and freshly ground pepper, to taste

4 teaspoons dry white wine

4 teaspoons fresh lime juice

2 teaspoons olive oil

1. Preheat oven to 450°. Lay out 4 pieces of 12-inch-long aluminum foil on a work surface. Coat the center of each piece of foil with about 1 teaspoon butter. Place about 6 tomato slices, overlapping, on each piece of foil and continue to layer all remaining ingredients, evenly divided, on top of each other on the foil in the order listed. Fold the foil together for each, crimping the edges to seal into snug packages.

2. Place on a baking sheet and cook about 15 to 18 minutes, or until the fish is opaque but still moist inside and just barely flakes when tested with a fork. (Test one for doneness. Reclose to serve.) Serve hot, in the package.

Whole Trout Baked in Foil
Trucha Empapelada

Makes **4 servings**

Cooking foods in foil is very popular in Mexico, for both home cooks and chefs. Instead of the classic way of wrapping and steaming in corn husks or banana leaves, or leaves from the maguey plant, foil offers an alternative that's quicker and easier. The aromas and flavors of the real leaves may be missing, but foods cooked in foil are aromatic, juicy, and very delicious. Fish is exceptionally good cooked this way. Whole trout from a fish market are already cleaned and weigh about 1 pound.

4 whole scaled and cleaned trout (about 1 pound each), rinsed

Salt, to taste

4 medium tomatoes, cored and sliced

1/2 cup thinly sliced white onion

2 jalapeño chiles, seeded, veins removed, and sliced into thin strips

12 fresh epazote leaves, or substitute fresh cilantro sprigs

4 teaspoons unsalted butter

4 teaspoons dry white wine

1. Preheat oven to 375°. Lay out 4 pieces of 12-inch-long foil, each large enough to completely wrap 1 fish. Season each fish inside and out with salt. Lay 1 fish in the center of each piece of foil. Layer the tomatoes, onion, chiles, and epazote evenly among the fish. Put 1 teaspoon butter on top of each. Drizzle 1 teaspoon of wine over each fish. Fold the foil over the fish and crimp the edges to make a snug package.

2. Put the 4 packages on a baking sheet and cook in the center of the oven 22 to 25 minutes, or until the fish is opaque inside and just barely flakes when tested with a fork. (Test one for doneness. Reclose to serve.) Serve hot in the foil packages.

Baked Whole Snapper
Huachinango al Horno

Makes **4 servings**

Serving a large whole fish is always dramatic. In Mexico's coastal cities the fish vendors, an integral part of public markets, always have whole fish. North of the border you may have to order whole fish from a good fish market. I find that red snapper, Pacific snapper, or rockfish are good choices for baked fish, but any whole fish that you like or that is available works in this recipe. Have the fishmonger scale and clean the fish. Serve with Mexican Rice (page 472).

¹/₄ **cup olive oil, plus extra to brush on the pan**
**1 3- to 4-pound scaled and cleaned whole snapper
   or rockfish, rinsed**
6 medium garlic cloves, mashed
**1 teaspoon dried oregano (Mexican variety
   preferred), crumbled**
1 teaspoon salt
¹/₄ **teaspoon freshly ground pepper**
¹/₄ **cup dry white wine**
Lime wedges

1. Preheat oven to 450°. Line a large rimmed baking pan with aluminum foil. Brush foil with oil. Make 4 crosswise slashes to the bone on each side of the fish.

2. In a bowl, the garlic, oregano, salt, pepper, wine, and ¼ cup of oil until smooth. Rub the mixture all over the inside and outside of the fish. Lay the fish on the foil in the baking pan.

3. Cover with foil and bake 25 minutes. Uncover and bake until the top browns a little, another 8 to 10 minutes. Remove the pan from the oven and let the fish stand 8 to 10 minutes. It can be somewhat awkward to remove the fish from the pan without it splitting, so serve from the pan, if you wish. Or use 2 wide spatulas to carefully lift the fish onto a large platter. Remove the top skin, if desired, by inserting the knife blade under the skin to lift gently off. (The skin will separate easily from the cooked fish.) Using two forks, separate the fish into portions and serve with lime wedges.

Sautéed, Fried, and Grilled Whole Fish and Fillets

Red Snapper Veracruzana
Huachinango Veracruzana

Makes 4 servings

The state of Veracruz is long and thin with a coastline of more than 400 miles along the Gulf of Mexico. Inland, the mountains predominate. From the foothills come vanilla, coffee, apples, and pears. Citrus and bananas grow in abundance in the coastal lowlands. There is great variety, but it's the seafood that first comes to mind when thinking about the foods of Veracruz.

Red snapper prepared in the Veracruz style, is a favorite all over Mexico. The flavors of capers, green olives, and olive oil reflect the Spanish influence in this famous dish, which is often prepared with a whole fish as well as individual fillets. Jalapeño chiles, originally from the area around Jalapa, the capital of the state of Veracruz, add their spicy taste to the dish. Many Mexican cooks prefer large capers to small ones. You may use either kind. If red snapper is not available, other white fish fillets, such as Pacific snapper or rock cod, can be substituted.

4 skinless red snapper or other white fish fillets (about 1 1/2 pounds)
1 tablespoon fresh lime juice
1/2 teaspoon salt
2 tablespoons olive oil
1 medium white onion, chopped
3 medium garlic cloves, minced
3 medium ripe tomatoes, peeled and chopped
4 jarred pickled jalapeño chiles (en escabeche), seeded and cut in strips, 1/8-inch wide
8 pimento-stuffed green olives, sliced crosswise
1/2 teaspoon dried oregano (Mexican variety preferred), crumbled
1/4 teaspoon dried thyme
1/4 teaspoon ground cinnamon (Mexican canela or Ceylon cinnamon preferred)
2 tablespoons drained capers (large or small)
2 tablespoons chopped fresh flat-leaf parsley

1. Place fish fillets in a single row on a large plate. Sprinkle with lime juice and salt. Let stand about 10 minutes.

2. In a medium nonstick skillet, heat the oil over medium heat. Add the fish and cook 2 minutes per side. Remove to a plate. In the same pan, cook the onion stirring, about 3 minutes, or until it begins to brown. Add the garlic and cook, stirring, about 1 minute. Add the tomatoes, jalapeños, olives, cinnamon, oregano, and capers. Bring to a boil. Reduce the heat to low.

3. Carefully return the fish to the pan and gently spoon the sauce over the fish. Simmer until the fish is opaque inside and just barely flakes when tested with a fork, 6 to 8 minutes. Serve hot, sprinkled with parsley.

Sautéed Red Snapper with Mushrooms
Huachinango con Hongos

Makes **4 servings**

I enjoyed this dish during lunch with friends in a small seaside restaurant along the Pacific coast near Puerto Vallarta. The cook had made good use of fresh mushrooms that were available at the public market, and even though mushrooms are not a basic food in the region, modern Puerto Vallarta has ingredients from everywhere. If you like mushrooms, you'll love this dish. Any firm white fish fillets, such as rock cod, sea bass, or even halibut, may be substituted for the snapper; the freshest being the best choice.

2 tablespoons unsalted butter, at room temperature

1 jarred pickled jalapeño chile (en escabeche), seeded and finely chopped

1 tablespoon tomato paste

1/4 cup loosely packed chopped fresh cilantro

4 (6- to 7-ounce) red snapper or other white fish fillets, each about 3/4-inch thick

1/4 teaspoon salt, or to taste

1/8 teaspoon freshly ground pepper, or to taste

2 tablespoons olive oil

1/2 medium white onion, thinly sliced

8 medium white or brown mushrooms, thinly sliced

2 scallions, including 2 inches of green, sliced into thin rounds

1 medium garlic clove, chopped

1/2 cup canned fat-free reduced-sodium chicken broth

1 medium tomato, seeded and cubed

1. In a medium bowl, blend together with a fork the butter, jalapeños, tomato paste, and cilantro to make a paste.

2. Season the fish with the salt and pepper. Heat the oil in a nonstick skillet over medium-high heat, and fry the fish 3 to 4 minutes per side, or until golden brown on the outside and opaque but still moist inside when tested with a fork. Remove the fish to a platter, cover, and reserve.

3. To the same skillet add the onion, mushrooms, scallions, and garlic. Cook, stirring, 2 minutes over high heat. Stir in the butter mixture, and add the broth. Continue cooking over high heat until the sauce reduces slightly, about 2 minutes. Adjust seasoning. Add the fresh tomato and heat through, about 1 minute. Spoon the sauce over the fish. Serve hot.

Sautéed Snapper Fillets in Tomato and Mushroom Sauce
Huachinango Entomatado

Makes **4 servings**

Chef Francisco Cisneros of Guaymas restaurant in Tiburon, California, shared this recipe. The restaurant offers fresh seafood dishes from Guaymas, Mexico, a fishing village on the Sea of Cortez. Serve the fish over cooked white rice.

¹/₂ **cup Basic Fish Stock (page 215) or canned chicken broth**

¹/₂ **cup Tomato–Jalapeño Chile Butter (page 18)**

2 tablespoons olive oil

4 (6- to 7-ounce) snapper fillets, each about ³/₄-inch thick

¹/₂ **medium white onion, thinly sliced**

1 medium garlic clove, finely chopped

¹/₄ **teaspoon dried oregano (Mexican variety preferred), crumbled**

8 medium mushrooms, thinly sliced

1 medium tomato, seeded and finely chopped

¹/₂ **green bell pepper, cut into thin strips**

Cilantro sprigs

Lime wedges

1. Prepare the fish stock if using homemade. Meanwhile, prepare the tomato-chile butter. Then, preheat the oven to 375°. Heat the oil in a large nonstick skillet over medium-high heat and fry the fish about 2 minutes per side or until it is lightly browned, but not cooked through.

2. Transfer the fish to an ovenproof baking dish and finish cooking in the oven until the fish is opaque but still moist inside and just barely flakes when tested with a fork, 8 to 10 minutes.

3. Meanwhile, in the same skillet, cook the onion over medium heat until it softens, about 3 minutes. Add the garlic and oregano. Cook 1 minute. Add remaining ingredients. Cook, stirring, over medium-high heat 3 minutes more.

4. Stir in the reserved tomato-chile butter and continue to cook about 2 to 3 minutes more, or until the sauce thickens slightly. To serve, place 1 fish fillet on each of 4 plates. Spoon the cooked sauce over the fish on each plate. Garnish the plates with cilantro and lime wedges. Serve hot.

Sautéed Snapper Fillets with Banana Salsa
Huachinango con Salsa de Plátano

Makes **4 servings**

Fresh Pacific snapper or other fish fillets go very well with a salsa made of ripe bananas. The sweetness of the bananas is balanced by the tartness of lime juice. Crunchy red bell pepper and spicy serrano chile add contrast and texture, and fresh mint adds a refreshing note to the salsa. I like to serve this unusual combination with black beans. The beans can be cooked a day ahead and reheated. A plate of crisp raw vegetables such as cucumbers, radishes, and carrots are a good addition to the meal.

Banana Salsa (page 40)

2 tablespoons olive oil

4 (6- to 7-ounce) snapper fillets, each about ³/₄-inch thick

¹/₄ **teaspoon salt, or to taste**

¹/₈ **teaspoon freshly ground pepper, or to taste**

1 tablespoon finely chopped fresh parsley

1. Prepare the banana salsa. Cover and refrigerate. (The salsa is best made no more than 1 hour before serving.)

2. Heat the oil over medium heat in a large nonstick skillet and fry the fish 3 to 4 minutes per side, or until golden brown on the outside and opaque but still moist inside and just barely flakes when tested with a fork. Season with salt and pepper. Sprinkle with parsley and serve with the banana salsa.

Sautéed Snapper with Lime Cream Sauce
Huachinango con Crema de Limón
Makes 4 servings

Zihuatanejo and Ixtapa on the Pacific coast in the state of Guerrero, are popular seaside getaways only 4 miles apart. Zihuatanejo, with its wide bay, has a long history as a trading port. In the early 1500s, Spanish ships loaded timber and other products in the harbor to be sent to Asia via the Philippines, and returning vessels carried spices, rice, fabrics, and the first coconut palms from the Philippines. Ixtapa was developed in the 1970s to be a luxurious vacation destination with a string of resort hotels along a stretch of beautiful white beaches.

Fish fillets with rich lime cream sauce is a modern dish from the dining room of the Sheraton-Ixtapa hotel.

4 (6-ounce) Pacific snappers, or other firm
    white fish fillets

1/2 teaspoon salt, or to taste

1 tablespoon olive oil or vegetable oil

1 tablespoon unsalted butter

3 thinly sliced green onions, including 3 inches
    of the green

1 medium garlic clove, minced

1/4 cup lightly packed chopped fresh cilantro

1/2 serrano chile, minced with seeds

1/4 cup canned fat-free reduced-sodium chicken broth

1/2 cup heavy cream

2 tablespoons fresh lime juice

1. Preheat the oven to 200°. Season the snapper fillets with salt. Heat the oil in a large nonstick skillet over high heat. Cook the fish about 3 minutes per side or until it is golden brown on the outside, opaque but still moist inside, and just barely flakes when tested with a fork. Transfer to a platter. Keep warm in the oven.

2. Melt the butter in the same skillet and cook the onions, garlic, cilantro, and chile over medium-heat until wilted and fragrant, about 1 minute. Add the broth and cream. Bring to a boil and cook, stirring, until the sauce reduces and thickens, about 2 minutes. Stir in the lime juice. Adjust salt. Serve the fish hot, with the sauce spooned on top.

Grilled Sea Bass in Red Chile Marinade
Robalo Asado en Adobo
Makes 4 servings

One of the newer and easiest ways to cook boneless fish fillets is on a stovetop grill pan. The raised ridges on the pan make an attractive pattern on the fish. A nonstick skillet can also be used. The spicy red chile paste in this dish colors the exterior of the fish in beautiful contrast to the white interior and hits the taste buds with hot flavor. Other firm white fish fillets, such as swordfish or halibut, are also excellent in this recipe. Mango-Avocado Salsa (page 39) goes well with the fish.

3 to 4 tablespoons Red Chile Paste (page 20)

4 (6- to 7-ounce) sea bass fillets, each about
    3/4-inch thick

2 teaspoons olive oil

1. Prepare the adobo. Then, trim the skin off the fish, if any, and thinly spread the chile paste all over the flesh. Cover and let marinate at least 1 hour and up to 6 hours.

2. Heat a stovetop grill pan or nonstick skillet over medium heat. Brush the pan and the fish lightly with the olive oil. Lay the fish on the hot pan, and cook about 4 to 5 minutes per side, or until the fish has nicely browned grill marks on the outside, is opaque but still moist inside, and just barely flakes when tested with a fork. Serve hot.

Sautéed Sea Bass with Pasilla Chile Sauce
Robalo con Salsa de Chile Pasilla

Makes 4 servings

Sea bass or other firm white fish, such as sword-fish or halibut, are my choices for this unusual dish from the Pacific coast of Mexico. The fish is served hot on a bed of crisp chopped lettuce with the room-temperature sauce spooned over the top. The temperature contrasts of the com-ponents make it important to serve the dish as soon as it's assembled, or the lettuce will lose crispness and the fish will start to cool. (The sauce can be made up to 5 days ahead. Store, covered, in the refrigerator until shortly before serving. Chop the lettuce ahead and refrigerate until ready to assemble the dish.) Black beans and fried plantains go very well with the fish.

4 (6- to 7-ounce) sea bass fillets,
    each about ³/₄-inch thick

2 tablespoons fresh lime juice

¹/₄ teaspoon salt

Pasilla Chile Sauce (page 26)

1 tablespoon vegetable oil

2 cups chopped lettuce, such as romaine
    or iceberg

2 medium tomatoes, thinly sliced

1. Put the fish fillets on a plate. Drizzle with lime juice and sprinkle with salt. Cover and refrigerate about 30 minutes. Prepare the chile sauce while the fish marinates.

2. Heat the oil over medium heat in a large non-stick skillet and cook the fish 3 to 4 minutes per side, or until it is lightly browned on the outside, opaque but still moist inside, and just barely flakes when tested with a fork. Serve the fish on a bed of chopped lettuce with the sauce spooned on top. Garnish with sliced tomatoes.

Sautéed Sea Bass with Corn Mushroom
Robalo con Cuitlacoche

Makes 4 servings

Cuitlacoche *(also spelled* huitlacoche*) is a gray-to-black fungus, somewhat like a mush-room, that grows on corn ears during the rainy season in Mexico.* Cuitlacoche *is very popular in cooking and is used extensively the way mushrooms are. The exotic mushroom-like taste reminds some people of truffles, while others just say the taste is exquisite, but hard to describe. I agree with both. Chef Felix Trejo of El Campanario restaurant in San Miguel de Allende shared this recipe for fresh sea bass that he serves on a bed of* cuitlacoche.

In the United States, canned cuitlacoche *can be found in some Mexican markets. Of course, nothing beats fresh, so keep your eye out for it since it may become more available as more people discover its exotic rich flavor. (See Mail-Order Sources for Ingredients, page 620.)*

1 (about 8-ounce) can cuitlacoche

3 teaspoons unsalted butter

¹/₂ medium white onion, finely chopped

1 small garlic clove, finely chopped

1 tablespoon chopped fresh epazote leaves,
    or 1 teaspoon dried epazote

¹/₄ teaspoon dried oregano (Mexican variety
    preferred), crumbled

¹/₂ teaspoon salt, or to taste

¹/₈ teaspoon freshly ground pepper, or to taste

3 teaspoons olive oil

4 (6- to 7-ounce) sea bass fillets,
    each about ³/₄-inch thick

1 medium tomato, seeded and finely diced

¹/₂ avocado (Hass variety preferred), peeled and
    finely diced

1 tablespoons fresh lime juice

1. Drain the excess liquid from the can of cuitlacoche, but do not rinse. Coarsely chop the cuitlacoche and reserve it in a bowl.

2. Heat the butter in a medium skillet and cook the onion until transparent, about 3 minutes. Add the garlic, epazote, and oregano. Cook, stirring, 2 minutes. Add the reserved cuitlacoche, ¼ teaspoon of the salt and the pepper. Simmer the mixture, stirring frequently, 4 to 5 minutes, to blend the flavors. Reserve in the pan off heat.

3. Heat the olive oil in a large nonstick skillet over medium-high heat. Add the fish and cook 3 to 4 minutes per side, or until it is golden brown on the outside, opaque but still moist inside, and just barely flakes when tested with a fork. Season with the remaining ¼ teaspoon of salt. Reheat the cuitlacoche mixture and divide it equally among 4 serving plates and top each with 1 fish fillet. Sprinkle the fish with the diced tomato and avocado and drizzle with a little lime juice. Serve hot.

Seared Tuna Steaks with Roasted Tomato Sauce
Atún Asada con Salsa de Jitomate Casera

Makes **4 servings**

La Capilla, *an elegant restaurant in San Miguel de Allende turns out intriguing* nueva cocina *dishes and continental dishes as well. For this dish, the tuna was firm, fresh, and perfectly cooked. Tuna is best when cooked until both sides are seared and the inside is still pink and tender. You can cook it longer, but the tuna will be dryer and less flavorful. The tomato sauce can be made ahead and reheated.*

Basic Roasted Tomato Sauce (page 42)
4 (6-ounce) tuna steaks, each about ³/₄-inch thick
2 teaspoons olive oil
¹/₄ teaspoon salt, or to taste
Freshly ground pepper, to taste
Lime wedges
Cilantro sprigs

1. Prepare the tomato sauce. Reserve in the pan off heat, or if made ahead, transfer to a covered container and refrigerate for up to 3 days.

2. Brush the tuna with oil and season with salt and pepper. Heat a stovetop grill pan or a non-stick skillet over medium-high heat. Cook the fish about 3 minutes per side or until it is lightly browned on the outside and until barely pink inside. (If you prefer tuna to be opaque inside, cook the first side 4 minutes, and the second side 3 minutes, or until barely opaque inside.)

3. Reheat the sauce. Serve the tuna with a little sauce spooned over each serving. Garnish with lime wedges and cilantro sprigs. Pass the remaining sauce at the table.

Seared Tuna Steaks with Yellow Chile Salsa
Atún con Salsa de Chile Guëro

Makes **4 servings**

Ensenada is a port city on the Pacific coast of Baja where fishing is an important industry. The fish market is filled with stalls selling stacks of just-caught tuna and many other varieties of seafood. When you see great looking fresh tuna in your store or market, try this delicious combination of pan-grilled or fried tuna steaks with yellow chile and tomatillo salsa.

Yellow Chile Salsa (page 33)
4 (6-ounce) tuna steaks, each about ³/₄-inch thick
¹/₂ teaspoon salt
1 tablespoon olive oil

1. Prepare the yellow salsa. If made ahead, cover and refrigerate until shortly before serving. Season the tuna with salt and brush all over with olive oil.

2. Heat a large stovetop grill pan or nonstick skillet over medium-high heat. Add the tuna and cook about 3 minutes per side or until it is lightly browned on the outside and still pink inside. Serve hot with the salsa. (If you prefer tuna to be opaque inside, cook the first side 4 minutes, and the second side 3 minutes, or until barely opaque inside.)

Seared Tuna with Oregano and Garlic
Atún Asada con Oregano y Ajo

Makes **4 servings**

El Campanario restaurant in San Miguel de Allende takes pride in its fresh fish offerings. Before you order, a large tray of fresh fish of the day is brought to the table for inspection. I ordered tuna steak with this bold and fabulous

oregano and garlic sauce. In Mexico, a molcajete (traditional basalt mortar) would often be used to mash the sauce ingredients, but in the United States you can use a regular mortar and pestle or mash the garlic with a garlic press or the side of a heavy-bladed chef's knife, then mix it with the other ingredients.

Maggi is a concentrated seasoning extract that's used a lot in Mexico to enhance flavors in sauces, soups, and stews; look for it in Mexican markets here or substitute Worcestershire sauce; it's not the same but adds good flavor.

1 tablespoon dried oregano (Mexican variety preferred), crumbled
1 large garlic clove, finely chopped
1 teaspoon Maggi seasoning extract or Worcestershire sauce
¹/₂ teaspoon salt
2¹/₂ tablespoons extra-virgin olive oil
1 tablespoon fresh lime juice
1 tablespoon finely chopped fresh flat-leaf parsley
¹/₄ teaspoon freshly ground pepper, or to taste
4 (6-ounce) tuna steaks, each about ³/₄-inch thick

1. With a mortar and pestle, mash the oregano, garlic, Maggi, and salt together to make a paste and scrape it into a small bowl. Add 2 tablespoons of the olive oil, lime juice, parsley, and pepper. Whisk well to blend and set aside.

2. Heat a large nonstick skillet over medium-high heat. Brush the tuna on both sides with the remaining ¹/₂ tablespoon of oil. Cook the tuna about 3 minutes per side or until it is lightly browned on the outside and still pink inside. (If you prefer tuna to be opaque inside, cook the first side 4 minutes, and the second side 3 minutes, or until barely opaque inside.) Transfer the fish to 4 plates. Add the garlic sauce to the skillet. Cook, stirring, about 45 to 50 seconds. Spoon over the fish and serve.

Grilled Spiced Tuna Steaks with Red Peppers and Jicama
Atún Asada con Chiles Dulce y Jicama

Makes **4 servings**

Yucatán dry spice rub lends a bold and spicy taste to tuna steaks that are quickly seared in a stovetop grill pan. The sautéed red bell pepper and jicama makes the tuna different, delicious, and decidedly new in style.

2 tablespoons Yucatán Dry Spice Rub (page 21)
4 (6-ounce) tuna steaks, each about ³/₄-inch thick
1 tablespoons olive oil
¹/₂ teaspoon salt, or to taste
Red Bell Peppers and Jicama (page 431)

1. Prepare the spice rub and measure out 2 tablespoons. (The remaining spice rub keeps indefinitely in a covered container stored with other spices.) Brush the tuna on both sides with the oil. Season lightly with salt. Put the tuna steaks on a large plate. Season each steak evenly with the spice rub and press to rub it in. Let the tuna stand for about 10 minutes.

2. Meanwhile, prepare the peppers and jicama. Keep warm. Heat a stovetop grill pan over medium-high heat until hot. Put the fish on the pan and cook about 3 minutes per side, or until it is lightly browned on the outside and still pink inside. (If you prefer tuna to be opaque inside, cook the first side 4 minutes, and the second side 3 minutes, or until barely opaque inside.) Transfer the fish to serving plates. Top each tuna steak equally with the red peppers and jicama. Serve at once.

Grilled Swordfish with Tomato and Caper Sauce
Pez Espada Asada con Salsa de Jitomate y Alcaparras

Makes **4 servings**

Along the Pacific Coast and Baja regions of Mexico, locally-caught swordfish is prepared in just about every way. For this recipe, the fish can be grilled over coals or on a stovetop grill pan. The accompanying sauce can be made while the fish marinates.

4 (6-ounce) swordfish steaks
¹/₄ cup dry white wine
1 tablespoon fresh lime juice
1 teaspoon Maggi seasoning extract or
**   Worcestershire sauce**
1 medium garlic clove, mashed
1 tablespoon olive oil, plus extra to brush on the fish
1 teaspoon unsalted butter
¹/₄ medium white onion, chopped
2 medium tomatoes, peeled and finely chopped
2 teaspoons drained small capers
1 serrano chile, minced with seeds
2 tablespoons chopped fresh cilantro
¹/₂ teaspoon salt, or to taste
¹/₈ teaspoon freshly ground pepper, or to taste

1. Put the swordfish in a large glass baking dish. Mix the wine, lime juice, Maggi, and garlic in a small bowl and pour over the fish. Turn the fish to coat with the marinade. Cover and refrigerate about 1 hour.

2. Meanwhile, heat the oil and butter in a medium skillet over medium heat and cook the onion until it starts to brown, about 4 minutes. Add the tomatoes, and cook, stirring, until most of the juices evaporate. Add the capers, serrano chile, cilantro, ¼ teaspoon of the salt, and pepper. Cook 1 minute. Set aside.

3. Prepare an outdoor grill, or preheat a grill pan. Sprinkle lightly with the remaining salt, and brush with olive oil. When the grill is ready, or the pan is heated, grill the fish about 4 minutes on each side or until it is lightly browned on the outside, opaque inside, and just barely flakes when tested with a fork. To serve, reheat the sauce and spoon over the grilled fish.

Grilled Swordfish with Tomato-Orange Salsa
Pez Espada Asada con Salsa de Jitomate Naranja

Makes 4 servings

Tomatoes and oranges make a unique salsa. The idea for this combination comes from La Capilla Restaurant in San Miguel de Allende.

2 navel oranges, peeled, white pith removed, and diced
1 medium tomato, seeded and diced or chopped
2 tablespoons finely chopped white onion
2 tablespoons finely chopped fresh mint
1 tablespoon finely chopped flat-leaf parsley
1 serrano chile, minced with seeds
2 teaspoons unseasoned rice vinegar
1/4 teaspoon sugar
1/4 teaspoon salt, plus extra for the fish
4 (6-ounce) swordfish steaks, each about 3/4-inch thick
2 teaspoons olive oil
1 large garlic clove, pressed

1. In a medium bowl, toss together the oranges, tomato, onion, mint, parsley, chile, vinegar, sugar, 1/4 teaspoon of the salt. If made ahead, cover and refrigerate up to 4 hours. Bring to room temperature before serving.

2. Brush the fish with oil and rub with garlic. Sprinkle lightly with salt. Cover and refrigerate about 30 minutes.

3. Prepare an outdoor grill or preheat a stovetop grill. Grill the fish about 4 minutes per side, or until it is browned on the outside, opaque but still moist inside, and just barely flakes when tested with a fork. Serve hot with the salsa spooned on top of each serving. Pass remaining salsa at the table.

Sautéed Fish Fillets with Golden Garlic and Lime
Pescado al Mojo de Ajo

Makes 4 servings

Very fresh white fish fillets, such as red snapper, rock cod, or sole are wonderful with golden bits of garlic. Fish cooked this way is popular along the Pacific coast and in the state of Sonora.

4 (6- to 7-ounce) white fish fillets, such as snapper or cod, each about 3/4-inch thick
2 teaspoons fresh lime juice
1/4 teaspoon salt, or to taste
1/4 cup olive oil
4 medium garlic cloves, finely chopped
1 tablespoon vegetable oil
1 tablespoon chopped fresh cilantro
Lime wedges

1. Rub lime juice over the fish and sprinkle with salt. In a small skillet, heat the olive oil over medium heat and cook the garlic, stirring, until it begins to brown lightly, about 2 minutes. (Take care not to burn, or the garlic will be bitter.) Remove from the heat and reserve in the pan.

2. Heat the vegetable oil in a large nonstick skillet and cook the fish about 3 to 4 minutes per side or until it is lightly browned on the outside, opaque but still moist inside, and just barely flakes when tested with a fork. Serve hot with some of the browned garlic and a drizzle of the oil spooned over each fillet. Sprinkle with cilantro. Garnish with the lime wedges.

Sautéed Fish Fillets with Avocado and Tomatillo Sauce
Pescado con Salsa de Aguacate y Tomatillo

Makes 4 servings

Firm fish fillets topped with an avocado sauce containing tomatillos makes an unusual and very pretty presentation. Mahimahi, sea bass, or cod, are good choices. Surround the fish with colorful vegetables, such as red and yellow peppers with zucchini. Tiny roasted red potatoes also taste great with the avocado sauce.

Avocado and Tomatillo Sauce (page 24)
4 (6- to 7-ounce) white fish fillets, each about
    ³/4-inch thick
¹/4 teaspoon salt, or to taste
¹/8 teaspoon freshly ground pepper, or to taste
2 teaspoons olive oil
2 teaspoons unsalted butter
Fresh cilantro or flat-leaf parsley

1. Prepare the avocado sauce. Cover and refrigerate. Season the fish lightly with salt and pepper.

2. In a large nonstick skillet, heat the oil and butter over medium-high heat. Cook the fish about 3 to 4 minutes per side, until it is golden brown on the outside, opaque but still moist inside, and just barely flakes when tested with a fork. Serve hot, with the sauce spooned on top. Garnish with cilantro or parsley. Pass the remaining sauce at the table.

Sautéed Fish Fillets with Orange Butter Sauce
Pescado con Naranja

Makes 4 servings

Any white fish fillets can be used for this frankly fancy dish. Pacific snapper is often used along Mexico's west coast, and it's excellent with the orange sauce. Oranges and other citrus juices are used in sauces and marinades throughout the country. Mild rice vinegar compliments the sauce and tastes similar to mild Mexican vinegar. Adding a bit of tequila is my idea.

³/4 cup fresh orange juice
1 tablespoon unseasoned rice vinegar
1 tablespoon olive oil
4 (6- to 7-ounce) white fish fillets, each about
    ³/4-inch thick
¹/4 teaspoon salt, or to taste
¹/8 teaspoon freshly ground pepper, or to taste
1 tablespoon tequila
2 tablespoons cold unsalted butter, cut into 4 pieces
2 tablespoons chopped fresh cilantro

1. In a small saucepan, boil the orange juice and vinegar until reduced to about ¹/3 cup. Reserve off heat.

2. Heat the oil in a large nonstick skillet and cook the fish 3 to 4 minutes per side or until it is golden brown on the outside, opaque but still moist inside, and just barely flakes when tested with a fork. Season with salt and pepper. Remove the fish to a serving platter.

3. Add the tequila to the skillet and bring to a boil, scraping up any browned bits. Add the reserved orange juice reduction to the same skillet and bring to a boil. Immediately reduce the heat to low and add the butter, 1 piece at a time, whisking just until melted. Remove from the heat and stir in the cilantro. Spoon the sauce over the fish. Serve at once.

Sautéed Fish Fillets with Poblano Chile Sauce

Pescado con Salsa de Chile Poblano

Makes 4 servings

This wonderful creamy poblano chile sauce from La Cava Restaurant in Mexico City works well with any firm white fish fillets.

2 large poblano chiles, roasted and peeled (page 8)
2 tablespoons vegetable oil
1/2 cup chopped white onion
1 medium garlic clove, chopped
1/2 teaspoon dried oregano (Mexican variety preferred), crumbled
2 tablespoons chopped fresh cilantro
1 small serrano chile, chopped with seeds
1/4 cup canned reduced-sodium chicken broth
1/4 cup heavy cream
1 teaspoon salt, or to taste
4 (6- to 7-ounce) white fish fillets, such as sea bass, each about 3/4-inch thick

1. Prepare the chiles. Then, cut out and discard the stem end of the chiles. Cut open the chiles and remove the seeds and veins. Rinse the chiles, blot with paper towels and cut them into strips. Chop them and put them in a blender. Heat 1 tablespoon of the oil in a medium nonstick skillet, and cook the onion, garlic, and oregano until the onion begins to brown, 3 to 4 minutes.

2. Scrape the skillet contents into the blender. Add the cilantro, serrano chile, broth, cream, and 1/2 teaspoon of the salt. Blend until smooth, creamy, and green in color. Transfer the sauce to a small saucepan, and simmer for 2 to 3 minutes to blend the flavors. Reserve off heat.

3. In the same nonstick skillet, heat the remaining 1 tablespoon of oil. Sprinkle the remaining 1/2-teaspoon of salt on the fish, and cook 3 to 4 minutes per side, or until it is lightly browned on the outside, opaque but still moist inside, and just barely flakes when tested with a fork. Reheat the reserved sauce. Serve the fish at once with the sauce spooned on top.

Sautéed Fish Fillets with Olive Salsa

Pescado con Salsa de Aceitunas

Makes 4 servings

A piquant olive salsa served with fish fillets is reminiscent of the flavors of Veracruz. Mexican Rice with Carrots (page 473) goes well with the fish and salsa.

8 pimiento-stuffed green olives, finely chopped
1 medium tomato, finely chopped
1 hard-cooked large egg, peeled and finely chopped
2 tablespoons minced white onion
1 1/2 teaspoons unseasoned rice vinegar
1/4 cup loosely packed chopped fresh cilantro
3 tablespoons extra-virgin olive oil
4 (6- to 7-ounce) white fish fillets, each about 3/4-inch thick
1/4 teaspoon salt, or to taste
1/4 teaspoon freshly ground pepper, or to taste

1. In a bowl, mix the olives, tomato, egg, onion, vinegar, cilantro, and 2 tablespoons of the oil. Cover and refrigerate about 1 hour or up to 6 hours.

2. In a large nonstick skillet, heat the remaining tablespoon of oil over medium heat and cook the fish, 3 to 4 minutes per side or until it is lightly browned on the outside, opaque inside, and just barely flakes when tested with a fork. Season with salt and pepper. Serve the fish with the salsa spooned on top.

Sautéed Fish Fillets with Plantains
Pescado con Plátanos Machos

Makes 4 servings

A spicy citrus marinade with fiery habanero chile infuses the fish with flavor and a hint of heat in the style of Yucatán. (Use protective gloves when handling the hot habanero chile.) Sautéed plantains accompany the fish, and plantains are easy to find these days in supermarkets or Latin-American grocery stores.

3 tablespoons olive oil

1 large garlic clove, finely chopped

2 tablespoons fresh lime juice

1 tablespoon fresh orange juice

1 habanero chile, quartered and seeded, veins removed

1 teaspoon brown sugar

1/2 teaspoon salt

1/8 teaspoon freshly ground pepper, or to taste

4 (6- to 7-ounce) white fish fillets, such as snapper, each about 3/4-inch thick

1 tablespoon unsalted butter

2 medium plantains, halved crosswise, peeled, and quartered lengthwise

Lime wedges

1. In a large shallow glass baking dish, mix together 2 tablespoons of the oil, and the garlic, lime and orange juices, chile, brown sugar, salt, and pepper. Let stand at room temperature 25 minutes.

2. Meanwhile, preheat the oven to 200°. Melt the butter in a large nonstick skillet over medium heat and cook the plantain pieces, turning, until golden brown on all sides, 4 to 6 minutes total. Season lightly with salt. Transfer to a plate and keep warm in the oven.

3. Remove the fish from the marinade, discarding the marinade. Blot the fish with paper towels. In a clean, large nonstick skillet, heat the remaining tablespoon of oil. Put the fish in the pan and cook about 3 minutes per side, or until it is lightly browned on the outside, opaque but still moist inside, and just barely flakes when tested with a fork. Serve the fish hot with the plantains.

Fried Fish in a Fluffy Egg Coat
Pescado Frito Capeado

Makes 4 servings

Fresh fish fillets are dipped in an airy fluffy egg batter and fried in the same way that chiles rellenos are battered and fried. This is a common way to prepare boneless fish fillets in Mexico. Pan-Roasted Tomatillo Sauce (page 35) or Fresh Salsa Mexicana (page 24) are good with the fish.

2 large eggs, separated

4 (6- to 7-ounce) white fish fillets, such as snapper or rock cod, each about 3/4-inch thick

1/4 teaspoon salt, or to taste

1/2 cup vegetable oil

1/4 cup all-purpose flour

In a medium bowl, beat the egg whites with an electric mixer until stiff and shiny. Beat in the egg yolks on low speed just until blended. Set aside. Sprinkle the fish lightly with salt. Heat the oil in a medium skillet until hot. Dust the fish all over with flour and dip in the egg batter. Fry about 3 minutes per side or until golden brown on the outside and opaque but still moist inside. Serve hot.

Ensenada Fried Fish Fillets with Lime Vinaigrette
Pescado Frito Ensenada con Vinagreta de Limón

Makes **4 servings**

Fried fish fillets come to the table in many ways all over Mexico. In Ensenada and the Baja peninsula, fish is often dusted with flour before being fried, a practice not as common in other regions of Mexico. The fried fillets, hot from the pan, are served with a cool lime vinaigrette. In Ensenada, a bottled hot sauce would be on the table to add to your taste. Crisp French fries might also accompany the fish.

3 tablespoons fresh lime juice
1/4 teaspoon grated lime zest
2 tablespoons minced red onion
1/2 teaspoon ground cumin
3/4 teaspoon salt, or to taste
1/4 cup olive oil
1/3 cup all-purpose flour
1/8 teaspoon freshly ground pepper, or to taste
4 (6- to 7-ounce) white fish fillets, such as snapper, rock cod, or sole, each about 3/4-inch thick
1/4 cup vegetable oil for frying
Chopped fresh cilantro

1. In a small bowl whisk together the lime juice, zest, onion, cumin, 1/4 teaspoon of the salt, and olive oil.

2. In a pie plate, mix the flour, pepper, and remaining 1/2 teaspoon of salt. Dredge the fish fillets in the flour. Shake off the excess. In a large skillet heat the oil over medium-high heat until hot and cook the fish, 2 fillets at a time, about 3 to 4 minutes per side, or until it is golden brown on the outside, opaque but still moist inside, and just barely flakes when tested with a fork. Drain on paper towels. Serve the fish with the vinaigrette poured on top of each piece. Sprinkle each serving with cilantro.

Fried Whole Fish
Pescado Frito

Makes **4 servings**

In or near any fishing port or village, fried fish will be served. Small, whole fresh fish need little adornment, and to fry it crisps up the skin and keeps the meat moist. Accompany the fish with pickled jalapeño chiles, fresh salsa, and French fries.

4 small scaled and cleaned whole fish, such as rock fish, snapper, or mackerel, rinsed
2 tablespoons all-purpose flour
1/2 teaspoon salt, or to taste
3 whole garlic cloves
Vegetable oil for frying
2 small limes, thinly sliced into circles

1. With a sharp knife, score each fish by making 3 diagonal cuts along the sides. Dust lightly with flour and sprinkle with salt.

2. Heat 1/2 inch of oil over medium-low heat in a large heavy frying pan. Fry the garlic until golden brown, about 3 minutes. Remove the garlic and discard. Fry the fish, 2 at a time, about 8 to 10 minutes, or until golden brown on the outside, opaque through to the bone, but still moist inside when tested with a knife. Drain on paper towels. Arrange 3 lime slices on each fish and serve.

Sautéed Halibut with Orange and Mint Sauce
Halibut con Salsa de Naranja y Yerbabuena

Makes **4 servings**

Halibut goes very well with citrus and mint, as do many of the firm white fish that are common in Mexico. This orange sauce is simple to make and tastes so good that you'll want to make it often. Citrus juices are widely used, especially with fish and poultry, in many parts of Mexico, and halibut works really well with the sauce. Serve with Mexican Rice (page 472).

¹/₂ cup fresh orange juice

1 teaspoon grated orange zest

1 tablespoon finely slivered mint leaves

1 teaspoon sugar

1 tablespoon unseasoned rice vinegar

¹/₈ teaspoon crushed red pepper

1 teaspoon cornstarch

1 tablespoon unsalted butter

1 tablespoon olive oil

4 (6- to 7-ounce) halibut steaks

¹/₂ teaspoon salt, or to taste

¹/₈ teaspoon freshly ground pepper, or to taste

1. Put the orange juice, rind, mint, sugar, vinegar, crushed pepper, and cornstarch in a small saucepan. Mix well and bring to a boil. Cook, stirring, until the sauce thickens slightly, 3 to 4 minutes. Remove from heat and stir in the butter.

2. In a nonstick skillet, heat the oil and cook the halibut, 4 to 5 minutes per side or until it is golden brown on the outside, opaque but still moist inside, and just barely flakes when tested with a fork. Reheat the sauce over low heat. Serve the fish hot with the sauce spooned on top.

Spanish-Style Salt Cod
Bacalao a la Vizcaina

Makes **4 servings**

The Spanish brought dried cod to Mexico in the 1500s. Mexican cooks adopted the fish into local preparations, and it is now a tradition in Mexico to serve this classic dish from the Basque region of Spain, the day after Christmas. In Oaxaca, the dish is called Bacalao Navideño, *where it's served on Christmas Eve.*

In the United States, dried salt cod can be found in many supermarkets, and in Italian or Latin-American markets. It's essential to soak the salt cod in cold water for many hours, changing the water several times to remove the saltiness and the strong smell. If the fish has been heavily salted and is hard as a board, it will take 20 to 24 hours to soften. A lightly cured fish will be a bit flexible and will soften in about 12 hours. If properly prepared, salt cod is excellent and worth the effort.

1 pound salt cod

2 tablespoons olive oil

1 medium onion, finely chopped

3 large garlic cloves, finely chopped

3 medium tomatoes, peeled and finely chopped

¹/₄ teaspoon dried crushed red pepper

2 tablespoons dry sherry

4 small red potatoes (about 1 pound), boiled, peeled, and quartered

¹/₄ cup finely chopped parsley

8 pimiento-stuffed green olives, cut in half crosswise

3 jarred pickled jalapeño chiles (en escabeche), seeded and cut into thin strips

1. Put the cod in a nonmetal bowl. Cover with water and soak (covered) 12 to 24 hours, changing the water 3 to 4 times until the fish is reconstituted. Drain and cut the fish into 4 pieces. Put the fish in a 3-quart saucepan, cover with water and bring to a boil. Cook 1 minute. Drain. Remove and discard skin and bones. Shred the fish and reserve in a bowl.

2. In a large skillet, heat the oil over medium heat and cook the onion and garlic until they start to brown, about 3 minutes. Add the tomatoes, crushed pepper and sherry. Bring to a boil and cook, stirring frequently, until the sauce thickens, 4 to 5 minutes. Add the cod and the remaining ingredients. Bring to a boil; then reduce heat to low, cover and simmer 20 to 25 minutes, or until the fish is tender.

Sautéed Shark with Fiery Cilantro-Mint Sauce
Tiburón en Salsa de Cilantro-Yerbabuena

Makes **4 servings**

Commercial marketing of shark has come into its own in recent years, and it's now available in many United States fish markets and some supermarkets as well. Fresh fish markets in Mexico regularly offer shark of whatever variety is caught along its extensive shoreline. Cazón (dogfish) is used in the Yucatán along the Caribbean coast. Other shark species, such as mako shark and thresher shark are frequently marketed in Mexico and the United States. Here, markets generally sell shark as steaks that are firm and very low in fat, and very similar to swordfish. This tangy sauce goes well with the mild flavor of shark. The sauce can be made ahead.

4 (6-ounce) shark steaks, trimmed of any skin
2 teaspoons fresh lime juice
1 medium garlic clove, mashed
Fiery Cilantro-Mint Sauce (page 30)
2 tablespoons olive oil
¹/₂ teaspoon salt

1. Put the shark on a plate and rub with the lime juice and garlic. Let stand about 20 minutes.

2. Meanwhile, prepare the sauce. Then, in a large skillet, heat the oil over medium heat until it shimmers. Pat the fish dry with paper towels and put in the pan. Cook about 4 to 5 minutes per side or until it is lightly browned on the outside, opaque but still moist inside, and just barely flakes when tested with a fork. Serve hot with a little of the sauce spooned over the fish.

Sautéed Skate with Fresh Salsa
Skate con Salsa

Makes **2 servings**

Skate is a small species of ray—a flat-bottomed kite-shaped fish found in many places around the world, and fairly common in the Sea of Cortez in Baja, Mexico. Until recently it was seldom exported, even though it's a popular food in Europe and parts of Asia. Now, the wings, the edible part, are occasionally available, skinned, in specialty fish markets in the United States. The firm white meat is similar to scallops and in Mexico is usually sautéed in butter and served with a simple sauce and crusty rolls.

Fresh Salsa Mexicana (page 24), or purchased
2 (about 6-ounce) skinned skate fillets
¹/₄ teaspoon salt, or to taste
Freshly ground pepper, to taste
2 tablespoons unsalted butter

Prepare the salsa, if using homemade. Then, season the skate with salt and pepper. Melt the butter in a large skillet over medium-high heat. Add the skate and cook 2 to 3 minutes per side or until golden brown on the outside and opaque but still moist inside, and just barely flakes when tested with a fork. Serve hot with fresh salsa.

Sautéed Squid with Almonds
Calamares Cancún

Makes 4 servings

*Sautéed squid with a quick pan sauce includ-
ing toasted almonds is an appealing, creative dish
from Cancún, on the east coast of the Yucatán
peninsula in the state of Quintana Roo. Cancún
became a resort area in the 1970s. Before that,
though, this region where the Mayan Indians once
lived, was relatively undeveloped until the beginning of the twentieth century. Now, native Mayan
dishes and Mexican foods from every region are
prepared in this popular tourist mecca.*

*If you find whole fresh squid, ask the fish-
monger to clean it for you. If fresh squid is not
available, frozen squid bodies or frozen rings
will do quite well. Small bay scallops are also
very good as a substitute for squid.*

*Serve this with crusty oval Mexican sand-
wich rolls (bolillos) or French bread.*

1½ pounds fresh squid, cleaned, or frozen and
    thawed squid bodies
½ teaspoon salt, or to taste
2 tablespoons olive oil
1 tablespoon unsalted butter
2 tablespoons dry vermouth or sherry
2 teaspoons fresh lime juice
2 tablespoons chopped fresh cilantro
⅓ cup finely chopped toasted almonds
Lime wedges

1. Rinse the squid bodies and cut into rings
about 1-inch wide. Pat dry with paper towels.
Season with salt. Heat the oil in a large nonstick
skillet over medium-high heat and sauté the
squid in 2 batches, stirring, until the squid is just
barely opaque, about 2 minutes. (Do not overcook, or the squid will toughen.) Using a slotted
spoon immediately remove the squid to a plate.

2. Melt the butter in the same pan and add the
remaining ingredients. Cook, stirring, until reduced
by half, about 2 minutes. Scrape the pan sauce
over the squid and serve at once with lime wedges.

Grilled Salmon with Mango-Avocado Salsa
Salmon Asada con Salsa de Mango y Aguacate

Makes 4 servings

*Farm-raised salmon allows us in the United
States to prepare this wonderful fish year-
round, and salmon has recently become popular
in Mexico. The pink flesh goes beautifully with
this new-style salsa. Because salmon fillets are
delicate and may fall apart, you can use a
hinged fish rack to hold them on the grill.*

Mango-Avocado Salsa (page 39)
1 salmon fillet (about 1½ to 2 pounds)
2 teaspoons olive oil
2 teaspoons fresh lime juice
¼ teaspoon salt, or to taste

1. Prepare the salsa. Cover and refrigerate.
Prepare an outdoor grill or preheat a stovetop
grill pan. Oil the grill grate or pan.

2. Pat the fish dry with paper towel. Brush the
fish with the oil and drizzle with the lime juice.
Season with salt. Grill the fish about 4 minutes on
one side, until the salmon has nicely browned
grill marks on the outside. Brush the top with
additional oil before turning to prevent sticking.
Cook 2 to 3 minutes more until the fish is barely
opaque inside and just barely flakes when tested
with a fork. Divide the salmon into serving
pieces, and spoon about 1 tablespoon salsa over
each serving. Serve at once. Pass the remaining
salsa at the table.

Sautéed Salmon with Creamy Corn Sauce and Toasted Pumpkin Seeds
Salmon con Crema de Elote y Pepitas

Makes **4 servings**

Mexicans have taken to salmon in a big way. When I made a research trip during the last stages of writing this book, I discovered that nearly every restaurant in the capital city doing elegant Mexican cooking had salmon on the menu. I was told that most of the salmon is imported from Canada and Chile, since salmon is not from Mexican waters. Sautéed salmon fillets team perfectly with a luscious corn sauce in a dish made with Mexican ingredients and French techniques.

¹/₄ cup raw hulled pumpkin seeds
1 tablespoon unsalted butter
2 tablespoons finely chopped white onion
1 large ear of fresh corn, kernels cut off
³/₄ cup canned fat-free reduced-sodium chicken broth
1 serrano chile, chopped with seeds
¹/₂ teaspoon salt, or to taste
2 tablespoons heavy cream or half and half
2 tablespoons olive oil
4 (5- to 6-ounce) skinned salmon fillets
2 tablespoons chopped fresh cilantro

1. Heat a small skillet over medium heat and toast the pumpkin seeds, stirring and tossing frequently, until they are aromatic and start to pop around in the pan, about 3 minutes. Transfer to a bowl. When the pumpkin seeds are cool, chop coarsely and set aside.

2. In a saucepan, melt the butter over medium heat and cook the onion, stirring, until translucent, about 3 minutes. Add the corn, ½ cup of the chicken broth, and ¼ teaspoon of the salt. Cook over medium heat until the corn is tender, about 6 minutes.

3. Transfer the corn mixture to a blender. Add the serrano and remaining ¼ cup of broth and blend until smooth, about 1 minute. Pour the sauce through a strainer into a clean saucepan. Press to release all the liquid. Discard debris. Stir the cream into the sauce and heat through. Adjust salt. Reserve over low heat in the pan.

4. In a large nonstick skillet, heat the olive oil over medium-high heat. Add the salmon and cook about 2 to 3 minutes per side or until it is browned on the outside, barely opaque inside and still moist, and just barely flakes when tested with a fork. Put 1 piece of salmon on each of 4 serving plates. Spoon some of the warm corn sauce across each piece of salmon. Sprinkle lightly with cilantro the toasted pumpkin seeds. Serve hot.

Pan-Fried Trout with "Drunken" Sauce
Trucha con Salsa Borracha

Makes **4 servings**

Trout are caught from a number of streams and rivers in Mexico and are most often grilled outdoors over glowing coals or fried in a skillet. Trout fishing is part of my heritage, and my Dad was an expert fly fisherman. We often fished together, even after I became an adult. We didn't know about "drunken sauce"(one including beer, tequila, or other alcohol) until I started traveling in Mexico, and now I love cooking trout this way. Fresh boned trout is widely available in fish markets just about everywhere in the United States.

"Drunken" Sauce (page 34)
4 (8- to 10-ounce) trout fillets
1 teaspoon salt, or to taste
Freshly ground pepper, to taste
2 tablespoons olive oil or vegetable oil

1. Prepare the sauce. Reserve in a serving bowl at room temperature. Put the trout on a large baking sheet. Season with salt and pepper inside and out. Let stand about 10 minutes.

2. Heat the oil in a large nonstick skillet over medium heat. Cook the trout, 2 at a time, about 5 to 6 minutes per side or until browned on the outside, opaque but still moist inside, and just barely flakes when tested with a fork. Spoon a little of the sauce over the fish, and serve hot, with the rest of the sauce passed at the table.

Pan-Fried Trout with Guacamole
Trucha con Guacamole

Makes **4 servings**

Farm-raised trout are available as skinned, boneless fillets in most quality fish markets in the United States, making this dish easy and affordable year round. We had an excellent trout prepared like this in Guadalajara. Tiny red potatoes accompanied the trout. As an alternative, the trout can be served chilled as a first course.

Classic Guacamole (page 23)
4 (8- to 10-ounce) trout fillets
1/2 teaspoon salt, or to taste
4 tablespoons olive oil
2 tomatoes, cut into wedges
1 lime, cut into wedges

1. Prepare the guacamole, cover tightly and refrigerate until ready to serve. Season the trout with salt.

2. In a large nonstick skillet, heat the oil over medium heat until it shimmers. Cook the trout fillets 3 to 4 minutes per side or until it is lightly browned on the outside, opaque but still moist inside, and just barely flakes when tested with a fork. Serve the fish on individual serving plates

with some guacamole spooned on top. Garnish with wedges of tomato and lime. Pass remaining guacamole at the table.

Batter-Fried Catfish with Chopped Radish Salad
Pescado Frito con Ensalada de Rábanos

Makes **4 servings**

Catfish are caught in the lakes and rivers in some parts of Mexico, and they are used a great deal in the state of Jalisco. Farm-raised catfish are available in most fish markets in the United States. The meat is white and mild. It takes very well to simple pan-frying, just the way it's done in rural Mexico. Serve hot from the pan with lime wedges and a crisp salad.

Chopped Radish Salad (page 175)
Seafood Cocktail Sauce (optional)
4 (6- to 7-ounce) skinned catfish fillets
1 teaspoon salt, or to taste
1/4 teaspoon freshly ground pepper, or to taste
2 tablespoons olive oil
2 tablespoons unsalted butter
1/2 cup all-purpose flour
Lime wedges

1. Prepare radish salad and cocktail sauce, if using. Season the fish with salt and pepper.

2. In a large nonstick skillet, heat the oil and butter over medium-high heat until the butter foams. Dredge the fillets, 1 at a time, in the flour. Pat off excess and place in the hot pan. Cook the fillets, in batches, about 2 minutes per side, or until golden brown on the outside and opaque but still moist inside. Transfer the fish to individual serving plates. Serve with lime wedges to squeeze the juice on the fish, and spoon a portion of the salad on the side. If using the cocktail sauce, pour it into small condiment bowls to pass at the table, if desired.

Shellfish

Shrimp in Garlic Sauce I
Camarónes al Mojo de Ajo I

Makes 4 servings

Nogales, in the state of Sonora on the Arizona-Mexico border, is one of the oldest border towns in Mexico. It has been an important trade route since 1880 and is now a popular gateway for visitors entering Mexico. When my husband and I lived in Phoenix many years ago, we traveled to Nogales as day visitors to shop and to eat fresh shrimp in butter-rich garlic sauce at La Roca restaurant. (Our Arizona friends tell us that La Roca is still there and the shrimp are as good as ever.)

A huge portion of shrimp, from Guaymas on the Sea of Cortez, was piled in the center of a large plate, with rice on one side and a slim wedge of iceberg lettuce with Thousand Island dressing on the other. This is my interpretation of La Roca's garlic shrimp. Serve over Mexican Rice (page 472).

1½ pounds (24 to 30) large shrimp, peeled and
    deveined, with tails removed

4 tablespoons olive oil

¾ teaspoon salt

Freshly ground pepper, or to taste

5 tablespoons unsalted butter, at room
    temperature

6 large garlic cloves, minced

3 tablespoons dry white wine

3 tablespoons fresh lime juice

1. Blot the shrimp dry with paper towels. Heat 2 tablespoons of the oil over medium-high heat in a skillet large enough to hold half of the shrimp in one layer. When the oil shimmers, place half of the shrimp in the pan using tongs. Season with half of the salt and a little pepper. Cook 1 to 2 minutes, or until the shrimp turn pink on the bottom. Turn and cook the second side until the shrimp are pink and curled, 1 to 2 minutes. With tongs, remove the shrimp to a bowl. Reserve. Repeat with remaining shrimp, oil, and salt.

2. Reduce heat to medium. Add the butter to the pan and stir in the garlic. Cook, stirring, until the garlic starts to brown, 1 to 2 minutes. Stir in the wine and cook 30 seconds. Return all of the shrimp to the pan. Add the lime juice. Toss to coat the shrimp with the sauce. Transfer the shrimp to a serving plate and serve at once.

Shrimp in Garlic Sauce II
Camarónes al Mojo de Ajo II

Makes 4 servings

Sometimes foods go so well together, every cook has a favorite way of preparing them. Such is the case with shrimp cooked with garlic in Mexico. Several years ago, when I took a group to Puerto Vallarta for a cooking vacation, the house manager of the home we rented really loved to cook. This is his recipe, which has red pepper, oregano, and a common seasoning extract called Maggi, but no wine, as the other version does.

1½ pounds (24 to 30) large shrimp, peeled and
    deveined, with tails on

3 tablespoons extra-virgin olive oil

½ teaspoon dried oregano (Mexican variety
    preferred), crumbled

6 large garlic cloves, minced

½ teaspoon salt, or to taste

¼ teaspoon dried crushed red pepper

1 teaspoon Maggi seasoning extract or
    Worcestershire sauce

3 tablespoons fresh lime juice

Lime wedges

1. Put the shrimp in a medium bowl. Add 1 tablespoon of the oil and oregano. Toss to coat the shrimp. Heat the remaining oil in a large heavy skillet over medium-high heat until it shimmers. Add the garlic and cook, stirring, until it starts to turn golden, about 1 minute. Add the shrimp all at once and cook, stirring, until the shrimp are pink and curled, about 2 to 3 minutes total.

2. Add the salt, crushed pepper, Maggi, and lime juice. Cook, stirring 1 minute. Serve the shrimp at once, scraping the juices from the pan over the shrimp. Garnish with lime wedges.

Shrimp in Pumpkin Seed Sauce
Camarónes en Pipian

Makes **8 servings**

This is a classic Mexican shrimp dish that's excellent for entertaining. Sauces flavored and thickened with pumpkin seeds goes back to the cooking traditions of Aztecs in central Mexico. This sauce is enriched and made more modern with the addition of cream and butter. Serve with Mexican Rice (page 472) and soft warm corn tortillas.

2 pounds (36 to 44) medium shrimp in the shell

4 cups water

¹/₂ teaspoon salt

¹/₄ tablespoon freshly ground pepper, or to taste

¹/₂ teaspoon cumin seeds

¹/₂ teaspoon dried oregano (Mexican variety preferred), crumbled

¹/₂ medium white onion

1 cup hulled raw unsalted pumpkin seeds

¹/₂ cup loosely packed fresh cilantro

2 serrano chiles, coarsely chopped with seeds

2 tablespoons unsalted butter

¹/₂ cup heavy cream

1. Place the shrimp in a large saucepan with the water, salt, pepper, cumin, oregano, and onion. Bring to a boil, over medium heat. Reduce heat to low and simmer until the shrimp are pink and curled, about 3 minutes. With a slotted spoon, lift the shrimp and onion from the cooking liquid. Save the cooking liquid to use for the sauce base. Set the onion aside on a plate.

2. When the shrimp are cool enough to handle, peel and devein. Put the shrimp shells in the pan of cooking liquid. Put the cleaned shrimp in a bowl and set aside. Bring the liquid with shrimp shells to a boil, reduce the heat to low, cover and simmer 10 minutes. Pour the shrimp broth through a strainer into a bowl. Reserve the broth and discard the shells.

3. In a dry skillet, toast the pumpkin seeds, stirring constantly, until they pop about in the pan and are aromatic. Spread the seeds out on a plate to cool; then grind to a powder in a spice grinder. (I use a coffee grinder reserved for spices.)

4. Put 2 cups of the shrimp broth into a blender jar. Add the ground pumpkin seeds, reserved onion, cilantro, and serranos. Blend until smooth.

5. In a large saucepan, melt the butter over medium heat. Pour in the blended sauce and cream. Bring to a boil; then reduce heat to low, and cook, stirring frequently, about 8 minutes. Stir in the shrimp. Heat through. Adjust seasoning, if needed. Serve hot.

Shrimp in Red Chile Sauce
Camarónes en Salsa de Chile Rojo

Makes 4 servings

This is a wonderful dish with a spicy, flavorful sauce made by thickening the shrimp cooking broth with puréed chiles and masa harina (the flour for making corn tortillas). The sauce is typical of West Central Mexico in the states of Michoacan and Jalisco. Serve over white rice.

2 cascabel chiles, cut open and seeded

1 large ancho chile, cut open and seeded, veins removed

1¹/₂ cups canned fat-free reduced-sodium chicken broth

¹/₂ cup water

¹/₂ white onion, sliced

¹/₂ small celery rib, sliced

2 cilantro sprigs

1 teaspoon dried oregano (Mexican variety preferred), crumbled

1 bay leaf

1 pound (18 to 22) medium shrimp in the shell

2 medium garlic cloves, peeled and thinly sliced

1 tablespoon masa harina (flour for corn tortillas)

¹/₂ teaspoon ground cumin

¹/₂ teaspoon salt, or to taste

1. In a small skillet, toast the chiles on both sides until blistered in spots, 30 to 40 seconds. (Take care not to let them burn.) Put the toasted chiles into a small bowl and cover with hot water. Soak about 20 minutes.

2. Meanwhile, in a medium saucepan bring to a boil the broth, water, onion, celery, cilantro, oregano, and bay leaf. Add the shrimp and cook over low heat until pink and curled, 3 to 4 minutes.

3. Pour the broth through a strainer into a bowl and reserve. Remove the shrimp, peel, devein, and reserve in a separate bowl. Discard the debris left in the strainer. Rinse the saucepan and return the broth to the pan.

4. Lift the chiles out of the soaking water and put them into a blender jar. Add the garlic, masa harina, cumin, and ¹/₂ cup of the broth from cooking the shrimp. Blend as smooth as possible. Pour the sauce through a strainer into the broth remaining in the pan.

5. Bring the broth to a boil, then reduce the heat to low and simmer, stirring frequently, until the sauce thickens and the flavors blend, about 10 minutes. (The sauce will still be thin.) Add the shrimp to the sauce. Heat through completely. Serve hot.

Grilled Shrimp Skewers
Brocheta de Camarónes

Makes 4 servings

A seasoned basting sauce makes these skewered grilled shrimp extra tasty. Serve with refried beans, fresh corn, salsa, and bolillos (oval Mexican sandwich rolls) for an informal outdoor meal. (If using wooden skewers, soak in water for 1 hour before using.)

1 pound (16 to 20) large shrimp, peeled and deveined

2 tablespoons unsalted butter, at room temperature

2 tablespoons fresh lime juice

2 medium garlic cloves, mashed

1 tablespoon pure ground ancho or pasilla chili powder (or substitute chili powder)

¹/₂ teaspoon ground cumin

¹/₄ teaspoon salt, or to taste

1. Thread the cleaned shrimp onto metal or previously soaked wooden skewers. Place skewered shrimp on a tray. In a small bowl, combine the butter with the lime juice, garlic, ground chili powder, cumin, and salt. Brush about half of the mixture all over the skewered shrimp. Cover and refrigerate about 30 minutes. (Save the remaining mixture to brush on the shrimp as it cooks on the grill.)

2. Prepare an outdoor grill and grease the grill rack or preheat the broiler. Place the shrimp skewers on the hot grill or under a hot oven broiler and cook 2 to 3 minutes per side, turning once and brushing with the remaining basting sauce. Cook until the shrimp are pink and begin to curl, 2 to 3 minutes more. Serve hot.

Shrimp with Peppers and Cheese
Camarónes con Pimientos y Queso
Makes **4 servings**

Manzanillo, on the Pacific coast in the tiny state of Colima, is probably best known for the posh Las Hadas resort made famous by the movie "10." The beautiful tropical setting and sandy beaches draw tourists from everywhere. The seafood is another big draw. Lobster and shrimp are a specialty, grilled over mesquite coals. Marlin and dorado are also highly esteemed, and sports fishermen come from far and near to take part in a yearly tournament, from which much of the catch is released back to help preserve the species.

This is my version of a creative brothy shrimp dish with sweet peppers that I ate here. Serve it in shallow soup bowls with soft tortillas. Add a plate of Mexican Rice (page 472) and Basic Refried Beans (page 462) to complete the meal.

2 tablespoons olive oil
1 tablespoon unsalted butter
1 large white onion, sliced lengthwise
2 red bell peppers, sliced in strips ¹/₂-inch wide
1 green bell pepper, sliced in strips ¹/₂-inch wide
3 medium tomatoes, peeled, seeded, and diced
³/₄ cup canned fat-free reduced-sodium chicken broth
1 pound (18 to 22) medium shrimp, peeled and deveined, with tails removed
¹/₂ teaspoon salt, or to taste
2 to 3 jarred pickled jalapeño chiles (en escabeche), seeded, veins removed, and thinly sliced
Crumbled cotija or mild feta cheese

1. In a large skillet, heat the oil and butter over medium heat. Add the onion and cook, stirring, until translucent, about 2 minutes. Add the red and green peppers. Cook, stirring, until crisp-tender, about 3 minutes. Add the tomatoes and chicken broth.

2. Bring to a boil, then add the shrimp and cook until pink and curled, about 5 minutes. Add the salt and pickled chiles. Divide the shrimp mixture equally among 4 shallow soup bowls. Sprinkle with cheese. Serve at once.

Shrimp with Tomatoes and Cheese
Camarónes con Jitomates y Queso

Makes 4 servings

After years of careless growth and declining tourism, Acapulco has made major efforts to beautify and clean up its beaches and other tourist attractions. Good Mexican specialties can be found in many restaurants, and it's fun exploring them. Su Casa is a great find. It sits on a hillside with a beautiful view and serves a fine selection of seafood, such as this impressive modern shrimp dish. Serve with white rice.

2 tablespoons olive oil

1/2 large white onion, thinly sliced in half rings

3 large tomatoes, peeled, seeded, and finely diced

4 large garlic cloves, finely chopped

2 jalapeño chiles, seeded, veins removed and chopped

1 pound (16 to 20) large shrimp, peeled and deveined

2 tablespoons finely chopped fresh oregano or 1/2 teaspoon dried oregano (Mexican variety preferred), crumbled

2 to 3 dashes hot pepper sauce, such as Tabasco

1/2 teaspoon salt, or to taste

1/2 cup crumbled cotija cheese

Heat the oil in a large heavy skillet over medium-high heat and cook the onion, stirring, until it starts to brown, about 4 minutes. Add the tomatoes, garlic, and jalapeños. Stir until the tomatoes are juicy and bubbling, 3 to 4 minutes. Add the shrimp and cook, turning and stirring, until pink, curled, and cooked through, about 4 minutes. Stir in the oregano, hot pepper sauce, and salt. Cook 1 minute. Divide among 4 plates and sprinkle each serving with cheese. Serve hot.

Crab and Scallop Cakes
Pastelitos de Jaiba y Callos

Makes 12 small cakes

La Capilla restaurant in the historic center of San Miguel de Allende is elegant with a sophisticated creative menu. This is my adaptation of the crab and scallop cakes served with chipotle mayonnaise that caught my attention. Any fresh or frozen crabmeat can be used, but canned crab just won't do. If you can get it, Dungeness crab is best.

Chipotle Mayonnaise (page 18)

1/2 pound fresh cooked crabmeat, picked over, or thawed, if frozen

4 large sea scallops, sliced in half across the grain and finely chopped

1 tablespoon olive oil

1/4 cup finely chopped white onion

1/4 cup finely chopped red bell pepper

1 serrano chiles, minced with seeds

1 teaspoon dried oregano (Mexican variety preferred), crumbled

1 tablespoon Maggi seasoning extract or Worcestershire sauce

1/4 teaspoon salt, or to taste

1/8 teaspoon freshly ground pepper, or to taste

3 tablespoons mayonnaise

1 large egg, lightly beaten

1 1/2 cups fine dry bread crumbs

1/4 cup corn oil or safflower oil

Cilantro sprigs

1. Prepare the chipotle mayonnaise. Reserve in a bowl. Then, put the crabmeat and chopped scallops in a large bowl. Cover and refrigerate.

2. In a medium skillet, heat the oil over medium heat and cook the onion until softened, about 2 minutes. Add the red pepper and cook until barely tender, about 2 more minutes. Transfer to the bowl with the crab and scallops. Add all of the remaining ingredients, except the bread crumbs, oil, and cilantro. Mix very well. Add ¾ cup of the bread crumbs and mix again.

3. With your hands, form the crab mixture into 12 small cakes, about ¾-inch thick. Put the remaining bread crumbs on a plate. Coat the cakes on both sides with the crumbs and place in a single layer on a platter. Cover and refrigerate 1 hour or up to overnight.

4. Heat the oil in a medium skillet over medium-high heat. Cook the crab-scallop cakes about 3 minutes per side, or until crisp and brown outside and cooked through, about 3 minutes per side. Serve on individual plates with chipotle mayonnaise. Garnish each plate with cilantro sprigs.

Blue Crabs with Salsa and Chipotle Mayonnaise
Jaibas con Salsa y Mayonesa de Chipotle

Makes 2 servings

Blue crabs are found along the coast of the Gulf of Mexico. The popular little crustaceans are served boiled, fried, stewed, in soups, tortas, (sandwiches), and tacos. Blue crabs are often sold live in many fish markets throughout the United States. Most people like to make an informal feast of eating blue crabs, served with only lime, simple condiments, good bread, and lots of napkins. Plan about 3 to 6 crabs per person, depending on crab size. Live crabs should be cooked and eaten the day they are purchased. Chipotle mayonnaise is spicy. Plain mayonnaise may be substituted, if desired.

Fresh Salsa Mexicana (page 24), or purchased
Chipotle Mayonnaise (page 18), or plain
    mayonnaise
8 to 10 live blue crabs
Lime wedges

1. Prepare the salsa and mayonnaise. Then, bring a large pot of water to a boil. Using tongs, drop the crabs in the boiling water, one by one. Cook until the crabs are bright red, about 4 to 5 minutes.

2. Drain in a colander and serve right away, or cool, refrigerate, and eat within 2 to 3 hours. Serve with lime wedges, salsa, mayonnaise, and bread.

Note: To eat, twist off the claws, break open and pick out the meat. Grasp the top shell by the edges and pull it away from the body. Turn crab over and lift off the triangular piece of shell. Remove the soft spines underneath. Discard the feathery gills and intestines. Break the body into pieces and pick or suck the meat out.

Broiled Oysters, Guaymas Style
Ostiones estilo Guaymas

Makes 4 servings

Guaymas is an active seaport town on the Gulf of California. Commercial fishermen routinely bring in boatloads of shrimp and oysters to be marketed locally or exported. During one of our trips to Guaymas we had broiled oysters like this made with the fresh catch.

Most fish markets in the United States will have fresh oysters in season. Oysters must be very fresh with shells tightly closed. If purchased without shells, the oyster liquid should be clear. If it is milky in color, do not use them. Serve fresh corn tortillas and a bowl of fresh salsa with the oysters.

24 medium-size fresh oysters
2 tablespoons vegetable oil
1/3 cup minced white onion
2 medium garlic cloves, finely chopped
2 tablespoons fresh lime juice
**1/4 teaspoon Maggi seasoning extract or
   Worcestershire sauce**
1/4 teaspoon crushed red pepper
1/4 teaspoon salt, or to taste

1. To shuck the oysters, hold each oyster upside down, using a potholder to protect the holding hand. Put the tip of an oyster knife near the hinge and between the shells and press the knife-holding hand down to separate the shells. Once the shell is opened, slide the knife along the top shell to cut connector muscle. Remove top shell. Then slide knife under the oyster and it will come free. Leave the oysters in the bottom shell, and pour the oyster liquid into a bowl and reserve. Discard the top shells. Put the oysters in their shell on a large baking sheet.

2. Preheat the oven broiler. In a small skillet, heat the oil over medium heat and cook the onion and garlic until softened, 3 to 4 minutes. Remove the pan from the heat. Stir in the reserved oyster liquid, lime juice, Maggi, red pepper, and salt. Spoon about 1 teaspoon of the mixture over the oysters and run under the broiler until the edges of the oysters begin to curl, 2 to 3 minutes. Serve hot.

Grilled Lobster Tails
Langosta a la Parilla

Makes 4 servings

When I think of lobster, I remember the succulent grilled lobsters I've enjoyed in Puerto Vallarta. They were simply grilled and eaten with melted butter and a squirt of fresh lime juice. Add fresh salsa, guacamole, crusty bread, and cold Mexican beer for a great meal. Frozen lobster tails are widely available in the United States and are easier to handle than whole lobster. Spiny lobsters—also called rock lobsters—are lobsters without claws, and the tails have moist, dense meat, perfect for grilling.

**4 spiny (or rock) lobster tails (1/2 pound each),
   thawed if frozen**
3 teaspoons olive oil or vegetable oil
1/2 teaspoon salt, or to taste
Freshly ground pepper, to taste
Unsalted butter, melted
Lime, cut into wedges

1. Prepare an outdoor grill, then grease the grill rack. With scissors, cut lengthwise down the center of the back of each lobster shell; then, using a heavy sharp knife cut through each shell to slice the lobster tails in half. Brush the cut side with oil.

2. Lay the lobster tails on the grill, cut side down and cook about 3 to 4 minutes per side, or until the lobster meat is opaque but still juicy in the thickest part, and is just firm when pressed gently with your finger. Serve hot in the shell with melted butter in condiment cups, and lime wedges to squirt the juice on the lobster.

Note: Cook uncovered if using a charcoal fire. Cook covered if using a gas grill.

Scallops with Chipotle Tomato Sauce
Callos con Salsa Chipotle de Jitomate

Makes **4 servings**

A brown-shelled scallop called chocolata, *found along the coast of the Sea of Cortez in Baja, Mexico, was used in this dish, but scallops from anywhere go well with this spicy fresh tomato sauce (large sea scallops work best). Canned* chipotle chiles en adobo *can be found in the Mexican section of most supermarkets or in Mexican markets. This dish goes well with Corn with Cheese (page 418).*

1 tablespoon olive oil

1/2 medium white onion, finely chopped

2 medium garlic cloves, finely chopped

1/2 teaspoon dried oregano (Mexican variety preferred), crumbled

4 medium tomatoes, peeled and chopped

1 canned chipotle chile en adobo, finely chopped

1/4 cup loosely packed chopped fresh cilantro

3/4 teaspoon salt, or to taste

1 pound (26 to 30) sea scallops

1/2 cup all-purpose flour

2 tablespoons corn oil

1. In a medium saucepan, heat the olive oil over medium heat and cook the onion, stirring, until softened, about 3 minutes. Add the garlic, oregano, and tomatoes. Bring to a boil and cook until the mixture thickens, 4 to 5 minutes. Add the chile, cilantro, and 1/4 teaspoon of the salt. Cook 1 minute. Cover and reserve in the pan off heat.

2. Blot the scallops with paper towels and put on a plate. In a shallow bowl mix the flour and remaining 1/2 teaspoon of salt. Dredge the scallops in the flour and shake off excess. Heat the corn oil in a large nonstick skillet and cook the scallops 1 to 2 minutes per side, or until golden on the outside and opaque but still moist inside. (Do not overcook or the scallops will toughen.)

3. Reheat the sauce and spoon a little in the center of 4 serving plates. Place an even number of scallops on top of the tomato sauce on each plate. Serve at once.

Scallops with Corn, Zucchini, and Tomatoes
Callos con Colache

Makes **4 to 6 servings**

In this dish, large sea scallops are nestled on a colorful bed of colache, *a classic combination of garden-fresh vegetables that's prepared in most regions of Mexico. Serving the scallops on top of* colache *is a wonderful blend of old and new cooking styles. Small individual bowls of black beans can be served on the side.*

Corn, Zucchini, and Tomatoes (page 418)

1 pound (26 to 30) sea scallops

1/2 teaspoon salt, or to taste

2 tablespoons unsalted butter

Lime wedges

1. Prepare the vegetable mixture. Reserve in the pan off heat. Then, season the scallops with salt and pepper. Heat the butter in a large skillet over medium-high heat and cook the scallops 1 to 2 minutes per side or until golden on the outside and opaque but still moist inside.

2. Reheat the vegetables and spoon evenly in the center of 4 serving plates. Place a portion of scallops on top of the vegetables on each plate. Garnish with lime wedges. Serve at once.

Scallops with Melon Salsa
Callos con Salsa de Melon

Makes **4 to 6 servings**

Large sea scallops are a luxury well worth the price when prepared in this nueva cocina *style. I serve the scallops on a bed of yellow rice with the salsa spooned over and around the scallops. It's both beautiful and delicious.*

Yellow Rice with Peas (omit the peas) (page 475)
Melon Salsa (page 40)
1 pound (26 to 30) sea scallops
1/2 cup finely ground yellow cornmeal
1/2 teaspoon salt, or to taste
1/4 teaspoon freshly ground pepper, or to taste
1/4 cup corn oil

1. Preheat the oven to 200°. Prepare the yellow rice recipe (without the peas). Cover and keep the rice warm in the oven. Prepare the salsa. Reserve.

2. Blot the scallops with paper towels and place on a plate. In a small bowl mix the cornmeal, salt, and pepper. Dredge the scallops in the cornmeal. Pat off excess. Put the scallops on wax paper as they are coated.

3. Heat the oil in a large nonstick skillet over medium heat until oil shimmers. Add the scallops and cook about 1 to 2 minutes per side, or until golden brown on both sides and just cooked through. Drain on paper towels. Put a portion of the rice in the center of 4 plates. Arrange the scallops equally on the rice. Garnish with the salsa. Serve at once.

Broiled Scallops with Spinach
Callos con Espinaca

Makes **4 servings**

My sister, Dorothy Davis, contributed this recipe from her kitchen in Mulege, Baja, Mexico where she and her husband live most of the winter. Dorothy is an artist and spends much of her time drawing and painting, but she has a great interest in Mexican food as well. Scallops are plentiful near Mulege, and fresh produce, including spinach, can be purchased right from the growers.

1 (16-ounce) package spinach leaves, well rinsed
1 medium garlic clove, finely chopped
Salt and freshly ground pepper, to taste
1/4 cup Mexican crema or sour cream
1/2 cup shredded Oaxaca or Monterey Jack cheese
1 tablespoon olive oil
12 large sea scallops (about 3/4 pound)

1. Put the spinach in a large pot with 1 tablespoon of water. Cover and cook until the spinach is wilted and bright green, about 3 minutes. Transfer the spinach to a large bowl. Add the garlic, salt, and pepper. Mix well and cool 10 minutes. Mix in the crema.

2. Grease a 9- or 10-inch glass pie plate or round ovenproof earthenware platter and spread the mixture in it. Sprinkle the cheese on top. Set aside.

3. Preheat the oven broiler. Slice scallops in half lengthwise, and pat dry with paper towels. Brush the scallops all over with oil and season lightly with salt. Arrange the scallops in a single layer on top of the spinach. Cook under the broiler until the scallops are golden brown on the topside, opaque inside, and the cheese is melted, 3 to 5 minutes. (Watch carefully to prevent burning.) Serve hot.

Mixed Seafood, Campeche Style
Pescado Mixta estilo Campeche

Makes **6 servings**

Campeche, a historic town on the Yucatán peninsula, is also an important fishing port with a large fleet of shrimp boats and an excellent fish market. During a visit with a culinary group led by Mexican cuisine authority Diana Kennedy, we attended a fiesta within the walls of a fortress that was built in the 1600s to protect the town against raiding pirates. The event featured regional foods and entertainment, and the array of dishes to choose from was quite astounding. This is a simplified version of a sautéed mixed seafood dish from that amazing feast. Serve the seafood over rice. Saffron is very expensive, but only a tiny bit is needed. I used imported saffron from Spain and look for the brightest red threads for best quality.

Sauce

1 tablespoon olive oil
1 large green bell pepper, finely chopped
¹/₂ medium white onion, finely chopped
1 medium carrot, peeled and diced (¹/₄ inch)
1 pound plum tomatoes, cored and chopped
3 medium garlic cloves, thinly sliced
¹/₄ teaspoon crushed saffron threads
¹/₂ teaspoon salt

Seafood

3 tablespoons olive oil
12 large shrimp (about ³/₄ pound), peeled and deveined
12 oysters or sea scallops, to suit your preference
¹/₃ pound prepared squid rings, fresh or frozen
Salt and freshly ground pepper, to taste

1. To prepare the sauce, heat the oil in a large skillet. Add the pepper, onion and carrot and cook over medium-low heat, stirring, 5 minutes. Remove from the heat and reserve in the pan.

2. In a blender, purée the tomatoes, garlic, and saffron until smooth. Press the mixture through a strainer into the pan with the peppers, then discard the pulp. Add the salt and return to medium-low heat. Simmer, uncovered, until the vegetables are tender, about 5 minutes.

3. To prepare the seafood: in another large skillet, heat the oil over medium heat and cook the shrimp, stirring, until pink and curled, about 2 to 3 minutes. Using a slotted spoon, transfer the shrimp to the pan with the peppers.

4. In the same skillet used to cook the shrimp, cook the oysters (or scallops), turning once, until lightly browned and just cooked through, 2 to 3 minutes. Transfer to the pan with the shrimp and peppers.

5. In the same skillet used to cook the shrimp and oysters, cook the squid, stirring, until just cooked, about 1 minute. Add to the other ingredients. Reheat, stirring frequently, until completely heated through, 3 to 4 minutes. Season with salt and pepper. Serve hot.

Vegetables

Corn 417

Mexican Corn on the Cob

Corn with Chipotle Butter

Corn with Cheese

Corn, Zucchini, and Tomatoes

Corn and Cabbage

Corn with Epazote
and Poblano Chiles

Hominy, Corn, and
Poblano Chiles

Corn Pancakes

Savory Corn Cake

Peppers 421

Stuffed Chiles with Cheese

Stuffed Chiles with
Minced Beef

Stuffed Chiles with
Shredded Spiced Chicken

Stuffed Chiles with Turkey

Stuffed Chiles with Fish

Stuffed Chiles with
Mashed Potatoes

Stuffed Chiles with
Refried Beans

Stuffed Anaheim Chiles
with Goat Cheese

Stuffed Chiles with
White Beans

Stuffed Poblano Chiles
in Walnut Sauce

Pickled Ancho Chiles
Stuffed with Guacamole

Green Chile Strips

Poblano Chile Strips with
Fried Onions

Green Chile Strips with
Onions and Mushrooms

Green Chile Strips in
Cream with Cheese

Red Bell Peppers and Jicama

Squash 431

Chayote and Carrots

Chayote and Tomato
with Cheese Topping

Chayote Casserole with
Ground Pork

Baked Stuffed Chayote

Grilled Zucchini

Sautéed Shredded Zucchini

Zucchini with Onions
and Cheese

Zucchini and Mushrooms
with Epazote

Zucchini and Carrots
with Tomato

Zucchini Pancakes

Zucchini Pudding

Squash Blossoms Stuffed
with Cheese

Winter Squash with Greens

Carrots 438

Carrot and Jicama Sticks

Carrot Pudding

Carrots and Potatoes in
Ancho Chile Sauce

Cauliflower 439

Cauliflower Fritters

Cauliflower with Cotija Cheese

Cauliflower with Tomatillo
and Sweet Pepper Salsa

Cauliflower with Tomatoes
and Poblanos

Chard 441

Chard with Poblano Chiles

Chard and Hominy

Chard with Pickled Red Onions

Chard with Potatoes

Chard with Chickpeas

Potatoes and Sweet Potatoes 444

Fried Potatoes with
Poblano Chile Strips

Fried Potatoes with
Tomatoes and Jalapeños

Pan-Roasted Potatoes
and Carrots

Potatoes in Ranchera Sauce

Chipotle Mashed Potatoes

Potatoes Steamed with Herbs

Baked Potatoes
Stuffed with Corn

Potato and Chile Gratin

Roasted Potatoes and Onions
with Yellow Chile Salsa

Roasted Potatoes and Onions,
Yucatán Style

Potato Masa Cakes
with Vegetables

Baked Sweet Potatoes
with Pumpkin Seeds

Sweet Potatoes with
Cream and Chipotle Chile

Other Vegetables 450

Asparagus with Mushrooms

Broccoli with Red Onion
and Cumin

Broccoli with Onions
and Sweet Potatoes

Eggplant Stuffed with
Shredded Chicken

Eggplant with Ranchera Sauce

Green Beans with Mushrooms

Mushrooms and Poblano Chiles
in Guajillo Sauce

Mushrooms, Tomatoes,
and Chiles

Purslane with Mushrooms

Portobello Mushrooms
Stuffed with Refried Beans

Fried Plantains

Plantains Stuffed with Beans

Grilled Fresh Cactus

Grilled Green Onions

Baked Tomatoes Mexicana

Mixed Vegetables,
Mexican Style

Onion, Zucchini, and Rice
Casserole

Life in every village, town, and city in Mexico pulsates around the public markets. The huge colorful displays of vegetables and fruits give testament to the abundance of produce that grows year round in the temperate climate. Daily marketing is still an important part of everyday life, especially in smaller towns and villages. All the indigenous vegetables and fruits, including corn, tomatoes, bell peppers and chiles, beans, squash, potatoes, cactus, jicama, avocados, guavas and cactus fruit, and a variety of herbs and wild greens, share market stalls with an impressive number of other produce introduced from Europe and Asia. Broccoli, cabbage, cauliflower, cucumbers, radishes, turnips, beets, oranges, melons, lemons, and much more provide the Mexican table with a huge selection all year round.

The vegetable dishes in this chapter incorporate the most important produce items used in Mexican cooking. Many of the recipes are traditional, while others reflect the trend toward new ways of using fresh vegetables. As Mexican cuisine evolves in the twenty-first century, home cooks and restaurant chefs alike are aware of healthful eating habits and are trying new ways to cook vegetables, such as cooking until just tender for brightest color, flavor, and texture, and reducing the fat in which vegetables are cooked.

Chiles rellenos—stuffed chiles—is probably the most well known Mexican vegetable dish. Of course, there are numerous variations. You'll find many of them here—sample them all and pick your favorite! The stuffed chiles can be coated with an egg batter (or not) and fried (or baked)—the choice is the cook's, as are the fillings—from cheese to beans to meats.

Chiles are also not the only vegetable suitable for rellenos; chayote, potatoes, even squash blossoms are stuffed with delicious fillings.

Other wonderful vegetable dishes include simple classics like Corn with Chipotle Butter (page 417), Chayote (a gourd similar to squash) and Tomato with Cheese Topping (page 431), and Cauliflower Fritters (page 439). Among the new-style vegetable dishes are Baked Potatoes Stuffed with Corn (page 446), Eggplant with Ranchera Sauce (page 453), and Broccoli with Red Onion and Cumin (page 450).

Although a few ingredients may require some searching, the recipes are simple enough to incorporate into your Mexican meals or any menu.

Corn

Mexican Corn on the Cob
Elotes

Makes 4 servings

Fresh ears of corn on the cob are cooked in steaming tubs of boiling water and sold by street venders all over Mexico. The corn is painted with mayonnaise and coated with cheese and a sprinkling of chili powder. Try this popular street snack at home.

4 large ears fresh corn, shucked (save 4 large leaves)
1/4 cup mayonnaise
1 teaspoon fresh lime juice
1/2 cup finely shredded cotija or mild feta cheese
1 tablespoon purchased chili powder

Bring a large pot of water to a boil. Cook the corn until tender, about 5 minutes. While the corn cooks, mix the mayonnaise and lime juice in a small bowl. Drain the corn. Brush the hot cooked corn with mayonnaise and sprinkle with cheese and chili powder. Serve each ear of corn hot, placed on top of a fresh corn leaf.

Corn with Chipotle Butter
Elote con Mantequilla de Chipotle

Makes 4 servings

Fresh corn spread with fiery, smoky-flavored chipotle butter brings a smile to lovers of corn and of spicy hot food. Advise your guests to taste with caution!

1/4 cup (1/2 stick) unsalted butter, at room temperature
1 small garlic clove, mashed
1 1/2 teaspoons mashed canned chipotle chile en adobo
4 large ears fresh corn, shucked
2 teaspoons olive oil
1/4 teaspoon salt, or to taste

1. In a medium bowl work together the butter, garlic, and chipotle to make a smooth paste. Form the mixture into a neat mound or log shape on a small serving plate. Refrigerate until shortly before using.

2. In a large pot of boiling water, cook the corn until barely tender, about 3 minutes. Drain and cool under running water to stop the cooking. Cut the kernels off the cobs.

3. In a medium skillet, heat the olive oil over medium heat. Add the corn and salt. Cook, stirring, until completely heated through, about 2 minutes. Serve hot with the chipotle butter, to be added at the table.

Corn with Cheese
Elote con Queso

Makes **4 servings**

When corn is fresh and sweet, try this special side dish. It's great with grilled meats and poultry. The texture, of the dish, similar to a porridge, comes from puréeing part of the corn and mixing it with the remaining whole kernels. There is no special ratio of purée to kernels, since the size of corn cobs vary.

6 large ears fresh corn, shucked
1/2 cup whole milk
2 tablespoons unsalted butter
1/2 teaspoon ground cumin
1/2 teaspoon salt, or to taste
Freshly ground pepper, to taste
1/4 cup grated cotija or Parmesan cheese

1. Cut the kernels off the cobs. Put 1 cup of the in a blender with the milk and purée until smooth.

2. Put the remaining corn kernels in a medium saucepan; then carefully scrape the cobs with the dull side of the knife blade to extract the milky corn pulp.

3. Add the corn pulp and the blended corn mixture to the pan. Add the butter, cumin, salt, and pepper. Bring to a boil over medium heat; then reduce the heat, cover, and simmer, stirring frequently, until the corn thickens, 5 to 6 minutes. Serve hot sprinkled with the cheese.

Corn, Zucchini, and Tomatoes
Colache

Makes **4 servings**

A classic Mexican combination that's best made with seasonal garden-fresh vegetables.

1 tablespoon olive oil or vegetable oil
1 teaspoon unsalted butter
1/2 medium white onion, finely chopped
3 ears fresh corn, shucked
2 medium zucchini, diced into 1/2-inch pieces
1 large ripe tomato, peeled and finely chopped
1 tablespoon chopped fresh cilantro
1/2 teaspoon salt, or to taste
Freshly ground pepper, to taste

1. In a large wide saucepan, heat the oil and butter over medium heat. Add the onion and cook, stirring, until the edges start to brown, about 5 minutes.

2. Cut the kernels off the cobs. Add the corn, zucchini, and 2 tablespoons of water. Cook, stirring, until the vegetables are crisp-tender, 4 to 5 minutes. Add the remaining ingredients and cook until the tomatoes release their juices. Simmer the mixture about 3 minutes. (To keep the bright colors, don't overcook.) Serve hot.

Corn and Cabbage
Elote y Col

Makes **4 servings**

Sautéed cabbage and corn is a quick way to add a serving of everyday vegetables to a main dish. Fresh salsa can be added to the vegetables during the last minute of cooking, if desired. The cabbage and corn combination goes well with roasted meats and poultry.

2 tablespoons unsalted butter

1/4 white onion, chopped

1/2 head of cabbage, chopped into 1/2-inch pieces

1 1/2 cups corn kernels (from about 2 ears of corn), or thawed, if frozen

1 jalapeño chile, seeded and finely chopped

1/2 teaspoon salt

Melt the butter in a large skillet over medium heat. Add the onion and cook until softened, about 3 minutes. Add the cabbage and cook, stirring, until wilted, 3 to 4 minutes. Add the corn, jalapeño, and salt. Cook, stirring frequently, until the corn is tender, about 3 minutes. Serve hot.

Corn with Epazote and Poblano Chiles

Elote con Epazote y Chiles Poblanos

Makes **4 servings**

Epazote, *a native Mexican herb that's now cultivated, is now more available in the United States. Try its intriguing taste in this easy corn dish and serve it with saucy meats or enchiladas. If you can't find fresh* epazote, *look for dried* epazote *in Mexican grocery stores, or in some supermarkets in Latin-American neighborhoods.*

4 large ears fresh corn, shucked

2 tablespoons unsalted butter

1/4 cup finely chopped white onion

2 tablespoons finely chopped fresh epazote leaves, or 1 tablespoon dried epazote

1 fresh poblano chile, seeded and finely chopped

1/4 teaspoon salt, or to taste

Freshly ground pepper, to taste

1. Bring a large pot of water to a boil. Drop in the ears of corn and simmer until barely tender, about 3 minutes. Drain and cool under running water. Cut off the corn kernels. Discard the cobs. Put the kernels in a bowl.

2. Melt the butter in a skillet over medium heat and cook the onion, epazote, and poblano, stirring, until the onion softens, 3 to 4 minutes. Add the reserved corn, salt, and pepper. Heat through completely. Serve hot.

Hominy, Corn, and Poblano Chiles

Pozole, Elote, y Chiles Poblanos

Makes **4 servings**

Hominy—corn kernels treated to remove the skins and often made into a stew or soup of the same name—is popular in the American southwest and throughout much of Mexico, where it's commonly called pozole. *Hominy is sold precooked in cans, which simplifies making this recipe. I like to use white hominy for this dish for color contrast with the yellow corn kernels and green poblano chiles. Serve as a side dish with fish, pork, or chicken.*

2 teaspoons olive oil

1/4 cup finely chopped white onion

1/2 teaspoon dried oregano (Mexican variety preferred), crumbled

1 (15-ounce) can white hominy, drained and rinsed

1/2 cup canned fat-free reduced-sodium chicken broth

1 1/2 cups corn kernels, fresh or thawed, if frozen

2 fresh poblano chiles, roasted and peeled (page 8) and neatly diced (about 1/3 inch)

1/4 teaspoon salt, or to taste

1. Heat the oil over medium heat in a medium deep skillet, or wide saucepan. Add the onion and oregano. Cook, stirring, until the onion is softened, about 3 minutes.

2. Add the hominy and chicken broth. Cook until the liquid is reduced to about 2 tablespoons, about 3 to 4 minutes. Stir in the corn, poblanos, and salt. Cook until the corn is tender, about 3 minutes. Serve hot.

Corn Pancakes
Tortitas de Elote

Makes **about 16 small pancakes**

Fresh corn makes irresistible little pancakes, to accompany entrées, such as sauced meat or poultry dishes, or as a quick snack topped with salsa. The batter is easy to make and quick to cook.

2 medium ears corn, shucked

¹/₄ cup milk

1 large egg, beaten

¹/₂ cup all-purpose flour

¹/₄ cup yellow cornmeal

1 teaspoon baking powder

1 teaspoon sugar

¹/₂ teaspoon salt

1 tablespoon vegetable oil

1. Cut the kernels from the corn cobs, and scrape the cobs to release the corn milk. Put in a bowl. Stir in the milk and egg. In another bowl, mix the flour, baking powder, and salt. Stir the dry ingredients into the corn mixture and mix well.

2. In a medium nonstick skillet, heat the oil over medium heat. Spoon about 2 tablespoons of batter into the oil to form a small pancake. Repeat and cook about 3 pancakes at a time about 1 to 2 minutes on each side, or until golden brown. Serve hot.

Savory Corn Cake
Torta de Elote

Makes **4 servings**

There are many traditional corn cakes, both sweet and savory. This one is moist and rich and tastes of sweet corn and butter. Serve it warm alongside saucy meats and beans, such as Chicken and Green Chile Stew (page 306) or Oven-Barbecued Beef (page 342). The cake will keep refrigerated for 2 to 3 days, and can be reheated in the oven or microwave.

1¹/₄ cups all-purpose flour

³/₄ teaspoon salt

1¹/₂ teaspoons baking powder

1¹/₄ cup fresh corn kernels, fresh or thawed, if frozen

¹/₄ cup milk

¹/₄ cup unsalted butter, at room temperature

2 tablespoons vegetable oil

3 tablespoons sugar

2 large eggs, separated

1. Position oven rack on upper third level. Preheat oven to 350°. Grease an 8-inch-square baking pan and line the bottom with parchment or waxed paper. In a large bowl, mix the flour, baking powder, and salt. Reserve.

2. In another bowl, using an electric mixer, beat the butter, oil, and sugar until fluffy. Add the egg yolks. Beat well. Beat in the blended corn. Add the dry ingredients and mix well. In a separate bowl, beat egg whites to soft peaks. Fold into the batter.

3. Turn the batter into the prepared pan and smooth the top. Bake 30 minutes or until a tester inserted into the center comes out clean. Let stand in the pan on a rack 10 minutes. Cut into 4 squares and then cut each square from corner to corner into triangles. Serve warm.

Note: If the top appears too pale when the cake is done, brown briefly, 30 to 45 seconds, under a hot broiler to make the top a little crusty. Watch carefully to prevent burning the top.

Peppers

Stuffed Chiles with Cheese
Chiles Rellenos con Queso

Makes **6 servings**

Dark green poblano chiles, roasted, peeled, and stuffed with cheese, then coated with a fluffy egg batter and fried are probably the most widely known of all the chiles rellenos. In most regions of Mexico poblano chiles are used for rellenos, but Anaheim and fresh New Mexico chiles are often used in the north. They also work very well.

Tomato Sauce for Stuffed Chiles (page 43)
6 fresh poblano or Anaheim chiles, roasted and peeled (page 8)
2 cups shredded Monterey Jack cheese
1/2 cup all-purpose flour
4 large eggs, separated
1/4 teaspoon salt
Vegetable oil for frying, such as corn oil

1. Prepare tomato sauce and keep warm. Prepare the chiles. Then, with a small sharp knife cut a slit lengthwise from the stem end to within 1-inch of the tip of each roasted and peeled chile. Keep the stems intact. Cut out the seed pod and rinse the chiles under running water to wash out the remaining seeds. Pat the chiles dry with paper towels.

2. Stuff each chile with a quarter of the cheese. Reshape and secure the opening with toothpicks. Put all but 1 tablespoon of the flour on a plate. Dust the stuffed chiles with flour and reserve on a plate.

3. Put the egg whites in a large bowl, and with an electric mixer (or by hand) beat until foamy. Add the salt and beat to stiff peaks. Beat in the egg yolks, at slow speed 1 at a time. Beat in the reserved 1 tablespoon of the flour.

4. In a heavy medium skillet, heat about 1 cup of oil until hot (375°). One at a time, dip the chiles into the egg batter to coat. Place a chile gently with two wooden spoons or tongs into the hot oil. Cook, turning once, until golden brown, about 2 minutes per side. Drain on paper towels. Repeat with remaining chiles. Remove toothpicks. Serve hot with the tomato sauce spooned over the chiles.

Stuffed Chiles with Minced Beef
Chiles Rellenos con Picadillo

Makes **6 servings**

Picadillo is a popular filling for chiles rellenos. It is made of minced pork, beef, or chicken, combined with onions, tomatoes, herbs, spices, and sometimes nuts, raisins, or other fruit. It's quite common in Mexico to serve two rellenos together, one filled with picadillo *and another with cheese (see preceding recipe on page 421).*

Tomato Sauce for Stuffed Chiles (page 43)
1¹/₂ cups minced pork or beef (Minced Spicy Pork, page 347)
6 fresh poblano or Anaheim chiles, roasted and peeled (page 8)
¹/₂ cup all-purpose flour
4 large eggs, separated
¹/₄ teaspoon salt
Vegetable oil for frying, such as corn oil

1. Prepare the tomato sauce. Reserve, covered, off heat. Prepare the beef filling. Reserve. Prepare the chiles. Then, with a small, sharp knife cut a slit lengthwise from the stem end to within 1-inch of the tip of each roasted and peeled chile. Keep the stems intact. Cut out the seed pod and rinse the chiles under running water to wash out the remaining seeds. Pat the chiles dry with paper towels.

2. Stuff each chile with about ½ cup of picadillo. Reshape and secure the opening with toothpicks. Put all but 1 tablespoon of the flour on a plate. Dust the stuffed chiles with flour and reserve on a plate.

3. Put the egg whites in a large bowl, and beat with an electric mixer or by hand until foamy. Add the salt and beat to soft peaks. Beat in the egg yolks one at a time. Beat in the reserved 1 tablespoon of the flour.

4. In a heavy medium skillet, heat about 1 cup of oil until hot (375°). One at a time, dip the chiles

into the egg batter to coat. Place a chile gently into the hot oil with 2 wooden spoons or tongs. Cook, turning once, until golden brown, about 2 minutes per side. Drain on paper towels. Repeat with remaining chiles. Serve with the tomato sauce spooned over the chiles.

Stuffed Chiles with Shredded Spiced Chicken
Chiles Rellenos con Picadillo de Pollo

Makes **6 servings**

When I travel in Mexico I'm always tempted by the many different versions of chiles rellenos. *Sometimes they are fried in a fluffy egg batter and sometimes there is no batter at all. Both ways are common. The first time I ate this* relleno *stuffed with chicken* picadillo *was in San Miguel de Allende and it's one of my favorites.*

Tomato Sauce for Stuffed Chiles (page 43)
2 cups (¹/₂ recipe) Minced Spicy Chicken (page 272)
6 large fresh poblano chiles, roasted and peeled (page 8)
¹/₂ cup all-purpose flour
4 large eggs, separated
¹/₄ teaspoon salt
Vegetable oil for frying, such as corn oil

1. Prepare the tomato sauce. Reserve, covered, off heat. Prepare the chicken. Reserve. Then, prepare the chiles. With a small sharp knife cut a slit lengthwise from the stem end to within 1-inch of the tip of each roasted and peeled chile. Keep the stems intact. Cut out the seed pod and rinse the chiles under running water to wash out the remaining seeds. Pat the chiles dry with paper towels.

2. Stuff each chile with about ½ cup of the reserved picadillo. Reshape and secure the opening with toothpicks. Put all but 1 tablespoon of the flour on a plate. Dust the stuffed chiles with flour and reserve on a plate.

3. Beat the egg whites in a large bowl with an electric mixer or by hand until foamy. Add the salt and beat to soft peaks. Beat in the egg yolks, 1 at a time. Beat in the reserved 1 tablespoon of the flour.

4. In a heavy medium skillet, heat about 1 cup of oil until hot (375°). One at a time, dip the chiles into the egg batter to coat. Place a chile gently into the hot oil with 2 wooden spoons or tongs. Cook, turning once, until golden brown, about 2 minutes per side. Drain on paper towels. Repeat with remaining chiles. Reheat the sauce. Serve with the tomato sauce spooned over the chiles.

Stuffed Chiles with Turkey
Chiles Rellenos con Pavo

Makes **6 servings**

In this modern rendition of stuffed poblano chiles I turned to the flavors of Veracruz and seasoned the cooked turkey with capers, raisins, cinnamon, allspice, and cloves, and also added toasted pine nuts. You can use meat from the Basic Cooked Turkey Breast (page 311) or roasted turkey meat from a deli.

Tomato Sauce for Stuffed Chiles (page 43)
6 large poblano chiles, roasted and peeled
**   (page 8)**
1 tablespoon olive oil
1 medium white onion, finely chopped
1 medium garlic clove, finely chopped
6 ripe plum tomatoes, peeled and finely chopped
1/2 teaspoon dried oregano (Mexican variety
**   preferred), crumbled**
1/4 teaspoon ground cinnamon (Mexican canela
**   or Ceylon variety preferred)**
1/4 teaspoon ground cloves
1/8 teaspoon ground allspice
3 cups shredded or chopped cooked turkey meat
3 teaspoons raisins
3 teaspoons drained small capers
3 teaspoons toasted pine nuts

1. Prepare the tomato sauce. Reserve covered off heat. Prepare the roasted chiles. With a small sharp knife cut a slit lengthwise from the stem end to within 1-inch of the tip of each roasted and peeled chile. Keep the stems intact. Cut out the seed pod and rinse the chiles under running water to wash out the remaining seeds. Put the chiles on a plate and set aside.

2. Preheat the oven to 350°. Heat the oil in a medium skillet and cook the onion and garlic until softened, 3 to 4 minutes. Add the tomatoes and cook, stirring, until most of the juices cook away, 2 to 3 minutes. Add the remaining ingredients and mix well.

3. Stuff each prepared chile with ½ cup of the turkey mixture. Lay the chiles in a rectangular baking pan, cover loosely with foil and bake until heated through, 20 to 25 minutes. Reheat the sauce. Pour about ¼ cup sauce on each of 4 serving plates. Place 1 chile on each plate and serve hot.

Stuffed Chiles with Fish
Chiles Rellenos con Pescado

Makes **6 servings**

Cooks from Veracruz, which hugs the Gulf of Mexico, are known for preparing fish every way imaginable, including using it to stuff chiles that are then topped with fresh tomato sauce. It's delicious.

Tomato Sauce for Stuffed Chiles (page 43)
**6 large poblano chiles, roasted and peeled
   (page 8)**
**1 pound fresh fish fillets, such as rock cod or
   snapper**
2 cups water
1/2 cup dry white wine
1 medium white onion, sliced
2 parsley sprigs
1 tablespoon olive oil
2 medium tomatoes, peeled and chopped
2 medium garlic cloves, finely chopped
2 teaspoons drained capers, chopped
**1/2 teaspoon dried oregano (Mexican variety
   preferred), crumbled**
1/2 teaspoon salt, or to taste
1/8 teaspoon freshly ground pepper, or to taste

1. Prepare the tomato sauce. Reserve in the pan off heat. Prepare the chiles. Then, with a small sharp knife cut a slit lengthwise from the stem end to within 1-inch of the tip of chile. Keep the stems intact. Cut out the seed pod and rinse the chiles under running water to wash out any remaining seeds. Pat the chiles dry with paper towels. Set aside.

2. Cut the fish fillets into 4-inch pieces. In a large skillet, bring water and wine to a boil. Add the fish, onion, and parsley. Reduce the heat, cover, and simmer until the fish is just opaque and just barely flakes when tested with a fork, 8 to 10 minutes, depending on thickness of the fish. Reserve

the fish on a plate. When cool enough to handle, remove the skin and bones from the fish and discard. Break fish into pieces with your fingers and reserve on a plate.

3. Preheat the oven to 375°. Chop the remaining onion. Heat the oil in a nonstick skillet over medium heat and cook the onion until softened, about 3 minutes. Add the remaining ingredients. Cook, stirring, until the tomato juices reduce and the mixture is nearly dry, 4 to 5 minutes.

4. Remove from the heat. Add the reserved fish. Stir gently to mix. Stuff the chiles equally with the fish mixture and place on a baking sheet. Cover with foil and bake until completely heated through, about 15 to 20 minutes. Reheat the sauce. Serve hot with the sauce spooned over the chiles.

Stuffed Chiles with Mashed Potatoes
Chiles Rellenos de Papas

Makes **6 servings**

Creamy mashed potatoes taste wonderful nestled in roasted green chiles. There is no batter or frying for this relleno, *a common preparation. Bright yellow corn scattered around the chiles makes a super presentation.*

Tomato Sauce for Stuffed Chiles (page 43)
**6 large poblano chiles, roasted and peeled
   (page 8)**
**6 small (about 1 pound) boiling potatoes,
   peeled and sliced**
1 large garlic clove, thinly sliced
1/3 cup milk
**3 tablespoons unsalted butter, at room
   temperature**
3 tablespoons crumbled cotija or mild feta cheese
1/2 teaspoon salt, or to taste
**1 cup cooked corn kernels, fresh (from about
   1 medium ear) or thawed, if frozen**

1. Prepare the sauce. Reserve covered, off heat. Prepare the chiles. Then, with a small sharp knife cut a slit lengthwise from the stem end to within 1-inch of the tip of each roasted and peeled chile. Keep the stems intact. Cut out the seed pod and rinse the chiles under running water to wash out the remaining seeds. Pat the chiles dry with paper towels. Set aside on a plate.

2. Preheat the oven to 350°. In a medium saucepan, cook the potatoes and garlic, in water to cover, over medium heat until the potatoes are tender, about 10 minutes. Mash the potatoes and garlic with the milk, butter, cheese, and salt until smooth.

3. Stuff each chile with about ½ cup of the mashed potatoes then close to reshape. Lay in an oiled baking dish. Cover loosely with foil and bake until hot, about 25 minutes. Reheat the sauce. To serve, spoon a pool of sauce on each of 4 serving plates and lay a stuffed chile in the center of each plate. Surround with a border of corn. Serve hot.

Stuffed Chiles with Refried Beans
Chiles Rellenos de Frijoles Refritos

Makes 6 servings

A beautiful garden restaurant, Nuu Luu, overlooking Oaxaca City, serves traditional Oaxacan food. I especially liked the chiles rellenos *stuffed with black beans. Any kind of refried beans can be used, but black beans would be used in Oaxaca.*

Tomato Sauce for Stuffed Chiles (page 43)

6 fresh poblano chiles, roasted and peeled (page 8)

3 cups Basic Refried Beans (page 462), or canned

½ cup Fresh Salsa Mexicana (page 24), or purchased salsa

½ cup shredded Monterey Jack cheese

1. Prepare the tomato sauce. Reserve covered, off heat. prepare the chiles. Then preheat the oven to 350°. With a small sharp knife cut a slit lengthwise from the stem end to within 1-inch of the tip of each roasted and peeled chile. Keep the stems intact. Cut out the seed pod and rinse the chiles under running water to wash out the remaining seeds. Pat the chiles dry with paper towels.

2. Mix the refried beans with the salsa and stuff each chile with about ½ cup of the beans and top each with ¼ cup of the cheese. Lay the chiles in a rectangular baking pan, cover loosely with foil and bake until hot and the cheese is melted, 20 to 25 minutes. Reheat the sauce. Serve hot with the tomato sauce spooned over the chiles.

Stuffed Anaheim Chiles with Goat Cheese
Chiles Rellenos con Queso de Chiva

Makes 6 servings

Long green Anaheim chiles are usually quite mild, but occasionally can be spicy. Look for bright green, fresh, unblemished chiles that are firm. Avoid soft and wrinkled chiles. Stuffed with goat cheese and served on a pool of tomato sauce, they make an exceptional first course.

Tomato Sauce for Stuffed Chiles (page 43)

12 fresh Anaheim or California long green chiles, roasted and peeled (page 8)

6 ounces soft goat cheese, cut into 12 equal pieces

1 cup corn kernels, fresh (from about 1 medium ear), or thawed, if frozen

1. Prepare the tomato sauce. Reserve, covered, off heat. Prepare the chiles. Then, with a small sharp knife, slit the chiles open from stem end to within 1½ inches of the tip, keeping the stem intact. Discard the seeds and rinse to dislodge any remaining seeds. Blot with paper towels and lay the chiles on a plate.

2. Preheat the oven to 350°. Tuck a piece of goat cheese inside each chile. Arrange the chiles in a single layer on a baking sheet and bake until heated through, about 20 minutes.

3. Cook the corn in a small pot of boiling water until barely tender, about 3 minutes. Reheat the tomato sauce and divide among 4 serving plates. Lay 2 chiles on the sauce on each plate. Garnish with corn.

Stuffed Chiles with White Beans
Chiles Rellenos con Frijoles Blancos

Makes 6 servings

The filling for this recipe is very good made with convenient canned white beans, and that's what I normally use for stuffing bright green poblano chiles.

Tomato Sauce for Stuffed Chiles (page 43)

6 large poblano chiles, roasted and peeled (page 8)

1 tablespoon olive oil or vegetable oil

1 medium onion, finely chopped

1 medium garlic clove, finely chopped

3 (15-ounce) cans small white beans, drained and rinsed

1 teaspoon dried oregano (Mexican variety preferred), crumbled

½ teaspoon dried thyme

⅓ cup canned fat-free reduced-sodium chicken broth

Salt and freshly ground pepper, to taste

½ cup crumbled queso fresco (fresh Mexican cheese) or mild feta cheese

1. Prepare the tomato sauce. Reserve, covered, off heat. Prepare the chiles. Then, put 1 roasted and peeled chile on a work surface. Using a small sharp knife cut a slit to open the chile from the stem end to within 1-inch of the tip. Carefully cut out the seed pod and discard. Gently rinse under running water to wash out remaining seeds. Repeat with the remaining chiles.

2. In a nonstick skillet, heat the oil over medium-low heat and cook the onion and garlic slowly, stirring frequently, until softened, but not browned, about 3 to 4 minutes. Add the beans. With the back of a wooden spoon mash a few of the beans to help thicken the mixture. Add the oregano, thyme, and chicken broth. Bring to a boil and cook, stirring, until the liquid is reduced and the beans hold their shape on a spoon. Season with salt and pepper. (Since the beans already contain sodium, more salt may not be needed.) Cool the beans in the pan.

3. Preheat oven to 350°. Spoon the filling equally into each prepared chile, packing well to reshape the chile. Place the filled chiles in a single layer, cut side up, in a rectangular baking pan. Cover with foil. Bake until completely heated through, about 25 minutes. Reheat the sauce and spoon over the top of each chile. Sprinkle with cheese. Serve.

Stuffed Poblano Chiles in Walnut Sauce
Chiles en Nogada

Makes **6 servings**

Mexico's colors are reflected in this stunning and festive dish from the city of Puebla that commemorates Mexico's Independence Day on September 16. The chiles are served almost everywhere in and around Puebla during the walnut harvest. Chiles en Nogada *is made by stuffing dark green poblano chiles with* picadillo— *an intriguing mixture of ground meat, onions, tomatoes, jalapeños, olives, raisins, dried fruits, and spices. The warm chiles are served with a cool creamy walnut sauce and brilliant red pomegranate seeds on top. If you make the dish in parts and start a day or two ahead, it's manageable.*

6 large poblano chiles, roasted and peeled (page 8)

3 cups minced pork or beef (Minced Spicy Pork, page 347)

Walnut Sauce (page 52)

1 pomegranate

Italian flat-leaf parsley sprigs

1. Prepare the poblano chiles. With a small sharp knife, slit each chile lengthwise, with stems intact, to within 1 inch of the bottom end. Carefully cut out the seed pod. Rinse the chiles under cold running water to remove the remaining seeds. Pat dry with paper towels and put on a plate. Cover and refrigerate until ready to stuff, up to 2 days ahead.

2. Prepare the picadillo. Cover and refrigerate until ready to stuff the chiles, up to 2 days ahead. Then, prepare the walnut sauce. Cover and refrigerate until ready to use, up to 1 day ahead.

3. Preheat the oven to 350°. Grease a baking sheet. To assemble, stuff each chile until plump with about ½ cup picadillo and close to reshape. Put the stuffed chiles on the baking sheet with the cut side up showing some of the stuffing. Cover with a loose tent of aluminum foil and bake until completely heated through, about 25 minutes.

4. Meanwhile, cut the pomegranate in half with a sharp knife. Reserve one half for another use. With the remaining half, separate the pomegranate seeds from the skin within a bowl of cold water in the sink (to prevent splattering of juices). Place the seeds in a small bowl. To serve, put 1 stuffed chile on each of 4 serving plates, spoon about ¼ cup walnut sauce over each chile and scatter about 1 tablespoon pomegranate seeds on top. Garnish with parsley sprigs.

Pickled Ancho Chiles Stuffed with Guacamole
Rellenos de Chiles Anchos en Escabeche con Guacamole

Makes 6 servings

Miguel Ravego, a Mexican-American chef with roots in Sonora in northern Mexico, introduced me to marinated ancho chiles. Stuffing them makes them irresistible, and guacamole within the marinated chile is one of my favorite versions.

6 large blemish-free ancho chiles of equal size

1¹/₂ cups red wine vinegar

1¹/₂ cups water

2¹/₂ tablespoons dark brown sugar

2 bay leaves

¹/₂ teaspoon allspice berries or ground allspice

4 whole cloves

³/₄ teaspoon dried oregano (Mexican variety preferred), crumbled

3 (about 3-inches-long) fresh mint sprigs

3 tablespoons olive oil

Classic Guacamole (page 23)

Sour cream

Chopped fresh cilantro

1. Wipe the chiles with a damp paper towel to remove dust. In a hot dry skillet, warm the chiles briefly until they soften and are pliable. Slit the chiles down one side, seed, and devein, leaving the stems intact. Reserve.

2. In a medium saucepan, bring to a boil the vinegar, water, brown sugar, bay leaf, allspice, cloves, and oregano. Remove the pan from the heat. Add the reserved chiles, fresh mint, and olive oil. Cover and marinate, turning gently, once or twice, for 6 to 8 hours at room temperature.

3. About 45 minutes before serving, prepare the guacamole. Drain the chiles, pat them dry, then stuff equally with the guacamole. (The marinated chiles are fragile, so handle very gently to prevent tearing them.) Place 1 stuffed chile on each of 4 serving plates. Drizzle with sour cream and sprinkle with chopped cilantro. Serve within 30 minutes to prevent the guacamole from turning brown.

Green Chile Strips
Rajas de Chiles

Makes 4 to 6 servings

Roasted and peeled fresh green chiles cut into strips are called rajas, *and are combined with other vegetables, stirred into egg and meat dishes, and used as a garnish. Poblano chiles are the most popular and common chile to be used for* rajas, *but Anaheims and other large fresh peppers are also prepared in the same way. Here, as is common, the chile strips are briefly sautéed.*

4 large poblano chiles, roasted and peeled (page 8)

1 tablespoon vegetable oil

¹/₂ teaspoon salt, or to taste

1. Prepare the chiles. Then, cut out the stem end section of the chiles. Discard the stems and cut the chiles open. Remove the seeds and veins. Rinse the chiles, blot with paper towels, and cut into thin strips (about 2 inches × ¼ inch).

2. Heat the oil in a medium skillet over medium heat and cook the chile strips until shiny and heated through, about 1 to 2 minutes. Season with salt.

Poblano Chile Strips with Fried Onions
Cebollas Fritas con Rajas

Makes **4 servings**

Onions and thin strips of roasted poblano chile are served as a team all over Mexico. Roasted chile strips are so common that they're simply known as rajas *(for "strips" or "slices"). Together, use them to top steaks, chicken, or fish. Put them inside sandwiches, tacos, or enchiladas. With this great team, you'll win a lot of fans!*

3 poblano chiles, roasted, peeled, and seeded (page 8)

2 tablespoons vegetable oil

1 large white onion, peeled and sliced

1/2 teaspoon dried oregano (Mexican variety preferred), crumbled

1/2 teaspoon salt

Prepare the chiles. Then, cut them into thin strips, about 2 inches × 1/4 inch. In a medium nonstick skillet, heat the oil over medium-high heat. Add the onion and cook, stirring, over medium heat until the onion begins to brown, 4 to 5 minutes. Add the chile strips and oregano. Cook, stirring, 1 minute. Season with salt. Serve hot.

Green Chile Strips with Onions and Mushrooms
Rajas con Cebollas y Hongos

Makes **4 servings**

It's common to see street vendors everywhere in Mexico cooking a variety of enticing foods from their temporary carts and simple stands, especially in the evening when people are out strolling through plazas and parks. This tasty concoction is like a Mexican stir-fry that's wrapped inside tortillas or stuffed into sandwich rolls. The combination is also terrific as a topping for hamburgers and steaks. Sometimes I add diced tomato at the last minute.

2 large poblano chiles, roasted and peeled (page 8)

2 tablespoons vegetable oil or olive oil

1 medium white onion, thinly sliced

12 medium white or brown cremini mushrooms, sliced

1/2 teaspoon dried oregano (Mexican variety preferred), crumbled

1/2 teaspoon salt, or to taste

Freshly ground pepper, to taste

1. Prepare the chiles, then cut out the stem end section of the chile. Discard the stems and cut the chiles open. Remove the seeds and veins. Rinse the chiles, blot with paper towels, and cut into thin strips (about 2 inches × 1/4 inch).

2. In a large skillet, heat the oil over medium heat and cook the onion, stirring, until limp, 3 to 4 minutes. Add the mushrooms and oregano. Cook, stirring, until the mushrooms release their juices and brown slightly. Add the reserved chile strips, salt, and pepper. Heat through completely. Serve hot.

Green Chile Strips in Cream with Cheese
Rajas en Crema con Queso

Makes **4 servings**

Rajas, *roasted and peeled poblano chiles cut into thin strips, are a common accompaniment to just about any meat or seafood dish. This delectable version with Mexican crema or sour cream and cheese is a little more elaborate.*

4 poblano chiles, roasted and peeled (page 8)

2 tablespoons unsalted butter or olive oil

1 medium white onion, thinly sliced

$^1/_2$ teaspoon salt, or to taste

1 cup Mexican crema or sour cream, thinned with milk

1 cup grated asadero or Monterey Jack cheese

1. Prepare the chiles. Then, cut out the stem end section of the chile. Discard the stems and cut the chiles open. Remove the seeds and veins. Rinse the chiles, blot with paper towels, and cut into thin strips (about 2 inches × ¼ inch).

2. Melt the butter over medium heat in a large skillet and cook the onion, stirring, until limp and softened, about 4 minutes.

3. Add the reserved chile strips, salt, and cream. Cook, stirring, until completely heated through and bubbling, about 3 minutes. Transfer to a shallow bowl. Sprinkle with cheese and serve at once.

Red Bell Peppers and Jicama
Chiles Dulce y Jicama

Makes **4 servings**

Red bell peppers are often called sweet peppers, chiles dulces, *and they are available in markets throughout Mexico. Jicama, a large, often round root vegetable with brown skin and crisp white flesh is seldom cooked, but in the new style of cooking* (nueva cocina), *Mexican chefs are discovering different ways of presenting traditional ingredients. When cooked, the jicama sticks resemble thin strips of French fries. This simple dish of red peppers and jicama are a striking pair to serve with fish or chicken.*

2 teaspoons olive oil

1 teaspoon unsalted butter

1 red bell pepper, cut into thin strips, about $^1/_3$-inch wide × 2-inches long

$^1/_2$ medium jicama, peeled and cut into thin strips, about $^1/_3$-inch wide × 2-inches long

$^1/_2$ teaspoon salt

$^1/_4$ teaspoon freshly ground pepper

1 tablespoon minced fresh parsley

In a nonstick skillet, heat the oil and butter over medium-high heat and cook the pepper and jicama, stirring frequently, until just limp, 3 to 4 minutes. Stir in the salt, pepper, and parsley. Serve hot as a side vegetable or as a garnish for grilled fish or chicken.

Squash

Chayote and Carrots
Chayote y Zanahorias

Makes **4 to 6 servings**

Since most flights within Mexico connect in Mexico City, I often spend the night at one of the airport hotels before an early morning flight the next day. One evening, my grilled chicken entrée served at the hotel restaurant included these perfectly prepared vegetables. They were not fancy, but fresh, pretty, and very tasty.

Chayote is a pale green pear-shaped member of the squash family with a mild taste it is now available in most supermarkets in the United States and in the same way as summer squash.

1 large chayote
3 large carrots, peeled and sliced on the diagonal into ovals
1 tablespoon unsalted butter
1/2 white onion, thinly sliced
1/2 teaspoon salt, or to taste

1. Cut the chayote in half lengthwise and cook in a large pot of boiling water until tender, about 25 minutes. Meanwhile, in another medium pot of boiling water, cook the carrots until tender, about 10 minutes. When the vegetables are tender drain and cool under running water.

2. Peel the chayote and slice thinly crosswise. In a large skillet, melt the butter over medium heat and cook the onion, stirring, until limp and tender, about 4 minutes. Add the sliced chayote, carrots, and salt. Stir gently to coat with the butter and heat through completely, about 2 minutes. Serve hot.

Chayote and Tomato with Cheese Topping
Chayote y Jitomate con Queso

Makes **4 servings**

Chayote is a pale green, pear-shaped squash commonly served in Mexico that is used in the same way as other summer squash. It has a mild pleasant taste. In this recipe, the chayotes are boiled until tender, then topped with a tomato sauce and cheese and finished in the oven.

2 large chayotes
2 tablespoons vegetable oil
1/2 medium white onion, chopped
2 medium garlic cloves, finely chopped
2 medium tomatoes, peeled and chopped
1/2 teaspoon dried oregano (Mexican variety preferred), crumbled
1/4 teaspoon dried thyme
1/2 teaspoon salt, or to taste
1 cup shredded Monterey Jack or cheddar cheese

1. Cut the chayotes in half lengthwise. Bring a large pot of water to a boil, and cook the chayotes until tender, about 25 minutes. Drain and reserve.

2. Preheat the oven to 375°. Grease an 8-inch square glass baking dish. Heat the oil in a medium skillet. Cook the onion and garlic until softened, about 3 minutes. Add the tomatoes, oregano, thyme, and salt. Bring to a boil and cook over medium-high heat, stirring frequently, until the juices are reduced and the mixture is nearly dry. Remove from the heat and reserve.

3. Peel the cooled chayotes and slice lengthwise about ½ inch thick. Arrange in a single layer in the baking dish. Spread the tomato sauce over the chayotes and top with the grated cheese. Bake, uncovered, until hot and the cheese is melted and bubbly, about 20 minutes. Serve hot.

Chayote Casserole with Ground Pork

Chayote en Cazuela con Puerco

Makes 4 servings

Chayotes are related to squash and are indigenous to Mexico. Here the chayote is baked in a creamy sauce with ground pork for a light main dish.

2 medium chayotes, quartered lengthwise

1 tablespoon olive oil

¹/₂ pound lean ground pork

¹/₂ medium white onion, coarsely chopped

¹/₂ red bell pepper, coarsely chopped

¹/₂ teaspoon dried thyme

¹/₂ teaspoon salt, or to taste

¹/₈ teaspoon freshly ground pepper, or to taste

¹/₂ cup heavy cream

1 tablespoon bread crumbs

¹/₂ cup shredded manchego or mild cheddar cheese

1. In a large pan of salted boiling water, cook the chayotes over medium heat until tender, about 25 minutes. Drain and cool under running water. Peel off the thin skin and slice crosswise. Reserve in a bowl.

2. Preheat oven to 350°. Grease an ovenproof casserole dish. Heat the oil in a skillet and cook the ground pork until no longer pink. Add the onion and red pepper. Cook, stirring, until tender, about 5 minutes. Add the reserved chayote and the remaining ingredients, except the cheese. Stir to mix. Bring to a boil and cook for 1 minute.

3. Transfer the vegetables to the casserole dish. Sprinkle the cheese on top. Bake until completely heated through and the cheese is melted, about 20 minutes. Serve hot.

Baked Stuffed Chayote

Chayote Relleno

Makes 4 servings

This is a traditional chayote dish that's prepared throughout Mexico. It can be served as a first course or as a side dish to meats and poultry.

2 medium chayotes, halved lengthwise

1 tablespoon olive oil or unsalted butter

1 medium white onion, chopped

2 medium garlic cloves, finely chopped

1 medium tomato, finely chopped

2 tablespoons bread crumbs

¹/₂ teaspoon salt, or to taste

¹/₂ teaspoon dried oregano (Mexican variety preferred), crumbled

1 tablespoon chopped fresh flat-leaf parsley

¹/₂ cup shredded cheddar cheese

1. Bring a large pot of water to a boil and cook the chayotes until tender when pierced with the tip of a sharp knife, about 25 to 30 minutes. Drain and cool. Scoop out the centers of the chayotes with a melon-baller, leaving a ¹/₂-inch edge with the shell. Reserve the shells and coarsely chop the flesh.

2. Preheat the oven to 350°. Heat the oil in a large skillet and cook the onion and garlic until softened, about 3 minutes. Add the tomato and cook until the juices reduce and the mixture is nearly dry. Stir in the chopped chayote, bread crumbs, salt, and oregano.

3. Spoon the mixture into the reserved shells. Mix the parsley and cheese together and divide it evenly over the stuffed shells. Press lightly to make the cheese stick. Put the shells on a foil-lined baking sheet and bake until heated through and the cheese is melted, 20 to 25 minutes. Serve hot.

Grilled Zucchini
Calabacitas Asadas

*Makes **4 servings***

Grilling green or yellow zucchini (or a combination of both) is an excellent way to cook this versatile vegetable that's always available. Cook on a stovetop grill pan, or grill outdoors if you already have a hot grill going. Serve with poultry, meats, or fish.

6 to 8 small zucchini
1 to 2 tablespoons olive oil
Salt and freshly ground pepper, to taste

Rinse the zucchini and pat dry. Trim off the ends. Thinly slice lengthwise. Brush both sides with oil. Heat a grill pan over medium heat until hot enough to make a few drops of water sizzle. Lay the zucchini slices on the pan. Season with salt and pepper, and cook until grill marks appear on the bottom, about 3 minutes. Turn and cook until crisp-tender and still bright green around the edges. Arrange the zucchini on a serving plate. Serve hot or warm.

Sautéed Shredded Zucchini
Calabacitas Rallados

*Makes **4 servings***

Zucchini retains its bright green color and a bit of crunch in this new-style vegetable dish. The zucchini is sprinked with chopped fresh oregano and crumbled cotija cheese. Try it with Grilled Chicken Breasts with Ancho Chile Sauce (page 274).

2 tablespoons olive oil
2 tablespoons finely chopped white onion
4 medium zucchini, coarsely shredded
1 teaspoon finely chopped fresh oregano
  or ¹/₂ teaspoon dried oregano (Mexican
  variety preferred), crumbled
¹/₈ teaspoon freshly ground pepper, or to taste
¹/₂ teaspoon salt
1 tablespoon crumbled cotija cheese

Heat the oil in a large nonstick skillet and cook the onion until slightly softened, but not browned, about 2 minutes. Add the zucchini and oregano. Cook, stirring, until zucchini is limp and hot, with bright green edges, about 4 minutes. Season with black pepper and salt. Sprinkle with cheese.

Zucchini with Onions and Cheese
Calabacitas con Cebollas y Queso

Makes **4 servings**

Here's a quick, satisfying side dish for busy cooks. I like this one with roasted or grilled meats. Oaxaca-style string cheese is now available in many supermarkets. Any good white melting cheese can be substituted, such as mozzarella.

1 tablespoon unsalted butter
1 tablespoon vegetable oil
1 medium white onion, finely chopped
1 large garlic clove, minced
4 medium zucchini (about 1 pound), cut into
    1/2-inch pieces
1/2 teaspoon ground cumin
1/4 teaspoon dried oregano (Mexican variety
    preferred), crumbled
1/4 teaspoon salt, or to taste
1/8 teaspoon freshly ground pepper, or to taste
1/2 cup small strips Oaxaca string cheese

1. In a medium skillet, melt the butter with the oil until hot. Cook the onion and garlic, stirring, until the onion is limp, about 4 minutes. Add the zucchini, cumin, oregano, salt and pepper. Cook until the zucchini is crisp tender, about 3 minutes.

2. Transfer the vegetables to an ovenproof casserole dish. Scatter the cheese over the top, and run under a preheated broiler until the cheese melts, 2 to 3 minutes. Serve at once.

Zucchini and Mushrooms with Epazote
Calabacitas con Hongos y Epazote

Makes **4 servings**

If fresh epazote is not available to flavor the vegetables use fresh oregano. It adds a different flavor, but is equally good with the vegetables.

3 teaspoons olive oil
4 medium zucchini, cut crosswise into 1-inch pieces
1/2 teaspoon salt, or to taste
1/2 pound small white mushrooms, quartered
2 medium garlic cloves, minced
1 tablespoon slivered fresh epazote leaves
1 small fresh red jalapeño or Fresno chile, seeded,
    veins removed, and very finely chopped

1. In a large nonstick skillet, heat 2 teaspoons of the oil over medium-high heat. Add the zucchini and cook, stirring, until crisp-tender and the edges turn bright green. Season with 1/4 teaspoon of the salt and transfer to a bowl.

2. In the same skillet, add the remaining teaspoon of oil. Add the mushrooms, garlic, and epazote. Cover and cook, stirring frequently, until the mushrooms release their juices and are tender, 3 to 4 minutes. Return the zucchini to the pan. Add the chile. Cook, stirring, until completely heated through, 1 to 2 minutes. Serve hot.

Zucchini and Carrots with Tomato
Calabacitas y Zanahorias con Jitomate

Makes **4 servings**

El Campanario, a beautiful and stylish restaurant in a restored eighteenth-century building in San Miguel de Allende, serves this bright mix of fresh vegetables with stuffed chicken breast. The vegetables also go well with other meats or grilled fish.

2 medium carrots, peeled and finely diced
    (¼ inch)

1 tablespoon olive oil

¼ medium white onion, finely chopped

2 medium zucchini, cut into ¼-inch dice

1 medium tomato, peeled, seeded, and
    finely chopped

1 tablespoon chopped fresh cilantro

¼ teaspoon salt, or to taste

⅛ teaspoon freshly ground pepper, or to taste

1. In a medium saucepan, cook the carrots in boiling water to cover until crisp tender, about 3 minutes. Drain and rinse under cold running water to stop the cooking. Reserve in a bowl.

2. Heat the oil in a skillet over medium heat. Add the onion and cook, stirring, until translucent, about 3 minutes. Add the zucchini and reserved carrots. Cook, stirring frequently until the zucchini is crisp tender, 3 to 4 minutes. Add the tomato, cilantro, salt, and pepper. Cook, stirring until completely heated through, 1 to 2 minutes. Serve hot.

Zucchini Pancakes
Tortas de Calabacitas

Makes **4 servings**

Sometimes these vegetable pancakes are taken on picnics and eaten cold. I like them best hot, right out of the pan, served with meat or chicken. The pancakes are also excellent for breakfast with chorizo sausage or ham. For the best results, squeeze the watery juices from the zucchini before stirring it into the batter.

2 cups (about ¾ pound) shredded zucchini

½ cup all-purpose flour

1 teaspoon baking powder

½ teaspoon salt

2 large eggs, beaten

1 jarred pickled jalapeño chile (en escabeche),
    seeded and finely chopped

1 tablespoon olive oil

1. Wrap the shredded zucchini in a clean tea towel and squeeze to remove most of the moisture. In a medium bowl mix together the flour, baking powder, and salt. Add the eggs, zucchini, and jalapeño. Mix well.

2. Heat the oil in a medium nonstick skillet over medium heat. When the oil is hot, spoon enough batter into the pan to make pancakes about 3 inches in diameter. Cook until lightly browned on both sides, about 2 minutes per side. Cook in batches, adding extra oil to the pan if needed. Serve hot or at room temperature.

Zucchini Pudding
Budín de Calabacitas

Makes 6 servings

Baked vegetable casseroles containing flour, eggs, and milk are called budínes *in Mexico. Serve this as a vegetarian entrée or to accompany saucy meat dishes. If you like tongue-tingling flavors, the* budín *is really good with Chipotle and Tomatillo Sauce (page 49).*

1/4 cup all-purpose flour
1/4 cup yellow cornmeal
1 teaspoon baking powder
1 1/2 tablespoons olive oil
1/2 cup white onion, finely chopped
3/4 pound medium zucchini, trimmed and cut into small dice
1/2 teaspoon dried thyme
1/2 teaspoon salt
1/8 teaspoon crushed red pepper
2 large eggs
1/2 cup low-fat milk
1/2 cup sour cream or yogurt
1/2 cup shredded Monterey Jack or cheddar cheese

1. Preheat the oven to 350°. Grease a square 8-inch baking dish. In a small bowl mix together the flour, cornmeal, and baking powder. Set aside.

2. Heat the oil in a large skillet over medium heat, and cook the onion until softened, about 3 minutes. Add the zucchini, thyme, salt, and crushed red pepper. Cook, stirring, until the zucchini is crisp-tender, about 2 minutes. Reserve in the pan off the heat.

3. Beat the eggs in a large bowl until blended. Beat in the milk, sour cream, and 1/4 cup of the cheese. Add the dry ingredients. Mix well. Add the zucchini mixture. Mix well. Transfer to the baking dish. Sprinkle the top with the remaining 1/4 cup of cheese. Bake until the budín is set and a tester inserted in the center comes out clean, about 35 minutes. Cut into squares and serve hot.

Squash Blossoms Stuffed with Cheese
Rellenos de Flor de Calabazas

Makes 4 servings

Squash blossoms are very fragile and need to be used the day they are purchased. The blossoms can be trimmed and stuffed with cheese ahead of time, but the beaten egg batter and frying must be done just before serving. The accompanying tomato sauce can be made ahead. Look for squash blossoms in season in farmer's markets, and in Mexican or Italian markets.

Tomato Sauce for Stuffed Chiles (page 43)
8 large squash blossoms
4 (1/4-inch-thick) slices Monterey Jack cheese
1/2 cup all-purpose flour
2 large eggs, separated
1/4 teaspoon salt
Vegetable oil for frying

1. Prepare the tomato sauce. Cover and reserve. Then, remove the green petals at the base of the squash blossoms and trim the stems to 2 inches. Reach into the center of the blossoms and pinch off the stamens. Rinse the blossoms gently and lay on a clean tea towel to dry.

2. Cut the cheese into pieces to fit inside the blossoms and gently fill each blossom. Overlap the petals of the fragile blossoms carefully to enclose the cheese. (They are limp and delicate and will stay closed.) Gently dust the filled blossoms with flour and lay on a plate.

3. In a medium bowl, beat the egg whites with the salt until stiff. Add egg yolks, 1 at a time, and continue beating just until well blended. In a medium nonstick skillet heat oil to a depth of about 1 inch over medium heat. When the oil shimmers, dip the stuffed blossoms into the beaten egg batter and place gently and carefully into the hot oil. (Your fingers will probably be covered with batter.) Cook until golden brown, about 1 minute per side. Drain on paper towels. Reheat the tomato sauce. Serve the cooked blossoms hot with the sauce spooned alongside.

Winter Squash with Greens
Calabaza con Quelites

Makes 4 to 6 servings

Any greens can be used in this recipe, such as chopped beet tops or chard, but packaged baby spinach is so convenient that I usually choose spinach. In Mexico, there are a number of native greens (quelites) *that are gathered locally in the regions where they grow, such as lamb's quarters,* romeritos, *and* papalo—*varieties that are generally not available here. Wild sorrel and* verdolagas *(purslane) are other examples that may be available here.*

Hominy, specially processed dried corn, is often used for a stew-type dish called pozole, *but can be used in vegetable medleys as well. Canned hominy is precooked for easy use.*

1 (2-pound) butternut squash
2 tablespoons olive oil
1 cup chopped white onion
1/4 teaspoon crushed red pepper
1 (15-ounce) can white hominy, drained and rinsed
1 (6-ounce) package fresh baby spinach
1/2 teaspoon salt, or to taste

1. Using a large heavy knife, cut the squash in half, lengthwise. Scoop out the seeds. Peel off the skin, then cut the squash into 1/2-inch pieces.
2. Heat the oil in a large wide saucepan over medium heat. Add the squash, onion, and crushed pepper. Cook, stirring until the squash is barely tender, 10 to 12 minutes. Add the hominy and cook 2 minutes. Add the spinach and cook, stirring, until the spinach is wilted, 4 to 5 minutes. Season with salt. Serve hot.

Carrots

Carrot and Jicama Sticks
Zanahoria y Jicama

Makes 4 servings

Jicama, a large round root vegetable with brown skin and white flesh, is not often served as a cooked vegetable, but it's really wonderful quickly sautéed in butter. Carrots make a perfect mate for the jicama. The vegetables can be cooked together for the same length of time when both are cut into skinny sticks.

1 teaspoon vegetable oil

2 tablespoons unsalted butter

3 medium carrots, peeled and cut into thin sticks, ¼-inch × 2 inches

1 medium jicama, peeled and cut into thin sticks, ¼-inch × 2 inches

½ teaspoon salt, or to taste

⅛ teaspoon freshly ground pepper, or to taste

In a large nonstick skillet, heat the oil and butter until the butter sizzles. Add the carrots and jicama. Toss to coat with the butter. Cover and cook, stirring frequently, until the vegetables are crisp-tender, 6 to 8 minutes. Season with salt and pepper. Serve hot.

Carrot Pudding
Budín de Zanahoria

Makes 6 servings

Vegetable puddings are called budínes in Mexican cooking and are often served as a separate course with a sauce. This carrot pudding is baked in a pie plate and cut in wedges to be served on the entrée plate with a saucy meat dish, such as Pork Stew from Puebla (page 356) and Lamb in Red Chile Stew (page 370).

⅛ cup cornmeal or bread crumbs

⅓ cup all-purpose flour

1 teaspoon baking powder

1 teaspoon sugar

¼ teaspoon ground cumin

¼ teaspoon ground allspice

2 tablespoons unsalted butter

3 medium carrots (10 ounces), peeled and coarsely grated

½ teaspoon salt, or to taste

2 large eggs

½ cup whole milk

½ cup grated Monterey Jack cheese

1. Grease an 8-inch pie plate. Sprinkle with corn meal or fine bread crumbs. Set aside. Preheat the oven to 350°. In a bowl, mix flour, baking powder, sugar, cumin, and allspice. Set aside.

2. Melt the butter in a skillet over medium heat and cook the carrots, stirring frequently, until limp, about 5 minutes. Stir in the salt. Remove from the heat and cool.

3. In a medium bowl, beat together the eggs and milk. Add the carrots, cheese, and dry ingredients. Mix well. Transfer to the pie plate. Bake 25 minutes, or until set and barely browned on top. Cut in wedges and serve hot.

Carrots and Potatoes in Ancho Chile Sauce
Zanahorias y Papas en Salsa de Chile Ancho

Makes **4 servings**

Here's a versatile and classic combination of cooked cubed carrots and potatoes mixed with mild red chile sauce that's baked in the oven until the flavors mingle and the vegetables start to brown. Serve as a side dish with just about anything, or try with a poached or fried egg sitting in a nest of the vegetables for brunch. The vegetables are also wonderful rolled inside a tortilla with tomatoes and shredded lettuce for a vegetarian taco or burrito.

**1 cup Ancho Chile Sauce for Enchiladas (page 48)
plus more if needed**
4 medium carrots, peeled and cut into ¹/₂-inch dice
**4 medium red or white potatoes, scrubbed and
diced (¹/₂ inch)**
1 tablespoon olive oil or vegetable oil
1 medium onion, coarsely chopped
¹/₂ teaspoon salt, or to taste

1. Prepare the chile sauce. Reserve in the pan off heat. In a large pan of boiling salted water, cook the carrots and potatoes until crisp-tender, about 5 minutes. Drain and transfer to an ovenproof casserole dish. Stir in 1 cup of the chile sauce. Reserve.

2. Preheat the oven to 350°. Heat the oil in a medium skillet over medium heat and cook the onion, stirring, until softened, 3 to 4 minutes. Add to the casserole dish. Add the salt. Stir to mix the ingredients. If the mixture seems dry, stir in an additional ¼ cup of the chile sauce. Bake until the vegetables are tender and starting to brown, about 30 minutes. Serve hot.

Note: Extra chile sauce may be refrigerated or frozen for later use.

Cauliflower

Cauliflower Fritters
Buñuelos de Coliflor

Makes **4 servings**

Sometimes cauliflower is prepared this way, with small pieces of cheese tucked between pieces of cauliflower, but instead, you can crumble a little cheese over the fritters after frying, if you wish. It's customary to serve the cauliflower as a separate course with Ranchera Sauce (page 44). It is also a wonderful side dish to accompany main-course meat or poultry dishes.

Ranchera Sauce (page 44)
**1 small cauliflower (about 1 pound),
cut into medium florets**
¹/₂ cup all-purpose flour
³/₄ teaspoon salt, or to taste
2 large eggs, separated
Vegetable oil for frying
¹/₃ cup crumbled cotija or mild feta cheese

1. Prepare the ranchera sauce. Reserve in the pan off heat. Cook the cauliflower in a large pot of boiling water until crisp-tender, about 2 minutes. Drain and cool at once in cold running water to stop the cooking. Drain well and pat dry with paper towels. Set aside.

2. Put the flour in a pie plate and mix in ½ teaspoon of the salt. In a deep-fryer or heavy saucepan heat oil over medium heat to a depth of 2 inches until the oil shimmers.

3. Meanwhile, beat the egg whites with the remaining ¼ teaspoon of salt until stiff. Beat in the yolks, one at a time, until well blended. Dredge the florets in the flour and dip into the egg batter a few at a time. Fry in batches until golden. Drain on paper towels. Reheat the sauce. Serve the fritters right away with ranchera sauce poured over the top and sprinkled with grated cheese.

Cauliflower with Cotija Cheese
Coliflor con Queso Cotija

Makes **4 servings**

A great deal of cauliflower is grown in Mexico. This simple dish of buttery cauliflower sprinkled with cheese is quite common and very good. Cotija cheese is available in many supermarkets or Mexican markets.

1 medium cauliflower (about 1¹/₂ pounds), cut into florets
1 tablespoon unsalted butter, at room temperature
1 tablespoon olive oil
¹/₂ teaspoon salt, or to taste
¹/₃ cup crumbled cotija cheese
2 teaspoons finely chopped fresh parsley or cilantro

Cook the cauliflower in a large pan of boiling water until barely tender, about 4 minutes. Drain and return to the pan while hot. Add the butter, olive oil, and salt. Stir very gently to melt the butter and coat the cauliflower. Transfer to a shallow serving bowl or platter. Sprinkle with the cheese and parsley. Serve hot.

Cauliflower with Tomatillo and Sweet Pepper Salsa
Coliflor con Tomatillo y Salsa de Chile Dulce

Makes **4 servings**

Here's a simple vegetable dish that makes a full presentation. It goes very well with Fried Fish in a Fluffy Egg Coat (page 397), Seared Tuna with Oregano and Garlic (page 392), or just plain grilled fish fillets.

Mild Tomatillo and Sweet Pepper Sauce (page 37)
1 medium cauliflower (about 1¹/₂ pounds), cut into florets
1 tablespoon olive oil or unsalted butter
¹/₂ teaspoon salt, or to taste

Prepare the salsa and reserve in a bowl. Cook the cauliflower in a large pan of boiling water until barely tender, 3 to 4 minutes. Drain and return to the pan. Add the olive oil and the salt. Mix gently. Serve the cauliflower hot or at room temperature with the sauce spooned on the top.

Cauliflower with Tomatoes and Poblanos
Coliflor con Jitomates y Rajas

Makes **4 servings**

A striking dish of white cauliflower with red tomatoes and green poblano chiles has the colors of the Mexican flag. Pork Roast with Peanut Mole (page 354) goes well with the vegetables, or for a simpler main dish, try Ground Pork Patties (page 347).

2 poblano chiles, roasted and peeled (page 8)
1 tablespoon unsalted butter
$1/2$ medium white onion, chopped
6 plum tomatoes, peeled, seeded, and diced
$1/2$ teaspoon ground cumin
$1/2$ teaspoon salt, or to taste
1 medium cauliflower (about $1^1/2$ pounds),
    cut into florets
2 tablespoons cotija or other mild cheese

1. Prepare the chiles. Then, cut out the stem end section of the chiles. Discard the stems and cut the chiles open. Remove the seeds and veins. Rinse the chiles, blot with paper towels, and cut into thin strips (about 2 inches × ¼ inch).

2. Melt the butter in a medium skillet and cook the onion, stirring, until softened, 3 to 4 minutes. Add the tomatoes, cumin, and ¼ teaspoon of the salt. Bring to a boil and cook until the tomatoes thicken, 3 to 4 minutes. Cover to keep warm.

3. Cook the cauliflower in a large pot of boiling water until crisp-tender, 3 to 4 minutes. Drain the cauliflower and arrange it on a serving platter. Sprinkle with the remaining salt. Spoon the reserved tomato sauce over the cauliflower and top with the chile strips. Sprinkle with crumbled cotija cheese. Serve hot.

Chard

Chard with Poblano Chiles
Acelgas con Rajas de Chile

Makes **4 servings**

Swiss chard often serves as a wrapping for tamales (see Tamales Wrapped in Swiss Chard, page 154), and is added to stewed vegetable dishes. Chard can often be overcooked. I prefer it cooked until just tender. It's wonderful served with Barbecued Pork Steaks Marinated in Red Chile Paste (page 350).

2 poblano chiles, roasted and peeled (page 8)
1 large bunch Swiss chard, rinsed and stemmed
2 tablespoons olive oil
1 medium white onion, chopped
2 medium garlic cloves, finely chopped
2 medium tomatoes, peeled and diced
$1/2$ teaspoon dried thyme leaves
$1/2$ teaspoon salt, or to taste
$1/8$ teaspoon freshly ground pepper, or to taste

1. Prepare the chiles. Then, cut out the stem end section of the chiles. Discard the stems and cut the chiles open. Remove the seeds and veins. Rinse the chiles, blot with paper towels, and cut into thin strips (about 2 inches × ¼ inch).

2. Cut the chard leaves crosswise about ½-inch wide. Put into a large saucepan and add ½ cup water. Cover and bring to a boil. Reduce the heat to low and simmer until the leaves are cooked down and tender, about 8 minutes. Drain the liquid left in the pan and set aside off heat.

3. In a medium nonstick skillet, heat the oil over medium heat and cook the onion and garlic, stirring, until they begin to brown, 3 to 4 minutes. Add the tomatoes and thyme. Cook, stirring, until bubbling and juicy, 2 to 3 minutes.

4. Transfer the mixture to the pan with the chard. Add the chile strips, salt, and pepper. Heat through, over medium-low heat. Adjust seasoning. Serve hot.

Chard and Hominy
Acelgas y Pozole
Makes 4 to 6 servings

Nueva cocina *(the new way of cooking)* is evident in many exciting and creative dishes. In the market in Guanajuato, I noted beautiful red and green chard, and I got the idea to use the striking colors of red chard and yellow hominy for a side dish that goes exceptionally well with pork.

4 teaspoons olive oil
1 medium white onion, finely chopped
2 medium garlic cloves, finely chopped
2 bunches red chard, rinsed, stems trimmed,
    and chopped
1/2 teaspoon salt, or to taste
Freshly ground pepper, to taste
2 (15-ounce) cans yellow hominy, rinsed very well
    and drained
1/2 teaspoon ground cumin
1/2 teaspoon Maggi seasoning extract or
    Worcestershire sauce
1/4 cup canned chicken broth or water

1. In a large saucepan, heat 2 teaspoons of the oil over medium-low heat. Add 1/2 of the chopped onion and the garlic. Cook, covered, stirring frequently, until the onion is limp, but not brown, 4 to 5 minutes. Add the chard, pushing it down into the pan, and 1/4 cup of water. Raise the heat to medium and cook, covered, stirring once or twice, until the chard is wilted and tender, but still retains its bright color, about 10 minutes. Season with salt and black pepper. Reserve in the pan off heat.

2. In a medium saucepan, heat the remaining 2 teaspoons of oil and cook the remaining onion, covered, until tender, about 5 minutes. Add the hominy, cumin, Maggi seasoning, and broth or water. Bring to a boil, then reduce heat to low, cover and simmer until completely heated through, 4 to 5 minutes. To serve, mound the chard in the center of a round serving platter. Surround the chard with a border of hominy. Serve at once.

Chard with Pickled Red Onions
Acelgas con Cebollas en Escabeche
Makes 4 servings

Chard is used in homey soups and stews and also as a wrapper for tamales. It's also wonderful as a side dish with roasted pork or lamb. Pickled red onions add a nice touch of color and flavor.

Pickled Red Onions (page 19)
2 large bunches Swiss chard, rinsed well
1 tablespoon vegetable oil or olive oil
1 large garlic clove, finely chopped
1/2 cup canned fat-free reduced-sodium
    chicken broth
1 teaspoon salt, or to taste
1/8 teaspoon freshly ground pepper, or to taste

1. Prepare the pickled onions. Reserve. Cut the thick center rib out of the chard leaves and discard. Coarsely chop the leaves and put them into a large saucepan. Add 3/4 cup of water, cover, and cook until wilted and tender, about 10 minutes. Drain well.

2. Return the pan to the heat and add the oil and garlic. Stir well to mix. Add the chicken broth, salt, and pepper. Bring to a boil, stirring, and cook over high heat until the liquid has evaporated. Stir in the red onions. Heat through and serve hot.

Chard with Potatoes
Acelgas con Papas

Makes **4 servings**

Chard is a staple in Mexican home cooking. It is raised in agricultural areas and in family gardens in many parts of Mexico. Chard with white or red stems can be used for this recipe.

2 medium potatoes, peeled and cut into
    3/4-inch pieces
1 tablespoon plus 2 teaspoons olive oil
1/2 medium white onion, chopped
2 medium garlic cloves, finely chopped
1 large jalapeño chile, seeded, veins removed,
    and chopped
1 large bunch Swiss chard, rinsed well, stemmed,
    and coarsely chopped
1/2 teaspoon salt, or to taste
1/8 teaspoon freshly ground pepper, or to taste

1. Cook the potato in water to cover until tender, but not soft, about 4 minutes. Drain and reserve in a bowl.

2. In a large saucepan, heat 1 tablespoon of the oil over medium heat and cook the onion, garlic, and jalapeño until the onion is translucent, 3 to 4 minutes. Add the chard, pushing it down into the pan. Add 1/3 cup water. Cover and cook, stirring once or twice, until the chard is wilted and tender, 8 to 10 minutes. Add the reserved cooked potato, the remaining oil, salt and pepper. Stir to mix. Serve hot.

Chard with Chickpeas
Acelgas con Garbanzos

Makes **4 servings**

Chard, one of the healthy cruciferous vegetables, is a good source of iron, and vitamins A and C. Choose chard with leaves that look tender and fresh with crisp stems. The large green leaves are used as tamale wrappers in many regions of Mexico, and in soups or in nourishing vegetable dishes like this one. Chickpeas add richness to make this a wonderful filling dish.

1 large bunch Swiss chard, rinsed well, stemmed,
    coarsely chopped
1 tablespoon vegetable oil or olive oil
1 medium white onion, chopped
2 medium garlic cloves, chopped
1 large tomato, peeled and chopped
1 1/2 cups cooked chickpeas (garbanzo beans),
    canned or homemade, drained
1/2 teaspoon salt, or to taste

1. Put the chard into a large saucepan. Add 3/4 cup water, cover, and cook until wilted and tender, about 10 minutes. Drain well, transfer to a bowl and reserve.

2. Rinse and dry the saucepan, and in it heat the oil over medium heat. Add the onion and garlic. Cook until they begin to brown, 4 to 5 minutes. Add the tomato, chickpeas, and the reserved chard. Season with salt and pepper. Bring to a boil, and cook, stirring frequently, until completely heated through, 4 to 5 minutes. Serve hot.

Potatoes and Sweet Potatoes

Fried Potatoes with Poblano Chile Strips
Papas Fritas con Rajas

Makes **4 servings**

Potato fans really take to this combination of potatoes, onions, and green chile strips from northern Mexico, fixed the way Mexican ranch-hands cook them on the range. This everyday dish is great for breakfast, brunch, or dinner, at home or camping. Mexicans like the flavor lard imparts to the fried potatoes, and you may, too.

**3 large poblano chiles, roasted and peeled
    (page 8)**
**4 medium unpeeled red potatoes
    (about 1¹/₂ pounds)**
2 tablespoons vegetable oil or lard
1 medium white onion, thinly sliced
¹/₂ teaspoon salt, or to taste
¹/₈ teaspoon freshly ground pepper, or to taste

1. Prepare the chiles and set aside. Then, in a medium saucepan, boil the potatoes in water to cover until barely tender. Cool under running water. Peel, and cut into ¾-inch pieces. Set aside. Remove the seeds and veins from the chiles and cut them into thin strips. Set aside.

2. In a large nonstick skillet, heat the oil over medium heat and cook the onion until softened, 3 to 4 minutes. Add the potatoes, chile strips, salt, and pepper. Raise the heat to medium-high and cook until the potatoes are lightly browned, stirring frequently, so they don't stick, about 10 minutes. Add more oil, if needed. Serve hot.

Fried Potatoes with Tomatoes and Jalapeños
Papas Fritas con Jitomates y Jalapeños

Makes **4 servings**

Food stall cooks and street vendors in Mexico sometimes prepare potatoes this way, then wrap them in tortillas for tacos. The fried potatoes are braised in broth until soft and served with a topping of sour cream, chopped tomatoes, and pickled jalapeño chiles. This is a great side dish for grilled meat and poultry.

2 tablespoons vegetable oil
**3 medium baking potatoes, peeled and cut into
    ¹/₂-inch dice**
¹/₂ medium white onion, chopped
¹/₂ teaspoon salt, or to taste
¹/₈ teaspoon freshly ground pepper, or to taste
**¹/₂ cup canned fat-free reduced-sodium
    chicken broth**
¹/₂ cup sour cream, thinned with 1 tablespoon milk
2 medium tomatoes, finely chopped
**2 jarred pickled jalapeño chiles (en escabeche),
    seeded and finely chopped**

1. In a large nonstick skillet, heat the oil over medium-high heat and cook the potatoes and onion, stirring frequently, until the potatoes are almost tender and start to brown.

2. Stir in the salt and pepper. Add the broth. Reduce the heat to low, cover the pan and simmer until the potatoes are soft and the liquid is absorbed. (If the liquid cooks away before the potatoes are soft, add a little more broth and continue cooking until the potatoes are tender.) Mound the potatoes on a warm serving platter. Drizzle with sour cream and scatter the tomatoes and chiles over the top. Serve hot.

Pan-Roasted Potatoes and Carrots
Papas y Zanahorias Asadas

Makes **4 servings**

Pan-roasting is a frequent technique used in the Mexican kitchen to enhance the flavor of everyday foods. Cumin and cilantro give these vegetables a little Mexican flair.

4 medium carrots (¹/₂ pound), peeled and cut into ³/₄-inch pieces

2 medium unpeeled red potatoes (³/₄ pound), scrubbed and cut into ³/₄-inch pieces

2 tablespoons unsalted butter

¹/₂ teaspoon ground cumin

¹/₄ teaspoon salt, or to taste

2 tablespoons chopped fresh cilantro

1. In a medium pan of boiling water, cook the carrots, uncovered, until crisp-tender, about 3 minutes. Scoop out with a slotted spoon, and put into a bowl. Add the potatoes to the same pan of boiling water, and cook until barely tender, about 4 minutes. Drain the potatoes and add to the bowl with the carrots.

2. Melt the butter in a large skillet, over medium heat. Add the carrots, potatoes, cumin, and salt. Cook, covered, stirring frequently, until the vegetables are tender, 4 to 5 minutes. Remove the lid, raise the heat to high, and cook the vegetables until they start to brown, about 4 minutes. Stir in the cilantro. Serve hot.

Potatoes in Ranchera Sauce
Papas en Salsa Ranchera

Makes **4 servings**

A bubbling cazuela *(casserole) of tender potatoes slowly cooked in tomato-rich* ranchera *sauce is a dish from northern Mexico's beef country to serve with grilled steaks.*

Ranchera Sauce (page 44)

4 large potatoes, peeled and sliced crosswise (about 2 pounds)

2 tablespoons olive oil

¹/₂ teaspoon salt, or to taste

¹/₈ teaspoon freshly ground pepper, or to taste

¹/₃ cup crumbled cotija or mild feta cheese

1. Prepare the sauce. Reserve in the pan off heat. Preheat the oven to 375°. Put the sliced potatoes in a large bowl. Add the oil, salt, and pepper and toss to coat the potatoes. Transfer to an ovenproof casserole dish and roast the potatoes, uncovered, in preheated oven for 30 minutes.

2. Reheat the sauce and pour over the potatoes. Cover and cook until the potatoes are very tender, about 35 to 40 minutes more. Sprinkle with the cheese and serve hot.

Chipotle Mashed Potatoes
Papas al Chipotle

Makes **4 servings**

A mixture of creamy-soft mashed potatoes and smoky chipotle chiles is a Mexican-American favorite and an easy dish you'll love.

2¹/₂ pounds Yukon gold potatoes, peeled and sliced
¹/₂ cup whole milk, or more if needed
2 teaspoons mashed canned chipotle chiles en adobo
1 tablespoon low-fat sour cream
³/₄ teaspoon salt, or to taste

1. Put the potatoes in a large saucepan and cover by about 2 inches with cold water. Bring to a boil and cook, partially covered, until the potatoes are very tender, 15 to 20 minutes. Drain the potatoes into a colander and return them at once to the pan.

2. With a potato masher, mash the hot potatoes with the milk. Add the chiles, and sour cream. Mash until fluffy. Add more milk, if needed. Stir in salt, and taste. Adjust as needed. Serve hot.

Potatoes Steamed with Herbs
Papas Empapeladas

Makes **4 servings**

Steaming foods in banana leaves, corn husks, or other kinds of food wrapper is one of the techniques used to cook foods in Mexico. Modern cooks and restaurant chefs, too, frequently use foil as a convenient way to steam many different foods. Tiny red potatoes are found in markets throughout Mexico, and they are excellent steamed with fresh herbs. Our red potatoes are usually a bit larger, so I cut them in half.

1 piece of foil, large enough to hold all the potatoes
1 tablespoon unsalted butter
12 small unpeeled red potatoes (about 2 pounds), scrubbed and halved
1 medium onion, thinly sliced
2 tablespoons finely chopped fresh oregano
1 tablespoon finely chopped fresh parsley
2 teaspoons olive oil
¹/₂ teaspoon salt, or to taste
¹/₄ teaspoon pepper, or to taste

1. Lay a large piece of foil on a flat surface. Spread the butter on the foil in the center. Slightly lift the foil edges to prevent the potatoes from rolling off and put the potatoes on the foil. Top with the remaining ingredients. Fold the foil like an envelope and make a tight seal to prevent any water from getting inside.

2. Bring about 1 cup of water to a boil in the bottom of a steamer. Place the potato package on the steamer rack, cover, reduce the heat to medium-low and cook over boiling water about 20 minutes, or until the potatoes are tender. Transfer the potatoes to a bowl with the steaming juices. Serve hot.

Baked Potatoes Stuffed with Corn
Papas Rellenos con Elote

Makes **4 servings**

This modern dish is adapted from a recipe by Patricia Armida of Mexico City. In the original recipe the potatoes were boiled before being mashed. I prefer to bake the potatoes for better flavor and better texture to hold the stuffing.

4 medium baking potatoes, scrubbed
2 tablespoons unsalted butter
¹/₄ cup milk
2 cups cooked fresh corn kernels (from about 2 large ears)
¹/₄ cup grated manchego or Monterey Jack cheese
³/₄ teaspoon salt, or to taste
¹/₈ teaspoon pepper, or to taste

1. Preheat the oven to 375°. Bake the potatoes until soft when tested with a knife, about 1 hour. Leave the oven on. While still warm but cool enough to handle, cut the top third off each potato horizontally. Scoop out the potato in the bottom section and put into a large bowl. Save the shells.

2. Mash the potatoes with the butter and milk. Mix in the cooked corn, cheese, salt, and pepper. Stuff the potato shells equally with the mashed potato mixture. Bake the stuffed potatoes until piping hot all the way through and lightly browned on top, 20 to 25 minutes.

Potato and Chile Gratin
Papas y Chile Ancho Al Horno

Makes 4 servings

Sliced potatoes baked in ancho chile and cream sauce is a modern dish using traditional ingredients. Serve with any kind of grilled fish, meat, or poultry.

2 ancho chiles

1 small garlic clove, minced

1 cup canned fat-free reduced-sodium chicken broth

1/2 cup heavy cream

1/2 teaspoon salt, or to taste

1/4 teaspoon freshly ground pepper, or to taste

3 baking potatoes (2 pounds), peeled, quartered lengthwise, and thinly sliced crosswise

1. Wipe the chiles with damp paper towel to remove any dust and cut them open. Remove the stems, seeds, and veins. In a dry skillet, over medium heat, toast the chiles until aromatic, about 6 to 8 seconds on each side. Put the chiles in a bowl and barely cover with hot water. Soak for 20 minutes.

2. Transfer the chiles to a blender and discard the water. Add the garlic and chicken broth. Blend for 1 minute to a smooth purée. Add the cream, salt,

and pepper. Pulse just to mix. Reserve in the blender jar.

3. Preheat the oven to 375°. Brush an 8-inch-square baking dish with vegetable oil. Arrange the sliced potatoes in the dish. Pour the chile mixture evenly over the potatoes. Bake uncovered until the potatoes are tender, and the sauce is bubbling, about 45 minutes. Serve hot.

Roasted Potatoes and Onions with Yellow Chile Salsa
Papas y Cebollas Al Horno con Salsa de Chile Guëro

Makes 4 servings

When you want a no-fuss but flavorful side dish to accompany any roasted or grilled meat, this is for you. The salsa can be made ahead and the potatoes and onions roast to perfection while you prepare the rest of the meal. Mexican markets sell lots of small red potatoes, about egg size, and that's what works best for this dish.

Yellow Chile Salsa (page 33)

12 small unpeeled red potatoes (about 2 pounds), scrubbed and halved

1 medium white onion, peeled and quartered lengthwise

2 tablespoons olive oil

1 teaspoon salt

1/8 teaspoon freshly ground pepper, or to taste

Prepare the salsa. If made ahead, cover and refrigerate until shortly before serving. Preheat the oven to 350°. In a large mixing bowl, toss the potatoes and onion with the olive oil to coat well. Place in a baking dish large enough to arrange potatoes in a single layer. Sprinkle with salt and pepper. Roast until very tender and browned, about 45 minutes. Serve hot. Accompany with the yellow chile salsa.

Roasted Potatoes and Onions, Yucatán Style
Papas y Cebollas Yucatán al Horno

Makes **4 servings**

The Yucatán spiced seasoning condiment, achiote rojo (achiote paste), that contains ground annatto seeds, oregano, cinnamon, cloves, allspice, cumin, and vinegar, is used to infuse the vegetables in this dish with typical Yucatán flavors. The seasoning paste is available in 3½-ounce packages in Mexican and Latin American markets.

1 tablespoon achiote rojo (packaged seasoning paste)

2 plum tomatoes (about 2 pounds), peeled and quartered

2 tablespoons fresh orange juice

8 small white boiling onions, peeled and halved root to stem

12 small red potatoes, scrubbed and halved

1 tablespoon olive oil

¹/₂ teaspoon salt, or to taste

Preheat oven to 350°. Put the seasoning paste, tomatoes, and orange juice in a blender and blend until smooth. Put the onions and potatoes in an ovenproof casserole dish. Add the seasoning mixture, oil, and salt. Turn to coat the vegetables. Cover and bake about 20 minutes. Remove the cover and continue to cook until the liquid is absorbed and the vegetables are browned and tender, 25 to 30 minutes. Serve hot.

Potato Masa Cakes with Vegetables
Tortitas de Papa y Masa con Verduras

Makes **4 servings**

Adobe Restaurant in Tlaquepaque, a village near Guadalajara, has a very inventive and modern menu, including this dish. Serve as a vegetarian entrée or with a small steak. Fresh Tomatillo Sauce (page 34) is served on the side.

Fresh Tomatillo Sauce (page 34) (optional)

1 tablespoon olive oil

1 medium white onion, finely chopped

1 small carrot, cut into ¹/₄-inch dice

2 small zucchini, cut into ¹/₄-inch dice

¹/₂ red bell pepper, neatly diced, about ¹/₄ inch

1 jalapeño chile, seeded, ribs removed, and minced

¹/₂ cup fresh corn kernels (from about 1 ear)

¹/₂ teaspoon salt, or to taste

¹/₈ teaspoon freshly ground pepper, or to taste

2 teaspoons unsalted butter

Potato Masa Cakes (page 114)

1. Prepare the salsa, if using. Then, in a large skillet, heat the oil over medium heat and cook the onion, stirring, until softened, about 3 minutes. Add the carrot and cook, stirring, 1 minute. Add the zucchini, red pepper, jalapeño, and corn. Cook, stirring, until the vegetables are tender, about 4 minutes. Stir in the salt, pepper, and butter. Reserve in the pan off heat.

2. Prepare the potato masa cakes. To serve, reheat the vegetables. Place 1 potato cake in the center of each of 4 serving plates. Divide the vegetable mixture over each cake. Serve with green salsa, if desired.

Baked Sweet Potatoes with Pumpkin Seeds
Camotes al Horno con Pepitas

Makes **4 servings**

Creative chefs are using native sweet potatoes (camotes) in new ways, and this mix of mashed sweet potatoes with toasted pumpkin seeds is an inspired combination that goes perfectly with pork and poultry.

4 medium orange-skinned sweet potatoes (often labeled yams); (about 1 pound)

¼ cup raw hulled pumpkin seeds

2 to 3 tablespoons unsalted butter

½ teaspoon salt, or to taste

⅛ teaspoon freshly ground pepper, or to taste

1. Preheat the oven to 400°. Scrub the potatoes and pierce each one a few times with a thin-bladed knife to prevent them from popping open while baking. Place on a 9- × 12-inch foil-lined baking pan and bake about 1 hour, or until very soft.

2. Meanwhile, in a dry skillet over medium heat, toast the pumpkin seeds until they are lightly browned and pop around in the pan. Remove to a bowl and reserve.

3. When the potatoes are done, remove from the skins and mash with the butter. Season with salt and pepper. Stir in the toasted pumpkin seeds. Serve hot.

Sweet Potatoes with Cream and Chipotle Chile
Camotes con Crema de Chipotle

Makes **4 servings**

Orange-skinned sweet potatoes with bright orange flesh, are best for this unusual recipe that I developed. The smoky tasting and feisty chipotle chile flavors the creamy sauce that coats the tender pieces of potato. Maggi is a seasoning extract that's popular in Mexico and can be found in Mexican markets in the United States. It deepens and enhances the taste of the dish.

1 tablespoon olive oil

¼ medium white onion, finely chopped

½ teaspoon Maggi seasoning extract or Worcestershire sauce

4 medium orange-skinned sweet potatoes (often labeled yams); (about 1 pound), peeled and cut into ¾-inch pieces

½ cup canned fat-free reduced-sodium chicken broth

¼ cup heavy cream

1 to 2 teaspoons chipotle salsa, or the sauce from canned chipotle chiles en adobo

¼ teaspoon salt, or to taste

⅛ teaspoon freshly ground pepper, or to taste

1. In a large skillet, heat the oil over medium-low heat and cook the onion, stirring, until limp and starting to brown, 4 to 5 minutes. Add the Maggi and stir to blend. Add the yams and broth. Bring to a boil, then reduce the heat to medium-low, cover and simmer until the yams are almost tender, 8 to 10 minutes.

2. Add the cream, chipotle sauce, salt, and pepper. Cook uncovered, stirring, until the sauce reduces and thickens and the yams are very tender. Serve hot.

Other Vegetables

Asparagus with Mushrooms
Esparragos con Hongos

Makes **4 servings**

Asparagus is not commonly used in the Mexican kitchen, but with the advent of nueva cocina, asparagus is sometimes used in upscale Mexico City restaurants. Teamed with mushrooms, asparagus makes a beautiful presentation served with Baked Chicken with Serrano Chile Cream Sauce (page 280).

1 pound fresh asparagus

¹/₂ teaspoon salt, or to taste

2 tablespoons olive oil

¹/₂ large white onion, thinly sliced

¹/₂ pound small white mushrooms, quartered

¹/₂ teaspoon ground cumin

¹/₈ teaspoon crushed red pepper

1. Preheat oven to 200°. Trim the tough ends from the asparagus. Bring a large pot of water to a boil. Add the asparagus. Cook, uncovered, until the asparagus is crisp-tender and still bright green, 6 to 8 minutes. Drain and cool under running water to stop the cooking. Put on a serving plate and sprinkle with ¼ teaspoon of the salt. Keep warm in the oven.

2. Heat the oil in a skillet over medium heat. Add the onion and cook until softened, about 3 minutes. Add the mushrooms, cover and cook, stirring frequently, until they release their juices and are tender, 3 to 4 minutes. Add the cumin, red pepper, and remaining ¼ teaspoon of salt, or to taste. Remove the asparagus from the oven and spoon the mushrooms and onion on top, leaving the green tips showing. Serve hot.

Broccoli with Red Onion and Cumin
Brocoli con Cebollas y Comino

Makes **4 servings**

Huauzontle *is an ancient green vegetable with a flavor similar to broccoli that grows in Puebla and other adjacent areas in central Mexico.* Huauzontle *is unavailable or very rarely marketed in this country. However, broccoli is grown in Mexico and is frequently used in Mexican cooking, sometimes as a substitute for* huauzontle *and works well in this dish.*

1¹/₂ tablespoons olive oil

1 medium red onion, thinly sliced

1 medium garlic clove, finely chopped

1 teaspoon ground cumin

1 teaspoon cider vinegar

¹/₂ teaspoon salt, or to taste

¹/₈ teaspoon freshly ground pepper, or to taste

1 tablespoon unsalted butter

1 pound broccoli, trimmed and cut into short lengthwise spears

1. In a skillet heat the oil over medium heat. Cook the onion and garlic, stirring, until the onion is limp, about 4 minutes. Add the remaining ingredients and cook for 1 minute. Reserve in the pan off heat.

2. Bring a large skillet or wide deep saucepan of water to a boil. Add the broccoli and cook, uncovered, until crisp-tender and still bright green, 6 to 7 minutes. Drain well and transfer to a serving platter or shallow bowl. Spoon the onions on top. Serve hot.

Broccoli with Onions and Sweet Potatoes

Brocoli con Cebollas y Camotes

Makes **4 servings**

Proving that simple can often be best, this stunning vegetable combination of only three ingredients, plus salt, pepper, and olive oil ranks right up there as one of the prettiest and tastiest vegetable dishes I've ever eaten. In Mexico huauzontle, *a vegetable with a taste similar to broccoli, might be used, but it's still a rarity in this country. Serve the vegetables next to Stuffed Chicken Breasts with Black Bean Sauce (page 297), and you've got a winning dinner.*

2 medium orange-skinned sweet potatoes (often labeled yams); (about 1 pound), peeled and cut into ³/₄-inch pieces

1 tablespoon plus 2 teaspoons olive oil

1 teaspoon salt

¹/₄ teaspoon freshly ground pepper, or to taste

1 pound broccoli, stems trimmed and cut into short lengthwise spears

¹/₂ large white onion, thinly sliced

1. Half fill a large deep skillet with water and bring to a boil, over medium-high heat. Add the sweet potatoes and cook, uncovered, until tender, about 10 minutes. Drain and put the hot sweet potatoes into a bowl. Add 1 tablespoon of the oil, ½ teaspoon of the salt, and ⅛ teaspoon pepper. Toss gently to coat. Cover and keep warm.

2. In the same skillet, again pour water to about half full, and bring to a boil. Add the broccoli and onion. Cook, uncovered, until crisp tender, about 5 minutes. Drain. Add the remaining 2 teaspoons oil, the remaining ½ teaspoon salt, and ⅛ teaspoon or more pepper. Turn gently to coat. Arrange the broccoli and onion on one side of a shallow bowl or serving plate and snuggle the sweet potatoe pieces next to them. Serve hot.

Eggplant Stuffed with Shredded Chicken

Berenjenas Rellenos con Pollo Deschebrada

Makes **4 servings**

Eggplant is grown in Mexico and available in many markets for home cooks. A few restaurants offering nueva cocina—creative dishes combining old and new Mexican food traditions—have begun adding Mexican-style eggplant to their menus. In Puebla, I had small thin pieces of fried eggplant served with a green salad. In Guanajuato, baked eggplant halves were stuffed with tomatoes, pickled jalapeños, onions, and shredded chicken, as in this dish.

Shredded Chicken (page 271)

1 large eggplant

1 teaspoon salt

3 tablespoons olive oil

1/2 medium white onion, finely chopped

2 medium tomatoes, peeled and finely chopped

1 to 2 jarred pickled jalapeño chiles (en escabeche), seeded and finely chopped

1/2 teaspoon dried oregano (Mexican variety preferred), crumbled

1/2 teaspoon ground cumin

1/4 cup grated manchego or asiago cheese

2 tablespoons bread crumbs

2 tablespoons finely chopped fresh parsley

1. Prepare the shredded chicken. Cover and refrigerate. Cut the eggplant in half lengthwise. With a sharp knife, score the cut side of the eggplant, but do not cut through the skin. Sprinkle the cut sides with 1/2 teaspoon of the salt, turn cut side down and let sit for 20 minutes. Rinse the eggplant and pat dry with paper towels.

2. Preheat the oven to 375°. Rub 2 tablespoons of the oil all over the eggplant and place on a baking sheet. Cover with foil and bake in preheated oven until tender, about 30 minutes. Remove from the oven and cool. When cool enough to handle scoop out the eggplant pulp, leaving the skin and about 1/2 inch of pulp intact. Reserve the eggplant shells. Finely chop the pulp with a knife and reserve.

3. Heat the remaining tablespoon of oil in a skillet and cook the onion, stirring, until it starts to brown, about 4 minutes. Add the tomato, jalapeño, oregano, cumin, and reserved chopped eggplant. Cook, uncovered, stirring frequently, until the mixture thickens, 12 to 15 minutes. Stir in the reserved shredded chicken.

4. Fill the eggplant halves with the chicken stuffing. Place on a foil-lined baking sheet. Mix the cheese, bread crumbs, and parsley. Sprinkle on top of the eggplant shells. Bake in preheated oven until the eggplant shells are soft and the filling is hot and golden brown on top, about 25 minutes. Serve hot or at room temperature.

Eggplant with Ranchera Sauce
Berenjena Ranchera

Makes **4 servings**

Years ago I first noticed beautiful purple egg-plants at the market in San Miguel de Allende. It occurred to me that it would be terrific with ranchera sauce, so this recipe is the result of my inspiration. Be sure to select firm eggplant with shiny unblemished skin. Serve Basic Refried Beans (page 462) as an excellent side dish with the eggplant.

Ranchera Sauce (page 44)
1 large eggplant, cut into 8 round slices
    ($1/2$-inch thick)
$1/2$ teaspoon salt, or to taste
$1/2$ cup all-purpose flour, on a plate
2 large eggs, well beaten, in a shallow bowl
$1/2$ cup fine dry bread crumbs, on a plate
Vegetable oil for frying
1 cup shredded Monterey Jack cheese

1. Prepare the ranchera sauce and reserve off heat in the pan. Sprinkle the eggplant rounds with salt. Dredge the eggplant in flour, pat off excess, then dip in beaten egg to coat. Press each round into the crumbs, coating completely. Put the rounds on a platter lined with waxed paper. Refrigerate at least 1 hour, or up to 6 hours.

2. Shortly before serving, heat oil to a depth of about ½ inch in a large nonstick skillet over medium-high heat until the oil shimmers. Fry the eggplant rounds until golden brown on both sides, 2 to 3 minutes per side. Drain on paper towels and then put the rounds on a baking sheet. Reheat the sauce and spoon about 2 tablespoons sauce on each round. Top equally with shredded cheese. Run under a hot oven broiler to melt the cheese, 1 to 2 minutes. Serve hot and pass remaining ranchera sauce at the table.

Green Beans with Mushrooms
Ejotes con Hongos

Makes **4 servings**

Green beans are often put into soups and stews in traditional Mexican cooking, but here is one of the newer ways to present fresh green beans as a side dish.

1 pound small fresh green beans, ends trimmed
1 tablespoon olive oil
$1/2$ medium white onion, thinly sliced
$1/2$ pound fresh white mushrooms, thinly sliced
1 small garlic clove, finely chopped
$1/2$ teaspoon salt, or to taste
2 plum tomatoes, cored and finely diced

1. In a medium saucepan of boiling water cook the beans, uncovered, until crisp-tender, about 6 minutes. Drain and rinse with cold running water to stop the cooking. Reserve.

2. In a large nonstick skillet, heat the olive oil over medium heat and cook the onion, mush-rooms, and garlic, stirring frequently, until the mushrooms start to brown, 6 to 8 minutes. Add the reserved green beans and salt. Cook, stirring, until completely heated through, 3 to 4 minutes. Transfer to a serving bowl. Scatter the diced tomatoes on top. Serve hot.

Mushrooms and Poblano Chiles in Guajillo Sauce
Hongos y Poblanos en Salsa de Guajillo

Makes **about 3 cups**

This is an outstanding combination to serve with grilled meats, or as a filling for enchiladas or crepes. I also use it in mini-amounts to fill Masa Shells for Sopes (page 107) and serve as an appetizer.

2 large poblano chiles, roasted and peeled (page 8)
Guajillo Chile Sauce with Cream (page 50)
3 tablespoons olive oil
1 1/2 pounds mushrooms (use a mixture of portobello, cremini, and white mushrooms), halved and thinly sliced
1/2 medium white onion, finely chopped
1/4 cup finely chopped fresh epazote leaves, if available, or cilantro
1/2 teaspoon salt, or to taste
1/4 teaspoon freshly ground pepper, or to taste
Finely crumbled or grated cotija cheese

1. Prepare the chiles. Then, cut out the stem end section of the chiles. Discard the stems and cut the chiles open. Remove the seeds and veins. Rinse the chiles, blot with paper towels, and cut into thin strips, then into dice. Then prepare the guajillo chile sauce. Reserve.

2. Heat the oil in a large nonstick skillet over medium-high heat. Add the mushrooms, poblanos, and onions. Cook, stirring, until the moisture has cooked away. Stir in the epazote, salt, and 1 cup of the reserved guajillo chile sauce. (Save the extra sauce for another use.) Cook the mushroom mixture until completely heated through, 3 to 4 minutes. Sprinkle top with cheese. Serve hot or as directed in your recipe.

Mushrooms, Tomatoes, and Chiles
Hongos, Jitomates, y Chiles

Makes **4 servings**

A tasty trio of sautéed mushrooms, tomatoes, and fiery little serrano chiles can be spooned over steaks, chickens, or hamburgers as a terrific topping, or served on the side to accompany enchiladas. For a traditional flavor, a good-quality lard lends authenticity to the dish.

1 tablespoon vegetable oil or lard
1/2 medium white onion, chopped
1/2 teaspoon dried oregano (Mexican variety preferred), crumbled
1 pound mixed mushrooms, cremini and white, thinly sliced
2 medium tomatoes, peeled, seeded, and finely chopped
2 serrano chiles, minced with seeds
2 tablespoons chopped fresh parsley
1 tablespoon chopped fresh epazote leaves, if available
1/2 teaspoon salt, or to taste

1. In a large nonstick skillet, heat the oil or lard over medium heat and fry the onion and oregano. Cook, stirring until the onion begins to brown, about 5 minutes.

2. Add the mushrooms and cook, partially covered, stirring occasionally, until the mushrooms are tender and starting to brown, 8 to 10 minutes. Add the remaining ingredients. Raise the heat and cook until completely heated through, 3 to 4 minutes. Serve hot.

Purslane with Mushrooms
Verdolagas con Hongos

Makes **4 servings**

For an excellent vegetarian entrée, combine the meaty texture of brown mushrooms with purslane (verdolagas), a succulent plant with fleshy green leaves and a mild almost lemony taste, that's used in cooked dishes or raw in salads. This vegetable that's so widely used in Mexico is slowly being discovered north of the border. It's worth looking for in farmer's markets or Latin-American markets.

1 tablespoon vegetable oil

$1/2$ medium onion, finely chopped

2 medium garlic cloves, chopped

$1/2$ teaspoon dried thyme

$1/2$ pound cremini mushrooms, quartered

$1/2$ teaspoon dried oregano (Mexican variety preferred), crumbled

1 large tomato, peeled and chopped

3 cups (12 ounces) purslane, thick stems removed

$1/2$ teaspoon salt, or to taste

$1/4$ teaspoon freshly ground pepper, or to taste

Heat the oil in a wide saucepan and cook the onion until it begins to brown. Add the garlic, thyme, oregano, and mushrooms. Cook, stirring frequently, until the mushrooms give up their juices, 3 to 4 minutes. Add the tomato, purslane, salt, pepper, and 2 tablespoons of water. Bring to a boil; then reduce the heat to low, cover, and simmer until the vegetables are tender, 10 to 12 minutes. Serve hot.

Portobello Mushrooms Stuffed with Refried Beans

Rellenos de Hongos Grande con Frijoles Refritos

Makes **4 servings**

All kinds and sizes of mushrooms grow in Mexico and Mexicans are experts at preparing stuffed vegetables. Mushrooms are a natural with their ready-made depression to hold the filling. Serve as a substantial starter course.

1 cup Basic Refried Beans (page 462)

2 teaspoons olive oil plus extra to brush on the mushrooms

1 medium white onion, chopped

1 medium tomato, cored and finely chopped

1 serrano chile, minced with seeds

$1/2$ teaspoon dried oregano (Mexican variety preferred), crumbled

Salt, to taste

4 portobello mushrooms (each top about 3-inches wide)

$1/4$ cup canned fat-free reduced-sodium chicken broth

$1/2$ cup shredded Monterey Jack or Oaxaca cheese

2 tablespoons chopped fresh cilantro

1. Prepare the refried beans. Heat 1 cup in a saucepan, cover, and keep warm. The beans should be thick and quite dry. In a skillet, heat 2 teaspoons of oil over medium heat and cook the onion, stirring, until it softens, 3 to 4 minutes. Add the tomato, chile, and oregano. Cook until the tomato juices reduce and the mixture thickens, about 3 minutes. Season with salt. Transfer to a bowl and reserve.

2. Remove the stems from the mushrooms. With a melon-baller, scoop out the black gills. Wipe the mushrooms with a damp paper towel. Rub the mushrooms all over with olive oil. Heat a large nonstick skillet over medium heat and place the mushrooms, cavity side down, in the pan. Add the broth, cover and cook for 5 minutes, then turn and cook for 3 to 4 minutes, or until the mushrooms are tender when pierced with a small sharp knife. Drain the juices from the mushrooms and save for another use, if desired.

3. Preheat the oven to 375°. Place the mushrooms, cavity side up, on a baking sheet. Sprinkle with salt. Stuff each mushroom cavity with about $1/4$ of the refried beans. Top each with $1/4$ of the tomato mixture and $1/4$ of the cheese. Bake until heated through and cheese is melted, 6 to 8 minutes. Sprinkle with cilantro. Serve hot.

Fried Plantains
Plátanos Machos Fritos

Makes 4 servings

Plantains are large firm "cooking bananas" with a mild flavor. They are ready to eat when the skin is almost black and slightly soft when pressed lightly. Plantains are popular all over Mexico, especially along the gulf coast and in tropical and sub-tropical regions where many varieties of bananas are grown, including the sweet regular eating bananas and small varieties of sweet plátano dedo (finger bananas).

2 large ripe plantains
2 tablespoons vegetable oil
¼ teaspoon salt, or to taste

Cut off both ends of the plantains and peel. Cut lengthwise in strips or crosswise on the diagonal into ovals, about ⅓-inch thick. Heat the oil in a large nonstick skillet and fry the plantains, turning, until golden, about 2 to 3 minutes. Drain on paper towels. Season with salt. Serve warm.

Plantains Stuffed with Beans
Rellenos de Plátanos Machos

Makes 12 small patties

Starchy "cooking bananas," plantains, or plátanos machos, are used extensively in the southern coastal regions of Mexico. In the states of Tabasco and Veracruz, we ate plantains in some form almost every day. Serve these little patties as a first course or side dish. For this recipe, the plantains are not yet ripe, and still firm to the touch. The skins should be partly yellow and mottled with a little brown.

2 plantains, peeled and sliced crosswise in 2-inch pieces
1 large egg, beaten
2 tablespoons all-purpose flour
½ teaspoon salt
1 cup Basic Refried Beans (page 462), or canned
Vegetable oil for frying
1½ cups shredded lettuce
½ cup Mexican crema or sour cream

1. Put the plantain pieces in a medium pan and add hot water to cover. Bring to a boil and cook, partially covered, until tender, about 10 minutes. Drain and cool. When cool, purée in a food processor. Add the beaten egg, flour, and salt. Pulse 3 to 4 times to blend. If the mixture is sticky, add a little more flour.

2. Form the mixture into 12 balls. With a thumb, poke a hole and fill each ball with about 2 teaspoons refried beans. Mold the batter to enclose the beans into fat cigar shaped patties. Heat oil to a depth of about 1-inch over medium heat in a medium nonstick skillet until it shimmers. Fry the patties, turning once, until golden brown on both sides. Serve hot on a bed of lettuce and top with a dollop of crema.

Grilled Fresh Cactus
Nopales Asada

Makes 4 servings

It's usually the texture of nopales that people object to, but chefs Rick Bayless and Mark Miller made me aware of grilling whole cactus paddles as a way to eliminate the sticky juices. I've found that if an outdoor grill is not available, a stovetop grill pan works well for cooking whole cactus paddles. For grilling, purchase thin, firm paddles about 5 to 6 inches long. If the thorns are still attached, they must be carefully removed. (See Preparing Cactus Paddles page 10.) Cactus paddles are found in the vegetable section of Mexican markets and many supermarkets.

4 medium cactus paddles, 4 to 6 inches long
2 teaspoons vegetable oil or olive oil
¹/₄ teaspoon salt, or to taste
¹/₈ teaspoon freshly ground pepper, or to taste

1. Prepare an outdoor grill, if using. If the cactus paddles still have thorns, with gloves on, remove all the thorns from the cactus by scraping them off with a sharp knife (but don't remove the skin); then trim off about ¼ inch all around the edge of the paddle. Rinse and dry with paper towels. Brush both sides of the cactus with oil. Season with salt and pepper.

2. Preheat a stovetop grill pan if using. Grill the cactus paddles until they are tender and marked by the grill, about 3 to 5 minutes per side, depending on the size. Serve 1 grilled paddle to each person, or cut into strips and serve from a plate as a side dish.

Grilled Green Onions
Cebollitas Asadas

Makes **4 servings**

Fresh Mexican green onions with larger bulbs than our common supermarket variety are often grilled whole and served with carne asada. *Mexican markets in the United States sometimes carry the Mexican variety, but our regular green onions work fine. Nowadays grilled green onions like this sometimes appear with* fajitas *in the United States.*

8 large green onions with green part attached
1 tablespoon vegetable oil
1 tablespoon fresh lime juice
¹/₄ teaspoon salt, or to taste

1. Prepare an outdoor grill or stovetop grill pan. Cut about 2 inches of the green ends off the onions, and trim the shaggy root ends, leaving a tiny bit to hold the onion together.

2. Brush the onions all over with vegetable oil and place them on the hot grill. (If the green part starts to burn, put a piece of foil under them.) Cook the onions until tender, turning once or twice, about 6 to 8 minutes. Sprinkle with lime juice and season with salt.

Baked Tomatoes Mexicana
Jitomates al Horno

Makes **4 servings**

From Monterrey, Mexico, in the state of Nuevo Leon, comes this unusual tomato preparation that goes well with grilled meats or chicken. The best tomatoes for this dish should be large and ripe, but still firm, with good red color.

3 large tomatoes, cored and cut into ¹/₂-inch slices
2 serrano chiles, finely chopped with seeds
2 green onions, including 2 inches of green, finely chopped
¹/₄ cup crumbled cotija or mild feta cheese
¹/₄ cup Mexican crema or sour cream
1 tablespoon finely chopped fresh parsley

Preheat the oven to 450°. Grease a baking sheet. Lay the tomato slices on the baking sheet in a single layer. In a small bowl, mix the chiles, onions, and cheese. Sprinkle equally over the tomatoes. Bake until juices bubble, 8 to 10 minutes. Add a dollop of sour cream on top of each tomato slice, and sprinkle with parsley. Serve at once.

Mixed Vegetables, Mexican Style
Verduras Mixta Mexicana

Makes **4 servings**

Serve Mexican-style mixed vegetables with grilled or roasted meat, poultry, or fish.

1 medium zucchini, cut into ¹/₂-inch pieces
1 cup small cauliflower florets
1 cup fresh corn kernels (from about 1 medium ear), or thawed if frozen
2 tablespoons olive oil
1 medium white onion, sliced
1 medium garlic clove, finely chopped
1 serrano chile, minced with seeds
1 medium tomato, peeled and finely chopped
1 teaspoon ground cumin
¹/₂ teaspoon salt, or to taste
¹/₄ teaspoon freshly ground pepper, or to taste
1 tablespoon chopped fresh cilantro

1. In a large saucepan of boiling salted water cook the zucchini, cauliflower, and corn until crisp-tender, about 2 minutes. Drain and transfer to a platter.

2. Heat the oil in a medium skillet over medium heat and cook the onion until limp, about 4 minutes. Add the remaining ingredients, except the cilantro. Cook, stirring, until the tomato is hot and bubbling, about 2 minutes. Spoon over the vegetables. Sprinkle with cilantro. Serve hot.

Onion, Zucchini, and Rice Casserole
Sopa Seca de Cebolla, Calabacitas, y Arroz en Cazuela

Makes **6 servings**

Sopa seca, or dry soup, usually means a dish made with rice or pasta in a similar way to soup, but in which the liquid is absorbed or evaporates completely, so the result is "dry." Sopa secas are traditionally served as a separate course, often after a "wet" soup, or as a side dish or light meal. I serve this sopa seca with grilled or sautéed meats or poultry. It can be made ahead and reheated.

2 tablespoons olive oil
2 tablespoons fine bread crumbs
4 medium white onions, halved and thinly sliced
2 medium zucchini, coarsely shredded
¹/₂ cup long-grain white rice
1 cup shredded manchego or Monterey Jack cheese
1³/₄ cups whole milk or half and half
1¹/₂ teaspoons canned or jarred chipotle chile sauce, or the sauce from canned chipotle chiles en adobo
³/₄ teaspoon salt

1. In a small bowl mix 1 teaspoon of the oil with the bread crumbs. Set aside. Heat the remaining oil in a large wide saucepan over medium heat. Add the onions and cook, stirring about 1 minute. Reduce the heat to low, cover, and cook slowly, stirring frequently, until limp, but not brown, about 10 minutes. Add the zucchini. Cook, stirring, for 1 minute. Remove the pan from the heat and reserve.

2. Preheat oven to 350°. Grease an ovenproof baking dish. Put 2 cups water in a small saucepan and bring to a boil. Add the rice and boil, uncovered, for 5 minutes. Drain, but don't rinse. Stir the rice into the onion mixture. Add the cheese, milk, chipotle sauce, and salt and mix well.

3. Transfer rice mixture to the baking dish. Bake, covered, 20 minutes. Remove the cover and continue to bake another 20 minutes, or until the liquid is absorbed, the onions are very tender when pierced with the tip of a sharp knife, and the top is lightly browned. Serve hot.

Beans, Rice, and Pasta

Bean Dishes 461

Basic Pot Beans

Basic Refried Beans

Pinto Beans with Fried Onions

Ranch Beans with Bacon

Horsemen's Beans

Red Beans and Pork Chili

Beans with Chorizo, Chiles, and Tequila

Black Beans Yucatán

Black Beans with Diced Pork, Yucatán-Style

Black Beans and Rice

Yucatán Puréed Black Beans

Quick Refried Black Beans

White Beans with Roasted Garlic

White Beans and Carrots with Green Onion

Basic Chickpeas

Chickpeas with Spinach

Fresh Fava Beans

Lima Beans with Toasted Pumpkin Seeds

Rice Dishes 472

Basic White Rice

Mexican Rice

Rice with Carrots

Rice with Corn

Tomatillo-Cilantro Rice

Green Rice

Rice with Pine Nuts

Yellow Rice with Peas

Rice with Chickpeas

Rice with Plantains

Rice with Mixed Vegetables

Rice with Squash Blossoms

Rice with Mushrooms and Poblano Chiles

Red Rice with Chicken

Rice with Minced Pork or Beef

Rice with Sausage and Cabbage

Rice with Ham and Pineapple

Rice with Shrimp and Corn

Rice with Crab, Yucatán Style

Pasta Dishes 482

Vermicelli with Mushrooms

Vermicelli with Chicken Meatballs

Vermicelli with Turkey

Together, beans and rice have long been staples in the Mexican diet, and they are cooked in dozens of inventive and inviting ways. Beans, in particular, are a crucial part of Mexican meals, and a pot of beans bubbles daily on nearly every stove.

There are dozens of bean varieties, colors, and sizes grown and then sold in every public market in the country. The variety is quite amazing to those who see it for the first time. Pinto beans, and pink, red, and brown beans are more prevalent in the north, giving way to a preference for black beans in much of central Mexico and in the south. White beans, too, appear in regional dishes in many parts of Mexico.

Rice came to Mexico through an important trade route established to avoid or withstand pirate attacks during the 1560s. Heavily armed galleons sailed between Manila in the Philippines and Acapulco, carrying goods and products of all kinds to Mexico, including rice.

Rice is commonly cooked in water or broth and served plain, or seasoned with tomatoes, onions, herbs, and spices—the preparation that's referred to as Mexican rice. Vegetables, meat, or seafood also often get mixed with rice to create main dishes.

Rice is frequently served as a "dry soup"(*sopa seca*), because it completely absorbs the liquid in which it is cooked. The rice is sautéed first in oil to enhance flavor before the liquid is added, as in a pilaf or risotto.

Pasta is a lesser-known ingredient of Mexican cooking, and may have been introduced when a large number of Italian, German, and Swiss farmers settled in central Mexico around San Miguel de Allende in the late 1700s. Pasta, usually in the form of vermicelli (*fideos*), is also made into *sopa seca*, using the same technique as for rice. *Fideos* are often topped with cheese and baked, or the pasta can be served directly from the pan it was cooked in as soon as the liquid is absorbed and the pasta is tender.

Sopas secas are generally served as a separate course following the "wet soup" (*sopa aguada*) course or as a light entrée.

The bean, rice, and pasta recipes in this chapter will add great flavor and variety to all your Mexican meals. They can accompany the main dish, or be a separate course, or serve as a one-dish meal. However they are incorporated, beans and rice, together or apart, are satisfying dishes for your Mexican menus.

Bean Dishes

Basic Pot Beans
Frijoles de Olla

Makes **6 to 8 servings**

A simmering pot of beans, called frijoles de olla, *is basic to Mexican cooking. It's easy to make, but does take a watchful eye to avoid scorching the beans. The finished pot of soupy beans are delicious just as they are, or can be used as a base for other bean dishes. Cook beans 1 day ahead for best flavor. Presoaking is not required. Mexican cooks rarely soak beans before cooking, and I do follow their method. (See sidebar.)*

1 pound dried beans, pinto, red, black, white, or other

1 bay leaf

1 teaspoon dried oregano (Mexican variety preferred), crumbled

2 teaspoons salt, or to taste

1. Pick over dried beans carefully and remove any pebbles or debris. Place in a large strainer or colander and rinse thoroughly under cold tap water.

2. Place the beans in a large pan with water to cover by about 2 inches. Bring to a boil over medium high heat, then turn heat to medium-low, add bay leaf and oregano. Cook, covered, stirring occasionally, about 1 to 1½ hours, or until beans are tender and the liquid thickens. Check the water level during cooking. There should always be about ½ inch water above the surface of the beans. Add hot water, when needed, about ¼ cup at a time.

3. When the beans are tender, add salt, remove the bay leaf, and serve hot with the bean broth. To store, cool, then cover the beans and refrigerate up to 3 days, or freeze up to 3 months.

Making Beans Easier to Digest

Although it is not the Mexican way, some people prefer to soak beans and discard the water before cooking to make them easier to digest. To soak beans, cover with 2 inches of water. Boil gently about 5 to 8 minutes. Cover and set aside to soak 2 to 4 hours. Drain, and add fresh water to cover by 2 inches and cook as instructed in the bean recipes.

If you do throw out the soaking water, be aware that some of the nutrition contained in the beans will be lost. Black beans, in particular, will also lose some of their wonderful black color.

In some regions where epazote is used to cook black beans, it is said that the herb has properties that help reduce the "gassy" effects of beans. There are also consumer products sold here in markets and drug stores, such as Beano, that may help make beans easier to digest.

Basic Refried Beans
Frijoles Refritos

Makes **about 5 cups**

Refried beans that are prepared at home from beans you have cooked yourself are absolutely delicious. You may never be tempted to use canned refried beans again. I often make up a big batch and freeze the beans in small containers for later use.

Lard is rendered from fresh pork fat and it imparts a wonderful creaminess and rich flavor to refried beans. It's easy to make, if you wish, and contains half the cholesterol of butter, so a little lard isn't that bad. The beans can be varied in many simple ways. You can add chopped cooked onion and garlic, or melt cheese over the top when serving. Ground cumin or dried epazote or oregano may be added for extra flavor.

Basic Pot Beans (page 461), any type
1/3 to 1/2 cup Basic Fresh Lard (page 19)
  or vegetable oil
Salt and freshly ground pepper, to taste

1. Cook pot beans until the liquid thickens and the beans are very tender. To fry the beans, heat a large heavy skillet over medium heat and add the lard or oil. When the lard is melted and hot, add about 1 cup of cooked beans and about 1/2 cup of the broth, too. Stir and mash as the beans cook and thicken. Gradually add all of the beans, and all of the remaining broth, mashing and stirring continuously, until the broth is reduced and the beans are thick enough to hold their shape.

2. When the beans are very thick and the juices have cooked away, add salt and pepper. The beans are ready to use, or to refrigerate or freeze for later use.

Pinto Beans with Fried Onions
Frijoles con Cebollas Fritos

Makes **8 servings**

We dug into a platter of these exceptional beans served as a side dish at a small restaurant in Zihuatanejo, a fishing village and vacation destination on the Pacific coast. The beans are cooked with onion and garlic until very tender, then partially mashed with fried caramelized onions. The garlic becomes creamy soft and mellow when cooked with the beans.

1 pound dried pinto beans
2 medium white onions, finely chopped and
  divided evenly
10 medium garlic cloves, peeled and thinly sliced
1 teaspoon dried oregano (Mexican variety
  preferred), crumbled
1 teaspoon salt, or to taste
1/4 cup lard, corn oil, or safflower oil
1/8 teaspoon freshly ground pepper, or to taste
1/2 cup finely crumbled cotija or mild feta cheese

1. Pick over dried beans carefully and remove any pebbles or debris. Place in a large strainer or colander and rinse thoroughly under cold tap water.

2. Put the beans, half of the onions, the garlic, and the oregano in a large pot. Add water to about 2 inches above the level of the beans. Bring to a boil, uncovered. Reduce the heat to low, cover, and cook the beans until tender, about 1½ to 2 hours. Add more water during cooking if the liquid thickens before the beans are tender. When the beans are tender, add the salt and continue to cook until the liquid thickens and the beans are soft. Turn off the heat and let the beans stand in the pot.

3. Heat the lard or oil in a large deep skillet over medium heat and cook the remaining onion, stirring, until golden brown and caramelized. Reduce the heat if the onion browns too fast. Take care not to burn it. Add 2 cups of the beans and mash with a bean masher or wooden spoon until thick and smooth. Add the remaining beans and cook, stirring, until the mixture is thick and creamy. Most of the beans should remain whole. Stir in the pepper, then adjust seasoning. Transfer the beans to a deep platter or large shallow bowl. Sprinkle with cheese and serve.

Ranch Beans with Bacon
Frijoles Rancheros

Makes **8 servings**

Typical of northern Mexico's home-style cooking, where ranches and farms are prevalent, these tasty beans go especially well with barbecued meats. Here in the United States, I serve them with Mexican-American Corn Bread (page 519) and Yucatán Cabbage Salsa (page 38).

1 pound pinto beans

2 bay leaves

1 teaspoon dried oregano, crumbled

$^1/_2$ pound sliced bacon, cut crossways in $^1/_2$-inch pieces

1 medium onion, finely chopped

2 jalapeño chiles, stemmed, seeded, veins removed, and chopped

1 teaspoon ground cumin

1 (14-ounce) can ready-cut tomatoes

$^1/_2$ teaspoon salt, or to taste

$^1/_8$ teaspoon freshly ground pepper, or to taste

1. Pick over dried beans carefully and remove any pebbles or debris. Place in a large strainer or colander and rinse thoroughly under cold tap water.

2. Put the beans in a large pot, and add fresh tap water to cover by 2 inches. Add the bay leaf and oregano. Bring to a boil, uncovered, over medium high heat, then turn heat to low, cover and simmer 1½ to 2 hours, stirring occasionally, until the beans are tender and the broth begins to thicken. (Add additional hot water during cooking, if the liquid thickens before the beans are tender. Do not let beans boil dry.)

3. Meanwhile, in a medium skillet, cook the bacon over medium heat until crisp, about 3 minutes. Add the bacon to the beans. Discard all but 1 tablespoon of the bacon fat, and cook the onion and cumin in the remaining bacon fat, stirring, about 1 minute. Add the tomatoes, salt and pepper. Cook, uncovered, about 3 minutes.

4. Add the tomato mixture to the beans and cook, stirring frequently, over low heat until the broth is thick, about 10 minutes. Add salt, if needed. (The amount of salt in the bacon will determine if extra salt is needed.) Serve hot, or cover and refrigerate for up to 3 days.

Horsemen's Beans
Frijoles Charros

Makes 8 servings

Traditional frijoles charros are cooked with tomatoes, onion, and serrano chiles. In this version, bacon is added to enrich and flavor the beans. Charros refers to the skilled horsemen from Jalisco and other nearby states, who wear elaborate outfits and huge sombreros beautifully decorated with silver. Their horses are similarly bedecked. There is a popular Charros festival in the city of Colima every February that continues for fifteen days with rodeos, bullfights, music, food, and dance. Frijoles charros are served in fondas and restaurants throughout the region. The beans are also called "cowboy beans" in other northern regions, such as Monterrey and in the state of Nuevo Leon.

1 pound pink beans

1 bay leaf

1/2 pound sliced bacon, cut crosswise into 1-inch pieces

1 large white onion, chopped

2 medium garlic cloves, chopped

1 serrano chile, finely chopped, including seeds

1 teaspoon dried oregano (Mexican variety preferred), crumbled

3 medium tomatoes, peeled and chopped, or 1 (15-ounce) can ready-cut tomatoes

1/2 teaspoon salt, or to taste

Freshly ground pepper, to taste

1. Pick over dried beans carefully and remove any pebbles or debris. Place in a large strainer or colander and rinse thoroughly under cold tap water.

2. Put the beans in a large pot. Cover with about 2 inches of water. Bring to a boil and add the bay leaf. Reduce the heat to low, cover and cook the beans, stirring occasionally, until tender, about 1½ to 2 hours. (Add more water if liquid thickens before the beans are tender. Do not let the beans boil dry.)

3. In a skillet, cook the bacon until crisp. Remove and drain on paper towels. Pour off all but 1 tablespoon of the bacon fat, and in the same pan, cook the onion and garlic, stirring, until the onion begins to brown, 3 to 4 minutes.

4. When the beans are tender, add the bacon and the skillet ingredients to the beans along with the serrano and tomatoes. Continue cooking the beans, uncovered, until the broth thickens, about 20 to 25 minutes. Season the beans with salt and pepper. Serve in individual bowls.

Red Beans and Pork Chili
Frijoles y Puerco con Chili

Makes 8 servings

Chili beans are among the favorite Mexican-American dishes in the United States that probably came across the Mexican border via Texas, where the beans are made with pork or beef. The beans in this hearty, full-meal dish are cooked with chunks of tender braised pork in a spicy tomato sauce of chili powder, herbs, and spices.

1 pound cooked red beans (Basic Pot Beans, page 461)

3 pounds boneless pork, cut into 1-inch pieces

3 tablespoons all-purpose flour

1 teaspoon salt, or to taste

2 tablespoons vegetable oil

1 large white onion, chopped

4 large garlic cloves, thinly sliced

3 medium tomatoes, peeled and chopped

2 large jalapeño chiles, seeded, veins removed, and chopped

1 teaspoon Worcestershire sauce

1/4 cup purchased chili powder

2 teaspoons ground cumin

1 teaspoon dried oregano (Mexican variety preferred), crumbled

1 cup canned beef broth

1. Prepare the red beans. While they are cooking, pat the pork dry with paper towels. Mix the flour and salt. Dust the pork lightly with the flour and shake off excess.

2. Heat the oil in a large saucepan over medium heat and brown the pork, in batches, without crowding, 3 to 4 minutes, then transfer to a bowl. Add the onion and garlic to the pan. Reduce heat to low, cover and cook, stirring frequently, until the onion is limp, 5 to 6 minutes. Add the remaining ingredients, except the broth. Bring to a boil, stirring, and cook 1 minute, scraping up any bits from the bottom of the pan.

3. Return the pork to the pan with the accumulated juices. Add the broth, bring to a boil, cover, reduce heat to low, and simmer, stirring occasionally, until the pork is tender, about 1 hour.

4. When the beans are tender and their broth has thickened, stir the beans into the pork. Bring to a boil; reduce heat to low and simmer, uncovered, 8 to 10 minutes to blend flavors. Adjust seasoning and serve.

Beans with Chorizo, Chiles, and Tequila
Frijoles de Fiesta

Makes 8 servings

Celebrations in Mexico naturally call for plenty of food. A friendly taxi driver in Guadalajara, in the state of Jalisco, told me how to make this fiesta bean dish. As he drove, he talked and I took notes. This pot of beans is fit for any convivial gathering.

Adding tequila to the beans (and to many other dishes) is common in Jalisco, where almost all of the tequila in Mexico is produced.

1 pound cooked red beans (Basic Pot Beans, page 461)

4 ancho chiles, toasted and seeded (page 9)

1 teaspoon dried oregano (Mexican variety preferred), crumbled

2 medium tomatoes, peeled and chopped .

1/2 cup canned chicken broth

2 bay leaves

1 teaspoon salt, or to taste

1/2 pound fresh bulk chorizo, or packaged, with casings removed, crumbled

1 medium white onion, chopped

2 tablespoons tequila

Chopped fresh cilantro, for garnishing

1/2 cup crumbled queso fresco (fresh Mexican cheese)

1. Prepare the beans. While the beans cook, soak the toasted chiles in hot water to cover 20 minutes. Transfer to a blender, discarding the soaking water. Add the oregano, tomatoes, and chicken broth. Blend as smoothly as possible.

2. When the beans are tender, add the puréed mixture to the pot of beans. Add the bay leaves and salt. Cover the pot and continue to simmer the beans over low heat.

3. In a large skillet, fry the chorizo until brown and cooked through, about 4 minutes. Pour off excess grease. Add the chorizo to the simmering beans. In the same skillet, fry the onion, stirring, until it starts to brown, 3 to 4 minutes. Add to the beans along with the tequila. Cook the beans until the broth reduces and thickens and the beans are very tender, 25 to 30 minutes. Remove the bay leaves. Serve the beans in shallow soup bowls. Sprinkle with chopped cilantro and crumbled cheese.

Black Beans Yucatán
Frijoles Negro Yucatecan

Makes **6 to 8 servings**

Black beans, cooked in the Yucatán style, are seasoned very simply and are quite "soupy." I prefer to serve them in individual bowls to be eaten with a main dish. The herb, epazote, *is essential to the authentic flavor, but if it's not available, just leave it out. The beans will still be very good. For this recipe, I use the quick-soak method as a variation to cook the beans, but do not drain off the soaking water. I often use sea salt for cooking and usually bring some home from Mexico. If you don't have it, use ordinary table salt.*

1 pound dried black beans

1 teaspoon dried oregano (Mexican variety preferred), crumbled

1 bay leaf

1 medium white onion, finely chopped

3 medium garlic cloves, thinly sliced

1 sprig epazote, about 6 inches long

1 teaspoon sea salt

1. Pick over dried beans carefully and remove any pebbles or debris. Place in a large strainer or colander and rinse thoroughly under cold tap water.

2. Put the beans in a large pot, and cover by 2 inches with water. Bring the beans to a boil, uncovered, and cook them for about 5 minutes. Cover and let the beans soak off the heat for about 20 to 25 minutes.

3. Bring the beans to a boil again. Add the oregano and bay leaf. Cover the pan, reduce the heat, and simmer the beans, stirring occasionally, until the beans are barely soft, about 45 minutes. Add the onion, garlic, epazote and salt. Add hot water ½ cup at a time, when needed, to keep the

beans from boiling dry. Cook until the beans are very soft, and the broth thickens, about 1 more hour. Remove the bay leaf and the epazote. Adjust seasoning. Serve hot.

Black Beans with Diced Pork, Yucatán-Style
Frijoles Negro con Cerdo estilo Yucatán

Makes **4 to 6 servings**

Merida, the capital of Yucatán features a mix of colonial and modern architecture. This recipe for black beans with tidbits of pork comes from El Anfitrión restaurant in Merida. Serve the dish like a stew, with good crusty bread or fresh tortillas. Garnish the beans with Radish Salsa (page 34).

2 cups dried black beans

1 tablespoon lard or vegetable oil

1½ pounds boneless pork, cut into 1-inch pieces

1 medium white onion, finely chopped

2 large garlic cloves, finely chopped

12 fresh chopped epazote leaves, or 1 teaspoon dried epazote

1 tablespoon chopped fresh cilantro

2 bay leaves

½ habanero chile, seeded (wear protective gloves)

1 teaspoon salt, or to taste

1. Pick over dried beans carefully and remove any pebbles or debris. Place in a large strainer or colander and rinse thoroughly under cold tap water.

2. Put the beans in a large pot with 6 cups of water. Bring to a boil, then reduce the heat to low, and simmer until the beans are tender, about 1½ to 2 hours.

3. Meanwhile, in a large nonstick skillet, heat the lard or oil and brown the pork. Add the remaining ingredients and cook, stirring, until the onion is softened, about 5 minutes. Add 1 cup of water. Bring to a boil, then reduce the heat to low, cover and simmer for 30 minutes. When the beans are tender, add the pork mixture to the beans. Cook, uncovered, until the liquid thickens and the flavors blend, about 20 to 25 minutes. Remove the bay leaves and habanero chile. Adjust seasoning. Serve hot.

Black Beans and Rice
Moros y Cristianos

Makes **6 to 8 servings**

Black beans and rice is a popular dish in Veracruz and shows the strong influence of Spanish food in the region. (The recipe name comes from Spain and refers to the long period when Muslim Moors ruled over predominately Christian Spain.) Depending on the cook's preference, sometimes the beans are partially cooked and then raw rice and liquid are added while the beans finish cooking, or, as in this recipe, both beans and rice are fully cooked separately and then combined for a few minutes to blend the flavors. The dish should be rich and moist, but not soupy.

¹/₂ pound (¹/₂ recipe) Basic Pot Beans (page 461) with black beans

1 tablespoon plus 2 teaspoons olive oil

1 cup long-grain white rice

2 cups canned chicken broth or water

1 medium white onion, chopped

2 medium garlic cloves, finely chopped

1 jalapeño chile, seeded, veins removed, and finely chopped

1 teaspoon ground cumin

¹/₂ teaspoon dried oregano (Mexican variety preferred), crumbled

Salt, to taste

1. Prepare black beans. When the beans are tender but not mushy, remove from the heat and reserve in their liquid.

2. Meanwhile, in a saucepan, heat the oil over medium heat. Add the rice and stir to coat with the oil. Cook, stirring frequently, until the rice is aromatic and beginning to brown. Add the broth or water all at once. Bring to a boil, then reduce the heat to low, cover and cook until the rice is tender and the liquid is absorbed, 18 to 20 minutes. Let the rice stand 10 minutes.

3. While the rice cooks, heat the remaining 2 teaspoons oil in a large saucepan and cook the onion until it starts to brown, about 3 minutes. Add the garlic, chile, cumin, and oregano. Cook, stirring, 2 minutes. Add 2 cups of the reserved cooked beans and ¹/₂ cup of their broth to the onion mixture. Add the cooked rice and stir gently to mix with the beans. Add salt. Cook about 5 minutes to heat through. If the mixture is not moist, add ¹/₂ cup additional bean broth. (Cover and refrigerate extra beans for another use.)

Yucatán Puréed Black Beans
Frijoles Colados

Makes **about 3 cups**

Many Yucatán cooks push the cooked beans through a wire strainer to purée the beans in the traditional way, but some prefer as I do, to purée the beans in a blender. A food processor can also be used. Try to cook the beans a day ahead for the best flavor. If fresh epazote is not available, dried epazote can usually be found in Latin-American markets.

¹/₂ pound dried black beans
¹/₂ medium white onion, chopped
1 teaspoon dried oregano (Mexican variety preferred), crumbled
1 (4- to 5-inch) sprig of fresh epazote or 1 teaspoon dried epazote
1 habanero chile, or 2 serrano chiles, whole (wear protective gloves)
2 tablespoons lard or vegetable oil
¹/₂ teaspoon salt, or to taste

1. Pick over dried beans carefully and remove any pebbles or debris. Place in a large strainer or colander; rinse thoroughly under cold tap water.
2. Put the beans, onion, epazote, and whole chile in a large pot. Add water to cover by 2 inches. Bring to a boil, then reduce the heat to low, partially cover and simmer until the beans are very tender, about 1½ to 2 hours depending on the age of the beans. If water reduces to the level of the beans before they are tender, add more water and cook until the beans are tender. Remove the epazote and whole chile. Add the lard or oil and the salt.
3. Purée the beans in a blender or food processor until thick but not too smooth. There should be some texture. Reheat shortly before serving. If beans thicken too much as they stand, add hot broth or water to achieve the desired consistency. To store, cover and refrigerate up to 3 days or freeze up to 3 months.

Quick Refried Black Beans
Frijoles Refritos Pronto

Makes **6 servings**

Convenient canned black beans are used in this recipe to make refried beans when there is no time to start from scratch.

3 tablespoons corn oil
¹/₂ medium onion, chopped
2 medium garlic cloves, finely chopped
1 teaspoon ground cumin
1 teaspoon dried oregano (Mexican variety preferred), crumbled
¹/₈ teaspoon crushed hot red pepper
1 cup canned ready-cut tomatoes, with the juices
2 (15-ounce) cans black beans, drained, but not rinsed

1. In a medium skillet, heat 1 tablespoon of the oil over medium high heat, and cook the onion and garlic, stirring, until the onion softens, about 3 minutes. Stir in the cumin, oregano, red pepper, tomatoes, and beans. Transfer the mixture to a food processor and pulse 8 to 10 times to make a coarse purée.
2. In a large skillet, heat the remaining 2 tablespoons of oil over medium heat. Add the bean mixture and bring to a boil, stirring constantly. Turn the heat to low and cook, uncovered, stirring frequently, 6 to 8 minutes, or until the liquids have reduced and the beans are thick enough to hold a mounded shape on a wooden spoon.

White Beans with Roasted Garlic

Frijoles Blanco con Ajo Asada

Makes 6 servings

Beans of many colors and sizes are an integral part of daily meals in most Mexican homes, so it was not surprising to have smooth, puréed white beans served with my entrée at the elegant Restaurant El Sacramonte *in Guadalajara.*

$1/2$ pound ($1/2$ recipe) dry white beans
    (Basic Pot Beans, page 461)
6 large garlic cloves, unpeeled
3 tablespoons unsalted butter
1 medium white onion, chopped
$1/2$ teaspoon dried oregano (Mexican variety
    preferred), crumbled
$1/2$ teaspoon dried marjoram
$1/2$ teaspoon ground cumin
Bean broth from cooking the beans, as needed
$1/2$ teaspoon salt, or to taste
$1/4$ teaspoon crushed red pepper
3 tablespoons finely chopped fresh parsley

1. Prepare the white beans. While the beans are cooking, roast the garlic cloves in a small dry skillet over medium heat until flecked with brown and slightly soft. Remove the papery skin and reserve.

2. When the beans are tender, using a slotted spoon, transfer the beans to a food processor or blender. Reserve the cooking broth.

3. Preheat oven to 325°. In a medium skillet, melt the butter over medium-low heat and cook the onion slowly, stirring frequently, until soft and translucent, 5 to 6 minutes. Add the oregano, marjoram, and cumin. Cook, stirring, 1 minute. Transfer to the processor with the beans. Add the

reserved roasted garlic and purée to a thick smooth mixture, adding just enough bean broth to achieve a consistency that holds its shape on a spoon. Add the salt and red pepper. Pulse 3 to 4 times to mix.

4. Transfer the puréed beans to an ovenproof baking dish and bake 20 to 25 minutes or until completely heated through. Sprinkle with chopped parsley and serve hot.

White Beans and Carrots with Green Onions

Frijoles Blancos y Zanahorias con Cebollinas

Makes 4 servings

In Veracruz, white beans and carrots are paired with tiny green onions called cebollinas. *The combination is very tasty, and I find that in the United States, substituting green onions for the unavailable* cebollinas *works just fine.*

2 medium carrots, peeled and cut into $1/4$-inch dice
2 cups cooked small white beans, canned or
    homemade, drained but not rinsed
1 tablespoon extra-virgin olive oil
4 green onions, thinly sliced crosswise
$1/2$ teaspoon ground cumin
$1/2$ teaspoon salt, or to taste
$1/8$ teaspoon freshly ground pepper, or to taste
1 tablespoon finely chopped fresh parsley

In a medium saucepan, boil about ¾ cup water and cook the carrots until crisp tender, about 3 minutes. Drain the carrots and return to the same pan. Add the cooked beans, olive oil, onions, cumin, salt, and pepper. Cook over medium-low heat until bubbling and completely heated through, 4 to 5 minutes. Stir in the parsley.

Basic Chickpeas
Garbanzos

Makes 3 cups cooked beans; about 6 servings

Chickpeas are grown and widely used through-out Mexico. Mexican cooks soak chickpeas overnight to reduce cooking time and to help loosen the skins so they will rub off easily after they are cooked, a traditional technique that I follow. It is not necessary to rub off the skins, but the beans have a smoother texture and taste without them.

It is very easy to cook dried chickpeas. Of course, it does take time to cook any beans from scratch, but the results are worth the extra effort, for the beans will have better flavor. Dried chickpeas require very little attention while they cook, but plan ahead and allow time to soak the beans overnight in the traditional way.

1 cup dried chickpeas (garbanzo beans)
1/2 teaspoon salt

1. Put the chickpeas in a strainer or colander and rinse under cold tap water. Drain and put into a bowl. Add hot water to about 1 inch above the level of the beans. Cover and soak overnight.

2. Put the soaked beans and the soaking water into a large pot. Add 2 more cups of water and the salt. Bring to a boil, then reduce the heat to low, cover and simmer until the beans are tender, but not mushy, about 1½ hours. Cool the beans in the broth; then scoop chickpeas out of the broth, about ¼ cup at a time, and rub off the thin outer skins with your fingers and discard them. Put skinned chickpeas into a bowl. Repeat until all are skinned, then return all the chickpeas to the broth. The beans are ready to use, or cover and refrigerate, in their broth, for up to 3 days.

Chickpeas with Spinach
Garbanzos con Espinaca

Makes 4 servings

This is a modern side dish with Spanish roots that goes well with grilled fish fillets, pork, or chicken. De arbol chiles are dried and can be easily crumbled into pieces with your fingers.

2 tablespoons olive oil
1 medium red onion, thinly sliced
2 medium garlic cloves, finely chopped
1 teaspoon ground cumin
1 de arbol chile, crumbled, or 1/4 teaspoon crushed red pepper
2 (15-ounce) cans chickpeas (garbanzo beans), drained and rinsed, or 3 1/2 cups drained home-cooked chickpeas
1 (10-ounce) package of fresh spinach leaves
2 tablespoons white wine vinegar
1/2 teaspoon salt, or to taste
1/8 teaspoon freshly ground pepper, or to taste

In a large nonstick skillet, heat the oil over medium heat and cook the onion until softened, 3 to 4 minutes. Add the garlic, cumin, chile, chickpeas, and ⅓ cup water. Bring to a boil; then add the spinach and cook, stirring until the spinach is wilted and tender, 6 to 8 minutes. Add the vinegar, salt, and pepper. Stir to combine. Serve hot.

Fresh Fava Beans
Fabas

Makes **about 1 cup fava beans;**
serves 4 to 6 as a garnish

Shelling then peeling fresh fabas (fava beans, or broad beans) is a tedious task, but it improves their texture. Fava beans are added to soups and stews. Mix them with fresh corn and sweet red peppers for a side dish or add them to green salads or white rice.

This basic recipe describes how to cook and peel fresh fabas that are available seasonally in some supermarkets and farmer's markets in the United States. In Mexico, when fava beans are in season, great boxes and piles of the beans in their pods appear in public markets everywhere.

1 pound unshelled fresh fava beans
1/4 teaspoon salt, or to taste
1 tablespoons olive oil

Shell the beans. In a large pot of boiling salted water cook the fabas until tender, 12 to 15 minutes. Drain and cool under running water. Remove the thin outer skin by pinching the beans; the skins usually slip off easily. Put the peeled beans in a bowl. Add salt and oil. The beans are ready to use.

Lima Beans with Toasted Pumpkin Seeds
Tok-cel

Makes **4 servings**

Credit for this Yucatán side dish with its native Indian name goes to Herberto (Bruce) Ucan, born and raised in the Yucatán, and now owner, with wife Laura, of The Mayan Gypsy, a restaurant in Louisville, Kentucky. Lima beans originated in Peru and spread throughout the New World. Raw, unsalted pumpkin seeds are used frequently in Mexican cooking and can be found in most health food stores and gourmet stores in the United States.

1/2 cup raw, unsalted pumpkin seeds
1 (10-ounce) package frozen lima beans
2 tablespoons olive oil
2 tablespoons fresh lime juice
1/2 teaspoon salt, or to taste

1. In a medium, dry skillet, over medium heat, toast the pumpkin seeds, stirring and tossing, until they begin to pop around in the pan, about 2 minutes. Cool the seeds in a bowl, then chop coarsely and set aside.

2. Cook the lima beans according to the directions on the package. Drain. Heat the olive oil in the same skillet used for toasting the pumpkin seeds. Add the lima beans, and cook, stirring, 1 minute. Stir in the chopped pumpkin seeds, lime juice, and salt. Heat through and serve hot.

Rice Dishes

Basic White Rice
Arroz Blanco

Makes **4 servings**

To cook a small amount of white rice the Mexican way, I use a heavy, stainless steel 2-quart saucepan with a cover. The raw rice is sautéed in oil, then simmered slowly in hot water or broth, like a pilaf.

1 tablespoon vegetable oil

1 cup long-grain white rice

1/2 teaspoon salt

2 cups water or canned fat-free reduced-sodium chicken broth

1. Heat the oil in a 2-quart wide saucepan or deep skillet. When the oil shimmers, add the rice and cook, stirring, until the rice is opaque and starts to change color, but doesn't brown, about 5 minutes. Add the liquid all at once, stir and bring to a boil.

2. Reduce heat to low, cover and simmer until the liquid is absorbed and the rice is tender, 18 to 20 minutes.

3. Remove the pan from the heat and let the rice stand 5 minutes. Stick a fork into the bottom of the pan to check for remaining moisture. If just dry on the bottom, fluff the rice with the fork and serve. If not, cover and let stand 5 more minutes. Serve hot.

Mexican Rice
Arroz a la Mexicana

Makes **4 servings**

Rice cooked in broth with tomatoes, onion, and garlic is a classic rice dish, with variations, throughout Mexico. It goes well with so many things; try it with Chicken with Black Bean and Avocado Salsa (page 283), or Seared Tuna with Oregano and Garlic (page 392).

2 tablespoons corn oil, olive oil, or other vegetable oil

1 cup long-grain white rice

1/2 medium white onion, finely chopped

2 medium garlic cloves, finely chopped

1/2 teaspoon ground cumin

1/4 teaspoon salt

1/4 pound plum tomatoes, peeled and finely chopped

2 cups canned fat-free reduced-sodium chicken broth

2 tablespoons chopped fresh cilantro

1. In a 4-quart saucepan, heat the oil over medium heat. Add the rice and cook, stirring, until golden, about 4 minutes. Add the onion, garlic, cumin, and salt. Cook, stirring, until the onion softens, about 3 minutes. Add the tomatoes and cook until the juices evaporate and the mixture is nearly dry, 3 to 4 minutes. Add the broth all at once and stir to settle the rice. Bring to a boil.

2. Reduce the heat to low, cover, and simmer until the liquid is absorbed and the rice is tender, 18 to 20 minutes. Remove from the heat and let stand 6 to 8 minutes. Fluff the rice and stir in the cilantro. Serve hot.

Rice with Carrots
Arroz con Zanahorias

Makes **4 servings**

White rice steamed with tiny bits of carrot, onion, and garlic is a common way to cook rice. Serve as a side dish.

2 tablespoons olive oil
2 tablespoons finely chopped white onion
1 cup long-grain white rice
1/2 medium carrot, peeled and finely diced or chopped
1 small garlic clove, finely chopped
1/4 teaspoon ground cumin
1/4 teaspoon salt, or to taste
2 cups hot tap water

1. In a wide 2-quart saucepan heat the oil over medium heat. Add the onion and rice. Cook, stirring, until the rice is opaque and starts to change color, but doesn't brown, about 3 minutes. Add the carrot, garlic, cumin, and salt. Cook 1 minute. Add the water all at once, and stir to settle the rice. Bring to a boil.

2. Reduce the heat to low, cover and simmer until the liquid is absorbed and the rice is tender, 18 to 20 minutes. Serve hot.

3. Remove the pan from the heat and let the rice stand 5 minutes. Stick a fork into the bottom of the pan to check for remaining moisture. If just dry on the bottom, fluff the rice with the fork and serve. If not, cover and let stand 5 more minutes. Serve hot.

Rice with Corn
Arroz con Elote

Makes **4 servings**

Rice and corn are often combined in Mexican cooking, and they are perfect partners for a satisfying side dish, particularly with saucy meat or poultry entrées. Rice and corn are also used as a filling for chiles rellenos.

1 tablespoon vegetable oil
1 cup long-grain white rice
2 cups hot tap water
2 medium ears fresh corn
1 tablespoon unsalted butter
1/2 teaspoon salt
1/2 teaspoon ground cumin

1. Heat the oil in a 2-quart wide saucepan or deep skillet. When the oil shimmers, add the rice and cook, stirring, until the rice is opaque and starts to change color, but doesn't brown, about 5 minutes. Add the liquid all at once, stir and bring to a boil.

2. Reduce heat to low, cover and simmer until the liquid is absorbed and the rice is tender, 18 to 20 minutes.

3. Remove the pan from the heat and let the rice stand 5 minutes. Stick a fork into the bottom of the pan to check for remaining moisture. If just dry on the bottom, fluff the rice with the fork and serve. If not, cover and let stand 5 more minutes.

4. Meanwhile, cook the corn in a large pot of boiling water, 5 minutes. Cool under cold running water. Cut off the kernels and discard the cobs. Add the corn kernels, butter, salt, and cumin to the rice. Mix gently and serve hot.

Tomatillo-Cilantro Rice
Arroz de Tomatillo y Cilantro

Makes **4 servings**

Cilantro takes on a different, mild taste when cooked. The intriguing subtle flavor of this rice has made it a favorite at my house. Patricia Amtmann, owner of an import business in Mexico City, told me how to prepare this dish, and I worked out the recipe. The rice pairs nicely with a main course of Shrimp with Tomatoes and Cheese (page 408).

2 medium tomatillos (2 ounces), husked, rinsed, and chopped

¹/₂ cup lightly packed coarsely chopped fresh cilantro

2 cups canned fat-free reduced-sodium chicken broth

1 tablespoon olive oil

1 cup long-grain white rice

2 green onions, including 2 inches of green stalk, chopped

¹/₄ teaspoon salt, or to taste

1. Put the tomatillos, cilantro, and 1 cup of the chicken broth into a blender and blend until smooth. Pour into a 2-cup liquid measuring cup and add enough of the remaining chicken broth to total 2 cups liquid. Reserve.

2. In a wide 2-quart saucepan, heat the oil over medium heat until hot. Add the rice and cook, stirring, until the rice coloris opaque and starts to change color, but doesn't brown, 4 to 5 minutes. Add the scallions and salt. Cook 1 minute. Pour in the reserved 2 cups puréed cilantro–chicken broth mixture. Bring to a boil.

3. Reduce heat to low, cover, and cook 18 to 20 minutes, or until the liquid is absorbed and the rice is tender. Remove from the heat, cover, and let sit 5 minutes. Stick a fork into the bottom of the pan to check for remaining moisture. If just dry, fluff with a fork and serve. If not, cover and let stand 5 more minutes.

Green Rice
Arroz Verde

Makes **4 servings**

Green rice gets its color and much of its flavor from puréed green chiles, parsley, and cilantro. The rice is very good with grilled fish fillets or chicken. For color and flavor accent on the plate, add a spicy fresh tomato salsa.

1 large poblano chile, roasted, peeled, and seeded (page 8)

¹/₂ cup loosely packed chopped fresh cilantro

2 tablespoons chopped fresh parsley

¹/₂ teaspoon dried oregano (Mexican variety preferred), crumbled

1 medium garlic clove, pressed

1³/₄ cups canned fat-free reduced-sodium chicken broth

1 tablespoon olive oil or vegetable oil

2 tablespoons white onion, finely chopped

1 cup long-grain white rice

¹/₂ teaspoon salt, or to taste

¹/₈ teaspoon freshly ground pepper, or to taste

1. Prepare the chile. Chop the chile and put into a blender. Add the cilantro, parsley, oregano, garlic, and the chicken broth. Blend until smooth. Reserve in the blender.

2. Heat the oil in a 2-quart saucepan over medium heat. Add the onion and rice. Stir to coat with oil and cook, stirring, until the rice and onion are fragrant and begin to color, 3 to 4 minutes. Add the puréed chile mixture all at once. Stir to incorporate evenly into the rice. Bring to a boil.

3. Reduce the heat to low, cover and cook 18 minutes, or until the rice is tender, but still moist, and the liquid is absorbed. Add the salt and pepper. Stir gently with a fork, cover, and let sit 5 minutes before serving.

Rice with Pine Nuts
Arroz con Piñones

Makes **4 servings**

Rice dishes such as this are called dry soups (sopas secas) *because they feature an ingredient that is cooked in liquid, like a soup; but the rice is then cooked until the liquid is completely absorbed, or until "dry." Dry soups are usually served as a separate course. In the United States, we often eat rice as a side dish with the main course; serve it the way you prefer. Toasted pine nuts give the rice a rich flavor.*

1 tablespoon plus 1 teaspoon vegetable oil

2 tablespoons pine nuts

1 cup long-grain white rice

2 tablespoons finely chopped onion

3 cups canned fat-free reduced-sodium chicken broth

1/4 teaspoon salt, or to taste

1 tablespoon chopped fresh cilantro

1. Heat 1 teaspoon of the oil in a small skillet, and toast the pine nuts, stirring, until pale golden brown, about 1 minute. Immediately remove the toasted nuts to a plate to stop the toasting. (Pay close attention: the nuts can burn quickly.)

2. Heat the remaining tablespoon of oil in a large pan over medium-high heat, and cook the rice and the onion, stirring, until aromatic, about 3 minutes. Add the broth and salt. Bring to a boil. Reduce the heat to low, cover and simmer the rice until the liquid is absorbed and the rice is tender, 18 to 20 minutes. Remove the pan from the heat and let the rice stand 5 minutes. Stick a fork into the bottom of the pan to check for moisture. If just dry on the bottom, fluff the rice with the fork. If not dry, cover and stand 5 more minutes. Stir in the pine nuts and cilantro.

Yellow Rice with Peas
Arroz Amarillo

Makes **4 servings**

Achiote (annatto) *seeds' color infuse into the cooking oil to give this Mexican rice its typical yellow hue, elusive aroma', and subtle flavor that's typical in Yucatán and along the Gulf coast of Mexico. The red-orange seeds can be found in Latin-American food stores, or in the Mexican section of most supermarkets.* Achiote *is used all over Mexico for this popular variation on rice, and it often contains fresh mint (but omit it if you like).*

2 tablespoons vegetable oil

1/2 tablespoon achiote seeds

1/2 medium onion, minced

1 medium garlic clove, minced

1 cup long-grain white rice

2 cups canned reduced-sodium chicken broth

1/4 teaspoon salt, or to taste

1/8 teaspoon freshly ground pepper, or to taste

1/2 cup cooked fresh or thawed frozen peas

1 1/2 teaspoons finely chopped fresh mint (optional)

1. In a small saucepan, heat the oil over medium heat. Add the achiote seeds and cook until the seeds sizzle and the oil is a rich gold color, about 1 minute. Remove the pan from the heat. Strain the yellow oil into a large saucepan and discard the seeds.

2. Heat the achiote oil over medium heat. Add the onion and garlic. Cook, stirring, until softened, about 2 minutes. Add the rice and cook, stirring, until the grains are yellow and aromatic, about 3 minutes. Stir in the chicken broth, salt, and pepper. Bring the rice to a boil.

3. Reduce heat to low, cover, and cook 18 to 20 minutes, or until the rice is tender and the liquid is absorbed. Remove pan from heat. Scatter the peas and mint over the top, but do not stir. Cover and let the rice stand 5 minutes. If just dry, fluff the rice with a fork then gently stir the peas and mint, if using, into the rice. Serve hot.

Rice with Chickpeas

Arroz con Garbanzos

Makes **4 servings**

Chickpeas, also called garbanzo beans, are used in soups and salads, and in this case added to rice for a hearty side dish. It's a full-flavored combination that goes well with grilled meats and fresh salsa. This calls for the convenience of canned chickpeas but you can also use freshly cooked—see Basic Chickpeas (page 470).

1 (8-ounce) can chickpeas (garbanzo beans), rinsed and well drained

2 tablespoons olive oil

1 cup long-grain white rice

¹/₄ large white onion, chopped

2 large garlic cloves, very thinly sliced

¹/₂ teaspoon salt, or to taste

1³/₄ cups canned fat-free reduced-sodium chicken broth

2 tablespoons chopped fresh parsley

¹/₂ teaspoon dried oregano (Mexican variety preferred), crumbled

¹/₄ teaspoon crushed red pepper

1. Put a paper towel in a small bowl and add the chickpeas to drain them of all moisture. Reserve. In a wide 2-quart saucepan, heat the oil over medium heat. Add the rice, onion, garlic, and salt. Cook, stirring frequently, until the rice is opaque and starts to change color, but doesn't brown and onion start to brown, 4 to 5 minutes.

2. Add the remaining ingredients and the reserved chickpeas. Stir once or twice to mix. Bring to a boil, reduce heat to low, cover, and simmer until the rice is tender and the liquid is absorbed, 18 to 20 minutes. Remove from the heat and let the rice stand 5 minutes. If just dry, fluff rice with a fork and stir gently to mix. Serve hot.

Rice with Plantains

Arroz con Plátano Machos

Makes **4 servings**

Plantains are cooking bananas, a species that are bigger, firmer, and less sweet than bananas, that are grown in Mexico and Central America. Ripe plantains have nearly black skins and give slightly when pressed lightly with your fingers. This is a very common way to serve rice, especially along the Gulf coast of Mexico, and it's among my favorite rice dishes. The rice presentation is a little more elaborate here, but you can simply spoon the rice onto a dish, if you prefer.

Basic White Rice (page 472)

1 tablespoon minced fresh parsley

¹/₂ teaspoon salt, or to taste

1 tablespoon unsalted butter

1 tablespoon vegetable oil

1 large ripe plantain, peeled and cut crosswise, about ¹/₄ inch thick

1. Preheat the oven to 200°. In a medium bowl, mix the hot cooked rice, parsley, and ¼ teaspoon of the salt. Pack the rice into a round-bottomed 2-cup capacity bowl, then. Invert the rice onto the center of a large serving plate. Keep warm in the oven.

2. In a medium skillet, heat the butter and oil over medium heat. Cook the plantain rounds until golden brown on both sides, about 5 minutes total. Sprinkle with the remaining ¼ teaspoon of salt. Arrange the plantain pieces around the rice dome, and serve hot.

Rice with Mixed Vegetables
Arroz con Verduras Mixta

**Makes 4 servings as a side dish
or 2 main dish servings**

This modern rice dish with a crown of colorful sautéed vegetables makes an excellent vegetarian main dish or a side dish to accompany meats, poultry, or fish. Red Fresno chiles, also called chiles caribe, *are about 2 inches long, wider at the stem end, tapering to a point at the tip. They are fiery hot with a thick flesh, and are often mistaken for red jalapeños. The two chiles can be used interchangeably. (Use kitchen gloves when handling the chiles.)*

Mexican crema is available in Latin-American markets and many supermarkets.

2 tablespoons olive oil

1 cup long-grain white rice

1 teaspoon salt, or to taste

2 cups water

¼ chopped onion

1 large garlic clove, finely chopped

2 small (4-ounce) zucchini, cut into ½-inch dice

1 large ear of corn, kernels cut off

½ teaspoon dried oregano (Mexican variety preferred), crumbled

¼ teaspoon ground cumin

1 red Fresno chile, seeded, veins removed, and finely diced (⅛ inch)

½ cup Mexican crema or sour cream

Chopped fresh cilantro

1. In a 2-quart saucepan, heat 1 tablespoon of the oil over medium heat. Add the rice, and stir frequently until the rice is opaque and aromatic, about 5 minutes. Add ½ teaspoon salt and the water. Stir once to settle the rice and bring to a boil.

2. Reduce heat to low, cover and simmer until the liquid is absorbed and the rice is tender, 18 to 20 minutes. Turn off the heat, fluff the rice with a fork, cover and let stand 85 minutes. Stick a fork into the bottom of the pan to check for remaining moisture. If just dry on the bottom, fluff the rice with the fork.

3. Meanwhile, in a large nonstick skillet, heat the remaining tablespoon of oil over medium heat. Add the onion and cook, stirring, until the onion is translucent, about 3 minutes. Add the garlic, zucchini, corn, oregano, cumin, red chile, and ¼ cup of water. Cook, stirring, until the liquid has boiled away, and the vegetables are crisp-tender, 4 to 5 minutes. Mound the rice in the center of a warm round serving platter. Spoon the vegetables around the rice. Drizzle thinned crema or sour cream over the rice and sprinkle with chopped cilantro. Serve hot.

Rice with Squash Blossoms
Arroz con Flor de Calabacitas

Makes **4 servings**

At one of the food stalls in the Oaxaca market, I stopped to admire a large cazuela (casserole dish) of rice with exquisitely fresh squash blossoms, sitting on a counter awaiting the day's customers. Cooked, chopped blossoms were mixed with the rice and a few fresh blossoms were placed around the bowl. It was beautiful! Squash blossoms are available in season in many farmer's markets. I created this recipe at home to match the memory.

1/4 pound (10 to 12) squash blossoms

2 tablespoons olive oil

1/4 cup white onion, finely chopped

1 cup long-grain white rice

**2 cups canned fat-free reduced-sodium
    chicken broth**

1 tablespoon unsalted butter

1/2 teaspoon salt, or to taste

1. To prepare the blossoms, cut off the stems and remove the green petals at the base of the flowers. Pinch off the stamen inside the blossoms. Rinse gently and gently shake off excess water. Chop crosswise about ½ inch thick and then lengthwise the same. Reserve.

2. In a wide 2-quart saucepan, heat the oil over medium heat and cook the onion, stirring, until the onion softens, about 3 minutes. Add the rice and cook, stirring, until the rice is opaque and starts to change color, but doesn't brown, about 3 minutes. Add the broth. Bring to a boil, then reduce the heat to low, cover, and simmer until the liquid is absorbed and the rice is tender, about 18 to 20 minutes. Remove pan from heat and let rice stand 5 minutes. Then fluff with a fork.

3. While the rice cooks, melt the butter in a skillet until it foams. Add the reserved squash blossoms and salt. Cook, stirring, over medium heat, until the blossoms are tender and the juices are absorbed, 6 to 8 minutes. When the rice is cooked, gently fold the cooked blossoms into the rice. Serve hot.

Rice with Mushrooms and Poblano Chiles
Arroz con Hongos y Poblanos

Makes **4 servings**

Wild mushrooms are gathered in huge numbers during the rainy season—from June to September—in Mexico. The high mountain forests surrounding Mexico City are noted for a great variety of wild mushrooms.

If available, use wild mushrooms, or as alternatives, brown cremini mushrooms or the larger portobellos are excellent for this dish.

1 tablespoon olive oil

1/4 medium white onion, finely chopped

1 large garlic clove, finely chopped

**6 ounces mushrooms, cleaned, trimmed,
    and coarsely chopped**

**1 large poblano chile, roasted and peeled
    (page 8), and cut into 1/2-inch squares**

1 cup long-grain white rice

2 cups canned fat-free reduced-sodium chicken broth

1/4 teaspoon salt, or to taste

1/4 teaspoon freshly ground pepper, or to taste

1 tablespoon chopped fresh flat-leaf parsley

1. In a wide 2-quart saucepan heat the oil over medium heat and cook the onion, stirring, until translucent, 3 to 4 minutes. Add the garlic, mushrooms, and poblano. Cook, stirring frequently, until the mushrooms give up their moisture and start to brown.

2. Add the rice and cook, stirring, 3 minutes. Add the broth all at once. Stir briefly to level the rice. Bring to a boil; then reduce the heat to low, cover and simmer until the rice is tender and the liquid is absorbed, about 20 minutes. Turn off the heat. Add the salt, pepper, and parsley. Fluff gently with a fork. Cover and let stand 8 to 10 minutes. Serve hot.

Red Rice with Chicken
Arroz Rojo con Pollo

Yummy! (handwritten)

Makes 4 servings

Ancho chile and tomato add flavor and color to this home-style rice dish. The rice should still be slightly moist when it's finished cooking. For a complete meal, serve the rice as a main dish with Cabbage and Orange Salad (page 183).

1 large ancho chile, rinsed and seeded, veins removed

2 medium garlic cloves, finely chopped

1/2 medium white onion, chopped

2 Roma tomatoes, peeled and chopped

1/4 cup water

2 tablespoons vegetable oil

4 skinless boneless chicken breast halves, cut into 1-inch pieces

2 cups hot water

1 cup long-grain white rice

2 teaspoons dried oregano (Mexican variety preferred), crumbled

2 tablespoons capers, drained

1/2 teaspoon salt, or to taste — *1 1/2 T* (handwritten)

2 tablespoons crumbled cotija cheese, or substitute mild feta cheese

1 tablespoon chopped fresh flat-leaf parsley

1. Soak the chile in a bowl of hot water about 20 minutes; then put it in a blender jar with the garlic, onion, tomatoes, and water. Blend until smooth. Reserve in the blender. *↳ or chicken broth* (handwritten)

2. In a large, wide pan, heat the oil until it shimmers, and stir-fry the chicken until no longer pink

inside, about 2 to 3 minutes. Remove the chicken to a plate. In the same pan, add the blended chile sauce, and cook, stirring, 2 minutes. Pour in the hot water; then add the rice, oregano, capers, and salt. Stir to mix, and bring to a boil.

3. Reduce heat to low, cover and simmer 15 minutes. The rice should be almost tender and still moist. Put the chicken pieces on top of the rice. Cover and continue cooking 5 more minutes. Remove from heat and let the rice stand 6 to 8 minutes. Transfer the rice to a shallow serving bowl or platter. Sprinkle the top with cheese and parsley. Serve hot.

Rice with Minced Pork or Beef
Arroz con Picadillo

Makes 8 servings

Picadillo—a mixture of ground beef or other meat, cooked with onion, tomato, chiles, raisins, herbs, and spices—cooked with rice makes a terrific do-ahead casserole for informal meals or to add to a buffet when entertaining. Picadillo is also a common filling for chiles rellenos, tamales, and tortillas.

4 cups (double recipe) Basic White Rice (page 472)

Minced pork or beef (Minced Spicy Pork, page 347)

2 tablespoons finely chopped fresh parsley

1. Prepare rice. Then, prepare picadillo with ground pork or beef. When the rice is cool, gently mix in the cooked picadillo. Transfer the mixture to an ovenproof earthenware casserole dish or glass baking dish. The dish may be made ahead to this point, covered and refrigerated for up to 1 day.

2. Shortly before serving, preheat the oven to 350°. Warm the casserole until hot all the way through, 20 to 25 minutes. Sprinkle with parsley. Serve hot.

Next time (handwritten)
– make in a rice cooker (handwritten)
– ~~use salt~~ put blender contents directly into rice cooker w/o heating it. Total Water/broth = 1 1/2 c. (handwritten)

Rice with Sausage and Cabbage
Arroz con Salchichas y Col

Makes 4 servings

Rice cooked with onions, tomato, and cabbage, and embellished with rounds of cooked smoked sausage, is a dish with strong Spanish characteristics. The Spanish connection began in 1519, nearly 500 years ago, when Cortéz landed at Veracruz. During the centuries that followed, many food contributions from Spain and Europe integrated with native Indian foods to create the cuisine of today. Linguica sausage is one of those food connections that's now made in Mexico, and in the United States as well. The sausage is available in many supermarkets or Latin-American markets. Grapefruit, Orange, and Avocado Salad (page 185) goes well with this satisfying rice dish.

2 teaspoons olive oil

1/2 medium white onion, chopped

1/4 head of cabbage, shredded

1 medium tomato, peeled and finely chopped

1/2 teaspoon dried oregano (Mexican variety preferred), crumbled

1/4 teaspoon salt, or to taste

Freshly ground pepper, to taste

1 cup long-grain white rice

2 cups canned chicken broth or water

1 pound smoked sausage links, such as Portuguese linguica, cut into 1/4-inch rounds

1 tablespoon chopped fresh parsley or cilantro

1. In a 2-quart, wide saucepan, heat the oil over medium heat and cook the onion until translucent, 3 to 4 minutes. Add the cabbage and cook, stirring, until wilted, 2 to 3 minutes. Add the tomatoes, oregano, and salt. Cook, stirring frequently until the tomato juices cook away and the mixture is nearly dry, 3 to 4 minutes. Add the rice and broth. Bring to a boil, uncovered. Stir to level the rice, reduce the heat to low, cover, and cook 18 to 20 minutes or until the liquid is absorbed and the rice is tender. Turn off the heat and let the rice stand 5 minutes.

2. Meanwhile, in a medium nonstick skillet, cook the sausage rounds until completely cooked and lightly browned, about 5 minutes. When the rice is cooked, fluff with a fork and transfer to a serving platter or shallow bowl. Arrange the sausage on top. Sprinkle with parsley. Serve at once.

Rice with Ham and Pineapple
Arroz con Piña y Jamón

Makes 4 servings

There's an excellent restaurant in Hotel Las Manitas in Cuernavaca, about an hour from Mexico City in the small state of Morelos. The genteel setting and Sunday lunch is something special, with Mexican families dining in the garden or on the terrace. This pretty rice dish with pineapple was featured on the buffet when we were there on one of several visits. This is my interpretation of the dish.

2 tablespoons plus 2 teaspoons olive oil

1 cup long-grain white rice

1/2 cup pineapple juice, canned, or thawed, if frozen

1 1/2 cups water

1/4 teaspoon salt, or to taste

1 cup diced or chopped cooked ham

1/2 red bell pepper, neatly diced (about 1/4 inch)

1 large jalapeño chile, seeded, veins removed, and finely chopped

1/4 teaspoon allspice

1 tablespoon white wine vinegar

1 tablespoon brown sugar

1 cup pineapple chunks, fresh or canned

Mint or cilantro sprigs

1. In a wide, heavy 2-quart saucepan, heat 2 tablespoons of the oil over medium heat. Add the rice and cook, stirring, until the rice is opaque and starts to change color, 3 to 4 minutes. Add the pineapple juice and water all at once. Add the salt. Stir to level the rice and bring to a boil. Reduce heat to the lowest setting, cover and simmer until the liquid is absorbed and the rice is tender, 18 to 20 minutes. Turn off the heat and let the rice stand about 5 minutes.

2. Meanwhile, in a small skillet, heat the remaining 2 teaspoons of oil and cook the ham, pepper, and chile, stirring, 2 minutes. Add the remaining ingredients, except the pineapple chunks. Cook until the sugar melts, about 30 seconds. When the rice is cooked, fluff with a fork and turn out on a serving platter. Spoon the ham mixture over the top. Garnish the edge of the platter with the pineapple chunks and mint or cilantro sprigs. Serve hot.

Rice with Shrimp and Corn
Arroz con Camarónes y Elote

Makes **4 servings**

Rice dishes called sopas secas, *(dry soups) are usually substantial dishes made with rice and other ingredients such as seafood, meat, or vegetables, and commonly served as a separate course, but you can also serve it as a side dish. This rice dish is adequate for a light meal accompanied by a salad. You can also start the meal with Black Bean Soup (page 248).*

2 plum tomatoes, peeled and chopped
2 medium garlic cloves, chopped
2 tablespoons chopped fresh cilantro
1 serrano chile, minced with seeds
1/2 teaspoon dried oregano (Mexican variety preferred), crumbled
1/2 teaspoon ground cumin
1 teaspoon salt, or to taste
1/8 teaspoon crushed red pepper
1 cup canned chicken broth
1 cup water
2 tablespoons olive oil
1 cup long-grain white rice
1/2 medium white onion, finely chopped
1 cup fresh or frozen corn kernels
1/3 pound (8 to 11) small cooked peeled shrimp

1. In a blender, purée until smooth the tomato, garlic, cilantro, serrano chile, oregano, cumin, salt, crushed pepper, broth, and water. Reserve in the blender jar.

2. In a 2½-quart saucepan, heat the oil over medium heat. Add the rice and onion and cook, stirring, until they begin to color, about 4 minutes. Pour the reserved tomato and broth mixture into the pan all at once. Stir to level the rice. Bring to a boil, then reduce the heat to low, cover, and cook 18 to 20 minutes, or until the rice is tender and the liquid is absorbed.

3. Meanwhile, in a small saucepan, cook the corn and boiling water to cover, 1 to 2 minutes, until tender. Drain. When the rice is done turn off the heat. Let rice stand 5 minutes. Fluff it with a fork, then gently stir in the shrimp and corn. Cover and let stand 8 to 10 minutes. Serve hot.

Rice with Crab, Yucatán Style
Arroz con Jaiba, estilo Yucatán

Makes **4 servings**

This Yucatán rice and crab dish, flavored with the red seasoning paste called achiote, is satisfying enough to make a meal, with the addition of a salad. The red seasoning paste, pressed into blocks and wrapped in plastic, is available in Mexican grocery stores.

2 small plum tomatoes (4 ounces), peeled and chopped

2 medium garlic cloves, chopped

1 serrano chile, minced with seeds

1 tablespoon prepared achiote seasoning paste

¹/₂ teaspoon dried oregano (Mexican variety preferred), crumbled

¹/₂ teaspoon salt, or to taste

¹/₄ teaspoon freshly ground pepper, or to taste

1 cup canned fat-free reduced-sodium chicken broth

³/₄ cup water

2 tablespoons olive oil

1 cup long-grain white rice

¹/₂ medium white onion, finely chopped

¹/₃ pound cooked crab meat, picked over and drained, if wet

¹/₂ cup cooked fresh or thawed frozen peas

1. In a blender, purée the tomato, garlic, serrano chile, achiote paste, oregano, salt, and pepper until smooth. Add the broth and water. Blend well. Let stand in the blender jar. In a 2-quart saucepan, heat the oil over medium heat. Add the rice and onion. Cook, stirring, until the rice and onion start to color, 3 to 4 minutes.

2. Pour the mixture in the blender into the pan all at once. Stir in the crab. Reduce heat to low, cover and cook until the rice is tender and the liquid is absorbed 18 to 20 minutes. Remove the pan from the heat. Fluff the rice with a fork. Gently stir in the peas. Cover and let stand 8 to 10 minutes.

Pasta Dishes

Vermicelli with Mushrooms
Fideos con Hongos

Makes **4 servings**

This is real comfort food! Mexican pasta dishes with fideos *means a dish made with vermicelli. These fall into the "dry soup" category of dishes that apply most often to rice, and which are usually served following the "wet soup" course for a traditional midday meal.*

Mexican cooks first sauté the vermicelli, as they do rice, until just golden, and that's a bit tricky. The cook must work quickly to prevent burning the pasta. The sauce and pasta are combined and then baked until well done. Serve separately, or as part of a main course with grilled meat or chicken.

3 tablespoons olive oil or vegetable oil

1 (8-ounce) package vermicelli coils

¹/₂ medium onion, finely chopped

2 medium garlic cloves, finely chopped

¹/₄ pound mushrooms, thinly sliced

2 medium tomatoes, peeled and chopped

1 jalapeño chile, seeded, veins removed, and finely chopped

2 tablespoons chopped fresh cilantro

2¹/₄ cups canned fat-free reduced-sodium chicken broth

¹/₂ teaspoon salt, or to taste

Freshly ground pepper, to taste

¹/₂ cup crumbled cotija cheese, or grated Parmesan cheese

1. Preheat oven to 350°. In a large skillet, heat the oil over medium heat. Fry the vermicelli coils, turning with tongs or two wooden spoons, until partially golden, about 2 minutes. (Work quickly and watch the color change to prevent burning the pasta.)

2. Transfer the vermicelli to an ovenproof casserole dish. In the same skillet, cook the onion until softened, about 3 minutes. Add the garlic and mushrooms. Cook, stirring, until the mushrooms release their juices, 3 to 4 minutes. Add the remaining ingredients, except the cheese, and bring to a boil. Pour over the vermicelli in the casserole dish. Gently press the pasta into the sauce. Cover with foil and bake 20 to 25 minutes, or until the vermicelli is tender and the liquid has been absorbed. Sprinkle with cheese and serve hot.

Vermicelli with Chicken Meatballs
Fideos con Albondigas de Pollo

Makes **4 servings**

Bellinghausen restaurant in Mexico City, a restaurant begun by German immigrants but which serves authentic traditional and modern dishes, has been a long-time favorite for me and my husband. We usually go for comida, *Mexico's midday meal, and always dine on the patio. Vermicelli in red sauce topped with a huge meatball is a popular item on the menu. I make small chicken meatballs instead of large beef meatballs for my version of the dish. Of course, ground beef can be substituted, if desired.*

Basic Cooked Tomato Sauce (page 42)
¼ cup olive oil
2 tablespoons minced white onion
2 tablespoons minced red bell pepper
1 jalapeño chile, seeded, veins removed, and minced
1 teaspoon ground cumin
1 teaspoon dried oregano (Mexican variety preferred), crumbled
½ pound ground chicken
2 tablespoons dry bread crumbs
2 tablespoons milk
½ teaspoon salt, or to taste
1 (8-ounce) package vermicelli coils
2 tablespoons chopped fresh cilantro

1. Prepare the tomato sauce. Reserve in the pan off heat. In a nonstick skillet, heat 2 teaspoons of the oil and cook the onion, red pepper, chile, cumin, and oregano over medium-low heat until the vegetables are softened, about 5 minutes. Transfer to a bowl and let cool.

2. Add the chicken, bread crumbs, milk, and salt. Mix well with your hands and roll into 2-inch meatballs. Wipe out the same skillet with paper towels, and heat 2 teaspoons of the oil over medium heat. Cook the meatballs, turning, until barely brown (they will not be cooked through), about 4 minutes. Reserve in the pan.

3. Preheat the oven to 350°. Heat the remaining oil in a large skillet over medium heat. Fry the vermicelli coils, turning with tongs or two wooden spoons, until partially golden, about 2 minutes. (Work quickly to prevent burning the pasta.)

4. Transfer the vermicelli to an ovenproof casserole dish. Pour the reserved tomato sauce over the vermicelli and gently press the pasta into the sauce. Cover with foil and bake in preheated oven 15 minutes. Remove the cover and arrange the meatballs on top of the pasta. Bake, uncovered, an additional 15 minutes, or until the meatballs are completely cooked through. Sprinkle with cilantro and serve.

Vermicelli with Turkey
Cazuela de Fideo con Pavo

Makes **4 servings**

Mexican home cooks are skilled at preparing economical, satisfying dishes for their families. A few vegetables and diced leftover turkey with fideos (vermicelli) makes a tasty meal. (If you don't have leftover turkey, buy cooked turkey breast from a deli.) This dish is popular with my cooking students. For a quick, filling meal, serve with a salad and purchased spicy green salsa.

3 tablespoons olive oil or vegetable oil

1 (8-ounce) package vermicelli coils

1/2 medium onion, finely chopped

1/4 pound tomatillos, husked, rinsed, and chopped

2 medium garlic cloves, finely chopped

1 teaspoon dried oregano (Mexican variety preferred), crumbled

1/2 teaspoon ground cumin

2 1/4 cups canned fat-free reduced-sodium chicken broth

1 cup diced or shredded cooked turkey

3 tablespoons chopped fresh cilantro

1/2 teaspoon salt, or to taste

1/8 teaspoon freshly ground pepper, or to taste

3/4 cup shredded Oaxaca or Monterey Jack cheese

1. Preheat oven to 350°. In a large skillet, heat the oil over medium heat. Fry the vermicelli, stirring with two wooden spoons, until partially golden, about 2 minutes. (Work quickly to prevent burning the pasta.) Transfer the pasta to an ovenproof casserole dish.

2. In the same skillet, cook the onion until softened, about 3 minutes. Add the tomatillos, garlic, oregano, and cumin. Cook, stirring, 2 minutes. Add the remaining ingredients, except the cheese, and bring to a boil. Pour over the vermicelli in the casserole dish. Gently press the pasta into the sauce to mix. Cover with foil and bake 20 minutes. Sprinkle with the cheese, and bake 5 more minutes, or until the cheese is melted. Serve hot.

Eggs *and* Breakfast Dishes

Egg Dishes 487

Mexican Scrambled Eggs

Scrambled Eggs with Chorizo

Eggs with Green Beans
and Chorizo

Eggs with Ground Beef
and Salsa

Ham and Potatoes with Eggs

Eggs with Shredded Dried Beef

Scrambled Eggs in
Tomatillo Sauce

Scrambled Eggs with
Avocado and Tomatoes

Scrambled Eggs with Cactus

Stuffed Chiles with
Scrambled Eggs and Bacon

"Lost" Eggs

Eggs in Ranchera Sauce

Eggs "Drowned" in
Tomato Sauce

"Divorced" Eggs

Eggs with Ham, Tomatoes,
and Peppers

Eggs with Steak and Onions

Potatoes and Chorizo
with Baked Eggs

Poached Eggs in
Tomato Chile Sauce

Black Bean Omelet

Zucchini Omelet

Cactus Omelet

Potato Omelet, Mexican Style

Shrimp and Spinach Omelet

Rice Casserole with Eggs

Savory Breakfast Cheesecake

Tortillas with Eggs,
Chorizo, and Cheese

Eggs, Motul Style on Tortillas

Bacon and Egg Quesadillas

Egg and Tortilla Casserole

Tortilla Casserole with
Eggs and Red Chile Sauce

Breakfast Dishes with Tortillas and Bread 503

Breakfast Tacos with
Potatoes and Chorizo

Breakfast Bean and
Cheese Tacos

Tortillas Topped with Pork
and Potatoes

Crisp Rolled Tortillas with Ham

Beef and Cheese Quesadillas

Potato Masa Cakes
with Spicy Pork

Bean and Melted
Cheese Sandwiches

Melted Cheese and
Green Sauce on Toasted Rolls

Toasted Rolls with Refried
Beans and Bacon

Banana Breakfast Burritos

Sweet Fried Bread

Fruit 509

Breakfast Fruit Plate

Banana and
Mandarin Fruit Cup

Pineapple Boats

Yogurt and
Tropical Fruit Starter

exicans make the most of their mornings—often eating twice before noon. Many Mexicans have a first breakfast (*desayuno*) at home, and a second breakfast (*almuerzo*) about eleven o'clock that is often enjoyed in a restaurant or in the public market cafes (*fondas*). *Desayuno* usually consists of coffee and *pan dulce* (Mexican sweet rolls) and *almuerzo* is a more hearty meal of juice, fresh fruit, egg and meat dishes, tortilla dishes, hot chocolate, and bread and rolls.

Few countries have as inspired an array of breakfast creations as Mexico does. Eggs are made in dozens of delicious ways for morning meals. Fruit juices and fruits are always fresh. Napkin-lined baskets brimming with fresh rolls and breads are often on the table, and tortillas are often employed to wrap up tasty fillings for a hearty meal.

In the sixteenth century the Spanish brought the first chickens to Mexico, and in time they became part of village life everywhere. The hens provided a steady supply of eggs that greatly enriched the country's cuisine. Now, nearly 400 years later, Mexican egg dishes are among the best in the world. Scrambled eggs with chorizo, salsa, and warm tortillas are a classic combination, and can be interpreted in various delicious ways. Omelets with potatoes or black beans or even cactus make satisfying morning meals. And with the kick of some chiles, you are sure to be wide awake as you start your day.

Mexican cooks also seem to wake up with a sense of humor, for they serve "Lost" Eggs (page 492), "Divorced" Eggs (page 493), and other dishes with unusual titles, which often derive from a whimsical presentation.

Mexican breakfasts or festive brunch buffets are great ways to entertain and because much of the work can be done ahead, you can enjoy the gathering, too.

Egg Dishes

Mexican Scrambled Eggs
Huevos Revueltos ala Mexicana

Makes **2 servings**

Eggs scrambled with onion, tomato, and chiles are ubiquitous all over Mexico. Black beans, or some other variety, and a few crisp tortilla wedges are usually served with the eggs.

1 tablespoon unsalted butter or vegetable oil
1/4 medium white onion, finely chopped
4 large eggs, beaten
1 small tomato, seeded and finely chopped
1 serrano chile, minced with seeds
1 tablespoon chopped fresh cilantro
1/4 teaspoon salt, or to taste

1. Heat the butter or oil in a medium nonstick skillet over medium heat. Sauté the onion, stirring, about 30 seconds. Add the beaten eggs, and cook, stirring to scramble, until almost set, but still moist, about 1 minute.

2. Quickly, add the tomato, serrano chile, cilantro, and salt. Cook, stirring slowly, until the eggs are set and the fresh ingredients are heated through, about 1 minute. Serve at once.

Scrambled Eggs with Chorizo
Huevos Revueltos con Chorizo

Makes **4 servings**

Eggs with chorizo, Mexico's spicy sausage, are eaten everywhere in Mexico. Some of the packaged chorizo in the United States is very fatty and produces more grease in the pan than flavorful bits of spicy sausage, so look for a butcher shop that prepares its own chorizo, *or try the recipe for Mexican Pork Sausage (page 348). Serve this hearty breakfast with warm tortillas and green salsa.*

Fresh Tomatillo Sauce (page 34), or purchased green salsa
1/2 pound fresh bulk chorizo, or packaged, with casings removed
1/4 medium onion, finely chopped
8 large eggs, beaten
2 tablespoons chopped fresh cilantro
Salt, to taste

1. Prepare sauce, if using homemade. Then, heat a large nonstick skillet over medium heat. Crumble the chorizo into the skillet and cook, stirring frequently, until brown and completely cooked, about 10 minutes. Drain excess fat, if needed.

2. Add the onion and cook, stirring, until softened, about 4 minutes. Stir in the eggs and cook, stirring slowly until scrambled and set, about 2 to 3 minutes, to desired doneness. Stir in the cilantro. Add salt, if needed. Serve at once with salsa on the side or passed at the table.

Eggs with Green Beans and Chorizo

Huevos con Ejotes y Chorizo

Makes **4 servings**

A skillet full of scrambled eggs with fresh green beans and spicy chorizo sausage is a complete meal in a pan. This is an egg dish made for a late breakfast (almuerzo), *that's eaten about 11 o'clock in Mexico. Business people often gather in restaurants for this meal. The early breakfast* (desayuno) *taken at home, usually consists only of coffee and* pan dulce *(sweet roll). Packaged chorizo can be greasy, so if you prefer, use bulk chorizo from a butcher, or substitute Mexican Pork Sausage (page 348). Add fresh salsa and some black beans to the meal, if you're feeding big appetites.*

¹/₄ pound small fresh green beans, cut in ¹/₂-inch lengths

¹/₈ teaspoon salt, or to taste

2 teaspoons vegetable oil

2 tablespoons finely chopped white onion

¹/₄ pound fresh bulk chorizo, or packaged, with casings removed

4 large eggs, beaten

1. Bring a small pot of water to a boil and cook the green beans until tender, 6 to 8 minutes. Drain well, season with salt, and set aside.

2. Heat the oil in a medium skillet over medium heat and cook the onion until softened, 3 to 4 minutes. Add the chorizo, breaking it into pieces, and cook until brown and completely cooked. Stir in the green beans. Cook 1 minute. Add the eggs. Cook, stirring slowly, until scrambled and set, 2 to 3 minutes or to desired doneness. Serve at once.

Eggs with Ground Beef and Salsa

Huevos con Carne Molida

Makes **4 servings**

In Puerto Vallarta, my husband and I ate this wonderful, hearty breakfast of eggs with ground beef, served with green tomatillo salsa and warm tortillas on the side. This is an easy breakfast that I like to serve to overnight guests. It's always a hit. Add a Breakfast Fruit Plate (page 509) to start.

Tomatillo and Arbol Chile Salsa (page 35), or purchased tomatillo salsa

2 teaspoons olive oil

³/₄ pound lean ground beef

4 green onions, sliced crosswise

1 medium tomato, peeled and finely chopped

³/₄ teaspoon salt, or to taste

¹/₄ teaspoon freshly ground pepper, or to taste

1 tablespoon unsalted butter

6 large eggs, beaten

¹/₂ cup sour cream

1. Prepare the salsa, if using homemade. Then, in a large nonstick skillet, heat the oil over medium heat and cook the meat, stirring, until brown and cooked through, about 4 minutes. Add the onions, tomato, ½ teaspoon of the salt, and the pepper. Cook, stirring, until the tomato juices are bubbling, about 3 to 4 minutes. Reserve in the pan off heat.

2. In another skillet, heat the butter over medium heat until it foams. Add the eggs and remaining salt. Cook, stirring slowly, to scramble. When the eggs begin to hold together, in about 2 to 3 minutes, transfer to the ground beef mixture. Stir gently to combine. Divide among 4 serving plates. Drizzle each serving with a portion of sour cream and about 1 tablespoon of green salsa. Pass extra salsa at the table.

Ham and Potatoes with Eggs
Huevos con Jamón y Papas

Makes **4 servings**

Many cultures enjoy the combination of fried potatoes, ham, and eggs, but in Mexico they're likely to be served with refried beans and salsa. Homemade beans and salsa are definitely best, if time permits.

2 cups Basic Refried Beans (page 462),
    or canned refried beans
Fresh Salsa Mexicana (page 24),
    or purchased salsa
1 large potato, peeled and cut into ¹/₄-inch dice
2 teaspoons unsalted butter
1 teaspoon vegetable oil
¹/₂ medium white onion, finely chopped
1 cup chopped cooked smoked ham
8 large eggs, beaten
¹/₂ teaspoon salt, or to taste
¹/₈ teaspoon freshly ground pepper, or to taste

1. Prepare refried beans and refrigerate, if made ahead. Heat the beans and keep warm in a 200° oven. Prepare salsa, if using homemade.

2. Then, in a medium pan of boiling water, cook the potatoes until tender, about 4 minutes. Drain and cool under running water. Drain again and set aside.

3. Heat the butter and oil in a large nonstick skillet and cook the onion until softened, about 3 minutes. Add the potatoes and cook until golden brown, about 5 minutes. Stir in the ham.

4. Pour the beaten eggs into the skillet, and cook, stirring slowly until scrambled and just set, 3 to 4 minutes, or to desired doneness. Season with salt and pepper. Divide evenly among 4 plates with a portion of refried beans on the side. Garnish with salsa. Serve hot.

Eggs with Shredded Dried Beef
Huevos con Machaca

Makes **4 servings**

Mexican dried beef (machaca) is a staple in northern Mexico. It goes into tacos, burritos, and gets mixed together with eggs for a robust breakfast. Prepare the machaca *a day ahead.*

1 cup (¹/₂ recipe) Mexican Dried Beef (page 330)
2 tablespoons vegetable oil
¹/₄ medium onion, finely chopped
1 jalapeño chile, seeded, veins removed,
    and finely chopped
1 medium tomato, cored and finely chopped
¹/₄ teaspoon salt, or to taste
¹/₈ teaspoon freshly ground pepper, or to taste
6 large eggs, beaten
2 tablespoons chopped fresh cilantro
2 tablespoons crumbled queso fresco
    (Mexican fresh cheese)

1. Prepare the dried beef a day ahead. Cover and refrigerate. Bring to room temperature before using. Heat the oil in a medium skillet.

2. Cook the onion and chile, stirring, until softened, 3 to 4 minutes. Stir in the shredded beef, tomato, salt, and pepper. Add the beaten eggs and cook, stirring to scramble, until just set, about 2 to 3 minutes or to desired doneness. Divide the eggs among four serving plates. Sprinkle with cilantro and cheese. Serve hot.

Scrambled Eggs in Tomatillo Sauce
Huevos Revueltos en Salsa Verde

Makes 4 servings

If you like cooked green sauce made with tomatillos, called salsa verde, *you'll love fluffy mounds of scrambled eggs bathed in the flavorful, slightly tart sauce. This is just the way cookbook author Patricia Quintana made them for me one morning in her Mexico City home. Serve with soft, warm tortillas.*

Basic Cooked Tomatillo Sauce (page 46)
1 tablespoon unsalted butter
2 teaspoons vegetable oil
6 large eggs, beaten
¼ teaspoon salt, or to taste

1. Prepare the green sauce. Reserve off heat. In a large nonstick skillet, heat the butter and oil over medium heat. Add the eggs and salt and cook, stirring slowly to scramble, then push them into small mounds. Cook until just set, about 2 to 3 minutes. With a large spoon, transfer the mounds of scrambled eggs to a plate.

2. Pour the reserved green sauce into the same skillet and bring to a boil. Reduce heat to low and carefully spoon the eggs into the sauce so that they keep their free-form mounded shapes. Cook until heated through, about 1 minute. Serve at once.

Scrambled Eggs with Avocado and Tomato
Huevos Revueltos con Aguacate y Jitomate

Makes 2 servings

Mexican scrambled eggs come in many great variations. This is one of my favorite combinations from Oaxaca. The eggs are served with black beans on the side.

1 tablespoon unsalted butter
½ medium white onion, finely chopped
4 large eggs, beaten
¼ teaspoon salt, or to taste
Freshly ground pepper, to taste
1 medium tomato, seeded and chopped
½ avocado (Hass variety preferred), peeled, pitted, and cut into ½-inch pieces

1. In a large nonstick skillet, melt the butter over medium-high heat and cook the onion, stirring, 1 minute. Reduce heat to low, cover, and cook until tender, 3 to 4 minutes.

2. Add the beaten eggs, salt, and pepper. Cook, stirring slowly to scramble, until the eggs are just set, about 1 to 2 minutes. Add the tomato and avocado. Stir gently to mix and remove the pan from the heat. Serve hot.

Scrambled Eggs with Cactus
Huevos Revueltos con Nopalitos

Makes 2 servings

Cactus is very common in Mexican cuisine and is used in most regions. It has a slightly tart taste that goes well with eggs. This version is from central Mexico. In Oaxaca, the same dish would include finely chopped tomatoes and a hefty amount of serrano chiles cooked with the eggs. For convenience, I use strips of cactus (nopalitos) *from a jar in this recipe. (Whole cactus leaves, or paddles, are called* nopales *and are generally sold fresh.) Bottled* nopalitos *are easy to find in Mexican grocery stores and many supermarkets. Be sure to buy the ones packed in water and not in brine. The color and texture will be much better.*

2 tablespoons unsalted butter

2 tablespoons chopped white onion

1/2 cup jarred cactus strips, drained and rinsed

4 large eggs, beaten

1/4 teaspoon salt, or to taste

1/8 teaspoon freshly ground pepper, or to taste

1 large tomato, sliced

2 tablespoons crumbled cotija cheese

Melt the butter in a medium skillet over medium heat, and cook the onion and cactus strips until the onion is softened, about 3 minutes. (The cactus strips will retain their texture as they cook with the onion.) Add the eggs and stir slowly to scramble. Cook until set, about 2 to 3 minutes, or to desired doneness. Season with salt and pepper. Serve with sliced tomato on the side and scatter cheese over all.

Stuffed Chiles with Scrambled Eggs and Bacon
Chiles Rellenos con Huevos Revueltos y Tocino

Makes 4 servings

Many people don't realize that there are lots of ways to prepare chiles rellenos *besides stuffing them with cheese and frying them in egg batter.* Chiles rellenos *means stuffed chiles and just about anything can go inside, and the chiles can be coated with an egg batter, or not. In this recipe, the scrambled eggs and bacon go inside the roasted chiles, and Ranchera Sauce (page 44) is spooned on top.*

For a special occasion, brunch, or late breakfast, you'll dazzle your guests with this impressive chile relleno *plate. The sauce can be made ahead and reheated. The chiles can be roasted and peeled in advance, and the bacon can be cooked ahead, too. The rest of the work goes pretty fast and is done shortly before serving. Serve with warm tortillas. Sliced avocado and orange segments may be added to each plate, if desired.*

Ranchera Sauce (page 44)

1/2 pound sliced bacon

4 large poblano chiles, roasted and peeled (page 8)

8 large eggs

1 tablespoon whole milk

1/4 teaspoon salt, or to taste

2 teaspoons unsalted butter

1 teaspoon vegetable oil

1. Prepare the ranchera sauce. Reserve, covered, in a pan off heat. In a large nonstick skillet, cook the bacon over medium heat until crisp and brown. Drain on paper towels. Crumble the bacon and reserve on a plate.

2. Prepare the chiles. (Keep the stems intact.) With a small sharp knife, cut a slit lengthwise from the stem end to within 1½ inches of the narrow end. Carefully remove the seed pod and seeds. Rinse under running water to wash out remaining seeds. Pat dry with paper towels. Reserve on a plate.

3. Preheat oven to 300°. In a bowl, beat the eggs with a fork until well combined. Add the milk and salt. Beat to mix. Heat the butter and oil in a large nonstick skillet and cook the eggs, stirring slowly to scramble, until just set, about 3 minutes. Stir in the crumbled bacon and cook about 20 seconds more. Fill the chiles equally with the egg mixture and arrange on a baking sheet. Put in the oven to keep warm.

4. Reheat the sauce until it comes to a boil. To serve, place 1 stuffed chile in the center of each of 4 serving plates. Spoon some of the heated sauce on top of each serving, letting it pool onto the plate.

"Lost" Eggs
Huevos Perdidos

Makes **4 servings**

These eggs are beaten and stirred into simmering red chile sauce. The eggs disappear into the sauce, hence the name "lost" eggs. The saucy eggs partner well with sausage, ham, or bacon. The delicious chile sauce includes the subtle flavors of cinnamon and allspice, which add complexity and depth. Serve with split, buttered, and toasted bolillos *(oval Mexican sandwich rolls) or French rolls, to dip into the tasty sauce as you "search" for the eggs.*

Ancho Chile Sauce for Enchiladas (page 48)
¹/₄ teaspoon ground cinnamon (Mexican canela or Ceylon variety preferred)
¹/₈ teaspoon ground allspice
4 large eggs, beaten

Prepare the chile sauce. If made ahead, reheat in a medium saucepan. Add the cinnamon and allspice to the cooked sauce and simmer about 5 minutes to blend the flavors. Slowly stir the eggs into the simmering sauce and continue stirring slowly until the eggs are cooked and "lost in the sauce," about 3 minutes. Divide among 4 shallow bowls. Serve hot.

Eggs in Ranchera Sauce
Huevos Rancheros

Makes **4 servings**

It's easy to please egg fans by serving huevos rancheros, *Mexico's world-renowned egg dish. If you make the sauce ahead of time, the dish is easy to manage.*

2 cups Basic Refried Beans (page 462), or canned
Ranchera Sauce (page 44)
2 tablespoons vegetable oil
4 (6- to 7-inch) corn tortillas
4 large eggs, beaten
¹/₄ cup crumbled cotija or mild feta cheese
¹/₄ teaspoon salt, or to taste
1 avocado (Hass variety preferred), peeled and sliced

1. Prepare the beans, if making homemade. Prepare the ranchera sauce. If made ahead, reheat the beans and put the sauce in a saucepan and bring to a boil. Remove from the heat, cover, and keep warm.

2. Heat the oil in a medium nonstick skillet and fry the tortillas briefly, 1 at a time, until soft and hot, about 10 seconds on each side. Drain on paper towels. In the same skillet, cook the eggs over medium heat until sunny-side up—with the whites set and opaque and the yolks still soft, about 2 minutes. Sprinkle lightly with salt. To assemble, put 1 tortilla on each of 4 plates. Top each tortilla with 1 egg, and spoon the hot ranchera sauce over each serving. Sprinkle with crumbled cheese. Add refried beans and avocado slices to each plate. Serve at once.

Eggs "Drowned" in Tomato Sauce
Huevos Ahogados

Makes **4 servings**

Ahogada *means drowned, and in this dish the eggs are typically poached directly in simmering tomato sauce. I prefer to cook the eggs to order in a skillet and then spoon the heated tomato sauce over the eggs at the moment of serving. Serve with soft, corn tortillas, or bolillos (oval Mexican sandwich rolls), split, buttered, and toasted under the broiler, to dip into the sauce.*

3 cups (1¹/₂ recipe) Tomato Sauce for Tortas (page 44)

2 teaspoons vegetable oil

2 teaspoons unsalted butter

8 large eggs (2 eggs per person)

¹/₄ teaspoon salt, or to taste

1 to 2 jarred pickled jalapeño chiles (en escabeche), seeded and cut into strips

Chopped fresh cilantro

Prepare the tomato sauce. Cover and keep warm. In a large nonstick skillet, heat the oil and butter over medium heat until hot. Cook the eggs in the preferred style (scrambled, fried, or poached) to the desired doneness. Season with salt and transfer to individual shallow soup plates or serving plates. Pour about ½ cup of heated tomato sauce over each serving. Garnish with the chile strips and chopped cilantro. Serve hot.

"Divorced" Eggs
Huevos Divorciados

Makes **4 servings**

This cleverly named dish is satisfying and filling, with plenty of contrasting flavors and colors. The name refers to the way the eggs and sauces are separated from each other on the plate and kept from mingling by the black beans in the middle. Each cooked egg is put on a crisp fried tortilla and separated or "divorced" by the refried beans. Green sauce accompanies one egg and red sauce the other. The fried tortillas and both sauces can be made ahead. All that's left is to fry the eggs to your preference.

2 cups Basic Refried Beans (page 462)

Basic Cooked Tomatillo Sauce (page 46)

Basic Cooked Tomato Sauce (page 42)

¹/₃ cup vegetable oil

8 (6- to 7-inch) corn tortillas

2 tablespoons unsalted butter or vegetable oil

8 large eggs

Salt, to taste

1. Prepare the refried beans. If made ahead, reheat shortly before using. Prepare the tomatillo and tomato sauces. Heat them in separate pans. Heat the oil in a medium skillet, over medium heat. Fry the tortillas, turning once or twice, until crisp, 1 to 2 minutes. Drain on paper towels. Discard the oil.

2. In the same skillet, heat the butter or oil and fry the eggs to desired doneness. Season lightly with salt.

3. On each of 4 plates, place 2 tortillas, separated. Spoon a line of beans between the tortillas. On each plate, put about ¼ cup of green sauce on one tortilla and ¼ cup of red sauce on the other. Top each tortilla with a fried egg. Serve at once.

Eggs with Ham, Tomatoes, and Peppers
Huevos Pisto Manchago

Makes **4 servings**

Progresso was once an important seaport for the state of Yucatán, on the Gulf coast of Mexico. When henequen, the fiber similar to sisal used for making rope, twine, and rugs, was in great demand, cargo ships from everywhere docked at the amazingly long wharf extending two kilometers into the shallow sea. Magnificent mansions once owned by wealthy henequen traders are now being restored as vacation homes and the town shows signs of expanding tourism.

My husband and I once made an early morning drive there to avoid the searing heat of midday. We had almuerzo (late breakfast) at El Cordobés, promoted as the oldest restaurant in Yucatán. My tasty egg dish had Spanish roots with Mexican additions. What follows is the recipe I reconstructed from that day.

1 tablespoon olive oil

1/2 medium white onion, finely chopped

1 medium garlic clove, minced

2 medium tomatoes, peeled and chopped

1 cup diced smoked ham

2 to 3 *guëro* (yellow) chiles or substitute jalapeños, seeded, veins removed, and cut into strips

1/2 teaspoon salt, or to taste

1/8 teaspoon freshly ground pepper, or to taste

4 large eggs

1 tablespoon finely chopped fresh parsley

8 (6- to 7-inch) corn tortillas

1. In a medium skillet, heat the oil over medium heat and cook the onion until it starts to brown, about 4 minutes. Add the garlic, tomatoes, and 1/4 cup of water. Bring to a boil and cook about 2 minutes.

2. Add the ham, chiles, salt, and pepper. Reduce the heat to low and simmer 5 minutes so the flavors can blend. Cover and keep warm. Meanwhile, warm tortillas in a hot dry skillet or on a comal, 1 at a time, turning once or twice until soft and hot, about 20 seconds. Stack and wrap in a clean kitchen towel or foil to keep warm and put in a basket.

3. Fry or poach the eggs to desired doneness. To serve, divide the sauce among 4 serving plates. Top each serving with 1 cooked egg. Sprinkle with parsley. Serve hot with warm corn tortillas.

Eggs with Steak and Onions
Huevos con Bistec y Cebollas

Makes **4 servings**

In Durango, a state in northwestern Mexico, steak is highly regarded, and Durango-style steaks, served with eggs, is a dish that's perfect for brunch or hearty breakfasts. The spicy sauce and onions that tops the eggs and steak is an eye opener just about any morning! These steaks are very thinly sliced, as Mexican meats often are, so ask a butcher to slice them for you. This dish is usually served with eggs "sunny-side up," but you can make them to your preference.

3 medium tomatoes, peeled and quartered

2 canned chipotle chiles en adobo, coarsely chopped

3 tablespoons vegetable oil

1 large white onion, thinly sliced

4 (4- to 5-ounce) thinly sliced sirloin steaks, 1/4-inch thick, trimmed of all fat

Salt and freshly ground pepper, to taste

4 large eggs

1. Put the tomatoes and chiles in a blender and blend to a course purée. Reserve in the blender. Heat 1 tablespoon of the oil in a heavy skillet over medium heat and cook the onions, stirring, until they start to brown, about 4 minutes. Transfer the onions to a bowl.

2. Preheat the oven to 200°. Cook the steaks in the same hot skillet, 1 to 2 minutes per side. Season with salt and pepper. Put the steaks on a platter. Add the reserved tomato purée to the same hot skillet, and cook, scraping up any browned bits from the pan, until bubbling and hot, about 3 minutes. Stir in the onions to coat with the sauce. Season to taste with salt. Pile the onions on the steaks and keep warm in the oven.

3. Heat the remaining oil in a clean nonstick skillet over medium heat. Break the eggs into the hot oil and fry until the whites are set and the yolks still soft, or to desired doneness. Season with salt. Divide the eggs, steaks and onions among 4 serving plates. Serve at once.

Potatoes and Chorizo with Baked Eggs
Papas y Chorizo con Huevos al Horno

Makes 4 servings

Here's a fabulous dish, to bake and serve in individual casserole dishes or ramekins, that works well for a festive brunch. The entire dish, except for the final breaking and baking of the eggs, can be done the day before. Serve with a tropical fruit cocktail and a basket of Mexican pan dulces *(sweet buns) purchased from a bakery (or if time permits and make Mexican Sweet Buns, page 527).*

2 baking potatoes (about 1¼ pounds), peeled
½ pound fresh bulk chorizo, or packaged, with casings removed
¼ medium white onion, finely chopped
¼ teaspoon salt, or to taste
Fresh Salsa Mexicana (page 24), or purchased salsa
4 large eggs
1 cup shredded Monterey Jack cheese

1. Cut the potatoes into small dice, about ¼ inch. Set aside. Heat a large nonstick skillet over medium heat. Break the chorizo into small bits (if in casings, remove the casings), and cook until it begins to brown and the fat is cooked out. Add the diced potatoes, onion, and salt. Cover and cook, stirring frequently, over medium-low heat, until the potatoes are tender, about 15 minutes.

2. Divide the potato mixture among 4 individual ovenproof casserole dishes or ramekins. (Recipe can be done to this point one day ahead. Cover and refrigerate.)

3. Prepare salsa, if using homemade. If made ahead, remove casserole dishes from the refrigerator 1 hour before baking. Preheat the oven to 375°. Bake until the potato mixture is hot all the way through, 15 to 18 minutes.

4. Remove casserole dishes from the oven and make an indentation with a spoon in the center of each casserole. Break an egg into the indentation. Sprinkle shredded cheese equally over the eggs. Return the casseroles to the oven and bake until the eggs are cooked as desired and the cheese is melted, about 15 minutes. Serve hot with fresh salsa.

Poached Eggs in Tomato Chile Sauce
Huevos en Rabos de Mestiza

Makes **2 servings**

This is a typical morning dish of eggs poached in fresh tomato sauce with chile strips and cheese, that comes from central Mexico. Even though the Mexican name suggests that the eggs are dressed in rags (rabos), it's a delicious and handsome dish. The eggs are often served in shallow earthenware bowls with bolillos (oval Mexican sandwich rolls).

2 poblano chiles, roasted, peeled, and seeded (page 8)

1 pound ripe tomatoes, peeled and chopped

2 teaspoons vegetable oil

¹/₂ medium white onion, thinly sliced

¹/₂ teaspoon salt, or to taste

4 large eggs

2 ounces Monterey Jack cheese, thinly sliced

1. Prepare the chiles and cut them into strips. Then, put the tomatoes and ½ cup water in a blender and blend until smooth. Reserve.

2. In a wide, deep skillet, heat the oil over medium heat and sauté the onion until softened, about 4 minutes. Add the reserved tomato purée, chile strips, and salt. Bring the sauce to a boil; then reduce the heat to medium-low, and simmer, partially covered, about 10 minutes to blend the flavors.

3. Add the eggs, taking care not to break the yolks. Lay the cheese on top. Cover the pan and simmer until the eggs are set, about 4 minutes, or cook to desired doneness. Carefully divide the sauce between two shallow bowls with an egg and cheese on top. Serve hot.

Black Bean Omelet
Huevos Tirados

Makes **4 (single) servings**

Locals and tourists alike flock to Café de la Parroquia in Veracruz. It's famous for its café con leche specialty and its breakfast dishes.

Breakfast at La Parroquia also features tirados, the region's well-known egg dish, and my favorite from Veracruz. In this version, each omelet is cooked as a single serving and the beans are folded into the eggs at the last moment.

Cooking one omelet at a time is very easy and goes fast, but if you wish to make one large omelet, use a large (12-inch) non-stick skillet and use all of the ingredients at the same time, following the instructions for the single-serving omelet, and increasing the cooking time. Cut the large omelet in quarters to serve.

1 cup drained, cooked black beans (Basic Pot Beans, page 461), or canned

Fresh Salsa Mexicana (page 24)

8 eggs (extra-large, if possible)

4 tablespoons vegetable oil

¹/₄ cup finely chopped onion

4 teaspoons unsalted butter

1. Prepare the beans and salsa, if using homemade. Then, preheat oven to 200°. Break 2 of the eggs in a small bowl and beat well with a fork. Heat 1 tablespoon of the oil in an 8-inch nonstick skillet over medium heat, and cook 1 tablespoon of the onion about 1 minute.

2. Add 1 teaspoon of the butter, and when melted, pour in the beaten eggs. Cook about 20 seconds, then use a fork and lift and push the edges of the eggs toward the center. Tip the pan, allowing the runny eggs to go to the edge and under the partially cooked eggs. Cook until the surface is nearly set, about 3 minutes.

3. Spoon ¼ cup of the beans on the surface, fold over like an envelope, and cook to desired doneness. Invert the omelet onto a serving plate. Keep warm in the oven. Repeat, making 1 omelet at a time, with the remaining ingredients. Serve the omelets hot, with fresh salsa on the side.

Zucchini Omelet
Omelet de Huevo con Calabacitas

Makes **2 servings**

Pale green squash called calabacitas *that are rounder than our darker green zucchini, is the native squash often used in Mexican cooking. Although* calabacitas *can be found in some places in the United States, I often use zucchini, which is more readily available. This recipe serves two, but for single-serving omelets, divide the ingredients and cook separately.*

4 large eggs

2 teaspoons milk

¼ teaspoon salt, or to taste

2 tablespoons vegetable oil or butter

¼ cup finely chopped white onion

2 small plum tomatoes, peeled and finely chopped

1 cup finely diced zucchini

1 serrano chile, minced with seeds

2 thin cheese slices, cheddar or Monterey Jack

1. In a small bowl, beat the eggs with the milk and salt. Set aside. In a medium nonstick skillet, heat the oil over medium heat. Add the onion and cook, stirring, 1 minute. Add the tomato and cook until the juices cook away, about 1 minute. Add the zucchini and serrano chile. Cook, stirring, until the zucchini edges turn bright green, about 45 seconds.

2. Spread the zucchini out flat on the surface of the pan, and pour in the beaten eggs. Shake and tilt the pan to level the eggs. Cover, and cook until the eggs are set, about 4 minutes. Lay the cheese

on half of the omelet and using a large spatula, fold in half and cook about 30 seconds, or to desired doneness. Slide the omelet onto a plate. Cut in half and serve at once.

Cactus Omelet
Omelet de Nopalitos

Makes **4 servings**

A fluffy omelet filled with diced cactus strips (nopalitos) and cheese is a delicious breakfast treat. Buy jarred cactus that's packed just water. Also, check the cactus color. The best ones are the brightest green with the clearest liquid. Avoid cactus in cans and cactus packed in brine.

1 cup jarred cactus strips, drained and rinsed

½ tablespoon vegetable oil or olive oil

½ cup finely chopped onion

1 to 2 jalapeño chiles, seeded, veins removed, and minced

½ teaspoon salt, or to taste

Freshly ground pepper, to taste

2 tablespoons unsalted butter

8 large eggs, beaten

1 cup shredded Oaxaca or Monterey Jack cheese

1. Cut the cactus strips into ¼-inch dice and set aside. In a medium nonstick skillet, heat the oil and cook the onion until translucent, about 3 minutes. Add the jalapeño and reserved diced cactus. Season with salt and pepper. Reserve in the pan off heat.

2. In a large (12-inch) nonstick skillet, melt the butter until it sizzles. Swirl the pan to distribute the butter. Pour in the beaten eggs. Cook about 30 seconds, then use a fork to lift and push the edges of the eggs toward the center, tipping the pan to allow the uncooked eggs to run to the edges and under the cooked eggs. Cook until the surface is nearly set, about 3 minutes.

3. Spoon the cactus filling over half of the eggs. Add the cheese. Using a large spatula, fold in half and cook about 30 seconds, or to desired doneness. Invert onto a plate, cut into quarters, and serve at once.

Potato Omelet, Mexican Style
Tortilla Espanole, Estilo Mexicana
Makes 2 to 4 servings

If you are familiar with the wonderful Spanish potato and egg dish called tortilla español, *you'll love this dish. It is a round omelet with the ingredients mixed into the eggs, rather than being folded in at the end of the cooking. It is cut into wedges to eat. In Mexico, it is usually served for a late breakfast* (almuerzo), *but I think it's great around the clock. The flavors of this dish are nearly the same as the Spanish potato omelet, but the chiles give it a zesty Mexican touch.*

Although the omelet is traditionally flipped to cook both sides, the omelet can also be browned under a broiler. But try flipping; it's easier than you think.

1 poblano chile, roasted, peeled, and seeded (page 8)
1/4 cup olive oil
2 medium potatoes, peeled, and thinly sliced crosswise
1 medium onion, finely chopped
1/2 teaspoon dried oregano (Mexican variety preferred), crumbled
1/2 teaspoon salt
4 large eggs

1. Prepare the chiles, then dice them. Then, in a medium nonstick skillet, heat the oil over medium heat. Add the potatoes, onion, and oregano. Cook, partially covered, stirring frequently, until the potatoes are tender, about 10 minutes. Stir in the diced chile and salt. Set aside off heat.

2. In a large bowl, beat the eggs. Add the cooked potatoes to the eggs and mix to combine. Reheat the skillet. (If the potatoes stuck to the skillet when cooked, wipe the pan clean and add fresh oil.) Add the egg and potato mixture to the hot skillet. Spread out flat. Cook, shaking the pan occasionally to prevent the omelet from sticking, until the eggs are nearly set on top and the bottom is browned, about 5 to 6 minutes.

3. Put a large plate over the skillet. Using potholders, with 1 hand on the plate and the other holding the skillet, flip over the skillet, turning the uncooked side of the omelet onto the plate. Slide the omelet back into the skillet and cook the second side until browned. Cut the omelet into wedges and serve hot or at room temperature.

Shrimp and Spinach Omelet
Tortilla de Camarónes y Espinaca
Makes 4 to 6 servings

Everywhere along the beautiful seacoast in the state of Veracruz, shrimp is enjoyed in many ways. This dish from Tampico is served in wedges like a Spanish potato tortilla (tortilla español) *or an Italian* frittata. *It's suitable for any meal of the day. Although this dish is usually flipped to cook both sides, here it is browned under the broiler, a simpler method with an omelet containing multiple ingredients.*

3 tablespoons olive oil
1/2 medium white onion, finely chopped
1/2 medium red bell pepper, finely diced or chopped
1 to 2 serrano chiles, finely chopped with seeds
3 cups chopped fresh spinach, rinsed and dried
1 teaspoon salt
1/2 pound (36 to 40) cooked tiny bay shrimp, patted dry if moist
8 large eggs, beaten

1. Preheat the oven broiler. Place oven rack about 6 inches from the broiler coils. Heat the oil in a large nonstick frying pan and cook the onion, red pepper, and serranos, stirring, until softened, 4 to 5 minutes. Add the spinach and salt. Cook, stirring, until the spinach is limp and the liquid has cooked away. Stir in the shrimp and level the ingredients in the pan.

2. Pour the eggs evenly over the spinach and shrimp mixture. Tilt the pan to cover the surface but do not stir. Reduce the heat to low and cook until the eggs are set around the edge, and the bottom is browned, 4 to 5 minutes. Put the pan under the broiler until the top is set and lightly browned, about 2 minutes. Cut into wedges and serve hot.

Rice Casserole with Eggs
Arroz al Horno con Huevos

Makes **4 servings**

Unusual and inventive egg dishes are a specialty of the Mexican kitchen. Serve this rice and baked egg casserole for a late breakfast or brunch.

The rice may be a bit crusty around the edge of the pan. That's good; most people like that part! Room-temperature eggs are called for in this recipe because they will bake more evenly and faster than cold eggs. Sliced avocados and salsa are perfect to serve with the casserole. A fresh fruit cup is a refreshing starter for the meal.

2 teaspoons olive oil

2 teaspoons unsalted butter

1/2 medium white onion, finely chopped, (about 1/2 cup)

1 cup long-grain white rice

3/4 teaspoon ground cumin

2 cups canned fat-free reduced-sodium chicken broth

1/2 teaspoon salt, or to taste

4 large eggs, at room temperature

3/4 cup shredded Monterey Jack cheese

1. Preheat oven to 350°. In a deep skillet with an ovenproof handle, heat the oil and butter, over medium heat. Add the onion and cook, stirring, until the onion is softened, about 3 minutes. Add the rice and cumin. Cook, stirring frequently, until the rice starts to color, about 3 to 4 minutes. Add the broth and salt. Stir to combine the ingredients.

2. Cover the skillet with aluminum foil and bake until the liquid is absorbed and the rice is tender, about 20 minutes. Remove the pan from the oven and uncover.

3. With a spoon, make 4 circular indentations in the rice. Break 1 egg into each hollow. (It's perfectly okay for the whites to run together.) Sprinkle cheese over the top, leaving the yolks showing, and return the pan to the oven.

4. Cook, uncovered, until the whites of the eggs are set and the yolks are still soft, 10 to 12 minutes. Carefully scoop a portion of rice with 1 egg on top for each serving. Serve at once.

Savory Breakfast Cheesecake
Torta de Queso para Desayuno

Makes 6 servings

Cheesecake for breakfast or brunch is not traditional, but this savory version goes very well with tropical fruit salads and is right at home at a modern Mexican-style late morning meal.

1 cup fine bread crumbs

3 tablespoons unsalted butter, melted

1 (1 pound) block cream cheese, at room
    temperature

1/2 pound aged manchego or asiago cheese,
    grated

4 large eggs

1 tablespoon minced fresh oregano

1/8 teaspoon crushed red pepper

1/4 teaspoon salt

1. Preheat oven to 350°. In a bowl, mix the bread crumbs and melted butter. Grease an 8-inch springform pan and press the crumbs into the bottom and a bit up the sides of the pan. Set aside.

2. In a large bowl with an electric mixer beat the cheeses together until smooth. Beat in the eggs, 1 at a time, beating well with each addition. Add the oregano, red pepper, and salt. Pour into the prepared pan and bake until puffed, golden brown, and set in the center.

3. Remove cake from the oven and let stand 10 minutes before removing the ring. After 10 minutes run a thin knife blade around the inside rim to loosen the cheesecake; then remove the ring and cool the cheesecake about 20 minutes before cutting. Serve warm.

Tortillas with Eggs, Chorizo, and Cheese
Huevos Tapatios

Makes 4 servings

Mexicans are masters at creating interesting egg dishes. The people from Guadalajara and the state of Jalisco are called Tapatios, *loosely translated, meaning they are the "tops," and proud of their heritage. They can also be proud of this dish. It's delicious and filling for breakfast, brunch, or anytime.*

Fresh Salsa Mexicana (page 24), or purchased salsa

1/2 pound fresh bulk chorizo, or packaged,
    with casings removed

2 tablespoons finely chopped onion

4 (6- to 7-inch) corn tortillas

1 tablespoon vegetable oil

4 large eggs, beaten

Salt, to taste

1 cup shredded Oaxaca or Monterey Jack cheese

1 avocado (Hass variety preferred), peeled,
    seeded, and diced

1. Prepare salsa, if using homemade. Then, in a medium skillet over medium heat, cook the chorizo, breaking it into pieces as it cooks, until it starts to brown. Add the onion and cook until translucent and the chorizo is completely cooked. Keep warm in the pan.

2. In a medium nonstick skillet, warm the tortillas, 1 at a time, until pliable and hot. Wrap in a clean kitchen towel to keep warm.

3. In the same nonstick skillet heat the oil over medium heat and fry the eggs to your preference. Season with salt. Sprinkle 1/4 cup of cheese on top of each egg. Cover the pan about 30 seconds to melt the cheese. To serve, place 1 warm tortilla on each of 4 plates. Spoon a portion of the chorizo on each tortilla and top with an egg. Garnish each plate with avocado and salsa. Serve at once.

Eggs, Motul Style on Tortillas
Huevos Motuleños

Makes 4 servings

This colorful Yucatán egg dish appears on restaurant menus all over the region. It is a satisfying meal of beans, eggs, ham, peas, and golden plantains served on a crisp tortilla (tostada) and topped with a spicy tomato sauce. It is wonderful for a brunch or late breakfast, called almuerzo in Mexico. Most of the parts can be made ahead, so the final cooking and assembly are easy.

2 cups cooked Black Beans Yucatán (page 466), drained and mashed
Yucatán Tomato Sauce (page 44)
4 Crisp-Fried Whole Tortillas (page 86)
1 fried plantain (see recipe, page 456)
2 tablespoons vegetable oil
¹/₂ cup fresh or frozen peas
4 large eggs
¹/₂ cup diced cooked ham

1. Prepare the beans, then the tomato sauce, and keep both warm. Fry the plantains, then in a separate pan, fry the corn tortillas. Set both aside.

2. Just before assembling the dish, Bring a small pan of water to a boil. Add the peas and cook 1 to 2 minutes. Drain.

3. In a medium nonstick skillet, heat 2 tablespoons oil over medium heat and fry the eggs "sunny-side up"—until the whites are set and the yolk is still soft, or to desired doneness.

4. Lay 1 crisp tortilla on each serving plate. Spread about ½ cup of mashed beans on each tortilla. Spoon 2 to 3 tablespoons of tomato sauce on top of the beans. Place a cooked egg on top and garnish each serving with ham, peas, and plantains. Serve at once.

Bacon and Egg Quesadillas
Quesadillas de Tocino y Huevo

Makes 2 servings

These breakfast quesadillas of tortillas filled with scrambled eggs, bacon, and cheese are quick and easy to make. This recipe, made with flour tortillas is from northern Mexico, where flour tortillas are frequently used. (In the central and southern regions, corn tortillas are by far the preferred tortilla.) The bacon can be cooked a day ahead to make it even quicker. You can serve them with red or green salsa; sometimes both are offered. Try Tomatillo and Chipotle Chile Sauce (page 36) or Pan-Roasted Red Salsa (page 30), or use prepared salsa, to save time.

1 tablespoon unsalted butter
2 green onions, chopped
4 large eggs, beaten
4 slices cooked crisp bacon, broken into small pieces
2 (8- to 9-inch) flour tortillas
¹/₂ cup shredded Oaxaca or Monterey Jack cheese
Vegetable oil

1. In a large nonstick skillet, melt the butter over medium-high heat and cook the onion, stirring, about 15 seconds. Add the beaten eggs and cook, stirring, until barely set. Stir in the bacon. Remove the pan from the heat.

2. Put the tortillas on a flat surface and spoon half of the eggs on each tortilla. Top equally with cheese. Fold the tortillas in half. Brush lightly with oil.

3. Wipe out the same skillet and heat over medium heat. Toast the quesadillas until lightly browned on both sides, about 1 minute per side. Serve hot.

Egg and Tortilla Casserole
Cazuela de Huevos

Makes 6 servings

Dry tortillas are never wasted in Mexico, but are used in many ways, from making crisp chips to layering in casseroles like this one. Serve for breakfast, brunch, or an informal lunch or supper.

2 teaspoons olive oil or vegetable oil
1/2 medium onion, finely chopped
6 medium tomatillos, husked, rinsed and finely chopped
1/2 teaspoon salt
1/2 teaspoon ground cumin
1 (7-ounce) can chopped green chiles
4 or 5 (6- to 7-inch) corn tortillas, halved and cut in 1-inch-wide strips
2 cups coarsely shredded Oaxaca or Monterey Jack cheese
8 large eggs
1/3 cup whole milk
1/4 red bell pepper, finely diced or chopped
2 green onions, finely chopped

1. Preheat oven to 350°. Grease a 9-inch square baking dish. In a skillet, heat the oil and cook the onion, stirring, until softened, about 3 minutes. Add the tomatillos, salt, cumin, and 1/4 cup of water. Bring to a boil and cook, uncovered, until the tomatillos are soft and pale green, 5 to 7 minutes. Remove from the heat and mix in the chiles.

2. Spread half of the chile mixture in the bottom of the baking dish. Layer half of the tortilla strips and half of the cheese on top. Repeat the layers with the remaining chile mixture, tortillas, and cheese.

3. In a bowl, beat the eggs and milk together. Pour evenly over the tortilla mixture. Sprinkle the top with the red pepper and green onions. Bake, uncovered until puffy and set in the center, about 35 to 40 minutes. Let stand 5 to 8 minutes. Cut into squares and serve hot.

Tortilla Casserole with Eggs and Red Chile Sauce
Chilaquiles con Huevos

Makes 4 servings

Homey casseroles called chilaquiles *are made of crisp fried tortilla strips or triangles mixed with sauces and other ingredients. This breakfast version features eggs and red chile sauce.*

Basic Red Chile Sauce (page 47)
6 (6- to 7-inch) corn tortillas, cut into strips, about 1/2-inch wide
Vegetable oil for frying
3 large eggs, beaten
1/2 teaspoon salt, or to taste
1/4 cup grated queso fresco (fresh Mexican cheese)
1/3 to 1/2 cup sour cream (optional)

1. Prepare the red chile sauce and keep warm. Pour oil into a large deep skillet to a depth of about 1/4 inch. When the oil is hot, fry the tortilla strips, in batches, until golden brown. Drain on paper towels.

2. Pour off all but 1 tablespoon of the oil from the skillet. Add the beaten eggs and salt. Cook, stirring, until just beginning to set, about 2 minutes. Add the tortilla strips and the heated chile sauce. Mix gently until the tortillas soften and absorb the sauce, about 2 minutes. Sprinkle the top with cheese and drizzle with sour cream, if desired. Serve hot.

Breakfast Dishes with Tortillas and Bread

Breakfast Tacos with Potatoes and Chorizo
Tacos de Papa y Chorizo

Makes **8 tacos**

Crisp rolled tacos filled with potatoes and chorizo sausage, served with Mexican scrambled eggs and fresh tropical fruits (Breakfast Fruit Plate, page 509), make a memorable brunch. Packaged chorizo sausage can be greasy, so if you can't find good quality at a butcher or gourmet store, substitute Mexican Pork Sausage (page 348).

1 cup (1¹/₂ recipe) Basic Cooked Tomatillo Sauce (page 46)
¹/₂ pound fresh bulk chorizo, or packaged, with casings removed
¹/₄ medium onion, finely chopped
2 medium boiled potatoes, peeled and finely diced or chopped
¹/₄ teaspoon salt, or to taste
Oil for frying tortillas
6 (6- to 7-inch) corn tortillas
¹/₂ cup sour cream

1. Prepare the tomatillo sauce. Then, fry the chorizo in a nonstick skillet over medium heat, breaking it into small pieces; cook until browned, about 3 to 4 minutes. Add the onion and cook until softened, about 3 minutes. Stir in the potatoes, salt, and ¹/₂ cup of the tomatillo sauce. Reserve off heat.

2. In another medium skillet, heat about 2 tablespoons of oil until it shimmers. One at a time, dip the tortillas in the hot oil just until limp, about 10 seconds. Drain on paper towels. Put about 2 tablespoons of the filling on one soft warm tortilla. Roll tightly and secure with a toothpick. Repeat until all tortillas are filled and rolled.

3. Add about 2 more tablespoons of oil to the same skillet used for softening the tortillas and fry the tacos, seam side down, until crisp and browned. Turn and fry the second side. Drain on paper towels. Arrange the tacos on a plate. Garnish with remaining tomatillo sauce and sour cream. Serve hot.

Breakfast Bean and Cheese Tacos
Tacos de Frijol y Queso para Desayuno

Makes **4 servings**

Yes, airport food can be inspirational! In Puerto Vallarta, before a morning departure, some friends and I ate breakfast in the airport's restaurant and we all agreed that the black bean taco was worth duplicating at home. Soft corn tortillas were folded in half, not rolled, after being filled with well-seasoned black beans and cheese, and ranchera sauce was spooned on top. Eat these tacos with a knife and fork.

2 cups Basic Pot Beans (page 461), or canned
Ranchera Sauce (page 44)
1 tablespoon olive oil or vegetable oil
¹/₄ medium white onion, finely chopped
1 medium tomato, peeled and finely chopped
1 serrano chile, finely chopped with seeds
¹/₂ teaspoon dried oregano (Mexican variety preferred), crumbled
8 (6- to 7-inch) corn tortillas
1¹/₂ cups shredded Monterey Jack cheese

1. Prepare the beans, if making homemade. Then, prepare the ranchera sauce. Set aside and keep warm.

2. In a medium saucepan heat the oil over medium heat and cook the onion until it starts to brown, 3 to 4 minutes. Add the tomato, serrano, and oregano. Cook, stirring, until the tomato juices reduce, about 4 minutes. Add the beans and cook, stirring frequently, until thickened, about 5 minutes.

3. In a dry skillet over medium-high heat, warm the tortillas, 1 at a time, until limp. Cover the tortillas with a clean kitchen towel to keep soft and warm until all are heated.

4. To assemble, put about ¼ cup beans on half of each tortilla, add about 2 tablespoons of cheese, then fold in half. Put 2 filled and folded tortillas on each of 4 plates. Spoon heated ranchera sauce on top, sprinkle with the remaining cheese, and serve at once.

Tortillas Topped with Pork and Potatoes
Picaditas de Cerdo y Papas

Makes **4 small servings**

This is one of my favorite picaditas—*a regional specialty of Puebla, a fascinating colonial city with a rich history that is also known for its wonderful cuisine. The exquisite hand-painted Talavera-style pottery and tiles come from Puebla, and the historic tiled kitchen in the Convent of Santa Rosa, where* Mole Poblano *was invented, is located here, too.*

Picaditas—corn tortilla dough pressed into small tortillas then pinched to form a cup for fillings—are commonly served for breakfast. I based this recipe on the picadita I had at El Balcon café in Puebla.

Basic Corn Tortilla Dough (page 133)
1 medium potato, peeled and diced (about ¹/₂ inch)
1¹/₂ tablespoons vegetable oil or olive oil
¹/₂ medium white onion, finely chopped
8 ounces thinly sliced pork sirloin (¹/₄ inch)
¹/₂ teaspoon salt, or to taste
¹/₄ teaspoon dried oregano (Mexican variety preferred), crumbled
1 cup red salsa, purchased or homemade
Crumbled cotija cheese, or substitute mild feta cheese

1. Prepare 4 fresh corn tortillas. Heat a medium dry skillet or Mexican comal (skillet) over medium-high heat. Put 1 tortilla on the pan. Cook until it loosens easily from the pan, about 45 seconds. Turn and cook 40 seconds. Remove from the pan and pinch up a ¹/₃-inch edge all around. Return to the pan, flat side down. Cook 35 seconds. Transfer to a plate. Cover to keep warm. Repeat with remaining tortillas. Stack, covered, on the same plate.

2. Put about 1 cup of water in a small saucepan, add the potato and bring to a boil. Cook until tender, about 4 minutes. Drain and reserve in a bowl. Heat 1 tablespoon of the oil in a medium skillet over medium-high heat. Cook the onion, stirring, until it starts to brown, about 3 minutes. Transfer to a plate.

3. Cook the steak in the same pan until browned on both sides and just cooked through, 2 to 3 minutes on each side. Remove the meat to a cutting board and chop coarsely.

4. Return the meat, onion, and potato to the pan. Add the remaining ¹/₂ tablespoon of oil, salt and oregano. Cook, stirring, 2 minutes. To assemble, spread 2 tablespoons of the salsa on each picadita. Top each with about 3 tablespoons of the meat mixture. Sprinkle with cheese. Serve at once, with additional salsa.

Crisp Rolled Tortillas with Ham
Taquitos de Jamón

Makes **8 taquitos**

Here, flour tortillas are rolled into cylinders (taquitos) in the style of northern Mexico. The tortillas are layered with thinly sliced deli-style smoked ham and cheese before being rolled. The taquitos are then lightly fried and served for breakfast. I like them with Mexican Scrambled Eggs (page 487). Taquitos can be assembled ahead and fried shortly before serving. They can also be cut into pieces and served as appetizers.

Chihuahua cheese is very popular in Mexico and is made by Mennonites who settled in the state of Chihuahua in 1921. There are now about twenty Mennonite communities, called camps (campos) in the region. They make cheese and cultivate crops on their farms. If you can't find Chihuahua cheese, mild cheddar is a good substitute.

8 (6- to 7-inch) flour tortillas
8 (¹/₁₆-inch-thick) round ham slices (about 6 inches in diameter)
2 cups shredded Chihuahua or mild cheddar cheese
Oil for frying

1. In a dry nonstick skillet, warm the tortillas, 1 at a time, until soft and flexible, about 20 seconds. Stack and wrap in a kitchen towel to keep soft. Lay 1 tortilla on a flat surface. Put a slice of ham on the tortilla and top with ¼ cup of cheese. Roll tightly and secure with toothpicks. Put on a plate and cover to keep soft. Repeat until all are rolled.

2. In the same skillet, heat about 2 tablespoons of oil over medium heat, and fry the taquitos 2 or 3 at a time until the cheese is melted and the tortillas are crisp and golden, about 1 minute. Drain on paper towels. Serve at once.

Beef and Cheese Quesadillas
Quesadillas de Carne y Queso

Makes **4 servings**

In Northern Mexico flour tortillas are often used as well as corn tortillas for tortilla snacks. Serve this popular ground beef and melted cheese quesadilla made with flour tortillas for an informal breakfast or brunch. The tortillas can be filled and folded ahead of time and then lightly fried until crisp just before serving. Accompany the quesadillas with guacamole and a dollop of sour cream.

2 tablespoons vegetable oil, plus extra for frying the quesadillas
¹/₂ medium white onion, finely chopped
¹/₂ pound lean ground beef
¹/₄ teaspoon dried oregano (Mexican variety preferred), crumbled
¹/₄ teaspoon ground cumin
Pinch crushed red pepper
1 cup canned diced tomatoes in their juice
Salt, to taste
4 (8- to 9-inch) flour tortillas
1¹/₃ cups shredded Chihuahua or mild cheddar cheese

1. In a medium nonstick skillet, heat 2 tablespoons of oil over medium heat. Add the onion and cook, stirring, until softened, 3 to 4 minutes. Add the beef, breaking it up into bits, and cook, stirring, until it starts to brown, 4 to 5 minutes. Add oregano, cumin, and crushed red pepper. Stir to mix with the meat. Add the tomatoes and cook until the juices reduce and the mixture is nearly dry, about 5 minutes. Season with salt.

2. Heat a large dry nonstick skillet over medium heat, and warm the tortillas, one at a time, turning once or twice, until soft and limp, about 20 seconds. Wrap in a clean kitchen towel to keep moist and soft. (This prevents the tortilla from cracking when it's folded.) Put 1 tortilla on a flat work surface. Spread ⅓ cup of the meat mixture half the tortilla and top with ⅓ cup cheese. Fold in half. Press lightly to flatten and put on a baking sheet. Cover with a piece of plastic wrap to prevent drying out. Repeat with the remaining tortillas and fillings. (Can be made ahead to this point, covered with plastic wrap and refrigerated up to 3 to 4 hours before frying.)

3. Preheat oven to 200°. In a large nonstick skillet, heat about 2 tablespoons oil over medium heat until it starts to shimmer. Put 1 quesadilla in the skillet and fry, turning once, until golden brown on both sides and the cheese is melted, about 1 to 2 minutes on each side. Drain on paper towels. Keep warm in the oven. Repeat until all are fried. Serve hot.

Potato Masa Cakes with Spicy Pork
Tortitas de Masa con Picante Puerco
Makes **4 servings**

Freshly cooked ground pork seasoned with herbs and spices and piled on crisp potato masa cakes makes an unusual and satisfying breakfast or brunch. Chunks of fresh pineapple and mango go well with the pork and potato cakes. For a more substantial meal, add refried beans to the plate. A meal like this would be served at almuerzo *(late breakfast) around 11 in the morning.*

1 tablespoon olive oil
¹/₂ **medium white onion, finely chopped**
³/₄ **pound fresh ground pork**
¹/₂ **teaspoon salt**
¹/₂ **teaspoon dried oregano (Mexican variety preferred), crumbled**
¹/₂ **teaspoon ground cumin**
¹/₄ **teaspoon dried thyme**
¹/₈ **teaspoon ground allspice**
2 **plum tomatoes, cored and finely chopped**
Potato Masa Cakes (page 114)
¹/₄ **cup crumbled cotija or feta cheese**

1. In a skillet, heat the oil over medium heat and cook the onion until softened, 3 to 4 minutes. Add the pork and cook, breaking the meat into bits with a wooden spoon until no longer pink, about 4 minutes. Add the salt, oregano, cumin, thyme, allspice, and tomatoes. Cook, stirring, until the mixture is completely cooked, about 5 minutes. Reserve in the pan off heat.

2. Prepare the potato masa cakes. To serve, reheat the pork. Place 1 potato cake on each of 4 serving plates. Top equally with the heated pork mixture. Sprinkle each serving with crumbled cheese. Serve at once.

Bean and Melted Cheese Sandwiches
Molletes
Makes **4 servings**

Molletes *are open-face sandwiches made on oval Mexican sandwich rolls called* bolillos. *The rolls are split and topped with refried beans and cheese. The molletes are baked to melt the cheese and are served hot, usually for breakfast, with salsa on top or on the side. They are also an excellent quick snack any time of the day.*

Fresh Salsa Mexicana (page 24), or purchased salsa
1 cup Basic Refried Beans (page 462), or canned
4 oval Mexican sandwich rolls (bolillos) or other 6-inch sandwich rolls, split in half
2 tablespoons unsalted butter, softened
1 cup shredded Monterey Jack cheese

1. Prepare salsa and beans if using homemade. Then, preheat the oven to 400°. Heat the beans in a small saucepan. Cut the rolls in half lengthwise. Pinch out a bit of the soft center to make a cavity in the rolls. Butter each half, and spread with about 2 tablespoons of beans. Top each half equally with cheese.

2. Put the sandwiches on a large baking sheet, and bake about 5 minutes, or until the cheese is melted. Serve hot with a dollop of salsa on top, or on the side.

Melted Cheese and Green Sauce on Toasted Rolls
Bolillos Tostada de Queso y Salsa Verde

Makes 4 servings

This is a take-off on a popular melted cheese and bean combination that's served on toasted bolillos *(oval Mexican sandwich rolls). French-style rolls can be substituted. I serve these filled rolls for brunch or a late breakfast, and do they ever disappear! The rolls can also be cut into pieces and served as an appetizer with drinks.*

Fresh Tomatillo Sauce (page 34), or 1½ cups
   purchased green salsa
4 oval Mexican sandwich rolls (bolillos) or other
   6-inch sandwich rolls
Unsalted butter or margarine (optional)
2 cups shredded medium Asadero or Chihuahua
   cheese, or substitute cheddar cheese

1. Make the tomatillo sauce, if using homemade. Preheat the oven broiler. Split the rolls in half lengthwise. Spread lightly with butter, if desired. Toast under broiler until golden, 3 to 4 minutes.

2. Spread about 1 generous tablespoon of the salsa on each toasted half roll. Top each half roll with about ¼ cup of cheese. Place all the rolls on a baking sheet and run under broiler until the cheese melts, 1 to 2 minutes. Serve hot.

Toasted Rolls with Refried Beans and Bacon
Bolillos Tostado con Frijoles Refritos y Tocino

Makes 4 servings

My husband and I have enjoyed years of pleasurable breakfasts at the hotel Mision de Los Angeles *in Oaxaca City while sitting at our favorite table in a sunny corner of the dining room. Toasted* bolillos *(oval Mexican rolls) are topped in a variety of ways. They're just as good for lunch as for breakfast.*

1 cup Basic Refried Beans (page 462), or canned
Fresh Salsa Mexicana (page 24), or purchased
   salsa
4 oval Mexican sandwich rolls (bolillos) or other
   6-inch sandwich rolls
Unsalted butter (optional)
12 slices crisp cooked bacon, crumbled

1. Prepare the beans and the salsa, if using homemade. Then, preheat the oven broiler. Slice the rolls in half lengthwise. Spread the cut sides with butter, if desired, and lay on a baking sheet. Toast under the broiler until the butter is melted and the rolls are lightly toasted.

2. Spread the toasted sides with refried beans and top evenly with the crumbled bacon. Serve the rolls with fresh salsa on the side.

Banana Breakfast Burritos
Burritos de Plátano para Desayunos

Makes 4 servings

Flour tortillas wrapped around warm buttery bananas with brown sugar syrup poured on top is my own Mexican breakfast creation. If you like bananas, you'll love these burritos.

Brown Sugar Syrup (page 583)

4 medium ripe but firm bananas

2 tablespoons sugar

1 teaspoon ground cinnamon (Mexican canela or Ceylon variety preferred)

2 tablespoons unsalted butter (plus more, if needed)

4 (8- to 9-inch) flour tortillas

Oil for frying

1. Prepare the sugar syrup and reserve in the pan off heat. In a small bowl mix the sugar and cinnamon. Peel the bananas and cut in half lengthwise.

2. In a large (12-inch) nonstick skillet melt the butter and cook the bananas, in batches, turning once, until light brown on both sides. Remove the bananas to a plate. Sprinkle with cinnamon-sugar. Reserve on the plate.

3. In a clean, dry large nonstick skillet, warm the tortillas, 1 at a time, turning, until soft and pliable. Stack and cover to keep warm.

4. To assemble, put 2 banana halves on half of each tortilla and fold into half-moons.

5. In the same skillet, heat about 2 tablespoons of vegetable oil. Put the folded tortillas in the hot oil, 1 or 2 at a time, and cook until light brown and crisp on both sides, 20 to 30 seconds for each side. Add more oil if needed.

6. Reheat the syrup. Transfer the burritos to serving plates. Pour about 2 tablespoons of the warm syrup over each burrito and serve at once. Pass remaining syrup at the table.

Sweet Fried Bread
Torrejas

Makes 4 servings

Mexico's answer to French toast is made with thick slices of bolillos *(oval Mexican rolls), or slices of baguette. In my view* torrejas *is even better than French toast!*

Brown Sugar Syrup (page 583)

1³/₄ cups milk

1 cinnamon stick (Mexican canela or Ceylon variety preferred)

¹/₄ cup sugar

12 (³/₄-inch-thick) slices oval Mexican sandwich rolls (bolillo), from about 4 (6-inch) bolillos or French rolls

3 large eggs, beaten

Oil for frying

1. Prepare the sugar syrup. Reserve in the pan off heat. In a medium saucepan, boil 1½ cups of the milk, cinnamon stick, and sugar, stirring frequently, until the sugar dissolves, 3 to 4 minutes. Let cool.

2. Put the bread in a single layer in a large oven-proof glass baking dish. Remove the cinnamon stick and pour the cooled milk over the bread, pushing the bread gently into the milk. Let stand 15 minutes.

3. In a heavy skillet, heat oil to a depth of about ¼-inch. In a pie plate, thoroughly mix the eggs with the remaining ¼ cup of milk. Carefully dip the soaked bread into the beaten eggs and fry in the hot oil until golden brown, about 2 minutes on each side. Add more oil to the pan, if needed. Put the *torrejas* on serving plates. Reheat the sugar syrup and spoon it generously over the *torrejas*. Serve at once.

Fruit

Breakfast Fruit Plate
Plata de Frutas

Makes 4 servings

*Mexico is a country blessed with an abundance
of fresh fruits year round, so the morning selections are really a treat. Artistically arranged
fruit plates are served everywhere—in homes,
at fondas (market stalls), and in plain and
fancy hotel dining rooms, on the coast and
inland. Usually, four or five kinds of fruit are
peeled, sliced, and arranged on each individual
plate. This recipe is just a guide. Include any
tropical fruits you prefer, such as mangos,
papayas, melon, or pineapple, in your plata
de frutas. Oranges, grapefruit, and kiwis are
also bright and tasty additions and are easy to
find in the United States. Select the best fruits
of the season.*

**2 ripe bananas, cut into 1/4-inch-thick
    oblong rounds**

**1 medium cantaloupe, quartered, seeded, peeled,
    and thinly sliced**

**1/2 medium honeydew melon, quartered, seeded,
    peeled, and thinly sliced**

12 strawberries, whole or sliced

1 lime, sliced

Arrange the bananas and melons in overlapping
rows on 4 serving plates. Garnish with strawberries and lime slices. Refrigerate for about an
hour. Serve cold.

Banana and Mandarin Fruit Cup
Taza de Plátano y Mandarina

Makes 4 servings

*Sliced bananas and seedless mandarin segments
simmered in brown sugar syrup are served
warm and make a distinctly pleasing addition
for breakfast or brunch. Select bananas that are
ripe, but not soft, and seedless mandarins or
tangerines for this dish. The fruit can be prepared ahead and gently reheated before serving.
Serve after a spicy main dish such as Eggs in
Ranchera Sauce (page 492) or Mexican
Scrambled Eggs (page 487).*

1/2 cup lightly packed light brown sugar

1 cup water

**2 small ripe bananas, peeled and cut crosswise
    about 1/2-inch thick**

**2 seedless mandarin oranges or tangerines,
    peeled and separated into segments**

1 tablespoon unsalted butter

1/2 teaspoon pure vanilla extract

**Ground cinnamon (Mexican canela or Ceylon
    variety preferred)**

1. In a medium saucepan, stir together the sugar
and water. Bring to a boil over medium heat, then
reduce the heat to low and cook, stirring frequently, about 3 minutes or until the syrup thickens slightly.

2. Add the bananas and mandarins. Stir gently to
coat with the syrup. Simmer 1 minute or until
the bananas just soften. Add the butter and stir
gently until the butter melts, 20 to 25 seconds.
Serve warm in small dessert bowls. Sprinkle
lightly with cinnamon, if desired.

Pineapple Boats
Barcas de Piña
Makes 4 servings

Just about every resort hotel in Mexico dazzles the eye with beautiful breakfast buffets. Pineapple boats laden with chunks of tropical fruits and decorated with exotic blossoms are often part of the tempting array of morning delights, and they are easy to make at home, too.

1 large ripe pineapple, with leaves attached
1 large ripe mango, peeled and cut into
    bite-size pieces
2 oranges, peeled and cut into bite-size pieces
2 ripe bananas, peeled and cut into bite-size
    pieces
1 kiwi, peeled and cut into bite size pieces
    (optional)
1/2 cup red or green seedless grapes
Fresh mint sprigs
Lime wedges

1. Cut the pineapple in half lengthwise keeping the leaves attached. Carefully cut out the fruit as close to the rind as possible, taking care to keep the outside shells intact. Reserve the shells. Cut the pineapple into bite size pieces and put them in a large bowl.

2. Add the mango, oranges, bananas, kiwi, and grapes to the bowl. Mix gently and mound the fruits in the reserved shells. Place the pineapple boats on a large serving platter. Decorate with mint sprigs and garnish with lime wedges. Serve cold.

Yogurt and Tropical Fruit Starter
Frutas y Yogurt
Makes 4 servings

In the town of Coatepec, near Jalapa, is a gorgeous hotel—the Posada Coatepec. There, I ate a healthful and delicious fruit and yogurt starter at breakfast, very much like this recipe. Serve in pretty bowls or large stemmed glasses to lend a "resort" ambiance to your breakfast. Be sure to inspect each berry for freshness.

1 large mango, peeled and diced
1 ripe banana, peeled and diced
1 cup fresh berries of choice, such as raspberries,
    blueberries, blackberries
2 (8-ounce) cups of plain or vanilla yogurt
1 (8-ounce) cup strawberry yogurt
4 large whole strawberries, for garnish

In a medium bowl, mix the mango, banana and berries together. Set aside. In the bottom of each of 4 serving bowls, put a portion of the plain or vanilla yogurt. Spoon the fruits equally over the yogurt. On the top of each serving add about 2 tablespoons of the strawberry yogurt, and place a strawberry in the center. Store in the refrigerator for at least an hour. Serve cold.

Biscuits, Muffins, *and* Breads

Although tortillas are the true "daily bread" for Mexicans, rolls and sweet breads are eaten frequently as well. Many different kinds of breads are enjoyed as a morning treat with coffee, tea, or hot chocolate. Oval-shaped Mexican sandwich rolls (*bolillos*) are also used to make delicious sandwiches and to accompany soups and many saucy dishes.

Bread (*pan*) made from wheat flour was introduced to Mexico by the Spanish in the 1500s and was further developed during the French occupation of 1864 to 1867. Bread baking has continued as an art and a highly respected occupation. In the best bakeries (*panaderias*) in the country, master bakers still instruct upcoming bakers by the apprenticeship method. Most bread baking in Mexico is done in bakeries, but there are a few special breads that can be adapted for home bakers. The results are still very good even though home kitchens lack the brick-lined ovens that give many of the breads their special texture and chewy quality.

During my many years of travel in Mexico, I have often visited local bakeries and still marvel at the skill with which they produce so many delightful shapes and varieties of bread and rolls, each one with its own name depicting something real or imagined.

One eye-catching bread, *Pan de los Muertos* (Bread of the Dead, page 525), is a round loaf decorated with dough-shaped crossbones for Day of the Dead (All Saints or All Souls Day) in November, a holiday honoring deceased loved ones. There are also delicately sweet everyday breads (*pan dulces*) such as the curved horn-shaped flaky rolls called cow horns (*cuernos*), round rolls cut and raised in the center and crusted with sugar called volcanoes (*volcans*), rolls with a carved shell design on top (*conchas*), and soft sweet rolls twisted to resemble bow-ties (*corbatas*).

Other special breads include Oaxacan Bread (page 526), which is soft and rich and usually eaten with hot chocolate for breakfast or as a snack in the evening, and Three Kings Bread (page 524), a glazed wreath-shaped bread filled with nuts and candied fruits, made for celebrations on January 6.

To get you started, this chapter begins with recipes for biscuits and muffins that are popular for breakfast or for a snack. There are also recipes for quick breads, which you can make for brunch or a treat anytime, such as Pumpkin Bread with Sunflower Seeds (page 518) and Mango-Pecan Quick Bread (page 519). A whole-wheat breakfast cookie is included here too because it is often eaten with rolls and biscuits. (Other popular cookies are in the Desserts chapter, pages 530 to 583.)

In addition to the specialty breads, wonderful additions to your Mexican baking repertoire are the several types of rolls you can use for sandwiches (*tortas*), with breakfast dishes, or to accompany stews. These breads are too good to pass up, so to simplify your efforts, the recipes call for quick-rising yeast and a food processor to make the dough.

Baking can be very satisfying and baking Mexican breads truly adds to the authentic experience of cooking and eating the Mexican way.

Biscuits and Muffins

Mexican Biscuits
Bisquets de Mexico

Makes **about 16 biscuits**

Mexican biscuits are rich and slightly sweet. When ordered in a restaurant the biscuits are sometimes split, buttered, and toasted under a broiler until the butter melts and the edges begin to turn golden. They are irresistible. Serve hot with honey or jam.

3 cups all-purpose flour
2 tablespoons sugar
4 teaspoons baking powder
1 teaspoon salt
¹/₂ cup cold unsalted butter or solid vegetable shortening
2 large eggs, beaten
²/₃ cup whole milk

1. Preheat the oven to 425°. In a large bowl whisk together the flour, sugar, baking powder, and salt. Cut in the butter or shortening until the mixture is crumbly. (This can be done in a food processor.) Then return the dry ingredients to the bowl.

2. Remove a scant 2 tablespoons of the beaten eggs to a small bowl and set aside. Mix the remaining egg with the milk. Make a well in the center of the dry ingredients and add the milk mixture all at once. Stir with a fork until combined. With your hands, work the dough together and turn the dough onto a lightly floured work surface. Knead gently 8 to 10 turns until the dough just holds together.

3. Roll out the dough with a lightly floured rolling pin to about ¾-inch thick. Cut into rounds with a 2½-inch biscuit cutter. Gather the scraps, roll and cut. Put the biscuits on an ungreased baking sheet. Brush the tops with the reserved beaten egg. Bake until golden brown, 12 to 14 minutes. Serve warm from the oven. If made ahead, biscuits can be split, buttered, and toasted under a broiler.

Pumpkin Biscuits
Bisquets de Calabaza

Makes **12 biscuits**

In the city of Zacatecas there are some wonderful cookies, breads, and biscuits made with whole-wheat flour and topped with nuts and seeds. The biscuits here were inspired by all the sampling I've done. These golden yellow biscuits are really good while still warm from the oven, spread with sweet butter and jam or honey.

2 to 3 tablespoons hulled green pumpkin seeds
1²/₃ cups all-purpose flour
1 tablespoon sugar
2¹/₂ teaspoons baking powder
¹/₂ teaspoon salt
6 tablespoons cold unsalted butter, cut into pieces
¹/₂ cup canned unsweetened solid-pack pumpkin
¹/₄ cup cold whole milk

1. In a small dry skillet, toast the pumpkin seeds, tossing, until they start popping in the pan, 2 to 3 minutes. Transfer to a bowl and reserve.

2. Preheat the oven to 425°. In a food processor put the flour, sugar, baking powder, and salt. Pulse to combine. Add the cold butter and process to resemble crumbs.

3. Transfer to a large mixing bowl. Add the pumpkin and milk. Mix just until the ingredients come together. Using your hands, gather the dough into a ball and place on a lightly floured work surface. Knead gently 8 to 10 turns until the dough holds together.

4. Pat the dough into a ¾-inch-thick rectangle about 6 × 8 inches. Cut into 12 2-inch squares. Top the biscuits with toasted pumpkin seeds, pushing them well into the dough, or they will fall out after baking. Arrange the biscuits on a baking sheet and bake about 15 minutes or until golden brown. Serve warm or at room temperature.

Muffins with Cinnamon-Sugar Topping
Muffins con Canela y Azucar

Makes 6 small muffins

Panaderias *(bakeries) all over Mexico make these cupcake-like muffins. I often buy one on my morning walks, to enjoy with coffee. Mexicans use what is called "true" cinnamon* (canela), *also known as Ceylon cinnamon, rather than the cassia variety.* Canela *has a much softer bark, which is easier to grind and has a mellower, sweeter flavor. In the United States, you can find ground* canela *cinnamon in the Mexican section of most supermarkets.*

2 tablespoons sugar

1 teaspoon ground cinnamon (Mexican canela or Ceylon variety preferred)

1 cup all-purpose flour

1¼ teaspoons baking powder

¼ teaspoon salt

¼ cup (½ stick) unsalted butter, at room temperature

⅓ cup sugar

1 large egg

⅓ cup plus 2 teaspoons milk

½ teaspoon pure vanilla extract

1. In a small bowl, mix together the sugar and cinnamon. Preheat the oven to 375°. Butter 6 ⅓-cup muffin cups.

2. In a medium bowl, whisk together the flour, baking powder, and salt. In another bowl, with an electric mixer, beat together the butter and sugar until fluffy about 1 minute. Add the egg and beat well. On slow speed, mix in the dry ingredients alternately with the milk and vanilla until combined.

3. Spoon the batter into the muffin cups until they are about ⅔ full. (Any extra batter can be baked in a small custard cup.) Sprinkle each muffin with about ½ teaspoon of the cinnamon sugar.

4. Bake until lightly browned, 15 to 20 minutes, or until a tester inserted in the center comes out clean. Remove pan from the oven, and invert muffins on a rack. The muffins are best served warm from the oven.

Pecan Muffins
Muffins de Nuez

Makes 12 small muffins

Muffins are made in some Mexican bakeries and served in many hotel dining rooms. Although they are not a traditional part of the cuisine, they go very well with Mexican brunches and breakfasts. The pecans (pecana *in Spanish but often just referred to in Mexico as* nuez, *meaning nut), and vanilla are native to Mexico and are often used in baked goods.*

Camille Tarantino, a friend who has traveled with me to Mexico, developed this recipe from our memories of muffins at a bakery in Oaxaca. The prune purée called for in this recipe adds moistness and rich dark color to the muffins (and a side benefit is that it's a more healthful muffin with less fat and calories).

1 cup all-purpose flour

½ cup sugar

2 teaspoons baking powder

½ teaspoon baking soda

1 teaspoon ground cinnamon (Mexican canela or Ceylon variety preferred)

⅛ teaspoon ground allspice

⅛ teaspoon ground cloves

¼ teaspoon salt

½ cup pecan pieces

2 large eggs, beaten

½ cup milk

½ cup prune purée

1 teaspoon pure vanilla extract

4 tablespoons butter, melted

1. Preheat the oven to 350°. Butter 12 ⅓-cup muffin cups. In a food processor fitted with the metal blade, put all of the dry ingredients and pulse 8 to 10 times to blend. Add the pecans and process until the nuts are finely ground, 10 to 12 seconds. Transfer to a large mixing bowl. Add the remaining ingredients and stir with a wooden spoon until just mixed.

2. Spoon the batter into the muffin cups until they are about ⅔ full. Bake until browned on top and a tester inserted in the center comes out clean, 15 to 18 minutes. Invert the muffins onto a rack. Serve warm or at room temperature.

Walnut and Apple Muffins
Muffins de Nuez y Manzana

Makes 12 small unmolded muffins

I stopped in a small Mexico City bakery in the Polanco district one day, and was intrigued by a large tray of nut muffins that were made by dropping the dough on to a baking sheet instead of baking it in muffin tins. They looked like round soft bumpy cookies, even though the sign on the display said "muffin de nuez". Whatever you'd like to call them, these soft, cookie-like muffins are very good. I liked the idea, and worked out this version at home. I used walnuts, as the bakery did (although the general word nuez *for nut is used), but you can substitute pecans, if you wish.*

1⅓ cups all-purpose flour
1 teaspoon baking powder
½ teaspoon ground cinnamon (Mexican canela or Ceylon variety preferred)
¼ teaspoon ground allspice
¼ teaspoon salt
½ cup dark brown sugar
¼ cup (½ stick) unsalted butter, at room temperature
1 large egg
¼ cup applesauce or apple butter
½ teaspoon pure vanilla extract
⅔ cup chopped walnuts

1. Preheat the oven to 375°. Grease 2 baking sheets. In a medium bowl mix together the flour, baking powder, cinnamon, allspice, and salt. Set aside.

2. Put the sugar and butter in a food processor. Process until fluffy, about 10 seconds. Add the egg. Process about 15 seconds. Add the applesauce and vanilla. Process 5 seconds. Add the dry ingredients and pulse 10 to 12 times to mix well. Scrape the dough into a bowl. (The dough should be stiff enough to hold its shape, but not dry.) If too dry, add applesauce 1 to 2 teaspoons at a time. If too moist, add 1 tablespoon flour at a time and pulse again. Stir the nuts into the batter.

3. Drop by generous tablespoons onto the prepared baking sheets. Bake until brown on the bottom and lightly browned on top, 10 to 12 minutes. Cool in the pan on a rack. Store in a sealed plastic bag. The muffins can be frozen and reheated, straight from the freezer, in a microwave.

Quick Breads

Baja Fig Bread
Pan de Higo estilo Baja

Makes **1** small (**7**¹/₂- × **3**³/₄-inch) loaf

When the missions were established in Baja, Mexico and north into California, the Franciscan friars planted and cultivated fruits and vegetables. Fig trees thrived in the desert climate and figs are still grown in the region. Use dried California mission figs for this quick breakfast bread that's my own creation. The bread is also good thinly sliced and spread with cream cheese.

1 cup whole-wheat flour
¹/₂ cup all-purpose flour
¹/₂ teaspoon baking powder
¹/₂ teaspoon baking soda
¹/₂ teaspoon ground cinnamon (Mexican canela or Ceylon variety preferred)
¹/₄ teaspoon salt
1 large egg, beaten
¹/₂ cup orange juice
3 tablespoons plain yogurt or sour cream
1 tablespoon dark brown sugar
1 tablespoon canola oil or vegetable oil
2 teaspoons pure vanilla extract
³/₄ cup finely chopped California mission figs

1. Preheat oven to 350°. Grease 1 small (7½- × 3¾-inch) loaf pan and line with parchment or wax paper. In a large bowl, whisk together the whole-wheat flour, all-purpose flour, baking powder, soda, cinnamon, and salt. Make a well in the center.

2. In a medium bowl, mix together the egg, orange juice, yogurt, sugar, oil, vanilla, and figs. Pour the wet ingredients into the well of the dry ingredients and stir together just to combine. Do not over mix. (The batter will be thick.)

3. Spoon the batter into the prepared pan, and level the top. Bake in preheated oven about 35 minutes, or until a tester inserted in the center comes out clean. Turn the bread out onto a wire rack. Cool at least 30 minutes. Slice and serve.

Banana Bread
Pan de Plátano

Makes **2** (**9**- × **5**- × **3**-inch) loaves

When time allows, Mexicans prepare and enjoy leisurely breakfasts at home just as we do. Banana bread fits nicely into a modern Mexican breakfast or brunch. Do as the Mexicans do, and serve this bread with a special plate of tropical fruits (Breakfast Fruit Plate, page 509, or Pineapple Boats, page 510).

Undiluted, thawed orange juice concentrate, as called for in the recipe, has a more intense orange flavor than diluted or fresh-squeezed. Fresh-squeezed juice may be used, if you like.

2 cups all-purpose flour
1 teaspoon baking powder
1 teaspoon baking soda
¹/₄ teaspoon ground allspice
¹/₄ teaspoon salt
2 cups mashed bananas (about 3 medium bananas)
1 cup sugar
2 large eggs, beaten
¹/₂ cup (1 stick) butter, melted and slightly cooled
2 tablespoons frozen orange juice concentrate, thawed or fresh-squeezed orange juice
1 tablespoon milk
¹/₂ teaspoon pure vanilla extract
³/₄ cup chopped pecan pieces

1. Preheat oven to 350°. Grease two 9- × 5- × 3-inch loaf pans and line with waxed paper or parchment paper. In a large bowl mix flour, baking powder, baking soda, allspice, and salt. In a medium bowl mix the mashed bananas, sugar, and eggs. Add the butter and mix well. Add the banana mixture to the dry ingredients and mix very well.

2. Stir in the orange juice, milk, and vanilla. Fold in the pecans.

3. Spoon half of the batter into each loaf pan. Bake 15 minutes; then reduce the oven temperature to 325° and bake 45 more minutes, or until browned on top and a tester inserted in the center comes out clean. Cool on a rack before slicing and serving.

Carrot Quick Bread
Pan de Zanahoria

Makes 1 (7¹/₂- × 3³/₄-inch) loaf

Quick breads are becoming more common in Mexico, often served in colorful napkin-lined baskets. They are wonderful additions to a Mexican brunch. I was especially impressed by the whole-wheat baked goods in Zacatecas, a beautiful colonial city in north-central Mexico with a rich history.

Zacatecas was a thriving mining center in the eighteenth century, when gold and silver mining brought growth and prosperity to the area. This high-altitude city (at 8,100 feet), and the hilly terrain, makes exploring through the cobblestone streets a "breath-taking" experience, *but Zacatecas is well worth seeing. I love the view from La Bufa, the hill that towers over the city, or by taking a ride on the* teleferico *(cable car) that also affords a fantastic view. This is also a grain-growing region, and whole-grain bakery products are common.*

1 cup all-purpose flour

¹/₂ cup whole-wheat flour

¹/₂ cup plus 1 tablespoon sugar

2¹/₂ teaspoons baking powder

¹/₂ teaspoon ground cinnamon (Mexican canela or Ceylon variety preferred)

¹/₄ teaspoon salt

1 large egg

¹/₂ cup whole milk

2 tablespoons vegetable oil

1 teaspoon pure vanilla extract

¹/₂ cup peeled and finely shredded carrots

1. Preheat oven to 350°. Grease a 7½- × 3¾-inch loaf pan and line with waxed paper or parchment paper. In a large bowl, whisk together the flours, sugar, baking powder, cinnamon, and salt. Make a well in the center. In a small bowl mix the egg with the milk, oil, and vanilla. Pour the wet ingredients into the well of the dry ingredients and add the carrots. Stir just to combine. Do not over mix. (The batter will be thick.)

2. Spoon into prepared loaf pan and bake 40 to 45 minutes, or until a tester inserted in the center comes out clean. Cool on a rack about 5 minutes before removing from the pan. Serve warm or at room temperature.

Pumpkin Bread with Sunflower Seeds

Pan de Calabaza con Pepitas

Makes 1 (8¹/2- × 4¹/2-inch) loaf

Add a sweet pumpkin loaf with crunchy sunflower seeds to a late Mexican breakfast or brunch. I came up with this recipe after being inspired by creative Mexican uses of the native ingredients of pumpkin, sunflower seeds, and vanilla.

2 cups all-purpose flour

1 cup sugar

1 teaspoon baking soda

1 teaspoon ground cinnamon (Mexican canela or Ceylon variety preferred)

¹/2 teaspoon ground allspice

¹/4 teaspoon ground nutmeg

2 large eggs, lightly beaten

1 cup canned pumpkin purée

¹/2 cup vegetable oil

¹/2 teaspoon pure vanilla extract

³/4 cup dry-roasted sunflower seeds

1. Preheat oven to 350°. Grease an 8½- × 4½-inch loaf pan and line with parchment or wax paper. In a large bowl, whisk together the flour, sugar, soda, cinnamon, allspice, and nutmeg. Make a well in the center. In a small bowl, mix the eggs, pumpkin, oil and vanilla. Add the pumpkin mixture to the well in the dry ingredients and stir until combined. The batter will be thick. Stir in the sunflower seeds.

2. Spoon the batter into the prepared pan and bake in the oven 50 to 60 minutes, or until a tester inserted into the center comes out clean. Turn the bread out onto a rack to cool. Slice to serve. The bread may be frozen in a sealed plastic freezer bag up to 3 months.

Whole-Wheat Breakfast Bread

Desayuno Pan Integral

Makes 1 small loaf (7¹/2- × 3³/4-inch pan)

Rancho La Puerta is a world-class spa located in Tecate, Mexico, just 40 miles from San Diego, California. The food is top class, too. This bread is an adaptation of a hearty, healthy loaf that's often served with fruit and yogurt at breakfast. I prefer mine with apricot or raspberry jam.

1¹/4 cups whole-wheat flour

¹/4 cup all-purpose flour

1¹/2 teaspoons ground cinnamon (Mexican canela or Ceylon variety preferred)

¹/2 teaspoon baking powder

¹/2 teaspoon baking soda

¹/4 teaspoon salt

1 large egg, lightly beaten

¹/2 cup pineapple or apple juice

2 tablespoons sour cream or yogurt

2 tablespoons dark brown sugar

2 tablespoons canola oil or vegetable oil

2 teaspoons pure vanilla extract

1. Preheat the oven to 350°. Spray 1 small loaf pan (3¾- × 7½-inch) with vegetable oil spray. In a large bowl, whisk together the flours and the cinnamon, baking powder, baking soda, and salt. Make a well in the center.

2. In a medium bowl, mix together the egg, pineapple juice, sour cream, sugar, oil, and vanilla. Add the wet ingredients to the well in the dry ingredients and fold together just to combine. Do not over mix. (The batter will be very thick.)

3. Spoon the batter into the prepared pan, level the top, and bake about 35 minutes, or until a tester inserted in the center comes out clean. Turn the bread out onto a wire rack. Cool at least 30 minutes. Slice and serve.

Mango-Pecan Quick Bread
Pan de Mango y Pacanas

Makes **1 (9- × 5-inch) loaf**

Mangos are abundant in Mexico and enjoyed in many ways. Quick breads are great for breakfast or for a treat with coffee, tea, or hot chocolate.

³/₄ **cup pecan pieces**

³/₄ **cup sugar**

1¹/₄ **cups all-purpose flour**

1¹/₂ **teaspoons baking powder**

¹/₄ **teaspoon baking soda**

1 **teaspoon ground cinnamon (Mexican canela or Ceylon variety preferred)**

¹/₂ **teaspoon salt**

¹/₄ **cup vegetable oil**

¹/₄ **cup milk**

1 **large egg**

1 **teaspoon pure vanilla extract**

1 **(1-pound) ripe mango, peeled and cut into ¹/₂-inch cubes**

1. Preheat oven to 350°. Grease a 9- × 5-inch loaf pan. Line the bottom with parchment or wax paper.

2. In a food processor fitted with the steel blade, process the pecans and sugar until the nuts are finely ground. Add the flour, baking powder, soda, cinnamon, and salt. Process until combined. In a bowl mix together the oil, milk, egg, and vanilla. Pour through the feed tube and pulse 5 to 6 times to combine.

3. Remove the batter to a large bowl and fold in the mango. Turn the batter into the prepared pan, smooth the top, and bake or until a tester inserted in the center comes out clean, 45 to 50 minutes. Cool the bread in the pan on a rack 10 minutes. Remove from the pan and cool completely before cutting. The bread is best after it sits for 6 to 8 hours.

Mexican-American Corn Bread
Pan de Elote Americana

Makes **6 servings**

American-style corn bread with a Mexican touch goes well with many Mexican foods, like Ranch Beans with Bacon (page 463), Pork and Green Chiles (page 358), or Beef, Vegetable, and Red Chile Stew (page 344). Here's a simple version to try.

1 **cup yellow cornmeal**

1¹/₂ **teaspoons baking powder**

¹/₄ **teaspoon baking soda**

¹/₄ **teaspoon salt**

1 **(8¹/₂-ounce) can creamed corn**

1 **(4-ounce) can chopped green chiles**

2 **large eggs, lightly beaten**

¹/₄ **cup milk**

¹/₄ **cup vegetable oil**

1¹/₂ **cups shredded cheddar cheese**

1. Preheat oven to 350°. Grease a square 8-inch baking pan. Line the bottom with parchment or waxed paper. In a large bowl mix the cornmeal, baking powder, soda, and salt. Add the corn, chopped chiles, eggs, milk, oil, and 1 cup of the cheese. Stir to mix well.

2. Transfer the batter to the prepared baking pan. Sprinkle the remaining ½ cup of cheese on top. Bake 30 minutes, or until the corn bread is golden brown on top and a tester inserted in the center comes out clean. Cut in squares. Serve hot or at room temperature.

Whole-Wheat Breakfast Cookies
Galletas Integral

Makes about 22 to 24 (3-inch) cookies

Zacatecas, capital of the state of the same name, is a beautiful colonial city in north-central Mexico. On one visit, I found a wonderful bakery filled with appealing breads and cookies, many of which were made with whole-wheat flour. Large, round cookies, much like these, topped with sunflower seeds, pecans, or sesame seeds, were great for breakfast or to munch on with late morning or afternoon tea or coffee. Traditionally, the seeds and nuts are pressed into the dough in a decorative pattern.

1 cup dark brown sugar

1/2 cup (1 stick) unsalted butter, at room temperature

2 large eggs, in separate bowls

1/4 cup milk

1 teaspoon pure vanilla extract

1 1/4 cups whole-wheat flour

1 1/4 cups all-purpose flour

2 teaspoons baking powder

1/4 teaspoon salt

1/2 cup hulled green pumpkin seeds, dry-roasted salted sunflower seeds, chopped pecans, or sesame seeds (or a combination)

1. Preheat the oven to 375°. Put the sugar and butter in a food processor and process until fluffy, about 10 seconds. Add 1 of the eggs. Process about 30 seconds. Add the milk and vanilla. Process about 10 seconds. In a large bowl mix together the whole-wheat flour, all-purpose flour, baking powder, and salt. Add to the processor and pulse about 10 times to mix well. Transfer the batter to the same large bowl.

2. With your hands, form about 2 tablespoons of dough into 3-inch circular disks about 1/2-inch thick. Put on a greased cookie sheet. Put about 1 teaspoon of the seeds or pecans, separately, on each cookie. Press lightly with your fingers to push the seeds or nuts into the dough.

3. In a small bowl, beat the remaining egg with a fork until well blended. Brush a little beaten egg on top of each cookie to glaze the cookies. Bake until golden brown and cooked through, about 10 to 12 minutes. Cool on a rack. Serve warm or at room temperature. Store the cookies at room temperature in a sealed plastic bag for 3 to 4 days.

Yeast Breads

Oval Mexican Sandwich Rolls
Bolillos

Makes **12 rolls**

The art of yeast baking was introduced to Mexico by the Spanish in the 1500s, and the French brought other baked goods later, during the reign of Emperor Maximilian in the 1860s. The oval rolls called bolillos *are by far the best known and most consumed daily yeast breads in Mexico. The rolls are baked twice daily in most* panaderías *(bakeries) all over the country to ensure freshness.*

Bolillos are eaten in a variety of ways, any time of the day. At breakfast, they are eaten with butter, jam, and honey, or split, covered with beans and cheese and toasted. They are used for an enormous variety of sandwiches (tortas), *and also eaten with soups, stews, and entrées for midday meals* (comida), *or supper* (cena). *Mexican Bread Pudding (page 565) is also made with* bolillos.

This recipe comes from Evie Lieb, an expert bread baker and instructor in Sacramento, California. Evie adapted her recipes to use a food processor because it makes working the dough easier. (You can also use a standing mixer with a dough blade.) Another efficient step is using quick-rising granulated yeast. If you measure the temperature of the warm liquid with an instant-read food thermometer before adding the yeast to it, you can ensure that the yeast will rise.

Although at home you can't precisely duplicate the chewy, crusty bread produced in Mexico's brick-lined steam ovens, you can create a steam effect in the oven by placing a pan of boiling water on the bottom shelf of the oven, resulting in a more chewy, textured bread.

4 cups bread flour

2 teaspoons quick-rising active dry yeast

4 teaspoons sugar

2 teaspoons salt

1 tablespoon canola oil or vegetable oil

1⅓ cups water plus 2 cups

¼ cup cornmeal

1. Grease 2 insulated baking sheets. Place flour, yeast, sugar, and salt in bowl of food processor fitted with the plastic dough blade, and process briefly to combine. In a glass measuring cup in the microwave, or in a small saucepan on the stove, heat the ⅓ cup water with the oil to 125° on an instant-read thermometer. With the machine running, add the liquid to the dry ingredients, pouring only as fast as it can be absorbed. Process 40 seconds, or until a homogeneous dough forms. If the dough is too dry, add water a little at a time, or if the dough is too sticky, add flour a little at a time.

2. Remove dough to a work surface and knead by hand until it becomes more elastic, about 1 minute. Cover the dough with plastic wrap and let rest 20 minutes.

3. Cut dough into 12 pieces and flatten each portion into a 4-inch circle. Then fold the top edge toward you, covering ⅔ of the circle. Press firmly to seal. Then fold lower half over, envelope style, and pinch the seam along its length to seal tightly. Form into a football shape, tapering the ends.

4. For each roll, dip the seam side in the cornmeal and place seam side down on the baking sheets. Cover lightly and let rise until doubled, 45 minutes to 1 hour, or until an impression remains in the dough when lightly pressed with your finger.

5. Meanwhile, preheat oven to 450° and set oven racks on the two lowest positions. Place a shallow heavy baking pan on the lower shelf. On the stove, boil the 2 cups of water and keep hot for later use. (You may not need all of it.)

6. When the rolls are ready, cut a 1-inch-deep, lengthwise slash in the top of each roll with a sharp, thin-bladed knife. Open the oven and pour about ¼ cup of the hot water into the hot pan in the oven (being careful of the resulting steam). Place the pans of rolls on the upper shelf. (Bake in batches, if necessary.) Lower heat to 400°. After 3 minutes, pour another ¼ cup hot water into the oven pan.

7. Bake 13 to 15 more minutes, or until the rolls are pale golden and sound hollow when tapped. Remove rolls to a rack to cool. Rolls are best the day they are baked, or they may be frozen in a sealed plastic freezer bag up to 3 months.

Quick Mexican Sandwich Rolls
Bolillos Rapido

Makes **12 rolls**

Use this really easy and fast way that I developed to make Mexican-style rolls called bolillos. *(You can also use a mixer with a dough blade.) The rolls are excellent for making Mexican sandwiches* (tortas).

1 package quick-rising active dry yeast

1¼ cup lukewarm water

1 tablespoon vegetable oil or olive oil

2 teaspoons sugar

3¼ cups all-purpose flour

1 teaspoon salt

¼ cup cornmeal (optional)

1. Grease 2 baking sheets. In a small bowl stir the yeast into ¼ cup of the lukewarm water. Stir in 1 teaspoon of the sugar. Let stand until foamy, about 5 minutes.

2. Put the flour, salt, and remaining teaspoon of sugar in a food processor fitted with the steel

blade. Pulse 4 to 5 times to blend. Pour in the yeast mixture. With the lid on and the processor running, add the oil to the remaining cup of warm water and pour through the feed tube. Process until dough forms and cleans the side of the bowl, with a few pieces whirling around the bottom. Process for 1 minute. (Dough should be soft and slightly sticky.) If too sticky, add flour, 1 tablespoon at a time, to achieve a soft, less-tacky dough.

3. Cut dough into 12 pieces and flatten each portion into a 4-inch circle. Then fold the top edge toward you, covering ⅔ of the circle. Press firmly to seal. Then fold lower half over, envelope style, and pinch the seam along its length to seal tightly. Form into a football shape, tapering the ends.

4. For each roll, dip the seam side in the cornmeal and place seam side down on the baking sheets. Cover lightly and let rise until doubled, 45 minutes to 1 hour, or until an impression remains in the dough when lightly pressed with your finger.

5. Preheat oven to 375°. With a sharp, thin-bladed knife, make a lengthwise cut about ½ inch deep on top of each roll. Bake rolls (in batches, if necessary) until they are lightly browned and sound hollow when tapped, 20 to 25 minutes. Cool on a rack. The rolls are best the day they are baked, or they may be frozen in a sealed plastic freezer bag up to 3 months.

Flat Mexican Sandwich Rolls
Teleras

Makes **8 sandwich rolls**

Teleras are flat, rectangular rolls that are common in central Mexico to use for tortas *(sandwiches). At the Libertad Market in Guadalajara, vendors entice passerby with huge trays of freshly prepared* tortas, *made with* teleras, *ready to be purchased and eaten on the go. The* tortas *contained an assortment of layered fillings, such* as refried beans, shredded chicken, pork, or beef, tomatoes, avocados, and lettuce, and salsa, mayonnaise, and pickled chiles. The teleras are made with the same dough as bolillos, except the rolls are shaped differently.

Quick Mexican Sandwich Rolls, preceding recipe (page 522)

1. Make the Quick Mexican-Style Rolls dough and divide the dough into 8 equal pieces.

2. Cover and let the dough rest 10 minutes to relax the gluten. With hands, form each piece into a 3- × 4 ½-inch rectangle. Arrange 2 inches apart on a large baking sheet. Cover and let rise in a warm, draft-free place until doubled in size, about 45 minutes.

3. Preheat oven to 375°. Using the rounded handle of a long wooden spoon, firmly press 2 indentations lengthwise in each roll. (Finished rolls will have 3 rounded humps across the top.) Bake until pale brown and sound hollow when tapped, about 20 to 25 minutes. Cool completely on a rack before using. Best the day they are baked, or rolls may be frozen in a sealed plastic bag up to 3 months.

Whole-Wheat Rolls
Bolillos Integral

Makes **8 rolls**

When visiting Zacatecas, a colonial city, my husband and I tried some whole-wheat Mexican-style rolls from a local bakery. The rolls had a crisp crust, a soft but chewy center and a nutty flavor. I developed this from that great memory (and some notes). This is very easy and quick to make, and the dough requires no kneading. I often make them for Mexican tortas *(sandwiches).*

1¹/₂ cups warm water (about 120°)
2 packages quick-rising active dry yeast
1 teaspoon salt
1 tablespoon sugar
2 cups whole-wheat flour
1¹/₂ cups all-purpose flour

1. In a large mixing bowl, put ½ cup of the warm water. Stir in the yeast and let stand 5 minutes. Add the remaining 1 cup of water, salt, sugar, and the whole-wheat flour. Beat the dough vigorously by hand about 2 minutes. Add the all-purpose flour and mix well. The dough will be thick and sticky, so grease your hands, then form it into a ball. Place the dough in a large greased bowl. Cover with plastic wrap and let the dough rise until doubled in size, and a dent remains when poked gently with a finger, about 45 minutes.

2. Preheat the oven to 400°. Grease an insulated baking sheet. Flour your hands and punch down the dough. Transfer the dough to a lightly floured work surface and roll it into a fat rope. Cut the dough into 8 equal pieces. Form each piece into an oval shaped roll and taper the two ends.

3. Place rolls on the baking sheet and let rise 20 minutes. Cut a lengthwise slit in the top of each roll with a sharp, thin-bladed knife and place the baking sheet of rolls in the oven. Bake 20 to 25 minutes, or until lightly browned on top. Transfer to a rack. Brush very lightly with oil. Cool. The rolls are best the day they are made or they may be frozen in a sealed plastic freezer bag up to 3 weeks.

Pan Tip for Baking Bread

When making rolls and bread, it's best to use an insulated baking sheet to prevent the bread from browning too much. If you don't have an insulated sheet, use 2 lightweight baking sheets stacked together.

Three Kings Bread
Rosca de los Reyes

Makes 2 small rings

Three Kings Bread is served on Epiphany, on January 6, the religious holiday in the Christian faith that honors when the birth of the infant Jesus was said to have been revealed to the three kings and the world. The bread is shaped like a wreath with a tiny china doll, symbolizing the infant Christ, baked inside. The wreaths are filled with candied fruits and nuts and glazed with icing. The person who gets the doll in his or her portion of sweet bread is traditionally designated to give a party on February 2, the religious holiday, Candelaria, *or* Candlemas Day.

Evie Lieb, a breadmaker and bread-baking teacher in Sacramento developed this delicious sweet bread recipe, and often uses a plastic doll if a china doll is not available. Cut a small plug from each baked ring, insert a little plastic doll and replace the cutout plug. Do this before the bread is glazed, and no one will be the wiser. Have handy an ovenproof glass bowl or a can to place in the center of the ring while it bakes, to prevent the dough from spreading and closing the center hole. (The dough can also be made with a standing mixer.)

Dough

4¹/₂ cups bread flour

2 teaspoons quick-rising active dry yeast

6 tablespoons sugar

1¹/₂ teaspoons unsalted salt

Grated zest of 1 lemon

2 teaspoons grated orange zest

1 cup milk

6 tablespoons butter

2 large eggs, beaten

Filling

8 candied cherries, cut into eighths

4 tablespoons chopped toasted walnuts

4 tablespoons dark raisins

8 wedges or rings of dried pineapple, cut into small pieces

1 large egg, beaten

Icing

3 tablespoons half and half or whole milk

2 cups sifted confectioners' sugar

¹/₂ teaspoon pure vanilla extract

Candied fruit, for decoration

2 tiny dolls, china or plastic (optional)

1. Make the dough: Place the flour, yeast, sugar, salt, and grated zest in a food processor fitted with a plastic dough blade. Pulse to combine.

2. In a glass measuring cup in a microwave, or in a small pan on the stove, heat the milk and butter to 120° to 125°. (The butter does not have to be completely melted). With processor running, add the liquid to the dry ingredients, pouring through the feed tube only as fast as it can be absorbed. Add the 2 beaten eggs in the same way. When incorporated, process about 40 seconds, or until the dough is homogeneous. Remove dough from the bowl and knead by hand 1 minute.

3. Place dough in a greased plastic bag large enough to accommodate the dough when it doubles, or in a greased bowl. Squeeze out the air and seal, leaving room for the dough to rise (or cover bowl with plastic wrap). Let rise until doubled in size and a dent remains when poked gently with a finger, about 45 minutes. Dough can be refrigerated for up to 24 hours at this point. (If refrigerated, allow the dough to come to room temperature before proceeding.)

4. Line an insulated baking sheet with parchment paper. Divide dough in half. Roll out one portion to a 6- × 15-inch rectangle. Over the rectangle, scatter half of the cherries, walnuts, raisins, and pineapple, leaving a 1-inch border along one long side. Put a piece of waxed paper over the surface of the rectangle and with a rolling pin press the filling into the dough.

5. Roll up tightly from the filled long side to the unfilled 1-inch border. Pinch tightly all along the seam to seal, and bring the ends together to form a ring. Pinch the edges to seal together. Repeat process for the second piece of dough.

6. Place the rings on the baking sheet. To keep the ring shape while baking, place in the middle of each ring a small, ovenproof glass bowl, or empty can, greased on the outside to prevent it from sticking to the dough. Cover the rings with plastic and let rise until double, about 45 minutes to 1 hour.

7. Preheat oven to 375°. When doubled, glaze the rings with beaten egg and bake 22 to 25 minutes, or until they sound hollow when tapped (or the internal temperature reads 200° on an instant-read thermometer.) Remove the can or bowl from the centers. If wreaths brown too fast before they are done, cover with foil, and continue baking. Cool completely on a rack before glazing.

8. Whisk together the icing ingredients, and when the ring has cooled, drizzle each ring with half of the mixture, allowing it to run down the sides. Before the icing dries, decorate the tops with candied fruits. The bread keeps about 2 days, or can be frozen in sealed plastic freezer bags up to 3 months. Return to room temperature before eating.

Bread of the Dead
Pan de los Muertos

Makes 1 large round loaf

Day of the Dead (Dia de los Muertos) *is commemorated all over Mexico each year with special traditions and foods. It is celebrated on November 2 and is the time when Mexicans honor the spirits of deceased relatives and friends.*

Preparations for the event begin weeks before, including making an altar to welcome the dead, and preparing special decorations, candies, and foods. This delicious bread is one of the important traditions. The top is decorated with "bones" formed from the bread dough, and often sprinkled with cinnamon-sugar or colored sugar crystals. Evie Lieb, an accomplished baker from Sacramento, shared this recipe, which simplifies the process by using a food processor to make the dough. (A standing mixer with a dough blade can also be used.)

3$^{1}/_{3}$ cups all-purpose flour
1 package quick-rising active dry yeast
1$^{1}/_{2}$ teaspoons anise seeds
1$^{1}/_{8}$ teaspoons salt
$^{1}/_{3}$ cup plus $^{1}/_{2}$ cup sugar
$^{1}/_{3}$ cup unsalted butter
$^{3}/_{4}$ cup milk
1 whole large egg
1 large egg yolk
1$^{1}/_{2}$ teaspoons ground cinnamon (Mexican canela or Ceylon variety preferred)
1 large egg white, beaten

1. Place the flour, yeast, anise seeds, salt, and $^{1}/_{3}$ cup of sugar in bowl of food processor fitted with the steel blade. Pulse briefly to combine ingredients. In a microwave-proof glass measuring cup, or in a small saucepan on the stove, heat the butter with the milk to 120° to 125°. (Butter does not have to be completely melted.)

2. With the processor running, add the liquid to the dry ingredients, pouring only as fast as the liquid can be absorbed. In a small bowl, beat together the whole egg and the egg yolk and add to the dough through the processor feed tube. Process 40 seconds to 1 minute. The dough should be soft and not stick to the sides of the bowl.

3. Remove the dough to a clean, dry work surface. With a scraper, gather the dough and knead briefly until smooth and elastic. Do not add flour unless the dough sticks to the work surface or your hands. Put the dough in a greased plastic bag or bowl large enough to accommodate the dough when it doubles. Seal the bag, pressing out the air but allowing room for the dough to rise (or cover the bowl with plastic wrap), 45 minutes to 1 hour.

4. Mix together the cinnamon and ½ cup sugar in a small bowl. When the dough has doubled, punch down and remove from the bag. Set aside ⅓ of the dough. Shape the remaining larger piece of dough into a ball and put it on a clean work surface. Cup hands and draw the edges under the ball, rotating the ball several times until the top is smooth. Pinch together the part underneath and press the top with your palm to flatten the ball slightly.

5. Line an insulated baking sheet with parchment paper. Shape the reserved ⅓ piece of dough into two 6-inch ropes and flatten the ends of each piece to resemble the ends of bones. Using a sharp, thin-bladed knife, cut a cross in the top of the round loaf. Brush the tops of the "bones" with the beaten egg white and dip them in the cinnamon-sugar mixture to coat evenly. Place the "bones" on the crosscut, one over the other, to form an "X" and press firmly to anchor.

6. Transfer the loaf to the baking sheet. Cover the bread lightly with a sheet of plastic wrap and let rise just until a dent remains when a finger is poked gently into the loaf, about 20 to 30 minutes.

7. Preheat oven to 350°. Brush the surface of the bread, but not the bones, with the beaten egg white. Cut small diagonal slashes with a sharp knife around the underside of the loaf to allow expansion of the dough while baking without splitting the surface.

8. Bake in the oven 30 to 40 minutes, or until it sounds hollow when tapped. If the bread browns too much during baking, cover with a piece of foil and continue baking until done. Remove bread to a rack. The bread can be stored 2 days at room temperature, wrapped in plastic, or frozen in a sealed plastic freezer bag for 3 months.

Oaxacan Bread
Pan de Yema

Makes **about 12 medium-size rolls**

In Oaxaca, two bustling city center markets are just a couple of blocks from the main zócalo (plaza). The bread stalls and fondas *(food stalls) are in the Mercado 20 de Noviembre. There are rows and rows of tables piled with rolls and breads of about any size to suit your fancy. The round egg bread* (pan de yema) *is a specialty of Oaxaca, traditionally eaten with a cup of hot chocolate into which the lightly sweetened bread is dipped. This version of the rolls can be made whatever size you wish.*

¼ cup (½ stick) unsalted butter, at room temperature

1 cup milk

½ cup sugar

1 teaspoon salt

2 packages quick-rising active dry yeast

¼ cup warm water (about 120°)

4 to 4½ cups all-purpose flour

4 large egg yolks, beaten

1 whole large egg, beaten separately from the yolks

1. In a saucepan, heat the butter, milk, sugar, and salt, stirring frequently, until the sugar dissolves and the butter melts. Cool to lukewarm (about 110°).

2. In a large bowl, dissolve the yeast in the warm water and stir in the lukewarm milk mixture. Add 2 cups of the flour and mix to a smooth batter. Stir in the beaten large egg yolks and the remaining 2 cups of flour. Add additional flour gradually until the dough holds together, but is still a bit sticky. Do not knead. Transfer to a large oiled bowl, and turn to coat with oil. Cover with a damp kitchen towel and let rise until doubled in size, about 1½ to 2 hours.

3. With floured hands, punch down dough. Place on a very lightly floured work surface and knead about 10 times, just enough to make the dough smooth and elastic. Pat into a ball. Cover and let stand 15 minutes to relax the dough.

4. Preheat the oven to 400°. Grease an insulated baking sheet or line with parchment paper. Cut the dough into 12 equal pieces, or depending on the size bread you want, cut the dough into equal pieces. Form each piece into a ball.

5. Place each ball on the baking sheet and flatten the rolls with the palm of your hand. Let the rolls rise 20 minutes. Brush the rolls with the beaten egg to glaze. Bake 12 to 15 minutes, or until it is browned and sounds hollow when tapped. Cool on a rack for about 30 minutes. Store 2 days at room temperature in a sealed plastic bag, or freeze in a sealed plastic freezer bag for up to 3 months.

Mexican Sweet Buns
Pan Dulces

Makes **18 sweet buns**

Mexican sweet rolls are made in hundreds of shapes and sizes throughout Mexico, each with its own name according to what it represents. The basic yeast dough for many of the sweet buns (pan dulces) in Mexico is the same, but variations are made by the use of more sugar, different spices, or eggs.

This recipe describes how to design three different sweet buns, a shell (concha), a crosshatch pattern (rosca), and a corn ear (elote).

Evie Lieb, an excellent baker and teacher, developed this simplified recipe and the technique for the designs. Usually, special molds are used to create the standard designs for sugar toppings, but they are not easy to find. The method here works very well, and the resulting buns are delicious served warm for breakfast or anytime.

4 cups all-purpose flour

1 package quick-rising active dry yeast

¹⁄₂ cup sugar

1¹⁄₄ teaspoons salt

¹⁄₄ cup water

¹⁄₂ cup milk

¹⁄₂ cup (1 stick) unsalted butter

2 large eggs, beaten

Topping or Filling

¹⁄₂ cup all-purpose flour

¹⁄₄ cup unsweetened cocoa powder

¹⁄₂ cup sugar

1 teaspoon ground cinnamon (Mexican canela or Ceylon variety preferred)

4 tablespoons cold butter, cut into small cubes

2 large egg yolks

1. To prepare the dough, place flour, yeast, sugar, and salt in food processor fitted with the plastic dough blade. Pulse to combine well. In a glass measuring cup in the microwave, or on a small pot on the stove, combine and heat the water, milk, and butter to 120° to 125°. (The butter doesn't have to be completely melted.)

2. With the processor running, add the heated liquid to the flour mixture, pouring only as fast as the liquid can be absorbed. Add the beaten eggs the same way. Once the eggs are incorporated, process 1 minute until a homogeneous soft dough is formed. If the dough is sticky, add 1 to 2 tablespoons of flour, or if the dough is too firm and dry, add 1 to 2 tablespoons of water. Remove the dough to a working surface and knead by hand 1 minute.

3. Place the dough in a greased plastic bag or bowl large enough to accommodate the dough when it doubles. Seal the bag, pressing out the air, but leaving space for the dough to rise (or cover the bowl with plastic wrap). Let the dough rise until doubled in size and a dent remains when a finger is gently poked into the dough, about 30 minutes, or in the refrigerator up to 24 hours.

4. Meanwhile, make the topping-filling: Clean the food processor, then place all of the topping ingredients in the processor fitted with the steel blade and pulse until the mixture resembles coarse crumbs. Reserve in a bowl.

5. When the dough has doubled, punch it down and divide into thirds. Cover and let rest 15 minutes. If refrigerated, once removed let rest until soft enough to shape.

6. Cut each third of the dough into 6 equal portions. Form each portion into a small ball and let rest 5 minutes to relax the dough. With hands or a rolling pin, flatten each ball to a 3 inch round, or ovals, if making corn ears. (See below.) Repeat until all 18 balls (or ovals) are formed.

7. Place parchment paper on 2 insulated baking sheets. Place 9 rounds of dough in staggered rows on each baking sheet.

8. To make the shell or cross-hatch design: With your hands, firmly compress 2 tablespoons of the topping mixture into a disc, then flatten to about 8 inches wide. Using a wide spatula, carefully transfer the topping disc to the surface of 1 bun and press it gently into the dough so it adheres to the top of the bun. With a sharp, thin-bladed knife, cut a decorative curved shell or crosshatch pattern through the topping to the top of the dough. Repeat with remaining dough and topping.

9. To make ears of corn shapes: Roll the dough portions into ovals about 3- × 6-inches. Place 2 tablespoons of sugar filling on top of each oval and press firmly, leaving a narrow border. Roll the ovals gently from the narrow end and place seam side down on the baking sheet as described in Step 7. With a sharp, thin-bladed knife make cuts ½ inch apart on the top of each bun perpendicular to the length and deep enough to penetrate the filling. Cover pans of rolls with plastic wrap and let rise until puffy and light, about 20 minutes.

10. Place oven racks in the lower half of the oven. Preheat the oven to 350°. Place 1 pan of buns on the rack placed on the second level from the bottom of the oven until lightly browned, about 22 minutes. Remove from the oven and cool on a rack. Place the second pan of buns on the same lower rack and bake until golden brown, about 22 minutes. Remove from the oven and cool on racks. The buns are best the day they are made or freeze them in sealed plastic freezer bags up to 3 months. The buns reheat well.

Mexican Pizza

Pizza Mexicana

Makes 2 (12-inch) pizzas

Mexicans love pizza. I first ate pizza there nearly thirty years ago, in Leon, Mexico, where I attended cooking school. I was surprised that pizza was even available. Nowadays, it is everywhere in so many variations that giving it a Mexican twist is a great blending of favorite cooking traditions.

Several years ago I made this Mexican pizza with my cooking class, and it was quite a hit. The cornmeal adds texture and crispness to the crust. The dough is made in a food processor with quick-rise yeast, so the whole process takes less than an hour. The pork topping is a favorite, but use this dough with any toppings you like. It can be made ahead, or while the pizza dough rises.

1 package quick-rising active dry yeast

¹/₂ cup warm water (about 110°)

2¹/₂ cups all-purpose flour

¹/₂ cup yellow cornmeal

1 teaspoon sugar

1 teaspoon salt

¹/₂ cup lukewarm water

2 tablespoons vegetable oil

Topping

1 pound fresh ground pork

¹/₂ cup finely chopped white onion

¹/₂ teaspoon dried oregano (Mexican variety preferred), crumbled

¹/₂ teaspoon ground cumin

1 medium tomato, peeled, seeded, and finely chopped

2 tablespoons bottled spicy red salsa

¹/₄ teaspoon salt, or to taste

2 cups lightly packed Monterey Jack cheese

6 green onions, cut in thin rounds, including the green

4 jarred pickled jalapeño chiles (en escabeche), seeded and cut into thin strips

Optional garnishes: sour cream, sliced olives, diced avocado

1. Dissolve the yeast and ¹/₂ teaspoon of the sugar in the warm water. Set aside until it bubbles, about 5 minutes. In a food processor, place flour, cornmeal, sugar, and salt. Add the yeast mixture.

2. Put the warm water and oil in a cup, and, with the processor running, pour this through the feed tube. Process 60 seconds. Dough should clean the sides of the bowl as it processes.

3. Transfer the dough to a greased bag or bowl, turning to grease the dough all over. Press down and cover with plastic wrap (or seal the bag). Let rise in a warm place until doubled in size, 25 to 30 minutes.

4. Meanwhile, prepare the pizza topping. In a medium skillet, cook the pork, breaking it into bits as it cooks. Add the onion, oregano, and cumin. Cook, stirring, 2 minutes. Add the tomato, salsa, and salt. Cook, stirring, until the mixture is nearly dry. Drain off excess grease as necessary. Cool off heat until ready to use.

5. Preheat the oven to 425°. Grease two baking sheets. Punch down the dough. Divide in half. Shape each half into a ball. Place each on a baking sheet. Using your hands, pat dough into 12-inch circles. Dough will be resilient, so keep patting it into shape, making the edges slightly thicker.

6. Spread the cooled cooked topping over each circle of dough. Then add the cheese, onions, and jalapeño chiles. Bake 15 to 20 minutes. Add optional garnishes. Serve at once.

Desserts

Flans and Puddings 560

Mexican Coffee Flan

Coconut Flan

Pumpkin Flan

Chocolate Flan

Orange Custard

Mexican Vanilla Pudding

Coconut Pudding

Coffee Pudding

Rice Pudding

Mexican Bread Pudding

Custard Bread Pudding

Sweet Potato Pudding
with Nuts

Ice Creams 568

Vanilla Ice Cream

Chocolate Ice Cream

Coffee Ice Cream

Mexican Caramel Ice Cream

Almond Ice Cream

Coconut Ice Cream

Watermelon Ice Cream

Cherimoya Ice

Fruit Desserts 572

Mangos with Strawberries

Grilled Pineapple

Broiled Pineapple

Pineapple with Mint

Bananas Victoria

Caramelized Bananas with
Mexican Eggnog Sauce

Plantains with Vanilla Sauce
and Pecans

Strawberries with
Mexican Eggnog

Strawberries and Bananas
in Walnut Sauce

Oranges and Strawberries
with Tequila

Peaches and Strawberries
with Vanilla Pudding

Peaches with Vanilla Ice Cream

Blackberry Parfaits

Plums in Orange Sauce

Fresh Figs with Cheese

Figs in Brown Sugar Syrup

Baked Apples

Poached Guavas

Guava Paste with
Cream Cheese

Sauces and Icings 581

Chocolate-Cinnamon
Dessert Sauce

Creamy Caramel Dessert Sauce

Rum Butter Sauce

Strawberry Dessert Sauce

Banana Cream Dessert Sauce

Chocolate Icing

Cream Cheese Frosting

Brown Sugar Syrup

Sweetened Whipped Cream

In pre-hispanic Mexico, sweets consisted mainly of native fruits, honey-sweetened tamales, and corn drinks. When the Spanish came to Mexico in the 16th century, bringing with them sugar, butter, eggs, cream, and wheat flour, the possibilities increased dramatically. Spanish nuns lived and worked in the convents that were part of the newly built churches and cathedrals, and they are credited with creating the first rich Mexican desserts. They brought with them European baking techniques and their own recipes from Spain, and they made the first Spanish-style puddings, custards, cakes, and pastries.

Later, when France occupied Mexico for a brief period in the 1860s, the French court introduced more rich pastries and crisp rolls and breads. Now they are part of Mexican culinary culture and Mexicans especially enjoy sweets for *marienda*— a time to relax with a late afternoon coffee, tea, or hot chocolate, and a pastry or other treat.

Recipes for traditional and contemporary cakes, puddings, cookies, ice creams, and other desserts are included in this chapter. Traditional and regional classics include Three Milks Cake from central Mexico (page 537), Sweet Corn Cake from Veracruz (page 538), and the Yucatán Heavenly Almond Cake (page 536). Other favorite sweets, like Mexican Coffee Flan (page 560), Rice Pudding (page 565), Mexican Caramel Crepes (page 557), Mexican Wedding Cookies (page 545), and Mexican Bread Pudding (page 565) are made throughout Mexico, and fresh fruit desserts, such as Mangos with Strawberries (page 572), and Plums in Orange Sauce (page 578), are eaten everywhere.

When it comes to cookies, there are many to munch on any time of day. Among them you'll find Crispy Pecan Cookies (page 544), Pumpkin Cookies (page 547), Piggy Brown Sugar Cookies (page 546), and Cinnamon-Walnut Cookies (page 543). Also among the favored sweets are exceptional ice creams (*helados*), sherbets, and refreshing ice bars (*paletas*), made from puréed sweetened fruits. There are dozens of enticing flavors, including rich and creamy chocolate, almond, coconut, and even watermelon ice cream.

Here's to satisfying your sweet tooth and to sweet endings for your Mexican meals!

Cakes

Mexican Chocolate Cake
Torta de Chocolate

Makes 1 (9-inch) round cake; 8 to 10 servings

Chocolate is one of Mexico's food gifts to the world. I used Mexican chocolate to develop this cake; I prefer Mayordomo or Guelaguetza brands from Oaxaca, which are not available in the United States, but Ibarra or Abuelita brands are widely available in our markets and they are fine for the cake. (See Mail-Order Sources for Ingredients, page 620, for Mayordomo or better yet, go to Oaxaca!)

³/₄ cup all-purpose flour

1 teaspoon baking powder

¹/₂ teaspoon baking soda

¹/₄ teaspoon salt

1 teaspoon ground cinnamon (Mexican canela or Ceylon variety preferred)

2 tablets (4 ounces) Mexican chocolate (such as Ibarra), chopped into pieces

³/₄ cup sugar

¹/₃ cup boiling water

3 large eggs

¹/₄ cup (¹/₂ stick) unsalted butter, at room temperature

¹/₃ cup sour cream

1 teaspoon pure vanilla extract

Chocolate Icing (page 582)

¹/₂ cup chopped pecans

1. Preheat oven to 350°. Grease the bottom of a 9-inch round cake pan. Line the pan with a circle of parchment or wax paper. Grease the paper and sides of the pan. In a small bowl, mix the flour, baking powder, soda, salt, and cinnamon. Set aside.

2. Put the chocolate pieces and sugar in a food processor. Process until chocolate is finely chopped. With machine on, pour the boiling water through the feed tube, processing until the chocolate is melted. Add the eggs. Process 20 seconds. Scrape down the sides of the bowl. Add the butter, sour cream, and vanilla. Process 20 seconds. Add the reserved flour mixture and pulse 6 to 8 times, or just until mixed. Turn the batter into prepared cake pan.

3. Bake 30 to 35 minutes, or until a cake tester inserted in the center comes out clean.

4. Meanwhile, prepare the icing. When the cake is done, let it cool in the pan on a rack 5 minutes. Invert the cake to unmold, remove the paper, and cool on the rack. When the cake is completely cool, frost with the icing. Decorate with chopped nuts. Store cake, well covered at room temperature for 3 days, or freeze for about 1 month.

Chocolate and Almond Cake
Pastel de Chocolate y Almendra

Makes 1 (8-inch) round cake; 8 to 10 servings

Chocolate desserts are not very common in Mexico, but many fine restaurants offer chocolate cakes. San Angel Inn restaurant in Mexico City makes a cake similar to this recipe. This cake doesn't require Mexican chocolate, which comes prepared with cinnamon and sugar already added. You can serve this cake plain as a snack cake, or make it more festive by including a dollop of whipped cream, a drizzle of chocolate-cinnamon sauce, and a few berries for garnish.

6 ounces sliced almonds (about 1²/₃ cups), toasted

4¹/₂ ounces semisweet chocolate, chopped

1 teaspoon ground cinnamon (Mexican canela
       or Ceylon variety preferred)

¹/₄ teaspoon salt

5 large eggs, separated

¹/₂ teaspoon pure vanilla extract

6 tablespoons sugar

Chocolate-Cinnamon Dessert Sauce (optional)
       (page 581)

Sweetened Whipped Cream (optional) (page 583)

Fresh berries (optional)

1. Preheat the oven to 350°. Grease the bottom of an 8-inch round cake pan. Line the pan with a circle of parchment or wax paper. Grease the paper and sides of the pan. Put the almonds in a large nonstick skillet and toast, stirring frequently, until aromatic and barely colored, 3 to 4 minutes. Transfer to a plate and let cool.

2. Put the cooled nuts, chocolate, cinnamon, and salt in a food processor and finely grind. Reserve. In a medium bowl, blend the egg yolks, vanilla, and 3 tablespoons of the sugar with an electric beater or mixer until pale and thickened, about 3 minutes. With a wooden spoon, mix in the reserved nut mixture.

3. In a clean large bowl with clean beaters, beat the egg whites to soft peaks. Add the remaining 3 tablespoons of sugar and beat until stiff. Mix about ¹/₃ of the beaten whites into the reserved nut mixture to lighten, and then gently fold in the remaining whites.

4. Transfer the batter to the prepared baking pan and bake 35 minutes, or until a skewer inserted in the center comes out clean.

5. If using the sauce, make it while the cake is baking. When the cake is done, let it cool in the pan on a rack for about 10 minutes.

6. Meanwhile, prepare the whipped cream if using. Turn out the cake and remove the paper. Invert onto a plate. You can decorate the cake while whole with the cream, sauce, and berries, or cut the cake into wedges and top each piece just before serving.

Chocolate-Banana Cake
Pastel de Chocolate y Plátano

Makes 1 (8-× 11-inch) cake; about 12 to 16 servings

Guests of all ages and generations go for this sumptuous cake. It's a modern take on dessert with New World ingredients—chocolate, vanilla, and pecans—and certainly an appropriate finish for a Mexican meal. Serve with ice cream or whipped cream.

2 cups sifted cake flour

2 tablespoons unsweetened cocoa powder

1 teaspoon baking soda

1 teaspoon ground cinnamon (Mexican canela
       or Ceylon variety preferred)

¹/₂ teaspoon salt

2 small ripe bananas

³/₄ cup whole milk

²/₃ cup packed dark brown sugar

¹/₄ cup dark corn syrup

3 tablespoons vegetable oil

1 tablespoon pure vanilla extract

³/₄ cup chopped pecans

1. Preheat the oven to 400°. Grease an 8- × 11-inch glass baking dish. In a large bowl, whisk together flour, cocoa, baking soda, cinnamon, and salt. Set aside.

2. In a medium bowl, mash the bananas. Add the milk, sugar, corn syrup, oil, and vanilla. Mix very well. Add the banana mixture to the dry ingredients and stir gently with a rubber spatula until the dry ingredients are moistened. Do not overmix.

3. Turn the batter into the prepared baking dish. Sprinkle the nuts evenly over the top. Bake 18 to 20 minutes or until a cake tester inserted in the center comes out clean. Let the cake cool completely in the pan on a rack about 30 minutes. Cut into squares and serve.

Mexican Pecan-Honey Cake
Torta de Miel y Pacanas

Makes 1 (9-inch) round cake; 8 to 10 servings

This delicious honey-soaked cake contains native nuts and honey, both of which are used extensively in Mexican sweets. Serve the cake alone or with sliced mango, bananas, or other tropical fruits.

1/2 cup pecans

1 cup all-purpose flour

1 1/2 teaspoons baking powder

1/2 teaspoon ground cinnamon (Mexican canela or Ceylon variety preferred)

1/4 teaspoon ground allspice

1/4 teaspoon salt

1/2 cup (1 stick) unsalted butter, at room temperature

3/4 cup sugar

3 large eggs

1/2 cup milk

Honey Syrup

1/4 cup sugar

1/3 cup water

1/2 cup dark honey

2 teaspoons fresh lemon juice

1. Preheat oven to 350°. Grease the bottom of a 9-inch round cake pan. Line bottom with a circle of parchment or waxed paper. Grease the bottom and sides of the pan. Put pecans in the food processor and with brief pulses process until finely ground.

2. Transfer the nuts to a medium bowl and thoroughly mix with the flour, baking powder, cinnamon, allspice, and salt. Reserve.

3. Wipe out the food processor with a paper towel. Process the butter and sugar until light and fluffy, about 15 seconds. Scrape down sides of bowl. Add eggs and process about 10 seconds. Add milk and process about 5 seconds. Scrape down the sides of the bowl. Add the reserved flour and nut mixture. Pulse 10 to 12 times, or until blended to a smooth batter. Do not overmix.

4. Transfer the batter to the prepared cake pan. Bake 30 to 35 minutes, or until tester inserted in the center of the cake comes out clean.

5. Meanwhile, prepare the syrup. In a small saucepan, boil sugar and water about 1 minute. Stir in honey and lemon juice. Reserve.

6. When cake is done, cool cake in the pan on a rack 5 minutes. Then invert onto the rack. Remove liner. Invert cake again right-side up onto a plate and spoon syrup gradually over the warm cake. (The syrup will be absorbed into the cake.) Allow to sit about 30 minutes before serving to allow absorption; serve at room temperature. Store, covered, at room temperature for 4 to 5 days.

Yucatán Heavenly Almond Cake
Torta de Cielo

Makes 1 (9-inch) round cake; 8 servings

Finely ground almonds add a rich texture to this traditional Yucatán cake, served for weddings, birthdays, fiestas, and other "uplifting" occasions. Beaten egg whites folded into the cake add cloud-like airyness too. Served with whipped cream and puréed fruit sauces or fresh berries.

6 ounces blanched whole almonds

1 cup sugar

1/2 cup all-purpose flour

1/2 teaspoon baking powder

1/2 teaspoon salt

6 large eggs, separated

2 tablespoons dark rum

1 teaspoon pure vanilla extract

Sifted confectioners' sugar

1. Preheat oven to 350°. Grease the bottom of a 9-inch springform pan. Line the bottom with a circle of parchment or wax paper. Grease the paper and the sides of the pan. Dust with flour and tap out excess. In a food processor, grind the almonds with the sugar to a fine, mealy consistency. Add the flour, baking powder, and 1/4 teaspoon of the salt. Pulse 6 to 8 times to mix.

2. With an electric mixer beat the egg whites until foamy. Add the remaining 1/4 teaspoon of salt and continue beating to stiff peaks. Beat in the egg yolks, 1 at a time on low speed, until the yolks are incorporated. Fold in the reserved almond mixture. Gently stir in the rum and vanilla.

3. Pour the batter into the prepared pan. Bake 25 to 30 minutes, or until golden brown and a tester inserted in the center of the cake comes out clean. Cool the cake in the pan on a rack about 5 minutes. (The cake will sink a little as it cools.)

Remove the ring from the pan and remove the paper from the bottom. Transfer the cake to a serving plate. Shortly before serving, dust the cake lightly with confectioners' sugar. Cut into wedges and serve.

"Drunken" Cake
Torta Borracha

Makes 1 (9-inch) round cake; 8 to 10 servings

Because this cake is so liberally doused with rum, calling it "drunken" seems quite appropriate, but this is no ordinary rum cake. Your family and friends will love it! The sweet rum syrup soaks in for a wonderfully moist cake. Serve it with fresh berries and whipped cream.

6 large eggs, separated

1 1/2 cups all-purpose flour

1 teaspoon baking powder

1/4 teaspoon salt

3/4 cup sugar

1/2 cup (1 stick) unsalted butter, melted

1 teaspoon pure vanilla extract

Rum Syrup

1 1/2 cups sugar

1 cup water

1/2 cup dark rum

1. Preheat oven to 350°. Grease and flour a 9-inch round cake pan. Put the egg whites in a large mixing bowl. Put the egg yolks in a small bowl. In a separate medium bowl mix the flour, baking powder, and salt.

2. With an electric beater or mixer, beat the egg whites until foamy and white. Add 1/4 cup of the sugar. And beat until shiny and soft peaks form. With the same beater, in a separate bowl beat the yolks with the remaining sugar until thick, pale yellow, and fluffy. Add the yolks to the beaten whites, and using low speed, blend 5 seconds.

3. With a rubber spatula, in 3 additions, fold the flour mixture carefully into the egg mixture. Drizzle the melted butter and vanilla over the batter, and stir gently to blend ingredients into a smooth batter.

4. Pour the batter into the prepared cake pan. Bake 25 to 30 minutes, or until the cake is golden brown on top, and a tester inserted in the center of the cake comes out clean.

5. When done, remove the cake from the oven, and let stand in the pan on a rack 5 minutes. (Don't cool cake.) Meanwhile, prepare the rum syrup. In a medium pan, stir together the sugar and water. Bring to a boil, stirring, to dissolve the sugar; then reduce heat to low and simmer 2 minutes. Remove from the heat, and stir in the rum.

6. Gradually spoon the hot rum syrup over the hot cake until it is all absorbed. Cool at least 1 hour before serving. Cut the cake in wedges while in the pan and serve at room temperature or cold. Store the cake, well covered, in the refrigerator up to 3 days.

Three Milks Cake
Pastel de Tres Leches

Makes 1 (9- × 13-inch) cake; 12 servings

Everyone who tries this cake nearly swoons in ecstasy! This recipe comes from Martha Lopez, from Guadalajara, the mother of my friend Fernando Elizalde, of Café Terra Cotta in Tucson, Arizona. Mexican women often serve this cake with coffee when they invite friends for marienda *(refreshment break) in the afternoon. The cake is a classic, and is made in many regions. Señora Lopez tops her cake with meringue frosting, but I serve the cake with sweetened whipped cream and seasonal fresh berries, mango, or peaches. Mexican cooks often add a bit of rum, sherry, or cognac to the cake, if they happen to have it.*

2 cups all-purpose flour

3 teaspoons baking powder

6 large eggs, separated, at room temperature

1¹/₂ cups sugar

2 teaspoons pure vanilla extract

¹/₂ cup whole milk, at room temperature

Three Milks Sauce

1 (12-ounce) can evaporated milk

1 (14-ounce) can sweetened condensed milk

¹/₂ cup half and half

2 tablespoons rum, sherry, or cognac (optional)

1 cup Sweetened Whipped Cream (page 583), (optional)

Ground cinnamon (optional)

1. Preheat oven to 325°. Grease a 9- × 13-inch glass baking dish. In a medium bowl, mix the flour and baking powder. In a large bowl, with an electric beater or mixer, beat the egg whites until stiff. Continue beating and gradually add the sugar until the sugar dissolves and the whites are thick and shiny.

2. Gradually beat in the yolks and vanilla. Beat on low speed 3 minutes. Beat in the flour mixture alternately with the milk until the batter is smooth.

3. Turn the batter into the prepared pan. Bake in preheated oven 40 to 45 minutes, or until a tester inserted in the center of the cake comes out clean.

4. Remove the cake from the oven and cool in the pan on a rack to lukewarm, about 20 minutes. Meanwhile, make the sauce. In a deep bowl, thoroughly whisk all of the ingredients together.

5. When the cake is cooled a bit, prick the top of the cake all over with a skewer and gradually spoon the sauce over the cake and leave it to soak 30 to 40 minutes. Refrigerate at least 2 hours and up to overnight. Just before serving prepare whipped cream, if using. Cut the cake in squares and serve cold, topped with sweetened whipped cream, if using. Dust lightly with cinnamon, if desired. The cake keeps refrigerated for up to 3 days.

Mexican Pound Cake
Marquesote

Makes **2 small loaves**

Mexican bakeries nearly always have freshly baked loaves of a simple pound cake to take home and serve with fresh fruits and sauces or ice cream. I bake the cake in two small loaf pans, so I can use one right away and freeze the other for later use. To make one loaf, use a 9- × 5-inch loaf pan.

³/₄ cup (1¹/₂ sticks) unsalted butter
³/₄ cup sugar
3 large eggs
1 teaspoon pure vanilla extract
1¹/₄ cups all-purpose flour
1 teaspoon baking powder
¹/₄ teaspoon salt

1. Preheat the oven to 350°. Grease and flour 2 small loaf pans (8½ × 4½ × 2½ inches). In a large bowl, with an electric beater or mixer, combine butter and sugar until light and fluffy, 3 to 4 minutes. Beat in the eggs, one at a time, beating well after each addition. Add the vanilla and beat until blended.

2. In a small bowl, whisk together the flour, baking powder, and salt. Using a wooden spoon or flexible rubber spatula, stir the dry ingredients into the egg mixture just until combined.

3. Transfer the batter to the prepared baking pans. Bake about 25 to 28 minutes, or until a tester inserted in the center comes out clean. Cool in pans on a rack to lukewarm, about 10 minutes. Remove the cakes from the pans and cool completely. Serve at room temperature. Store, well-wrapped in plastic, at room temperature, up to 5 days, or freeze wrapped and secured in a sealed freezer bag for 3 months.

Sweet Corn Cake
Pastel de Elote

Makes **1 (8-inch) round cake; 6 to 8 servings**

This recipe is inspired by a sweet, moist corn cake that I had at a restaurant in Veracruz. From my sketchy notes describing the cake, my friend, Marsi Atkinson, a fine baker, recreated this divine cake for me. Eat it plain, lightly dusted with sifted confectioners' sugar, or adorned with fresh berries and a dollop of whipped cream.

1¹/₄ cups all-purpose flour
1 teaspoon baking powder
¹/₄ teaspoon salt
1 cup fresh corn kernels (from about 1 large ear of corn), or thawed frozen corn kernels
¹/₄ cup milk
¹/₂ teaspoon pure vanilla extract
¹/₄ cup (¹/₂ stick) butter, at room temperature
¹/₄ cup vegetable oil
¹/₂ cup granulated sugar
¹/₄ cup brown sugar
2 large eggs, separated
2 tablespoons sifted confectioners' sugar (optional)

1. Preheat oven to 350°. Grease the bottom of an 8-inch round cake pan. Line the bottom of the pan with a circle of parchment or wax paper. Grease the paper and the sides of the pan. In a small bowl, mix together the flour, baking powder, and salt. Reserve.

2. In a blender, purée the corn with the milk and vanilla. Reserve. In a large bowl, beat the butter, oil, sugar, and brown sugar until smooth and fluffy. Add the egg yolks and beat well to mix. Beat in the corn mixture. Add the dry ingredients and stir to mix. In a separate medium bowl, beat the egg whites to soft peaks. Fold the egg whites into the batter.

3. Turn the batter into the buttered baking pan. Bake 30 minutes, or until a tester inserted in the center of the cake comes out clean. Cool the cake in the pan on a rack, about 1 hour before cutting. Cut in wedges to serve. Dust with confectioners' sugar, if desired.

Rice Flour Cake with Cheese
Pastel de Harina de Arroz y Queso

Makes 1 (8-inch) cake; 6 to 8 servings

This is a fine-textured cake with a slightly tangy taste. It is ideal to serve with fresh fruit and any kind of dessert sauce. I purchased a similar cake from a countryside cheese shop and bakery in the state of Veracruz. The recipe has been adapted for a food processor; you'll be amazed at how easy it is to make.

Rice flour can be found in Latin-American markets and health food stores. Rice flour is used in both sweet and savory baked goods in Mexico. Similar cakes that contain dry cheese are also made in Guatemala and in other Latin-American cultures.

^{1}/$_2$ **cup (1 stick) unsalted butter, at room temperature**

^{3}/$_4$ **cup sugar**

2 large eggs

^{1}/$_4$ **cup whole milk**

^{1}/$_2$ **teaspoon pure vanilla extract**

^{1}/$_4$ **cup very finely crumbled cotija cheese**

^{3}/$_4$ **cup rice flour**

1 teaspoon baking powder

1. Preheat oven to 350°. Grease an 8-inch round cake pan and line the bottom with a circle of parchment or wax paper. Grease the paper and the pan sides. Put the butter and sugar in a food processor and process until soft and fluffy, about 20 seconds. Scrape down the sides of the bowl as needed. Add the eggs and process about 10 seconds. Add the milk, vanilla, and cheese. Process about 5 seconds. In a small bowl, whisk together the flour and baking powder. Add to the processor and pulse 6 to 8 times to blend.

2. With a rubber spatula, scrape the batter into the prepared baking pan and level the top. Bake about 30 minutes, or until golden brown and the center springs back when touched lightly with your fingers. Cool the cake in the pan on a rack about 8 minutes. Remove from the pan and cool completely. Store, well wrapped at room temperature, up to 3 days.

Lime Cake
Pastel de Limón

Makes 1 (8-inch) round cake; 6 to 8 servings

The lime glaze on this simple single-layer cake gives a nice tartness to balance the sweet cake. Limes, mainly the small Key lime, are grown and used daily in the Mexican kitchen, often adding flavor to sweets. Serve this single-layer cake with fresh fruit and whipped cream to end any Mexican meal. I like puréed mango folded into sweetened whipped cream as a topping for the cake.

1¹/₃ cups cake flour
¹/₂ teaspoon baking powder
¹/₈ teaspoon salt
1 teaspoon grated lime zest (from about 1 lime)
1 cup sugar
3 large eggs
¹/₃ cup whole milk or half and half
1 tablespoon rum
4 tablespoons (¹/₂ stick) unsalted butter, melted and cooled

Lime Glaze

¹/₃ cup plus 1 tablespoon sifted confectioners' sugar
¹/₃ cup fresh lime juice (from about 3 limes)

1. Preheat oven to 350°. Grease the bottom of an 8-inch round cake pan. Line with a circle of parchment or wax paper. Grease the paper and sides of the pan. In a medium bowl whisk together flour, baking powder, and salt. Set aside.

2. In a large bowl mix the zest and sugar. Add the eggs and beat with an electric beater or mixer until foamy and pale, about 1 minute. On low speed, beat in the milk and rum.

3. Using a rubber spatula, gently stir in the flour mixture in 3 additions until the batter is smooth. Fold in the cooled butter until thoroughly mixed.

4. Transfer the batter to the prepared pan. Bake 25 minutes, or until the cake is golden brown and a tester inserted in the center of the cake comes out clean. Cool the cake in the pan on a rack 5 minutes.

5. Meanwhile prepare lime glaze. In a small bowl mix the sugar and lime juice until smooth. (Lay parchment paper under the rack to catch dripping glaze.)

6. Turn cake out on the rack. Remove the liner and invert again so cake is right side up. Spoon glaze over the cake while it's hot and let it dribble down the sides of the cake. Serve at room temperature. Store, covered, at room temperature up to 3 days.

Pineapple Cake
Pastel de Piña

Makes 1 (8-inch) square cake; about 9 servings

For a sweet ending, try this super-moist contemporary pineapple cake, adapted from a recipe in Cocina Facil (Easy Cooking), *a Mexican food magazine, the next time you throw a Mexican party. It's simple to make and your guests will love it. Top the cake with ice cream or whipped cream.*

1 cup all-purpose flour
¹/₂ cup plus 2 teaspoons sugar
1 teaspoon baking soda
¹/₄ teaspoon salt
1 cup canned crushed pineapple with juice
1 large egg, beaten
¹/₂ teaspoon pure vanilla extract

1. Preheat the oven to 325°. Grease an 8-inch-square baking pan and dust with flour. In a large bowl, whisk together the flour, sugar, baking soda, and salt. In a medium bowl, mix the pineapple, egg, and vanilla. Add to the dry ingredients and mix well.

2. Pour the batter into the prepared pan. Bake until dark golden brown on top and a tester inserted into the center of the cake comes out clean, about 30 minutes. Remove the cake from the oven to a rack and cool completely in the pan. Cut the cake into squares and serve directly from the pan. Store, covered, at room temperature up to 3 days.

Vanilla Cupcakes
Pastelitas de Vainilla

Makes **12 cupcakes**

Vanilla-flavored white cupcakes without frosting are almost certain to be available in whatever bakery you might pop into all over Mexico. These sweet little cakes are a quick treat to nibble anytime, on the street, in the car, or to take on a picnic. If you prefer, top them with frosting.

2 cups all-purpose flour
2¹/₂ teaspoons baking powder
¹/₄ teaspoon salt
¹/₄ cup (¹/₂ stick) unsalted butter, at room temperature, or vegetable shortening
1 cup sugar
1 large egg
³/₄ cup milk
1 teaspoon pure vanilla extract

1. Preheat the oven to 375°. Grease a cupcake pan, or line with paper cups. In a medium bowl, whisk together the flour, baking powder, and salt. Reserve.

2. Put the butter and sugar in a food processor and process until creamy, 10 to 15 seconds. Add the egg and process until fluffy, about 15 seconds. Add the milk and vanilla. Process until smooth, 8 to 10 seconds. Add the dry ingredients and pulse 4 to 6 times until just combined.

3. Fill 12 muffin cups about ⅔ full. Bake until raised and golden brown on top and a toothpick inserted in the center of the highest cupcake comes out clean, about 20 minutes. Transfer to a rack to cool Store, covered, in a dry cupboard up to 3 days.

Cookies

Almond-Walnut Cookies
Galletas de Nuez

Makes **about 20 cookies**

These crescent-shaped cookies are delicate and rich, very much like one of my favorite crispy little cookies in Mexico City.

¹/₄ pound whole almonds
¹/₄ pound walnut pieces
1 cup sugar
1 teaspoon baking powder
1 tablespoon fine bread crumbs
¹/₂ teaspoon cinnamon (Mexican canela or Ceylon variety preferred)
1 large egg

1. Preheat oven to 350°. Grease a cookie sheet. Put the nuts and sugar into a food processor and blend until fine, 10 to 15 seconds. Add the baking powder, bread crumbs, and cinnamon. Process 5 seconds. Add the egg and process to form a paste, about 5 seconds.

2. Roll walnut-size pieces of dough into thin rope shapes, then shape into crescents and put on the cookie sheet about 1 inch apart. Bake until golden brown, about 12 to 15 minutes. Transfer to a rack. Cool completely. Store, covered, at room temperature, up to 5 days, or freeze in a sealable plastic freezer bag up to 3 weeks.

Almond Macaroons
Macaroon de Almendras

Makes **about 16 cookies**

Macaroons made of coconut or almonds are found in bakeries all over Mexico.

1 cup slivered blanched almonds
2/3 cups sugar
1 tablespoon all-purpose flour
Pinch salt
1 large egg white
1/4 teaspoon pure almond or vanilla extract
Confectioners' sugar
16 whole almonds

1. Preheat the oven to 350°. Line a cookie sheet with parchment. In a food processor, grind the slivered almonds, sugar, flour, and salt until fine, 10 to 15 seconds. Add the egg white and extract. Blend until well mixed, 6 to 8 seconds. The dough will be a bit sticky.

2. Roll the dough into 16 balls about 1-inch in diameter, and arrange about 2 inches apart on the cookie sheet. Slightly flatten the balls. Dust lightly with confectioners' sugar. Press 1 almond into the top of each cookie. Bake 12 to 14 minutes, or until pale golden. Transfer to a rack. Cool completely. Keep the macaroons in an airtight container at room temperature 3 to 4 days.

Mexican Almond Cookies
Galletas de Almendra

Makes **about 30 cookies**

It's a tradition to enjoy small crisp cookies with afternoon coffee or tea. I've been refreshed many times with coffee and cookies like these at the Salon de Te in Mexico City. Lime zest adds a wonderful flavor to these buttery cookies.

The dough for these cookies needs to be cold and firm to roll into balls that are not sticky, and for the cookies to bake properly and hold their shape.

1/2 cup slivered blanched almonds
3/4 cup sugar
1/4 teaspoon salt
1/2 cup (1 stick) unsalted butter, at room temperature
1 large egg
1/2 teaspoon grated lime zest
1 teaspoon pure vanilla extract
1 1/4 cups all-purpose flour

1. In a food processor, blend the almonds with 2 tablespoons of the sugar and the salt until finely ground, about 15 seconds. Transfer to a bowl. Put the butter and the remaining sugar in the processor. Process 15 seconds, or until creamy. Add the egg and process 15 seconds. Add the ground almonds, lime zest, and vanilla. Process 10 seconds. Add the flour and pulse to blend well, 5 to 6 times. Transfer the dough to a bowl, cover, and refrigerate about 4 hours, or until firm and cold.

2. Preheat the oven to 375°. Grease a large cookie sheet or line with parchment paper. Remove the dough from the refrigerator, and roll into walnut-size balls. Place about 1 inch apart on the cookie sheet. Bake until the cookies are browned around the edges and the tops are rounded and still white, about 12 minutes. Transfer the cookies to a rack. When cool, store, covered, about a week, or freeze in a sealed plastic freezer bag for about 3 weeks.

Cinnamon-Walnut Cookies
Galletas de Azucar y Nuez

Makes **about 24 cookies**

Mexican cinnamon, called canela, or true cinnamon, is mild, with a light floral aroma. The cinnamon can be found in cellophane packages in most supermarkets. I use a food processor for this recipe, but an electric mixer can also be used.

2 cups all-purpose flour

1 tablespoon ground cinnamon (Mexican canela or Ceylon variety preferred)

$1/4$ teaspoon salt

$3/4$ cup ($1^1/2$ sticks) unsalted butter, at room temperature

1 cup sugar

1 large egg

$1/2$ teaspoon pure vanilla extract

$1/2$ cup finely chopped walnuts

1. In a medium bowl, whisk together the flour, cinnamon, and salt. In a food processor, process the butter and sugar until light and creamy, about 1 minute. Add the egg and vanilla. Process until fluffy, about 30 seconds. Add the dry ingredients, and pulse until the dough comes together, about 25 seconds. Add the nuts and pulse 6 to 8 times to mix with the dough. Transfer the dough to a bowl, cover and refrigerate until firm enough to handle, about 1 hour.

2. Preheat the oven to 350°. Grease 2 large cookie sheets or line with parchment paper. Shape the dough into 1½-inch balls with your hands. Place the balls onto the cookie sheets, about 1 inch apart. Put cookie sheets in refrigerator about 5 minutes. Flatten each ball with the bottom of a glass to about ¼-inch thick. Bake 15 minutes or until the cookies are light brown and crisp around the edges. Transfer to a rack to cool. When cool, store, covered, about a week, or freeze in a sealed plastic freezer bag for 3 weeks.

Chocolate Pecan Cookies
Galletas de Chocolate y Pacanas

Makes **30 small cookies**

In Mexico, chocolate is primarily used for a hot beverage, but I discovered small chocolate cookies topped with pecans in a bakery in Guanajuato. Use high-quality unsweetened chocolate, and not Mexican chocolate for the cookies. Mexican chocolate doesn't melt smoothly enough.

$1/2$ cup (1 stick) unsalted butter, at room temperature

1 cup firmly packed dark brown sugar

2 ounces unsweetened chocolate, melted

1 large egg, beaten

$1/4$ cup milk

$1/4$ teaspoon pure vanilla extract

$1^3/4$ cup all-purpose flour

1 teaspoon baking powder

$1/4$ teaspoon baking soda

$1/8$ teaspoon salt

30 pecan halves

1. Preheat oven to 375°. Grease 1 large or 2 medium cookie sheets or line with parchment. In a large bowl, with an electric beater or mixer beat the butter and sugar together until creamy, about 1 minute. Beat in the melted chocolate and egg. Add the milk and vanilla. In a medium bowl whisk together the flour, baking powder, soda, and salt. Stir into the creamed mixture and mix well.

2. Drop by rounded tablespoons about 1 inch apart onto the cookie sheets. Press 1 pecan half into each cookie. Bake about 10 minutes, or until lightly browned and just firm to the touch. If using 2 cookie sheets, rotate on the oven racks midway through for even baking. Transfer to racks to cool. Store, covered, at room temperature 3 to 4 days, or freeze in sealed freezer bags 3 months.

Crispy Pecan Cookies
Galletas de Pacanas

Makes **about 16 cookies**

These easy-to-make cookies harden quickly after they are removed from the oven, so be sure to bake them on parchment paper or a well-greased, heavy cookie sheet, to prevent breaking or sticking to the pan. Grind the pecans in a food processor until they are as fine as crumbs, but not pasty. The cookies are great with coffee or served with fresh peaches or strawberries.

1/2 **cup pecans**
1 **large egg white**
2/3 **cup sifted powdered sugar**
1/2 **teaspoon pure vanilla extract**
1/4 **teaspoon salt**

1. Preheat the oven to 350°. Place pecans in a food processor and process until finely ground, about 20 seconds. Grease a cookie sheet or line with parchment paper.

2. In a large bowl, with an electric beater or mixer, beat the egg white to stiff peaks, then gradually beat in the sugar. Beat in the vanilla and salt until the dough is well combined, about 30 seconds. With a rubber spatula, thoroughly mix in the pecans. The dough will be very thick and sticky.

3. Drop cookies by teaspoons about 1 inch apart onto the cookie sheet. Bake 15 minutes, or until the cookies are lightly browned and firm to the touch. Transfer the cookies to a rack. Cool completely. They will stay nice and crisp up to 3 days, stored in a sealed plastic bag.

Pecan Butter Cookies
Galletas de Mantequilla y Pacanas

Makes **about 36 cookies**

It's rare for me to pass a Mexican bakery without checking out the cookie trays. These little nut cookies are really easy to bake and wonderful to eat. I use the food processor to mix the dough.

1/2 **cup pecan pieces**
3/4 **cup sugar**
1/4 **teaspoon salt**
1/2 **cup (1 stick) unsalted butter, at room temperature**
1 **large egg**
1 **teaspoon pure vanilla extract**
1 1/4 **cups all-purpose flour**

1. Put the pecans, 2 tablespoons of the sugar, and salt in a food processor. Process until the nuts are finely ground, about 20 seconds. Transfer the nut mixture to a small bowl. Put the butter and remaining sugar in the processor and process about 15 seconds, or until creamy. Add the egg and process 15 seconds. Add the reserved nuts and vanilla. Add the flour and pulse 6 to 8 times until blended. Transfer the dough to a bowl, cover and refrigerate for 2 to 3 hours, until cold and firm.

2. Preheat the oven to 375°. Grease one large or two medium cookie sheets or line with parchment paper. Roll the chilled dough into walnut-size balls. Place about 1 inch apart on the cookie sheet. Bake 12 to 14 minutes, or until the cookies are lightly browned around the edges and the tops are slightly rounded and still light in color (If using 2 cookie sheets, rotate on the oven racks midway through for even baking.) Transfer to a rack.

Pecan Bars with Chocolate Crust
Postre de Pacanas y Chocolate

Makes **about 24 bars**

These delicious nut bars with a crumbly chocolate crust make a wonderful treat to complete a Mexican meal. Look for Mexican canela in cellophane packages in the Mexican section of many supermarkets, for the subtle, mild flavor and authenticity used in Mexican baking.

1¼ cups all-purpose flour
1 cup sifted confectioners' sugar
⅓ cup unsweetened cocoa powder
1 teaspoon ground cinnamon (Mexican canela or Ceylon variety preferred)
1 cup (2 sticks) cold unsalted butter, cut into 1-inch pieces
1 (14-ounce) can sweetened condensed milk
1 large egg
1½ teaspoons pure vanilla extract
1½ cups chopped pecans

1. Preheat the oven to 350°. Lightly grease the bottom of a 13- × 9-inch baking dish. In food processor bowl, put the flour, sugar, cocoa, and cinnamon. Pulse 4 times to mix. Add the butter and pulse about 6 times until crumbly. Press dough firmly onto the bottom of the baking dish. Bake 12 minutes.

2. Meanwhile, in a medium bowl, mix together the sweetened condensed milk, egg, and vanilla. Stir in the nuts. Spread evenly over the baked crust. (Be careful of hot pan.) Bake 25 minutes or until the top looks caramel colored. Cool in the pan on a rack. Cut into bars.

Mexican Wedding Cookies
Polvorones

Makes **about 24 cookies**

*There are several versions of Mexican wedding cookies (*polvorones*) in different parts of Mexico. They are well-loved little sweets to serve at weddings and other special occasions. The name* polvorones, *comes from the word for dust (*polvo*) because of their light flaky texture and coating of sugar.*

½ cup (1 stick) unsalted butter, at room temperature
2 tablespoons sifted confectioners' sugar plus ½ cup for dusting
1 teaspoon pure vanilla extract
1 cup all-purpose flour
1 cup very finely chopped pecans or walnuts

1. Preheat the oven to 375°. In a large mixing bowl with an electric beater or mixer, beat the butter until fluffy, about 1 minute. Beat in the two tablespoons of confectioners' sugar and the vanilla until very smooth, about 1 minute. Add the flour and nuts. Beat on low speed just until well mixed. Refrigerate the dough about 25 minutes, just to firm it up a bit.

2. Form the dough into small balls about 1 inch in diameter and place on 1 large or 2 medium ungreased cookie sheets. Bake 15 minutes or until lightly browned. Cool the cookies on a rack 6 to 8 minutes, then roll the warm cookies in the remaining half cup of sifted confectioners' sugar. Store, covered, at room temperature, up to 3 or 4 days.

Piggy Brown Sugar Cookies
Puerquitos

Makes about 14 cookies

These whimsical, pig-shaped cookies are offered in bakeries throughout Mexico, and they're not just for children! I rarely make it past a window that displays a large tray of the pig cookies without purchasing one to eat on the spot or enjoy later with coffee or hot chocolate. The cookies are slightly soft in the center with a barely crisp crust and taste of cinnamon and brown sugar. Pig-shaped cookie cutters are available in most cookware stores. (You can, of course, cut the dough in whatever shape you choose.) I use a 4½-inch cutter, which is larger than most.

2 cups all-purpose flour
1¹/₂ teaspoons unsweetened cocoa powder
¹/₂ cup packed dark brown sugar
4 teaspoons baking powder
2 teaspoons ground cinnamon (Mexican canela or Ceylon variety preferred)
¹/₄ teaspoon salt
¹/₂ cup (1 stick) cold unsalted butter, cut into chunks
¹/₃ cup milk
¹/₂ teaspoon pure vanilla extract

Glaze

¹/₂ cup confectioners' sugar
2 teaspoons milk
¹/₈ teaspoon pure vanilla extract

1. Preheat oven to 400°. Grease 2 cookie sheets or line with parchment paper. In a food processor, blend together the flour, cocoa, sugar, baking powder, cinnamon, and salt, 5 to 10 seconds. Add the butter and process to a mealy mixture, 45 to 50 seconds. Add the milk and vanilla. Process until the dough comes together in a ball.

2. Remove the dough and form into a flat disk with your hands. Chill the dough in the refrigerator 30 minutes to make it easier to handle.) Dust both sides lightly with flour and roll out on a lightly floured work surface to about ¼-inch thickness. With a pig-shape cookie cutter, cut out cookies and place on cookie sheets. Gather the scraps and re-roll to make a few more cookies. Bake 10 to 12 minutes or until the tops are lightly browned. (Rotate the cookie sheet on the oven racks midway through for even baking.)

3. Meanwhile, prepare the glaze. In a small bowl, stir together the confectioners' sugar, the milk, and the vanilla until well blended.

4. When the cookies are done, leave them on the sheets and brush them lightly with glaze while they are still hot. Transfer to racks. When cool, store, covered, at room temperature, 3 to 5 days, or freeze in a sealed plastic freezer bag 3 to 4 weeks.

Coconut Cookies
Galletas de Coco

Makes about 24 cookies

Mexican bakeries (panaderias) offer a variety of cookies, and coconut is often among the selections. Toasting the coconut briefly in the oven gives the cookies an especially good taste.

³/₄ cup sweetened flaked coconut
²/₃ cups all-purpose flour
¹/₂ teaspoon baking soda
¹/₄ teaspoon salt
4¹/₂ tablespoons unsalted butter, at room temperature
¹/₄ cup packed light brown sugar
2 tablespoons granulated sugar
1 large egg
¹/₄ teaspoon pure vanilla extract

1. Preheat the oven to 375°. Spread the coconut on a baking sheet and toast until pale golden, 3 to 4 minutes. Cool coconut on a plate.

2. In a small bowl, mix together flour, baking soda, and salt. In a large bowl with an electric mixer, beat together the butter and the sugars until light and fluffy, about 2 minutes. Beat in the egg and vanilla. Using a wooden spoon or rubber spatula, stir in the flour mixture and coconut until well combined.

3. Drop by teaspoons about 1 inch apart on ungreased cookie sheets and bake on the middle shelves of the oven about 8 to 10 minutes or until golden. Cool 1 minute on the baking sheet, and then transfer to racks to cool completely. Store, covered, at room temperature about 4 to 6 days.

Banana Cookies
Pastelitas de Plátano

Makes **about 24 cookies**

Soft cookies are among my favorite treats to have with afternoon coffee or tea, and bananas go into sweet and savory foods in Mexico, including cookies like these. In Mexico, the late afternoon break for refreshment is called marienda, *a perfect time for these cinnamon-sugar-coated cookies.*

$1/3$ **cup butter, at room temperature**

$1/2$ **cup sugar**

1 ripe banana (6-ounce), peeled and mashed

$1/2$ **teaspoon pure vanilla extract**

1 large egg, lightly beaten

1 cup plus 2 tablespoons all-purpose flour

1 teaspoon baking powder

$1/4$ **teaspoon baking soda**

$1/2$ **teaspoon salt**

2 tablespoons sugar mixed with $1/2$ teaspoon cinnamon for topping

1. Preheat the oven to 400°. In a large bowl with an electric beater or mixer, beat the butter and sugar together until fluffy, 1 to 2 minutes. Blend in the mashed banana and vanilla. Beat in the egg. In a small bowl, thoroughly mix the flour, baking powder, soda, and salt; then stir into the banana mixture.

2. Drop by teaspoons onto ungreased cookie sheets, about 1 inch apart. Bake about 12 minutes or until lightly browned. (Rotate the cookie sheets

on the oven racks midway through for even baking.) When done, leave the cookies on the sheets and sprinkle lightly with the cinnamon-sugar while hot. Cool on racks. Store, covered, at room temperature, up to 3 days or freeze in sealed plastic freezer bags 3 to 4 weeks.

Pumpkin Cookies
Pasteles de Calabaza

Makes **about 20 cookies**

Pumpkin cookies are plump and soft. Enjoy them with Mexican Hot Chocolate (page 590), or afternoon coffee.

1 cup all-purpose flour

1 teaspoon baking soda

$1/2$ **teaspoon salt**

1 teaspoon ground cinnamon (Mexican canela or Ceylon variety preferred)

$1/4$ **teaspoon ground allspice**

$2/3$ **cup packed dark brown sugar**

6 tablespoons butter, at room temperature

$1/2$ **cup canned unsweetened solid-pack pumpkin**

1 large egg

1 teaspoon pure vanilla extract

$1/3$ **cup raisins**

1. Preheat oven to 375°. Grease a large cookie sheet or line with parchment. In a food processor, process the brown sugar, butter, pumpkin, egg, and vanilla. In a medium bowl, mix the flour, baking soda, salt, cinnamon, and allspice; then add into the pumpkin mixture and pulse until well blended. Transfer the dough to a bowl and stir in the raisins.

2. Drop the dough by heaping tablespoons about 2 inches apart onto cookie sheet. Bake 15 minutes, or until the cookies are light brown and springy to the touch. Store, covered at room temperature up to 3 days, or freeze in sealed plastic freezer bags for 3 to 4 weeks.

Pumpkin Spice Squares
Dulce de Calabaza

Makes **6 to 8 servings**

Pumpkins are grown throughout Mexico and used in both savory and sweet dishes. These pumpkin squares are excellent for a picnic.

2 large eggs
1 cup sugar
1/2 cup vegetable oil
1 cup canned unsweetened solid-pack pumpkin
1 cup all-purpose flour
1 teaspoon baking powder
1/2 teaspoon baking soda
1/4 teaspoon salt
1 teaspoon ground cinnamon (Mexican canela or Ceylon variety preferred)
1/4 teaspoon ground allspice
1/8 teaspoon ground cloves
1/2 cup chopped walnuts or pecans

1. Preheat oven to 350°. Grease an 8-inch square baking pan. In a large bowl beat the eggs, sugar, oil, and pumpkin. In a small bowl whisk together the remaining ingredients, except the nuts. Mix the dry ingredients into the pumpkin mixture. Stir in the nuts.

2. Transfer the batter to the baking pan. Bake about 25 minutes, or until a tester inserted in the center comes out clean. Cool completely in the pan on a rack. Cut into squares.

Pastries and Pies

Mexican Fried Sweet Pastries
Churros

Makes **about 12 (4-inch long) churros**

Churros *are common street food all over Mexico, and are normally sold from special stands or small shops with walk-up windows. My husband Bill and I bought our first churros in Morelia, in the state of Michoacan, during an evening stroll. The sweet golden pastries coated with sugar were sublime.*

Churros are also quite easy to make. The thick dough is traditionally pushed through a special utensil called a churrera *right into hot oil. I use a pastry bag with a large star tip. Wedges of fresh lime are added to the oil while it heats to give a subtle zest to the flavor of the churros.*

1 cup water
1 tablespoon sugar
1/2 teaspoon salt
1 cup all-purpose flour
1 large egg
Corn oil or safflower oil for frying
1 lime, quartered
3/4 cup sugar

1. In a medium saucepan, stir together the water, sugar, and salt. Bring to a boil over medium heat. Remove pan from the heat and add the flour all at once. Quickly beat with a wooden spoon to blend completely. Put the pan back on medium-low heat and continue beating until the mixture clings together and a film forms on the bottom of the pan, about 1 minute. Remove from the heat. Using an electric beater or mixer, beat the egg into the dough and beat until the egg is absorbed and the mixture is smooth.

2. In a medium heavy saucepan or wok, pour oil to a depth of about 1½ inches. Add the lime wedges. Heat the oil over medium-high heat to 400° (about 6 to 8 minutes), or until the oil shimmers and a small piece of dough sizzles immediately when put into the oil. With tongs or a slotted spoon, remove the lime wedges from the oil and discard.

3. Put the churro mixture into a pastry bag fitted with a #6 star tip. Force about a 4-inch length of dough through the tip directly into the hot oil. (If dough does not drop off with a quick twist of the bag, release one hand from the bag and carefully cut dough off with kitchen scissors.) Fry until golden. Drain on paper towels. Roll in sugar. Repeat until all churros are made. Serve at once, sprinkled with the sugar.

Crisp-Fried Pastries
Buñuelos

Makes 8 servings

To ensure good luck in the New Year, it's customary to eat crisp bunuelos *with brown sugar syrup from a clay bowl and then break the bowl. My husband and I have enjoyed this festive tradition several times when in Oaxaca during New Year's Eve. Shortly after the stroke of midnight, broken pottery is everywhere. (Thousands of rustic clay bowls are made especially for this celebration.) The* bunuelos *can be served with the syrup or simply sprinkled with cinnamon and sugar.*

1 cup all-purpose flour, plus more for kneading the dough

2 teaspoons sugar

¹/₄ teaspoon salt

¹/₄ teaspoon baking powder

1 large egg, beaten

¹/₄ cup milk

1 tablespoon unsalted butter, melted

Oil for frying

1 tablespoon sugar mixed with ¹/₂ teaspoon ground cinnamon (optional)

Brown Sugar Syrup (page 583), (optional)

1. In a large bowl, whisk together 1 cup of flour, the sugar, salt, and baking powder. In a small bowl, stir together the egg, milk, and melted butter. Add to the flour mixture and mix thoroughly. Turn out onto a lightly floured work surface. Sprinkle the dough with 2 tablespoons of flour and knead to make a soft smooth dough, 3 to 5 minutes.

2. Divide into 8 pieces and roll into balls. Cover the balls with a dry cloth and let rest 20 minutes. Place 1 ball on a lightly floured surface and with a rolling pin roll out to a round about ¹/₈-inch thick. Using your hands, gently stretch the dough to make it even thinner. Repeat with the remaining balls.

3. Pour oil to a depth of 1 inch in a large deep skillet. When the oil shimmers, and a small piece of dough sizzles at once, with a long-handled utensil carefully place 1 bunuelo in the hot oil. Fry briefly until the bottom is lightly browned, about 20 seconds. Scoop oil over the top, and turn over with tongs to fry the second side until crisp. Drain on paper towels. Repeat with remaining bunuelos. Prepare the cinnamon-sugar or syrup, if using. Sprinkle or pour over bunuelos and serve hot.

Apple-Raisin Turnovers
Empanadas de Manzanas y Pasas

Makes **about 16 turnovers**

Walk into a Mexican bakery and empanadas with an apple filling will probably be among the many choices of irresistible baked goods.

Sweet Pastry Dough for Turnovers (page 555)
1¼ cups peeled finely chopped cooking apples, such as Pippin or Golden Delicious
1 tablespoon water
⅓ cup sugar
1 tablespoon cornstarch
½ teaspoon ground cinnamon (Mexican canela or Ceylon variety preferred)
¼ teaspoon ground allspice
⅛ teaspoon salt
2 tablespoons raisins

1. Prepare the dough. Cover and refrigerate while making the filling. In a medium saucepan, mix the apples, water, sugar, cornstarch, cinnamon, allspice, and salt. Bring to a boil over medium heat, and cook, stirring, until the mixture is thick and clear, and the apples are tender, about 5 minutes. Stir in the raisins and set the mixture aside to cool.

2. When the filling is cool, preheat the oven to 400°. Place half of the reserved dough on a lightly floured work surface and roll out ¼-inch thick. Cut into 4-inch circles with a biscuit cutter or rim of a glass. Gather the scraps and re-roll. You should have 8 dough circles.

3. Put about 1 tablespoon filling in the center of each circle and fold in half. Moisten the edges with water and crimp the edges with a fork or fingers to seal.

4. Place on 2 ungreased baking sheets. Brush the tops with beaten egg white and bake until golden brown, about 15 minutes. Remove empanadas

and transfer to a rack to cool. Repeat rolling, filling, and baking the remaining half of the dough.

Pineapple Turnovers
Empanadas de Piña

Makes **about 16 turnovers**

While living in Phoenix, Arizona, some years ago, we frequently drove to Nogales, Mexico just steps across the border. I always went to a certain bakery for their excellent pineapple empanadas similar to these. The filling must be very thick or it will ooze out of the pastry during baking.

Sweet Pastry Dough for Turnovers (page 555)
1 (8-ounce) can crushed pineapple, drained of excess juice
1 tablespoon plus ½ teaspoon cornstarch
½ teaspoon ground cinnamon (Mexican canela or Ceylon variety preferred)
3 tablespoons sugar

1. Prepare the dough. Cover and refrigerate while making the filling. In a medium saucepan, mix the pineapple, cornstarch, cinnamon, and sugar. Bring to a boil over medium heat, and cook stirring until the mixture is thick and clear, 4 to 5 minutes. Transfer to a bowl and cool completely.

2. When the filling is cool, preheat the oven to 400°. Place half of the reserved dough on a lightly floured work surface and roll out ¼-inch thick. Cut into 4-inch circles with a biscuit cutter or rim of a glass. Gather the scraps and re-roll. You should have 8 dough circles.

3. Put about 1 tablespoon filling in the center of each circle and fold in half. Moisten the edges with water and crimp the edges with a fork or fingers to seal.

4. Place on 2 ungreased baking sheets. Brush the tops with beaten egg white and bake until golden brown, about 15 minutes. Remove empanadas and transfer to a rack to cool. Repeat rolling, filling, and baking remaining half of the dough.

Pumpkin Turnovers
Empanadas de Calabaza

Makes **about 16 turnovers**

Pumpkin turnovers have a filling somewhat like our pumpkin pie. This recipe can also be made with mashed sweet potatoes in place of the pumpkin.

Sweet Pastry Dough for Turnovers (page 555)
1¹/₄ cups canned unsweetened solid-pack pumpkin
¹/₄ cup dark brown sugar
¹/₄ teaspoon ground cinnamon (Mexican canela or Ceylon variety preferred)
¹/₄ teaspoon ground nutmeg
1 large egg white, beaten

1. Prepare the dough. Cover and refrigerate while making the filling. In a medium saucepan, mix the pumpkin, brown sugar, cinnamon, and nutmeg. Cook over medium-low heat until the sugar melts and the mixture thickens, about 10 minutes. Transfer the filling to a bowl and cool completely.

2. When the filling is cool, preheat the oven to 400°. Place half of the reserved dough on a lightly floured work surface and roll out to ¹/₄-inch thick. Cut into 4-inch circles with a biscuit cutter or rim of a glass. Gather the scraps and re-roll. You should have 8 dough circles.

3. Put about 1 tablespoon filling in the center of each circle and fold in half. Moisten the edges with water and crimp the edges with a fork or fingers to seal.

4. Place on an ungreased baking sheet. Brush the tops with beaten egg white and bake until golden brown, about 15 minutes. Remove empanadas and transfer to a rack to cool. Repeat rolling, filling, and baking the remaining half of the dough.

Banana Tart
Torta de Plátano

Makes **1 (9-inch) tart**

At the Salon de Te in Mexico City's well-known elegant district called the pink zone (Zona Rosa), there are many tempting pastries and other sweets to assuage late afternoon appetites. This is my version of its banana tart with bright strawberry glaze. Serve the tart the day it's made.

Sweet Pastry Shell (page 554)
4 ounces fresh cream cheese
¹/₂ cup whipping or heavy cream
1 tablespoon sugar
2 large egg yolks
¹/₂ teaspoon pure vanilla extract
3 ripe firm bananas, peeled and sliced in ¹/₄-inch rounds
1 tablespoon fresh lime juice
10 ounces frozen sweetened sliced strawberries, thawed
2 teaspoons cornstarch

1. Make the pastry shell and cool completely. Leave the oven at 375°. To make the filling, put the cream cheese in a food processor bowl and process to soften, about 8 seconds. Add the cream, sugar, egg yolks, and vanilla. Process until smooth, about 10 seconds. Pour into the cooled pastry shell.

2. Bake until barely set, 6 to 8 minutes. (The filling will still wiggle a little in the center.) Cool on a rack.

3. Arrange the banana slices in a circular pattern over the entire surface of the tart. (Use any extra banana slices for another purpose.) Brush the arranged bananas lightly with the lime juice. Set the tart aside.

4. Press the thawed berries through a strainer over a small saucepan, pressing well to extract all the pulpy juices. Discard the pulp in the strainer.

5. Stir the cornstarch and 1 teaspoon of water together in a small dish and stir into the berry pulp. Put the mixture in a small saucepan and bring to a boil over medium heat, stirring, until thickened and clear. Spoon the glaze carefully over the bananas, covering completely. Refrigerate the tart at least 1 hour or up to 6 hours before serving.

Lime Tart
Torta de Limón

Makes 8 servings

Contemporary Mexican desserts like this rich tart are now a part of the sweet scene in some upscale Mexico City restaurants.

Sweet Pastry Shell (page 554)
1 (14-ounce) can sweetened condensed milk
3 large egg yolks
1/2 cup fresh lime juice
2 large egg whites
1 tablespoon sugar
Sweetened Whipped Cream (page 583)

1. Prepare and the pastry shell. Reduce the oven temperature to 325°.In a large mixing bowl, whisk together the milk, yolks, and lime juice. Set aside. In another large bowl, beat the egg whites with an electric mixer until fluffy, about 30 seconds. Add the sugar and beat until shiny with soft peaks, 1 to 2 minutes. Fold the egg whites into the milk mixture until just combined. Do not overmix.

2. Pour the mixture into the crust. (It will be very full. If there is too much filling, bake extra in a custard cup.) Bake the tart until filling rises and a tester inserted into the center comes out clean, about 35 to 40 minutes. Transfer the tart to a rack and cool completely. Refrigerate at least 3 hours or overnight. Prepare the whipped cream then top the tart with the cream just before serving.

Lime Pie
Pay de Limón

Makes one 9-inch pie

Pastries and other sweets are often eaten in late afternoon for marienda, *a convivial time when people sit and enjoy pastries with coffee, tea, or hot chocolate. In the Zona Rosa of Mexico City, one of the main commercial districts in the city, I often take* marienda *at the Salon de Te, where I encountered a delicate lime pie very much like this one. To add color and elegance to the pie, sprinkle finely grated lime rind on the whipped cream, or add a few candied violets.*

Crust
1½ cups vanilla wafer crumbs
¼ cup (½ stick) unsalted butter, melted

Filling
5 large egg yolks, lightly beaten
1 cup plus 1 tablespoon sugar
1½ tablespoons cornstarch
½ cup fresh lime juice
3 tablespoons unsalted butter, at room temperature
3 large egg whites
⅛ teaspoon salt
Sifted confectioners' sugar, for dusting
Sweetened Whipped Cream (page 583)

1. Preheat the oven to 375°. In a bowl, mix the cookie crumbs and melted butter. Press the crumbs into a 9-inch pie pan. Bake 5 minutes. Remove the crust from the oven, and let cool. Leave the oven on.

2. Put the egg yolks, ½ cup of the sugar, cornstarch, lime juice, and butter in the top of a double boiler, and whisk thoroughly. Cook over simmering water, stirring constantly, until thick and smooth, about 10 minutes. Set aside and let the custard cool to lukewarm.

3. In a clean mixing bowl, with an electric beater or mixer, beat the egg whites with the salt to soft peaks. Gradually beat in the remaining sugar, continuing to beat the egg whites to stiff peaks, 2 to 3 minutes. Gently fold the lime custard into the egg whites, and spoon into the prepared pie shell. Level the surface.

4. Bake until filling is lightly browned and slightly raised, about 12 minutes. Transfer pie in the pan to a rack to cool completely. Refrigerate the pie about 8 hours, or overnight.

5. Remove the pie from the refrigerator shortly before serving, and dust with powdered sugar. Cut into wedges, and serve cold with whipped cream.

Pineapple Pie
Pay de Piña

Makes **6 to 8 servings**

The cook in my rented villa in Puerta Vallarta promised a surprise one evening. I remember how pleased she was when she presented her American-style pineapple pie to my tour group. The memory inspired this recipe.

Pie Crust (page 554)
1/2 cup sugar
2 1/2 tablespoons cornstarch
1/8 teaspoon salt
4 large egg yolks, beaten
2 cups whole milk
1/2 teaspoon pure vanilla extract
**1 cup drained canned crushed pineapple
    in heavy syrup**
1/8 teaspoon cream of tartar
3 tablespoons sifted confectioners' sugar

1. Preheat the oven to 350°. Bake the pie crust and reserve. Leave the oven on. In a saucepan, mix the sugar, cornstarch, and salt. Whisk in the beaten egg yolks, milk, and pineapple. Bring to a boil, whisking, over medium-low heat, until the mixture is thick and smooth, about 10 minutes. Stir in the vanilla. Set filling aside.

2. In a large bowl, beat 3 of the egg whites with the cream of tartar until foamy. Add the confectioners' sugar gradually while beating until the mixture is shiny with stiff peaks. Pour the warm filling into the baked pie crust.

3. Cover the filling with the beaten egg whites, spreading the meringue to contact the edge of the crust. Bake until the meringue is golden brown, 10 to 15 minutes. Transfer the pie to a rack to cool completely then refrigerate about 1 hour or up to overnight. Serve the pie cool, but not ice cold.

Pie Crust
Pastel por Pasteles

Makes 1 single crust for 8-inch pie

This is a classic pastry that's used for pies or turnovers in Mexican and American kitchens. The food processor makes blending the dough quick and easy work. The pastry can also be used for other single-crust pies or empanadas. It is not as sweet and delicate as the "cookie" type pastry shell that follows this recipe.

1¹/₈ cup all-purpose flour, plus more for dusting work surface

¹/₂ teaspoon salt

1 teaspoon sugar

¹/₂ cup (1 stick) cold unsalted butter, cut into pieces

3 to 4 tablespoons ice water

1. Preheat the oven to 425°. Put the flour, salt, and sugar in a food processor. Pulse 3 to 4 times to combine. Add the butter. Process until the mixture looks like cornmeal, about 10 seconds. Add the water all at once and process until the mixture clumps together; remove and form into a ball. Flatten into a disk, wrap in plastic, and refrigerate 15 minutes to relax the dough.

2. Roll out the dough on a lightly floured work surface to a 10-inch circle, about ⅛-inch thick. Transfer the dough to an 8-inch pie plate. Trim off the excess dough, leaving about ½-inch all around the rim. Crimp the edges with fingers or press with a fork. Prick the shell all over with a fork. Placed a piece of foil in the shell and weigh down with pie weights or dried beans.

3. Bake 12 minutes. Remove the foil and weights. Reduce the oven temperature to 350° and bake 10 to 15 minutes more or until the crust is golden brown. Cool completely on a rack before filling.

Sweet Pastry Shell
Pastel para Tortas Dulces

Makes 1 (9-inch) tart shell

A press-in cookie-type pastry shell is easy and especially useful for many dessert tarts, such as the Banana Tart (page 551).

1 cup plus 1 tablespoon all-purpose flour

2 tablespoons sugar

¹/₈ teaspoon salt

¹/₂ cup (1 stick) cold unsalted butter, cut into chunks

1. Preheat the oven to 375°. Put the flour, sugar, and salt in a food processor bowl and pulse 6 to 8 times to blend. Add the butter and process until the mixture looks like cornmeal, about 10 seconds. Remove the bowl from the processor base and remove the blade. Scrape the mixture directly into the tart pan.

2. Using your fingers, carefully spread the mixture over the pan bottom with a light touch. Press to fit the bottom and up the sides. Bake until golden brown, about 15 minutes. Cool completely on a rack before filling.

Sweet Pastry Dough for Turnovers
Empanadas Dulce

Makes dough for about 16 empanadas

This buttery, slightly sweet dough is excellent for all kinds of sweet empanadas.

2 cups all-purpose flour
2 tablespoons sugar
1/4 teaspoon salt
3/4 cup (1 1/2 sticks) cold unsalted butter, cut into small pieces
1 large egg yolk
1/4 cup ice water

1. Put the flour, sugar, and salt in a food processor bowl and pulse 6 to 8 times to blend. Add the butter and process until crumbly, 10 to 15 seconds.

2. In a small bowl, beat together the egg yolk and the water. Add to the flour mixture all at once, and process until the dough comes together. Remove the dough from the processor and divide in half for easier handling and form into 2 discs. Dust each lightly with flour. The dough is ready to use. Cover and refrigerate while making the filling. If not using right away, cover with plastic and refrigerate up to 3 days.

Savory Pastry Dough for Turnovers
Empanadas

Makes about 24 small turnovers

Empanadas, *both savory and sweet, are consumed all over Mexico. This dough is easy to manage and is suitable for savory (or sweet) fillings.*

2 cups all-purpose flour
1/4 teaspoon salt
3/4 cup (1 1/2 sticks) cold unsalted butter, cut into small pieces
1 large egg yolk
1/4 cup ice water

1. Put the flour and salt in a food processor bowl and blend for about 5 seconds. Add the butter and process until crumbly, 10 to 15 seconds.

2. In a small bowl, beat the egg yolk and water with a fork and add all at once to the flour mixture. Process until a dough forms and holds together. Remove the dough to a lightly floured work surface. Divide the dough in half for easier handling and form into discs. The dough is ready to use. Cover with plastic and set aside while making the filling. If not using right away, wrap completely in plastic and refrigerate up to 3 days.

Other Desserts and Sweets

Almond and Lady Finger Dessert
Postre de Almendra

Makes **8 small servings**

This old-fashioned sweet is one of the first Mexican desserts I made when I began to concentrate on Mexican cooking. It's rich and very sweet, but also very delicious. I learned it from Vicki Barrios, who once taught cooking classes in the San Francisco area in the mid-1970s. The dessert has Spanish influence with the flavor of Spanish sherry, but it's a home-style dessert in central Mexico.

1 cup slivered almonds

2 cups sugar

1 cup water

³/₄ cup dry sherry, such as amontillado

1 dozen lady fingers, purchased, split lengthwise

6 large egg yolks

1 teaspoon pure vanilla extract

Ground cinnamon (Mexican canela or Ceylon variety preferred)

1. In a dry skillet, toast the almonds, stirring until lightly browned. Transfer to a plate to cool; then finely grind the nuts. There should be some texture. Reserve.

2. Put the sugar and water in a medium saucepan and bring to a boil. Cook over medium heat 5 minutes. Remove the pan from the heat and stir in the sherry. Reserve.

3. Arrange the lady fingers on an oval platter. Spoon about ¼ cup of the sugar syrup over the lady fingers. Set aside.

4. In a medium bowl, thoroughly beat the egg yolks with a fork. Mix the reserved almonds into the yolks. Stir the egg mixture into the syrup in the saucepan. Cook over low heat, stirring constantly, until the mixture starts to thicken. Remove from the heat. Stir in vanilla and pour evenly over the lady fingers. Sprinkle lightly with cinnamon. Refrigerate about 2 hours or until cold. Serve in small dessert bowls.

Meringues
Merengues

Makes **8 servings**

Delicate sweet meringues are sold in many fancy bakeries in Mexico. They make an ideal dessert filled with ice cream and fresh fruit.

¹/₂ cup sugar

¹/₄ teaspoon cream of tartar

¹/₈ teaspoon salt

2 large egg whites

¹/₂ teaspoon pure vanilla extract

1. Preheat the oven to 250°. Line a cookie sheet with parchment paper. In a small bowl mix together the sugar, cream of tartar and salt. Set aside. In a medium bowl beat the egg whites with an electric beater or mixer until foamy, about 1 minute. Gradually beat in the sugar mixture until the egg whites hold stiff peaks, 4 to 5 minutes.

2. Drop meringue by heaped tablespoons onto parchment paper. Wet the spoon and use the back to make indentations in the centers to form a nest and to shape the meringues into rounds about 3 inches in diameter. Swirl the excess around the outer edges. Bake 45 minutes, or until dry, crisp, and barely colored. Cool completely before using. Store in an airtight container up to 3 days. If they soften, heat in a 250° oven about 5 minutes or until crisp.

Mexican Caramel Crepes
Crepas de Cajeta

Makes **6 servings**

Crepas de Cajeta is a very popular dessert just about everywhere in Mexico. Cajeta *is a Mexican caramel sauce produced in the town of Celaya in central Mexico. A common brand available in the United States is Coronado, made of either goat's or cow's milk and sold in 16-ounce jars. Both are common and very good.* Cajeta *also comes flavored with wine. I prefer plain. The wine gives the* cajeta *a slightly astringent taste.*

12 crepes (Basic Crepes, page 136)

¹/₄ cup (¹/₂ stick) unsalted butter

2 cups cajeta (Mexican caramel sauce) or Creamy Caramel Dessert Sauce (page 581)

¹/₂ cup heavy cream or half and half

¹/₂ teaspoon ground cinnamon (Mexican canela or Ceylon variety preferred)

1 cup chopped pecans

1. Prepare the crepes. Prepare the sauce, if using homemade. Preheat oven to 200°. Then, melt 2 tablespoons of the butter in a medium skillet over low heat. Place the crepes, 1 at a time, in the skillet, turning, to coat with the warm butter. Fold in quarters and place on a plate, over-lapping, as all the crepes are warmed. Cover with foil and put in the oven to keep warm.

2. Put the cajeta and cream in the same skillet, and simmer, stirring, until heated through. To serve, put 2 tablespoons of caramel sauce on each of 6 dessert plates. Arrange 2 crepes on each plate. Drizzle remaining caramel on top. Sprinkle with cinnamon and scatter the chopped pecans over the top. Serve warm.

Pecan Candy
Dulce de Pacanas

Makes **about 10 (2-inch) candies**

Whenever I pass the candy and sweets shops in the Mexico City airport, I select a treat or two. The soft, chewy pecan candies are a favorite of mine, and I was delighted to find a recipe by cookbook author Mark Bittman that I adapted to make the candy at home.

¹/₂ cup dark brown sugar

2 tablespoons unsalted butter

¹/₂ cup whole milk

1 tablespoon dark corn syrup

¹/₂ teaspoon pure vanilla extract

¹/₂ cup coarsely chopped pecans

1. Oil a baking sheet very well with vegetable oil to prevent candy from sticking. Put all of the ingredients in a medium heavy-bottomed sauce-pan and bring to a boil over medium-high heat. The candy will foam and bubble vigorously, so watch carefully to prevent boil-over. Adjust the heat as needed. Cook, stirring frequently, until thick enough to hold its shape when dropped by a spoon onto the baking sheet, about 12 to 15 minutes (245° on a candy thermometer).

2. Drop by tablespoons about 2 inches apart. The candies will be free-formed. Let sit in a cool dry place at least 6 hours or overnight. When no longer sticky, remove from the pan with a wide thin spatula. To store, wrap in wax paper and put in a covered container. The candy keeps well for 3 to 4 weeks, but is better eaten in a day or two.

Pumpkin Seed Hard Candy
Palanquetas de Pepitas

Makes **about 12 candies**

Caramelized sugar with pumpkin seeds is a common brittle candy found in sweet shops and sometimes sold by street vendors in Mexico. The shiny green hued brittle looks enticing, tastes good, and is really easy to make.

³/₄ cup hulled green pumpkin seeds, toasted
1 cup sugar
¹/₈ teaspoon salt
1 tablespoon unsalted butter

1. Grease a baking sheet. In a medium dry skillet, toast the pumpkin seeds, stirring, over medium heat until they begin to brown, pop around in the pan, and smell toasty. Transfer to a plate to cool.

2. Preheat oven to 200° and put the baking sheet in the oven to warm.(This will help the candy spread.) Put the sugar in a heavy medium skillet, and heat over medium heat, stirring frequently, until the sugar melts. Continue stirring until the melted sugar turns lightly golden brown, 3 to 4 minutes. Take care not to let the sugar get dark brown; once it starts to turn, it colors fast. Stir in the toasted pumpkin seeds, salt, and butter. (The seeds will probably make a popping noise.)

3. Immediately spread the mixture with the back of a spoon on the warm baking sheet. Work quickly because the caramel will begin to harden right away. Cool the brittle completely. Break into 12 free-form pieces and store, covered, at room temperature for several weeks.

Prunes Stuffed with Walnut Candy
Ciruelas Rellenas con Dulce de Nuez

Makes **about 30 candies**

These typical candy-like confections are delightful with a glass of port or other dessert wines. In California, we like them with a late-harvest riesling. The candies taste best if they "age" for a few days.

¹/₄ cup (¹/₂ stick) unsalted butter
¹/₂ cup brown sugar, packed
¹/₄ cup fresh orange juice
1 scant cup sifted confectioners' sugar
¹/₂ cup chopped walnuts
¹/₂ teaspoon pure vanilla extract
1 pound small pitted prunes

1. Put a small bowl of cold water next to the stove. Melt the butter in a heavy saucepan. Add the sugar and bring to a boil over low heat, stirring constantly, until the sugar dissolves and starts to bubble. Add the orange juice and bring to a brisk boil, stirring, until the mixture makes a soft ball in cold water, about 5 minutes. (Test by dropping a very small amount of the syrup off the spoon into the water, and if it holds together when you pinch it, its ready, or if it registers 236° on a candy thermometer.

2. Remove the pan from the heat and cool the syrup without stirring, until lukewarm, 6 to 8 minutes. Stir in the confectioners' sugar until completely blended. The mixture will be thick and stiff. Stir in the nuts and vanilla.

3. Using your hands, form the nut mixture into small rounds to stuff into the prunes. Arrange on a plate. Cover and let sit overnight at room temperature, or store in a covered container for 3 to 4 weeks.

Sweet Rice Flour Tamales
Tamales Canarios

Makes about 16 small tamales

During a festive tamale cena (supper) in the countryside near Puebla our culinary group was awed by an unexpected treat as we drove to our destination. Straight ahead, in the glow of an orange setting sun, was the magnificent active volcano, Popocatepetl, billowing with steam. We stopped to take photographs and to marvel at the sight as the sun dropped from view. One of our hostesses for the evening, Monica Mastretta from Puebla, prepared this unique sweet tamale as a surprise—another unexpected treat!

Rice flour can be found in Mexican markets and health food stores.

16 corn husks, plus extra to line the steamer
6 tablespoons unsalted butter
³/₄ cup sugar
3 large egg yolks
1 cup rice flour
1 teaspoon baking powder
¹/₈ teaspoon salt
1 large egg white
¹/₂ cup raisins

1. Soak the corn husks in warm water about 20 minutes. Pat dry and wrap in a damp towel. In a 2-piece large steamer kettle, put 2 cups of hot water in the bottom and place the steamer part on top. Line the top with extra corn husks.

2. With an electric beater or mixer, beat the butter and sugar until creamy, about 1 minute. Beat in the egg yolks, 1 at a time. In a bowl, mix rice flour, baking powder, and salt. Add to the butter mixture and beat to combine, 20 to 30 seconds. In another bowl, beat the egg white to soft peaks. Fold into the batter. The dough should just hold its shape on a spoon.

3. Lay 1 corn husk on a working surface and put 1 generous tablespoon of the batter in a 3-inch-long band, about 1-inch wide, in the center of the husk near the wide end. Put about 6 raisins on the batter and press them in. Fold the sides of the husk to overlap, but not too tight, to leave room for the batter to expand. Twist the pointed end in the opposite direction of the seam, and set aside, folded ends down. Repeat until all husks are filled.

4. Bring the water in the steamer to a boil. Lay the tamales on the corn husks in the top of the steamer, leaving space between so they can steam evenly. Cover with foil and a damp towel to prevent steam from dripping onto the tamales. Put on the lid and steam the tamales 25 to 30 minutes, or until the dough separates easily from the husk. Serve at once. To keep, freeze in a sealed plastic freezer bag 3 to 4 weeks. Re-steam directly from the freezer.

Flans and Puddings

Mexican Coffee Flan
Flan de Café

Makes 8 to 10 servings

Flan is probably the most popular of all Mexican desserts, and this coffee-flavored flan, with its silky texture, is my favorite. The recipe comes from my first cooking classes in Leon, Mexico, and I still follow the same recipe. Be sure to warm the pan in the oven; this makes it easier to coat the pan with the caramel. The flan needs time to firm up in the refrigerator, so prepare it ahead.

1 cup sugar
1 (12-ounce) can evaporated milk
1 (14-ounce) can sweetened condensed milk
1 cup whole milk
5 large eggs
1 large egg yolk
1 teaspoon pure vanilla extract
1 teaspoon instant coffee dissolved in 1 teaspoon boiling water
1 tablespoon brandy or rum

1. Preheat the oven to 200°. Warm a 9-inch round × 2-inch deep cake pan in the oven. In a heavy medium saucepan, cook sugar over medium heat, stirring frequently, until melted and golden brown, 5 to 8 minutes. Quickly pour caramelized sugar syrup into the warm cake pan. Using potholders to protect hands, tip the pan around to coat the bottom and about 1 inch up sides with the caramel syrup. Set aside.

2. Raise the oven to 325°. In a saucepan, bring about 2 cups of water to a boil. Meanwhile, place in a blender jar the three milks, the eggs, egg yolk, vanilla, coffee, and brandy. Mix on low speed 1 minute until completely mixed and smooth. (If

there is too much liquid, blend in 2 batches to prevent overflowing.)

3. Pour the custard into the caramel-lined pan, set the pan into a larger pan, and place them on the middle rack of the oven. Carefully pour boiling water into the larger holding pan to a depth of 1 inch. Bake uncovered, 30 to 35 minutes, or until custard is set and a thin knife blade inserted in the center comes out clean. Cool completely on a rack, then refrigerate, covered with plastic, about 8 hours or overnight.

4. To serve, run a thin knife around edge of pan between custard and pan. (Press the knife against the pan, not the custard.) Place a deep serving plate with a rim over the pan and invert to unmold the flan. Carefully lift up pan and allow syrup to run over the flan. Cut into wedges to serve.

Coconut Flan
Flan de Coco

Makes 8 to 10 servings

Sweet flans are probably Mexico's favorite desserts. This one is based on the coconut flan I had at Fonda el Refugio, in Mexico City, known for its authentic Mexican cooking. It needs time to set, so prepare it ahead.

1 cup sugar
1 (14-ounce) can sweetened condensed milk
2¹/₂ cups whole milk
5 large eggs
1 large egg yolk
1 teaspoon pure vanilla extract
³/₄ cup sweetened flaked coconut, chopped

1. Preheat the oven to 200°. Warm a 9-inch round × 2-inch deep cake pan in the oven. (This makes it easier to coat the pan with the caramel.) In a heavy medium saucepan, cook sugar over medium heat, stirring frequently, until melted and golden brown, 5 to 8 minutes. Quickly pour caramelized sugar syrup into the warm cake pan. Using potholders to protect hands, tip the pan around to coat the bottom and about 1 inch up sides with the caramel syrup. Set aside.

2. Raise the oven to 325°. In a saucepan, bring about 2 cups of water to a boil. In a blender, put the sweetened condensed milk, whole milk, eggs, yolk, and vanilla. Mix on low speed 1 minute. (Blend in batches, if necessary.) Add the coconut and pulse 4 to 5 times to blend.

3. Pour the custard into the caramelized pan, set the pan into a larger pan and place them on the middle rack of the oven. Carefully pour boiling water into the larger holding pan to a depth of 1 inch. Bake the flan 30 to 35 minutes or until the custard is set and a thin knife inserted in the center comes out clean. Remove from the water bath and cool completely on a rack, then refrigerate, covered with plastic, at least 8 hours or overnight before serving.

4. To serve, run a thin knife blade between custard and pan rim. (Press the knife against the pan, not the custard.) Invert onto a deep serving plate with a rim to unmold. Remove the pan carefully, allowing the syrup to run over the top of the flan. Cut into wedges and serve.

Pumpkin Flan
Flan de Calabaza

Makes **8 servings**

This is a wonderful dessert for a dinner party. Flans and puddings are common Mexican desserts and are made in different flavors. Pumpkin makes a denser flan than the traditional coffee-flavored flan, but it's also rich and delicious. Flans really don't need a garnish, but a dollop of whipped cream on top is nice. Make the flan one day ahead to allow it to set completely.

1 cup sugar
1 (14-ounce) can sweetened condensed milk
1½ cups whole or low-fat milk
1 cup canned unsweetened solid-pack pumpkin
6 large eggs
½ teaspoon salt
1 teaspoon ground cinnamon (Mexican canela or Ceylon variety preferred)
¼ teaspoon ground allspice
⅛ teaspoon grated nutmeg
2 tablespoons dark rum
1 teaspoon pure vanilla extract

1. Preheat the oven to 200°. Warm a 9-inch round × 2-inch deep cake pan in the oven. (This makes it easier to coat pan with caramel.) In a heavy medium skillet, melt sugar over medium heat, stirring frequently, until melted and golden brown. Quickly pour caramelized sugar syrup into the warm cake pan. Using potholders to protect hands, tip the pan around to coat the bottom and about 1 inch up sides with the caramel syrup. Set aside.

2. Raise oven to 325°. In a saucepan, bring 2 cups of water to a boil. In a large bowl, combine the remaining ingredients. Beat with a mixer on low speed about 1 minute until very smooth. Pour the custard into the cake pan.

3. Pour the custard into the caramelized pan, set the pan into a larger pan and place them on the middle rack of the oven. Carefully pour boiling water into the larger holding pan to a depth of 1 inch. Bake the flan 30 to 40 minutes, or until the custard is set, and a thin knife blade inserted into the center comes out clean. Cool completely on a rack, then refrigerate, covered with plastic, at least 8 hours or overnight.

4. To serve, run a knife between the custard and pan rim. (Press the knife against the pan, not the custard.) Invert onto a deep serving plate with a rim to unmold. Remove the pan carefully, allowing the syrup to run over the top of the flan. Cut into wedges and serve.

Chocolate Flan

Flan de Chocolate

Makes 8 to 10 servings

Luscious chocolate flan is not a standard flan in the Mexican kitchen, but it is emerging in nueva cocina. I developed this recipe at the request of several chocolate fans in my cooking classes. The flan is easy to make, but must be made a day ahead to set properly. The flan can be served alone in all its decadent glory, or garnished with fresh raspberries and a tiny dollop of whipped cream to make it extra-fancy.

1 cup sugar

1 (14-ounce) can sweetened condensed milk

1 (12-ounce) can evaporated milk

3 large eggs

2 large egg yolks

1/2 cup dark chocolate syrup, such as Hershey's

1 teaspoon pure vanilla extract or
    1 tablespoon rum

1. Preheat the oven to 200°. Warm the cake pan in the oven. (This makes it easier to coat the bottom of the pan with the caramel.) To make the caramel, put the sugar in a small heavy saucepan. Cook over medium heat, stirring frequently, until the mixture melts and turns golden brown, 5 to 8 minutes. (Watch closely as the sugar starts to melt to prevent burning.) Using potholders, remove the warm pan from the oven and pour the caramel into the pan. Tilt the pan several time to coat the bottom and about 1 inch up the sides of the pan. Set aside.

2. Raise the oven temperature to 325°. In a saucepan, bring about 2 cups of water to a boil. Meanwhile, put the 2 milks, eggs, chocolate syrup, and vanilla or rum into a blender. Blend on low-to-medium speed until the mixture is completely smooth and very well blended, about 1 minute. (Blend in batches, if necessary.) Scrape down the sides of the jar if needed and blend a bit longer.

3. Pour the custard into the caramelized pan, set the pan into a larger pan and place them on the middle rack of the oven. Carefully pour boiling water into the larger holding pan to a depth of 1 inch.

4. Bake about 40 minutes, or until the custard is almost set in the center and a thin knife inserted in the center comes out clean. Remove from the water bath and cool completely on a rack, then refrigerate, covered with plastic, at least 8 hours or overnight before serving.

5. To serve, run a thin knife blade between custard and pan rim. (Press the knife against the pan, not the custard.) Invert onto a deep serving plate with a rim to unmold. Remove the pan carefully, allowing the syrup to run over the top of the flan. Cut into wedges and serve.

Orange Custard
Flan de Naranja

Makes 4 servings

Spain contributed enormously to the desserts of Mexico, such as this lovely baked custard that's similar to flan, except it is not baked in caramel-coated cups. Spain brought oranges to Mexico, and groves have flourished in many regions, such as the coastal and lower elevation areas along both coasts. The small amount of cornstarch mixed with the sugar keeps the custards from curdling. The custards are best eaten the same day they are made.

2 large eggs
2 large egg yolks
¼ cup sugar
1 teaspoon cornstarch
**1 cup fresh orange juice (from 3 to 4 oranges),
    at room temperature**
1 teaspoon finely grated orange zest

1. Preheat the oven to 325°. In a saucepan, bring to a boil about 2 cups water for the water bath. Lightly butter 4 (6-ounce) custard cups. In a small bowl, mix very well the sugar and corn starch. Set aside. In a medium bowl, with an electric beater or mixer, beat the eggs and egg yolks to combine.

2. Add the sugar and beat at medium-to-high speed until the mixture is smooth, pale and creamy, about 3 minutes. Beat in the orange juice gradually until very well mixed. Stir in the zest.

3. Pour the mixture into the prepared custard cups. Place the cups into a large baking pan and carefully pour boiling water around the cups to come about half way up on the outside of the cups. Bake about 40 minutes, or until the custards are almost set in the center and a thin knife

inserted in the center comes out clean. Remove the cups from the water bath and cool completely on a rack, then refrigerate about 6 hours before serving. Serve chilled, directly from the cups.

Mexican Vanilla Pudding
Natillas

Makes 6 servings

Sometimes Mexican cooks serve this classic pudding with a sprinkle of cinnamon and toasted nuts or sherry-soaked raisins on top. Plain natillas (without garnishes) with its soft creamy consistency, like crème anglaise, is also divine spooned over cakes, fruits, or berries.

¾ cup sugar
3½ tablespoons cornstarch
¼ teaspoon salt
2 large eggs, separated
3 cups milk
1 tablespoon medium-dry sherry
1 teaspoon pure vanilla extract

1. In a heavy medium nonreactive saucepan, mix ½ cup of the sugar with the cornstarch and salt. Stir in the egg yolks until blended, and gradually whisk in the milk. Bring to a boil over medium heat, whisking constantly, and cook until thickened, about 6 to 8 minutes.

2. Remove from the heat and stir in the sherry and the vanilla. Transfer to a bowl. Cover with plastic wrap, pressing it directly on the surface of the pudding to prevent a skin from forming on top. Refrigerate until cold, at least 2 hours. (Natillas will have a creamy soft consistency.) Spoon into small dessert bowls and serve cold. Garnish, if desired. Pudding keeps, covered and refrigerated, up to 3 days.

Coconut Pudding
Cocada

Makes 4 servings

Cocada is made all over Mexico. It's traditional to flavor this Mexican dessert with sherry and decorate the top with toasted almonds.

1/4 cup sugar

2 tablespoons water

1 cinnamon stick (Mexican canela or Ceylon variety preferred)

1/2 cup (about 2 ounces) lightly packed sweetened flaked coconut

1/8 teaspoon salt

1 1/4 cups plus 1/4 cup whole milk

2 large eggs

1 tablespoon dry sherry, such as amontillado

1/4 teaspoon pure vanilla extract

Toasted slivered almonds, for garnish

1. In a medium saucepan, boil the sugar, water, and cinnamon stick 5 minutes. Remove the cinnamon stick. Add the coconut and cook, stirring, until all of the syrup is absorbed, about 5 minutes. Add the salt and 1 1/4 cups of the milk. Cook, over medium heat, stirring until the mixture comes to a boil, then turn off the heat and let the mixture sit in the pan while beating the eggs.

2. In a small bowl, beat the eggs with the remaining 1/4 cup of milk. Stir 1/2 cup of the hot pudding into the beaten eggs and then stir the egg mixture into the hot coconut mixture. Return the pan to the heat and cook, over low heat, stirring constantly, until the pudding is hot and thickens slightly, about 5 to 7 minutes. (Do not boil, or the pudding might curdle.) Stir in the sherry and vanilla. Pour into 4 individual serving dishes. Refrigerate at least 6 hours or overnight. Serve cold with toasted almonds scattered on top. Store covered in the refrigerator up to 3 days.

Coffee Pudding
Budín de Café

Makes 4 servings

Coffee-flavored flans and puddings are popular in Mexico. This one is flavored with coffee essence made from instant coffee. (If a stronger coffee flavor is preferred, instant espresso may be used.) Instant coffee is widely available in Mexico. Before instant coffee was available, a very strong brewed coffee would flavor the budín. Mexico produces a great deal of coffee that's grown in the highlands of southern Mexico. The pudding should be served the day it's made.

1/2 cup sugar

3 tablespoons cornstarch

1/8 teaspoon salt

3 large eggs, beaten

2 1/2 cups whole milk

1 tablespoon instant coffee powder, or instant espresso

1/2 teaspoon pure vanilla extract

Sweetened Whipped Cream (page 583) (optional)

1. In a medium saucepan, mix the sugar, cornstarch, and salt. In a medium bowl, thoroughly whisk together the eggs and milk and then whisk the eggs and milk into the sugar mixture in the saucepan.

2. Bring to a boil over medium heat. Whisk in the coffee and cook, stirring constantly, until the mixture is smooth and thick, 8 to 10 minutes. Stir in the vanilla. Divide the pudding among 4 dessert bowls. Refrigerate about 6 hours. Serve cold. Refrigerate, covered, up to 3 days.

Rice Pudding
Arroz con Leche

Makes 6 servings

Dessert puddings came to Mexico with the Spanish in the mid-1500s, along with many sweet desserts. Spanish nuns, using recipes and ingredients they were familiar with, prepared puddings, flans, and other sweets, just as they had done in Spain. Desserts like this are now part of Mexican meals throughout the country, and all of Latin-America as well. The pudding is best served the day it's made.

1/2 cup short- or medium-grain rice

1 cinnamon stick (Mexican canela or Ceylon variety preferred)

2/3 cup sugar

1/8 teaspoon salt

3 1/2 cups whole milk

1/2 teaspoon pure vanilla extract

1 tablespoon unsalted butter

1. In a 2-quart saucepan mix the rice, cinnamon stick, sugar, salt, and 1¼ cups of water. Bring to a boil; then reduce the heat to low and simmer, covered, until most of the water is absorbed, about 15 minutes.

2. Stir in the milk and cook, partially covered, over low heat, stirring occasionally to prevent sticking, until thickened and creamy, and the rice is very tender, about 1 hour. Discard the cinnamon stick. Stir in the vanilla and butter. Divide among 6 dessert bowls. Serve warm or at room temperature. Refrigerate, covered, if kept overnight.

Mexican Bread Pudding
Capirotada

Makes 8 servings

Mexico's bread pudding is dense, sweet, and wonderful. The addition of cheese to the pudding is very common, but surprises many unsuspecting tasters. Some cooks add an apple or pear, and some sweet versions even contain tomatoes. This recipe, from San Miguel de Allende, in central Mexico, calls for making the sugar syrup with piloncillo *(Mexican unrefined brown sugar) that has a mild molasses-like flavor. Use it, if possible, or substitute dark brown sugar. Serve warm with whipped cream, ice cream, or Rum Butter Sauce (page 581).*

1 large egg, beaten

1/2 cup milk

3 tablespoons unsalted butter, melted

6 cups cubed (3/4-inch) lightly toasted sweet French bread

1/2 cup coarsely shredded Chihuahua, or mild cheddar cheese

8 ounces piloncillo (Mexican unrefined brown sugar) or 1 cup packed dark brown sugar

3 cups water

1 cinnamon stick (Mexican canela or Ceylon variety preferred)

1/2 teaspoon pure vanilla extract

3/4 cup chopped pecans or walnuts

1/2 cup raisins

1 teaspoon ground cinnamon (Mexican canela or Ceylon variety preferred)

1. Preheat the oven to 350°. Grease a wide 2½-quart baking dish. In a large mixing bowl, beat together the egg, milk, and melted butter. Add the bread cubes and cheese. Toss well. Set aside.

2. In a medium saucepan, place the piloncillo or brown sugar, water, and cinnamon stick. Bring to a boil; then reduce the heat to low and simmer the syrup uncovered 5 minutes. Turn off the heat and remove the cinnamon stick. Stir in the vanilla.

3. In the greased baking dish, spread half of the bread mixture evenly over the bottom. Scatter pecans and raisins evenly over the bread. Cover with the remaining bread mixture. Sprinkle cinnamon on top. Pour the sugar syrup evenly over the surface. With the back of a spoon, press bread mixture gently to soak with syrup.

4. Bake 30 to 35 minutes, or until the top is lightly browned and the pudding is set.

Custard Bread Pudding
Budín de Pan

Makes 6 to 8 servings

Almost everyone likes bread pudding, but this one with strong Spanish influence, is my personal favorite. It's quite elegant with a very smooth custard. Start making the pudding a day ahead to allow for soaking the bread with the egg and milk custard. Serve warm with Strawberry Dessert Sauce (page 582) or Mexican Vanilla Pudding (page 563) and garnish the dessert with fresh berries, mangos, or peaches.

1 (16-ounce) day-old loaf of sweet French bread, sliced 1/2 inch thick

3 large eggs, plus 2 egg yolks

3 cups whole milk

2/3 cup sugar plus 1/3 cup for the topping

1 1/2 teaspoons pure vanilla extract

1/8 teaspoon salt

2 tablespoons unsalted butter, melted

1. Liberally grease a 9-inch square glass baking dish. Remove the crusts from the bread. Place a single layer of sliced bread in the baking dish. Cut the bread to fit closely and neatly together. Arrange a second bread layer over the first. Set aside.

2. In a mixing bowl, beat the eggs and yolks together with a fork. Add the milk, 2/3 cup of the sugar, vanilla, and salt. Mix very well. Pour the custard slowly over the bread, stopping once or twice to stir the custard mixture to prevent the sugar from settling to the bottom. When all of the custard has been poured over the bread, gently press the bread with the back of a wooden spoon into the custard to soak thoroughly. Place a piece of plastic wrap directly on the surface of the pudding and refrigerate overnight.

3. About 1 hour before baking, remove the pudding from the refrigerator. Preheat the oven to 350°. Bring 2 cups of water to a boil. Melt the butter and drizzle on top of the pudding. Sprinkle evenly with the remaining 1/3 cup of sugar. Place the pudding pan into a larger pan and place them in the middle of the oven. Pour boiling water into the larger holding pan to a height of 1 inch.

4. Bake, uncovered, 45 to 50 minutes, or until a tester inserted in the center comes out clean. The pudding will be puffed and barely brown. Remove the pudding and water bath from the oven.

5. Raise the oven rack one step closer to the broiler (or if your broiler is separate, simply heat the broiler). Put the pudding under the broiler and brown the top of the pudding briefly, 2 to 3 minutes, until evenly browned. Watch carefully and turn the pan around to brown evenly. Cool the pudding on a rack about 20 minutes. Cut into neat squares or rectangles and serve warm.

Sweet Potato Pudding with Nuts
Budín de Camotes con Nuez

Makes 6 servings

Alicia Franyuti, owner of the Hacienda de las Flores in San Miguel de Allende, planned several meals for my culinary group when we stayed at her charming hotel. This sweet potato pudding was one of the desserts prepared by her kitchen staff.

2 pounds orange-skinned sweet potatoes (often labeled yams), scrubbed but not peeled

¹/₄ cup honey

2 tablespoons dark brown sugar

3 tablespoons unsalted butter

1 teaspoon pure vanilla extract

¹/₂ teaspoon salt

2 large eggs, beaten

¹/₂ cup chopped pecans or walnuts

Brown Sugar Syrup (page 583)

Sweetened Whipped Cream (page 583) (optional)

1. Preheat the oven to 400°. Grease an 8-inch square baking dish. Cut the yams crosswise into 1-inch rounds. Bring a 3-quart saucepan of water to boil and cook the yams until tender, about 20 minutes. Drain.

2. While the yams are still warm, but cool enough to handle, peel and put in a large bowl. Mash well with a potato masher. Stir in the honey, brown sugar, butter, vanilla, and salt. Add the eggs and mix very well.

3. Transfer to the prepared baking dish. Sprinkle the nuts over the top. Bake until a tester inserted in the center comes out clean, 20 to 25 minutes.

4. Meanwhile, prepare syrup and keep warm. Prepare whipped cream, if using. Then, when pudding is done, serve it warm in small dessert bowls with warm syrup spooned over the top. Add a dollop of whipped cream, if desired. Any remaining sugar syrup will keep, refrigerated, in a covered container indefinitely.

Ice Creams

Vanilla Ice Cream
Helado de Vainilla

Makes **1 quart**

Rich and creamy vanilla ice cream is easy to make, and nearly foolproof if you use moist, good quality vanilla beans with a strong vanilla aroma. Mexican vanilla beans from the main vanilla orchid plantations in Papantla, in the state of Veracruz, are prized in Mexico, but any fine vanilla bean works very well.

2 cups whipping or heavy cream
1 cup whole milk
2/3 cup sugar
1 vanilla bean
4 large egg yolks, beaten

1. Split vanilla bean in half lengthwise with a thin-bladed knife. Put the cream, milk, and sugar into a medium saucepan. Scrape the seeds of the vanilla bean into the liquid and drop the vanilla bean into the pan. Stir, and heat until steaming. Add 1 cup of the hot cream to the egg yolks, beating thoroughly with a whisk. Pour the egg mixture into the pan with the remaining hot cream. Cook, stirring constantly, over medium-low heat until the custard thickens slightly and coats the back of a wooden spoon. (Do not allow the custard to boil or it will curdle.)

2. Remove the custard from the heat and pour through a strainer into a clean container. Add the vanilla bean to the container. Cool completely, then remove the vanilla bean, cover, and refrigerate at least 6 hours or overnight. Stir the mixture and transfer to an ice cream machine. Freeze according to the manufacturer's directions.

Chocolate Ice Cream
Helado de Chocolate

Makes **about 1 quart**

A good friend and occasional travel partner, Camille Tarantino, gets credit for developing this intense chocolate ice cream so reminiscent of the rich goodness of the Mexican original that inspired it.

2 large eggs
1 1/4 cups unsweetened cocoa powder
1 1/2 cups whole milk, warmed to steaming
3/4 cup sugar
1 1/4 cups whipping or heavy cream
2 1/2 teaspoons pure vanilla extract
1/4 teaspoon almond extract (optional)
1/4 teaspoon ground cinnamon (Mexican canela or Ceylon variety preferred)

1. Put the eggs and cocoa in a blender or food processor and pulse to mix. Gradually add the warmed milk through the lid opening. Pour into a medium saucepan. Whisk in the sugar, and cook over medium heat, stirring, until the sugar dissolves and the mixture thickens and coats the back of a wooden spoon, about 4 to 6 minutes. (Do not boil or it will curdle).

2. Cool to lukewarm; then stir in the cream, vanilla, almond extract, and cinnamon. Transfer to a clean container. Cover and refrigerate about 6 hours or overnight. Stir the mixture and transfer to an ice cream machine. Freeze according to manufacturer's directions.

Coffee Ice Cream
Helado de Café

Makes **about 1 quart**

During our shared trips to Mexico, Camille Tarantino and I seldom end a day without indulging in a scoop of ice cream. Camille developed the recipe for this yummy ice cream that contains no eggs. It reminds us of ice cream from our favorite ice cream shop, on a corner across from the main zocalo (plaza), in Oaxaca.

1¼ **cups milk**

2 **tablespoons instant coffee or espresso powder**

²/₃ **cup sugar**

3 **cups whipping or heavy cream**

2 **teaspoons pure vanilla extract**

In a medium saucepan heat the milk until steaming, but do not boil. Whisk in the coffee. Add the sugar and continue whisking until the sugar is completely dissolved. Cool to lukewarm. Add the whipping cream and vanilla. Whisk until completely mixed. Transfer to a clean container. Cover and refrigerate 6 hours or overnight. Stir the mixture and transfer to an ice cream machine. Freeze according to the manufacturer's directions.

Mexican Caramel Ice Cream
Helado de Cajeta

Makes **about 1 quart**

This ice cream is smooth and luscious! Cajeta is a thick caramel sauce or candy made from goat's milk or cow's milk in Celaya, a city in the state of Guanajuato. Cajeta is packed in jars with labels showing either a cow or a goat face. The product is similar to dulce de leche, *the Spanish name for a rich concoction made with sugar and cream. Cajeta is widely available in Mexican markets and in the Mexican section of many supermarkets.*

3 **cups whole milk**

2 **large egg yolks**

¹/₃ **cup sugar**

¹/₄ **teaspoon salt**

1¹/₂ **cups cajeta (Mexican caramel sauce)**

1. In a saucepan, mix the milk, yolks, sugar, and salt. Cook, stirring, over medium-low heat until it starts to steam and thicken enough to coat the back of a wooden spoon. (Do not boil, or it will curdle.)

2. Remove from the heat and continue whisking while adding the cajeta until fully incorporated. Transfer to a clean container, cover, and refrigerate at least 3 hours or up to overnight. The cajeta cools the mixture as it is stirred in. Transfer to an ice cream machine. Freeze according to the manufacturer's directions.

Almond Ice Cream
Helado Almendra

Makes **1 quart**

My friend Camille Tarantino has shared several trips to Mexico with me, and tasting the delicious ice creams has always been near the top of our list of things to do. Camille developed this creamy almond-flavored ice cream that we remembered after one of our trips. Toast the almonds until golden brown, but watch carefully and do not let them burn. To retain the smooth texture of the ice cream, the nuts are discarded after flavoring the custard. You can, of course, leave them in if you want a little nutty crunch in your ice cream.

2 cups whipping or heavy cream

2 cups whole milk

1 cup coarsely chopped toasted almonds (page 9)

2 teaspoons pure vanilla extract

1 teaspoon almond extract

3/4 cup sugar

4 large egg yolks

1. In a medium saucepan, bring to a boil the cream, milk, almonds, vanilla, and almond extract. Cook 2 minutes. Cover and let stand off heat 15 minutes to infuse the flavors.

2. Meanwhile, in a large mixing bowl, with an electric beater or mixer, beat the egg yolks until well combined. Gradually add the sugar, beating, until the yolks are pale and form a ribbon, about 4 minutes. Set aside.

3. Return the milk to a boil again; then pour the hot milk through a strainer into the bowl with the beaten yolks, stirring to combine. Discard the nuts.

4. Pour the mixture into a clean saucepan and cook over low heat, stirring, until the custard thickens and coats the back of a wooden spoon. (Do not boil or it will curdle.)

5. Immediately remove the pan from the heat and strain into a clean container. Cover and refrigerate the custard about 6 hours or overnight. Transfer to an ice cream machine. Freeze according to the manufacturer's directions.

Coconut Ice Cream
Helado de Coco

Makes **about 1 quart**

My good friend and premier ice-cream-maker, Camille Tarantino, was always ready and willing to test ice creams following our trips to Mexico. We made this simple one for a cooking class and everyone really loved the rich coconut flavor.

1 1/2 cups milk or half and half

3/4 cup sugar

1 (14-ounce) can coconut milk

1. Combine the milk and sugar in a saucepan. Gently warm over low heat, stirring, until the sugar dissolves. Remove from the heat and whisk in the coconut milk until smooth.

2. Transfer to a clean container, cover, and refrigerate about 6 hours or overnight. Stir the mixture and transfer to ice cream machine. Freeze according to the manufacturer's instructions.

Watermelon Ice Cream
Helado de Sandia

Makes **6 servings**

This recipe doesn't require an ice cream maker; it uses frozen chunks of watermelon and frozen strawberries (for extra body and color) combined with cream to make a smooth ice cream that is a real crowd-pleaser. Using a food processor makes it simple to prepare. The ice cream can be served directly from the processor bowl as soon as it's made, or it can be placed in the freezer for 30 minutes and then served. Make the dessert with the ripest, sweetest summer melon you can find.

4 cups watermelon chunks, seeded and cut into 1-inch pieces
1/2 (10-ounce) package frozen sweetened whole strawberries
1/2 cup heavy cream
1/4 cup sugar or more, to taste

1. Put the watermelon pieces on a baking sheet and freeze until solid. Transfer to a sealable plastic bag, secure, and keep in freezer until ready to use.

2. Remove the watermelon and the strawberries from the freezer about 5 minutes before processing. Cut the frozen berries into pieces. Place half of the watermelon in a food processor, fitted with the steel blade and process until finely chopped. Add the remaining watermelon and the berries. Pulse to break up.

3. Add the cream and 1/4 cup of sugar. Process until the mixture is smooth and creamy. Add more sugar, if needed. Scrape down the sides of the bowl and process another 5 seconds. Spoon into serving bowls and serve at once, or store in the processor and place in the freezer up to 30 minutes for the best texture.

Note: Mixture will freeze quite solid if left longer, but it can be processed again quite successfully if it becomes too hard.

Cherimoya Ice
Nieve de Cherimoya

Makes **4 servings**

Cherimoyas, *grown in Mexico's tropical zones, are large oval-shaped tropical fruits with a rich exotic taste reminiscent of pineapple, banana, and papaya. The fruit has a leathery green skin with overlapping indentations somewhat like thumbprints. The flesh is creamy white, with a texture like firm custard, somewhat like a soft pear, but smoother. The center is full of shiny black seeds. Ripe* cherimoyas *will give when pressed gently. Underripe fruit will ripen at room temperature. The fruit makes a wonderfully refreshing ice and is one of dozens of flavors to choose from in Mexico's many ice cream stands or shops.*

1 large ripe cherimoya (about 3/4 pound)
1/2 cup sugar
1/2 cup water
2 tablespoons frozen concentrate of pineapple or orange juice

1. Cut the cherimoya lengthwise into quarters. Peel the quarters and scoop out the seeds. Chop the fruit medium-fine. There should be about 1 1/3 cups.

2. In a small saucepan, mix the sugar and water. Bring to a boil and cook until reduced to 1/2 cup, 4 to 5 minutes. Cool completely.

3. Put the cherimoya and pineapple or orange juice into a blender and purée. When the sugar syrup is cool, add to the blender and mix briefly. Transfer the mixture to an ice cream machine and freeze, following the manufacturer's directions. To serve, let stand at room temperature to soften slightly.

Fruit Desserts

Mangos with Strawberries
Mangos con Fresas

Makes 4 servings

Delectable, juicy mangos are now mainstream fruits in the United States, thanks to wider cultivation. Mexico grows several varieties of mangos in all tropical parts of the country, and excellent strawberries are grown in central Mexico, especially in Irapuato in the state of Guanajuato, one of Mexico's most productive farming regions. When both of these fine fruits are in season, they can be teamed up for a simply beautiful dessert. Pass a plate of Cinnamon-Walnut Cookies (page 543) for an extra treat with the fruit.

Strawberry Dessert Sauce (page 582)
2 large ripe mangos
**12 whole fresh strawberries, trimmed and
    thinly sliced**
Fresh mint sprigs

1. Prepare strawberry sauce. Then, with a sharp, thin-bladed knife, peel the somewhat flatter half of each mango and cut a thick slice of the fruit away from the large flat pit, cutting as close as possible to the pit.

2. Turn the mango over and peel the other flat side, cutting a thick slice away from the pit, as before. Thinly slice the mango halves and arrange the slices among 4 dessert plates.

3. Spoon some strawberry sauce over each serving. Garnish with sliced berries and mint sprigs.

Grilled Pineapple
Piña a la Parrilla

Makes 6 to 8 servings

Pineapple is abundant all over Mexico, and the sweet fruit grills beautifully, so when you have hot coals left in the grill from other cooking, try grilling pineapple. Serve with a scoop of ice cream, if desired. For another method, use a stovetop grill pan.

1 whole fresh ripe pineapple (about 2 pounds)
1 tablespoon unsalted butter, melted
2 teaspoons honey

1. Prepare an outdoor grill. Cut the pineapple lengthwise right through the top leaves, leaving them intact, into 6 or 8 equal wedges. Mix the butter and honey in a small bowl. Grease the grill.

2. Lay the pineapple cut side down, about 6 inches above the coals. Grill until lightly charred, 2 to 3 minutes on each cut side of the wedges. If using a stovetop grill pan, heat the pan over medium heat and cook each pineapple wedge in the same manner, 3 to 4 minutes on each cut side of the wedges. Just before removing them from the grill (or pan), brush the pieces lightly with the butter and honey mixture. Serve warm.

Broiled Pineapple
Piña Asada

Makes **4 servings**

Broiled fresh pineapple emerges from the oven with a caramelized, sweet sugary crust for a different version than grilling over hot coals. It's sensational served warm, but perfectly good at room temperature, too.

1 whole fresh ripe pineapple (about 2 pounds)
2 tablespoons unsalted butter, melted
2 tablespoons light brown sugar

1. Cut about 1 inch off the top and bottom of the pineapple with a sharp heavy knife. Stand the pineapple on a flat work surface and with a smaller sharp knife, cut off the peel, a strip at a time, from top to bottom. Then, with a paring knife, dig out any "eyes" from the flesh. Turn the pineapple on its side and cut into 1-inch-thick slices.

2. Place the oven rack about 6 inches below the broiler unit. Preheat the broiler. Put the pineapple on a baking sheet. Brush the slices with melted butter.

3. Broil the pineapple until lightly browned, 5 to 6 minutes. Turn the slices over and brush with melted butter. Broil the second side until just starting to brown, 3 to 4 minutes. Sprinkle the slices lightly with brown sugar, and broil until the sugar melts, 1 to 2 minutes. Cut the pineapple rounds into bite-size (about 1-inch) pieces. Discard the core. Divide the pieces among 4 serving plates or small dessert bowls. Serve warm.

Pineapple with Mint
Piña con Yerbabuena

Makes **4 to 6 servings**

Fresh fruit is always an appropriate dessert following a Mexican meal. A thick juicy slice of cold pineapple flavored with mint has great eye-appeal and is very refreshing.

Casa de Los Tesoros, a hotel in the former silver mining city of Alamos, in the state of Sonora, served pineapple this way. Alamos, a National Historic Monument, is a popular tourist destination, where colonial architecture has been beautifully maintained.

1 whole fresh ripe pineapple (about 2 pounds)
1/2 cup finely chopped fresh mint
1/2 cup sugar
4 to 6 large fresh strawberries
4 to 6 mint sprigs

1. Cut about 1 inch off the top and bottom of the pineapple with a sharp heavy knife. Stand the pineapple on its end and, with a smaller, sharp knife, cut off the husk in strips from top to bottom all the way around. Then, with a paring knife, dig out any "eyes" from the flesh. Lay the pineapple on its side and cut crosswise into 6 (¾-inch-thick) slices and place on a plate.

2. Sprinkle sugar evenly over slices and divide the shredded mint evenly on top of each slice. Stack the sugared, minted slices, one on top of the other, and put the stack in a sealed plastic bag. Close securely. Refrigerate at least 6 hours or overnight, so the fruit macerates in the sugar and mint.

3. To serve, discard the shredded mint. Pour the collected juices through a strainer into a cup. Discard residue. Place 1 slice of pineapple on each of 4 plates with a strawberry in the center. Spoon some of the juice on each slice. Garnish with fresh mint sprigs. Serve cold.

Bananas Victoria
Dulce de Plátanos Victoria

Makes **4 servings**

Years ago, this banana dessert was on the menu of the beautiful Hotel Victoria in Oaxaca, Mexico. This is my version of the dessert.

¹/₂ cup chopped walnuts

3 tablespoons dark brown sugar

¹/₄ cup raisins

¹/₂ teaspoon ground cinnamon (Mexican canela or Ceylon variety preferred)

¹/₄ cup fresh orange juice

¹/₂ teaspoon pure vanilla extract

4 ripe bananas (short, plump bananas work best)

2 tablespoons unsalted butter, melted

1 pint vanilla ice cream

1. Preheat the oven to 350°. Put the walnuts in a medium bowl. Mix in the brown sugar, raisins, cinnamon, orange juice, and vanilla.

2. Peel the bananas. Cut lengthwise in half, and place them close together, cut side up, on a foil-lined baking sheet. Top the bananas evenly with the nut-raisin mixture. Drizzle the butter over all. Cover with another sheet of aluminum foil. Seal tightly. Bake 25 minutes, or until the bananas are soft and the sauce bubbles. Serve warm on dessert plates with ice cream.

Caramelized Bananas with Mexican Eggnog Sauce
Plátanos Dulce con Rompope

Makes **4 servings**

Mexican desserts are often sweet and rich just like this one. A small serving is exquisite and comforting. I like to add small, crisp chocolate cookie, such as Chocolate Pecan Cookies (page 543) to munch with the dessert. Rompope, the eggnog dessert sauce for the bananas, is very easy to make, or can be purchased in some specialty liquor stores.

2 cups (¹/₂ recipe) Mexican Eggnog Rum Drink (page 612), or purchased rompope

¹/₄ cup sugar

1 tablespoon unsalted butter

¹/₃ cup fresh orange juice

1 teaspoon fresh lime juice

2 medium firm-but-ripe bananas, peeled and sliced diagonally into ¹/₂-inch-thick pieces

1. Prepare ¹/₂ recipe eggnog drink, if using home-made. In a small, dry, heavy saucepan or nonstick skillet cook the sugar, stirring over medium heat until melted and golden brown. Remove the skillet from the heat. Stir in the butter and juices. (Some of the caramel may harden, but will melt again.)

2. Return pan to the heat and cook until blended and the caramel melts, 5 to 8 minutes. Add the bananas and turn to coat with the caramel. Cook 1 to 2 minutes until heated through and slightly softened. To serve, spoon 3 tablespoons rompope into each of 4 small dessert bowls. Divide the bananas evenly and spoon 2 to 3 tablespoons of the sauce over each serving. Serve warm.

Plantains with Vanilla Sauce and Pecans

Plátanos Machos con Natillas y Pecanas

Makes **4 servings**

Large, starchy cooking bananas called plantains are often sold when the skin is still green, but they are ripe when the skin is nearly black and the fruit feels slightly soft to the touch. When plantains are sautéed, they become golden brown and sweet. Regular sweet, yellow bananas can be used, but they should be firm and not too ripe.

2 cups (¹/₂ recipe) **Mexican Vanilla Pudding (page 563)**

3 medium-size ripe plantains

2 tablespoons unsalted butter

¹/₄ cup dark rum

2 tablespoons sugar

¹/₄ teaspoon ground cinnamon (Mexican canela or Ceylon variety preferred)

¹/₂ cup chopped pecans

1. Prepare ¹/₂ recipe of the vanilla pudding. Then, peel the plantains and slice on a diagonal into ovals about ¹/₄-inch thick. Melt the butter in a medium skillet over medium heat. Sauté the plantains, in batches, until golden brown on both sides. Arrange on 4 warm dessert plates.

2. In the same skillet, over medium heat, add the rum, sugar, and cinnamon. Stir to deglaze the skillet. Spoon the glaze over the warm plantains. Divide the plantains among 4 dessert plates. Spoon about ¹/₄ cup of vanilla pudding over each serving. Sprinkle with the pecans. Serve at once. (Cover and refrigerate any left over pudding for a midnight snack.)

Strawberries with Mexican Eggnog

Fresas con Rompope

Makes **4 servings**

Fresh strawberries were abundant in San Miguel de Allende during a winter visit several years ago, since Irapuato, the nearby strawberry capital of Mexico, was in full harvest. We enjoyed ripe, red berries topped with rompope, Mexico's well-known eggnog rum drink that's sold in liquor stores. It's also very easy to make your own. Rompope has a creamy texture like a liquidy vanilla custard.

2 cups (¹/₂ recipe) **Mexican Eggnog Rum Drink (page 612), or purchased rompope**

Sweetened Whipped Cream (page 583) (optional)

3 cups fresh strawberries, rinsed and hulled

¹/₄ cup sugar

Fresh mint sprigs

1. Prepare eggnog drink, if making homemade. Prepare whipped cream, if using. Then, put the cleaned berries in a bowl and toss gently with the sugar. Cover and refrigerate at least 30 minutes and up to 2 hours.

2. Divide among 4 dessert bowls. Pour ¹/₄ cup rompope into each serving. Add a dollop of whipped cream, if using. Garnish each serving with a mint sprig. (Leftover rompope keeps 3 to 4 weeks, refrigerated.)

Strawberries and Bananas in Walnut Sauce

Fresas y Plátanos en Nogada

Makes 4 servings

Simple fruit desserts often make just the right finish after a spicy meal. Sweet, juicy strawberries teamed with bananas are a pretty and delicious dessert when drizzled with creamy walnut sauce. Scatter a few chopped walnuts on top, if desired.

1 cup Walnut Sauce (page 52)
16 ripe red strawberries, hulled, rinsed, and sliced lengthwise
2 medium bananas, peeled and sliced on a diagonal into 1/4-inch-thick ovals
1/2 teaspoon sugar, or to taste
Coarsely chopped walnuts (optional)
Mint sprigs

1. Prepare walnut sauce. Then, on each of 4 dessert plates, arrange the strawberries and bananas in overlapping lines.

2. Taste the walnut sauce and add sugar to taste, if desired. Drizzle 1 to 2 tablespoons of the sauce over the fruit, but do not cover completely. Scatter chopped walnuts on top, if desired, and garnish each serving with a sprig of mint. The remaining walnut sauce can be passed at the table. (Leftover walnut sauce keeps, refrigerated about 5 days.)

Oranges and Strawberries with Tequila

Naranjas y Fresas con Tequila

Makes 4 servings

Cold, juicy oranges and bright red strawberries, mixed with a bit of tequila, make a memorable dessert or a festive starter for breakfast or brunch. (You may want to inform your guests that the fruit has a little kick.) Prepare the fruit a few hours in advance to allow the flavors to marry. Use seedless navel oranges to make this dish easier to prepare. Pink grapefruit segments are also an alternative for oranges. You would need 2 medium grapefruits.

4 large navel oranges
1 tablespoon sugar
1 tablespoon silver or gold tequila
1/2 tablespoon orange liqueur, such as Triple Sec or Grand Marnier
16 ripe strawberries
Fresh mint sprigs

1. Peel the oranges, and remove the white pith. Cut into bite-size pieces and put into a medium bowl. Add the sugar, tequila, and orange liqueur. Stir to combine. Cover and refrigerate about 4 hours, stirring occasionally, to distribute the juices.

2. About 1 hour before serving, rinse the strawberries and remove the stems and leaves. Cut the berries in half and add to the oranges. Serve cold in individual bowls with the juices. Garnish each serving with a sprig of mint.

Peaches and Strawberries with Vanilla Pudding
Melacatones con Natillas y Fresas

Makes 4 servings

Poached fresh peaches, nestled in heavenly vanilla pudding studded with bright juicy strawberries, is a dessert worth waiting for. Use wonderful ripe peaches. San Angel Inn, a great restaurant in Mexico City, matches fresh fruits with natillas, *the classic Mexican vanilla pudding. Whenever the dessert cart stops at my table, I'm tempted by this sweet dish. Peaches and strawberries are both grown in a variety of agricultural areas of Mexico.*

2 cups water

3/4 cup sugar

2 large ripe peaches, peeled, halved, and pitted

1 vanilla bean, or 1 teaspoon pure vanilla extract

Mexican Vanilla Pudding (page 563)

16 whole or sliced fresh strawberries

Fresh mint sprigs

1. In a wide 3-quart, nonreactive pot, bring the water and sugar to a boil over high heat, stirring to dissolve the sugar. Reduce the heat to low, add the peach halves and vanilla. Poach slowly, uncovered, until the peaches are barely tender when pierced with tip of a sharp knife, 10 to 20 minutes, depending on the ripeness of the peaches. Transfer the peaches and the syrup to a bowl. (Rinse and dry the vanilla bean. Store to use again.) Cover and refrigerate until cold, about 4 hours or overnight.

2. Make the pudding and chill until shortly before serving. To serve, spoon a serving of pudding into 4 dessert dishes. (Save remaining pudding for another use.) Place 1 peach half in each dish, rounded side up. Garnish each serving with strawberries and a sprig of mint.

Peaches with Vanilla Ice Cream
Melocotones con Helado

Makes 4 servings

When we first traveled to Mexico more than thirty years ago, peaches with ice cream, melocotones con helado, *were served in most fancy Mexico City restaurants. Invariably, the peaches were canned. On a recent trip to Mexico City, Chef Ricardo Muñoz Zurita introduced me to a variety of fresh peach grown in Mexico. It was small and ordinary looking, but very sweet. It revived the memory of those earlier peach desserts and how good they could be with fresh peaches. This dessert is a delicious way to enjoy ripe peaches, when in season, with ice cream and toasted nuts. Sometimes I drizzle chocolate syrup over the top.*

1 pint Vanilla Ice Cream (page 568), or purchased ice cream

4 ripe fresh peaches

1 teaspoon fresh lime or lemon juice

1/2 cup chopped toasted walnuts or pecans

1. Prepare ice cream in advance, if using homemade. Then, bring a large pot of water to a boil. Dip the peaches in, 1 at a time, until the skins loosen, about 10 seconds. Peel, pit, and cut the peaches in half. Put in a bowl. Add the lime or lemon juice. Toss gently to coat to help prevent the peaches from turning brown for a short time. Cover and refrigerate up to 2 hours.

2. Meanwhile, toast the nuts in a small, dry skillet over medium heat, stirring and shaking the pan, until fragrant and lightly toasted, 3 to 4 minutes. Serve the peaches cold, cut side up, in small dessert bowls with ice cream spooned into the cavities. Sprinkle lightly with nuts. Drizzle a little chocolate syrup on top, if desired.

Blackberry Parfait
Dulce de Zarzamora

Makes **4 servings**

Polanco is a beautiful zone in Mexico City, with mansions, fine restaurants, lots of great shops, and a wonderful open-air market with colorful, abundant produce and other food items. My husband and I love to stroll by all the vendors, and this recipe is a result of admiring baskets of luscious fresh blackberries that were in season during one of our trips.

**2 cups Vanilla Ice Cream (page 568), or purchased
    vanilla ice cream or frozen yogurt**
**4 cups fresh blackberries, or thawed unsweetened
    frozen berries**
¹/₂ cup sugar
1 tablespoon crème de cassis liqueur
1 cup Sweetened Whipped Cream (page 583)
Fresh mint sprigs

1. Prepare ice cream, if using homemade. Put the berries in a large bowl. Add the sugar and cassis. Toss to mix, cover and refrigerate at least 4 hours or overnight.

2. Prepare whipped cream. Then, shortly before serving, put ¼ cup sweetened berries in the bottom of each of 4 parfait or wineglasses. Spoon ½ cup ice cream on the berries. Add another ¼ cup of berries and top each serving with a generous dollop of whipped cream. Garnish with mint sprigs. Serve at once.

Note: Berry juice will seep into the ice cream, but it still looks and tastes great.

Plums in Orange Sauce
Ciruelas en Salsa de Naranja

Makes **4 servings**

Boxes of ripe red plums appeared in markets and on the street during an early summer trip to Mexico City. Many people were eating plums out of hand with juice dripping through their fingers. Mexicans love fresh fruits of every kind, and these little plums were clearly in season. Fresh plums are wonderful poached in orange juice and honey. These are served cold with the reduced poaching syrup poured on top. Add a dollop of whipped cream or a scoop of ice cream, if you like.

1 cup fresh orange juice
2 teaspoons fresh lime juice or lemon juice
¹/₂ cup honey
**1 cinnamon stick (Mexican canela or Ceylon variety
    preferred)**
12 ripe plums, cut in half and pits removed

1. In a saucepan, mix the orange juice, lime juice, and honey. Add the cinnamon stick and bring to a boil over medium heat. Add the plums, reduce the heat to low, cover and cook, turning the plums once or twice until they are tender, but not soft or falling apart, about 6 to 8 minutes, depending on the size and ripeness of the fruit.

2. Using a slotted spoon, transfer the plums to a bowl. Discard the cinnamon stick. Bring the liquid to a boil over medium-high heat and cook until reduced by about half. Pour the syrup over the plums, cover and refrigerate until cold, at least 1 hour and up to overnight. Serve cold.

Fresh Figs with Cheese
Higos con Queso
Makes **4 servings**

When Catholic missions were established in Baja, Mexico, in the 1500s, the Spanish Franciscan missionaries introduced figs to the region, where the purple-black Mission fig is still grown. Fresh figs are very perishable and are best eaten within a day or two of purchasing.

Figs and cheese are divine together. Mexican-style panela cheese, with a slightly spongy, but firm texture, is a perfect partner and has become widely available. Clusters of seedless grapes may be added to the arrangement, if desired.

12 fresh ripe figs
6 ounces panela cheese, cut into fat strips
(1/2 inch × 3 inches)

Cut the figs in half from stem to tip. Arrange the fig halves cut side up, alternating with the cheese on a serving plate.

Figs in Brown Sugar Syrup
Dulce de Higos
Makes **4 servings**

Early missionaries who settled in Baja planted fig trees and date palms, and many of these trees thrive even today. Fresh figs are a delicacy, and if not eaten out of hand, I think a simple compote is the one of best ways to enjoy this delightful fruit. Fresh ripe figs should be quite soft and eaten within a day or two of purchase.

12 fresh ripe figs
1/4 cup sugar
1/2 cup water
Brown Sugar Syrup (page 583)
Sweetened Whipped Cream (page 583) or ice cream

1. Preheat the oven to 350°. Prick each fig in 2 or 3 places with the tip of a small sharp knife. Place the figs standing up in a pie plate. Sprinkle with the sugar and drizzle the water over the tops. Bake, uncovered, basting 2 to 3 times with the liquid until completely heated through, 20 to 25 minutes.

2. Prepare the brown sugar syrup, and whip the cream, if using. To serve, divide the figs among 4 dessert dishes. Spoon the sugar syrup over the figs, letting it pool onto the dish. Add a dollop of whipped cream, if using, or ice cream.

Baked Apples
Manzanas al Horno
Makes **4 servings**

The state of Chihuahua supplies most of the apples that are grown in Mexico. Some are grown in other temperate regions of central Mexico, and apples are also imported from other countries. Drizzle the baked apples with warm Brown Sugar Syrup (page 583) or serve with vanilla ice cream.

Vanilla Ice Cream (page 568), or purchased
4 apples (such as Rome Beauty or Winesap),
rinsed and cut in half lengthwise
2 teaspoons raisins
2 teaspoons dark brown sugar
2 teaspoons unsalted butter
Ground cinnamon

1. Prepare the ice cream in advance, if using homemade. Then, preheat the oven to 350°. Using a melon-baller scoop out the center cores from the apples. Place the apples in an ovenproof baking dish. Fill each cavity with about 1/2 teaspoon raisins and 1/2 teaspoon brown sugar. Top each with 1/2 teaspoon butter and sprinkle lightly with cinnamon. Add 2 tablespoons water to the dish and cover with foil.

2. Bake until apples are tender, about 30 to 35 minutes, depending on the variety of apple. Remove from the oven and spoon any juices from the baking dish over the apples. Serve warm topped with a scoop of ice cream.

Poached Guavas
Guayabas en Almibar

Makes **4 servings**

Guavas are native to Mexico and are grown in many parts of the country, especially in the states of Michoacan and Jalisco. Look for guavas in Mexican markets or gourmet produce markets. Select small ripe, but still firm, guavas. They make a delightful dessert or breakfast treat when poached in a sugar syrup. The fruit can be served alone in the syrup, or dressed up, placed on a pool of vanilla pudding (Mexican Vanilla Pudding, page 563).

1¹/₂ cups water

³/₄ cup sugar

1 cinnamon stick (Mexican canela or Ceylon variety preferred)

¹/₂ teaspoon pure vanilla extract

8 ripe but still-firm guavas, stems removed

1. Put the water, sugar, and cinnamon stick in a medium saucepan and bring to a boil, stirring, over medium heat. Reduce the heat to low, cover and simmer 15 minutes.

2. Meanwhile, peel the guavas and cut them in half. Scoop out the seeds with a teaspoon. Discard the seeds and put the guava shells in the syrup. When the syrup returns to a boil, reduce the heat to medium-low, partially cover, and simmer until the fruit is tender, but not too soft, 8 to 10 minutes. Remove the cinnamon stick.

3. Transfer the fruit and syrup to a bowl and cool the fruit in the syrup. Stir in the vanilla. Serve cool in small bowls. If made ahead, cover and refrigerate up to 2 days. Remove from the refrigerator about 1 hour before serving.

Guava Paste with Cream Cheese
Ate de Guayaba con Queso

Makes **4 servings**

Fruit pastes (ates) are often eaten as desserts with cheese, as in this recipe, or sometimes sliced and eaten alone as an afternoon snack. Guava pastes have recently become more available in the United States in most Mexican markets and in some supermarkets. The small blocks of pastes are easy to cut into thin slices and have a sweet gumdrop kind of texture. Crisp butter cookies or crackers are often served with ate.

1 (3-ounce) package cream cheese

1 (4-ounce) package guava paste

Cut the cream cheese into 4 equal slices and cut the guava paste into 8 thin slices. Place 1 piece of cream cheese between 2 slices of guava paste. Serve at room temperature.

Sauces and Icings

Chocolate-Cinnamon Dessert Sauce
Salsa de Chocolate-Canela

Makes **about 2 cups**

Here's an easy sauce to serve with any number of desserts.

1 cup sifted confectioners' sugar
³/₄ cup half and half
¹/₂ cup semi-sweet chocolate chips
2 tablespoons unsalted butter
¹/₈ teaspoon ground cinnamon (Mexican canela or Ceylon variety preferred)

In a saucepan, mix together the sugar, half and half, chocolate chips, butter, and cinnamon. Cook over medium-low heat, stirring constantly, until the mixture simmers and the chocolate is completely melted, about 4 minutes. Transfer to a bowl and cool. Sauce keeps well, refrigerated, 2 to 3 weeks.

Creamy Caramel Dessert Sauce
Salsa Dulce para Postres

Makes **about 1¹/₂ cups**

This simple, creamy caramel sauce is an alternative to Mexico's similar rich sauce called cajeta. *There are many versions, some of which include goat's or cow's milk, or which have fruit purées folded in. This recipe is very basic and a quick version to make. Serve warm over ice cream (*helado*) or other desserts (*postres*), such as dessert crepes or unfrosted cakes.*

¹/₂ cup heavy cream
¹/₂ cup dark brown sugar
¹/₂ cup sugar
2 tablespoons unsalted butter
1 teaspoon pure vanilla extract

Put the cream and both sugars in a medium saucepan and cook slowly over low heat, until completely melted and the mixture comes to a boil, about 5 minutes. When completely melted, add the butter, whisking, until thoroughly combined and smooth. Remove the pan from the heat. Stir in the vanilla. Serve warm, or store in a covered container in the refrigerator up to 3 days.

Rum Butter Sauce

Makes **about 1¹/₂ cups**

Serve this sweet dessert sauce over bread pudding, baked apples, bananas, or simple cakes.

1 cup sugar
1¹/₂ tablespoons cornstarch
¹/₄ cup dark rum
¹/₂ teaspoon pure vanilla extract
2 tablespoons unsalted butter, at room temperature

In a medium saucepan, mix the sugar and cornstarch. Add 1 cup of water. Bring to a boil over medium heat, stirring, until thick and clear, about 3 minutes. Remove the pan from the heat and stir in the rum, vanilla, and butter. Serve the sauce hot or warm. (Store in a covered container in the refrigerator for up to a week.) Reheat shortly before using.

Strawberry Dessert Sauce
Salsa Dulce de Fresas
Makes **about 1 cup**

Strawberries are widely grown in Mexico. I use sweetened frozen strawberries for this easy strawberry sauce that can be made year round for a wonderful fresh tasting topping for fruit, such as Mangos with Strawberries (page 572), or over ice cream or cake.

1 (10-ounce) package frozen sweetened strawberries, thawed
1 teaspoon orange liqueur, such as Triple Sec or Grand Marnier, or orange juice
1 tablespoon Port wine, or ¹/₂ teaspoon pure vanilla extract

Thaw the berries completely overnight in the refrigerator. Put the thawed berries and all the juices in a strainer set over a medium bowl. Push the berries and most of the pulp through the strainer. Discard pulp. Stir in the orange liqueur, Port, or vanilla. Cover and refrigerate until shortly before serving, up to 3 days.

Note: If sweetened berries aren't available, add confectioners' sugar (to taste) to sauce after pressing pulp.

Banana Cream Dessert Sauce
Crema de Plátano
Makes **about 1¹/₂ cups**

Contemporary Mexican desserts are being presented in stylish new ways. I had a similar banana sauce with rum cake at Fuerte restaurant in Tlaquepaque. The sauce is also very good spooned over fresh tropical fruits.

1 ripe banana (about 4 ounces), peeled and sliced
¹/₄ cup pineapple juice
¹/₄ cup sifted confectioners' sugar
³/₄ cup cold whipping or heavy cream
¹/₄ teaspoon pure vanilla extract

1. Put the banana, pineapple juice, and sugar in a medium saucepan and cook over medium heat until the bananas are soft, about 3 minutes. Transfer to a food processor and purée until smooth. Transfer to a bowl, cover, and refrigerate until cold, about 1 hour.

2. Beat the cream to stiff peaks and fold into the cold banana purée. Stir in the vanilla. Cover and refrigerate until shortly before serving. (Can be made 1 day ahead.)

Chocolate Icing
Makes **About 1 cup**

Chocolate was one of Mexico's gifts to the world, and that remarkable product has been put to incredible use. Here's a simple chocolate icing to frost Vanilla Cupcakes (page 541) or Chocolate and Almond Cake (page 534). Use whatever high-quality brand of chocolate you prefer. Mexican chocolate tablets don't melt smoothly enough for this type of frosting.

3 ounces semisweet or bittersweet chocolate, coarsely chopped
¹/₂ cup sifted confectioners' sugar
3 tablespoons unsalted butter
¹/₂ teaspoon pure vanilla extract

1. In the top part of a double boiler, put the chocolate, powdered sugar, butter, and 1 tablespoon of water. Set the top of the double boiler over simmering water in the bottom of the boiler. The water should not touch the top part of the double boiler containing the chocolate.

2. Stir constantly until the mixture is melted and smooth, about 5 minutes. Stir in the vanilla. Transfer the chocolate to a bowl and cool until thickened to a soft spreading consistency. Use at once.

Cream Cheese Frosting

Makes **about 1¹/₂ cups**

When you need a quick and easy frosting to spread over cakes, cream cheese is the answer. I often use this frosting for Pineapple Cake (page 540) or Lime Cake (page 540).

1 (8-ounce) package cream cheese, at room temperature
6 tablespoons unsalted butter, at room temperature
1¹/₂ cups sifted confectioners' sugar
¹/₂ teaspoon pure vanilla extract

In a medium bowl, with an electric beater or mixer, beat the cream cheese and butter until smooth. Beat in the confectioners' sugar and vanilla. Spread the frosting over the cake. Use at once.

Brown Sugar Syrup

Makes **about 1¹/₂ cups**

Mexican dark brown sugar cones called pilon-cillo *are available in Mexican markets, or use regular dark brown sugar in this dessert sauce that is often spooned over baked puddings or other desserts. The syrup can be made ahead and stored in the refrigerator.*

1 cup packed dark brown sugar, or 4 (2-ounce) piloncillo cones
¹/₂ cup water
¹/₂ teaspoon pure vanilla extract

In a small saucepan, combine the sugar, water, and vanilla. Bring to a boil, over medium heat, stirring, to melt the sugar. Cook about 1 minute. Remove the pan from the heat and let stand about 10 minutes to thicken slightly. The sauce is ready to use, or cool and store in a covered container in the refrigerator indefinitely. Reheat the syrup before using.

Sweetened Whipped Cream
Crema Batida Dulce

Makes **1¹/₂ cups**

Use lightly sweetened cream to garnish cake slices, fruits, or other desserts, or to spread over the sides and the top of cakes. Cream can be whipped, covered, and refrigerated about 1 to 2 hours before using, to prevent separation.

1 cup cold heavy whipping cream
1¹/₂ teaspoons sugar
¹/₄ teaspoon pure vanilla extract

In a large bowl with an electric beater or mixer, whip the cream with the sugar to soft or stiff peaks, as preferred. Take care not to beat too much, or the cream will turn to butter. Stir in the vanilla.

Beverages

Coffee and Hot Chocolate 588

Mexican Coffee

Coffee with Milk

Mexican Cappuccino, Guanajuato Style

Coffee Olé

Coffee Popo

Mexican Hot Chocolate

Corn- and Rice-Based Drinks 592

Chocolate Masa Drink

Tamarind Masa Drink

Rich Pineapple Drink

Almond-Flavored Rice Drink

Melon Horchata

Fruit Drinks and Punches (Non-alcoholic) 594

Strawberry Cooler

Banana-Strawberry Drink

Banana-Mango Drink

Mango-Orange Punch

Watermelon Cooler

Fresh Jamaica Cooler

Tamarind Cooler

Pomegranate Cooler

Easy Pineapple Punch

Citrus-Mint Ice Tea Punch

Sparkling Limeade

Party Punches with Alcohol 598

Red Wine Punch

Guadalajara Red Wine Punch

White Wine Punch

Christmas Wine Punch

Tequila Punch in a Clay Bowl

Watermelon Rum Punch

Fermented Pineapple Drink

Many Mexicans still begin and end their day as their ancestors did—sipping warm drinks—such as hot chocolate, *atoles*, and coffee drinks, with recipes centuries-old, as well as modern variations of them. (Today, they are often served with light rolls, pastries, or tamales.) *Atole*, a warm drink that is said to date back to pre-Columbian times, is thickened with corn *masa*, and flavored with vanilla, cinnamon, fresh fruits—such as pineapple or locally grown tamarind pods—or the popular favorite version, with chocolate.

The warm climate in much of Mexico has also long been inspiration for the creation of many refreshing cold drinks (*bebidas*). A common sight along the streets and through the markets all over Mexico are vendors displaying huge glass jars filled with beverages in a rainbow of hues. These wonderful cool drinks called *aguas frescas* are blended fruits, water, and ice. Another type of soothing drink, called *licuado*, blends milk with fruits, sugar, and ice. There are recipes in this chapter for a number of these delightful drinks that are perfect to serve with warm weather meals and at any kind of fiesta.

Another type of *fresca* called *horchata* is made with blended rice or melon seeds and served cold. To the uninitiated, *horchatas* seem unusual, but they are worth trying; you will be surprised by how soothing and nourishing they are.

Mexicans love fiestas and special occasions of all kinds, and alcoholic drinks like *rompope* (Mexican Eggnog Rum Drink, page 612) go hand in hand with the festivities. Mexican resort and beach areas would also not be the same without specialty cocktails and fruity concoctions like margaritas or "Drunken" Pineapple Drink (page 606), served to toast the setting sun or to celebrate the good life.

Most of these drinks feature tequila or rum, which are locally produced. Some are made with wine into fruit punches. All are easy to make at home.

All of the tequila sold throughout the world comes from the state of Jalisco, or from two other designated places, Guanajuato and Tamaulipas, in Mexico, and is government-regulated to prohibit any other area from calling their product tequila.

Tequila and mezcal are both made from the juices of *agave* plants that have long sword-like leaves with tiny needle-like thorns along the outside edge. Blue agave (*agave azul*), the designated plant for tequila, grows primarily in the state of Jalisco. It takes 7 to 12 years for a plant to mature. When the plants are ready to harvest, skilled harvesters (*jimadores*) swiftly and deftly cut off the outer leaves with a machete, and then the plant is chopped off at its roots. Finally, with a razor-sharp half-moon-blade tool, the leaf stubs left on the plant are trimmed, exposing the heart, called *piña* (pineapple), because it resembles a giant pineapple.

The huge *piñas*, weighing from 40 to more than 100 pounds, are carried to the distillery where they are steam-cooked for 24 to 36 hours to convert the starches to sugar, and then crushed and pressed to extract the juice, called *agua miel* (honey water). The juice is fermented in huge vats to produce a clear liquid that's about 40% alcohol—the basic tequila.

Tequila, by Mexican law, must be made with blue *agave* and the most prized tequilas are made from 100% blue agave. Less expensive tequilas must contain at least 51% blue agave juices. Clear tequila is called silver (*plata*) or white (*blanco*) and is usually not aged. Gold (*oro*) tequila contains added coloring and flavorings and may or may not be aged for a short time. *Reposado* (rested) is aged for a minimum of two months up to one year in oak, and is usually sipped or taken as a shot from tiny glasses called *cabollitas*. *Añejo* (aged) must age for at least one year in government-sealed oak barrels. Aging mellows and matures the taste, making aged tequilas exceptionally smooth. *Añejo* is sipped from *cabollitas*, or even from a brandy glass. Tequila is also used in cooking, in a minor way, to add a subtle, fruity and intriguing flavor of *agave* to the food. With more people cooking *nueva cocina*—mixing traditional and modern ingredients and techniques—cooking with tequila is becoming more common.

Mezcal, like tequila, also comes from a variety of an agave plant called the *maguey*. The plant looks very similar, but lacks the distinctive blue color of *agave azul*. In taste and texture, mezcal is smoky and more coarse than tequila. Most mezcals come from the state of Oaxaca and are made on small farms (*palenques*) by local distillers.

Mexico produces a fair amount of wine, both white and red. There are wine-growing areas of Mexico in the states of Baja California, Aguascalientes, Coahuila, Hidalgo, Queretaro, and Zacatecas. A number of varietals are grown, including cabernet, chardonnay, pinot noir, and chenin blanc. Mexican wines have not yet reached an esteemed level in winemaking, however, they have improved in recent years and new growing regions are being cultivated all the time. Wine is often served with Mexican meals, and its popularity seems to be growing.

Rum, distilled from sugar cane, is also produced in Mexico. Bacardi, a well-known Cuban rum manufacturer, built a showcase distillery in 1956 in the state of Puebla. Another fine rum, Corsario Oro Especial, is produced in Atizipan de Zaragosa, a suburb of Mexico City, and rum also comes from the states of San Luis Potosi and Tamaulipas. A great deal of rum, both domestically produced and imported, goes into colorful tropical drinks.

Mexican brandy is considered to be quite good and goes into a number of after-dinner drinks. Two favorite labels are Presidente and Don Pedro Reserva Especial.

Mexico also makes many brands of well-known light and dark beers. The major breweries are in Monterrey and Mexico City, with independent breweries in other places, such as Montejo in the Yucatán Peninsula, and Moctezuma Brewery in Orizaba in the state of Veracruz.

When planning a Mexican meal or a party, you'll find plenty of beverage inspiration in this chapter. Salud!

Coffee and Hot Chocolate

Mexican Coffee
Café de Olla

Makes **4 servings**

Traditional Mexican coffee is brewed with cinnamon, cloves, and hard cones of brown sugar called piloncillo. *Coffee lovers enjoy this sweet brew at home, and in restaurants and coffee houses all over Mexico. Drink it for breakfast, during* marienda *(Mexico's coffee, tea, and sweets break), or at the end of a Mexican meal.* Piloncillo *can be purchased here in Latin-American markets and the Mexican section of many supermarkets.*

4 cups water
4 small (1-ounce) cones of piloncillo, or ¹/₂ cup packed dark brown sugar
2 cinnamon sticks (Mexican canela or Ceylon variety preferred)
3 whole cloves
³/₄ cup coarsely ground dark roast coffee

Put the water in a medium saucepan and add the sugar, cinnamon, and cloves. Bring to a boil, stirring, until the sugar is melted, about 5 minutes. Stir in the coffee, and remove the pan from the heat. Cover, and let steep 8 minutes. Strain the coffee through a coffee filter or a fine-mesh strainer into a heatproof coffee server. Serve at once.

Coffee with Milk
Café Con Leche

Makes **2 servings**

The restaurant and coffee house, La Parroquia, in Veracruz, is famous as the place to go for breakfast, and especially for café con leche. *The waiters whisk around the restaurant carrying two large beverage kettles, one with coffee, and the other with hot milk, and when you tap on your glass indicating the need for a refill, they deftly pour from both at the same time into your cup.*

When making this at home, freshly made strong coffee is important for the flavor because it is diluted with an equal amount of hot milk.

1 cup hot brewed espresso or strong coffee
1 cup milk
Sugar, optional

Brew the coffee shortly before serving. Heat the milk in a small pan over low heat until steaming, or alternatively, heat the milk in a microwave, if desired. For a more dramatic effect for a guest, pour half of the coffee and half of the milk simultaneously into each of two coffee cups. Or, pour the coffee and milk, one at a time into each cup. Stir to mix. Add sugar, if desired.

Mexican Cappuccino, Guanajuato Style
Cappuccino Guanajuato

Makes **2 servings**

Guanajuato is a historic colonial city in the central region of Mexico known as the Bajio. You enter this captivating city through long, twisting tunnels. Our hotel, Posada Santa Fe, was located on the Jardín Union, the most popular garden plaza in the city. Steep hills and narrow, winding streets are connected with stone steps or cobblestone walkways in all directions. We stopped for coffee near the Jardín Union and discovered this interesting twist to cappuccino. Coffee lovers will want to try this. To serve this the authentic way, use a 6- to 7-ounce heat-resistant glass coffee cup. To present the coffee to full effect, don't stir the ingredients: the layers will stay separated until stirred.

3 tablespoons Brown Sugar Syrup (page 583)

4 tablespoons Sweetened Whipped Cream (page 583)

²/₃ cup strong espresso-brewed coffee

1 cup hot milk (or steamed with an espresso machine, if available)

Unsweetened cocoa powder or ground cinnamon (Mexican canela or Ceylon variety preferred)

Prepare the sugar syrup and the whipped cream. Then, carefully pour the syrup, coffee, and milk, equally, in order, into two 6-ounce coffee cups. Top with a dollop of cream. Sprinkle with cocoa or cinnamon. Serve hot.

Coffee Olé
Café Olé

Makes **2 servings**

Linger after dinner with a hot and mellow cup of coffee spiked with aged tequila, coffee liqueur, and a dollop of whipped cream. The bartender who made this café olé (a favorite in Mexico City), said that the deep mellow flavor of aged tequila (añejo) makes a more balanced drink than other types of tequila, however, my husband and I think reposado (rested) is good, too.

Sweetened Whipped Cream (page 583)

1¹/₃ cups strong freshly brewed coffee

2 ounces tequila añejo (aged) or reposado

2 ounces coffee-flavored liqueur, such as Kahlua

Ground cinnamon (Mexican canela or Ceylon variety preferred) (optional)

Prepare the whipped cream. Then, pour the hot coffee into coffee mugs. Stir in the tequila and liqueur. Top with a dollop of whipped cream. Sprinkle lightly with cinnamon, if desired. Serve hot.

Coffee Popo
Café de Popo

Makes **2 servings**

This hot coffee drink is dedicated to the late Al Williams, who was born in Mexico, and became famous for the legendary Papagayo Room, a gourmet Mexican restaurant in San Francisco's Fairmont Hotel. Al and his wife, Katherine Williams, later ran a cooking school where I had some of my first lessons in Mexican cooking. The drink is named for the Mexican volcano, Popocatepetl, as Al said, "Hot below, snow-capped above."

Sweetened Whipped Cream (page 583)
3 teaspoons sugar, or to taste
2 lemon peel strips (2-inches long × 1/2-inch wide)
2 ounces añejo (aged) or reposado (rested) tequila
2 cups strong freshly brewed hot coffee

Prepare the whipped cream. Reserve. Put 1 teaspoon of sugar in each of 2 double old-fashioned glasses or coffee cups. Twist the lemon peels and drop 1 into each glass or cup. Add 1 ounce tequila to each, then fill the cups with hot coffee. Top each with whipped cream. Serve hot.

Mexican Hot Chocolate
Chocolate Mexicana

Makes **4 servings**

Just about everybody loves a steaming cup of Mexican hot chocolate. The round tablets of authentic Mexican chocolate are widely available in most supermarkets in the United States. The tablets weigh about 3 ounces and are already sweetened with sugar and flavored with cinnamon, vanilla, and sometimes ground almonds. Some of the best-tasting Mexican chocolate is processed in the states of Tabasco and Oaxaca, where there are many cacao plantations, and anyone who travels to those areas will want to bring home some of the special blends.

This drink is delightfully frothy. In Mexico, a molinillo (hand-made wooden chocolate beater) is the traditional tool to froth the hot chocolate, but you can use an electric beater or an immersion blender as well.

2 (6 ounces) tablets Mexican chocolate (such as Ibarra or Auelita brands), chopped or broken into pieces
4 cups whole or 2% milk

Put the chocolate and milk in a medium saucepan, and bring to a boil over medium heat, stirring, until the chocolate is melted, 5 to 6 minutes. Remove the pan from the heat and beat until frothy with an electric beater on slow speed. Serve hot.

Mexican Chocolate

An ancient story dating back to the Toltecs, a pre-Aztec native people, tells that the feathered serpent god, Quetzalcoatl, planted the first *cacao* trees in the tropical lowlands of Tabasco and Veracruz centuries before the discovery of the New World, and it was known as the "food of the gods." The precious beans spread into other regions, and when the Aztecs brought *cacao* beans into the Valley of Mexico, they called the unsweetened beverage made of the ground beans "bitter water." The roasted beans were ground and mixed with water, red chile, and vanilla.

Chronicles from Cortéz and other early voyagers described the drink and its great importance in the Court of Moctezuma. It was said to give strength and endurance to warriors and was also thought to be an aphrodisiac. The *cacao* beans were even used as currency. Spanish voyagers soon transported the new product to Spain, where the use of it changed from a bitter drink and for some of the famous *moles* (complex sauces) of Mexico, to flavoring sweet beverages, desserts, and the pleasurable sweet chocolate foods that we know today.

Mexican cuisine still embraces chocolate in a beverage, but now it's sweetened and flavored with cinnamon, vanilla, and ground almonds, and it's made with either hot water or milk. Chocolate desserts are made in European-style pastry shops, but are not commonly made at home.

Mexican chocolate is sold in solid disks and blocks. In the United States, the round tablets of chocolate are widely available in Mexican stores and many supermarkets. Two imported brands are Ibarra and Abuelita.

Higher quality, more refined Mexican chocolate made in the states of Tabasco and Oaxaca are not widely imported, but perhaps this will change, as more people travel, taste, and become aware of how good they are. I like *Comalcalco* from Tabasco, but have never seen it here. It's a real treat to visit the rows of chocolate shops in Oaxaca's central market where tasting is encouraged and expected. I always return home with purchases of *Guelaguetza* and *Mayordomo*, two of my favorite Oaxacan brands.

Corn- and Rice-Based Drinks

Chocolate Masa Drink
Champurrado

Makes **6 servings**

Atoles *are rich drinks usually thickened with masa, and flavored with spices, fruits, and in this case, chocolate. Such drinks have an ancient history and are still made in traditional homes and also sold in market food stalls. Champurrado is served steaming hot. Sweet tamales or Mexican* pan dulce *(sweet bread) are typical accompaniments. In the United States,* masa harina *and Mexican chocolate can be found in many supermarkets or in Mexican grocery stores. Even though Mexican chocolate already contains sugar and cinnamon, the* atole *needs extra sweetness and flavor from Mexican brown sugar (*piloncillo*) or regular brown sugar and additional cinnamon.*

¹/₄ cup masa harina (flour for corn tortillas)

2 cups cold water

1 tablet (2 ounces) Mexican chocolate, broken into pieces

¹/₂ teaspoon ground cinnamon (Mexican canela or Ceylon variety preferred)

2 small cones piloncillo, or 2 tablespoons dark brown sugar

¹/₂ teaspoon pure vanilla extract

1 cup whole milk

1. In a medium bowl, whisk to blend the masa harina with about ½ cup of the water. Add remaining water and whisk very well. Let stand about 5 minutes, whisking 3 to 4 times. Pour the masa-water through a fine-mesh strainer into a heavy-bottomed saucepan. Bring to a boil over low heat, whisking constantly, 6 to 8 minutes, or until thickened.

2. Add the chocolate pieces, cinnamon, and sugar to the masa mixture and continue whisking constantly until the chocolate is melted, about 5 minutes. Keep the heat low or medium-low to prevent scorching. Add the milk gradually, whisking all the while, and cook until the champurrado is creamy and steaming hot. Serve at once.

Tamarind Masa Drink
Atole de Tamarindo

Makes **4 servings**

This atole *(masa-thickened drink) is from the state of Michoacan. Tamarind was brought to Mexico from Asia by way of trading vessels from the Philippines, and the plant is grown widely in many areas of Mexico. The brown pod of the plant contains a sticky, very sour fruit with large seeds. It takes a lot of sugar to sweeten tamarind, but the resulting tart-sweet beverage is really very good. In the United States, tamarind paste is available in many Mexican or Asian markets in 14-ounce packages. The* atole *is served warm as an after-dinner finisher, or as an afternoon pick-me-up.*

2 cups water

8 ounces tamarind paste, separated into pieces

³/₄ cup dark brown sugar

3 tablespoons masa harina (flour for corn tortillas)

¹/₂ cup hot tap water

1. Put the 2 cups of water and the tamarind paste in a medium saucepan. Bring to a boil over medium heat, partially cover, lower the heat to medium-low and simmer the tamarind until the seeds separate from the pulp, 12 to 15 minutes. Pour the liquid through a fine-mesh strainer into a bowl, pressing, with a spoon to extract all of the juices and any pulp that passes through the strainer. Discard the seeds and pulp.

2. Pour the juice back into the saucepan. Add the sugar and bring to a boil. Cook over medium heat until the sugar is dissolved, 3 to 4 minutes. In a small bowl, mix the masa harina with the hot water and slowly stir it into the tamarind mixture. Bring to a boil, partially cover, and cook over medium-low heat, stirring frequently, until the juice thickens slightly, about 10 minutes. Serve warm in 3- to 4-ounce cordial glasses. Store in a covered jar, in the refrigerator, for 3 to 4 weeks.

Rich Pineapple Drink
Atole de Piña

Makes **about 6 servings**

My first pineapple atole *was served at the home of the mother of my tour guide in Oaxaca, who invited me to her home for* almuerzo *(late breakfast). This atole, thickened with cornstarch instead of masa, accompanied tamales—an authentic combination enjoyed in the morning, or as a late evening treat. These rich drinks called* atoles *can be an acquired taste, because we're not accustomed to thickened juices and the texture can be a bit grainy when made with* masa, *but I liked this one made with cornstarch and pineapple after the first sip! Cornstarch makes a smoother* atole *than those thickened with* masa harina.

1/4 cup cornstarch
1 cup cold water
1 quart milk
1 cup sugar
1 cinnamon stick (Mexican canela or Ceylon variety preferred)
2 cups chopped fresh pineapple

1. In a medium pan, mix the cornstarch with the water. Bring to a boil, stirring, until the water begins to thicken. Reduce the heat to medium-low.

Stir in the milk and sugar. Add the cinnamon stick. Cook, stirring, until the milk is hot and begins to steam. Remove the pan from the heat.

2. Purée the pineapple in a blender until smooth, then pour it through a fine-mesh strainer into the pan of milk. Return the pan to the heat, and cook, stirring frequently, until steaming, but do not boil. Remove the cinnamon stick. Serve at once.

Almond-Flavored Rice Drink
Horchata de Almendra

Makes **about 4 servings**

Horchata, *a cold, refreshing drink made with rice or melon seeds steeped in and mixed with water or milk, is made all over Mexico. I like this pleasant-tasting version with toasted almonds blended into the mixture.* Horchata *is sold on the street, in market food stalls, and in some restaurants. It is drunk as a quick refreshment anytime.*

2 tablespoons uncooked long-grain white rice
2 tablespoons finely ground toasted almonds
1/2 cup sugar
1/2 teaspoon ground cinnamon (Mexican canela or Ceylon variety preferred)
1 teaspoon pure vanilla extract

1. In a small bowl mix the rice with 1/2 cup water. In another small bowl mix the toasted almonds with 1/2 cup water. Let stand to soak, 1 hour.

2. Pour the rice and the soaking water into a blender jar and blend on high speed 1 minute. Pour through a fine-mesh strainer into a 1-quart glass container. Pour the almonds and the soaking water, the sugar, cinnamon, and vanilla into the same blender jar and blend on high speed 1 minute.

3. Pour through a fine-mesh strainer into the container with the rice. Stir in 1¾ cups of cold water. Refrigerate until cold. Serve over ice.

Melon Horchata
Horchata de Melon

Makes **about 4 servings**

This horchata, *a refreshing cold drink, is made from cantaloupe and is a favorite. It may seem strange to use the seeds along with the melon flesh, but that's the custom, and the resulting drink is very good. Another well-known* horchata *is made with rice.*

1 ripe cantaloupe
¼ cup fresh lime juice
2 cups water
1 tablespoon sugar, or to taste

Cut the cantaloupe in half. With a spoon, scoop out the flesh and seeds (there will be about 2 cups). Put the melon and seeds in a blender with the lime juice and sugar. Add 2 cups of cold water, and blend 1 minute, or until very smooth. Pour through a fine-mesh strainer into a glass container. Serve over ice.

Fruit Drinks and Punches (Non-alcoholic)

Strawberry Cooler
Fresca de Fresas

Makes **about 6 servings**

Try this agua fresca *(fresh fruit drink) when strawberries are in season. Be sure to use bright red ripe berries for the best flavor.*

4 cups fresh strawberries, hulled
1 to 2 cups cold water
3 teaspoons sugar, or to taste

In a blender place 2 cups fresh berries. Add 1 cup water, cover and blend. Add more water, if necessary, but just enough to blend to a smooth liquid of drinking consistency, but not too thin. Sweeten with sugar. Serve cold.

Banana-Strawberry Drink
Licuado de Plátano y Fresa

Makes **2 servings**

Licuados *are another type of fresca that's often blended with milk instead of water. Soft ripe fruit makes the most flavorful drinks. Bananas and sweet strawberries blended with milk or yogurt is great for breakfast. Mexican yogurt is very good and is sold there at many fruit drink establishments where you may choose either milk or yogurt in your licuado.*

1 large ripe banana, peeled and cut into chunks
8 to 10 red ripe strawberries, hulled and halved
2 cups cold low-fat milk or yogurt
2 teaspoons sugar

Put all of the ingredients in a blender and purée until smooth. Serve cold.

Banana-Mango Drink
Licuado de Plátano y Mango

Makes **2 servings**

Add cold milk to the fresh fruit in a blended drink, and it becomes a licuado, *another type of* fresca, *or fresh drink. This creamy, rich drink is delicious and satisfying.*

1/2 ripe mango
2 cups cold whole or low-fat milk
1 medium ripe banana, peeled and cut into chunks
1 tablespoon sugar

1. To peel and cut up the mango, cut 1/2 of the mango away from the flat oval seed with a sharp paring knife. Then lay the cut half on a flat surface, skin side down, and make cross-cuts on the fruit, separating the flesh into cubes. (Do not cut through the peel.) Push the fruit inside out and cut the cubes off the peel.

2. Discard the peel and put the pieces of fruit in a blender jar. Add the remaining ingredients and purée until smooth. Serve cold.

Mango-Orange Punch
Ponche de Mango-Naranja

Makes **about 4 servings**

Ponches *is the name given to thin fruit punches that contain blended fresh fruits and fruits juices. Sometimes tea, wine, or another beverage is added to the punch. Blend the fruit of a juicy sweet mango with fresh orange juice for a truly quenching summer drink.*

1 large ripe mango
2 cups fresh orange juice
Juice of one lime, or to taste
2 tablespoons sugar, or to taste
1 1/2 cups cold water

1. Peel 1/2 of the mango with a sharp thin-bladed knife. Cut the peeled half of the fruit away from the pit, cutting as close to the seed as possible. Turn the fruit over, holding it in the palm of your hand, and peel the remaining half. Cut that half away from the pit as before. Discard the seed. Cut the fruit into small pieces and put in a blender.

2. Add the remaining ingredients and purée as smoothly as possible. Pour the mixture through a fine-mesh strainer into a pitcher, pressing on the solids to release all the juices. Discard the pulp. Serve over ice cubes in tall glasses.

Watermelon Cooler
Sandia Fresca

Makes **about 4 servings**

Mexico produces the reddest, sweetest watermelons imaginable, and a fresca *made with watermelon is one of the most refreshing drinks on a hot day.*

6 cups watermelon chunks, seeds removed, or seedless watermelon, if bright red and ripe
2 teaspoons fresh lime juice

Purée the watermelon and lime juice in a blender until smooth. Pour over ice in tall glasses.

Fresh Jamaica Cooler
Jamaica Fresca

Makes 4 servings

Jamaica is a dried reddish-purple flower related to the hibiscus. The dried blossoms are steeped and sweetened to make a traditional cold drink with a bright cranberry color and a tart crisp flavor. Look for jamaica *in cellophane packages in Mexican markets, and in the Mexican section of some supermarkets.*

¹/₂ cup loose dried jamaica flowers
1 cup boiling water
4 cups cold water
¹/₄ to ¹/₂ cup sugar

In a medium nonreactive pan, put the jamaica blossoms in 1 cup of boiling water and simmer over low heat 3 minutes. Pour the mixture into a large glass container and add the cold water and ¼ cup sugar. Cover and steep 4 hours in the refrigerator. Pour through a fine-mesh strainer into a glass pitcher. Stir in additional sugar, if desired. Serve, over ice, in tall glasses. Store, covered, in the refrigerator up to 4 days.

Tamarind Cooler
Fresca de Tamarindo

Makes 4 servings

Dry, brown-colored tamarind pods are steeped in hot water for this distinctive tart-sweet beverage. The pods are found in Latin-American markets. Tamarind is also a popular flavoring for Mexican hard candy, and the hot drink made with tamarind paste (Tamarind Masa Drink, page 592).

1¹/₂ cups (about 8 ounces) tamarind pods
3 cups water
¹/₃ cup sugar

1. Break off and discard most of the outer bark of the tamarind pods. Rinse the pods and cut into small pieces. Put the pods in a medium saucepan and add the water. Bring to a boil, then reduce heat, cover, and simmer 10 minutes. Remove the pan from the heat and cool. Cover and refrigerate the mixture about 6 hours or overnight.

2. Pour the juice through a fine-mesh strainer into a pitcher or glass jar. Discard the tamarind. Add the sugar, and stir until dissolved. Pour into glasses, over ice, and serve.

Pomegranate Cooler
Fresca de Granada

Makes 4 to 6 servings

This drink spotlights the glorious color of the jewel-like seeds of the pomegranate. When pomegranates are abundant in the fall, surprise your family and friends with this refreshing thirst-quencher.

5 pomegranates
¹/₂ cup fresh orange juice
1 quart cold water
2 to 3 tablespoons sugar, or to taste

1. Cut open the pomegranates and break the fruit into sections. In the sink, in a bowl of cold water, pick out the small red seeds. Discard the thin white membrane between the sections. Put the seeds in a blender or food processor. Blend on low speed, or pulse to a coarse purée.

2. Pour through a fine strainer into a bowl to catch the juices. Discard the seeds. Add the orange juice and water. Sweeten to taste with sugar. Pour into a jar, cover and refrigerate until cold. Serve over ice.

Easy Pineapple Punch
Ponche de Piña

Makes **8 servings**

This is a convenient way to make a refreshing non-alcoholic punch for any occasion. Frozen pineapple juice takes out the work of preparing, peeling, and blending fresh pineapple, when in this case, frozen juice works very well. For the punch, dilute a 12-ounce container of frozen pineapple juice with only 2 cans of water, not 3 cans as directed on the container.

¹/₄ cup sugar

1 cup water

2 cinnamon sticks (Mexican canela or Ceylon variety preferred)

4 whole cloves

1 (12-ounce) can frozen pineapple concentrate diluted with 2 cans of water

1 cup fresh orange juice

1 lime, thinly sliced

In a small saucepan, simmer the sugar, water, cinnamon sticks and cloves about 10 minutes. Cool to room temperature. Remove the cinnamon sticks and cloves. Pour liquid into a large pitcher. Stir in the pineapple and the orange juices. Add the lime slices. Serve cold with ice cubes.

Citrus-Mint Ice Tea Punch
Ponche de Tea con Naranja y Limón

Makes **4 to 6 servings**

This quick and tasty iced tea punch with the added flavors of orange and lime juices is equally good with a meal or as an afternoon refreshment.

4 cups water

4 tea bags (black tea preferred)

8 small fresh mint sprigs

2 tablespoons sugar

³/₄ cup fresh orange juice

3 tablespoons fresh lime juice

Ice cubes

1. Pour the water into a medium saucepan and bring to a boil. Turn off the heat and add the tea bags, 4 sprigs of the mint, and sugar. Stir to dissolve the sugar and let steep 8 minutes. Cool to lukewarm, about 10 minutes.

2. Strain the orange and lime juice through a fine wire strainer into a pitcher. Remove the mint sprigs from the tea and pour the tea into the pitcher with the juices. Taste for sweetness. Put about 6 ice cubes in each of 4 tall glasses and fill each glass with punch. Garnish with the remaining mint sprigs. Serve cold.

Sparkling Limeade
Limónada

Makes **4 to 6 servings**

Nothing is quite as welcome as an ice cold glass of tangy, refreshing juice on a hot afternoon. Limes are the source of one of the best-loved and most common Mexican refreshers and the small Key lime (sometimes called Mexican limes) is the one used in Mexico.

To squeeze the juice, hand-held small lime squeezers are in every kitchen and sold in every market in Mexico. The hinged handles have cup-shaped depressions to hold cut limes. Close the handles, press firmly and the juice is extracted, leaving the seeds behind and the skins inverted. Simple and amazing! There are also larger sizes for oranges and grapefruit. The squeezers are available in some Mexican markets in the United States, and a new colorful enameled model is even sold in cookware shops here and in Mexico. You can also use a reamer or other juicer, if you prefer.

6 large limes
1 quart soda water
2 to 3 tablespoons sugar, or to taste

Squeeze the juice from 5 of the limes. Put the juice into a glass pitcher. Cut the remaining lime into very thin slices and add to the pitcher. Pour soda water over. Sweeten with sugar. Serve in tall glasses with ice cubes.

Note: If using the smaller Key limes, squeeze 11 limes, and slice an additional lime for the pitcher.

Party Punches with Alcohol

Red Wine Punch
Sangria Rojo

Makes **4 to 6 servings**

Here's one of the many ways to make sangria, the well-known red wine punch with Spanish roots that's also made all over Mexico—at home and in restaurants. Most of the wine vineyards are located in northern Mexico in the states of Baja California, Coahuila, Zacatecas, and Aguascalientes. Mexican red wines suitable for sangria include zinfandel, pinot noir, and blended red wines called vinos tintos. *There is no need to use a very expensive wine for sangria since the fruits mask much of the flavor. There are many ways to mix fruit and wine to make sangria, but using citrus fruits and juices is pretty classic. Sliced apples, pears, or peaches are also sometimes used in sangria.*

1 (750 ml) bottle dry red wine
1 cup fresh orange juice
2 tablespoons fresh lime juice
1/4 cup sugar, or to taste
1 (12-ounce) bottle club soda
1 orange, thinly sliced
1 lime, thinly sliced
Ice cubes

In a large glass container, stir together the wine, orange juice, lime juice, and sugar until the sugar is dissolved. Add the soda, orange, and lime slices. If time allows, let the sangria sit about 1 hour to blend the flavors. Pour into glasses over ice cubes.

Guadalajara Red Wine Punch
Sangria de Guadalajara

Makes **about 6 servings**

Sangria, *the refreshing red wine punch, is as popular in Mexico as in Spain, where it originated. This version was served at El Tapatio, a resort hotel outside Guadalajara. The ingredients are simplicity itself, and the two-color, layered effect is eye-catching. The idea is to pour the limeade first, directly into the glasses, over ice cubes, and float the wine on top. The drinker can stir the drink together or not, as desired. This is a great punch to serve with grilled steak or other red meats.*

1 (12-ounce) can frozen limeade concentrate, thawed
Ice cubes
1 (750 ml) bottle dry red wine

Pour the limeade concentrate into a glass pitcher, and dilute with water as directed. Stir well. Put 3 ice cubes in the bottom of each of 6 (8-ounce) wine glasses. Pour limeade over the ice cubes, halfway to the top in each glass. Slowly pour the red wine directly onto the ice cubes to within 1 inch of the glass rim. Add a stirrer to each glass, if desired. (The wine usually floats at the top of the glasses until stirred in.) Serve at once.

White Wine Punch
Sangria Blanca

Makes **6 servings**

White sangria is a very nice change from the usual red wine punch. It is especially appropriate for a special and festive luncheon. White sangria goes well with chicken or fish, or is good for sipping on a hot afternoon. In Mexico, chenin blanc or a blended vino blanco *(white wine) from the states of Baja California, Coahuila, Aguascalientes, or other growing regions would be used for the sangria. This is my version of white sangria that I sometimes make for cooking classes.*

1 bottle (750 ml) dry white wine
1/2 cup orange-flavored liqueur, such as Triple Sec or Cointreau
1/2 cup fresh orange juice
1/2 cup sugar
1 orange, thinly sliced
1 lime, thinly sliced
1 lemon, thinly sliced
1 1/2 cups club soda
6 small clusters of Thompson seedless grapes, about 5 grapes per cluster
Fresh mint sprigs

1. In a large pitcher, mix the wine, orange liqueur, orange juice, sugar, orange, lime and lemon slices. Cover and refrigerate until ready to serve, up to about 6 hours.

2. Shortly before serving, add the club soda. Pour the sangria over ice cubes into 6 stemmed glasses. Put a cluster of grapes over the rim of each glass and add a sprig of mint. Serve at once.

Christmas Wine Punch
Ponche Navideño

Makes 10 to 12 servings

Patricia Quintana of Mexico City, a cookbook author, instructor, and authority on Mexican cuisine, shared her recipe with me for Ponche Navideño. *This is my simplified version of her festive punch.*

The punch is served during the Christmas holidays and after Posadas (the re-enactment of Mary, with the infant Jesus, looking for shelter). My husband, Bill, and I joined one such Posada procession one evening in Oaxaca. We were given lighted candles to carry, and at the end of the walk the procession returned to a small plaza for Ponche Navideño and sweet fried pastries called Bunuelos (page 549).

Mexican cinnamon (canela) sticks are available in cellophane packages in Mexican markets and the Mexican section of many supermarkets.

4 quarts water

1 cup dry red wine

1 cup pitted dried prunes, halved

1 cup dried apricot halves

2 medium apples, cored and diced (about ¹/₂ inch)

1 small orange, pierced with 5 whole cloves

³/₄ cup raisins

¹/₂ cup packed dark brown sugar, or to taste

2 cinnamon sticks (Mexican canela or Ceylon variety preferred)

¹/₂ teaspoon whole allspice berries

Put all of the ingredients in a large stainless steel pot and bring to a boil. Reduce the heat to low and simmer, partially covered, 45 minutes. Discard the orange and cinnamon sticks. Serve the punch hot with a bit of the fruit in each cup.

Tequila Punch in a Clay Bowl
Cazuela

Makes 1 large serving

At the huge, lively square called Parian in Tlaquepaque, several restaurants and bars compete for customers by enticing passers-by to try certain specialties of the house. My husband, Bill, and I, and our friends, Donna and Don Luria from Tucson, Arizona, were delighted and amazed by a popular local punch simply called Cazuela. *Individual clay bowls, called* cazuelas *(traditionally used to cook savory casseroles and other foods) are filled to brimming with chunks of citrus fruits, grapefruit soda, tequila, and ice cubes. Two fat jaunty straws are poked into the punch for drinking. This typical refreshing drink is very popular and lots of fun!*

For each serving—which two can share—you'll need a 2-cup capacity shallow ceramic or glass bowl, about 7 inches in diameter at the top, with sloping sides. (Some individual pasta bowls are about the right size for this drink.)

2 ounces silver or gold tequila

6 ounces grapefruit soda

1 small lime, quartered with skin

¹/₂ small unpeeled orange, cut into 1-inch chunks

¹/₄ small unpeeled grapefruit, cut into 1-inch chunks

Ice cubes

Pour the tequila and grapefruit soda into the bowl. Add the pieces of citrus fruits. Let steep about 10 minutes. Add the amount of ice cubes needed to fill the bowl. Add 2 straws. Serve cold.

Watermelon Rum Punch
Ponche de Sandia y Ron

Makes **about 12 to 16 servings**

Summer picnics or backyard fiestas require something special to drink, like this watermelon punch, which is served right from the hollowed-out watermelon. You can offer sparkling water, to those who want to add a splash to the punch just before drinking. Put a bucket of ice next to the punch for self-service.

¹/₂ cup Simple Syrup (page 614)
1 large watermelon
2 cups pineapple juice
1 cup fresh orange juice
¹/₂ cup fresh lime juice
1¹/₂ cups rum, or more, if you like

1. Prepare the simple syrup and reserve amount needed. Store the rest in the refrigerator. Cut off the top third of the watermelon lengthwise. Scoop out all of the melon flesh, in chunks, from both pieces. Remove the seeds and discard the seeds and the top third of the shell. Put the melon flesh in a food processor or blender and purée until smooth.

2. With a large knife, cut off a thin strip of the larger hollow shell bottom so that shell will sit flat. Then, with a sharp knife, make short zig-zag cuts around the top edge of the shell to make an attractive rim. Reserve.

3. Pour the watermelon purée into a large glass container. Add the pineapple juice, orange juice, lime juice, rum, and syrup. Mix well, cover, and refrigerate until cold. Refrigerate the carved shell, too, if you have refrigerator space. Shortly before serving, pour the punch into the carved watermelon shell. Serve in punch glasses.

Fermented Pineapple Drink
Tepache

Makes **12 to 16 servings**

This drink is made all over Mexico. Older versions had the drink fermented with barley, which took two to three days to ferment. With beer, fermentation only takes 24 hours. When I served this drink to friends and cooking students, it was a hit. Piloncillo is Mexican raw sugar that's formed into hard cones or disks. If not available, dark brown sugar works fine. Canela is the type of cinnamon used in Mexico. Canela cinnamon sticks and piloncillo are both available in Mexican markets and in the Mexican section of some supermarkets.

1 whole fresh ripe pineapple (about 2 pounds)
2 quarts cold water
1 pound Mexican piloncillo or dark brown sugar
2 cinnamon sticks (Mexican canela or Ceylon variety preferred)
4 whole cloves
1 (12-ounce) bottle lager beer

1. Remove the top and bottom of the pineapple. Stand the pineapple on end and with a sharp knife, cut off the peel all the way around. With a paring knife, dig out the "eyes." Chop the pineapple coarsely and put the pineapple into a large glass container or crock and reserve.

2. In a large pan, bring to a boil the water, sugar, and spices. Boil over medium heat 15 minutes. Remove from the heat and cool until lukewarm, about 15 minutes. Pour the cooled sugar mixture over the pineapple. Add the beer. Cover and let stand at room temperature to ferment 24 hours.

3. Strain the mixture through cheesecloth or a fine strainer into a glass container. Serve over ice cubes in small 4-ounce juice glasses, or in wine glasses.

Mixed Alcoholic Drinks and Cocktails

Margarita Mexicana

Makes 2 servings

This recipe reflects my favorite method for making a margarita—the authentic Mexican version—plus a few options to suit your taste. The classic is made with a good-quality silver tequila, Mexican (Key) limes, and the orange-flavored liqueur, Cointreau. The glass is rimmed with salt, then the margarita is shaken with cracked ice and strained into the glass.

Of course, margaritas can be made to order. A common alternative is with no salt on the rim and poured on the rocks, instead of shaken with ice and strained.

There are many stories about the origins of the margarita. One story details that the margarita was invented at Rancho La Gloria in 1948 in Rosarita Beach, south of Tijuana, and that it was named after a movie actress Marjorie (Margarita, in Spanish) King, who often visited the area. Another story claims that the drink originated in Acapulco in the 1940s and was made by Margaret Sames, a wealthy woman whose husband named the drink after her. Whoever is the source, she is honored every day in Mexican restaurants around the world!

Silver tequila is traditionally used to make margaritas. The clear color mixes well with fresh lime juice and orange-flavored liqueur. Silver tequila is less expensive and complex than aged tequilas, and many margarita drinkers prefer to save the more expensive types for sipping and not mix or dilute them with other flavors. Of course, you can experiment and decide for yourself. Tequila is now so popular that

liquor stores everywhere stock several brands and all types—silver, gold, reposado, and añejo. Either Cointreau or Triple Sec can be mixed with the tequila. For my taste, fresh lime juice is imperative. If you don't have a cocktail shaker, a pitcher can be used to mix the drink.

Lime quarters, to rub on the glass

Salt to rim the glass; put in a saucer

Cracked ice (see Note)

3 ounces silver tequila

2 ounces fresh lime juice

1 ounce orange-flavored liqueur, such as Cointreau or Triple Sec

Rub the rims of the glasses with a lime quarter. Dip the glass rim in the salt, if using. Set the glass aside. Fill a bar shaker or small pitcher with cracked ice. Add tequila, lime juice, and liqueur. Shake several times or stir well, and strain into a cocktail glass, or serve on the rocks, if preferred.

Note: To crack ice cubes, put them in a heavy plastic bag, remove air from the bag, seal it, then put the bag on a cutting board. With a hammer or heavy rolling pin, gently break cubes into chips.

Frozen Margarita
Margarita de Mango Congelado

Makes **2 servings**

Smooth icy margaritas made with mangos, as well as other ripe, fresh fruit, are served in modern upscale restaurants and bars. I especially remember the one sampled at Jose Cuervo's beautiful distillery in Tequila, Mexico. If the mango is ripe and sweet the drinks will be great, so be sure to choose a perfect mango. You can also substitute 1 cup of another fresh fruit, such as hulled strawberries, or raspberries. An equal amount of frozen fruit can be substituted, if quality fresh fruits are not available. Serve before a festive warm-weather meal.

1 large ripe mango

1 cup cracked ice (see Note)

3 tablespoons gold or silver tequila

2 tablespoons Simple Syrup (page 614)

1 1/2 tablespoons orange-flavored liqueur,
   such as Cointreau or Triple Sec

1 tablespoon fresh lime juice

1. To prepare the mango, with a sharp thin-bladed knife, cut each half of the mango away from the flat seed, cutting as close as possible to the seed. Lay ½ of the mango on a flat surface, skin side down, and cut cross-hatches on the fruit side (separating the flesh into cubes), without piercing through the skin. Bend the skin inside out and cut the pieces of fruit away from the peel. Repeat with the other half of the mango.

2. Put the mango and the remaining ingredients in a blender and blend until very smooth. Taste for sweetness. Add more simple syrup, if needed. Divide the margaritas between 2 glasses and serve.

Note: To crack ice cubes, put them in a heavy plastic bag, remove air from the bag, seal it, then put the bag on a cutting board. With a hammer or heavy rolling pin, gently break cubes into chips.

Mexican Screwdriver

Makes **2 servings**

In Mazatlán and other resort towns along the Pacific coast, a Mexican Screwdriver is sometimes called a Sinaloa Screwdriver, after the name for the coastal state of Sinaloa. This bar drink is served in a heavy 10-ounce glass goblet with lots of cracked ice. As with most Mexican cocktails, serve with a salted or spicy snack, such as Spicy Roasted Cocktail Peanuts (page 130) or Toasted Pumpkin Seeds (page 130).

6 ounces tangerine juice, fresh or made from
   frozen concentrate

2 teaspoons orange-flavored liqueur,
   such as Cointreau or Triple Sec

3 ounces white or gold tequila

2 strips of fresh lime peel

Cracked ice (see Note)

Stir the tangerine juice, orange liqueur, and tequila together in the goblet. Add cracked ice to fill the glasses. Twist a lime peel over each glass and drop it in the glass.

Note: To crack ice cubes, put them in a heavy plastic bag, remove air from the bag, seal it, then put the bag on a cutting board. With a hammer or heavy rolling pin, gently break cubes into chips.

Tequila Salud

Makes 1 (2-ounce) serving

If a straight shot of tequila is a bit much for your taste, try a Tequila Salud that my husband, Bill, conjured up for me. When I sip tequila, my preference is reposado (rested), but if you have a favorite, use it. We always use 100% blue agave. Tequila Salud is best icy cold right out of the freezer, with a squirt of fresh lime. Salud!

**1 ounce 100% blue agave tequila, reposado
  or añejo**

1/2 teaspoon fresh lime juice

Pour the tequila into a thin (2-ounce) cordial glass, and put it in the freezer at least 1 hour. Remove the glass of tequila from the freezer and immediately add the lime juice. Serve immediately while icy cold.

Tequila and Soda Cocktail
Claro

Makes 2 servings

Tequila has become amazingly popular and many people have discovered how suave and varied the types of tequila can be. With this popularity, new mixed drinks pop up all the time. My husband came up with this way to enjoy tequila as a cocktail. It's colorless, so we named it claro *(clear). Serve with finger snacks before a meal.*

Ice cubes

3 ounces silver tequila

4 to 4 ounces soda water or seltzer

1/2 fresh orange slice

Fill an old-fashioned glass or a 6-ounce glass with ice cubes. Pour in the tequila and fill the glass with soda water. Give it a stir. Garnish with the orange slice. Serve.

Tequila and Grapefruit Cooler
Paloma

Makes 2 servings

Paloma *is a popular drink in Guadalajara and the surrounding area, known for the distilling of tequila from blue agave. My husband and I, and friends we traveled with, tasted our first* Paloma *at Herradura's tequila distillery in Amatitan, a village near the town of Tequila. This simple tequila and grapefruit drink is popular in Jalisco and along the Pacific Coast. We were very fortunate to be invited to the historical and highly esteemed distillery for a private tour, tequila tasting, and lunch. We enjoyed our* comida *outdoors in a beautiful courtyard, and sipped this refreshing drink.*

1/2 fresh lime

Salt, to rim the glass

Ice cubes

**2 ounces tequila (100% blue agave reposado
  preferred)**

1 (12-ounce) can or bottle grapefruit soda

2 fresh grapefruit wedges

2 fresh sprigs of mint

Moisten the top of a tall (about 10 or 12 ounce) glass with lime juice and dip in a saucer of salt to rim the glass. Fill the glass half full of ice cubes. Pour in the tequila and grapefruit soda. Stir. Place a grapefruit wedge on the glass rim and garnish with a sprig of mint. Serve cold.

Tequila Sour

Makes **2 servings**

Shake up a few tequila sours for your next party, or mix the sours in a pitcher and stir briskly.

2 ounces silver or gold tequila
2 ounces fresh lime juice
2 ounces Simple Syrup (page 614)
Cracked ice (see Note)
1 fresh orange slice, cut in half
2 Maraschino cherries

Put all of the ingredients, except the sliced orange and cherries, into a bar shaker or a 2-cup pitcher half filled with cracked ice. Cover and shake about 20 seconds, or stir briskly with a long-handled spoon. Serve over ice or strain into a sour glass or a wine glass. Garnish each glass with an orange slice and a cherry.

Note: To crack ice cubes, put them in a heavy plastic bag, remove air from the bag, seal it, then put the bag on a cutting board. With a hammer or heavy rolling pin, gently break cubes into chips.

Tequila Sunrise

Makes **2 servings**

This is a lovely drink to serve with brunch. Make each drink separately in stemmed wine glasses to show off the "sunrise" colors, which layer beautifully. Sometimes the colors blend together, but the drink still looks pretty, and most people stir to mix the drink anyway. It's said by some that if you pour the ingredients slowly over the back of a spoon into the glass,

this lessens the impact of the liquid falling in the glass and keeps each layer distinct. I've tried this and the results are pretty good. My usual method is to pour slowly right on top of the ice cubes. The ice cubes seem to have the same effect as the back of the spoon.

4 teaspoons grenadine
6 tablespoons silver or gold tequila
4 teaspoons fresh lime juice
1/2 cup strained fresh or frozen orange juice

Fill 2 (8-ounce) wine glasses one-third full with ice cubes. Without stirring, pour half of each ingredient, separately and slowly in the order they are listed, on top of the ice into each glass. Serve at once.

Watermelon and Tequila Cooler
Sandia y Tequila Fresca

Makes **2 servings**

This tall, cool, and refreshing drink with a kick of tequila is just the thing to end a hot day.

About 1/2 medium watermelon (about 2 pounds)
2 ounces silver or gold tequila
1/4 cup fresh lime juice
1/4 cup Simple Syrup (page 614)
Ice cubes

Cut the rind off the watermelon and remove the seeds. Cut enough chunks to measure 2 cups and put in a blender. Add the remaining ingredients and purée until smooth. Pour over ice in 2 tall glasses. Serve cold.

"Drunken" Pineapple Drink
Piña Borracha

Makes **8 servings**

Bring a little of the ambiance of Mexican seaside resort hotels to your home, by making this tempting drink for a party. Start this drink a full day before serving, and be sure your pineapple is very ripe and sweet. Serve the punch ice cold in sherry glasses like an aperitif or a liqueur.

1 whole fresh ripe pineapple (about 2 pounds)
2 cups silver or gold tequila
1 cup fresh orange juice

1. Peel the pineapple and remove the eyes. Cut lengthwise into quarters and cut into 1-inch pieces. Then, with a large sharp knife, coarsely chop the pineapple. Put the chopped pineapple, tequila, and orange juice in a large glass jar. Cover and refrigerate 24 hours.

2. Pour through a fine-mesh strainer into a clean glass pitcher or other glass container, and serve very cold.

Crazy Coconut Drink
Coco Loco

Makes **2 servings**

In Mexican beach towns like Acapulco, where coconut palms grow and coconuts are green and abundant, this drink is often made on the spot. The coconut is cracked open at the top with an ax or machete, tequila or rum is mixed with the fresh coconut milk inside, and it's served with a straw. Unless you have green coconuts easily accessible, you can use canned coconut milk. Aged tequilas, like reposado or añejo, are more expensive and not needed in mixed libations, so silver tequila is called for here.

Ice cubes
8 ounces canned coconut milk
2 ounces silver tequila or white rum

Fill 2 (8-ounce) glasses with ice cubes. Pour 4 ounces of coconut milk in each glass and add the tequila or rum. Stir. Serve cold.

Banana Tequila Smoothie
Plátano Tequila Suave

Makes **4 servings**

This appealing drink is made with tequila, but it's also equally refreshing without. Serve it for a late breakfast or brunch.

2 medium bananas, peeled and thickly sliced
2 cups fresh orange juice
2 tablespoons sugar
4 ounces silver or gold tequila
1 cup cracked ice (see Note)

Put all of the ingredients except for the ice in a blender jar and purée until smooth. Do this in two equal batches, if needed. Serve over crushed ice in stemmed glasses.

Note: To crack ice cubes, put them in a heavy plastic bag, remove air from the bag, seal it, then put the bag on a cutting board. With a hammer or heavy rolling pin, gently break cubes into chips.

Tequila Bloody Mary
Tequila Sangre de Maria

Makes **2 servings**

Some people, like me, like this version better than the classic one made with vodka. Quesadillas or crisp chips and guacamole go well with this drink.

2 cups spicy tomato juice, such as Snappy Tom, or plain tomato juice

3 teaspoons fresh lime juice, or to taste

1/8 teaspoon Worcestershire sauce

4 ounces silver or gold tequila

Cracked ice (see Note)

In a pitcher, mix all the ingredients together, except the ice. Pour over cracked ice into 2 double old-fashioned glasses.

Note: To crack ice cubes, put them in a heavy plastic bag, remove air from the bag, seal it, then put the bag on a cutting board. With a hammer or heavy rolling pin, gently break cubes into chips.

Brave Bull
Toro Bravo

Makes **2 servings**

A Brave Bull is a fashionable Mexican after-dinner drink on both sides of the border. Mexico produces the world's best coffee liqueur with flavors of chocolate and vanilla.

Cracked ice (see Note)

2 ounces tequila

2 ounces coffee-flavored liqueur, such as Kahlua

Fill 2 (6-ounce) glasses almost to the brim with cracked ice. Pour the tequila and liqueur over the ice. Stir well and serve.

Note: To crack ice cubes, put them in a heavy plastic bag, remove air from the bag, seal it, then put the bag on a cutting board. With a hammer or heavy rolling pin, gently break cubes into chips.

Mango, Pineapple, and Mezcal Drink
Bebida de Mango, Piña, y Mezcal

Makes **4 servings**

Mezcal is one of the alcoholic beverages made from the agave *plant commonly called* maguey *in Mexico. It has an earthy, smoky taste somewhat like tequila. Mezcal is mainly produced in small quantities in the state of Oaxaca by traditional methods in rustic stills. It is now being exported in limited amounts and interest in the product is growing. Some people know it from the worm (gusano) in the bottle, which is probably a sales gimmick, and may not add anything to the* mezcal, *although* gusanos *are considered a delicacy in the Oaxaca region. (Gusanos* live in the maguey *plants and have been gathered and eaten by native people for centuries.)*

Tourists love to buy mezcal *as a souvenir, and often develop a taste for this unique Mexican beverage. Sip it straight, or try this recipe of blended fruit and* mezcal.

1 large ripe mango

1 cup chopped fresh pineapple

1 cup fresh orange juice

1/2 cup mezcal

Ice cubes

1. To peel and cut up the mango, cut 1/2 of the mango away from the flat oval seed with a sharp paring knife. Then lay the cut half on a flat surface, skin side down, and make cross-cuts on the fruit, separating the flesh into cubes. (Do not cut through the peel.) Press the fruit inside out and cut the chunks off the peel. Discard the peel and put the fruit in the blender.

2. Add the pineapple, orange juice, and mezcal and purée until very smooth. Serve over ice in 6-ounce glasses.

Daiquiri

Makes **2 servings**

When I first traveled to Mexico 30 years ago, a Daiquiri was my favorite cocktail. Now that cocktails are popular again, so is the Daiquiri. Mexico produces some fine-quality rums, such as Bacardi which is distilled in Puebla, about 100 miles south of Mexico City. Other Mexican rums may not be widely available in United States liquor stores, so you can use the rum of your choice. I often buy a bottle in the Mexico City or Guadalajara airport before departing Mexico.

1 cup cracked ice (see Note)
2 ounces white rum
1/2 ounce Simple Syrup (page 614)
1/2 ounce maraschino cherry liqueur
Juice of 1 lime
2 thin slices of fresh lime

In a blender or cocktail shaker, thoroughly mix all of the ingredients, except the lime slices. Pour it through a fine-mesh strainer, then equally fill 2 (4-ounce) stemmed cocktail glasses and garnish each with a slice of lime.

Note: To crack ice cubes, put them in a heavy plastic bag, remove air from the bag, seal it, then put the bag on a cutting board. With a hammer or heavy rolling pin, gently break cubes into chips.

Mango Daiquiri
Daiquiri de Mango

Makes **2 servings**

Large, sweet mangos are now available almost everywhere. Their distinctive flavor mixed with rum makes a unique slushy frozen Daiquiri that's popular in Baja, along the coast of the Sea of Cortéz.

1 large ripe mango
3 ounces white rum
1 ounce fresh lime juice
1/2 ounce Simple Syrup (page 614)
1 cup cracked ice (see Note)
1 thin slice of lime, cut in half

1. Determine the slightly flat sides of the mango, and hold one of the flatter sides of the mango in the palm of your hand. Cut the top half of the mango away from the pit, cutting as close to the pit as possible. Make crosswise cuts in the fruit side, but do not cut through the skin. Bend the fruit backwards and cut off the scored pieces of fruit. Repeat with the remaining half of the mango.

2. Put the mango and the rest of the ingredients, except the sliced lime, in a blender. Blend until smooth and slushy. Pour equally into 2 (4-ounce) stemmed cocktail glasses. Garnish each glass with a half slice of lime, and serve at once.

Note: To crack ice cubes, put them in a heavy plastic bag, remove air from the bag, seal it, then put the bag on a cutting board. With a hammer or heavy rolling pin, gently break cubes into chips.

El Presidente Cocktail
Presidente

Makes **2 servings**

This rum cocktail has been a common drink in Mexico City and other major cities in Mexico for a long time, and it is still offered in upscale bars and restaurants.

2 jiggers white rum
1 ounce vermouth
1 teaspoon grenadine
Juice of 1 lime
3/4 cup cracked ice (see Note)

Put all of the ingredients in a blender or cocktail shaker. Shake well and pour equally into 2 (4-ounce) stemmed cocktail glasses.

Note: To crack ice cubes, put them in a heavy plastic bag, remove air from the bag, seal it, then put the bag on a cutting board. With a hammer or heavy rolling pin, gently break cubes into chips.

Little Bull
Toritos

Makes **4 servings**

This rich, luxurious drink was served at a seaside setting in Veracruz. A small bowl of spicy nuts and pumpkin seeds came to the table with the drinks. The drink can be made with a variety of tropical fruits, but I liked pineapple or mango the best. Peeled and ready-to-use containers of fresh pineapple and sometimes mango are available in many supermarket produce markets. They are a great convenience when making this drink.

1 cup chopped fresh pineapple or mango
1 cup water
¼ cup sweetened condensed milk
¼ cup dark rum
Ice cubes

Put all of the ingredients in a blender, except the ice, and blend until smooth. Half fill 4 (4-ounce) cocktail glasses with ice cubes. Pour the drink equally over the ice and serve at once.

Rum and Coke
Cuba Libre

Makes **2 servings**

Rum and Coca-Cola (Cuba Libre) was invented in a bar in Old Havana in 1898 following Cuba's War of Independence. A group of off-duty soldiers was having drinks and one ordered rum with Coca-Cola and lime juice. The story goes that they wanted a name for the drink, and someone called out, "Cuba Libre" for Cuba's freedom after the war. The drink later became popular throughout Mexico as "rum and Coke."

Cuba's famous Bacardi rum has been distilled in Mexico since 1956 when Barcardi built a distillation plant in the state of Puebla. The distinctive bottle is covered with fibers woven by Mexico's Texcoco Indians. Coca-Cola plants have been going strong in Mexico since the 1920s and Coke is a popular soft drink. Cuba Libres can be served with appetizers before a meal.

2 ounces dark rum
Coca-Cola (enough to fill the glass ¾ full)
4 to 6 ice cubes
2 lime wedges

In 2 short (4-ounce) bar glasses, divide the rum and cola equally and stir to mix. Add 2 to 3 ice cubes to each glass, and a squeeze of lime juice. Drop a lime wedge into each glass.

Rum Collins
Collins de Ron

Makes **2 servings**

A tall, cold Collins made with light rum is a popular poolside or bar drink in Mexico. It goes well with informal Mexican snacks such as Crisp Rolled Chicken Taquitos (page 92).

Ice cubes
2 ounces white rum
2 ounces Simple Syrup (page 614)
2 ounces lime juice
1 (12-ounce) bottle club soda

Fill two 8-ounce glasses with ice cubes. Pour half the rum, syrup, and lime juice into each glass. Add club soda to fill each glass. Stir briefly, and serve cold.

Pacific Gold Cocktail
Oro de Pacifico

Makes **2 servings**

Along the Pacific coast of Mexico, this drink is usually thought of as a "sun-downer." Tourists and locals gather in bars along the beach before having dinner to enjoy often-spectacular sunsets.

1 cup cracked ice (see Note)
6 ounces pineapple juice
4 ounces fresh grapefruit juice
2 ounces silver or white tequila
2 ounces white rum
2 ounces sweet coconut cream, such as Coco Lopez
2 mint sprigs

Put the ice in a blender jar. Add all of the remaining ingredients but the mint, and blend until smooth. Pour equally into 2 (10-ounce) Pilsner-style glasses. Add a straw and garnish with the mint. Serve cold.

Note: To crack ice cubes, put them in a heavy plastic bag, remove air from the bag, seal it, then put the bag on a cutting board. With a hammer or heavy rolling pin, gently break cubes into chips.

Papaya Cocktail
Coctél de Papaya

Makes **4 servings**

The fruit of large, football-shaped Mexican papaya is reddish-orange in color and blends easily to make a smooth, seductive cocktail that's quite elegant to serve before a Mexican dinner party.

Mexican papayas are often available in the United States, but the smaller, yellow Hawaiian papaya works well, too. Choose papayas that give slightly to the touch and have smooth unbruised skin. Serve the drinks in margarita or martini glasses.

1 Mexican papaya or 2 Hawaiian papayas
3 ounces white or dark rum
1/4 cup fresh lime juice, or to taste
2 teaspoons sugar, or to taste
1 cup cracked ice (see Note)

1. Cut the papaya in half. Scoop out the seeds with a spoon. Discard the seeds. Peel off the skin and coarsely chop the fruit. Put the chopped fruit in a blender.

2. Add the remaining ingredients to the blender and blend on high until thick and smooth. Divide among 4 (4-ounce) cocktail glasses, and serve at once.

Note: To crack ice cubes, put them in a heavy plastic bag, remove air from the bag, seal it, then put the bag on a cutting board. With a hammer or heavy rolling pin, gently break cubes into chips.

Rum Frappe
Frappe de Ron

Makes **2 servings**

Surprise a friend or party guests with this elegant drink, best enjoyed on warm nights. (Increase quantities as needed.) The recipe calls for orange sherbet but Mexican ices and sherbets come in a rainbow of wonderful flavors, including tangerine, lime, and grapefruit. Experiment to find your favorite.

4 rounded tablespoons orange sherbet
3 ounces dark or white rum

Put 2 rounded tablespoons of sherbet into each of 2 fluted champagne glasses. Add half of the rum to each glass and stir the contents of each glass slowly with a spoon, until the drink becomes smooth. Serve with a straw.

Rum and Pomegranate Cocktail
Granada Coctél

Makes **2 servings**

Pomegranates are grown in many parts of Mexico and the bright red seeds are used to garnish Stuffed Poblano Chiles in Walnut Sauce (page 427) and Christmas Eve Salad (page 188). The juice is often used as a refreshing beverage or added to drinks like this cocktail.

Some commercial grenadine syrups are flavored with pomegranate juice, but most are made of artificial flavors. You can make your own Pomegranate Syrup (page 615) or substitute grenadine. This is fun to serve for something different.

2 teaspoons Pomegranate Syrup (page 615)
    or grenadine syrup
4 ounces pineapple juice
3 ounces white rum
2 teaspoons fresh lime juice
Cracked ice (see Note)

Prepare pomegranate syrup, if using. Then, put all of the ingredients into a blender or cocktail shaker with cracked ice. Blend or shake well and strain equally into 2 (4-ounce) cocktail glasses. Serve cold.

Note: To crack ice cubes, put them in a heavy plastic bag, remove air from the bag, seal it, then put the bag on a cutting board. With a hammer or heavy rolling pin, gently break cubes into chips.

Planter's Punch
Ponche de Guayaba

Makes **4 servings**

Imagine yourself, pool-side at a Mexican resort, sipping a tall, cold tropical drink like this. That's the life!

Guava nectar or juice is found in cans, or as a frozen concentrate. Serve the drinks over ice in tall glasses for sipping. You can also serve the drinks with a Mexican sandwich such as Mexican Chicken Sandwich (page 119), or Shrimp and Avocado Sandwich (page 197), or Mushrooms and Epazote Tacos (page 94).

2 cups guava juice
1 cup frozen limeade
1 cup dark rum
Ice cubes
Mint sprigs
Lime slices

In a glass pitcher, mix guava juice, limeade, and rum. Fill 4 (8-ounce) glasses halfway with ice cubes, and pour punch over the ice. Garnish each glass with a sprig of mint, and add a slice of lime on the edge of the glass. If desired, add 2 straws to each glass. Serve at once.

Pineapple-Coconut-Rum Drink
Piña Colada

Makes **2 servings**

Piña coladas are enormously popular at Mexican seaside resorts. You know someone ordered one when you see a wedge of fresh pineapple decorating the glass and a bright red cherry perched on top. If you can't grab a plane and head south of the border, get in the vacation spirit by making these at home. Piña coladas are a popular beverage to serve with brunch.

4 ounces white rum
5 ounces pineapple juice
1 teaspoon fresh lime juice
2 ounces canned sweet cream of coconut, such as Coco Lopez
3/4 cup crushed ice
4 pineapple wedges
4 Maraschino cherries

Put all of the ingredients, except the pineapple wedges and the cherries, in a blender and blend on high speed until frothy and smooth. Divide between 2 (8-ounce) stemmed wine glasses. Skewer the pineapple wedges and cherries on cocktail picks to garnish the drinks. Serve.

Note: To crack ice cubes, put them in a heavy plastic bag, remove air from the bag, seal it, then put the bag on a cutting board. With a hammer or heavy rolling pin, gently break cubes into chips.

Banana-Coconut-Rum Drink
Plátano Colada

Makes **2 servings**

Mexican beach resorts are the most likely places to find fancy tropical drinks like this twist on the popular Piña Colada.

10 ice cubes
1 1/2 ripe bananas, peeled and cut into chunks
4 ounces canned sweet cream of coconut, such as Coco Lopez
1/2 cup pineapple juice
4 ounces dark rum
2 tablespoons fresh lime juice
2 mint sprigs

Put the ice cubes, bananas, coconut cream, pineapple juice, rum, and lime juice in a blender. Blend until very smooth. Divide between 2 (8-ounce) stemmed glasses. Garnish each glass with a mint sprig.

Mexican Eggnog Rum Drink
Rompope

Makes **about 4 to 6 servings**

Rompope is similar to eggnog and was intro-duced from Spain during the colonial era in Puebla. It is served for parties and as an after-dinner drink, but is especially popular around Christmas time. Rompope is quite easy to make, and it's well worth the short amount of time it takes to make at home.

Rompope is available commercially bottled and may be sold in some liquor stores, but it is not easy to find in the United States. Serve rompope in small glasses after dinner, or use it as a delicious sauce for fruit or cake desserts.

3 cups whole milk

1 cup sugar

1 cinnamon stick (Mexican canela or Ceylon variety preferred)

1 (2-inch) piece vanilla bean

6 large egg yolks, well beaten

1 cup dark rum

1. In a medium saucepan, put the milk, sugar, cinnamon stick, and vanilla bean. Bring to a boil and cook at a steady boil, stirring frequently, 5 minutes. Cool to lukewarm.

2. Stir the beaten egg yolks into the milk mixture. Return to the stove and cook over medium-low heat, stirring constantly until the mixture thickens. Remove from the heat. Discard the cinnamon stick and vanilla bean.

3. Stir in the rum. Whisk until frothy. Cool, then refrigerate and serve cold or, to store, pour into a sterilized glass jar and tightly close the lid. Keeps, refrigerated, 4 to 5 weeks.

Brandy Devil
Brandy Diablo

Makes **2 servings**

Mexico produces some very respectable brandy, and brandy is Mexico's second most popular distilled liquor. Grapes for brandy are grown in north-central Mexico in the states of Zacatecas and Aguascalientes. Good Mexican brandies include Don Pedro, Presidente, and Solera. Mexican brandy is sold domestically and also exported. A Brandy Devil is like a Brandy Old-Fashioned and is normally enjoyed before dinner.

2 ounces brandy

2 ounces dry vermouth

4 dashes Angostura bitters

Cracked ice (see Note)

2 strips thin orange peel

Put all of the ingredients, except the orange peel, into a cocktail shaker or in a pitcher with cracked ice. Shake (or stir) well and pour into cocktail glasses. Twist the orange peel over the glasses and drop them into the glass.

Note: To crack ice cubes, put them in a heavy plastic bag, remove air from the bag, seal it, then put the bag on a cutting board. With a hammer or heavy rolling pin, gently break cubes into chips.

Mexican Grasshopper

Makes **2 servings**

Mexico's wonderful creamy, coffee-flavored liqueur, known the world-over as Kahlua, is perfect in this sweet rich-tasting after-dinner drink. Mexican Grasshoppers are wonderfully satisfying and almost like liquid desserts. Sip slowly and enjoy!

1/2 cup crushed ice

2 ounces Kahlua or other coffee-flavored liqueur

2 ounces green crème de menthe

2 ounces whipping cream

Put ice in a blender. Add the Kahlua, crème de menthe, and cream. Blend until frothy and divide between 2 (4-ounce) stemmed cocktail glasses.

Other Drinks and Drink Basics

Sangrita I

Makes **2 cups (5 to 6 servings)**

Sangrita is a popular Mexican beverage made of orange juice, tomato juice, lime, grenadine, and Tabasco. It is traditionally sipped alongside straight tequila as an aperitif. Serve each person a 1-ounce shot of quality tequila, preferably an aged 100% blue agave tequila—and about 3 ounces of sangrita in a small narrow glass.

Sangrita can be purchased in a bottle, but it's fun and easy to make. There are different formulas for sangrita. This is my version made after many taste tests in Mexico. Another sangrita recipe follows, made without tomato juice. Serve some Spicy Roasted Cocktail Peanuts (page 130) or crisp tortilla chips to munch on with the drinks.

1 cup fresh orange juice
1/2 cup canned tomato juice
1/2 cup fresh lime juice
2 tablespoons grenadine syrup
4 to 6 dashes hot pepper sauce, such as Tabasco

Mix all the ingredients in a pitcher. Cover and refrigerate 1 to 4 hours. Pour through a fine-mesh strainer into a pitcher. Discard pulp. Serve in small glasses with tequila on the side. Keeps 3 to 4 days covered in the refrigerator.

Sangrita II

Makes **about 2 cups (5 to 6 servings)**

Here is another version of sangrita that is also common in Mexico. It does not contain tomato juice, which some people prefer. I also concocted this one from tasting different versions, reading labels on bottled sangrita, and asking bartenders' questions.

2 cups fresh orange juice
2 tablespoons fresh lime juice
1/4 cup grenadine
1/4 teaspoon cayenne pepper
1 teaspoon salt, or to taste

Put all of the ingredients into a jar. Stir thoroughly. Cover and store in the refrigerator up to 4 to 5 days.

Simple Syrup

Makes **about 2 1/2 cups**

Keep this ever-useful universal syrup in the refrigerator for sweetening all kinds of bar drinks.

2 cups water
1 cup sugar

In a saucepan, mix the sugar and water. Bring to a slow simmer, stirring, until the sugar is melted, about 3 minutes. Cool. Store in a glass jar, covered, in the refrigerator. It keeps indefinitely.

Pomegranate Syrup

Makes **about 2 cups**

The pomegranates displayed in Mexican markets usually show several beautifully cut samples of the fruits to entice shoppers with a view of the jeweled seeds held within. Pomegranate juices make a wonderful sweet-sour syrup to add color and sweetness to fruit drinks or cocktails. The juice can also be drizzled over fruit, such as mangos or peaches. Store in a covered jar or bottle in the refrigerator. It keeps for months.

4 large pomegranates
1 cup sugar

1. With a large, sharp knife cut the pomegranates in half and then break them into sections. Hold the sections in a bowl of cold water in the sink (to prevent juices from splattering), and pick out the red seeds, discarding the thin white membrane, and place them in a small bowl. Put the seeds in a blender or citrus juicer and blend about 5 seconds.

2. Pour the juice through a fine-mesh strainer into a nonreactive 1-quart saucepan. Discard the seeds and debris left in the strainer. Add the sugar to the juice and stir until dissolved, 2 to 3 minutes. Bring to a boil over medium heat, then reduce heat to medium-low and simmer, stirring frequently, 5 minutes. Cool completely. Pour into a jar or bottle, cover and refrigerate.

Mexican Cooking Glossary

Achiote: The reddish-orange seed of the annato tree used to season and color foods. A seasoning paste is also made from the seeds. Used extensively in the Yucatán region. (Can dye clothes, skin.)

Adobo: A chile-based paste to use as marinade or sauce.

Agua fresca: Beverage made with blended fruit, flavorings, and water.

Aguacate: Spanish for avocado, which are native to Mexico. Pear-shaped or round fruit with dark green to almost-black skin and soft cream-colored interior when ripe. Avocados (*aguacate*) are native to Mexico, and there are many varieties. Used for guacamole and other salads, and sauces.

Anaheim or California: Long, slender chile, light green in color. Ranges from mild to quite hot. Roast and peel before using in chiles rellenos, sauces, and vegetable dishes. Also canned as whole green chiles and diced green chiles.

Ancho: A dark red to almost-black dried poblano chile, with wrinkled skin. In some places it is called *pasilla*. Wide at the top and tapered toward the tip, and 3 to 4 inches long. Anchos are mild to hot. Used for sauces, or reconstituted then stuffed.

Antojito: Appetizer or snack. From the Spanish word *antojo*, meaning whim. Includes traditional small portions of street foods such as tacos, sopes, tostados, and burritos. Sometimes called *botana*.

Asada or asado: Broiled or grilled meat.

Atole: Thick drink or porridge usually made with ground corn.

Bebida: Alcoholic or non-alcoholic beverage or drink.

Banana leaves: Large flat leaves of the banana tree widely used in Mexico to wrap tamales, or other foods that are baked or steamed.

Bolillo: Oval-shaped Mexican sandwich roll (about 6 inches long), with crusty exterior and soft center. Often used for Mexican sandwiches called *tortas*.

Botana: Snack or appetizer. Also called antojito.

Budín: Pudding. Refers to sweet desserts and savory baked dishes.

Buñuelo: Fritter made with wheat flour.

Burrito: A filled and wrapped flour tortilla. Common in northern Mexico.

Cajeta: Thick caramel confection made with goat's or cow's milk and sugar. Long, slow-simmering produces caramel color and very sweet flavor.

California: Shiny dried chile with smooth red skin, 4 to 5 inches long, mild to slightly hot. Used in cooked sauces and ground into chili powders.

Canela: Also called Ceylon cinnamon; referred to as the pure or true cinnamon. Has a milder, sweeter flavor than Cassia variety common in the United States.

Carnita: Pork steamed and fried in lard. Popular filling for tacos.

Cascabel: Dried reddish-brown chile that's mildly hot with a nutty flavor. Round in shape and rattles when shaken.

Cazuela: Clay cooking vessel that's wider at the top than at the bottom.

Ceviche: Raw fish marinated and "cooked" in lime juice. The chemical action of the acid in the lime juice firms the flesh and turns it opaque, so the texture is as though cooked.

Chalupa: Corn tortilla dough formed into small oval or round with pinched-up rims. Fried and topped with filling for appetizers.

Champurrado: Chocolate atole (corn-based chocolate drink).

Chaya: Mayan green leafy plant found in the Yucatán. The tender greens are used like spinach or Swiss chard (the recommended substitutes).

Chayote: Pear-shaped, pale green vegetables related to squash. They are indigenous to Mexico and are also known as vegetable pears or mirlitons.

Cherimoya: Tropical dark green fruit with patterned skin that resembles thumbprints. Creamy white flesh with shiny black seeds. Used in sorbets and other desserts.

Chicharrón: Fried pork rind used as snack or garnish.

Chilaquile: Casserole made with day-old tortilla strips or wedges combined with eggs, sausage, or bits of chicken or meat, onion, and red or green sauce. Usually topped with crumbled cheese.

Chile: Term used for a large number of capsicum peppers—both fresh and dried—ranging from mild to extremely hot, that are used in cooking. Dried chiles are mainly used for cooked sauces. (See individual listings.) Chiles are also ground, and labeled "pure" with the name of the chile. Unless labeled pure, chili powder is a blend of ground chile and other spices.

Chile de arbol: Small, thin, dried red chile that's very hot. Used in table sauces and cooked sauces.

Chile relleño: Stuffed fresh or dried chile.

Chimichanga: Large flour tortilla, stuffed, folded, and fried.

Chipotle: Dried, smoked jalapeño chile with a brown leathery skin; it's very hot. Used canned in a seasoning mixture called adobo, and also puréed and made into a fiery chipotle sauce with a smoky taste. Chipotles are popular, and a little goes a long way.

Chorizo: Spicy Mexican pork sausage.

Churro: Rope-shaped, deep-fried fritter, from 4 inches to about 10 inches long, that is rolled in sugar while hot.

Cilantro: Green herb, also called Chinese parsley, that has a distinctive flavor essential in many fresh salsas and as a garnish.

Comal: A griddle made of clay, aluminum, iron, or steel. Used for toasting ingredients such as tomatoes, chiles, seeds, herbs.

Cotija cheese: Aged cheese; also called *queso añejo*.

Crema: Mexican cream that is thick and slightly sour, somewhat like French crème fraiche. It's used to garnish enchiladas, tacos, and other snacks.

Empanada: Sweet or savory pastry turnover.

Enchilada: Filled corn tortilla, folded, rolled, or stacked, and covered with sauce. Often baked.

Epazote: An important green herb—essential in some regions of Mexico—used in bean dishes, tamales, some sauces and stews, and other dishes. Used fresh and dried.

Escabeche: Meats, fish, or vegetables "pickled" in vinegar, oil, herbs and spices.

Flan: Baked custard made with milk and eggs. Originally from Spain.

Flauta: Corn tortilla rolled around filling and fried.

Frijoles refritos: Refried beans.

Garnacha: Yucatán appetizer made with small bowl-shaped corn tortilla dough that's fried and filled with beans and spicy meat or chicken mixtures.

Gordita: Appetizer made of corn tortilla dough that's shaped into patties, then baked on a comal or skillet, or fried and topped with beans, shredded meats, chicken, and just about anything.

Guajillo: Medium-to-long, dark red dried chile that's quite hot and very popular. Used extensively in cooked sauces.

Güero chile: Pale yellow, waxy, small hot chile. Also milder banana and Hungarian wax chiles, about 4 inches long; used in sauces, salads, and sometimes pickled.

Gusano de maguey: Small worm that inhabits agave plants. It is fried and eaten as a delicacy and also put into bottles of mezcal liquor.

Habanero: Small, very hot—maybe the hottest of all chiles—in shades of green, yellow, orange, and red. A lantern shape with indentations and irregularities. Closely related to the Scotch Bonnet chile.

Helado: Ice cream

Hierba Santa: Large leaf with an anise-like flavor used in sauces and as a wrap for steaming fish and sometimes tamales. Also called *hoja santa*, *momo*, and *acuyo* in some regions.

Horchata: Beverage made by grinding uncooked rice or melon seeds with water or juice.

Huevos rancheros: Breakfast specialty of eggs on tortillas topped with a tomato-based sauce (*salsa ranchera*).

Huitlacoche: (also *cuitlacoche*) A black fungus growing on corn during the rainy season. Used in crepes, soups, and with eggs.

Jalapeño: Dark green, plump hot chile about 2 to 3 inches long, with a rounded bottom. Used raw in salsas and cooked in sauces. Also pickled and canned.

Jicama: Large root vegetable with light brown skin and white flesh, shaped like a turnip, with a crisp sweet taste. Jicama is eaten raw, peeled and sliced, and is occasionally cooked.

Lard: Rendered pork fat.

Licuado: Beverage of blended fruit with milk, yogurt, or water.

Manchego cheese: Popular Spanish cheese made of sheep's milk; also made in Mexico with cow's milk.

Masa: Fresh dough made of specially processed dried corn used to make corn tortillas, tamales, and other masa dishes. Dried masa is also dehydrated into a flour called *masa harina*.

Metate: Three-legged stone used for grinding.

Mixiote: Thin membrane, like parchment, from the maguey plant. Used to wrap foods that are then cooked in a pit.

Molcajete: Stone mortar used for mashing and grinding.

Mole: *Nahuatl* word meaning sauce. Refers to a number of traditional complex sauces from different regions of the country.

Mulato: Dried, very dark, almost-black chile, very similar to and often mistaken for an ancho. Used in moles.

New Mexico: Long green chile resembling Anaheim, but hotter, and used in the same ways as Anaheims.

Nopales: Paddles from the prickly pear cactus that are eaten as a vegetable all over Mexico. Often cut into strips called *nopalitos* for cooking. The edible fruit of the plant is called a prickly pear, or *tuna*.

Pan de muerto: Special round loaf of sweet bread topped with decorative dough-shaped crossbones that is used for celebrating the Day of the Dead, which honors deceased family and friends.

Panela: Mild slightly soft cheese; often sliced as an appetizer.

Pasilla: Long, narrow, black chile that's also called *chile negro*. In some places the name *pasilla* is used for fresh poblano chiles and dried anchos.

Pibil: Refers to the pit-cooked foods of Yucatán.

Picadillo: Sautéed ground meat dish made with beef, pork, or chicken, and tomatoes, onions, garlic, and other regional flavorings. Often used as a stuffing.

Piloncillo: Unrefined cane sugar; shaped into cones or slabs.

Pipian: Stew, similar to mole, with ground pumpkin or squash seeds and nuts.

Plátano: A cooking banana, or plantain, also known as *plátano macho*. Plantains are fried, baked, or mashed. The skin turns nearly black when ripe. Also used to refer to a sweet eating banana.

Poblano: The most-used fresh green chile. Dark green and shiny with broad shoulders, tapering to a rounded or pointed bottom. Used extensively roasted, peeled, and stuffed for *rellenos*, and as a garnish when cut into thin strips or squares. Poblanos are also cooked in many dishes and puréed in many sauces.

Postre: Dessert

Pozole: Soup made with pork or other meat and treated dried corn, called hominy in the United States.

Quesadilla: Folded, grilled, or fried corn or flour tortilla filled with cheese, and sometimes other ingredients are tucked inside with the cheese.

Rajas: Strips of roasted and peeled poblano chiles.

Relleno: Any food that is stuffed. Most often used for stuffed chiles.

Rompope: Mexican cooked eggnog drink made with milk, sugar, egg yolks, vanilla, and rum.

Salsa verde: Cooked or raw green sauce.

Sangrita: A popular drink to accompany tequila made from orange juice, grenadine, chiles, and sometimes tomato juice.

Serrano: Small, slender, light green, hot-to-very-hot chile that used mainly in fresh salsas or cooked sauces. Often used interchangeably with jalapeños.

Sopa seca: "Dry soup"; refers to rice and pasta dishes. The liquid the rice or pasta begins cooking with is completely absorbed, making it dry.

Sope: Like gordita. Appetizer made of tortilla dough that's formed into small rounds with pinched-up rims, then fried and topped.

Tamal: Often spelled tamale. Tortilla dough filled with any kind of meat, vegetable, or fruit, then wrapped in corn husks, banana leaves, or other wrappings, and steamed.

Taco: Corn tortilla folded around a filling. Sometimes briefly fried.

Tamarindo: Brown pods from the tamarind tree. The inside of the pods makes a tart juice that's used to flavor beverages, candies, and sauces.

Taquito: Filled, rolled, and fried corn tortilla, similar to a flauta.

Tejolote: Pestle used for grinding in a molcajete (stone bowl).

Tinga: Special stew from the state of Puebla.

Tomatillo: Small green tart fruit with a papery hush that looks like a green tomato. Used in cooked and raw sauces and salsas throughout the country. Also called tomato verde in Mexico.

Torta: Mexican sandwich; also means a pie or tart.

Tortilla: Thin flat bread made of masa (specially treated dried corn). Corn tortillas are the most important bread in Mexico. Tortillas are also made of wheat flour, used more in northern Mexico.

Tostada: Fried corn tortilla chips, or whole fried tortillas used as an edible plate to layer with ingredients such as beans, lettuce, tomatoes, avocado, meats, and cheeses.

Yuca: Edible root from a tropical plant that's used like potatoes, mainly in Yucatán, Campeche, Quintana Roo, and Chiapas. Often made into fritters or chips.

Mail-Order Sources for Ingredients

Herbs of Mexico, 3903 Whittier Boulevard, Los Angeles, California 90023. Tel: (213) 261-2521. Many herbs and chiles.

Coyote Cucina Catalog, 1364 Rufine Circle #1, Santa Fe, New Mexico 87502. Tel: (800) 866-HOWL. Send for catalog—dried chiles, herbs, and spices.

CMC Company, P.O. Box 322, Avalon, N.J. 08202. Tel: (800) 262-2780. Website: www.thecmccompany.com Dried chiles, Mexican chocolate, avocado leaves, and dried herbs and spices.

Tierra Vegetables, 13684 Chalk Hill Road, Healdsburg, California 95448. Good source for dried chiles.

It's About Thyme, P.O. Box 878, Manchaca, Texas 78652. Tel: (512) 280-1192. Fresh plants and herbs, especially hierba santa and epazote; catalog available.

Adriana's Caravan, 409 Vanderbilt St., Brooklyn, New York 11218. Tel: (800) 316-0820. Website: www.adrainascaravan.com Many spices, herbs, and dried chiles. Mexican chocolate and Mexican vanilla beans.

Shepherd's Garden Seeds, 30 Irene St., Torrington, Connecticut 06790. Tel: (860) 482-3638. Good selection of garden seeds, including tomatillos, chiles, epazote.

Frieda's Finest, Tel: (714) 826-6100. Website: www.friedas.com Selection of fresh ingredients, such as banana leaves, cactus paddles, fresh chiles, and plantains. Expensive, but generally good quality.

Glen Burns Farms, 16158 Hillside Circle, Montverde, Florida 34756. Tel: (407) 469-4490. Huitlacoche available.

Pendery's, 304 E. Belknap, Fort Worth, Texas 76102. Tel: (800) 533-1870. Website: www.penderys.com Chiles, herbs, spices.

Penzey's Spices, Tel: (800) 741-7787. Website: www.penzeys.com Good selection of spices and herbs; also *canela* (cinnamon), labeled "Ceylon" cinnamon.

Seeds of Change, Tel: (888) 762-7333. Website: www.seedsofchange.com Hard-to-find seeds for purslane (*verdolagas*), epazote, and lambs quarters (*quelites*).

Cheese Express, Tel: (888) 530-0505. Website: www.cheeseexpress.com A good variety of Mexican cheeses.

Cacique Cheese Co., Box 729, City of Industry, California 91747. Tel: (818) 961-3399. A good selection of Mexican-type cheeses widely distributed in New York, Florida, Illinois, Arizona, and more. Call, or look in your area's dairy cases.

Chocolate Mayordomo de Oaxaca, Avenida Chapultepec 125, Oaxaca City, Oaxaca 68000. Fax: 011-52-951-611-02.

Index

Mexican recipe titles and terms are in *italics*.

Drink. *(cont.)*
  pineapple, fermented, 601
  pineapple, rich, 593
  pineapple-coconut-rum, 612
  tamarind masa, 592–93
"Drunken" Cake, 536–37
"Drunken" Chicken, 294–95
"Drunken" Pineapple Drink, 606
"Drunken" Sauce, 34
  pan-fried trout with, 402–3
Duck, dishes with, 320–22
Dulce, 83, 340, 430, 548, 557, 574,
  578, 579
Dumplings, masa, 135, 375
Durango Beef Stew, 344–45

E

Egg(s). *See also* Omelet
  bacon and, quesadillas, 501
  baked, potatoes and chorizo with,
    495
  coat, fried fish in, 397
  deviled, Mexican style, 130
  "divorced", 493
  "drowned" in tomato sauce, 483
  with green beans and chorizo, 488
  with ground beef and salsa, 488
  with ham, tomatoes, and peppers, 494
  "lost", 492
  Motul style on tortillas, 501
  poached, 496
  in ranchera sauce, 492
  rice casserole with, 499
  salad, green bean and, 176
  scrambled
    with avocado, tomato, 490
    with cactus, 490–91
    with chorizo, 487
    mexican, 487
    stuffed chiles with, 491
    in tomatillo sauce, 490
  with shredded dried beef, 489
  with steak and onions, 494–95
  -stuffed tortillas with pumpkin seed
    sauce, Yucatán, 104

and tortilla casserole, 502
tortilla casserole with red chile sauce
  and, 502
Eggnog
  Mexican, 575
  rum drink, 612–13
  sauce, Mexican, 574
Eggplant, dishes with, 452, 453
Ejotes con Hongos, 453
Elotes, 417–20
El Presidente Cocktail, 608
Emerald Salad, 170
Empanadas, 124, 550, 551, 555
Enchilada(s)
  ancho chile sauce for, 48
  beef, stacked, 142
  black bean, 141
  cheese, in red sauce, 138
  de Carne de Res, 142
  de Frijol Negro, 141
  de Mariscos, 141–41
  de Verduras, 143
  Rojas de Queso, 138
  Salsa de Chili en Polvo, 51
  sauce, chili powder, 51
  seafood, 140–41
  Suizas, 139
  Swiss, 139
  turkey, in green sauce, 140
  vegetable, 143
  Verde de Pavo, 140
Enfrijoladas, 144
Ensalada, 165–211, 403
Ensenada Fried Fish Fillets with
  Lime Vinaigrette, 398
Entomatadas, 43, 144
Epazote
  corn with poblano chiles and, 419
  mushroom and, tacos, 94
  onion, and chipotle turnovers, 124
  red chile broth, chicken and,
    222–23
  zucchini, mushrooms with, 434
Esparragos con Hongos, 450
Especias para Carne, 20
Estofado, 307, 308, 361

F

Fava bean(s)
  and Cactus Soup, 248
  fresh, 471
  salad, fresh, 208
  soup, 247–48
Fideos con Albondigas de Pollo, 483
Fideos con Hongos, 482–83
Fiery Cilantro-Mint Sauce, 30
  butterflied leg of lamb with, 367
  chicken and corn with, 283
  Cornish hens with, 323
  sautéed shark with, 400
Fig bread, Baja, 516
Figs, fresh, with cheese, 579
Figs in Brown Sugar Syrup, 579
Fish. *See also specific names*
  balls, appetizer, 84
  cocktail, marinated, 79
  fried, in egg coat, 397
  in Seven Seas Soup, 233
  shrimp, and oysters baked in
    packages, 384
  stock, basic, 215
  stuffed chiles with, 424
  tacos, 97
  tacos, red snapper, 98
  whole, fried, 398
Fish fillets(s)
  baked, with almonds, 380
  baked, with citrus-tequila sauce,
    380–81
  baked, with green chiles, 381
  baked fisherman style, 382–83
  baked in banana leaf, 382
  fried, with lime vinaigrette,
    ensenada, 398
  marinated fried, 80–81
  salad with avocado-tomatillo
    dressing, 206
  sautéed, 394–96
Flan, 560–63
Flank steak
  tequila-lime, with pickled red
    onions, 330

About the Author

Marge Poore is the author of five cookbooks, including *365 Easy Mexican Recipes*, *The Complete Chicken Breast Cookbook*, and *The Best Stove-Top Grill Pan Cookbook Ever*.

Poore is a graduate of Chico State University, Chico, California, with a Bachelor's degree in Education. During her 18-year teaching career, she made several moves with her husband, Bill, as his career assignments took them from California to Hawaii, Oregon, Arizona, and back to California, and she taught in elementary schools in each of those locations. In between moving from location to location, Poore and her husband made their first trips to Mexico, where they both became enthralled with the culture, people, folk art, crafts, and the cuisine of the country. Poore also began her study of Mexican cooking then.

She left her first career in elementary teaching and pursued her second career in culinary teaching, after she attended cooking school in Leon, Mexico, in 1978 to learn the basics of Mexican cooking. She has since traveled widely in Mexico and has taken classes from native cooks in Mexico City, Oaxaca, San Miguel de Allende, Merida, Villahermosa, and Veracruz. She has also taken classes from Mexican cooking authorities Diana Kennedy, Patricia Quintana, and Rick Bayless, to broaden her knowledge and hone her skills.

Poore has taught cooking classes all around the San Francisco Bay Area, Southern California, Oregon, Nevada, and Vancouver, British Columbia. She completed the tour leader program at the International Tour Management Institute in San Francisco and has led culinary tours to Mexico, Spain, the American Southwest, and New Orleans.

For twenty years, Poore was a partner of and participated in a popular summer program of cooking classes at Lake Tahoe, California. She has been a guest instructor for the Yosemite Chef's Holidays at the Ahwahnee Hotel in Yosemite National Park, the College of Marin, Santa Rosa Community College, and the Sonoma County Culinary Guild.

Poore has written articles for newspapers, Mexicana Airlines' in-flight magazine, and *Food and Wine* magazine. She is a member of the International Association of Culinary Professionals, The American Institute of Wine and Food, and the Sonoma County Culinary Guild.

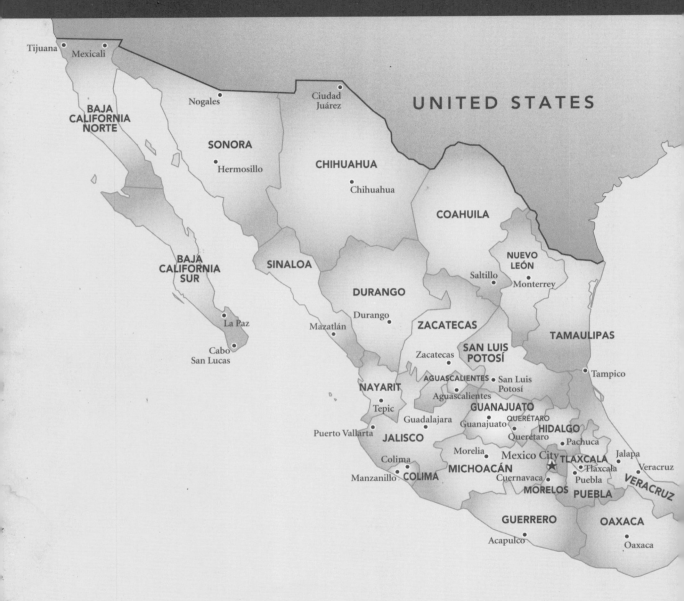

Tijuana
Mexicali

BAJA CALIFORNIA NORTE

Nogales

Ciudad Juárez

UNITED STATES

SONORA

Hermosillo

CHIHUAHUA

Chihuahua

COAHUILA

BAJA CALIFORNIA SUR

SINALOA

NUEVO LEÓN

Saltillo

Monterrey

DURANGO

Durango

La Paz

Mazatlán

ZACATECAS

SAN LUIS POTOSÍ

TAMAULIPAS

Cabo San Lucas

Zacatecas

AGUASCALIENTES

San Luis Potosí

Tampico

Aguascalientes

NAYARIT

Tepic

GUANAJUATO

QUERÉTARO

Guadalajara

Guanajuato

HIDALGO

Querétaro

Pachuca

Puerto Vallarta

JALISCO

Morelia

Mexico City ★

TLAXCALA

Jalapa

Colima

MICHOACÁN

Tlaxcala

Veracruz

Manzanillo

COLIMA

Cuernavaca

Puebla

VERACRUZ

MORELOS

PUEBLA

GUERRERO

OAXACA

Acapulco

Oaxaca